Europe's Crucial Years

The Diplomatic Background of World War I, 1902–1914

**The University Press
of New England**

Sponsoring Institutions

Brandeis University
Clark University
Dartmouth College
University of New Hampshire
University of Rhode Island
University of Vermont

Europe's Crucial Years

The Diplomatic Background of World War I, 1902–1914

by Dwight E. Lee

Published for Clark University Press by the

University Press of New England   Hanover, New Hampshire 1974

To

Commander John K. Thurston, U.S.N.

and Lucinda Lee Thurston

Preface

Twenty years ago I began this study of European diplomatic history from 1902 to 1914, but teaching and administrative duties greatly slowed my progress. The delays were fortunate, however, because over the past ten years monographs based upon previously unavailable sources have revised former interpretations. Utilizing them and the voluminous published sources where revisions have not yet been made, I have sought to strike a balance between a detailed exposition and a general or popular account. There are aspects of the period, notably economic and social developments, that I have left aside, but excuse myself on the grounds that Oron J. Hale's *The Great Illusion* well provides this background of diplomacy.

Because the origins of the First World War have been a highly controversial field, I owe my readers an explanation of my own approach to it. When I began my studies of European diplomacy in the first postwar decade, I was an ardent revisionist, believing that the war-guilt clause of the Versailles treaty did Germany a grave injustice and that by righting the record and properly analyzing the causes of the war a historian might make a contribution to world peace. As the years have gone by, however, my perspective has shifted, not merely because of the lapse of time but also because the world that we naively envisaged in 1920 has failed to unfold as we had hoped it would. The pursuit of national interests amid the almost continuous warfare since 1935 has rendered the historian more humble in his approach to the period before 1914. He can look upon it not only with less prejudice but also with greater empathy. I have therefore sought in this study to discover not who was guilty but what events and decisions led, often unwittingly, to a situation in which the only available recourse was war.

To the dozens of graduate students who were members of my seminar on the backgrounds of the First World War, I am greatly indebted for helping me to develop and clarify my interpretation of the period. I am also grateful to the American Philosophical Society for a research grant in the early stages of this work, and to the staffs of Widener Library at Harvard University and the Robert Hutchings Goddard Library at Clark University, especially Librarian Tilton M. Barron, Reference Librarian Marion Henderson, and Administrative Assistant Jean Perkins, for their unfailing courtesy and helpfulness. Finally I acknowledge with deep gratitude the aid of the late Mrs. Clara Brahm, whose skillful and sensitive translation of Russian materials enabled me to use sources that would otherwise have been closed.

Worcester, Massachusetts
October 1973

D.E.L.

Contents

Illustrations

Maps

The maps in this book were compiled by Douglas C. Smith and designed and executed by Norman T. Carpenter of the Clark University Cartographic Laboratory.

Abbreviations

A.A.	Auswärtiges Amt (German foreign office)
AHR	*American Historical Review*
APG	*Archiv für Politik und Geschichte*
ARB	*Austrian Red Book*
BD	*British Documents on the Origins of the War*
CEH	*Central European History*
CH	*Current History*
CHJ	*Cambridge Historical Journal*
DDF	*Documents Diplomatique Français (1871–1914)*
DDI	*Documenti Diplomatici Italiani (4th Ser., 1908–1914: 4 DDI)*
EG	*Europäische Geschichte*
EHR	*English Historical Review*
FA	*Foreign Affairs*
GP	*Die Grosse Politik der enropäischen Kabinette*
HJ	*Historical Journal*
HZ	*Historische Zeitschrift*
IBZI	*Die Internationalen Beziehungen im Zeitalter des Imperialismus*
JCEH	*Journal of Central European History*
JCH	*Journal of Contemporary History*
JMH	*Journal of Modern History*
KA	*Krasnyi Arkhiv*
KBM	*Kriegsschuldfrage-Berliner Monatshefte*
KD	Kautsky Documents (*Outbreak of the World War*, 1924)
LN	*Livre Noir*

MO	*Mezhdunarodny Otnosheniya* (Tr. as *IBZI*. See above)
ÖUA	*Osterreich-Ungarns Aussenpolitik*
PSQ	*Political Science Quarterly*
QDC	*Questions Diplomatiques et Coloniales*
RDM	*Revue des Deux Mondes*
RH	*Revue Historique*
RHGM	*Revue d'Histoire de la Guerre Mondiale*
SEER	*Slavonic and East European Review*
SR	*Slavonic Review*

Chapter 1

Introduction

In August 1914 a Continent-wide war for the first time since Water-
loo broke the peace. The Crimean war, the Franco-Prussian war, the
Russo-Turkish war of 1877–1878, the Italo-Turkish war of 1911–
1912, and the Balkan wars of 1912–1913 had been partial or peripheral
conflicts, while the Russo-Japanese war of 1904–1905, like the numer-
ous colonial brush fires, had not touched the Continent at all. The
holocaust of 1914–1918 that soon became a world war, the war-guilt
clause of the Versailles peace treaty, and the efforts to end war
through an international organization all spurred the search for the
"causes" of the break and for a culprit who could be blamed for it.
By the end of the first post war decade the searchers had reached a
consensus to divide the causes into "underlying" and "immediate,"
but they had failed to reach agreement between the sturdy revisionists, who controverted the Versailles dictum of Germany's guilt, and
their opponents, who upheld the peace conference verdict.

During the second postwar decade the greater perspective and the
flow of published documents helped to refine the conclusions of the
first decade that all powers were guilty of responsibility for the underlying causes, but that one, or one alliance group, was responsible
for the immediate causes. The rapid approach and outbreak of the
Second World War, however, along with concurrent refinements of
historical methods helped to dispel the illusions and the phraseology
about war "causes" that had warped the judgment of the earlier
searchers and tended to reaffirm the conviction that Germany was
after all an incorrigibly aggressive power whose ambitions accounted
for both wars. Luigi Albertini's thoroughly documented and cogently
reasoned three-volume work, *The Origins of the war of 1914*, which
appeared in the midst of the second conflagration, confirmed the Versailles verdict and thus confounded the revisionists. In the second upsurge of the war-guilt controversy that set German historians by the
ears in the 1960's, the question of causes largely disappeared and
the so-called Fischer school went further than Albertini in ascribing
the outbreak of the 1914 war to Germany. A European perspective,

however, has thus far been lost in the narrow concentration upon German guilt without as yet a new over-all approach to the question of why the war of 1914.

After more than a half century of fruitless efforts to eliminate war, the earlier definitions of the underlying causes of the first world war now appear to be specious. Sidney Bradshaw Fay, whose *Origins of the World War* may be regarded as the classic statement of the revisionist viewpoint, summarized them as the alliance system, militarism, nationalism, economic imperialism, and the newspaper press.[1] Others replaced the first by "international anarchy," the second by the armaments race, and the last by the upsurge of public opinion that thwarted the efforts of decision-makers to come to reasonable compromises and agreements.[2] Except for nationalism and the relatively new phenomenon of a public opinion whipped up by the expansion of the press into a mass medium inspired by nationalist sentiments, these "causes" may better be regarded as descriptions of international behavior patterns in a world of national sovereign states that knew no law but their own vital interests in security and well-being—a characteristic of international relations which those of the first postwar decade hoped was ended but which is still with us. Rather than seek underlying causes, we must look for the development of a situation that by 1914 made war the outcome of the July crisis after four previous crises in a single decade had been solved by peaceable means. Before beginning the story of the developments that led to war, however, we need to look at the character of European diplomacy in the period and sketch the outlines of international relations before 1902.

1. Fay, *Origins* (1929 ed.), I, 32–49. Full citations for each reference will be found either in the Bibliographical Essay or in the note in which the reference first appears.

2. For a handy collection of differing interpretations, see *The Outbreak of the First World War: Who or What Was Responsible?*, ed. Dwight E. Lee (3rd ed. Lexington, Mass., 1970). A recent essay is that of Joachim Remak, "1914—The Third Balkan War: Origins Reconsidered," *JMH*, XLIII (1971), 353–66; and a groundbreaking reply by Paul W. Schroeder, "World War I as Galloping Gertie: A Reply to Joachim Remak," *JMH*, XLIV (1972), 319–45. Arno J. Mayer, "Domestic Causes of the First World War," *Responsibility of Power* (eds. Leonard Krieger and Fritz Stern. Garden City, N.Y., 1967), pp. 286–300, calls attention to a neglected aspect.

1. *Théophile Delcassé and Wife (The Bettmann Archive)*

II.

Europe in 1900 was much closer in customs and outlook to 1850 than to 1950. Although changes had begun to appear which presaged a slowly mounting revolution in all phases of life, diplomacy retained the pattern of the nineteenth century. The diplomat, whether in foreign office or embassy, still worked within a framework of gentlemanly—aristocratic—methods and habits. Even if he was more conscious of economic factors in the burgeoning industrialism of the time than his predecessors of 100 or even 50 years before, his sovereign or chief executive still played an important role, and in Austria-Hungary and Russia a decisive one. Ceremonial and protocol still remained highly important when monarchical exchanges might foster or hinder negotiations or friendly relationships and when toasts at state banquets revealed the actual or hoped-for attitudes of one country toward another. There were signs, however, that bankers and big businessmen were intruding upon the inner sanctum of diplomatic activity, as was the journalist, who was becoming more influential in the shaping of public opinion.

As for international politics, Europe, which had reached its apogee as the economic, cultural, and political center of the world, must be defined as the six so-called "great powers"—Great Britain, France, Germany, Russia, Austria-Hungary, and Italy. Outside these countries, Japan in the Far East since 1895 and the United States in the West since 1898 were rising to the status of great powers but played only tangential roles in Europe's affairs. The other European nations either did not count in international politics or were drawn into them by reason of their helplessness, as was the case with the Ottoman empire and the rising Balkan states, or their special interests, such as Spain's in the Moroccan question.

The diplomacy of the 1890's, "the diplomacy of imperialism," had settled many international problems but had left unsolved others that were to form the *res gestae* of the crucial years after 1902. In Africa the boundaries between British and German colonies had been drawn, and the colonies of Belgium, Spain, and Portugal firmly rooted. Moreover, Egypt and the Sudan after the Fashoda crisis of 1898 were clearly marked out for British domination even though a final Anglo-French agreement was still to come. Tripoli and Morocco were still to be appropriated and the latter was to become the subject of the first major international crisis of the twentieth century. Signs had already appeared by 1901 that it was ripe for a European imperialist showdown.

In the Near and Middle East, the Armenian massacres of 1894–1895 and the Greco-Turkish War of 1897, triggered by the Cretan insurrection of 1896, had tested the venerable Concert of Europe and found it totally lacking in the Armenian question and inharmonious but still partially functioning in the Greco-Turkish imbroglio. Russia and Austria-Hungary had put the Balkan problems on ice in 1897, but the insurrectionary activities of the Internal Macedonian Revolutionary Organization (IMRO), the always latent rivalries of Italy and Austria-Hungary over the Balkans, and the eventual falling-out of Russia and Austria were to create serious international concerns and sometimes crises, not the least of which was that of 1914. Farther afield the economic and political ambitions of Germany, especially its projected Bagdad Railway, and the rivalries of Russia and England in revolution-ridden Persia created problems that led to irritating rivalries in the one case and compromise in the other.

With the Sino-Japanese war of 1894–1895 the Far East had become the most important area of great-power rivalries, but by the turn of the century, when the Boxer Insurrection evoked an impressive show of European and American concert, the spheres of influence of France, Britain, and Germany had been clearly laid out behind the false façade of the Open Door. Though Russia's claim to a sphere in Manchuria had been tacitly or openly acknowledged by Germany and France, the obvious rivalry there and in Korea of Russia and Japan was still to be settled by the triumph of the latter in the Russo-Japanese War.

The imperialistic rivalries over the unclaimed or dubiously claimed backward parts of the earth were played out within a framework of European alliances and alignments that had arisen and continued to exist basically because of European problems of security, hence of power, by virtue not only of empire but even more of military and naval capacity. Moreover, these alignments reflected purely European points of conflict, such as Alsace-Lorraine between France and Germany, the Balkans between Austria-Hungary and Russia, and the Straits of the Bosphorus and Dardanelles between Great Britain and Russia. Between 1891 and 1900 the Triple Alliance of Germany, Austria-Hungary, and Italy opposed the Dual Alliance of France and Russia, although the lines between any two members of the opposing groups were not inflexible, and interpenetration occurred. Great Britain, faithful to a long tradition especially dear to Lord Salisbury, prime minister 1895–1902, stood aloof from formal alliance commitments in "splendid isolation" but more often than not found herself cooperating with one or another of the Triplice. Shifts in the national policies of the members and in the structure of these groupings and a change in the postures of Italy, France, and Great Britain after the opening of the twentieth century constitute the most significant turn in international politics on the eve of the crucial years that ended with war in 1914.

For the revolution in international relations major responsibility must be assigned to Théophile Delcassé, French foreign minister. A Gambetta man who had come up through the familiar road of law, journalism, and politics, Delcassé became foreign minister in June 1898, to outlive five ministries and stay in office for seven years— a record in the Third Republic. A Southerner, a perfect gentleman who treated friends and adversaries alike with courtesy, Delcassé was astute, vigorous, and hard-working, though not highly imaginative nor colorful either in his correspondence or in his oratory. His greatest weakness was perhaps his vanity, which sometimes warped his judgment, and his greatest strength lay in his persistence and determination. Ambassadors and fellow ministers alike found him hard to deal with because of his penchant for secrecy. He did not lie, writes Joseph Caillaux, "but he deceived by his silences, and he also deceived by a flow of words behind which he concealed his patiently thought-through plans." Sir Edmund Monson, British ambassador in Paris, wrote in November 1900: "He always urges that he is not a diplomatist by profession, but he carries subterfuge to an extent which I have hardly ever met before in a Minister of Foreign Affairs."[3] Yet he inspired great loyalty, amounting almost to hero worship, among his staff, while he failed to win the confidence of many parliamentarians, and, excepting for Premier Waldeck-Rousseau (1899–1902) and President Loubet, had little to do with his colleagues in the ministries of which he was a member.

When Delcassé became foreign minister, he had already become a convinced expansionist whose attitude toward other powers was largely determined by his "preoccupation with France's future as a Mediterranean power."[4] He dreamed of a greater France across that sea, with an African hinterland southward to the Congo. In this vision

3. Joseph Caillaux, *Mes mémoires*, I 153; Monson to Lansdowne: Lord Newton, *Lansdowne*, p. 209.

4. Christopher Andrew, *Delcassé*, pp. 86–87.

he had the support of a colonial group in France who were already casting their eyes on Morocco as part of the French metropolis of the future. To achieve his goal he proposed to carry further the rapprochement already begun with Italy, if possible loosening her ties with the Triple Alliance, and to establish friendship with Spain. Beyond that he at first envisaged the cooperation of Germany in challenging Great Britain in Egypt and in winning Morocco. But when he and M. N. Muraviev, Russian foreign minister, sought the support of Germany for an intervention in the Boer war, and the ousting of Britain from Egypt (1900), he learned that the German price was a guarantee of the status quo in the European possessions of the three powers. No Frenchman, least of all Delcassé, could agree to reaffirm in this way the Treaty of Frankfurt. This episode marked a significant turn in Delcassé's thinking, for there is no evidence in the French documents that he ever again considered a rapprochement with Germany, believing that the sacrifice of Alsace-Lorraine would always be a condition of an accord with her. Though he professed to be pro-British when he took office, the French diplomatic defeat in the Fashoda crisis and his conviction that Great Britain would oppose his ambitions in Morocco kept him aloof from her until he was convinced that a barter of Morocco for Egypt was feasible.

Delcassé's first major move, however, after settling the Fashoda affair, was to tighten the Franco-Russian alliance, which to him was a cornerstone of French foreign policy. On his trip to St. Petersburg in August 1899 he and Muraviev agreed to extend the time limit of the alliance indefinitely in order to take advantage of a possible break-up of the Austro-Hungarian empire. The reshaping of the alliance, continued through military conferences and Delcassé's second visit to St. Petersburg in April 1901, was intended not to assure the return of Alsace-Lorraine to France but to guard against a German expansion to the Adriatic if the Dual Monarchy broke up, and to prevent a Russo-German agreement. Delcassé's further pursuit of his program with reference to Italy, Spain, England, and Morocco constituted a more revolutionary turn of events than the tightening of ties with Russia and will be dealt with in the following chapters.

Despite Delcassé's success with his ally, Russia's policy and conditions far from guaranteed her loyalty or usefulness to France throughout his term of office. The trouble with Russia, as either ally or foe, was her instability of policy; her government has been characterized as "organized anarchy." The tsar remained autocrat of all the Russias, and when he was a Nicholas II, decision-making lay in the hands of the most artful persuader. Nicholas II was not a simple man, but he was as slow-witted as he was well-meaning. He had an untrained mind, lacking in clear and precise grasp, coupled with a strong emotional loyalty to tradition and especially to his father, Alexander III. Thus he supported the Dual Alliance but at the same time, in matters not touching his position or his family, could be swayed by vigorous and persuasive personalities like Emperor William II, by such schemers as Bezobrazov, and by such imposters as the mesmerist Philip or the later "Holy man" Grigori Rasputin. Moreover, the tsar was capable of strong likes and dislikes, neither of which, as in the case of Sergei Witte, whom he came to hate or V. A. Sukhomlinov, war minister, who amused him, was based upon sound judgment or worth or objective recognition of inability or rascality. Since the ultimate political decisions thus lay in the hands of a man who lacked clarity of perception and firmness of will, both domestic and foreign policy tended either to reflect the dominant personality or group of the moment or to stumble along in familiar grooves.

At the turn of the century, Sergei Witte was the strong man whose activities impinged upon almost every area of governmental activity. In foreign relations Count Vladimir N. Lamsdorff, foreign minister upon the death of Muraviev in August 1900, counted for little in the diplomacy of Russia except as an honest, modest, hard-working, but mediocre public servant. He had been a loyal disciple of N. K. von Giers, who had pursued a Germanophile policy in the 1880's and like his former master was credited with a predilection for cooperation with Germany and Austria-Hungary rather than France. However that may be, he reflected the tsar's desire for peace and for the maintainance of the traditional Russian interest in the Balkans, two reasons perhaps why Nicholas II kept him in office despite the coolness toward him of the Dowager Empress Marie, who often influenced the likes and dislikes of her son.

In summary, not only had the Dual Alliance been held together but its character had been modified by the 1899 agreement and the subsequent military and diplomatic exchanges. The reason lay in both the persistence of France and the financial need of Russia. But the tsar and his foreign office remained on friendly terms with both Germany and Austria and were following a course in the Far East that was progressively to weaken Russia's position in Europe.

In the Triple Alliance, Germany was still, as in Bismarck's day, the dominant power, but internally and externally it was rapidly becoming quite a different Germany from the Reich that Bismarck had founded. By the end of the nineteenth century Germany was entering upon its greatest industrial and commercial growth, despite a recession for a couple of years in 1900 and 1901. The consequent strains upon the political and economic structure created domestic and foreign policy problems: the traditional agrarian, Prussian, military, and economic interest faced an industrial, commercial, naval challenge which industrial finance and developing technology presented. What would be the outcome? Inevitably Germany was expanding into world markets and the adjustment that had to be made would determine whether German foreign policy would retain the limited objectives of Bismarck or emerge into *Weltpolitik*. The conflict in domestic politics between the agrarians and the industrialists was in the process of solution by the turn of the century. By log-rolling tactics a policy of protection to satisfy the big land-holders who resented American and Russian competition, and naval expansion and *Weltpolitik*, supported by big banks, industry, and trade, united the traditional and the new in a coalition that dominated German policies. The inevitable repercussions upon Germany's foreign relations were not foreseen by political leaders nor by the responsible heads of State, Emperor William II and Chancellor Bernhard von Bülow.

Many students of German and world affairs at the opening of the twentieth century have blamed the kaiser for the unhealthy internal political developments and the dangerous foreign policy pursued. That by temperament and outlook he was ill-suited for the formulation and pursuit of a wise policy there can be no doubt. His shortcomings were obvious. He was a sensitive, insecure, and nervous man who sought in the greatness and power of Germany the satisfaction of his own love of glory. He could be charming, amiable, and cordial, but at the same time his dislike of slow, stiff, or very serious people warped his judgment of men and left him open to the Byzantinism that too often distorted his outlook and encouraged him in the sudden inspirations that more often than not led to complications in domestic or foreign politics. To an extent, he embodied in his own intellectual make-up the dilemma that Germany was facing: a feudalistic romanticism and a keen interest in the modern ideas that science and technology presented. Thus he scorned the constitution and parliament and yearned with great physical and mental vigor for power. Though more and more surrounded by military men, who encouraged him to look down upon the foreign office as muddle-headed, he espoused the navy from the start. He cannot be held responsible for German policy, and his marginal comments on foreign office correspondence should not be taken too seriously, but unfortunately his chancellors lacked the firmness of a Bismarck, with the result that his impetuosity and his penchants, especially for the navy, helped to direct Germany's course.

Count Bernhard von Bülow, foreign secretary 1897–1900 and chancellor, October 1900 to July 1909, was certainly not the man to deal with either the political tensions or the Emperor in a statesman-like way. He was basically a courtier and diplomat, suave, polished, and agreeable; though astute, he lacked the seriousness of purpose and firmness of method that the times required. While there can be no doubt of the Emperor's earnest loyalty to Germany, Bülow seemed loyal only to his own pride and ambition; "he clung to his career," said Philip Eulenburg, courtier and diplomat, "with every fibre of his being."[5] Scion of a Prussian noble family and thus heir of the aristocratic and military tradition, which he greatly admired, his classical education, his early experiences in Paris, his fondness for Italy and his marriage to an Italian countess all gave him an air of cosmopolitanism that helped to create the impression, especially upon foreign statesmen, that he had a profound knowledge of world problems. Yet his oratory and even his memoirs give the impression of showiness and superficiality. Aristocratic and snobbish in his tastes, a lover of jests and prurient gossip, he belonged to the new age as well as the old and owed his position in part to his willingness to go along with *Weltpolitik* and a big navy.

Bülow professed in his memoirs that he was determined to keep Germany out of war: "to provoke no one, but, at the same time, allow no one to tread on our feet."[6] Such a policy was easy to pursue under the conditions existing when he became foreign secretary in 1897, but by the time he became chancellor in 1900, when fundamental changes were occurring in the power relationships of the Continent and when unity of purpose had not yet been quite established at home, Bülow's formula was inadequate. He perforce embraced imperialism; he conceded tariff reform to the agrarians; he backed the exploitation of Asiatic Turkey already begun with the Bagdad Railway and other concessions, and the development of a first-class navy. Agrarian protection and the expansion of German interests in the Near East were bound to alienate Russia, whom he and the Emperor wanted to win back to close friendship, if not

5. Johannes Haller, *Eulenberg*, II, 306.
6. Bernhard von Bülow, *Memoirs*, I, 30.

alliance; and the naval policy was imcompatible with good British relations. Bülow never seemed to recognize the implications of the policy forced upon him by his domestic situation and his own predilections, but sought to stave off the consequences by diplomacy which too often took the form of huckstering.

In foreign relations Bülow was strongly influenced, at least down to 1906, by the "specter" or, as some said, the "weasel" of the Foreign Office, Baron Friedrich von Holstein. Even his friends, and he seems to have had very few, could not deny his egotistical and neurotic temperament, his unbalanced and morbidly suspicious nature. This lonely, secretive, but industrious official thought himself the repository of the old, the true Bismarckian, traditions. He wanted power, too, but not pomp, hence preferred to work behind the scenes, jealous of anyone who appeared to be opposed to him and unscrupulous and tortuous in his methods of ridding himself of fancied or genuine opponents. In the older tradition he tended to favor the army and therefore had little sympathy with the naval policy and its consequent estrangement of Britain. Bülow professed to "love that tragic nature of his."[7] He undoubtedly deferred to Holstein's judgment on many crucial questions and came to a complete understanding with him before acting on important matters. Whether from fear of Holstein's unscrupulousness or from genuine respect, Bülow's boast that he could get rid of Holstein in three months was never carried out, and it was only when Bülow was temporarily incapacitated by illness that Holstein finally left his post. Meanwhile, although Holstein was shrewd and highly intelligent, he misjudged the course that international politics was taking after 1901 and thus confounded rather than clarified Germany's proper course.

In the pursuit of world status, rather than the continental role of Bismarck's aim, political circumstances and personalities combined to shape the course of events. The combination of industrialists and agrarians created by clever political manipulation gave the government a big majority for Alfred von Tirpitz's second naval bill of 1900 and for the log-rolling counterpart, the tariff law of 1902 which Bülow introduced toward the end of 1900. Without seeming to note the implications of these measures, Bülow and the emperor followed a course that no longer fitted conditions. They sought to retain Russian friendship and if possible to stultify the Franco-Russian alliance by personal influence over the tsar and support of Russia's Far East-

7. Haller, *Eulenberg*, I, 324.

ern policy. While they refused to ally with England, they felt confident that England could never make friends with France or Russia, hence must ever be dependent upon Germany. They flirted with France when the Boer war (1899–1902) generally alienated Europeans as well as Americans from sympathy with Britain, but their basic policy was still that of Triple Alliance solidarity, even though Bülow professed in January 1902 that it was no longer an absolute necessity. It was, he explained, of greatest importance as a guarantee of peace and of the status quo, a tie between states which by their geographical situation and traditions had to live in *bon voisinage*.[8]

Austria-Hungary shared fully Germany's attitude toward the Triplice. At the turn of the century and for some years, Austria-Hungary had to pursue a peaceful and conservative foreign policy because of internal dissension, especially the clamor of the national minorities, and even the discontent of the Magyars at what seemed to them to be an unequal position in the Dual Monarchy. Under the circumstances outsiders and even Germans talked freely of the imminent dissolution of the Habsburg empire. While the government weathered the storm for the time being, it was in no position to undertake a vigorous and adventurous policy. Moreover, a conservative policy suited both the Emperor and his foreign minister. Like the tsar in Russia, Emperor Francis Joseph was the ultimate arbiter of foreign policy. Unlike either the tsar or the German kaiser, he was a methodical, orderly, and serious-minded monarch. He shared with them a high sense of honor and responsibility, but again was probably more concerned to keep the peace than either of them. He allowed his foreign ministers greater latitude in his declining years than he had earlier, but still insisted that they follow his directions. Indeed, since the foreign minister was his own choice, he was a man likely to reflect the purposes of his master.

Count Agenor Goluchowski, minister for foreign affairs from 1895 to October 1906, had not distinguished himself before his appointment by Francis Joseph. His lack of ambition led to the criticism that he was "lazy and superficial," but the German Foreign Office, except for Holstein, who hated him because of a social slight many years before, valued him as a "well-tried friend." Aside from their loyalty to the Dual Alliance with Germany, Francis Joseph and Goluchowski had fairly clearly defined negative policies: they would not allow any other power to occupy Albania and thus close the Adriatic;

8. *Fürst Bülows Reden*, ed. Johannes Penzler (3 vols. Berlin, 1907–1909), I, 245.

they would not permit the union of Serbia and Montenegro; they would oppose a Russian occupation of Constantinople, and Russian domination of the Balkans. This list testifies to their almost exclusive concern with the Balkans, where they had sought to maintain the status quo by agreements with Russia in 1897 and subsequently with Italy. They counted heavily upon maintaining friendly relations with Russia and would have preferred a league of the three emperors to the Triplice.

The Italian member of the Triple Alliance was going through as great an internal transformation as Germany and was reassessing its position in the alliance at the turn of the century. In particular, the resurgence of irredentism and the ambition, always latent, to play a role in the western Balkans and the Adriatic was building up grounds of irritation and even of tension with Austria-Hungary. Italy's "extra waltz" with France, as Bülow was to put it, is part of the story of the diplomatic revolution of 1902–1907. It is perhaps one reason why Francis Joseph of Austria placed greater value upon the Dual Alliance with Germany than upon the Triplice.[9]

III.

From this world of alliances and alignments Great Britain alone stood aloof among the great powers of Europe. Her domestic policy was relatively calm in the declining years of Queen Victoria, but the Boer War, October 1899 to May 1902, with its unexpected setbacks and difficulties, rocked the country and gave occasion for the expression of shrill condemnation of Britain in the continental press, especially that of Germany. Another noteworthy feature of the opening years of the twentieth century was the shift in governmental personnel. King Edward VII succeeded his mother on the throne in January 1901. Lord Salisbury relinquished the Foreign Office to Lord Lansdowne in November 1900, and the premiership to Arthur James Balfour in July 1902. Although King Edward took a more active part in the ceremonial functions of official entertainment and visits abroad and Lord Lansdowne was a much younger and more flexible man than Salisbury, events rather than personalities accounted for the slow and almost imperceptible change in British foreign policy from "splendid isolation" to entente and even, in the case of Japan, alliance.

9. For a fuller treatment of Italy, see chapter 2, below.

Lord Salisbury's emphasis upon "splendid isolation" had, in considerable measure, been based upon British public opinion, which made binding alliances impossible but did not preclude ententes. He had indeed on more than one occasion, and notably in 1887, secretly cooperated with European powers, most frequently with the Triplice. But after the fall of Bismarck, Germany's policy seemed unreliable; the formation and consolidation of the Franco-Russian alliance deepened the danger to British interests in the Far East and India; and the reactions to the Boer War underlined a danger, always present from 1894 and never closer than at the opening of the new century, for, as Sir Edward Grey later told the Committee of Imperial Defense, Great Britain might have to measure her sea power not against one or two powers but five. When the overtures to Russia in 1898 and the talks with Germany between 1899 and the end of 1901 failed to bring about collaboration with at least one European power as a firm continental friend, Britain turned to Japan. The policy pursued was undoubtedly "haphazard and without sufficient direction. . . . In a world dominated by alliances no such plan [as good relations with all] was feasible. The alternative, when once the basis was gone of the old cooperation with the Triple Alliance, was worked out piecemeal with little evidence of a general design."[10]

By the Anglo-Japanese Alliance of 30 January 1902, the two powers recognized the independence of China and Korea, but at the same time the special interests of each party—Britain in China and Japan in Korea—which it was permissible to defend against the aggressive action of any other power. If either power became involved with a third, the other would observe strict neutrality; but if any additional power or powers should join against one ally, the other would make war in common with its ally. Such a commitment was an innovation in British diplomacy and was recognized as such in the parliamentary debates upon its ratification.[11] Yet the advantages to Britain of an ally in the Far East, particularly a naval power, were obvious even though there was a good deal of grumbling in Britain that the burdens of the alliance were unequal. The revolution in British policy, however, did not so much concern the substance of its position as the method of achieving its goals, for Britain had tied her hands in the Japanese alliance with respect to a possible future contingency in a way that

10. Lillian Penson, "The New Course in British Foreign Policy," *Transactions of the Royal Historical Society*, 4th series, XXV (1943), 138.

11. For a recent cogent assessment of the significance of the Anglo-Japanese alliance, see C. J. Lowe, *The Reluctant Imperialists* (London, 1967), pp. 248–51.

Lord Salisbury had once declared she would never do. Moreover, the unforeseen significance of the alliance lay in its making the more imperative an entente with France if Britain were to safeguard herself from involvement with the Franco-Russian alliance, and in enabling Japan to fight Russia without interference.

The sharpest European reaction to the Anglo-Russian alliance came from France and Russia, who together issued a declaration, 20 March 1902, in which they, too, affirmed their interest in the integrity and independence of China, and asserted that if the actions of a third power or new troubles in China menaced their own proper interests there, they would counsel together as to the means of protecting them. Nevertheless, Delcassé made it clear a little later that he had no intention of extending the Franco-Russian alliance to the Far East, and as his subsequent negotiations with England and his attitude throughout the Russo-Japanese war showed, he was axious indeed to avoid any entanglements there. Germany was outwardly reserved but her cordial relations with Russia throughout 1902 could only have the same effect as the French cooperation in the declaration of March: to encourage Russia in the course that was to lead to the Russo-Japanese war.

In the background of the diplomatic revolution of 1902–1907 one additional factor loomed large: the widespread, constant, and sometimes virulent ill-feeling between Germany and England expressed especially in the press war of 1900–1901. Although this manifestation of public opinion was probably not a decisive influence on the policy formulation of either government, it undoubtedly "figured in the calculations of both British and German leaders," setting "limits to their mobility in negotiations.[12]

In Germany, beneath the surface of the strong anti-English agitation lay the drive for world power that was to have momentous consequences and that found its first significant expression in the naval bill of 1898. Admiral Tirpitz capitalized upon the longing for a "place in the sun" to establish a fleet that would give "Germany a measure of naval power against Great Britain," for, as Hans Delbrück later put it, the German navy was intended to change the power relationships of the world to the advantage of Germany by the elimination of British maritime supremacy. Tirpitz carefully concealed his ultimate objective in 1898, appealing to national and party sentiments,

12. Oron J. Hale, *Publicity and Diplomacy*, p. 189.

but openly proclaimed it in 1900.[13] By that time the outbreak and conduct of the Boer war had provided additional reasons for German indignation over Britain's imperial rule.

On the English side, the press war arose in part over the growing fear of the German industrial and commercial competition that became apparent in the years around 1900 when German industrial production and cartellization presented a challenge to British markets and transportation. The chorus of anti-German feeling, however, was not widespread and was characterized by the shrill tones of a few newspapers and periodicals. Resentment at the pro-Boer attitude of Germany, unlike the reaction to similar sentiments in other lands, lasted longer and left an indelible impression. By 1901, moreover, a few raucous voices, especially of *The Times* and the *National Review*, began to raise warning cries about the German naval program, which had passed almost unnoticed until then.

As far as the public in both England and Germany is concerned the high point of recrimination came with the Chamberlain-Bülow exchange. In a speech at Edinburgh, October 1901, Joseph Chamberlain, the colonial secretary, sought to defend Britain against the charges of cruelty in her treatment of the Boers and especially her use of concentration camps by alleging that she was no worse than others, and specifically mentioned German army behavior in the Franco-Prussian war. Bülow, in a Reichstag speech on 8 January 1902, retorted by what was, in effect, a personal attack upon Chamberlain and thus aroused other violent attacks by such men as Max Liebermann, a Pan-German member of the Reichstag. The whole affair was an unusually shocking example of vituperation in an age which as yet had not reached the refinements of international mudslinging which were developed by the mid-twentieth century. Bülow's advisers had in vain sought to dissuade him from his attack, but had greater success in moderating the tone of the press afterward. The British drew the conclusion from the affair that Germany was the enemy, as Sir Cecil Spring-Rice noted when he visited London a few weeks after the Bülow speech.[14]

Evidence of deep-seated resentment and mistrust continued to pile

13. On Delbrück and Tirpitz's aims: Ludwig Dehio, *Germany and World Politics in the Twentieth Century*, p. 79; Volker R. Berghahn, *Der Tirpitz-Plan*, Part I. For the domestic background and the significance of the fleet: J. C. G. Röhl, *Germany without Bismarck*, pp. 251–58; Jonathan Steinberg, *Yesterday's Deterrent*, ch. I.

14. Julian Amery, *Life of Joseph Chamberlain*, IV, 175–76.

up throughout 1902. After the signature on 31 May 1902 of the peace treaty that ended the Boer War, both the British and the German governments wished that the press warfare would cease, as it did in France and other countries. But a few publications in both England and Germany continued to snipe at each other and the debates in Germany over the tariff bill, the plans of Emperor William to receive the Boer generals touring Europe in the autumn (which had to be canceled), and the Venezuela intervention raised the excitement of the press to fever pitch once more.

The Venezuela affair illustrated the emotional and nonrational aspect of the Anglo-German press feud. The Venezuelan government had rejected arbitration of claims by Britain, Germany, and Italy arising out of damages incurred in the civil war of 1898–1902. From late 1901 the German government undertook negotiations by which it obtained the acquiescence of the United States in a show of force, if it refrained from any territorial acquisitions, and the agreement of the British government to a naval demonstration which eventually took the form of a blockade of Venezuelan ports from late December 1902 until mid-February 1903, when arbitration proceedings at the Hague got under way. Although the government acted in a spirit of cooperation and Germany especially leaned over backward to avoid the slightest appearance of any independent line of action, the press in both countries condemned any form of joint action. At first moderate, the German press reacted vigorously, especially after the United States joined in the press attack. Before the public clamor some British ministers tried to minimize the extent of cooperation, but Lansdowne publicly defended the policy and afterward German behavior as well. On the German side Count Paul von Wolff Metternich, ambassador in London, concluded that the best policy to pursue was to sit quietly and wait until the bitterness that had been aroused in wide circles of the English people faded away.

In the long run, the Anglo-German press wars at the turn of the century were of greater significance than the failure of Anglo-German alliance negotiations or the creation of the Anglo-Japanese alliance. Britain certainly had no more, probably fewer, points of conflict in the world with Germany than with France or Russia. Yet it made friends with them and failed to do so with Germany. The stereotypes that emerged at the turn of the century in the minds of public and statesmen were a very important factor—probably more important than economic competition—in preventing the continuation or the resumption of cordial relations. To the Germans, Great Britain was henceforth a grasping imperialist power, jealous of Germany's rightful place in the world; to the British, Germany was an aggressive, ill-mannered nation whose dearest desire was ruthlessly to climb to the top, crushing all opponents, if need be, on the way. It is true that moderate elements on both sides did not share these views and sought to combat them, but in moments of crisis they came to the fore, limiting if not directing the policies which the statesmen pursued. The short-run effect was to help produce the conviction in the minds of such Englishmen as Chamberlain and Lansdowne that Great Britain should not only abandon the policy of isolation, which the latter told the House of Lords in February 1902 was a thing of the past, but also look elsewhere than Germany for friends. They turned first to France. But the gaze of France, in 1902, was fixed upon Italy.

Chapter 2

Italy's "Extra Dance," 1902

In the struggle between France and Germany over Italy, the principal protagonists were Foreign Minister Théophile Delcassé and Ambassador Camille Barrère for the French, and Chancellor Count Bernhard von Bülow and his ambassadors, Count Karl Wedel and Count Anton Monts, for the Germans. Minor roles were played by British Secretary for Foreign Affairs Lord Lansdowne, and the Russian ambassador in Rome, Alexander Ivanovich Nelidov, by Count Agenor Goluchowski, Austro-Hungarian foreign minister, and his ambassador in Rome, Marius Baron von Friedenburg Pasetti. Italian Foreign Minister Marquis Visconti Venosta had prepared the ground for an Italo-French rapprochement and Giulio Prinetti, foreign minister in Premier Giuseppi Zanardelli's government, followed in his footsteps. He was later replaced by Tommaso Tittoni in Premier Giovanni Giolitti's ministry. Luigi Luzzatti, a financier and one-time minister, aided Barrère. Italy's ambassadors were Count Tornielli-Brusati di Vergano in Paris and Carlo Count Lanza in Berlin.

Next in importance to the consummation of the Entente Cordiale was Italy's modification of its diplomatic orientation, and it came first. From a "Triplice-true" power, Italy in the period of 1896 to 1902 became a power with a foot in both alliance camps, thus constituting an uncertain element in the calculations of the great powers. But the process of change began long before its culmination in 1902, and to a certain extent was based upon internal as well as external conditions.

I.

Italy's external relations in the 1890's began slowly to drift from hostility toward friendship with France. Economic interests, both commercial and financial, in part at least, helped to bring about the change, although it is an exaggeration to say that they alone accounted for it. In 1887, after the tariff war began between Italy and France and especially after 1891 when the Paris bourse was closed to Italian bonds, Germany had mainly supplied Italy with her needed capital and had achieved a preponderant position in industrial and commercial investments. After 1896, however, the Italian government under the leadership of such men as the Marquis di Rudini and Luigi Luzzatti turned to French banking circles, which had already begun quietly to buy up Italian securities. Also a series of steps occurred in the diplomatic field which paralleled the return of French influence in the private and public finances of Italy. The first move was the agreement over Tunis at the end of September 1896 by which Italy, in effect, recognized France's position there. Next, in November 1898, Luzzatti completed negotiations for a commercial treaty with France that ended the long tariff war and greatly increased Italian trade.

Following these events and the simultaneous drying up of German funds because of shortages at home, Paris regained its former predominant position as the banker of Italy. By May 1902 France was holding nearly 29 millions of Italian public securities to Germany's 10.39 millions. Thus Italy had to a certain extent become dependent upon the French market, although her own prosperity was reducing her dependence upon any outside financial support. There was some truth, however, in the remark of an Italian deputy that France did not have to make concessions to Italy in order to win her friendship, for she could drive Italy to economic ruin.[1]

The problem that Italy faced from the late 1890's, therefore, was how to improve diplomatic relations with France without antagonizing Germany and without estranging Great Britain, Italy's traditional friend but also potentially one of her most dangerous enemies. The Marquis Visconti Venosta, who was foreign minister for nearly two years, 1899 to February 1901, established the lines along which Italian policy was to operate for many years: maintenance of the Triple Alliance but agreements with other powers in order to reinsure Italy's special interests. The first fruit of this policy was the agreement of 14–16 December 1900, by which France declared her disinterestedness in Tripoli and Italy recognized the interests of France in Morocco

1. René Pinon, *L'Empire de la Méditerrané*, p. 49. Cf. Vittorio Raca, "L'Italie," *Le marché financier*, 1902–03 (Paris, 1903), p. 832; Jacob Viner, "International finance," *International Economics*, p. 63.

arising from "the proximity of her territory with that empire." If France should modify the political or territorial status of Morocco, Italy reserved the right "eventually to develop her influence with regard to Tripolitania-Cyrenaica."[2] The significance of this agreement lay not only in the seal it set upon the rapprochement of France and Italy, but also in the effect upon Italy's position in the Triple Alliance. Whereas up to this time Italy had relied upon the support of Germany to counter any expansion of France in North Africa, now, by coming to terms with France, Italy could dispense with German help, or at most regard it only as a reinsurance should friendship with France prove to be illusory. In other words, Italy by her own action had removed the necessity for Article IX of the Triple Alliance treaty, which had been included at Italy's own insistence in 1887.[3] Italy's allies, who had not been informed of the agreement of 1900 until a year later, tended to see it as directed against England, and well it might have proved to be had not Britain and Italy, and later Britain and France, drawn together.

Meanwhile, Italy's economic progress and her growing social and political stability tended to weaken the importance of the Triple Alliance in Italian eyes. Moreover, the alliance had been of no help whatever in Italy's dark days of the Adua disaster, 1896. Even more important was the re-emergence of irredentism by 1900 and the growing tension between Italy and Austria-Hungary over the Balkans, especially Albania and Montenegro. Visconti Venosta in the parliamentary debates of December 1900 asserted that Italy and Austria-Hungary had discussed their interests and had decided that their best protection lay in the maintenance of the status quo in Albania. He was referring to the verbal Monza agreement of 1897 that he then proceeded to put into writing by an exchange of letters with Count Goluchowski of Austria-Hungary in December 1900 and February 1901. If the existing state of affairs could not be preserved, the two countries were to attempt to see that modifications took the direction of autonomy, and in general they were to seek in common "the most appropriate ways and means to reconcile and to safeguard" their reciprocal interests.[4] Nevertheless popular agitation and Italian ef-

2. The texts in Alfred Francis Pribram, *Secret Treaties*, II, 240–45. The letters were signed on 4 January 1901, but predated.

3. By Article IX Germany and Italy were to maintain the status quo in North Africa, and if Italy were compelled to take action there, Germany had to support her: Pribram, *Secret Treaties*, I, 156–57.

4. Ibid., I, 196–201, and II, 114–15.

forts to develop economic and cultural ties with Albania and Montenegro kept the sense of conflict alive.

The Italo-Austrian conflicts of interest were a source of worry to Germany, to whom both powers turned in times of acute strain. Germany could do little, however, except to mediate as best she could, usually with some success because both partners in the Triplice recognized that in the last analysis they had to maintain the alliance as the only alternative to outright conflict. As for the Franco-Italian rapprochement, Bülow made light of it. Nevertheless, the question of the renewal of the Triple Alliance, which was discussed throughout 1901 and the first six months of 1902, became particularly significant because of the change in the Italian government and the strenuous efforts of France to prevent or to modify the character of Italy's relation to it.

II.

King Victor Emmanuel III was not fully trusted by his allies. The assassination of his father, King Humbert, in 1900 was regarded as a severe blow to the Triplice because the young king was thought to be under the influence of his wife, daughter of Prince Nicholas of Montenegro, and known to have Slavic leanings. The king, however, was too intelligent and too clever to embark upon a radical shift in foreign policy. He undoubtedly shared the ambition of many Italian leaders to achieve a more independent position within the Triple Alliance and to prepare Italy for a more active policy in the Eastern Mediterranean. Above all he intended to make a personal imprint upon Italian foreign policy, as he told William II, and gave special attention both to the policy pursued by his foreign minister and to affairs abroad on which he received reports from his own agents. His choice of a new head of the government after the cabinet crisis of February 1901 seemed at the time to reflect his intention to move away from the Triple Alliance toward closer ties with France.

Instead of naming Baron Sidney Sonnino, leader of the majority which had overthrown the previous government and considered to be a pro-Triplice man, the king chose Giuseppe Zanardelli to head a coalition of leftist groups and to carry out a program of badly needed internal reforms. Zanardelli was an old man who had begun his political career in the Risorgimento and was known for his aversion to Austria. While leadership in domestic policy tended to fall into the hands of his Minister of Interior, Giovanni Giolitti, who was to use his position to prepare the way for his own remarkable career as the unchallenged leader of Italian politics, foreign affairs went to Giulio Prinetti, a new man in government and without experience in diplomacy, but also a known Francophile. A businessman, head of a large bicycle factory in Milan, Prinetti was noted for his hot temper, his mordant tongue, and his "wild utterances" as well as for his great personal ambition. Though he, too, was a political conservative, he was a contrast in every other respect to his venerable predecessor, Visconti Venosta, a contrast that was the more significant not only because of Prinetti's complete lack of diplomatic experience, but also because he was the one conservative in a leftist cabinet and thus seemed the more conspicuous as the harbinger of a new alliance policy.

Actually, however, Prinetti, like the king and Zanardelli, was less concerned with a radical departure than with the achievement of Italian independence in determining her policy and in the expansion of Italian activity in the Mediterranean. Moreover, commercial and financial considerations, as well as political, provided a framework within which Prinetti had to work. The Zanardelli government placed great emphasis on continuing economic progress and was anxious to consolidate its financial position by reducing the interest rates on its foreign debts by a conversion operation. These objectives meant not only the renewal of commercial treaties with Germany and Austria-Hungary but also the continued support of France and its money market. Specifically, then, Prinetti and the Zanardelli government were committed to Visconti's phrase "independent ever, isolated never" and, in addition, to concern for Tripoli, the other shore of the Adriatic, an equal voice in the Eastern Question, advantageous trade treaties, and access to favorable money markets both for public and private investment. They took the not unreasonable position that membership in the Triple Alliance did not preclude friendships with other nations and pointed out that both Germany and Austria-Hungary had pursued a similar course, especially with reference to Russia. They also were sensitive to Italian public opinion, which in 1901 was swinging away from the Triple Alliance toward France.

Under Delcassé's direction French policy had been committed for some time to winning a solid entente if not an alliance with Italy. The Tripoli-Morocco agreement of December 1900 was but a half-way step toward the ultimate objective that Delcassé had in mind. While it provided for an Italian hands-off policy toward Morocco and thus constituted the first step toward French predominance there, it failed to achieve the other goal of weaning Italy away from the Triple Alliance. The French proposal in 1901—that in return for support of Italian rights in Tripolitania, Italy should assure France of her freedom from "all political and military obligations against her"—had been rejected by Visconti Venosta. Therefore, in 1901–1902, both Italy and France sought to fill the gaps in the 1900 agreement.

Delcassé in pursuing this goal had the dedicated collaboration in Rome of Camille Barrère, the ambassador there from 1898 to 1924. His acquaintances were divided in their opinions of him. The French thought of him as an ideal ambassador with a fine presence, a grand manner, a broad education, elegance of style, and that variety of interests in the fine arts and music that earned him the sobriquet of "prince of the Renaissance." They speak of his "firmness of character" and his "profound feeling" for the dignity of France, but to judge from his own despatches he might well be regarded as highhanded and overbearing. Prince Eulenburg, who had known Barrère at his post in Munich, called him "absolutely unscrupulous." Italians who knew him testified to his "fiery and nervous" temperament and his lack of moderation, but they also credited him with perseverance and sagacity, and recognized his ability in making his country and its policy popular in Italy.[5]

Part of Barrère's influence may be attributed to his relatively wise and moderate objectives in 1901–1902. After the formation of the Zanardelli government he took the position to which he adhered consistently: France, without contesting the right of Italy to contract engagements which she judged to be in her interests, expected Italy to make them in harmony with the amicable relations already established between the French and Italian peoples. More specifically, he insisted that if Italy renewed the Triple Alliance (and he soon learned that the king had decided to do so), she should eliminate any obligation to support German aggression against France.

In seeking this objective, Barrère attempted to bring Russian pressure to bear upon the Italian government, assuming that through the family ties of the two courts and perhaps the mediation of Prince Nicholas of Montenegro, King Victor Emmanuel might be influenced to accept the French viewpoint. Count Lamsdorff, however, doubted

<hr />

5. Jacques Chastenet, *Histoire de la troisième république*, III (Paris, 1955), 260; Léon Noël, *Camille Barrère*, p. 77; Haller, *Eulenberg*, I, 109; Enrico Serra, *Camille Barrère*, pp. 358–77.

the value of any attempt to influence Victor Emmanuel, who, he said, had a strong will and was not easily influenced. Barrère also relied upon the sympathy for France and influence upon Italian statesmen of three men: Visconti Venosta, Rudini, and Luzzatti, all three of whom had opposed an anti-French and pro-Triplice orientation and had been closely associated with the steps toward rapprochement with France. Of these, Luzzatti was his closest collaborator and was especially valuable in making known the financial stakes in Italo-French friendship. But Barrère did not confine his activities in Rome to diplomatic and political circles. He cultivated a wide array of friends and acquaintances, including even Donna Laura Minghetti, the mother-in-law of Chancellor von Bülow, and above all sought by every means, including a liberal use of funds, to enlist journalists in both Italy and France in the cause of "Latin sisterhood."

III.

In addition to French policy and the question of the Triplice the attitude of Great Britain was a factor in the Italian situation of 1901–1902. It was of secondary importance compared with the other two, but closely related to them. Italy had always been sensitive to the seapower of England, for with 80 percent of her boundaries consisting of seacoast, she could not disregard the most powerful Mediterranean fleet. From the founding of the Triple Alliance she had insisted upon good relations with England and even partnership; but she had been disappointed by the British attitude on more than one occasion, notably by the Anglo-French agreement of 1899 on boundaries in Central Africa affecting the hinterland of Tripoli-Cyrenaica. After the development of the Franco-Italian rapprochement, Italo-British coolness might lead to complications for Italy should France and England remain hostile to each other in the Mediterranean. On the other hand, Italy's allies counted upon Anglo-French enmity as essential in keeping Italy loyal to the Triplice, because they felt that Italy could not afford to antagonize her allies and Britain at the same time, and, if necessary, would choose Britain in preference to France.

From the spring of 1899, when the Anglo-French agreement on Africa was signed, until the opening weeks of 1902 Anglo-Italian relations were at a low ebb. In 1900 Britain rejected Italian requests for cooperation concerning Morocco and defense of the Italian coast.

Lansdowne explained the difficulty of arrangements with Italy if it were "true that the policy of Italy in the case of a European war" were to be "mainly determined by the advice she may receive from Germany . . ." On the other hand, Visconti Venosta was reported as saying that England treated Italy as a "quantité négligeable."[6]

In 1901, however, the British observed that Italy was consolidating her economic and political situation, and that relations between France and Italy were obviously on a firm, friendly basis. What seems to have convinced the British government that it should meet Italian wishes in a more conciliatory spirit was the announcement by Prinetti in the Italian chamber on 14 December of the French declaration of disinterestedness in Tripoli. Prinetti included in his statement the assertion that the amicable relations of the two countries had become such that they had permitted an exchange of explanations as clear as they were satisfactory on their interests in the Mediterranean. This evidence that if the British, too, professed disinterestedness in Tripoli the French would not move in removed one of the reasons for hesitancy that had existed earlier. On the other hand, uncertainty about the nature of the Italo-French agreement led the British to fear that Italy had committed herself to a French policy that would upset the status quo, and that Italian naval bases might be lost to England in case of a conflict in the Mediterranean. The coincidence of the contretemps between Bülow and Chamberlain with Prinetti's declaration and vigorous Italian complaints of British "neglect of Italy," as King Victor Emmanuel put it, emphasized the importance of mending fences in the Mediterranean basin. The first British move was the withdrawal in January 1902 of a proclamation that had angered Italy because it had placed the English and Italian languages on an equal footing in Malta but had provided for the abolition of Italian as one of the official languages by 1914. The Italian press received news of the withdrawal enthusiastically, and Prinetti felt encouraged to press for a British assurance concerning Tripoli.

Lansdowne throughout January failed to see any reason for changing the noncommittal attitude of 1899 and objected to Prinetti's desire for a declaration of disinterestedness in Tripoli, because such a declaration would conflict with the spirit of British treaty engagements with Turkey. Upon Prinetti's insistence, however, and his assurance that the other powers had given Italy a free hand in Tripoli,

6. Lord Newton, *Lansdowne*, p. 213; Serra, *L'Intesa mediterranea del 1902*, p. 29. Cf. James Linus Glanville, *Italy's Relations with England*, pp. 71–85.

Lansdowne finally approved a declaration on 7 March 1902 that met Italian wishes. The British statement, after denying any aggressive designs upon Tripoli and asserting that the British government desired the maintenance of the status quo, declared that if the status quo should be altered, any alteration "should be in conformity with Italian interests." This assurance was based upon the understanding that Italy would not enter any arrangement with other powers "of a nature inimical to British interests."[7]

From the Italian viewpoint, the British assurance and the evidence of good will toward Italy came just in time to strengthen the Italian government's hand at home, where a parliamentary crisis in early March threatened Zanardelli's position, and abroad in negotiations with Germany and Austria-Hungary. Also the accord of 1902, by virtue of its existence along with the Italo-French accords, reinforced the freedom of Italy from dependence upon the Triple Alliance. As for Great Britain, it helped to prepare the way for the Anglo-French entente over Egypt and Morocco.[8] In other words, the Anglo-Italian accord of 1902 represented a step toward a significant transition in European power alignments.

IV.

Nevertheless the renewed Anglo-Italian friendship and the understanding over Tripolitania were secondary in immediate importance to the outcome of the tug-of-war between France and the Triplice over the allegiance of Italy. The struggle had begun within a few weeks after the Zanardelli government took office in February 1901 and the first victory had gone to France.

In April an Italian naval squadron visited Toulon under the command of the Duke of Genoa in order to salute President Loubet, who was visiting southeastern France. The excuse for the visit was a return of courtesies displayed by the French fleet at Cagliostro in the previous year, but the whole affair, including a very cordial exchange of toasts between Loubet and the Duke of Genoa, had undoubtedly been very carefully written, directed, and produced by

7. Lansdowne to Currie, 3 February, 7 March 1902: *BD*, I, nos. 359, 360.
8. Serra, *L'Intesa mediterranea*, pp. 173–75, thinks that the Russo-French opposition to the Anglo-Japanese treaty and the explosive Macedonian situation (see below, ch. 8) may have spurred the British to re-establish good relations with Italy.

Barrère in order to emphasize and if possible accentuate the good feeling between Italy and France. Although the German ambassador at Rome, Count Karl Wedel, made light of the event, Bülow seemed to take it a little more seriously and was reported to have told his mother-in-law, Donna Laura Minghetti, that Italy had soon to make "a choice between marriage and concubinage."[9] Two months later, however, Prinetti managed to please both his allies and France when he indicated on 14 June in the budget debate that "the most intimate relations with France are perfectly reconcilable with the Triple Alliance," and commented that Toulon showed that between the Italian and French peoples there was now "a cordial friendship so natural between two nations, sisters by race, genius and culture."[10]

He had made the cordial remarks concerning France only after much prodding from France. The whole episode, indeed, showed how persistently and with what arguments Barrère and Delcassé pursued their objectives. Despite the alleged Francophilism of Prinetti, Barrère had been much disturbed by his public statements concerning the renewal of the Triple Alliance. Also, in conversation with A. I. Nelidov, the Russian ambassador and Barrère's good friend, Prinetti stressed the importance of the Triplice as an instrument of peace, and the compatibility of the two coexisting groups of powers. What alarmed Nelidov, and undoubtedly Barrère as well, was the foreign minister's assertion that he would renew the alliance without change, for both men were sure that there was a clause by which Italy was bound to help Germany against France and perhaps Austria-Hungary against Russia.

Barrère had already taken steps to impress upon Prinetti the necessity of eliminating from the Triple Alliance any clauses that might be offensive toward France. At his suggestion Delcassé spoke to Count Tornielli, the Italian ambassador, about the coming Italian budgetary debates and how closely France would follow them for any references to the Triplice. In unmistakable terms he told Tornielli that if Italy believed she had to renew the alliance, she would have to take care "to abolish the offensive obligations against France which do not conform either to our present excellent relations or the development that I sincerely want to work to give them." A reminder of what Italy owed and might yet owe to France then followed: Public opinion in France, Delcassé said, had manifestly favored the

9. Barrère to Delcassé, 16 April 1901: 2 *DDF*, I, no. 194.
10. Same to same, 21 June 1901: ibid., no. 293.

rapprochement, "and the characteristic rise of Italian bonds on the Paris bourse well indicated to what point they are convinced here that every cause of defiance, all the more of conflict, between Italy and us is henceforth suppressed."[11]

Undoubtedly Delcassé's allusion to the Italian securities on the Paris bourse—not the first nor the last time that he or Barrère played this gambit—helped to impress Prinetti, who took a more cordial tone when Barrère visited him on 9 June and even showed him part of the speech he was preparing for the chamber. Barrère was not the man, however, to be satisfied with such vague statements as Prinetti made on 14 June. He pressed Prinetti for a more explicit promise, apparently reminding him again that the quotation on Italian bonds depended upon French good will, and on 25 June obtained Prinetti's statement that the Italian government would not renew the Triple Alliance before the expiration of the existing treaty, namely two more years; and if the alliance should be renewed, it would not contain any clause "of a nature to awaken the susceptibilities of France or to menace its security directly or indirectly."[12] This was neither the first nor the last time that Prinetti was to contradict himself in his dealings with the two protagonists. Nor was the phrase "directly or indirectly" an innocuous one, for it was to become the crux of negotiations a year later.

Throughout the remainder of the summer and early autumn, Prinetti seemed completely oriented toward France. In July he suggested that some public declaration be made concerning Barrère's letter of 14 December 1900, but Delcassé refused for fear that a revelation about Tripoli would involve one regarding Morocco; he felt that the time was inopportune for that. At the end of October, however, Prinetti had good reason to reveal French promises concerning Tripoli, because French action in the Aegean was arousing considerable attention in Italy and might well raise questions of Italian interests in the Eastern Mediterranean. France had decided to make a show of force over the failure of the Porte to meet demands for payments to French companies, and had sent naval vessels into the Aegean. Prinetti professed to Wedel to be greatly irritated by this move, and asserted that if the French fleet occupied Mytilene or laid hands on the customs office at Smyrna, a storm would break out in Italy be-

11. Delcassé to Barrère, 7 June 1901: ibid., no. 273.
12. "Note sur les rapports de la France et de l'Italie depuis 1898," 28 August 1901: ibid., no. 376.

cause of the sensitivity of public opinion to any Mediterranean question. He could not take any official step until he knew what the French intended to do, but in the meantime he wanted to know what the views of Bülow were on steps to be taken on the basis of Article VI of the Triple Alliance treaty in case France should attack Turkish territory. He also would make the same request of Ambassador Pasetti of Austria-Hungary concerning the application of Article VII.[13] Bülow made a quieting answer, observing that Russia would hardly permit her ally to take serious action against Turkey; and when Wedel reported this view to Prinetti, he found the latter much quieter. The Italian Minister alleged that if a French occupation of Turkish territory became definitive, Italy would secure a base in the Western Mediterranean. He was not thinking at all of Tripoli, he asserted, because support of Turkish sovereignty there was an expressed interest of Italy's, but if some day Tripoli could not be Turkish then it could become only Italian, and therefore in case of necessity Italy had to be its protector. To this Bülow noted on Wedel's report, that if Tripoli should become French, Italy would either declare war on France, or go to Morocco, or proclaim the republic. "In any case it would be the end of the Dreibund."[14]

This exchange with his alliance partner revealed Prinetti's anxiety over Italian reactions to French moves in the Eastern Mediterranean, but probably the events in the Aegean were only a trigger to his deeper motivation: pressure upon his allies by the public declaration of French concessions. This time Delcassé consented to the statement which had been worked out between Prinetti and Barrère and which has already been mentioned (above, p. 26) in connection with Italo-British relations. Prinetti said on 14 December that the recent French naval demonstrations at Mytilene could not awaken any Italian susceptibilities, nor could it break the mutual confidence that had become the rule in the relations of the two governments. After explaining briefly the agreement with France, he concluded that the amicable relations of the two countries had become such as to permit "an ex-

13. By Article VI Germany and Italy undertook "to use their influence to forestall on the Ottoman coasts and islands of the Adriatic and Aegean seas any territorial modification which might be injurious to one or the other of the Powers signatory to the present treaty." By Article VII Austria-Hungary and Italy made the same pledge and added a provision for compensation if either had to modify the status quo by a temporary or permanent occupation of territory in the named regions: Pribram, *Secret Treaties*, I, 154–57.

14. Wedel to Bülow, Rome, 6 November 1901: *GP*, XVIII(1), no. 5682.

change of explanations as clear as they are satisfactory on their interests in the Mediterranean"; and that their views were in "perfect concordance" concerning their respective interests.[15] Although Prinetti, in accord with Delcassé's stipulation, had said nothing about Morocco, shrewd observers rightly jumped to the conclusion that Italy had given France a free hand there. This view was confirmed by Delcassé himself in an interview with an Italian journalist, which was published by the *Giornale d'Italia*, 3 January 1902, and by Barrère in his annual New Year's speech to the French colony in Rome.

Hardly had Prinetti made his public declaration of Franco-Italian agreement than he began to reassure the Triplice allies of Italy's loyalty. Naturally, both Berlin and Vienna had been disturbed by the implications of his statement, although both professed to be sure that Italy would not break away from the alliance. Prinetti could have taken a more dignified and trustworthy position had he confined himself to the kind of remark which his Ambassador in London made to Lord Lansdowne, "that because a Power belonged to the Triple Alliance, there was no reason why it should not occasionally make international arrangements on its own account. Prince Bismarck's understanding with Russia in 1886 was a case in point."[16] Instead Prinetti went so far as to say to Wedel on 26 December: "I can give you the solemn assurance, and I can do it in the name of the King, that I am quite ready to sacrifice the friendship of France for the Triple Alliance, but never the Triple Alliance for the friendship of France."[17] This categorical statement of loyalty to the alliance against the background of his relations with France can be explained on one of three bases: He meant what he said; he hoped by such a statement to prepare the ground for a more favorable reception of the modifications in the Triple Alliance which he wished to obtain; or he was deliberately two-faced in the conduct of his relations with foreign powers, saying to each one in turn what he thought would most please his interlocutor. The kindest interpretation is that, impetuous and inexperienced still in diplomacy as he was, he honestly thought that by his tactics he was observing Visconti Venosta's first rule of Italian policy: "Independent ever, isolated never."

Bülow was scarcely more honest than Prinetti in his well-known

15. Barrère to Delcassé, 3 December 1901: 2 *DDF*, I, no. 549; and 31 October, 1901: *Revue de Paris*, 1937, II, 747–49.

16. Lansdowne to Currie, 17 December 1901: *BD*, I, no. 353.

17. Wedel to Bülow, 26 December 1901: *GP*, XVIII(2), no. 5842.

Reichstag speech of 8 January 1902, when he made light of the Triple Alliance and asserted that Italy's "extra dance" should not alarm Germany any more than the flirtations of a faithful wife should cause uneasiness to her husband.[18] In diplomatic correspondence, Bülow sought to work upon Prinetti's fears over the Roman question which might be raised if a clerical government should take power in France. Bülow asked Eulenburg to hint to Count Nigra, the Italian Ambassador in Vienna and a supporter of the Triple Alliance, that even an anticlerical government in France would like to see the Pope's temporal power restored, because that would mean the end of Italian unity. Eulenburg was also to tell Nigra that at their last meeting Pope Leo XIII had asked Emperor William to give him back Rome, but that the Emperor had refused, saying that King Humbert was his friend. Fortunately for Bülow's reputation, he does not seem to have pursued such specious arguments, much less compelling as they were than Barrère's occasional reference to the importance for Italy of the Paris bourse.

Against this background of Italian amity with France but privately professed devotion to the Triplice, and German professed indifference to Italy's "extra dance" but homage to the Alliance as a gauge of peace among neighbors, negotiations for the fourth treaty of the Triple Alliance began, to extend from January 1902 until May. Prinetti from the first doggedly demanded that the commercial treaties between Italy and each of her allies be renewed, or that the renewal be assured along with the renewal of the Alliance; that both Germany and Austria-Hungary make declarations of their disinterestedness in Tripoli, as France had done and as Great Britain did in the course of the negotiations; that Germany as well as Austria-Hungary guarantee the status quo in the Balkans against the attempt of any great power to upset it and that Article VII be reworded in order to commit Italy and Austria-Hungary to promote the autonomy of the Balkan states as they had done in the case of Albania; fiinally (in order to fulfill his promise to Barrère that there would be nothing in the treaty of an offensive nature against France) that a preamble be drawn up and published stating the purely defensive character of the alliance. In the face of these demands, Bülow once asked for a delaration that Italy had not concluded an accord with any other state which would compromise the efficacy of the defensive clauses of the Triplice; but he did not press the point. For the most part, he and

18. Penzler, ed., *Fürst Bülows Reden*, I, 243, 245.

Goluchowski met every demand of Prinetti's with a flat no and insisted that the treaty be renewed without modification of any kind. Bülow argued that changes would arouse the press in all three countries and breed mistrust, and that it was essential to contribute to a feeling of peace and quiet in Europe to be able to assure other governments, especially the Russian, that the treaty had been renewed "completely without change." Also, though not explicitly clear but undoubtedly present in German thinking, there was the sense of rivalry with France for the loyalty of Italy. Bülow's insistence upon an unchanged treaty would keep the "weak" Prinetti, who was "too trustful" toward Barrère, faithful to the Triplice.[19]

After a meeting with Bülow in Venice on 28 March 1902, Prinetti gave up most of his previous demands and concentrated upon obtaining declarations of disinterestedness regarding Tripolitania and a promise of renewed commercial treaties. He told Wedel that in place of the published preamble which he had wanted, he would declare in Parliament that the treaty contained nothing hostile to France. Thus, thought Wedel, he would give the impression that for the love of France a modification had taken place.

It took more than a month after the Venice meeting and German pressure on both parties for Prinetti and Goluchowski to come to terms, or, it might better be said, before Prinetti decided he could get nothing more than an Austrian declaration of disinterestedness in Tripoli and a verbal promise concerning the Balkans and the maintenance of trade treaties. In the middle of April, Goluchowski informed Prinetti that he had to have a definite written statement before 6 May of his intention to renew the alliance, because on the 7th Goluchowski had to speak before the Delegations. At last, after a conference in Rome with Lanza and Nigra, who were both upholders of the Triplice, Prinetti on 3 May informed his two allies officially that Italy would renew the treaty. It was now his turn to refuse proposals of Berlin and Vienna that the renewal take the form of a protocol and that the protocol of 1891, which referred to the accession of England in terms no longer applicable, be omitted. Prinetti insisted that the actual text of the treaty be signed and that the protocol of 1891, despite its obviously unrealistic second paragraph covering England, also be signed. The allies yielded, Bülow remarking that the inclusion of the 1891 protocol "all the more clearly em-

19. Bülow, Memorandum, 12 January 1902; Bülow to Wedel, 9 March 1902: GP, XVIII(2), nos. 5715, 5731.

phasized" that the "treaty had been accepted without alteration." The actual signing of the documents did not take place until 28 June 1902, because in the budget debates of the Italian Parliament, terminated on the 24th, Prinetti wanted to be able to say, if asked, that the Triple Alliance had not yet been renewed and thus to avoid a possible storm that might arise from the Left if he announced that it had been signed. Two days later, 30 June, Ambassador Pasetti delivered the declaration that Austria-Hungary would not interfere with Italian action in Tripoli if the status quo could not be maintained.[20] This was the only "change" since 1891 which Prinetti could properly claim.

Meanwhile, for the first three months of these negotiations, Barrère made few direct moves to put pressure upon Prinetti, although he suggested directives for the French press in its handling of the Triple Alliance. He complained to Prinetti in late February that there had been nothing in the speech from the throne at the opening of Parliament concerning Italo-French relations and elicited from Prinetti a reiteration of his pledges to France. He sought in conversation with the Marquis di Rudini, the former premier who had taken the first steps toward rapprochement with France in 1896, to enlist his aid in bringing pressure to bear upon Prinetti to modify the terms of the Triplice. Although Rudini disliked Prinetti, Barrère hoped that they might be brought together through his good friend Luigi Luzzatti, and if that failed, that Visconti Venosta might be enlisted, again through Luzzatti, to counsel Prinetti. Finally, he inspired a statement by Delcassé to the French senate on 20 March, again emphasizing the good relations with Italy and at the same time paying a tribute to Prinetti, as one of "the eminent statesmen" who had worked to allay misunderstandings.[21]

Upon the eve of Prinetti's meeting with Bülow at Venice, however, Barrère felt that he had to strengthen Prinetti's resolve to bring the Triplice into line with Italo-French amity. Barrère was clearly a little fearful that Prinetti might not be quite capable of dealing with Bülow, for after all he was "not a Visconti Venosta," and he frankly sought to indicate to the foreign minister the advantages of his position. On the other hand, to judge from Barrère's report of the conversation, Prinetti was no longer confident that he could make any modifications in the Triple Alliance treaties. He therefore made two important

20. Pribram, *Secret Treaties*, II, 129–32.
21. 2 *DDF*, II, 218, note 2, and no. 57.

statements: If he signed the Triple Alliance, he would give to France and to Parliament assurances that would leave no doubt of the character and implications of that act. Here was the germ of the written exchanges of 30 June. In the second place, Prinetti told Barrère that there was nothing hostile to France in the treaty itself, only in the "annexes"; and *"Ceux-là doivent tomber et disparaître."*[22] Barrère underlined these words. Although at the time Barrère did not know the terms of the Triple Alliance treaty, he correctly guessed the content of Article II by which Italy had to support Germany if she were attacked by France, and assumed that Prinetti referred by "annexes" to military agreements which he hoped Italy would renounce, thus indicating that he had no convictions about Prinetti's ability to fulfill his declaration.

Upon Prinetti's return from his meeting with Bülow in Venice, Barrère was convinced that he had not tried hard enough to get modifications in the treaty text, but gained the impression that nothing decisive had occurred, whereas, as we know, Bülow had flatly told Prinetti that it was the treaty without change or nothing. In this connection there is a conflict of testimony about Prinetti's mood after the meeting. Both the German and the Austro-Hungarian ambassadors in Rome reported that he was highly satisfied ("befriedigt"), but Barrère said that he was "très mécontent" and later suggested that the Venice meeting determined Prinetti to make the accord with France.[23] It seems more probable that the pressure by his allies in April to make a decision before May 6 and the impossibility of fulfilling his promises to France in any other way led him inevitably to the accord of June.

Whatever the explanation, Barrère in April redoubled his efforts to pin Prinetti down by use of the press, of Delcassé's reminders to Tornielli, and of Italian friends. By the 10th he reported that Visconti Venosta had promised to come from Milan to Rome and talk with Prinetti and Zanardelli. Moreover, the line he was to take had been agreed upon in principle. Italy was to renew the Triple Alliance, obtaining what modifications or interpretations might be possible; then Italy and France were to exchange reciprocal pledges that they

22. Barrère to Delcassé, 26 March 1902: ibid., no. 168.

23. *GP*, XVIII(2), 562, note *, and Wedel to Bülow, 2 April 1902: ibid., no. 5740; Barrère, 8 *RDM*, III, 101. Maximilian Claar, "Zwanzig Jahre habsburgischer Diplomatie in Rome," *KBM*, XV (1937), 545, asserts that Bülow's refusal to make any change in the Triplice treaty gave Prinetti a "moral alibi" for his negotiations with France.

had no obligations to engage militarily against the other, and finally they were to modify their Mediterranean agreement so that either country could develop freely and under convenient circumstances its interests in Tripoli and Morocco respectively, i.e. neither had to wait upon the action or consent of the other. At the same time, Visconti Venosta developed a justification for such an arrangement which remained basic to Italian thinking on relations with the Triplice. By her accord with France, he reasoned, Italy would be giving Germany more than Berlin had a right to expect, for by her accord with France, Italy relieved Germany of her obligation (Article X) to support Italy in an armed conflict with France in the Mediterranean. On the other hand, by renewing the Triple Alliance, Italy was giving both Germany and Austria-Hungary the certainty that she would not join their enemies or take action in the Trentino and the Adriatic. Barrère rightly considered the Visconti proposal and argument an "interesting intervention" and concluded that it was certain that the "military acts emanating from the union of the three Powers'" would be "denounced."[24]

Learning a few days later that Bülow had told Prinetti at Venice that there could be no modification of the treaty and that Austria had given Prinetti a deadline for his decision, Barrère redoubled his own efforts to influence the Italian foreign minister. That Prinetti at last recognized his own inability to modify the treaty was clear from his talk with Barrère on 30 April, when he revealed also what was probably the key to the government's decision to renew the Triplice without any of the conditions which Prinetti had at first laid down. "A change in the formal text," he told Barrère, "requires a change of political orientation. That is not impossible, but it is extremely difficult." He continued to deny, however, that there had been a decision to renew the treaty (probably correct, although the actual decision must have been only a few hours away), or that there had been any negotiations for renewal, but only "conversations and exchanges of ideas," the outcome of which was still unclear. He talked of resigning. Barrère recognized a change in Prinetti's tone, but believed that together they could work out an accord that would satisfy France.[25]

After Goluchowski stated to the Austro-Hungarian Delegations on 7 May that the Triple Alliance would be renewed without modifications in "spirit or letter," Prinetti could no longer avoid the problem of squaring Italy with France. He admitted to Barrère on the 8th that

24. Barrère to Delcassé (2 despatches), 10 April 1902: 2 DDF, II, nos. 193–94.
25. Same to same, 20 and 30 April 1902: ibid., nos. 209, 225.

the renewal had been agreed upon and proceeded to discuss how to bring future Italo-French relations into accord with the Triple Alliance Treaty—a reversal of his former talk of making the Triplice conform with Italo-French amity. Barrère at once drew up the points which he felt should be covered in an agreement, and suggested a protocol as the proper form for it. He worked out the draft of the document with Luzzatti on 24 May. This draft followed the general pattern which Visconti Venosta had sketched out early in April, but left two points up in the air: the problem of a declaration of war as a result of provocation, and the duration of the agreement.

While the wording of the agreement, especially on these two points, was being negotiated between Rome and Paris, Prinetti, who had made his first public declaration in Parliament on 23 May, sent a formal declaration to Delcassé through Ambassador Tornielli that there was nothing directly or indirectly agressive toward France in the renewed Triple Alliance, and that there were no "protocols or additional conventions." Tornielli's refusal at first to deliver the declaration led to his exclusion not only from further negotiations but also from knowledge of the eventual text.[26] By 21 June Barrère and Prinetti had established the contents of their accord, but the latter now wanted to change the form by substituting for a protocol an exchange of letters. He said that the king found it repugnant to sign a "contre-traité" so soon after the signature of the Triple Alliance. Delcassé accepted the change in form but insisted upon a date not later than the end of the month. He also wanted to make a statement to the Chamber of Deputies and asked what Prinetti would approve. Although Barrère replied that Prinetti wanted him to avoid anything that would raise unpleasant questions from Italy's allies, and Delcassé submitted his statement to Prinetti, there is no indication in the published documents of the latter's explicit approval.

In the last days of June Barrère resorted once more to financial pressure to keep Prinetti to the sticking point. On 12 June the Italian Parliament had voted the issue of consols at 3½ percent in order to convert some of the previous 5 percent issues to the lower interest rate. Barrère telegraphed Delcassé not to permit the Paris bourse to handle the new issue until after the agreement with Italy had been made, and on 26 June told Prinetti that there would be no difficulty about the consols after the signature of the declarations. Four days

26. Tornielli to Delcassé, 4 June 1902: ibid., no. 277. For Tornielli's position, see ibid., nos. 278, 293, 332, 349.

later, after further minor changes in wording, they exchanged the letters which sealed the Italo-French accord.

Prinetti had hoped to avoid the public statement that the Triple Alliance had been renewed without change and had used vague phraseology in his own statements to Parliament, but the Wolff news agency in Germany, much to Prinetti's annoyance, announced the signature of the treaty on 28 June "without change." Moreover, according to Barrère, Bülow asked Lanza to send a message to Prinetti to defy the French, whose procedures masked *arrières pensées* and whose government might fall into nationalist hands. Therefore Barrère felt it the more necessary that Delcassé make his statement to the chamber as soon as possible, and prepare the press to comment on it with warmth toward Italy and coolness toward her allies in order to demonstrate the falsity of the news that the Triplice had been renewed without change, but that on the contrary it was "irremediably" decadent.[27]

Accordingly Delcassé told the Chamber of Deputies on 3 July that as a result of an exchange of views and declarations the French government was certain that

the policy of Italy in consequence of her alliance was not directed either directly or indirectly against France, that it could not in any case involve any menace for us, neither in diplomatic form nor by protocols or international military stipulations, and that in no case and under no form could Italy become either the auxiliary or the instrument of an aggression against our country.[28]

The basis for such a statement lay in Prinetti's declaration delivered by Tornielli on 4 June and in the letters and explanations which Barrère and Prinetti had exchanged on the 30th of June, but which had been dated 10 and 11 July and were to be replaced by letters dated 1 and 2 November in order that, if ever disclosed, they would not appear to have been exchanged within forty-eight hours of the Italian signature on the Triple Alliance treaty.

The letters followed the pattern already indicated. They changed the understanding of 1900 concerning Tripoli and Morocco from a declaration of disinterestedness to an approval of positive action by stating that "each of the two Powers can freely develop its sphere of influence in the above mentioned regions at the moment it deems op-

27. Barrère to Delcassé, 1 July 1902: ibid., no. 316.

28. Ibid., 386, note 1. Barrère to Poincaré, 10 March 1912: ibid., 692–99, is a summary of the negotiations of 1902.

portune, and without the action of one of them being necessarily subordinated to that of the other." They further established that in case either of them were "the object of a direct or indirect aggression on the part of one or more Powers," the other would maintain strict neutrality. Then came the stipulation upon which Delcassé was particularly insistent that "the same would hold good" in case either, "as the result of a direct provocation, should find herself compelled, in defence of her honor or of her security, to take the initiative of a declaration of war," although in this eventuality, a previous communication of intent was required in order that the other party could "thus be enabled to determine whether there is really a case of direct provocation." Each declared that "no protocol or military provision in the nature of an international contract which would be in disagreement with the present declarations exists or will be concluded by her." Finally, they agreed that, except for the "interpretation of the Mediterranean interests of the two powers" which had "a final character," the declarations would remain valid as long as neither notified the other of their modification.[29]

In the second set of letters, Barrère asked for and received a definition of "direct provocation." Prinetti stated that "direct" meant "that the facts capable of being eventually invoked as constituting the provocation must concern the direct relations between the Power provoking and the Power provoked." He added illustrations in an oral explanation which Barrère considered to be an "authentic commentary" and thus a part of the exchange. Examples of "direct provocation," said Prinetti, were the publication of a "faked despatch" by Bismarck in 1870, and the refusal of King William to receive Benedetti; the Schnaebele incident; and "certain vicissitudes of the Fashoda affair." Indirect provocation, on the other hand, he illustrated by the Hohenzollern candidature to the Spanish throne, and "such an indirect initiative in Far Eastern affairs as did not aim at one of the contracting powers, although that initiative could displease it and appear to be contrary to its direct interest." These written and oral exchanges Barrère later described as "not a *contre-traité*," but a "a *contre-partie* of the Triplice which it reduces to very little on the point which interests us the most."[30]

29. Barrère to Delcassé, 10 July 1902: ibid., no. 329; also Pribram, *Secret Treaties*, II, 248–55 (dated 1 November 1902).

30. Barrère to Delcassé, 20 July 1902: 2 *DDF*, II, no. 340; and Pribram, *Secret Treaties*, II, 254–57 (without explanations).

Ever since 1902 opinion has been divided as to the morality of Italian policy and the consistency or contradiction between the commitments to the Triple Alliance and those to France. Interpretations range from the judgment that the Italians "deceived everybody" to the statement that Italian conduct "even considering, or rather especially considering, the extreme measures of a pacific prudence taken in 1902, might have constituted a lesson in loyalty for everybody, Hohenzollern Germany to begin with." One Italian commentator has condemned the French accord as "a genuine bargain of Esau, one of the gravest errors of our foreign policy since 1848,"[31] while others have asserted that by it Italy reached an equilibrium between the central and the western powers and achieved elasticity of negotiation in a period when alignments were shifting. The supporters of Italian honesty usually point out that Italy had as much right as Germany to make agreements with other powers, and give the examples of Bismarck's reinsurance treaty with Russia, and Austria's agreements with Russia over the Balkans and neutrality in 1897 and in 1904. Few would contest such a right, but the question is: What was the effect of the French accord upon Italy's obligations and its international position?

First, in respect of the Triple Alliance, all interpreters agree that there was no textual violation as a result of the accords with France. Actually, the major effect upon the treaty was to nullify that part of Article X which obliged Germany to come to the aid of Italy if the latter should find it necessary to go to war with France because of her expansion in North Africa. Italy had insisted on this article in 1887, and Bismarck had paid the price in order to keep the alliance. Now the French accord rendered this article useless; but undoubtedly Prinetti, himself, who had not suggested or even hinted that Article X be dropped, was glad to have it as a reinsurance against a French change of policy. As far as the neutrality provision of the French accord was concerned, Italy was not in any case obliged to aid Germany unless she was attacked "without direct provocation," and thus had in no way violated the terms of the Triple Alliance. Even the case of a two-power attack upon one of Italy's allies (Article III) involved the question of "direct provocation," and again the French accord offered no conflict. Thus the only direct effect, even upon the "spirit" of the Triplice was the cancellation of one obligation which Italy herself had

31. Georges André Fribourg, *L'Italie et nous* (Paris, 1947), p. 157; Carlo Sforza, *Europe and the Europeans* (Indianapolis, New York, 1936), p. 142; Francesco Tommasini, *L'Italia alla vigilia della guerra*, I, 167.

insisted upon and which she no longer needed. A frank and direct statement to her allies of that change of policy would have been more honest but would not have changed the situation.

Looking at the French side of the negotiations, we can see that Prinetti had misled if not deceived Barrère, both when he talked of trying to modify the Triple Alliance treaty and when he asserted that there were no protocols or military commitments. There is no evidence in the published documents that Prinetti ever tried to change any of the articles which concerned war with France, not even Article X, as already noted. Moreover, the military convention of 1888, which provided for the use of Italy's Third army on the upper Rhine (though Schlieffen in March 1901 had relieved Italy of the obligation), still remained in force as far as Saletta, the Italian Chief of Staff, was concerned. To be sure the Foreign minister had no official knowledge of this convention and had not signed any such document. When in July, Austrian and German newspapers began talking of a military agreement, Prinetti said to the French Chargé d'Affaires: "Je ne sais s'ils ont existé dans le passé; je n'ai jamais voulu le savoir." It was possible, he admitted, that military conventions had existed between the general staffs, but he asserted again that there was nothing inside or outside the Treaty which obligated Italy to participate in the war operations of her allies.[32] Taken at its face value, this again was a lie, but in terms of the French accord and its promise of Italian neutrality if France were attacked or went to war as a result of "direct provocation," it was true.

Even with reference to the military convention the French were not entirely ignorant of its existence and content. On 1 May 1902 Lamsdorff sent to Ambassador A. I. Nelidov in Rome copies of the correspondence of April 1888 between the Italian Chief of Staff and Colonel Goiran who went to Vienna and Berlin in order to arrange for the transportation of the Italian army corps through Austria and southern Germany to the Upper Rhine. Nelidov conveyed their content to Barrère and expressed to Lamsdorff his pleasure at seeing them, because they confirmed the suspicion that there were military agreements.[33] Whether or not Barrère ever made use of his knowledge does not appear from the published French documents. Nelidov, however, found in them a good reason for trying with French help to prevent Italy from making similar military commitments to Austria,

32. Legrand to Delcassé, Rome, 29 July 1902: 2 *DDF*, II, no. 348.
33. "Agressivnye plany Italii, *KA*, LXXXVII (1938), 64–88.

which Goiran discussed with the Austro-Hungarian minister of war, as reported in the correspondence of 1888.

Apart from the questions of misrepresentation, there was a solid core of intent in Prinetti's policy, however maladroitly pursued, that was of major significance. Without the French accord, excepting the declarations concerning Morocco and Tripoli, Italy's policy would have been the same: friendship for France and membership in the Triple Alliance. The declarations concerning neutrality merely spelled out a position which Italy already enjoyed under the Triplice, i.e. a right to determine the issue of direct provocation should France attack Germany. But the accord emphasized this position and this right in a way which meant that a new set of relations had come into existence. Italy, by her accord with Great Britain as well as that with France, had reduced the Triple Alliance to continental importance and had sought to solve its Mediterranean aspirations in agreement, rather than in conflict, with France—a policy that Prinetti inherited. Though England, too, had been a partner of Italy and indirectly of the Triple Alliance in the Mediterranean, a further sign of the changing times was the continued cordial relations between Italy and England after the March declaration, alongside the cordial Italo-French relations. It might be argued that whereas Italo-English coolness from 1899 to 1902 had helped to bring about Italo-French rapprochement, the latter in turn helped to presage the Anglo-French entente. The change stands out the sharper if 1902 is contrasted with 1887. Then, when the Triple Alliance was renewed for the first time, there was an Anglo-German entente, an Italo-French hostility, and an Italo-Austrian truce. Now, in 1902, England and Germany were drifting apart, Italy and France were friends, and Italy and Austria were allied opponents. As Sir Rennell Rodd put it, the Italian rapprochement with France was "inevitable."[34]

The principal advantages to Italy in the new situation were a double guarantee of security and the continued flow of financial assistance from the French money market, without sacrificing, it was hoped, the commercial relations with Germany and Austria. On the other hand, the very weaknesses, economic and military, which forced Italy to pursue her policy of Triple Alliance *and* French amity, laid her open to continual pressures from both sides, less severe than those of the first six months of 1902 but nonetheless constant. Talk of greater mobility and greater independence from Triplice or German domina-

34. Rennell Rodd to Lansdowne, 9 July 1902: BD, I, no. 364.

tion was largely illusory as long as Italy was considered, as it was, a second-rate power. Its "greater mobility" carried with it the disadvantages as well as the advantages of a relatively weak power seeking safety in a balance of forces. This is part of the reason why a critic like the former Senator Albertini felt that Italy, by its promise of neutrality to France, had acted contrary to its own interests by giving an assurance to France which was "to prejudice irreparably her [Italy's] freedom of action in the case of a general conflagration and to prejudice it without adequate advantage . . . Italy would have had a very different claim to French gratitude if the neutrality proclaimed in 1914 had not already been promised by the pact of 1902, i.e. if it had not been a right on which Paris already reckoned."[35]

Yet given the Morocco-Tripoli deal with France and the expansionist desires of Italy which led to it, what else could Italy wisely do but go on to the neutrality pact with France which was the price she had to pay for financial support and continued friendly relations? Germany and Austria-Hungary clearly offered Italy nothing but disinterestedness in Tripoli and reinsurance against a French reversal of policy. They did not even guarantee the Italian government continued favorable trade relations. Besides, as the negotiations between Prinetti and Barrère developed, there arose the possibility that with the aid of French influence Italy might make an entente with Russia that would be to her advantage in the Balkans, where, as was clear by 1902, rivalry with Austria-Hungary was developing.

V.

The first steps toward an Italo-Russian rapprochement are not altogether clear but were apparently taken by Ambassador Nelidov and Barrère in Rome. They were anxious to associate France's ally with the newly created Franco-Italian accord and enjoined their respective foreign ministers to work for an Italo-Russian entente. Foreign Minister Prinetti was reported to be interested in it in order to counter possible Austrian activities in the Balkans. As a result of French and Russian cooperation and Italian compliance with their plans, King Victor Emmanuel III visited Tsar Nicholas II in July 1902, two months before he visited his own ally, William II. If the promoters of the king's meeting with the tsar expected to bring about an entente, they

35. Luigi Albertini, *Origins*, I, 131–32. Cf. Tommasini, *L'Italia*, I, 165–66.

were disappointed, for it was not until the tsar visited the king at Racconigi in 1909 that Italy and Russia concluded a Balkan agreement.

The episode of the king's visit to Russia was but one of many in the contest between France and Germany for Italy's favors. Until the autumn of 1903 France seemed to have bested Germany, but with the change of the Italian government in November 1903, Germany's prospects brightened. Giovanni Giolitti replaced Zanardelli as premier, and Tommaso Tittoni became minister of foreign affairs. The latter was reported to be a partisan of the Triple Alliance and of better relations with Austria-Hungary. He was a "Roman of the Romans," Bülow testified, and was "level-headed, cautious, and subtle." Barrère sized him up as "his sovereign's man, who would not dare anything against his views."[36] Barrère could congratulate himself that his old friend, Luigi Luzzatti, who had done so much to help him in 1902, became minister of the treasury in the same government. Giolitti may have put him there in order to assure the completion of a labor treaty under negotiation with France, and the continued listing of Italian bonds on the Paris bourse. However that may be, it was high time that a moderating influence was put upon the anti-Austrian feeling that was mounting in Italy.

In June 1903 irredentism had come to the fore over a disturbance at the University of Innsbruck which led to demonstrations at the University of Rome, compelling the government to close it. But the cry of "Trento e Trieste" grew ever louder. The manifestations of popular feeling worried both the German and the Austro-Hungarian governments, although Tittoni, in his first official statement in the Chamber on 15 December declared that the alliance ties between Austria-Hungary and Italy should be just as close as those between Germany and Italy. Also he said that Italy would remain true to the Triplice, which was a powerful guarantee of peace and no hindrance to the traditional friendship with England and to the happily renewed amity with France. At the same time, Austria-Hungary reassured Italy concerning her policy in the Balkans.

Despite Tittoni's good intentions he became involved in Franco-German rivalry over Italy in April 1904 when President Loubet visited Rome and Naples. Although by the time of this visit the background had greatly changed from that of 1902 because of the outbreak of the Russo-Japanese war in February and the announcement of the Entente

36. Bülow, Memoirs, II, 524; Barrère to Delcassé, 21 June 1904: 2 DDF, V, no. 239.

Cordiale in April, the event was nevertheless the capstone to the Franco-Italian accord of 1902. The Italian government's interests were clear and fairly simple. Italy wanted help from France in a more complete conversion of her debts in order to lower interest rates, and she wanted to prevent Austria-Hungary from taking advantage of Russian involvement in the Far East in order to strengthen her own position in the Balkans and particularly in Albania. Italy's policy has been described as one of maneuvering between the Triplice and France. This is true, but puts the emphasis in the wrong place. Throughout 1904 and especially in connection with Loubet's visit, Italy was more acted upon than acting. The whole affair is an excellent example of the shameless pressures exerted by the French on one side and the Germans on the other.

On the French side, Barrère obviously wanted to make the Italian need of loans a lever for further political agreements that a visit of President Loubet to Rome in April would celebrate. Delcassé, however, either because of caution or because of the impending entente with Great Britain, reduced Italian relations to second rank and at first refused to go along with Barrère's plans. Moreover, Delcassé and Loubet were reluctant to visit Rome because of the complications that might arise over relations with the Vatican. But Barrère by the end of January had made arrangements for the President's visit that would amply demonstrate great popular enthusiasm in Italy for French friendship. Delcassé had perforce to go along and thus to defy the clericals and the pope.

News of the French plans and fears that Italy might indeed be turning the harmless "extra dance" into "a whole cotillion with a kiss at the end"[37] gave Holstein and Bülow great uneasiness. They conjectured that Italy had made a reinsurance treaty that would make the Triplice inoperable against France. They felt that Italo-Austrian tension was dangerous and tried to convince the Italian government that Austria-Hungary had no expansionist ambitions in the Balkans, offering to mediate between Rome and Vienna. Bülow sensed, however, that the Loubet visit was a serious matter and might well jeopardize the future of the Triplice. He warned the Italian ambassador, Count Lanza, and ordered Count Anton Monts, who had succeeded Wedel as ambassador in Rome, to warn the Italian government that the behavior of Italy might compel him to go before the Reichstag in May and say that virtually no alliance relation existed between Germany

37. Reverseaux to Delcassé, Vienna, 5 May 1904: 2 DDF, V, no. 95.

and Italy any more; the festivities in honor of Loubet must not be greater than those for Kaiser William II, who expected to meet Victor Emmanuel III at Naples in March, and above all in toasts to Loubet the Triple Alliance had to be mentioned. This was the opening gun in the battle of the toasts which both Germany and France waged with all the diplomatic artillery at their command.

The Germans made the first moves. When Victor Emmanuel visited the kaiser on the *Hohenzollern* in Naples bay on 26 March, the king toasted his "faithful and dependable friend," saying that "the bonds, which for so many years tied the states together with their common alliance associate, were up to the present the strongest guarantee of the peace of Europe." He concluded with the wish that "these bonds" might ever continue to unite the two "in their common efforts toward peaceful progress in the future." The kaiser, of course, replied with an even more glowing tribute to the loyalty and unshakeable unity of the two peoples.[38]

Barrère protested the king's toast to the kaiser, alleging that it would make a bad impression on the French Parliament and would distress Delcassé. On the other hand, Monts in Rome thought he had obtained Tittoni's pledge that the Triplice would be mentioned in the toast to Loubet, and rumors reached Luzzatti that the Germans were plotting to bring about a crash in Italian securities in order to offset the cordiality of the welcome to Loubet. Barrère, however, continued undisturbed to prepare not only the public but also the government for the great event. When he learned that Tittoni had put into the toast to Loubet a reference to the Triplice, he required him to suppress it. Thus the French came out the victors in the second round of the battle. But that was not all. Despite Monts's demand that any later toasts should mention the Triplice, a toast at Naples, where Loubet and the king reviewed the French and Italian fleets, failed again to do so.

Naturally Italy's allies were irritated, as the Austro-Hungarians clearly showed; or were worried about possible further Italo-French agreements, as both Vienna and Berlin admitted; or were outraged by Italian conduct. Monts reported a fellow diplomat's remark that the Italians pursued "only a policy of mendicants."[39] In Berlin, although Tittoni had sought through Count Lanza to excuse himself by saying that he had promised only to do his best about the toasts (and Lanza

38. Arthur Singer, *Geschichte des Dreibundes*, pp. 151–52.
39. Monts to Bülow, 6 May 1904: *GP*, XX(1), no. 6415.

added that Barrère, so to speak, had held a pistol to the king's breast), Holstein and Bülow took a very pessimistic view of Italy's policy. The pro-French current was preponderant in Italy, said Holstein, and the Triplice nothing more than a *succès d'estime*. Nevertheless he and Bülow decided to put on a bold front, trying to save the situation through inspired press articles that would play down the Italian enthusiasm for France, through lectures to the Italian government on the dangers to the regime of French-inspired republicanism and socialism, and through indulgence for Italian expansionist ambitions in Tripoli.

Tittoni followed his earlier explanation with a categorical statement to Berlin that there was no treaty between Italy and France and that there was no need for one, "since a political agreement of a general nature is inconsistent with the spirit of our alliance treaties to which we want to remain sincerely faithful."[40] On the other hand, he sought to allay public suspicion of Austria-Hungary by reporting to Parliament his complete agreement with Goluchowski at their meeting in Abbazia on 14 April over the Balkans and especially Albania: they would continue to seek peace and the maintenance of the alliance through respect for the status quo. Goluchowski echoed his words in an address to the Austro-Hungarian delegations on 16 May.

Yet the tension between Italy and Austria-Hungary continued to be a cause for worry to them and to their common ally, Germany. Both countries sought to increase their military budgets, and active irredentist agitation continued in Italy, paralleled by student excitement in Trieste and Innsbruck and capped by the reference in a public speech by the president of the Italian Chamber of Deputies to "our Trent." The completion of a satisfactory commercial treaty, at long last, in September 1904 had no effect on the situation. Under the circumstances, Austria-Hungary can scarcely be blamed for signing on 15 October a neutrality treaty with Russia in case either became involved in an unprovoked war with a third party. This agreement, "largely aimed at Italy," was "eloquent testimony to the bad state of relations between Austria and Italy,"[41] and, incidentally, a shining example for Italian historians of how Italy's allies were no more loyal to the Triplice than Italy was.

Under these circumstances two topics continued to preoccupy German statesmen: the question of Italian loyalty to the Triplice, and the

40. Same to same, 12 May 1904: ibid., no. 6418.
41. Pribram, *Secret Treaties*, I, 236–39. Cf. F. R. Bridge, *From Sadowa to Sarajevo*, pp. 271–73.

problem of lessening the tension between her two allies. These were
the themes of conversation between Giolitti and Bülow at Homburg,
27 September 1904, when each sought to reassure the other. Again, in
February 1905, Giolitti and Tittoni jointly signed a statement, sent
through Lanza to Bülow, in which they formally denied that any
"political or military accord" had been made with France when Loubet
visited Italy. Bülow concluded that it was best to keep up the "façade
of the Triplice," because as long as the Italians were in it they would
be viewed with mistrust by hostile powers, but that in case of complications it would be an illusion to count upon active Italian cooperation—yet it would be an advantage if Italy remained neutral instead
of joining France.[42] The French, too, were a little uneasy about Italy's
policy. But for both Germany and France, relations with Italy had
sunk to a position of secondary importance by the end of 1904. For
Italy, however, the pattern of international relations which she was to
pursue with only slight deviations to 1914 had been set: Triplice
member, and French friend.

42. Bülow to William II, 5 March 1905: *GP*, XX(1), no. 6428.

Chapter 3

The Entente

Cordiale, 1904

Lord Lansdowne, British foreign secretary, and Paul Cambon, French ambassador in London, were the architects of the Entente Cordiale. On the British side those who supported the efforts to improve relations were Lord Cromer, consul-general in Egypt; Joseph Chamberlain, secretary for the colonies; Sir Thomas Barclay, an ardent francophile; Ambassador Sir Edmund Monson in Paris; and Sir Arthur Nicolson, British minister in Tangier. The principal French promoters of entente with Britain were Eugène Etienne, a deputy and leader of the colonial group; Baron Estournelle de Constant, a senator; and Foreign Minister Théophile Delcassé after months of hesitation. King Edward VII and President Emile Loubet provided a ceremonial façade for the Entente. In dealing with Spain over Morocco, Delcassé negotiated with Spanish Ambassador Fernando de Leon y Castillo. His agent in Morocco was Joseph Georges Saint-René Taillandier.

Long before the completion of the Franco-Italian accord of 1902, Delcassé had begun to work toward the realization of his major colonial ambition: The development of French preponderance in Morocco. Many cross-currents made the course at times uncertain, but the broad outlines of action had been adumbrated as early as the autumn of 1898 by the leaders of the colonial group in the Chamber of Deputies, who wanted to round out Greater France of the Mediterranean by the addition of Morocco.

I.

The *parti colonial*, with which Delcassé had been closely associated since its foundation in 1892, was not a formal organization but "a current of public opinion, uniting men of right and left," who were interested in the colonies. The most important committees of the group were the *Comité de l'Afrique Française*, with its mouthpiece the *Bulletin*, and the *Union Coloniale Française*. In 1903 a small group who had been most interested in Morocco formed the *Comité du Maroc*. The outstanding leader of the colonial party and of the committees, especially the last, was Eugène Etienne, a deputy from Oran since 1881 and twice under-secretary for colonies. He was another Gambetta man and a long-time friend of Delcassé's, with whom he kept in close touch even when they differed over policies. Etienne and his associates were flexible in the tactics they advocated for the development of Greater France, and as for Morocco were primarily interested in agreements with other interested powers which would give France a free hand there. They favored an agreement with Germany even after Delcassé had rejected the idea, and supported the Italian rapprochement. Etienne differed from Delcassé most radically between 1898 and 1903 in his advocacy of an understanding not only with Germany but also with Great Britain. He thought a deal should be made with the latter on the basis of an exchange of Egypt for Morocco. Here lay the germ of the subsequent entente cordiale, but Delcassé would not hear of it because he was convinced of England's implacable hostility to French aims in the sherifian kingdom.

A staunch supporter of French aspirations in Morocco and a believer in the colonial group's proposed barter of Egypt for Morocco was Paul Cambon, ambassador in London (1898–1920). His almost weekly cross-channel trips enabled him to keep in close touch with Delcassé, and at times, like Barrère in Rome, he initiated moves and prompted Delcassé on the best procedure in dealing with England. As the French minister and resident in Tunis (1882–1886), who set up the machinery for the protectorate, he had developed strong views of the desirability and the methods of French expansion into such areas as Morocco. As a diplomat his courtesy, tactfulness, and charm "seemed to come straight out of the eighteenth century,"[1] and made him a highly successful negotiator with the British, who recognized his pertinacity and adroitness and credited him with honesty and sincerity. Without resorting to the bullying methods of Barrère, hardly appropriate in London, Cambon achieved as much by shrewd tactics and strength of will. He was determined to make a deal with Britain, long before Delcassé approved the idea. Early in 1901 he broached the subject of Morocco to Lord Lansdowne as a possible compensation for French fishing rights in Newfoundland, but without results,

1. J. A. Spender, *Life, Journalism and Politics* (2 vols. New York, n.d.), I, 171.

2. *Paul Cambon (Culver Pictures)*

and by the opening of 1902 he was beginning to feel that action was urgently needed if France were not to lose out in the coveted area of Morocco.

The events of 1901 were important for the later emergence of the Entente Cordiale. The sultan's rule in Morocco was obviously becoming shaky because of financial difficulties and rising unrest among the tribes. In the alliance discussions between Great Britain and Germany an agreement over Morocco took a prominent place at least in the thinking of Joseph Chamberlain. But the Germans were not interested, nor did they respond to the sultan's appeals for help. The British, too, failed to respond to the sultan's pleas. Therefore, by default, the way was left open to France. At the same time Delcassé began to prepare for the ultimate pacific penetration of the country. In midyear he appointed Joseph Georges Saint-René Taillandier minister in Morocco to conduct a more active policy there. Delcassé's first achievement was a protocol, signed at Paris in July for the regulation of the border between Algeria and Morocco. Its terms were so vague and unsatisfactory in practice, however, that another accord of April 1902 was drawn up "establishing peace in the Sahara region by mutual support." Instead of tightening the frontier, the accord made the boundary even looser but emphasized the cooperation of France and Morocco in controlling the border tribes. In fact, because the sultan's agents were dependent upon French support, France had achieved a special position and a legal basis for political, economic, and military claims upon Morocco that no other power possessed.[2]

In 1902 Delcassé took steps to warn off Great Britain, whom he and Taillandier considered to be France's chief rival in Morocco, and to let the sultan know that he was to accept only French aid. At the same time he blessed the organization by Schneider-Creusot of a powerful and active agency that could promote French industrial and commercial interests in Morocco. Delcassé, however, was moving very cautiously. He even refused a loan in February 1902, although he agreed to one in November. Early in 1902 he had taken the position, with which Paul Cambon agreed, that the granting of any major concessions to foreigners by Morocco, such as railway or telegraph and telephone construction, would constitute a violation of the status quo, to which he professed to be devoted until he could clear the way for French freedom of action. He carefully distinguished between the in-

2. Henri Cambon, *Histoire du Maroc*, pp. 126–27. Cf. Carl Vincent Confer, "Divided Counsels in French Imperialism," *JMH*, XVIII (1946), 50–53.

ternational and the Franco-Moroccan questions, and proposed "to settle the former with each power separately and in turn, in order finally to possess complete freedom to settle the latter directly with Morocco."[3]

In pursuit of this plan, which had been foreshadowed as early as 1900, Delcassé proceeded in 1902 to press negotiations with Spain. His accord with Italy of June–July he regarded as the first step toward solving the international question. He had no intention of dealing with Germany, and until 3 February 1903 planned to offer Great Britain only the neutrality of Tangier and guarantees of commercial freedom. On the other hand, Spain could not be ignored, for she was eager to expand her holdings of Ceuta, Melilla, and offshore islands on the Mediterranean coast and her protectorate of Rio de Oro in the south, acquired by treaty with France in 1900. The Spanish leaders, however, could not make up their minds whether to build a continental alliance for protection against Great Britain, whose possible expansion at Spanish expense they feared, or make friends with her. The government of Francisco Silvela, leader of the conservatives, favored a close cooperation with France, backed by Russia or perhaps Germany, and from 1899 to 1901 dickered with France, but the government of Praxides Sagasta (March 1901 to December 1902), the liberal leader, while willing to make an agreement with France, wanted to do so in accord with Great Britain.

Nevertheless, in the summer and autumn of 1902 Delcassé ardently pursued negotiations with the Sagasta government through the Spanish ambassador in Paris, Fernando de Leon y Castillo. Three times he thought that he had reached agreement, only to be turned down by Madrid, as he thought, under pressure from Germany and Great Britain. He believed that Sagasta was about ready to sign a slightly modified proposal of 8 November when he fell from office on 3 December. By the draft convention of November, in the event that the status quo could not be preserved in Morocco, Spain was to have a sphere of influence in the south from Rio de Oro to the Sous River and in the north from the mouth of the Sebou River on the Atlantic coast to the Moulouya River on the Mediterranean, with the frontier so drawn as to include Fez. France was to have the rest of Morocco for her sphere. The Silvela government, which succeeded Sagasta's hesitated to sign the convention despite the extensive concessions to

---

3. Andrew, *Delcassé*, p. 138. See also ibid., pp. 264–65; Paul Cambon, *Correspondence*, II, 68–70.

Spain and Silvela's intimations before taking office that he would do so. Both Castillo in Paris and the new foreign minister, Buenventura Abarzuza, feared that without an accord with Britain a Franco-Spanish agreement might bring Spain into conflict with her. By the end of January, moreover, Delcassé had second thoughts about promising Fez to Spain and had decided that the road to Madrid lay through London. Accordingly he let negotiations lapse and on 6 April 1903 instructed Jules Cambon, who had become his ambassador to Spain in January, to treat "without haste, cautiously and methodically" the further attempts of Spain to negotiate with France and Russia. A month later Lansdowne tried to put to rest Silvela's concern over rumored Franco-British negotiations by assuring him that he would "not enter upon any fresh arrangement without knowledge of Spanish government."[4] In short, Spain had to await the conclusion of an accord between France and England but was not to be left out of the ultimate arrangements concerning Morocco.

II.

In London throughout 1902 Paul Cambon was testing the ground for an agreement with Great Britain. On the British side Lord Lansdowne, who had expressly acknowledged that the approach to an Anglo-Japanese alliance represented the admission "that we do not wish to stand alone,"[5] was nevertheless reserved toward Cambon's tentative approaches. In January they talked about Morocco, airing the suspicions on the one hand that Britain was contemplating concessions for railway and telegraph lines, and on the other that France was trying to establish her supremacy there. Lansdowne, like Sir Arthur Nicolson at Tangier, wanted a share in Moroccan development but denied that Britain was seeking exclusive privileges. Cambon asserted that France wanted to maintain the status quo, to which Lansdowne agreed. Cambon made it clear that France did not want Britain to expand her influence and interest in Morocco, while Lansdowne insisted that Britain had interests there. Thus some understanding between the two countries had to be reached if Delcassé was to achieve his goals.

On the English side opinion was moving toward a general agree-

4. Delcassé to J. Cambon, 6 April 1903: 2 *DDF*, III, no. 162; Lansdowne to Durand, 15 May 1903: *BD*, II, no. 350.

5. Lansdowne, Memorandum, 11 November 1901: *BD*, II, no. 92.

ment with France, now that the possibility of an Anglo-German understanding had disappeared. Joseph Chamberlain, who had been anxious
for a German alliance in the previous year, became thoroughly convinced in 1902 that none was possible and professed to be ready for
an understanding with France. He and Cambon talked about it unofficially and apparently touched upon the possibility of a deal involving Egypt and Morocco. A school of thought in the Admiralty was
ready to partition Morocco, letting France have what she wanted excepting for the area around Tangier. King Edward VII blessed the
idea of a general settlement with France and was ready to visit President Loubet as a gesture of good will, although he gave up the notion
for 1902 because of coronation plans. Yet no progress was made in the
spring and early summer because both powers, especially France, were
preoccupied with other matters, and, as noted above, Delcassé on the
French side was not yet interested in an accord with Britain.

The completion of the accord with Italy, however, and the fear that
the sultan of Morocco might develop relations with other powers to
the detriment of France moved the *Direction Politique* at the Quai
d'Orsay to make a careful evaluation of the situation on 15 July 1902.
As they saw it the obvious course was to come to an agreement with
Spain. Once in accord, France and Spain should offer to England a
collective guarantee of Tangier, and to both England and Germany
commercial liberty in Morocco. If necessary, compensation might be
found for both elsewhere in Africa. Other powers, which had but a
secondary interest anyway, would agree to such arrangements and
France and Spain could count upon the good will of Italy and Russia.[6]

Regardless of this memorandum, if indeed he had seen it, Paul
Cambon on 23 July raised the question of Morocco with Lord Lansdowne. He indicated that there was great danger that the complaisance
of the sultan toward the southern tribes who were arming against
France on the frontier, his susceptibility to the counsels of Kaid Maclean, a British favorite who was virtual commander-in-chief, and the
possibility of a situation arising that France would regard as a menace
all pointed to the necessity of an entente in order to avoid events that
might lead to a serious Anglo-French conflict. Lansdowne, protesting
that Maclean was but a noncommissioned officer and that Nicolson
(at Tangier) was loyally carrying out the British policy of maintaining
the status quo, declared that he was ready to discuss the subjects that
Delcassé might authorize "in the frankest possible manner." There

6. "Note sur la question marocaine," 15 July 1902: 2 *DDF*, II, no. 333.

was little more here than had been said on 22 January, but Cambon concluded that he had established the bases of an entente with England.[7]

When the two next discussed the possibilities of an accord, 6 August, Lansdowne had procured Prime Minister Arthur J. Balfour's approval of further talks, and, although Cambon had not received detailed instructions from Delcassé, he nevertheless went ahead to explain the French position. For the first time he introduced the subject of Siam into the discussion, suggesting that the agreement of 1896 should be clarified in such a way as to give France and Britain a greater control in their respective "spheres of influence"—a phrase that Lansdowne repudiated—and to protect Siam from German intrusion. As for Morocco, obviously of greater immediate concern, Cambon again alluded to the aspirations of the sultan's English employees. He hoped that a crisis would not arise but felt that it would be wise to discuss what action the two governments should take in the event of Morocco passing "into liquidation." Without explicitly saying so, Cambon represented the French aim as an ultimate partition between France and Spain and the internationalization of Tangier. Lansdowne emphatically rejected "any attempt to deal prematurely with the 'liquidation' of Morocco," because it would raise complications, reminding Cambon that other powers—Italy, Spain, and Germany—were concerned in Morocco. Without mentioning Italy, a point that Lansdowne found noteworthy, Cambon argued that although Germany in the past had sought concessions, she was not now "to the front there or elsewhere in the Mediterranean." Lansdowne postponed any official reply to Cambon's observations. According to Cambon, he did ask if the conversations should not be rounded out by talking of Newfoundland, and when Cambon suggested (for the third time in eighteen months) that French rights there might be traded for Gambia, Lansdowne declared that Britain could not give up Gambia but he would see about something else if France asked for it.[8]

For several reasons the opening for further discussion made on 23 July and 6 August was not entered in 1902. Lansdowne and his colleagues were undoubtedly scared by Cambon's mention of the ultimate "liquidation" of Morocco, and on 15 October Lansdowne not only told Cambon that he could not accept the view that Britain's only in-

7. Lansdowne to Monson, 23 July 1902: *BD*, II, no. 321; P. Cambon to Delcassé, 23 October 1902: *Correspondance*, II, 72–75.

8. P. Cambon to Delcassé, 9 August 1902: 2 *DDF*, II, no. 369; Lansdowne to Monson, 6 August 1902: *BD*, II, no. 322.

terest in Morocco was Tangier, but also said that he was not ready to discuss the liquidation of Morocco. Cambon asserted that France did not want a premature action but wanted only to discuss thorny points, agreement upon which would diminish the chance that liquidation would become necessary. At the same time he complained again of Kaid Maclean. Rumors in September at Paris and in Morocco that Britain was about to make a deal with France over Egypt and Morocco had led the sultan to send Maclean to London to seek support for Moroccan independence and a loan. Lansdowne let him know that British policy was firmly attached to the status quo and advised that he seek a loan from the three powers—France, England, and Germany. Lansdowne's explanations to Cambon concerning Maclean's mission and a secret French intelligence report lessened French anxiety, and the whole episode revealed that as yet Lansdowne was unwilling to give France a free hand in Morocco and was accepting Germany as an interested power along with France and England.[9]

In addition to Moroccan affairs, Lansdowne was in the thick of negotiations over Macedonia, the Straits question, the evacuation of Shanghai, over which differences developed with Germany, and Venezuela, where he arranged for joint action with Germany to the hesitation of members of the government and the irritation of public opinion. The Shanghai and Venezuela affairs helped to weight the scales against further cooperation with Germany and thus to influence Lansdowne's attitude toward agreements with France. Although the discussions of Morocco were in abeyance till the end of the year, Lansdowne and Cambon were involved in the Siamese question.

France and Britain each had a treaty with Siam and also a convention with each other, none of which had clearly defined their respective positions in Siam. The French colonial group was anxious to extend French controlled areas and to obtain exclusive rights over economic development in Siamese territory of the middle Mekong valley. The British, who thought their secret treaty with Siam of 1897 had given them a sphere of influence in the Malay region, found that Siam was threatening to make good her claim to suzerainty over certain Malay states with which England wanted to deal directly. Delcassé, during the summer and early autumn, negotiated a new frontier treaty with Siam that was signed on 7 October. But the surrender to Siam

9. Lansdowne to Monson, 15 October 1902: *BD*, II, no. 325; French intelligence report, 7 October, and P. Cambon to Delcassé, 23 October 1902: 2 *DDF*, II, nos. 429, 456.

without compensation of the port of Chantaboun, which France had occupied in 1893, angered the colonial group who regarded the surrender as constituting "an intolerable loss of face," and led to a bitter parliamentary wrangle that nearly caused Delcassé's fall. Because his own lack of interest in France's far eastern empire was not shared by the colonialists, he had to promise in February 1903 to renegotiate the treaty with Siam.[10]

Meanwhile in London, whenever Cambon talked about Siam, he found that Lansdowne did not seriously object to what France was trying to do, but did say that the treaty with Siam encroached upon the treaty rights of Great Britain and also put France in a privileged position which would enable her to dominate the central part of the Siamese kingdom. These criticisms, in view of Lansdowne's own secret treaty and negotiations, were obviously meant for the record, because Lansdowne refused to discuss Siam until after the British negotiations with the Malay states were completed and the Franco-Siamese treaty of 7 October was ratified. One point did emerge, however, from the conversations of October and November 1902, an apparent agreement that when they did come to an accord France and England would exclude any third power from intervention in the central part of Siam. Moreover, Cambon and Lansdowne tacitly agreed that whatever one power got in the way of special privileges or a sphere of influence would be balanced by similar and equal gains for the other. There the matter of Siam rested until Delcassé concluded another treaty with Siam (it was concluded in 1904) and the terms of the Entente Cordiale were being discussed in earnest.

While the discussions over Siam and the parallel negotiations with Spain were going on, events in Morocco again brought that country to the fore. In the autumn of 1902 a serious rebellion broke out, centering in the Northeast around Taza, where a pretender attracted a large following and for a time successfully resisted the sultan's efforts to suppress him. Great Britain in November prepared a squadron at Gibraltar to sail for Tetuan and Tangier if British subjects were endangered, and France, fearful of British unilateral action, readied a section of the Mediterranean fleet for possible action. Moreover, Delcassé put a good deal of pressure on French bankers to arrange a loan to the sultan, for he was fearful that other countries might step in and make conditions for loans that would be detrimental to his plans.

10. Andrew, *Delcassé*, pp. 257–58. On Britain and Siam, see J. Chandran, "Britain and the Siamese Malay States," *HJ*, XV (1972), 471–92.

A turn for the worse, however, in the Moroccan civil war and the necessity for French naval and military preparations along the coast and the Algerian frontier led Delcassé to authorize talks with Lansdowne. Cambon was to emphasize that France sincerely desired not to "go beyond the observation" of events in Morocco and to express hopes that Lansdowne would take the same position. Also, Cambon should remember the desire to maintain a privileged position for France in Morocco and to prevent the intervention of other powers. He was to tell Lansdowne about the French talks with Spain if Lansdowne gave him a favorable opening. The insistence upon the status quo and nonintervention was agreed upon orally between Delcassé and Cambon on the 29th. They also agreed that if intervention were necessary in order to protect Europeans, the three powers—France, Spain, and England—should work closely together. Cambon no doubt found all of this *fort bon* since Delcassé was slowly coming around to his view of relations with Britain.[11]

In his talk with Lansdowne on 31 December, Cambon was assured that Britain, too, did not want to interfere in Morocco, but only to protect her nationals if necessary. He also got Lansdowne's promise to concert with France in advance regarding the form of any contemplated intervention. In speaking of the French desire to keep the surveillance of Morocco limited to the three powers, Cambon was much more specific than Delcassé's written instruction with respect to the danger of German intervention, whose ambition to get a foothold in Morocco and the Mediterranean he elaborated in detail. Lansdowne agreed in principle to limit intervention to the three most interested powers, although he asserted that he had to reflect upon it further and speak to Balfour. In his own report of the discussion, Lansdowne was impressed with the change of tone since the talk of 6 August, from "liquidation" of Morocco to a policy of nonintervention and the maintenance of the status quo. Though Lansdowne himself did not note it, he too had changed his tone when he accepted the exclusion of Germany from Moroccan arrangements. This decision, qualified by further reflection, imperceptibly hardened as time went on, hence represented a significant step toward the entente with France.

The change of tone in the Cambon-Lansdowne talks, however, was paralleled by the more fundamental change of policy adopted by Delcassé in the course of January 1903. By the end of that month he had

11. Delcassé to P. Cambon, 30 December, and Cambon to Delcassé, 31 December 1902: 2 *DDF*, II, nos. 548, 552; Cambon, *Correspondance*, II, 85.

not only dropped the negotiations with Spain but also, as Cambon attested, had accepted the idea of a deal with Great Britain involving Egypt and Morocco. Important in bringing about this change was the dispelling of Delcassé's suspicions of British policy by the evidence he received in December and January that not only Lansdowne but also Chamberlain and King Edward VII, whom the French regarded as the three makers of British foreign policy, now definitely favored an understanding with France. Though probably not thought out in systematic Bismarckian fashion, there were also general considerations of international politics that dictated an entente with England. If the tension between Russia and Japan continued to increase, France might find herself in an embarassing position unless a conflict between the Dual Alliance and the Anglo-Japanese alliance could be avoided by an entente with Britain. Delcassé was also well aware of the dream of his mentor, Gambetta, of a Franco-British alliance, and hoped that it might be linked with the Dual Alliance, or at least might bring about an Anglo-Russian rapprochement. Furthermore, fear of Germany's designs in Morocco was heightened by the formation in October 1902 of a German Moroccan association that demanded a foothold in Morocco. A British entente would complement the Franco-Italian and eventually the Franco-Spanish accords in order to keep Morocco and the Mediterranean safe from German intrusion. More immediately effective in driving Delcassé toward a deal with Britain, however, was the constant pressure of the French colonial group exercised through Delcassé's close contacts with Etienne and the publicity of such journalists as Robert de Caix of the *Comité du Maroc*.

On the British side the danger of complications arising from the Moroccan civil war was a compelling reason for an agreement with France, which Nicolson at Tangier was urging by the end of 1902. Moreover, like France, Great Britain was apprehensive over developments in both the Far East and Near East. The reasons why Chamberlain had wanted an accord with Germany in 1901 were now even more compelling. Great Britain could not risk the potential hostility of three great powers—Russia, Germany, and France. The turn toward Germany in 1901 had long since been abandoned and replaced by a rift which the Venezuela affair of 1902–03 accentuated. An entente with France would eliminate a potential rival and perhaps open the road to Russia, who as yet seemed intractable. A more immediate practical matter was Cromer's reform project in Egypt, which could not be put into effect without French consent and approval. Although there is no specific documentary evidence of Cromer's urging an entente with France until the middle of 1903, he had undoubtedly discussed it while on leave in London in late 1902 and showed a keen interest in it when newspaper rumors of an Egyptian-Moroccan deal appeared in February 1903. Moreover, in Egypt he began to work for a local rapprochement with the French there.

Despite the recognition on both sides of the need for an entente, however, there was no progress toward it until July 1903. Paul Cambon, more eager than Delcassé to get on with negotiations, tried to hasten them by inspiring an article in *The Times* of 2 February 1903, date-lined Madrid but written by Morton Fullerton, a European correspondent who had been an assistant of the famous Henri de Blowitz. The article, after describing the position of the Spanish government in the Moroccan question, stated that toward the end of the previous summer Delcassé had made overtures to Lansdowne for a settlement of the Moroccan question, "in connection with the question of Egypt," and that the proposal "was not unfavorably received by Lord Lansdowne." The article concluded with a defense of Delcassé's policy, described as "nothing more or less than a proposal to England to leave France alone to secure the suzerainty of Morocco when and how she cared to do so by pacific penetration."[12] Two days after the article appeared, Paul Cambon assured Lansdowne that France was ready to deal with the Moroccan question any time. Although Lansdowne invited Cambon to recapitulate the proposals for an accord, he made no response and failed to renew discussions for another five months. Nor did Delcassé press for talks. When asked in the Chamber of Deputies, 11 March, with reference to *The Times* article, if he had linked Morocco and Egypt at any time, Delcassé replied: "That must have been in my sleep." To this Ribot remarked: "That is to say, while sleeping, Madame, we have had a narrow escape."[13]

In the first six months of 1903, however, public opinion in both France and England was slowly creating a favorable climate for an Anglo-French understanding. There were several factors here, of which the most important were the agitation for an arbitration treaty, the attitude of the French colonial group (noted above), the interests of the commercial and financial circles, and the rising fear of Germany in Great Britain.

The movement for an improvement in Anglo-French relations and

---

12. *The Times*, 2 February 1903, p. 5; Andrew, *Delcassé*, pp. 206–08.
13. 2 *DDF*, III, 183, note 1, and no. 63.

particularly for the negotiation of an arbitration treaty, which was led by Thomas Barclay, one-time president of the British Chamber of Commerce, and Baron d'Estournelle de Constant, French deputy and well-known advocate of peace, is too familiar to need description. Barclay himself has well told the story of his efforts, though with some exaggeration, and both Ambassador Monson in Paris and Cambon in London recognized the importance of these men in arousing public opinion and organizing parliamentary and business groups behind their drive to bring about good relations and an arbitration treaty. The latter objective was realized by the signature of a treaty in October 1903.[14]

The propaganda of Barclay and Estournelle appealed strongly to business and financial circles in both France and England. On the English side, one of the major reasons for support was the growing fear of German competition in world trade and the feeling that economically France was not a rival. Also, especially in 1903, banking circles in both France and England became interested in sharing the Russian loan market. The French were anxious to be relieved of the heavy burden of meeting Russian needs, and Witte wanted to find new sources of loans, such as the British market. To the Rothschilds on both side of the channel and their friends, the Anglo-French rapprochement was a necessary step toward an Anglo-Russian one which they envisaged. Moreover, the concept of an Anglo-French deal over Egypt and Morocco, occasionally mooted in the press since 1900, began to appear prominently in 1903, and some of the motivation for it was the financial advantage to both Britain and France.

In France, as in England, a wide range of feelings and interests accounts for the swing toward a rapprochement with Britain. Among the leftist groups Anglophile sentiments were related to an anti-Russian reaction in the years 1900–1903. The triumph of the anticlerical and staunchly republican majority at the polls in May 1902 undoubtedly confirmed the trend of thought away from tsarism and toward democratic England. On the other hand, high financial and colonialist circles, who were rightist in their politics, also favored better relations with England in order to further French expansion. Their outlook represented the beginnings of the new nationalism, which was to become a clearly defined movement by 1911. An ad-

14. Sir Thomas Barclay, *Thirty Years: Anglo-French Reminiscences* (Boston, New York, 1914), pp. 175–236. Cf. *BD*, II, nos. 352, 353; Joseph J. Mathews, *Egypt*, pp. 46–48.

ditional factor that turned Frenchmen toward England was the obvious anti-Germany sentiment there. Ambassador Metternich noted, 2 June 1903, that "without the estrangement of England and Germany a mood of Anglophilia would have been impossible in France . . ."[15]

A dramatic manifestation of Anglo-French cordiality occurred during King Edward VII's visit to Paris, 1–4 May 1903. Although at his first public appearance a few cries of "Vivent les Boers!" greeted him, by the time of his departure he had succeeded beyond all expectations in winning the hearts of the Parisians. He had also strengthened the belief of Delcassé and Loubet that an agreement with Britain was possible. Many writers then and since have exaggerated the king's role in the formation of the Entent Cordiale, naming him as one of its principal architects. On the other hand, such men as Lansdowne and Balfour, who worked with him, have rated his contribution to British diplomacy as low. What he did contribute to the Entente Cordiale was a keen interest in bettering Anglo-French relations and an ability through his tact and graciousness, and perhaps his reputation as a lover of good living, to endear himself to the French public. He helped to create an atmosphere within which the diplomats could effectively work.

Between Edward VII's visit to Paris in May and President Loubet's return visit to London, 6–9 July, announced on 27 May, the French and British press talked more cordially than before not only of rapprochement, but also of the points to be dealt with in an agreement, including Egypt. The *Dépêche Coloniale*, in two articles of 15 and 19 May, came out for the French renunciation of economic rights in Egypt and compensation in Morocco. *The Times* and other English papers commented favorably on these articles. In the July issue of the *National Review*, Etienne took the same line and suggested that discussions should embrace all outstanding colonial differences. Although Cambon and Lansdowne did not discuss the issues raised in the press, Cambon found the foreign secretary warmer about an accord and felt that there was no point in the exchange of visits unless an exchange of views on all issues followed it. He carefully arranged a program for Delcassé while in London with the president, placing him at the embassy dinner between Lansdowne and Chamberlain, who, he wrote Delcassé, was actually the government of England and was disgusted with the Germans. On the British side, only Lord Cromer in Egypt picked up the press talk of an Egyptian-

15. Metternich to Bülow, 2 June 1903: GP, XXVII, no. 5376.

Moroccan deal, and wrote Lansdowne that he wanted to discuss it with him when he came to London. The Cabinet by the opening of July was anxious to proceed with negotiations, and the public was ready for them. *Le Temps* declared that "the Franco-English rapprochement is a *fait accompli*," and urged that negotiations begin.[16]

The reasons why the British government was ready to begin negotiations were mixed. Chamberlain wanted primarily to check Germany, but Lansdowne and Balfour were mainly concerned about the Far and Middle Eastern situation. On 3 July 1903 the Japanese ambassador, Hayashi, told Lansdowne that Japan was going to approach Russia concerning their differences over Manchuria and Korea and that if the approach failed, Russia would be solely responsible for the consequences. He asked what steps Great Britain proposed to take in defense of her interests. The last thing Lansdowne wanted was embroilment with Russia, and there seemed to be but one way out of the danger, an entente with France which, he hoped, might lead to an entente with Russia. In addition, therefore, to the pro-French current of opinion in the British press and the possibility of a satisfactory transaction over Egypt and Morocco, the dread of war in the Far East made urgent the opening of serious talks with the French.

III.

The talk between Lansdowne and Delcassé on 7 July 1903 inaugurated the negotiations that were finally concluded on 8 April 1904. But before the two men met, a dress rehearsal of the opening scene occurred on 2 July, when Eugène Etienne visited Lansdowne at the foreign office. In view of their close association it is possible that Etienne was acting as an emissary of Delcassé's and that he reported the result of his conversation with Lansdowne. In it three things were notable: the omission among the issues Etienne raised of any mention of Egypt (which is singular in view of his article in the *National Review*); Etienne's emphasis upon the German menace to the peace of Europe that a Franco-British understanding could check; and the suggestion that perhaps France might help to influence Russia and

---

16. 11 July 1903, as quoted by Johan M. Goudswaard, *Some Aspects of the End of Britain's "Splendid Isolation," 1898–1904* (Rotterdam, 1952), p. 108.

thereby lessen Anglo-Russian tension. Although Lansdowne was obviously most interested in what Etienne had to say, making a lengthy report of it, he withheld comment and remarked only that it would give him great satisfaction to promote a reasonable "give and take arrangement between the two governments."[17] If reported to Delcassé, this remark could but encourage him in preparation for his own discussion with Lansdowne.

On 7 July when the two men got together, their discussion constituted only a preliminary review of the major points of difference—Morocco, Newfoundland, the New Hebrides, Siam, and Sokoto. For the first time in formal discourse Lansdowne brought up the question of Egypt. Delcassé treated it with reserve, since he was hopeful that a deal could be made without major concessions to Great Britain there. He and Lansdowne, however, voiced the same sentiments in favor of a comprehensive settlement of all differences. Lansdowne also agreed that France had a special position with respect to Morocco because of the Algerian border. In recognizing this peculiarly French interest, Lansdowne laid down three conditions to which he adhered throughout subsequent negotiations: England's interest in the Moroccan seaboard, on which there should be no fortifications; consideration of Spanish interests and consultation with Spain; and equality of opportunity for British commerce in Morocco. Delcassé readily agreed to meet these conditions while insisting that his policy in Morocco was based upon the maintenance of her independence and integrity. He left no doubt that a general settlement hinged upon what France obtained in Morocco. On all the points raised in the discussion both statesmen were cordial and conciliatory in their attitude.

The backgrounds and methods for the negotiations over these points in France and England were different. In France, Delcassé had behind him the colonial group headed by Etienne. So intent were they upon a free hand in Morocco that they were willing to give up much, though not more than was absolutely necessary. In England, Lansdowne had no pressure group but consulted the Cabinet at every important turn. He did have a one-man lobby in Lord Cromer, consul-general in Egypt, who had long wanted to free Great Britain's hands there in order to press forward with the reform program that he had formulated and that could only be effected if French resistance were ended. He had already begun to work actively toward financial

17. Lansdowne to Monson, 2 July 1903: *BD*, II, no. 356.

reforms that involved abolition of the *Caisse de la Dette*, an international commission which controlled Egyptian expenditures, and France knew of his plans unofficially. At every step in the negotiations after 7 July 1903, Cromer advised Lansdowne, enthusiastically supporting the attempt to come to an understanding with France, not merely to settle Egyptian difficulties but also as a possible stepping stone to an understanding with Russia and the easing of military and naval expenditures. He urged speed before the French conciliatory spirit changed, and his role entitles him to be included among the architects of the Entente Cordiale, not only because of his advice to Lansdowne but also because of efforts like the substitution of the native name "Kodok" for "Fashoda" in order to foster friendly French sentiment.

It is noteworthy that all the negotiations were carried on in London between Lansdowne and Paul Cambon, who acted not merely as a mouthpiece for Delcassé but as a plenipotentiary who kept a tight rein on discussions and at times prevented his chief from giving up too much in order to conclude the accords. The British ambassador in Paris, Sir Edmund Monson, who was never close to Delcassé, nevertheless played the important role of observer who supplied information to Lansdowne, evaluated proposals, and sometimes even suggested that Cambon was not quite representing his chief's views.

Little progress was made in negotiations up to 1 October 1903. Discussions of 29 July and 5 August revealed a major difference over Egypt, for France obviously wanted to dodge the question. After Lansdowne had made it plain that Britain had to have French approval to remain in Egypt as long as she liked, Cambon and Delcassé agreed, however, that they had to have an equivalent elsewhere and to raise their demands respecting Morocco. Another aspect of the pourparlers was the discussion of the German danger arising from her designs in Morocco. Cambon talked about the German desire for coaling stations there, apparently as a means of pressure upon Lansdowne to accept French views. Also Cambon revealed the French proposals to Spain that had not been agreed upon, and suggested how Lansdowne might answer possible Spanish inquiries concerning rumors of Anglo-French negotiations. It was not until after the summer holidays that Lansdowne on 1 October gave a full-length statement of his views on all points, including two that had not previously been mentioned—Zanzibar and Madagascar. His memorandum indicated agreement with France on Siam and Sokoto, and renounced British claims in Madagascar. He refused to consider a partition of the New Hebrides, and proposed that France withdraw her jurisdiction and post office from Zanzibar.

Three thorny questions stood out in Lansdowne's memorandum: Morocco, Egypt, and Newfoundland. As for the first, Lansdowne spelled out his three conditions of 7 July, emphasizing British freedom of trade in Morocco and the nonfortification of the coast from the Algerian border to Mazagan, whether in French or Spanish hands. He indirectly recognized the possibility of a liquidation of the sultan's rule, and in return for French acquiescence in British demands concerning Egypt would discuss with France similar concessions in Morocco. In addition to French recognition of the permanent British occupation of Egypt, he proposed the abolition of the *Caisse de la Dette*, and the conversion of the debt and the reorganization of railway administration, two projects dear to Cromer's heart, as Britain and Egypt should decide. On Newfoundland, Lansdowne accepted the French proposal that in return for the surrender of French treaty rights there, the fishing industry should be indemnified and France receive territorial compensation, but balked at the request for a guaranteed right to catch or buy bait. The questions of both bait and territorial compensation were to loom large in subsequent bickering.

The immediate French reaction to these proposals was to stress the primacy of the Morocco-Egypt axis and to maintain that the British had not given France an equivalent for their gains. They argued, as they continued to do until the accord was signed, that in giving France a free hand in Morocco, Britain was not giving something she possessed, whereas in Egypt France was asked to give up rights which she now enjoyed. Moreover, in Morocco France would still have to bargain with Spain, and that was likely to prove a difficult business. Delcassé and Cambon therefore suggested that England and France proceed in their respective areas gradually and by parallel advances. Lansdowne rejected this proposal and, pointing out that Great Britain had to deal with other powers too, felt that France should give an answer, yes or no, concerning the recognition of British permanency in Egypt.[18]

Before a formal reply was made to Lansdowne's memorandum, he and Cambon signed the arbitration treaty on 14 October 1903. The press in both countries received the treaty well, looking upon it as

18. Lansdowne to Monson, 7 October 1903: ibid., no. 370; P. Cambon to Delcassé, 11 October 1903: 2 DDF, IV, no. 7.

a symbol of Anglo-French rapprochement. The Dutch minister in London probably echoed a widespread opinion that the treaty confirmed a rapprochement "which has gradually become an Entente Cordiale."[19]

Although President Loubet expressed the belief that "this agreement would be followed by another of greater importance and more extensive and varied scope,"[20] the difficulties made negotiating arduous over the next two months. The French reply to Lansdowne's memorandum of 1 October reached him on the 26th. Delcassé at last agreed not to fix a term for the British occupation of Egypt. He also accepted Lansdowne's proposals regarding Siam, Zanzibar, Madagascar, and the New Hebrides, but raised serious questions concerning both Egypt and Morocco and insisted that France receive Gambia in return for her rights in Newfoundland. This demand proved to be the sticking point, still unsettled by mid-December when Lansdowne reported to the Cabinet that there was "no insuperable or even serious difficulty in connection with Egypt; and though Morocco still presents certain points of difference, it ought not to be hard to find a way through them." On the other hand, Newfoundland, he said, "presents the most embarrassing of the outstanding problems."[21]

Lord Cromer, who constantly stressed the vital importance of a settlement, was pleased with the progress of negotiations, and thought that "we were in reality asking for a great deal more than we offered in return."[22] Cambon agreed with him but felt that France was in a position "to be difficult" because "the English have more interest in making an arrangement with us for Egypt than we have in concluding one with them for Morocco." He noted, however, that English commercial circles had become greatly interested in Morocco and were pressing their demands on Lansdowne. Also the situation of the Cabinet was precarious, and an agreement with France would help to consolidate Lansdowne's position. Cambon remarked that "we have every interest in strengthening and maintaining him because who knows if we could settle with another."[23] Unwilling,

19. Goudswaard, *Some Aspects*, p. 111. For the treaty text: Barclay, *Thirty Years*, pp. 232–34; or 2 *DDF*, IV, no. 10.

20. Monson to Lansdowne, 22 October 1903: *BD*, II, no. 372.

21. Balfour to the king, 11 December 1903: Goudswaard, *Some Aspects*, p. 113.

22. Newton, *Lansdowne*, pp. 283–84; Marquis of Zetland, *Lord Cromer* (London, 1932), pp. 277–78.

23. P. Cambon to Delcassé, 18 November and 21 October 1903: 2 *DDF*, IV, nos. 89, 28; 23 October 1903: Cambon, *Correspondance*, II, 98–99.

however, to make concessions for the sake of agreement, Cambon sometimes raised the German danger of intervention in the western Mediterranean in order to persuade Lansdowne to accept French proposals.

By mid-January 1904 negotiations over the compensation for French rights in Newfoundland reached a deadlock, for Lansdowne's proffered substitutes for Gambia failed to satisfy Cambon and Delcassé. Cambon had been counting upon British eagerness to conclude the agreement and knew that Cromer was pressing for it. Delcassé, too, was anxious to finish, and Cambon conceived his own role to be that of putting on the brakes in order to avoid another fiasco such as those of the Spanish and Siamese negotiations. Cromer was truly worried lest a complete breakdown occur. He argued that it was "worth some sacrifice to avoid this" and urged speed. Sir Edmund Gorst, in Paris to complete the financial arrangements concerning Egypt, felt that "the spirit in which our government and the foreign office are negotiating is much too stiff. . . ."[24] Actually both sides were "too stiff" over the Newfoundland question. Although the outbreak of the Russo-Japanese war on 8 February 1904 might well have increased their desire to conclude the entente, they took two more months of haggling before signing the accords that constituted the Entente Cordiale.

Most of this time was taken up with the search for an arrangement concerning the Newfoundland problem which they could present to their parliaments and public as a bargain. The British had to take into account the views of the Newfoundland government as well as their own, while Delcassé found the minister of colonies exigent over proposed boundaries in Africa. The British categorically refused to cede Gambia, on which the French had insisted, but finally agreed to delimit the boundary so as to give France access on the Gambia River to navigable waters, to give additional slices of territory in northern Nigeria, and to cede the Isles of Los opposite French-held Conakry. Although the general lines of settlement had been drawn by the end of February, when Balfour reported hopefully to the king that the decision on Los would probably end the major difficulties, most of March was taken up with "sticking in all sorts of ignoble ruts," as Lansdowne put it.[25]

Besides unsolved questions of detail, other problems not only

24. Newton, *Lansdowne*, p. 289; Zetland, *Cromer*, p. 280.
25. Zetland, *Cromer*, p. 281.

caused trouble but constituted reasons for the conclusion of negotiations. Spain was becoming increasingly uneasy because of current
rumors and had to be reassured. Events in Morocco required action
there, especially in respect of finances. Delcassé wanted to clear the
way for a French loan late in February and sought British approval
for a unilateral French operation to which Lansdowne agreed. Both
governments were none too stable, and there were fears on both sides
that ministerial crises might prevent the conclusion of an agreement.
Nevertheless, at the last minute the French attempted revisions in
wording and substance which Lansdowne firmly refused to consider.
At length, however, with the help of Gorst, who shuttled between
London and Paris to help in drafting the agreement on Egypt and
the Khedivial decree that was to put its major provisions into effect,
the three instruments comprising the agreement were completed.
Lansdowne and Paul Cambon signed them at the Foreign Office in
London on 8 April 1904.

The form of the comprehensive agreement had been outlined by
Lansdowne and Cambon on 11 March.[26] The first instrument was a
"Declaration Concerning Egypt and Morocco," to which the Khedivial
decree was annexed. In the declaration France expressly stated that
she would not hamper the action of England in Egypt by asking
for a fixed term of occupation or in any other manner; on the other
hand, Great Britain recognized that in Morocco "it appertains to
France . . . to preserve order in that country, and to provide assistance." The promises were worded so that it appeared that there were
equivalents throughout. Both promised to maintain the political status
quo and to grant freedom of trade and equality in customs duties
for a period of thirty years. Britain's pledge to insure the free passage
of the Suez canal was offset by a provision not to erect fortifications
on the coast of Morocco "between, but not including, Melilla and
the heights which command the right bank of the River Sebou."
They both pledged to take account of Spain's special interests in
Morocco. The Khedivial Decree created a new set of laws regulating
the relations between the Egyptian government and the bondholders.
The *Caisse de la Dette* remained but was greatly restricted in its
functions, for the control of revenues was taken from it and placed
in the hands of the government, which meant in practice the British
advisers to the Khedive.

By five secret articles, eventually published in 1911, the two powers

26. The texts: *BD*, II, no. 417, or 2 *DDF*, IV, no. 389.

provided for possible future changes in Egypt and Morocco, again on a basis of reciprocity, by asserting that France would not "refuse to entertain" any proposals Great Britain might make for changes in "the system of the Capitulations or in the judicial organization of Egypt," and Britain agreed "to entertain the suggestions that the Government of the French Republic may make to them with a view of introducing similar reforms in Morocco." These innocuously worded pledges were supplemented by a delimitation of spheres of influence in Morocco for France and Spain, "whenever the Sultan ceases to exercise authority over it." Spain was to administer exclusively the coast from Melilla to the heights on the right bank of the Sebou, the zone within which fortifications were prohibited. Though there was no explicit pledge of mutual support, these secret articles not only provided for a future partition of Morocco, but also indirectly bound Great Britain to support it. The long-term implications of these secret articles made them the most significant provisions of the accord, a significance that the Balfour government failed to appreciate.

In a second instrument, a Convention, France and Britain settled the age-old disputes over the Newfoundland fisheries. The French gave up their rights of landing on the "Treaty" or "French" shore, first obtained in 1713, and were obliged to remove their property while retaining the right to fish in Newfoundland territorial waters. Britain had to indemnify individuals for property loss and to give France territorial compensation. After much haggling they had finally agreed upon a small slice of Gambia, a shift in the northern boundary of Nigeria giving France some 16,000 square miles and a more practicable route from the Niger to Lake Chad, and the Isles of Los commanding the harbor of Conakry in Guinea.

The third instrument was a declaration concerning Siam, Madagascar, and the New Hebrides. Unable to settle their differences in the New Hebrides, France and Britain postponed a settlement that was finally made in 1906. The British renunciation of protests concerning tariffs levied in Madagascar after its annexation by France in 1896 was traded against French withdrawal of jurisdiction and postal services from Zanzibar. Siam had already been settled before the signature of the declaration, France gaining a sphere of influence in the east and Britain one in the west. France had made a second treaty with Siam after the abortive one of 1903 in February 1904, which was ratified in November. Although the nationalists thought the second treaty differed little from the first, it was approved, wrote René Millet, a severe critic of Delcassé, almost unperceived "au milieu des feux d'artifice tirés en l'honneur de l'entente cordiale."[27]

IV.

Lord Lansdowne, in summing up the negotiations and agreements, expected the "cumulative effect" to be highly advantageous. He emphasized the comprehensiveness of the settlement that removed the sources of long-standing differences which had been "a chronic addition to our diplomatic embarrassments and a standing menace to an international friendship which we have been at pains to cultivate, and which, we rejoice to think, has completely overshadowed the antipathies and suspicions of the past." Moreover he felt that the accords had been to the mutual advantage of both Britain and France.[28]

The British press was almost unanimous in its praise of the accord with France, although there were some complaints about the relinquishment of Morocco to France, and especially about the guarantee of freedom of trade for only thirty years. Many remarked about the great change in Anglo-French relations that had occurred over such a short period since the tension only six years before of the Fashoda crisis. In the parliamentary debate, June 1904, liberal as well as conservative leaders welcomed the accord. Sir Edward Grey asserted that the agreement was "much more important . . . in the spirit in this case than in the letter, especially as regards to the future," and he hoped that the government would "lose no opportunity of making it a working model for other cases where it is possible to do so." He did not indicate whether he had in mind Russia, as Cromer and others did, or Germany. The only sour note was that of Rosebery who thought that the agreement with France was "much more likely to lead to complications than to peace."[29]

In France the press was generally favorable to the accord but less enthusiastic, and whereas in London the House of Commons passed the third reading of the ratifying bill by a voice vote, a con-

27. René Millet, *Notre politique extérieure de 1898 à 1905* (Paris, 1905), pp. 65–66. The text of the treaty: 2 *DDF*, IV, no. 270.

28. Lansdowne to Monson, 8 April 1904: *BD*, II, no. 416.

29. Sir E. Grey, *Speeches on Foreign Affairs, 1904–1914* (ed. Paul Knaplund. London, 1931), p. 21; Marquis of Crewe, *Lord Rosebery* (New York, London, 1931), p. 478.

siderable minority in the French chamber not only criticized the accord but also voted against it. Delcassé principally based his plea for the agreement on the grounds that it gave France dominance in Morocco, which would strengthen Algeria, and that Morocco under another power would be a menace. The extreme Left and Right were unhappy about the terms of the accord for different reasons, and already a breach was developing between Delcassé and the colonial group that was to facilitate his downfall a year later. They both wanted Morocco, but the colonial group wanted an accord with Germany, too, whose benevolence toward French imperialism under Bismarck they still attributed to the Bülow regime. Hence the insistence in some of the press that the accord was not directed against anyone. On the other hand, it was hailed as a stepping stone toward Anglo-Russian friendship. Still others—by the time of the parliamentary debate in November 1904, postponed till then in order to include the Franco-Spanish agreement—faced squarely the possible power implications of Anglo-French friendship. Paul Deschanel, president of the chamber and a close friend of Caillaux, asserted that it was the political and commercial threat of Germany that had led England to make the accord with France; hence, he said, "one was justified in [expecting] some permanent effects coming from that permanent cause."[30] On the whole, however, those who accepted the entente took it at its face value—it was not an alliance, and its value to France, aside from the removal of conflicts with England, remained to be seen.

Among the other European powers, Italy had reason to welcome the Entente Cordiale heartily because, in view of her relations established by the agreements of 1902 with both Britain and France, she no longer had to face the possibility of making a choice between them. More than one newspaper stressed this point. Although Loubet's visit to Rome took place after the announcement of the Anglo-French accord and Germany and France vied strenuously for Italy's allegiance, the fear expressed by Bülow and Goluchowski that Italy would flee the Triplice if England and France came to an understanding was not fulfilled.

In Russia, who had been forewarned of the entente in March, Lamsdorff cordially congratulated France and seemed to be sensible of the benefits that Russia might draw from Anglo-French friendship in the amelioration of Anglo-Russian relations. Thus he seemed to

30. Gabriel-Louis Jaray, "L'Accord entre la France et l'Angleterre," QDC, 16 November 1904, pp. 597–98.

reciprocate the sentiments of Lansdowne and Cromer in England and of several commentators in France. The Russian press, too, seemed to take a more friendly attitude toward England, and the ambassador in Paris, Nelidov, who had been intimate with Barrère in Rome, expressed his satisfaction in an interview published by *Le Temps*, in which he also hinted that the Russian government was likely "to regard as their friends the friends of their ally."[31] The Russo-Japanese war, however, and the British expedition to Tibet, noted by Paul Cambon as a stumbling block to better Anglo-Russian relations, made any likelihood of an immediate rapprochement remote, as the German minister in Lisbon rightly argued.

Of all the third powers, Germany's reaction to the Entente Cordiale and to the arrangements in Morocco was the most significant. Lansdowne and Cambon had feared that Germany might demand some area of the Atlantic coast, and Lansdowne, at least, seemed to fear that she might take umbrage at a Franco-British arrangement. Both Delcassé and Lansdowne gave Germany advance notice of the accord, the former informally on 23 March and the later formally on 6 April when Sir Frank Lascelles, British ambassador in Berlin, told Bülow that the agreement was not directed against Germany. Bülow then and later took the position publicly that the settlement of Anglo-French differences served the interest of world peace. Even when Bebel and others in the Reichstag spoke of an isolation of Germany. Bülow on 12 and 14 April presented an optimistic view of the situation and asserted that "we have no reason to fear isolation if we keep our sword sharp." He argued that "Germany is too strong. For us there are many possible combinations, and even if we remain alone, that would not be so frightful."[32] Privately, the kaiser estimated that the agreement was a valuable French achievement and that England had thereby gained a greater freedom of movement and hence need show less consideration for Germany. Bülow admitted that both France and England gained in international weight and in freedom of movement; and that Italy would be strongly attracted by the entente. But he tried to reassure the kaiser by predicting that the entente would cool down when Russo-Japanese peace negotiations began, because Britain would support Japan and France, Russia.

The fact was, as this correspondence and other discussions showed,

31. Monson to Lansdowne, 12 April 1904: *BD*, II, no. 418.
32. Penzler, ed., *Fürst Bülows Reden*, II, 84.

the German policy-makers were unprepared for the consummation of the entente. As far back as the spring of 1903 when rumors cropped up about an Anglo-French understanding, the German Foreign Office reasoned that France, as long as she clung to *revanche*, could not give up Russia, and an Anglo-French accord would loosen the ties between Paris and St. Petersburg. Both Holstein and Bülow seemed incapable of viewing Anglo-French relations as part of a continental complex, and they felt quite safe from any threat of a triple alliance against Germany. They also thought that Russia might put pressure on Paris to resist an accord with England, or might be led to resurrect the league of the three emperors, if French loyalty seemed shaken. Thus, as Bülow put it, they could take the whole thing "not at all suavely enough (*gar nicht pomadig genug*)."[33]

Now that the Entente Cordiale had actually been made, not only were the Germans unprepared for it, but they were ready to believe the worst about it. French and British newspapers that talked about the isolation of Germany and the possibility of an Anglo-Russian entente did not ease the situation. The kaiser's disappointment over his reception in Italy and the failure of a meeting with Loubet in April helped to increase his anxiety and to lead to a series of boastful and minatory speeches at Karlsruhe and Mainz in late April and early May. The assertion of Baron Greindl, the Belgian minister in Berlin, that he believed the Anglo-French agreement contained a secret clause with reference to the Rhine frontier alarmed Bülow, who questioned Metternich in London about it. Lansdowne told Metternich that the whole thing was a "perfect mare's nest."[34] Edward VII, too, when he visited the Emperor at Kiel in June sought to allay Bülow's fears by saying that no such particular arrangement as the Anglo-French agreement was necessary between England and Germany because there were no "concrete, conflicting political interests"; "patience and mutual tact" would "little by little bring back our peoples into the paths of better mutual understanding."[35] Unfortunately, the meeting did not reassure either party, because the kaiser and Bülow got the impression that Edward VII had aimed at the encirclement of Germany, and the king took away the impression that the only way to combat German plans was through her isolation. For the time being,

33. Bülow to Holstein, 3 April 1903: *GP*, XVIII(2), no. 5911.

34. Bülow and Metternich exchange of telegrams, 4 June 1904: *GP*, XX(1), nos. 6383–84.

35. Bülow, *Memoirs*, II, 33–34.

however, Germany sought what advantage she could from the Egyptian question and see-sawed for more than six months before making a strike over Morocco.

While Austria and Italy made little or no difficulty over their consent to the Khedivial decree by which Britain sought to free Egypt from the fetters of international financial control, and Russia acquiesced after Lansdowne had given assurances concerning the Younghusband expedition to Tibet, Germany attempted to make her agreement conditional upon the settlement of claims in Samoa and South Africa, and upon the betterment of commercial relations between Germany and Britain and Germany and Canada. Lansdowne was indignant at what he called "a great piece of effrontery," and refused to treat of anything outside Egypt itself.[36] The upshot of more than a month of negotiation was the agreement of 15–19 June by which Germany made pledges similar to those of France with respect to the Khedivial decree and British action in Egypt. Great Britain promised that German commerce in Egypt was to enjoy most-favored-nation treatment for thirty years; German rights arising from treaties, conventions, and usage would be respected; German schools would enjoy the same liberty as in the past; and German officials in the Egyptian services would not be placed at a disadvantage compared with British officials in the same services. Whether or not the German intention was to test the possibility of an entente with Britain or to show, as Holstein suggested, that Germany would not be led about by a previous Anglo-French decision, the effect of her demands was to convince the British once more that Germany was a higgling and difficult power with whom to deal. On the other hand, the winning of German consent to the Khedivial decree meant that, as Richard von Kühlmann, first secretary of the German mission in Tangier, observed, "The Egyptian question is dead, the Moroccan very much alive."[37]

While the Anglo-German negotiations were going on, Delcassé began to wrestle with Spain over an agreement. Great Britain had assured Spain that she would not be left out of arrangements concerning Morocco; and the kaiser, in March 1904, told the Spanish king at Vigo that Germany had no interest in Morocco and that Spain should come to an understanding with France. Nevertheless, throughout the Franco-Spanish negotiations, begun on 19 April, Ger-

36. Newton, *Lansdowne*, pp. 329–30.
37. Kühlmann, Memorandum, 1 October 1904: *GP*, XX(1), no. 6386.

many hovered behind the scenes hoping that she might participate in the arrangements over Morocco, but was never brought in, even though the Spaniards at times threatened to do so. In negotiating with France, Spain hoped that she could count on Great Britain to soften Delcassé's terms, but Lansdowne, though he occasionally made a plea for a specific point which Spain wanted, did so in a friendly spirit and without exerting pressure upon France.

The fact is that by April 1904 Delcassé had reversed his position of 1902. Then he envisaged a close cooperation with Spain and only a secondary consideration of Great Britain, but because Spain did not clinch the bargain then proposed, because the French colonial group opposed so large a concession to Spain, and finally because he made a deal with Great Britain that had cost France her former position in Egypt, he was now in 1904 determined to reduce to a minimum the Spanish share in the "pacific penetration" of Morocco and in an eventual partition. This minimum limited Spanish territory in northern Morocco to the neutral zone from Melilla to the Sebou River, as defined in the convention with Britain, and in the south deprived Spain of control over the Sous River valley. The accord with England had given Delcassé the whip hand, and to the chagrin of the Spanish government he used it throughout the negotiations.

From the first talks with Leon y Castillo in Paris, Delcassé sought to make the Spanish position in Morocco entirely subservient to the French. He not only denied Spain an equal partnership with France in relations with Morocco but even insisted that France would operate in the Spanish as well as in the French zones of influence. Moreover, he wanted to keep the accord secret for fear that publication would exasperate the sultan or arouse the Moroccans against France. Because Spain was not in a position to send an expedition to Morocco, France alone would have to repress such a movement. Throughout he insisted that France wished to maintain the status quo. The Spanish government, on the other hand, wanted the more extensive sphere of influence offered in 1902, a greater share in the administration of Morocco, publication of the agreement in order to satisfy the cortes, and an early date for the establishment of Spanish administration of their zone of influence. Yielding only on minor points, Delcassé at length completed the terms of a public declaration and of a secret convention, which he signed on 3 October 1904.[38]

38. Text of the agreement: 2 DDF, V, no. 358.

The public declaration simply announced Spanish adherence to the Anglo-French declaration of 8 April and a Franco-Spanish accord upon the rights and interests of France and Spain in Morocco. The secret convention, on the other hand, looked to the ultimate partition of the country between France and Spain. Article II, which delimited the Spanish sphere in the north so as to leave Fez well outside it, provided that for not more than fifteen years Spain would exercise the same rights respecting tranquillity and reforms as France, but only after a previous agreement with France before each action, whereas France would simply give Spain notice of any action that would affect the Spanish zone. By Article III, if the status quo became impossible to maintain, Spain was to act freely in her zone of influence. By Articles IV and V the boundaries of Ifni (ceded to Spain in 1860) and of the Spanish zone in southern Morocco were delimited and the provisions respecting the northern zone were applied to the southern. Other Articles forbade Spain to alienate or sell any of the areas assigned to her. If either party had to resort to military action, it was obliged to give notice to the other. Tangier was to retain its special character. In public works involving both the Spanish zone and the remainder of Morocco, French and Spanish contractors were to participate; and France would enjoy the same rights in the Spanish zone as Article II gave to Spain.

Thus Delcassé had got what he wanted: freedom to achieve a preponderant position in Morocco for the next fifteen years if, before that time, Morocco did not break up. The Spaniards were compelled to take second place in the meantime and to act in their zones only with the previous consent of France. It is small wonder that the convention had to be kept secret; but secrecy both here and in the accord with Britain had unfortunate effects. Germany, for example, mistrusted the secret provisions, overestimating the significance of the Anglo-French articles and underestimating that of the Franco-Spanish. Saint-René Taillandier was aghast at the prospect in Morocco, for he feared that the secrets would not be kept and that the maghzen, the sultan's government and entourage, would be alienated if it learned of them. But as Delcassé saw it, there was no choice, because he could not go ahead in Morocco without coming to terms with Spain, and the price, however reduced to a minimum, could not be advertised because it would reveal too clearly his ultimate objectives and arouse opposition, certainly from Germany.

V.

The assessment of the Entente Cordiale, of which the Franco-Spanish accord was but a subsidiary appendix, has been influenced so much by the subsequent course of events, especially the first Moroccan crisis a year later, that it is difficult to see the accord in its contemporary perspective. Certainly on the British side the entente was not directed against Germany. Nevertheless it is impossible to maintain that Lansdowne, Balfour, and their colleagues, including Edward VII, were not aware that trouble might well arise with Germany over its pointed exclusion from Morocco. Throughout the negotiations Paul Cambon had remarked upon the dangers of a German intervention, and Lansdowne had not demurred. Had the Balfour government been interested in a general pacification all over the world, it would not have rejected the German desire for a settlement even though the Germans expressed themselves in connection with the Egyptian question in a most clumsy and maladroit manner. The truth is that in the press of England as well as France and Germany, the entente was hailed as constituting the isolation of Germany. Sir Eyre Crowe's famous argument that the accord was nothing more nor less than the outcome of a desire to end friction between Britain and France and in no way menaced Germany needs to be watered down a good bit. For, as J. A. Spender testifies, Crowe's account of the accord is incomplete. To the French as well as to the Germans, the Entente Cordiale was bound to have European implications. England had wittingly or unwittingly plunged into the heart of European contention and had cast its vote on behalf of France.[39]

The major French concern over Germany was connected with the Moroccan question. Delcassé, throwing overboard the suggestion in his own office and the advice of Paul Cambon and of Ambassador Bihourd in Berlin and of the leaders of the colonial group that a forward move in Morocco required an understanding with Germany as well as with Spain and England, had decided that as long as he faithfully maintained the open door for commerce he need make no special effort to treat with Germany. But beyond Morocco, his desire to bring Great Britain and Russia together and his awareness of the

39. Crowe, Memorandum, 1 January 1907: *BD*, III, 397–99; J. A. Spender, *Fifty Years of Europe* (New York, 1933), pp. 220–21. Cf. Samuel R. Williamson, Jr., *Politics of Grand Strategy*, pp. 14–15.

power element in such problems as the Far Eastern and Near Eastern questions could not but make him welcome the entente with England as a blow to German *Weltpolitik*. In this sense the Entente Cordiale was to him not just a colonial settlement but also a diplomatic revolution. Yet neither he nor his collaborators, as far as the record shows, anticipated the crisis that was to occur in 1905. Nor did they look upon Britain as a reliable military assistant. The entente to the French was just that, valuable as it might be in aligning Great Britain on their side. Yet it meant that henceforth Paris—not Berlin or London—would control the relations between Germany and England, for whatever move either sought to make would inevitably be assessed in the light of the London-Paris relationship.

Contrariwise, what the Entente Cordiale itself was to become was largely dependent upon the German attitude. For years Germany had been in the comfortable position of a *tertius gaudens* between the Dual Alliance and Britain, but now that position had been destroyed. If she acquiesced quietly in the new order of things, the ties between England and France might remain tenuous, but if she sought to challenge the new alignment, she was likely to cement the ties more firmly.

Who got the better of the bargain in the Entente Cordiale of 1904? The French and even some Englishmen contended that it was Great Britain, because the accord sanctioned what in effect Great Britain already had in Egypt, while France had yet to make good her aspirations in Morocco. On the other hand, this situation put upon Britain a heavy moral responsibility to back France in Morocco if another power made difficulties there. Beyond that, the ultimate meaning of the Entente Cordiale was that "to get security in Cairo" Britain "would end up supporting French security on the Rhine."[40]

Such a consequence was still far away in 1904, and there were other realities, especially the Russo-Japanese War, to be brought into the picture in order to gain an understanding of the first test of the entente in 1905.

40. Archibald Paton Thornton, *The Imperial Idea and its Enemies* (London, 1959), p. 117. Cf. Erich Brandenburg, *Vom Bismarck zum Weltkrieg* (1939), p. 239.

Chapter 4

The Russo-Japanese

War, 1904–1905

In the background and conduct of the war with Japan the major
Russian figures involved were Tsar Nicholas II ("Nicky" to his
friend the kaiser); Sergei Iulievich Witte, finance minister till August
1903 and plenipotentiary at the Conference of Portsmouth in 1905;
Foreign Minister V. N. Lamsdorff; General A. N. Kuropatkin,
minister of war until 1904; and Admiral E. I. Alexeiev, viceroy
of the Far East. Russian ambassadors in key positions were Count
A. C. Benckendorff in London and A. I. Nelidov in Paris (formerly
in Rome). Marquis Taro Katsura headed the Japanese government
with Marquis Jutaro Komura as his foreign minister. His active
ambassadors were Shinichiro Kurino at St. Petersburg, Ichiro Motono
at Paris, and Viscount Tadasu Hayashi at London. German policy was
directed by William II ("Willy" in his correspondence with the tsar),
Chancellor Bülow, and Friedrich von Holstein, chief counselor in
the Foreign Office. It was implemented in Paris by Ambassador Prince
Hugo Radolin, and in London by Ambassador Count von Wolff-
Metternich. French Foreign Minister Théophile Delcassé's principal
aids were Maurice Paléologue at the Quai d' Orsay, Maurice Bompard
in St. Petersburg, and Paul Cambon in London, where Lord Lans-
downe headed the Foreign Office in Arthur James Balfour's ministry.

While alliances and alignments among the European great powers
were being modified by the Franco-Italian rapprochement and the
Anglo-French entente, a crisis was builidng up in the Far East between Russia and Japan. Their conflict of interests in Manchuria and
Korea was the only clash before 1914 to result in war between two
imperialistic powers; and the repercussions of their bloody engagement inevitably affected the international relations among the great
powers during and following their war.

I.

On the Russian side a political and economic push into the Far East had been under way ever since Sergei Iulievich Witte, minister of finance (1892–1903), had laid out his plans for the development of Russian power in Manchuria and North China. He was, to be sure, but the organizing genius who began to fulfill the dreams of Russian expansion that developed apace in the 1890's. Under him the Ministry of Finance slowly built up an economic empire which made it superior in Far Eastern affairs to the Foreign Office and even a rival of the War Ministry. While his objectives were fundamentally economic, utilizing railroad building, port development, mining, and banking as the instruments of power, they inevitably required close ties with the Chinese government and local administration in order to counter the rival imperialistic ambitions of other great powers. Moreover, the alluring concept of Russia's "manifest destiny," especially in Manchuria and Korea, led adventuresome men into policies and actions which Witte could not control, even though he had played a leading part in promoting Russia's expansionist ambitions.

Of most direct bearing upon the eventual armed clash with Japan were the intervention after the Sino-Japanese war of 1894–1895, the agreement with China in 1896 for an alliance and the building of the Chinese Eastern Railway across Manchuria, the subsequent building of the South Manchurian Railway, the acquisition of Port Arthur and of concessions in Korea, the occupation during the Boxer Rebellion of all key points in Manchuria, the aim of an exclusive monopoly over its resources, and finally the attempt from early 1901 to take advantage of the situation in order to establish political as well as economic control over Manchuria as a condition for the withdrawal of Russian occupation forces. Russia's formal adherence to the open door policy and the principle of the integrity of China seemed to be belied by her apparent objectives, and gave other powers, especially the United States, Great Britain, and Japan, grounds for vigorous protests against Russian moves in 1901–1902.

In fact the Russian government found itself caught on the horns of a dilemma. Through both Foreign Minister V. N. Lamsdorff and Witte, Russia had pledged in 1900 that as soon as peace returned after the Boxer rebellion and the security of the Manchurian railroads had been assured, she would withdraw her troops from Chinese territory, provided, said Lamsdorff's circular, "such action did

3. Nicholas II and William II (The Bettmann Archive)

not meet with obstacles caused by the proceedings of other Powers."[1]
In that last clause lay the other horn of the dilemma: if evacuation
meant leaving the field to Japan, the United States, and other powers
to penetrate Manchuria economically and thus to compete with Russia, then the dream of establishing preponderance in Manchuria
would vanish. Pledged to evacuate but fearful of the consequences of
expansion, Russia had little choice. Expansion might bring war with
Japan, but that eventually was unthinkable for Witte and others in
the Russian government. At length, faced with such events as the
Anglo-Japanese alliance of February 1902 and the determined stand
of the United States against Russia's economic pretensions in Manchuria, Russia hastily negotiated a treaty of 8 April 1902 with China
by which Manchuria was to be evacuated in three stages to be completed in eighteen months. Although the first stage was carried out in
southern Manchuria, the second and third, because of a conflict of
views within Russian governing circles, were never acted upon. The
conflict arose not simply over what policy to pursue in the Far East,
but also over the leadership in implementing the policy.

For several years opposition to Witte had been growing, but up
to the latter part of 1902 had achieved little success. The active leader
of the major rival group was A. M. Bezobrazov, a former guardsman
with several influential friends who introduced him at court. He
was a man of imagination, a persuasive talker, and something of
a swashbuckler who, according to V. K. Plehve, minister of the
interior and another opponent of Witte's, knew "how to read Nicholas II's mind better than his ministers and had made himself advocate of a policy that was in reality the synthesis of the sovereign's
secret desires."[2] The vehicle of Bezobrazov's operation was the Yalu
River timber concession stretching some 1,800 square miles over
northern Korea from the Tiumen River to the mouth of the Yalu.
As he and his friends saw it, Witte had been mistaken in relying
upon the compliance of China to sanction the developing Russian
interests, for China was recalcitrant toward Russia and impotent
under the pressure of other powers. Therefore, using the Yalu concession as a bulwark in Korea against Japanese expansion, Russia
should rely upon a combination of the Dual and Triple Alliances to
back her against the other great powers and proceed to establish
domination over Manchuria and eventually Korea.

1. Andrew Malozemoff, *Russian Far Eastern Policy*, p. 146.
2. General Moulin to André, 6 October 1904: 2 *DDF*, V, no. 364.

In the rivalry with the Bezobrazovists, or "Koreans" as they were sometimes called, Witte had the support of Lamsdorff and the minister of war, General A. N. Kuropatkin. The tug-of-war between this "mangy triumvirate," as their opponents called them, and the "Koreans" swayed back and forth in 1902–1903, with the tsar now favoring one side and now the other. In August 1903, however, he pushed both Bezobrazov and Witte out of their positions of influence and established the Viceroyalty of the Far East under Admiral Alexeiev, reputedly a "Korean" who was to direct military, economic, and diplomatic affairs in the whole area east of Lake Baikal. Witte was relieved of his post as Minister of Finance and was appointed chairman of the committee of ministers, an almost wholly honorary position. By this time Japan, although increasingly aroused by the activities of the Yalu Timber Company in Korea and Russian efforts to gain Chinese acquiescence in her domination of Manchuria, was ready to come to an understanding with Russia.

The Japanese had not been idle while Russia was attempting to expand her economic and political hold on Manchuria and Korea. The intervention of the three European powers after the Sino-Japanese war of 1894–1895 led Japan to build up her armaments to the point where she could compete with the great powers and at the same time to pursue a policy of safeguarding her interests on the mainland by cautious exploitation of the weaknesses of China. Japan directed her main drive toward Korea. There she established commercial and industrial rights in the South, enjoyed a great expansion of trade, and gave financial assistance to the Korean court by means of loans. Although plans for railway building went slowly, Japan had become the dominant power in Korea by 1900, supplanting Russia, who had maintained a lead up to 1898 but had then largely withdrawn.

But Japan, in its watchfulness at every sign of Russian expansion, was concerned not only that no other power gain preponderance in Korea but also that none secure a position that might threaten Japan's interests there. Yet despite rapid progress in armament, elder statesmen like Marquis Yamagata, one-time premier and influential in the councils of Marquis Katsura's government, which took office in June 1901, believed that Japan had to move cautiously lest she be subjected to another setback like that of 1895. Moreover, Japan needed help from other powers. Hence the alliance with Great Britain, consummated on 30 January 1902. The Katsura government included among its objectives the establishment of a protectorate over Korea.

Katsura himself thought that "if Manchuria comes into [Russia's] clutches, it will inevitably extend into Korea and will not end until there is no room for us." While he advocated thinking in terms of a "temporary peace," hence of short-term friendship with Russia, he, like Yamagata and his foreign minister Komura, believed in the inevitability of an eventual clash.[3] Time was an important element in their calculations because they were convinced that once the Trans-siberian Railway was completed, it would be too late to stop the Russians. Although there was a difference of opinion in Japan about how to deal with Russia, the Katsura government decided to negotiate with her despite the poor prospects of a satisfactory agreement in view of past and present Russian policy.

In Russia at the same time there was some feeling that because a war with Japan would be a great misfortune, the complete relinquishment of Korea would be the lesser of two evils. Witte took this position and Lamsdorff supported him, but they wanted to retain a hold on Manchuria and ultimately to get Korea. Thus both Japan and Russia were insincere in approaching one another, Japan in broaching the idea of a deal because Korea alone would not satisfy her, and Russia in entertaining the notion of trading Korea for Manchuria when there was no intention of giving up the former permanently. In December 1902 Russia replaced A. P. Izvolsky at Tokyo by Baron Roman R. Rosen, *persona grata* to the Japanese, in the hope of bringing about some understanding over Korea, and in June 1903 Japan decided to make an approach to Russia.

II.

In deciding upon negotiations with Russia, Japan occupied a relatively favorable international position. She enjoyed the moral support of the United States, who had protested the attempts of Russia to exact guarantees from China of a preponderant Russian position in Manchuria. Washington's deep-seated suspicions of Russia gave the impression that the United States was to be reckoned among Russia's adversaries, but Japan well knew that the United States would not risk war nor directly aid Japan, although by 1903 she had tacitly conceded to Japan a preponderant position in Korea.

3. Katsura and Komura, Memoranda: Ian H. Nish, *The Anglo-Japanese Alliance*, pp. 381–85.

As for Japan's ally, Great Britain, her attitude in 1903 was ambiguous. Britain had failed to act vigorously in protesting Russian demands upon China in April, and Lansdowne was hopeful of reaching an entente with Russia over central Asia. The upshot of exchanges with the Japanese in July was concern that Japan not conduct negotiations with Russia in such a way as to suggest any impairment of the Anglo-Japanese alliance, and that she keep Britain informed. Nevertheless, the existence of the alliance meant that Japan was assured of support should a third power intervene on behalf of Russia.

On the other hand, Russia could not rely on French aid against Japan, for by August, Delcassé had decided upon an accord with Great Britain in order to improve not only Anglo-French relations, but Anglo-Russian as well. Also, Germany since 1901 had declared more than once that she was neutral respecting Far Eastern questions, and the kaiser had sent word to the tsar that he had to keep his hands free in order to cover Russia's rear in Europe. Although Russia in 1903 hoped for more active support, the kaiser refused to make any promises. Fortunately Russia's relations with Austria-Hungary, with whom she was attempting to solve the Macedonian question, were good.

A little more than a month after the Japanese decision to approach Russia, the ambassador in St. Petersburg, Kurino, obtained Lamsdorff's agreement to negotiate, and on 12 August presented Japan's first proposal. The terms were one-sided and undoubtedly intended as an extreme statement of Japanese desires, but nevertheless embodied an objective already adopted in June: a mutual engagement to respect the independence and integrity of the Chinese and Korean empires; recognition of the "dominant interests" of Japan in Korea and of "those special interests of Russia in railway enterprises in Manchuria." Thus while Japan was to have virtually unrestricted rights in Korea, Russia was to be limited in Manchuria to "special interests" in the railways, clearly not an equal exchange but intended to safeguard Japan in Korea from the danger of a preponderant Russia position on its border.[4]

Following the Japanese statement in August, negotiations proceeded at a snail's pace. Russia insisted that they take place in Tokyo,

---

4. The available texts of the Russo-Japanese exchanges differ in wording but not in substance. I have followed John Albert White, *The Diplomacy of the Russo-Japanese War*, pp. 106ff.

where Rosen, in contact with Admiral Alexeiev at Port Arthur, would carry the burden of discussion. Because Russian draft proposals were shuttled back and forth among the tsar, Lamsdorff, Alexeiev, and Rosen, the replies to Japan were long delayed. Russian moves in the autumn of 1903, moreover, increased Japan's suspicion of her policy. The appointment of Alexeiev as Viceroy of the Far East ("a thunderbolt to disturb the East," said the United States minister in Tokyo),[5] a new set of demands upon China, the reoccupation of Mukden instead of the scheduled withdrawal of occupation troops—all confirmed Japan's conviction that Russia was planning to annex Manchuria.

At the same time something of a rift between Great Britain and Japan seemed to be opening. Although Japan had informed England of the negotiations, there had been no consultation. Lansdowne, however, not only let Japan know his views but also sought to exercise a moderating influence upon both parties, for he was feeling his way toward an entente with Russia that he hoped might help to solve the Manchurian problem. But Japan refused to accept Lansdowne's views, and Lamsdorff's expressed willingness to discuss the Far East came to nothing because he was no longer primarily responsible for the conduct of negotiations.

Meanwhile, Russo-Japanese exchanges made no progress toward agreement, each doggedly insisting upon terms that the other refused to consider. Also, long delays continued to occur between Japanese notes and Russian answers, not only because of cumbersome communication among the Russians but also because the debate within the Russian government continued over policies and interests. For example, Kuropatkin throughout November and December tried in vain to persuade his colleagues and the tsar to take northern Manchuria and abandon the rest. In addition, the lines of authority between Lamsdorff and Alexeiev remained indistinct, and Lamsdorff confessed to Kuropatkin that he did not expect any outcome of the negotiations because Alexeiev made demands as if the Japanese had already been conquered. Lamsdorff's pessimism proved to be well justified. By mid-January 1904, when the Japanese military began to think that it would be better if war came at once, the positions taken by Russia and Japan were virtually unchanged from those of the previous autumn. Japan still insisted upon her basic demands

5. Griscom to Secretary Hay, 8 December 1903: Alfred L. P. Dennis, *Adventures in American Diplomacy*, p. 383.

in respect to Korea and Manchuria, while Russia continued to ignore them, persisting in her original view that Russian treaty rights in Manchuria were not subjects for a bilateral agreement with Japan.

The great powers had watched the developing deadlock without interfering. In December 1903 Lansdowne suggested to Cambon "that it was the duty of our two governments . . . to do all in their power to keep the peace." Cambon agreed that they should "pour as much cold water as possible on the embers."[6] Although intermittent discussions continued throughout December, Lansdowne's desire to find some way to mediate between Russia and Japan was vetoed by Prime Minister Balfour, who was backed by the Cabinet in his view that Great Britain should do nothing to prevent war or to help Japan, except under the terms of the alliance. Japan herself made it clear in January 1904 that mediation would be unwelcome, for it would not lead to a permanent settlement and might enable Russia to make further delays to the military disadvantage of Japan. Russia, too, did not want mediation, but instead asked Delcassé to enlist Lansdowne in an effort to moderate Japan's demands, although he was not to use the words "mediation" or "good offices." Delcassé, however, made no headway with the Japanese and British ambassadors with whom he discussed the proposal.[7]

By this time both Japan and Russia were preparing for war. Japan on 14 January formed a high military council to direct military operations, and the tsar permitted Alexeiev to prepare for mobilization and the movement of troops to the Yalu. On 28 January a conference under the chairmanship of Grand Duke Alexei Aleksandrovich decided after a hot debate to yield on two of Japan's points, but not on the matter of giving a pledge to Japan to respect Chinese integrity. That Japan regarded as a sine qua non. The Russian proposal, however, is of academic interest only because it was sent to Port Arthur for transmittal to Tokyo on the very day, 3 February, that the Jananese government decided upon war. The emperor approved the decision on the 4th. On the 6th Admiral Togo dispatched transports to Korea, and Komura telegraphed Kurino in St. Petersburg to break

6. Lansdowne to Monson, 11 December 1903: *BD*, II, no. 259; P. Cambon to Delcassé, 11 December 1903: 2 *DDF*, IV, no. 121. Whether Lansdowne was assured of French neutrality is a moot question. Cambon's correspondence makes it doubtful. See Cambon to Delcassé, 8 February 1904: 2 *DDF*, IV, no. 246; and Cambon to his son, 26 December 1903: *Correspondance*, II, 102–04.

7. Bompard and Delcassé exchange of telegrams, 12–13 January 1904: 2 *DDF*, IV, nos. 169, 171–72.

off diplomatic relations. These Japanese actions spelled the end of negotiation, and it is doubtful whether the outcome would have been different if Japan had received the last Russian proposal, which still fell short of her minimum demands.

At the last moment the Russian government appealed to Great Britain to undertake mediation. While Lansdowne felt that the Japanese demand for a declaration regarding the integrity of China was excessive, he told Benckendorff that any kind of intervention was impossible because Japan would not accept it. The tsar himself at a council meeting of 8 February regarded mediation as too late. He had already on the previous day authorized Alexeiev to order mobilization, and as a result of decisions taken by the council telegraphed him that if the Japanese fleet with a landing force crossed the 39th parallel on the Korean west coast, he might attack it without waiting for the first shot. As it was, the Japanese fired the first round when their torpedo boats launched an attack on Russian naval vessels at Port Arthur on the night of 8–9 February. The formality of declarations of war followed on 10 February 1904.

At the outbreak of war the powers were concerned over the position of China. Upon a suggestion from Germany, the United States issued a circular note proposing the preservation of the "administrative entity of China," a phrase designed to get around the awkward fact that the war might be fought on Chinese soil in Manchuria. The powers agreed to this proposal and one by one made known their own neutrality, thus finally clearing away the clouds of suspicion, particularly concerning Britain and France. For Delcassé, who had worked with Japanese Ambassador Motono to bring about an agreement between Japan and Russia, the outbreak of war was unexpected, for he had told the council of ministers as late as 5 February that peace could be kept. The Germans, on the other hand, had long anticipated the war and thought that it would strengthen Russia's position in the Far East and deprive France of Russian help in Europe. Britain, even though neutral, "kept the ring" for Japan, because her maritime strength prevented any other power from intervening.

III.

Upon the outbreak of war not even Great Britain and the United States, who had sympathized with Japan in her opposition to Russia, expected a Japanese military victory. Japan, who needed loans even more urgently than Russia, therefore had to pay 6 per cent on the first loan floated in New York and London in May 1904. As Japanese victories over Russia mounted—the Yalu in May, Liao-yang in August, Port Arthur in January 1905, and Mukden in March—confidence in Japan's ultimate success rose and she was able to contract a loan at the end of March 1905 at 4.5 percent. The crowning blow to Russia came with the destruction of the fleet in the Tsushima straits at the end of May 1905. Meanwhile the diplomatic situation was unfavorable to Russia, who had entered the war with only Germany playing the role of firm friend. Her ally, France, bent upon completing the entente with Britain, observed a strict neutrality, modified to "benevolence" only when circumstances of competition with Germany for Russian loyalty required it. Public opinion in France at the outset approved strict neutrality, although the Left openly denounced Russia.

As the war progressed, British opinion tended to cool toward Japan. At the outset the government was determined to observe strict neutrality. As Japan won her initial victories, doubts arose as to the wisdom of applauding the victory of an Asiatic over a European power, and the consequences of a Japanese victory for the balance of power in the Far East. Moreover, the government continued to talk of the possibility of a rapprochement with Russia until irritations arising from the activities of Russian naval vessels during the summer and autumn of 1904 put an end to it for the duration of the war. In any case the Russian court and the tsar himself were so anti-British that there was little hope of improvement in diplomatic relations while the war lasted. That relations did not deteriorate dangerously was owing to the Russian decision not to send the Black Sea fleet through the Straits, a move secretly advocated by the kaiser and one that Balfour and Lansdowne had agreed to resist. The Dogger Bank incident in October 1904 and the problem of coaling the Russian war ships, of which more below, might have created a serious crisis but failed to do so, thanks in considerable measure to the efforts of the French. Throughout the first year of the Russo-Japanese war, therefore, the conclusion of the Entente Cordiale and the British determination to keep out of the conflict meant that Britain was pushed closer to France, whose ambassador in London consulted with Lord Lansdowne "on all dangerous questions."[8]

The European power most directly involved diplomatically with

8. George Monger, *End of Isolation*, pp. 167–68.

the implications of the war was Germany. In 1904 Germany found herself increasingly uncomfortable because of the weakening of the Triple Alliance by Italy's rapprochement with France, signalized by the Loubet-Delcassé visit to Rome in April and by the conclusion of the Entente Cordiale, which the kaiser suspected was aimed at Germany. Even before these events underlined the deterioration of Germany's position, the kaiser had sought to establish close relations with Russia through personal contacts with the tsar. He had impressed the Russian emperor by his friendly attitude at Wiesbaden and Wolfgarten, 4 and 5 November 1903, and followed the meeting by letters and telegrams throughout 1904, in which constantly recurring themes were the "Crimean combination" of England and France, the anti-Russian machinations of the British, and the "Yellow Peril."[9]

The obverse of this coin was German-British relations which had become sharpened by the questions arising from the Russo-Japanese war and the increasing awareness in England from the time of the Venezuelan misadventure in early 1903 of the aggressive potentialities of the German fleet under construction. Each mistrusted the other because of their being on opposite sides in the Russo-Japanese war, but more important was the German mistrust of England arising from the feeling of isolation after the signing of the Entente Cordiale. Nevertheless, something of a short-lived detente occurred when Edward VII visited the kaiser during the regatta at Kiel near the end of June. The kaiser even reported to the tsar that "Uncle Bertie's" visit was going off well. At King Edward's suggestion a German squadron visited Plymouth on 11 July. Also Britain and Germany signed an arbitration treaty on the 12th. The press of both countries, however, either played down the exchanges as unimportant or continued to voice suspicion of each other. Both governments, on the other hand, had cause for irritation against Russia when in July a Russian cruiser stopped a German ship and removed postbags of correspondence for Japan at about the same time as the seizure of a British ship. A sharp protest by the kaiser to the tsar brought the promise to prevent such acts in the future. The incident led the British to feel that Germany might back them up in opposing Russian egress through the Straits, but they found the Germans reserved in their attitude toward the question.

The problem of coaling the Russian fleet found Britain and Ger-

9. A. N. Kuropatkin, *KA*, II, 93; *The Kaiser's Letters to the Tsar*, Ed. N. F. Grant, pp. 99, 118, 147, and *passim*.

many poles apart; and the coaling question became an important aspect of the kaiser's attempts to conclude an alliance with Russia. On 16 August 1904 Great Britain notified the belligerents that neither Russian nor Japanese naval vessels would be allowed to coal in British ports, because that would violate British neutrality. Almost a month later the *Berliner Tageblatt* reported an agreement between the Russian government and the Hamburg-America Company for the purchase of coal and its transportation to Far Eastern areas of conflict. In response to Japanese protests Bülow refused to admit that this private arrangement constituted an unneutral act, but he was sufficiently concerned to ask St. Petersburg what would happen if England took an unfriendly attitude toward Germany and aroused Japan. He commented that if Japan and England should make war, France would be tempted to pursue *revanche*. Such hypothetical questions indicated the suspicious frame of mind of the Germans concerning both England and France in the autumn of 1904. Lamsdorff, in reply to Bülow, did not think Japan was in a position to fight Germany, nor did he think that Britain wanted war.

The Dogger Bank incident on the night of 21–22 October when the Russian Baltic fleet on its way to the Far East fired upon Hull fishermen, brought matters among Great Britain, Germany, and Russia to a head. The British people were thoroughly aroused over the killing and wounding of fishermen and the sinking of trawlers. For a few days there seemed to be a real danger of war. The Admiralty had the Russian fleet followed as it left British waters and made preparations for destroying the "fleet of lunatics." Moreover, since the story was abroad that the Germans lay behind the trouble by warning the Russian government that Japanese mines and torpedo boats were awaiting the fleet as it emerged from the Baltic, the British public made little distinction in their anger between the Russian fleet and the Hapag coaling ships. Thanks to the coolness of Lansdowne, the intercession of Delcassé, and the energetic and untiring mediation of Cambon between Lansdowne and Benckendorff, Britain and Russia on 25 November agreed to an international commission of inquiry to sit in Paris and to report on where the responsibility lay and "the degree of blame attaching to the two high contracting parties or of other countries in case their responsibility shall be established by the inquiry."[10] The Commission rendered its report on 25 February 1905 that the Russian admiral was responsible

---

10. Andrew, *Delcassé*, pp. 247–48; Henri Cambon, *Paul Cambon*, p. 222; Monger, *End of Isolation*, pp. 171–75.

for firing upon the fishing vessels, but that his precautions and standing orders were not excessive under the circumstances and that when he discovered what was happening he personally attempted to prevent the trawlers from being fired upon. The report was obviously designed as a compromise between the British and Russian positions. The incident was closed on 9 March with the Russian payment of £65,000 as an indemnity due to the Hull fishermen.[11] Since by this time Port Arthur had fallen and within a couple of weeks the Japanese were to win the battle of Mukden, the British had little cause to fear Russian hostility.

Meanwhile a war scare developed between Britain and Germany. The British were convinced by this time that Germany was building a fleet in order to attack England, and also had formed a secret alliance with Russia against her. Aside from the known intimacy of the kaiser and the tsar, the Witte-Bülow negotiations in July of a tariff agreement constituted one basis for the rumor. Actually there was nothing more sinister in these negotiations than the Russian acceptance of unfavorable tariff terms in return for the right to secure loans in Berlin, but rumors flourished on all sides in the atmosphere of 1904. Bülow told Sir Frank Lascelles, the British ambassador in Berlin, of his impression that there was a strong party in England working for a war with Germany, and Lascelles admitted that *The Times* sowed distrust of Germany, and that Valentine Chirol, head of its foreign department and the soul of the campaign, was convinced of a secret German-Russian agreement. On the British side, indeed, intemperate articles in the press and suspicions arising from Germany's benevolent attitude toward Russia, coupled with the growing conviction of German hostile intentions in building a navy, accounted for the feeling of tension after the Dogger Bank incident.

In Germany, however, the fear of an attack by England, a "Copenhagening" of the fleet, was even more palpable than British fears of Germany. For the first time the German Foreign Office was frightened by the possibility of a war with Britain. Besides the British press articles, the Germans noted loose talk in British naval circles about the wisdom of attacking Germany before she had completed her fleet-building plans, and, what was more immediately important, the concentration of naval strength in home waters—part of the redis-

---

11. Amos S. Hershey, *International Law and Diplomacy of the Russo-Japanese War* (New York, 1906), pp. 236–38.

tribution of the navy that involved the development of a naval base at Rosyth on the north coast, planned for some months and submitted to Parliament on 12 December 1904. The German government called warships home from the Orient, canceled Christmas leaves, and summoned Ambassador Metternich to Berlin in December for consultations. Except for the press war, the British were unaware of the German alarm until Dr. Herman Paasche, a vice-president of the Reichstag, referred to the crisis in Anglo-German relations in a public speech on 4 January 1905. His statements greatly exaggerated the situation, for he alleged that the two countries had been on the verge of war. The tension and press agitation which lasted into February 1905 furnished fuel for both the British and the German navy leagues.

No one in Germany inveighed more bitterly against Britain than William II, who on 27 October 1904 telegraphed the tsar that the English press had been "threatening Germany" not to allow coal to be sent to the Russian fleet, and that it was "not impossible" that Britain and Japan might lodge a protest and " 'a sommation' to stop further work." The result, the kaiser continued, "would be the absolute immobility of your fleet and inability to proceed to its destination from want of fuel. This new danger would have to be faced in community by Russia and Germany together . . ." Continuing to advise Nicholas II, the kaiser suggested that France be reminded of her obligations, commented upon the Dogger Bank incident, again urged the tsar to order new ships of the line, and closed by expressing his assurance that "you can always rely on my absolute and faithful loyalty."[12]

In broadly hinting at an accord, the kaiser was acting in full agreement with Bülow and Holstein, although the Foreign Office had opposed a German-Russian alliance up to four months before and Tirpitz objected to it because he thought the danger of a clash with England would be heightened by it. Holstein on 25 October had already discussed the same proposals as the kaiser's with the Russian ambassador, Count von Osten-Sacken. At the same time he made a clumsy attempt to get France out of the Entente Cordiale and into a Russo-German alliance. The German feelers found the tsar in a receptive mood. In his reply to the kaiser of 29 October he opened with a reference to the Dogger Bank incident and continued:

12. The kaiser to the tsar, 27 October 1904: *GP*, XIX(1), no. 6118. Cf. Jonathan Steinberg, "The Copenhagen Complex," *1914: The Coming of the First World War* (New York, 1966), pp. 30–32.

I have not words to express my indignation with England's conduct . . . I agree fully with your complaints about England's behaviour concerning the coaling of our ships by German steamers . . . It is certainly high time to put a stop to this. The only way as you say would be that Germany, Russia, and France should at once unite upon an arrangement to abolish the Anglo-Japanese arrogance and insolence. Would you like to lay down and frame the outlines of such a treaty and let me know about it?

Thus, despite the objections of Lamsdorff, whom the tsar had consulted, Nicky responded eagerly to Willy's suggestion.[13]

The kaiser's reply of the 30th, drawn up by Bülow, inveighed against both the British and the French and enclosed the draft of a treaty by which the two parties promised to aid one another with all land and naval forces if either was attacked by a European power, and both were jointly to remind France of her obligations under the Franco-Russian alliance (Article I). They promised not to conclude a separate peace with any common adversary (Article II). Finally, coming to the point of departure for the proposed alliance, the pledge to aid each other would be valid in case the acts of one of the high contracting parties during the war, such as the delivery of coal to a belligerent, should give rise after the war to complaints by a third power of pretended violation of the rights of neutrals (Article III).[14]

The tsar returned the draft, 7 November, with a change in the first article, according to which he would take the necessary steps to associate France with the accord, and with the addition of a sentence to Article III according to which the accord was to "subsist in the face of difficulties which might arise at the time of the negotiations of peace between Russia and Japan."[15] The kaiser, 17 November, objected to the change in Article III, asserting that if this amendment were revealed, it might be inferred that instead of a defensive alliance, Germany and Russia had "formed a sort of chartered Company Limited for annexation purposes, possibly involving secret clauses for the private gain of Germany. It would be better merely to promise not to support any proposals for robbing Russia of the fruits of victory." Accordingly he offered changes in the wording of the preamble and offered a new Article III by which the treaty would remain in

13. The tsar to the kaiser, 29/16 October 1904: *GP*, XIX(1), no. 6119.

14. Bülow to the kaiser, 30 October 1904: ibid., no. 6120, enclosing a draft answer to the tsar.

15. The tsar to the kaiser, 7 November/25 October 1904: ibid., no. 6124.

force until denounced one year in advance. Thus the alliance was to continue beyond the end of the war. In the letter containing these proposed changes, which Bülow and Holstein had drafted, the kaiser urged a speedy conclusion of the accord and added the suggestion that Russia make a military demonstration on the Persian-Afghan frontier "for the sobering of England." He argued that "pressure on the Indian frontier from Persia will have remarkably quieting influence on the hot-headed Jingoes in London," and concluded: "God grant that we may have found the right way to hem in the horrors of war and give His blessing to our plans."[16]

But the tsar had second thoughts, prompted no doubt by Lamsdorff, about signing the treaty without notice to France. He wired, 23 November, that it would be advisable for France to see it. This suggestion called forth a perfervid plea not to inform France before signing the agreement, for France would give notice to her "friend (if not secret ally) England" and the outcome would "doubtless be an instantaneous attack by the two allied powers, England and Japan, on Germany in Europe as well as in Asia." Given British superior naval power, Germany would be crippled temporarily and the balance of power upset to the disadvantage of Russia. It would be maintained only by an agreement among Russia, Germany, and France. He preferred no treaty at all to informing France before signature. The tsar persisted, even offering a draft notice to France, 7 December, but in view of the German refusal to inform France before signing the treaty, the projected alliance was dead.[17]

At this juncture, however, a British stoppage (3 December) of a German ship from coaling at Cardiff because its cargo was believed to be destined for the Russian fleet brought the issue of coal deliveries to the fore again. Even Holstein began to believe in the possibility of a British attack, and the kaiser on a hunting trip in Silesia became more and more excited. Through instructions to the German ambassador in Russia, Count von Alvensleben, and a telegram from Willy to Nicky (7 December), Germany asked for "absolutely positive guarantees" of Russia's full support should coaling of the Russian fleet lead to war. The kaiser declared: "Should you be unable to guarantee me that you will loyally fight shoulder to shoulder with me, then I regret I must immediately forbid German

16. The kaiser to the tsar, 17 November 1904: ibid., no. 6125.
17. The tsar and kaiser exchange, 23/10 November and 24 November 1904: ibid., nos. 6126–27.

steamers to continue to coal your fleet." Accordingly, by a note to Alvensleben of 12 December 1904, Lamsdorff conveyed the assurances that Germany demanded.[18]

On 21 December Willy repeated to Nicky his refusal to take France into their confidence before they had come to a definite arrangement. No doubt he and Bülow hoped by this letter to reopen negotiations. If so, they were disappointed, for in his reply of 25 December the tsar referred to his pledge concerning coaling, but did not even mention the matter of the alliance. The kaiser gave vent to his chagrin in a letter of 28 December to Bülow in which he noted the negative result "after two months' honest work," and asserted that this was the first failure he had personally experienced since ascending the throne. He suggested that they must now cultivate America and Japan the more. "Paris must incidentally get a sock in the eye." He suspected that France had had wind of the negotiations and had frustrated them; "Delcassé is damnably skilful and very strong."[19]

The kaiser's conjecture about French knowledge of the negotiations was correct. Although the Quai d'Orsay had the key to the German embassy's code, their source of information about German-Russian relations was not German cables but St. Petersburg. They learned definitely of the kaiser's draft treaty from Minister of War Sakharov, who revealed the general contents to the French military attaché, General Moulin. Even before Moulin's report reached Paris, Delcassé received hints of what was going on, for Prince Radolin, the German ambassador, on Holstein's orders, told him that the Russo-Japanese war was likely to spread to Europe and that Germany would stand by Russia. Through the Spanish ambassador, Radolin let Delcassé know, in addition, that if there were war between Germany on one side and Japan and England on the other, there would be a Russo-German alliance within twenty-four hours; in that case France would have to choose. Radolin was further quoted as saying that Delcassé could alone keep peace and should counsel England to stop playing with fire.[20] Delcassé, who had already noted that to withhold aid from Russia was to incur the risk that Germany would win Russia

18. Bülow to Alvensleben, 6 December; the kaiser to the tsar, 7 December; and Lamsdorff to Alvensleben, 12 December 1904: ibid., nos. 6129–30, 6137.

19. The kaiser and tsar exchange, 21 and 25 December 1904; the kaiser to Bülow, 28 December 1904: ibid., nos. 6141, 6145–46.

20. Notes secrètes, 4 and 5 November, and Moulin to André, 17 November 1904: 2 DDF, V, nos. 424–26, 450.

over and thus end the Franco-Russian alliance, came to the conclusion, after discussing Radolin's and the Spanish ambassador's talks, that there was undoubtedly an accord between Berlin and St. Petersburg. He wondered what the French position would be if a general war broke out and Russia at the last moment admitted that she was tied to Germany. He concluded that as long as the Treaty of Frankfurt was unrevised, there could be no intimate collaboration with Germany, for that would mean accepting the loss of Alsace-Lorraine. This was the first time, writes Maurice Paléologue, that Delcassé had pronounced the names of Alsace-Lorraine in his presence.[21]

At the same time, 5 November 1904, Georges Louis, director of the political section at the Quai d'Orsay, sent Paléologue to London with notes on the recent talks in order to discuss them with Paul Cambon. As a result of Paléologue's briefing, Cambon concluded that they must work at London and St. Petersburg against the kaiser's intrigues, and tell the tsar that France would not accede to a combination against England. Accordingly, on the 7th Cambon gave Lansdowne his apprehensions concerning the situation. The latter had the impression that Germany was badly disposed toward Britain and was not acting in St. Petersburg in a pacific direction. He denied that the British fleet was "shadowing" the Baltic squadron and asserted that as soon as the Dogger Bank incident was settled, the squadron at Gibraltar would be removed in order to show that appeasement was complete. He was worried about the Russian Volunteer Fleet and asked why the Russians did not keep their ships at a distance from British trade routes and why their commanders were not given orders to be prudent with British vessels. To avoid conflict, he told Cambon, each must do his bit.[22]

Upon receiving Paléologue's report of his talk with Cambon, Delcassé observed that he saw what he had to do, but wondered if he had time for it, because he needed fifteen days to maneuver between London and St. Petersburg. He immediately wired to Russia Lansdowne's remarks about the Russian Volunteer Fleet; and on the following day (9 November) told Nelidov, the Russian ambassador, of Paléologue's mission to London, and then said that he knew of the private correspondence between William II and Nicholas II, and the proposed alliance directed against England into which they expected to force France. Delcassé declared that as long as he was

21. Maurice Paléologue, *Un grand tournant*, p. 164.
22. P. Cambon, Note secrète, 7 November 1904: 2 *DDF*, V, no. 433.

minister, France would not enter a coalition with Germany. If Russia contracted a special accord with Germany, France would look out for herself in other directions. Nelidov, protesting that Delcassé's information could not be true, could only guarantee the tsar's fidelity to the alliance. Although there are no explicit published references to instructions, Ambassador Bompard, who returned from a holiday to St. Petersburg on 21 November, apparently presented Delcassé's position to Lamsdorff and perhaps to the tsar as well. In any event, the tsar's first proposal to the kaiser to inform France about the draft treaty was dated 23 November.

The tsar assured Bompard when he talked with him that the alliance remained as solid as in the past. The French on their side attempted with some success to counteract the view in Russia that France had done little to help her and that Germany was her only loyal friend. They faithfully carried out the plans for placing port facilities in their African possessions, Madagascar, and Indochina at the disposal of the Baltic squadron as it journeyed to the Far East. Also they secured assurances of Russian readiness to give priority to French industries in procuring war materials. These services to Russia were largely owing to the persistence of Delcassé, for the French feeling of loyalty to the Dual Alliance was at a very low ebb. Delcassé stuck to the alliance, however, out of fear of Germany, and won the admiration of Russia, whose regard for France had dropped as low as the market there for Russian securities.[23] The kaiser was right to characterize Delcassé as "damnably skilful and very strong."

The events of November and December 1904 made doubly certain that there could be no Anglo-Russian rapprochement, much less an entente, as long as Russian officialdom and especially the tsar looked upon England as their undeclared enemy in the war with Japan. As for Germany and Britain, the war scare subsided, except for a brief flurry in February 1905, until its revival in the autumn of 1905. Count Metternich and the military and naval attachés in London helped greatly to allay German fears of a British attack. Despite the gloomy conjectures of Holstein and others that a quadruple alliance of Britain, Japan, France, and Russia was a possibility (a recurring theme in 1904–05),[24] suspicions and apprehensions on all sides tended

---

23. On the Franco-Russian exchanges, see ibid., nos. 435, 467, 471; Paléologue, *Un grand tournant*, pp. 170–71, 197–98; Andrew, *Delcassé*, pp. 231–32, 248–49.

24. See Kwang-Ching Liu, *JMH*, XVIII, 222–40; Andrew, *Delcassé*, p. 292.

to subside until the kaiser's Tangier coup at the end of March. Moreover, the fall of Port Arthur, 1 January 1905, and the Japanese victory at Mukden, early in March, brought to the fore the problem of peacemaking rather than wartime rivalries.

IV.

As early as June 1904 sporadic discussions of how to bring about peace began. From the first, President Roosevelt, for the United States, took an active part in testing the ground for it. He first offered his cooperation to France, and later, in August, made proposals to Germany of a plan for an internationalized and neutralized Manchuria. In July Baron von Eckardstein, former secretary of the Germany embassy in London, acted as an intermediary between Witte and Hayashi who were planning a meeting to discuss peace terms. King Edward VII also suggested himself as mediator between the belligerents. All of these tentative steps or proposals failed, mainly because of the tsar's obstinate determination to carry on the war in the expectation of an ultimate Russian victory—an expectation that the kaiser consistently encouraged. The same fate awaited a renewed Japanese attempt to open peace negotiations in January 1905.

After the battle of Mukden, however, both belligerents began to reassess their prospects for continuing the war. Russia from the time of Bloody Sunday, 22 January, was increasingly threatened by revolution at home, although opinion was divided as to the effect of a continuation of the war on the internal troubles. Also, Russia's financial outlook was increasingly gloomy, because the possibility of making further loans in either France or Germany was slim.[25] Men like Witte and the minister of finance, Kokovstov, who were especially aware of the country's economic situation, began in February to counsel peace on honorable terms. The Japanese likewise came to the conclusion that they were reaching the limits of their striking power as their lines of communication with the fighting front lengthened and their manpower began to be exhausted. Although they were able to conclude a loan in March, they decided in April to seek

25. On the anti-Russian feeling in France and Russian efforts to counteract it, see James William Long, "Russian Manipulation of the French Press, 1904–1906," *Slavic Review*, XXXI (1972), 343–54.

peace through the mediation of the United States, and made a request for the president's good offices on 25 April.

President Roosevelt had again actively promoted the idea of peace negotiations from mid-March, but had received little encouragement from any of the powers, including Russia, whom he had approached. Delcassé, on the other hand, received feelers from both Russia and Japan on 22 March to use his good offices in bringing about peace. Russia insisted that she should not be asked to cede territory, to pay a war indemnity, or to limit her armed forces in the Far East. Delcassé gave Ambassador Motono the first two conditions and assured him that he was in a position to bring Russia and Japan in touch with one another for the conclusion of peace. By mid-April, however, the Japanese had backed off, probably because of the military situation and especially the indecisive naval situation.[26] Great Britain scrupulously avoided any action that might be interpreted as interference by Japan, with whom she was negotiating a renewal of the alliance. Germany's principal concern from March to the end of May was to prevent a French or Anglo-French mediation that might result in the bugbear of the *Wilhelmstrasse*, the quadruple alliance of Russia, France, Japan, and Britain.[27]

The sinking of the Russian fleet at Tsushima, 27–28 May, however, and the increasing revolutionary activity in Russia convinced the kaiser that Russia should make peace in order to safeguard the monarchical principle and save Nicky from assassination. Thus Roosevelt, requested formally on 31 May by the Japanese to mediate "entirely on his own motion and initiative," found the kaiser willing to join him in urging Russian acceptance of a peace conference, which he proposed through the Russian ambassador in Washington and the United States ambassador in Russia. The urgings of William II on 3 June, prompted by his fears for the tsar and the desire to prevent a French mediation, an appeal of the national zemstvo congress on the same day, and the approval of 6 June by a military conference of steps toward peace persuaded Nicholas II to give his consent to a peace conference. Roosevelt issued a formal invitation to both governments to come together in order to ascertain the possibility of agreement on peace terms. The Japanese on 10 June and the Russians two days later accepted the invitation. Two weeks later

26. Andrew, *Delcassé*, pp. 292–96, describes these talks.
27. Ibid. Cf. *GP* XIX(2), nos. 6306–07.

they agreed upon Portsmouth, New Hampshire, as the site of the conference.

Before the conference opened on 9 August, there were three events that were related to the war but were also significant developments in European international relations: the secret Björkö treaty that was signed by Willy and Nicky on 24 July, the Taft-Katsura agreement of 29 July, and the renewal of the Anglo-Japanese alliance.

After the failure to win Russian agreement to the alliance proposal of October 1904, the kaiser and the German Foreign Office became absorbed in the mediation question and the first Moroccan crisis. There was a brief exchange with Russia in February-March 1905 over coaling of the Russian fleet beyond Madagascar, in which the kaiser washed his hands of the affair, alleging that providing coal was a private enterprise of the Hamburg-America lines; and also an abortive attempt by Bülow to reach an accord with Russia by which both powers would pledge not to seek any territorial advantage in case the Danubian Monarchy collapsed. But after the fall of Delcassé, 6 June, whom the kaiser had largely blamed for the failure of his plans in the previous autumn, and the agreement of France to a conference on Morocco, Bülow and Holstein approved the kaiser's proposal that he revive the idea of a combination of the Triple and Dual Alliances at a meeting with the tsar at Björkö. This project was to enable Germany to break out of the encirclement attributed to Edward VII, and the reason for moving at once was again the fear of the dreaded quadruple alliance once peace between Russia and Japan was concluded. Accordingly, Willy surprised Nicky on 24 July with a prepared draft of a treaty, and without difficulty persuaded him to sign it—a "turning point in the history of Europe," wrote the kaiser to Bülow, "thanks be to God."[28]

The treaty, similar to that of the previous year, provided that "if one of the two empires should be attacked by a European power, its ally would aid it in Europe with all its land and sea forces" (Article I), and the parties would not conclude a separate peace (Article II). The treaty was to come into effect upon the conclusion of peace between Russia and Japan (Article III), and at that time Russia would inform France and propose her adherence as an ally (Article IV). The kaiser summarized his dreams of the effects of the treaty, and incidentally his major interest in it, in a letter to

28. William II to Bülow, 25 July 1905: GP XIX(2), no. 6220.

Nicky of 26 September in which he asserted that the continental combine, flanked by America which would side with it, was

> the sole & only manner to effectively block the way to the whole world becoming John Bull's private property, which he exploits at his heart's content after having, by lies and intrigues without end, set the rest of the civilized nations by each other's ears for his own personal benefit.

Since the French were hypnotized by British cordiality and the Entente Cordiale, the tsar should have Nelidov remind France that her future lies "with us." He suggested that now that peace with Japan had been signed, the ambassadors of Germany and Russia should be instructed to work together in matters of general policy and thus impress the world that their relations were close, and at the same time prepare the French for the new orientation.[29] But again, William II was to see his dream shattered.

Bülow objected to the limitation of the treaty to Europe, arguing that Russia in her weakened condition was of no use to Germany there; and Holstein agreed that the only way Russia could help Germany would be to attack India or Persia, which the limitation to Europe prevented. When the kaiser defended the treaty and opposed revision, Bülow threatened to resign and made the occasion a means of firmly establishing his authority over the control of German policy. But neither he nor Holstein pressed for a revision of the wording of the treaty. As it turned out, the Russians again quashed the proposed alliance. Lamsdorff, with the help of Witte, who had supported the idea of a continental alliance but denounced the treaty when he read it, persuaded the tsar that it represented a betrayal of France. A cautious feeling-out of the French had revealed that they were no more ready to join in a combination with Germany than Delcassé had been in the previous autumn. Nicky so informed Willy on 23 November. The Kaiser was again furious over the collapse of his plans, and suspected the formation of an Anglo-French-Russian coalition that Edward VII had "cleverly wangled."[30]

Five days after the Björkö meeting Prime Minister Katsura of

---

29. Willy to Nicky, 26 September 1905: *Kaiser's Letters,* pp. 209–16.

30. William II to Bülow, 26 November 1905: *GP,* XIX(2), no. 6255; exchanges of Lamsdorff, Nelidov, and Osten-Sacken, 9 August to 27 October 1905: "Björkoe," Tr. Alfred von Wegerer, *KBM,* II, 477–95. Evidence concerning Witte's role is contradictory. Cf. E. J. Dillon, *Eclipse of Russia,* pp. 354, 393–97; A. Savinsky, *Recollections of a Russian Diplomatist,* p. 125; Haller, *Eulenberg,* II, 169–70.

Japan and Secretary of War William Howard Taft signed a memorandum by which Katsura gave positive assurance that Japan entertained
no aggressive designs on the Philippines, while Taft enthusiastically
approved a Japanese protectorate over Korea. This accord indirectly
affected European affairs by establishing an American counterpart
of the Anglo-Japanese alliance.

Although that alliance was not due to expire until 1907, both
Britain and Japan began to consider the renewal and expansion of
the treaty at the turn of the years 1904–1905. On the British side
the relation of the alliance to peace terms was an important point,
for it was thought that the Japanese peace terms might depend upon
whether or not Japan could count upon the continuance of the alliance as a safeguard against Russian revenge. In March 1905 Lansdowne and Ambassador Hayashi began to negotiate the renewal, and
to the former the events in the Far East, including relations with
Japan, were perhaps more important than the Moroccan crisis and
France. In the negotiations the Japanese desire to have a free hand
in Korea, in place of a guarantee of its independence as in the first
treaty, and the British wish to extend the alliance to India, wanted
in 1902 but not carried through, became the quid pro quo which was
accepted in principle in June but which required much discussion of
detail. From the start Lansdowne was anxious to have the approval
of the United States, which he obtained in late July; the British
ambassador in Washington conveyed President Roosevelt's blessing
upon the alliance in early August.[31]

The treaty of alliance was really a new one rather than a renewal,
for by it each party was to come to the aid of the other if attacked
by a single power, its scope was extended to India, and Japan received recognition of her paramount rights in Korea, provided the
measures of "guidance, control, and protection" there were not
inconsistent with the principle of the open door. Passing over the
advantages of this British pledge, Great Britain gained militarily
from the Japanese victory over Russia as well as the pledge of
Japanese assistance in a conflict over India. The battle of Tsushima
had virtually eliminated Russian naval competition, so that Great
Britain, as Admiral Fisher pointed out, disposed of a force of battleships "considerably superior" to that of the combined fleets of France,
Russia, and Germany. Furthermore, the alliance gave Great Britain

31. See Nish, *Anglo-Japanese Alliance*, chs. 15, 16; Monger, *End of Isolation*,
pp. 185–214.

the assistance of Japan in defending the frontiers of India without the necessity of making large-scale increases in the British standing army.

The effect of the alliance upon British relations with Russia was a matter of anxiety, for the hope of an entente upon the conclusion of the Russo-Japanese war had revived. Lansdowne, therefore, through both the French government and his own ambassador in St. Petersburg sought to convince the Russian government, without immediate success, that the alliance, as he communicated to Russia on 9 September, was not directed at Russia. No doubt the kaiser's counterpropaganda in connection with the Treaty of Björkö helped to keep alive the tsar's prejudices. The Anglo-Japanese alliance was published to the world on 27 September in order to help counteract the unpopularity in Japan of the Portsmouth peace terms.

Into the negotiations and crises of the Portsmouth peace conference we need not go.[32] Suffice it to say that the exertions of President Roosevelt, with the help of the kaiser in persuading the tsar to agree to acceptable terms, played a significant part in preventing a breakdown of negotiations in the latter days of August. The tsar's decision that he would not yield an inch of territory or pay a ruble of indemnity had to be revised in order to accommodate the cession of Sakhalin up to the 50th parallel, but the Japanese demand for an indemnity had to be given up in order to achieve the peace that the government badly needed. As it was, Japan secured control of Korea and southern Manchuria and the lease of Port Arthur, achievements that exceeded the demands upon Russia two years before, while Russia perforce retreated correspondingly from her former position in the Far East.

The effects of the war and peace upon Europe were principally confined to the weakening of Russia and the indirect strengthening of Great Britain. Not only the war but the revolutionary movement of 1905 meant that Russian power in the European balance was for the time being virtually nil. At the same time defeat in the Far East helped to turn Russian attention again to the Near East, ultimately with disastrous consequences. For Britain the emergence of her ally Japan as a continental power in Asia and the predominant naval power in the Far East afforded her the opportunity to concentrate British naval power largely in European waters and thus meet the rising challenge of Germany. France had already, before the end of the Russo-Japanese war, experienced the effects of her ally's weakness in the first Moroccan crisis.

32. See the excellent treatment by White, *Russo-Japanese War*, pp. 227–329.

Chapter 5

The First

Moroccan Crisis,

1905–1906

*Foreign Minister Théophile Delcassé ended his long tenure of office
in June 1905 to be followed by Maurice Rouvier, French premier
since January, who in turn was replaced by Léon Bourgeois in March
1906. At the Quai d'Orsay Maurice Paléologue continued to counsel
his superiors, while Paul Révoil became a special adviser on Morocco
and delegate to the Algeciras conference. Saint-René Taillandier
remained French agent in Morocco. Especially prominent among the
French ambassadors were Georges Bihourd in Berlin, Paul Cambon
in London, Camille Barrère in Rome, and Jean J. Jusserand in
Washington. The decision-makers in Germany were Chancellor
Bülow and Friedrich von Holstein, the éminence grise of the Foreign
Office. Ambassador Prince Radolin at Paris, Count von Tattenbach,
special agent in Morocco and delegate to the Algeciras conference,
and Ambassador Speck von Sternburg at Washington carried out
Berlin's orders. For Great Britain Sir Arthur Nicolson, minister in
Morocco and delegate to the conference of Algeciras, Ambassador
Sir Francis Bertie in Paris, and Sir T. H. Sanderson, permanent
undersecretary at the Foreign Office, worked under the direction of
Lord Lansdowne until December 1905 when Sir Edward Grey became
secretary for foreign affairs in the Liberal government of Sir Henry
Campbell-Bannerman. In the wings United States President T. R.
Roosevelt, Russian Foreign Minister Vladimir Nikolaievich Lamsdorff,
Sergei Witte, returning from Portsmouth, and Ambassador Count
von der Osten-Sacken at Berlin participated in the tangled skein
of negotiations. At Algeciras the venerable Visconti Venosta, long
since retired as foreign minister, represented Italy.*

Throughout the summer and autumn of 1904, while negotiating with
Spain and dealing with the problems raised by the Russo-Japanese war

and the German effort to win an alliance with Russia, Delcassé and his representative in Morocco, Saint-René Taillandier, worked on a program of reforms to be presented to the sultan and the maghzen (the court and government of Morocco). They succeeded in June in floating a loan by a French consortium, secured by the collection of customs in eight ports, and began police reforms, but encountered hostility on the part of the Moroccans and ill will among representatives of the other powers. Declassé, incurably optimistic, put through the chambers in November the ratification of the Entente Cordiale and the accord with Spain, declaring that the objective was French preponderance in Morocco and the augmentation of French power in the Mediterranean without alienating other nations. His goal was reflected in the press, which at times overplayed the character of French plans by indicating that Morocco was to become another Tunis, thus giving rise to charges of "Tunisification." Officially, however, in drawing up a program of financial, military, and economic reforms, stress was laid upon the example of Egypt rather than Tunis.[1]

After delays caused by the sultan's intransigence, Taillandier reached the Moroccan capital at Fez on 25 January 1905 and set to work to convince the Moroccans that the proposed reforms were necessary and that France alone could help achieve them. After a month of optimistic reports, however, he had to admit that the forces of opposition were mounting, and in another month that he had failed to secure any concrete agreement on the implementation of his proposals.

I.

Changes were occurring at home and abroad that were destined to frustrate Delcassé's plans. On 24 January 1905 Maurice Rouvier, minister of finance in the Combes government, became premier. He was a banker who had disagreed with some of Delcassé's policies in the past and was suspected of seeking to deal with Germany. Although there is no evidence that he actively opposed Delcassé's Moroccan policy until after the kaiser's visit to Tangier, he voiced his disapproval of Delcassé's disregard of Germany. The major change in the situation, however, came about as a result of the German decision to challenge French objectives and methods in Morocco. Here

---

1. See "Note . . . sur l'organisation des régions marocaines voisines de l'Algérie," October 1904: 2 DDF, V, no. 356.

4. Prince Bernhard von Bulow (The Bettmann Archive)

lay Delcassé's greatest error of judgment. He had adamantly refused to seek German approval of his Moroccan ambitions despite the urging of the colonialists and several of his own diplomatic corps, among whom his ambassador in Berlin, George Bihourd, was most insistent. The combination of disaffected colleagues and German encouragement of resistance to French plans ultimately led to Delcassé's downfall.

Delcassé, however, was not entirely to blame for taking a complacent attitude toward Germany in respect to Morocco, for both Ambassador Radolin privately and Bülow publicly in the Reichstag raised no objection to the Anglo-French accord of April 1904, nor for several months did Taillandier report any hostile German attitude or activity in Morocco. What Delcassé failed to note, as Bihourd did, was Bülow's emphasis upon German commercial interests there, which he said that Germany would protect. Beneath the surface the Germans were far from complacent. The government had sought since 1901 to participate in the economic development of Morocco, but up to the end of 1903 had found that German business circles were reticent to face the troubled conditions there. The government's reserve in dealing with the Moroccan question had not been shared by the *Morokkanische Gesellschaft*, the colonial society, and the Pan-German league, especially after 1902. All these groups demanded energetic action in Morocco and insisted upon the right to receive a morsel of the Moroccan heritage. Although German public opinion, aside from the colonial and Pan-German circles, reacted moderately to the French accords with Britain and Spain in 1904 and refused to envisage a crisis with France, it did demand negotiations that would guarantee Germany's economic interests. When France began to develop her plan of pacific penetration without seeking to negotiate with Germany, the idea developed that she was gravely menacing those interests and that Delcassé was deliberately directing his Moroccan policy against Germany. Therefore both the government and public opinion, disturbed over the future of the German position in Morocco, came to the conclusion that a riposte, too long delayed, was necessary.

For a long time the government had failed to act because of divided counsels. The kaiser had been indifferent toward the Moroccan question. He told the king of Spain at Vigo early in March 1904 that Germany had no territorial interest in Morocco, but wanted only equality of economic rights. On the other hand Bülow did not agree with the kaiser, and Lichnowsky, then a counsellor in the Foreign

Office, wrote: "We need a success in our foreign policy, because the Anglo-French agreement and the Franco-Italian rapprochement are generally viewed as our defeat."[2] Holstein in a memorandum of 3 June argued that Germany should insist upon recognition by France of her rights in Morocco, just as Great Britain had sought the consent of third parties to her changes in Egypt. He assumed that the French intended to annex Morocco or to shut out all others. Germany should take a stand for freedom of trade and the principle that no power infringed upon the interests of others without their consent. "Not only for material interests," he argued, "but even more to preserve her prestige, Germany must oppose the intended annexation of Morocco by France." Because Germany would be championing economic interests, even England's diplomatic support of France, pledged in Article IX of the April accord, would remain platonic; and other third parties would rally to Germany's side.[3]

Throughout the summer of 1904, however, Germany made no overt move to assert her economic rights in Morocco, for there was still no agreement as to how to proceed. The kaiser had his eyes fixed upon an alliance with Russia into which to draw France. Bülow, half persuaded to adopt some countermove to French policy, failed to formulate procedure. In October, however, two events hastened a decision. Delcassé completed his accord with Spain, but failed to open the talks with Germany that she had hoped for; and in Tangier Taillandier revealed to Richard von Kühlmann, the German chargé d'affaires, his projected mission to Fez for the purpose of establishing French predominance in Morocco. In addition, in November, the French prevented Morocco from buying war material from Germany, thus heightening the rivalry of Krupp and Schneider-Creusot, who were already competing for Turkish business with the backing of their respective embassies.

Even with this evidence of "Tunisification" the Germans were content merely to warn France of possible intervention in Morocco, expecting that they would scare Delcassé into talking with them. But at the end of December when, it will be remembered, the kaiser voiced his bitter disappointment over the failure of the alliance with Russia and ultimately France, Bülow and Holstein decided to change their tactics and engage France in a test of strength by which they would inflict a severe diplomatic defeat upon her. Russian military defeats

2. As quoted by Eugene N. Anderson, *First Moroccan Crisis*, p. 147.
3. Norman Rich, *Holstein*, II, 683–84.

in Manchuria and the known weakness of French military forces entered into their calculations, but they also had to be sure that the sultan of Morocco and the maghzen would go along with them. By the end of January 1905, Sultan Abdul Aziz, with the active encouragement of the German agent at the Fez consulate, Dr. Philip Vassel, had clearly indicated his desire to work with Germany against France, and by March, Vassel had blocked Taillandier's mission and had made considerable progress in establishing German influence at Fez. Believing that the time for a grand coup had come, Bülow and Holstein decided that the kaiser should land at Tangier, while on his Mediterranean cruise, and proclaim Germany's position. They announced his forthcoming visit in the press on 19 March. The kaiser protested this move, and in order to overcome his doubts of its wisdom, Bülow argued that if the announced landing were given up, Delcassé would say that Germany had yielded to French pressure, and the kaiser would certainly not want Delcassé to achieve such a triumph. On the other hand, if the kaiser were jubilantly received in Tangier, Delacassé would "be done for."[4]

By the end of March, Bülow and the Foreign Office had not worked out any firm policy concerning ultimate objectives and how to obtain them. Even the concept of a dramatic gesture by the kaiser may well have emanated from official and nonofficial Germans in Morocco. The widely voiced explanation of the decision is that the news of the Japanese victory at Mukden on 16 March opened a golden opportunity to challenge France whose ally would be powerless to help her. This explanation makes two assumptions that are scarcely tenable: first, that Germany wanted to provoke a war with France that no one —Holstein, Bülow, or the kaiser—contemplated;[5] and second, that the Germans had thought through what they wanted and how to get it. Another explanation is that the news of Taillandier's alleged assertion at Fez that France had the approval of all the powers for her reform program and was acting as the mandatory of Europe spurred the German government publicly to proclaim its opposition to France, for Germany had interests to protect and had not given her approval

---

4. Ibid., 694.

5. There is no consensus as to whether Germany wanted war in 1905, but I accept the view that Bülow and Holstein did not, although General Schlieffen may have contemplated war and Germany's aims and methods involved the risk of war. Cf. Rich, *Holstein*, II, 696–99; Gerhard Ritter, *The Schlieffen Plan*, pp. 96–112, 118–28; Gordan A. Craig, *From Bismarck to Adenauer* (Baltimore, 1958), pp. 42–44.

of French objectives. Undoubtedly the government took Mukden, the military weaknesses of France, and her claims of a mandate into account, but the decision to end the year-long waiting game arose from the situation in Morocco and Berlin. Germany now knew what France was demanding at Fez and that the sultan and the maghzen would cooperate to thwart her. Moreover, Holstein, who had believed strongly from the first that Germany should intervene, was once more after a period of absence the dominant policy-maker at the Foreign Office.

Although Holstein and Bülow had not drawn up a blue print of action, in the manner of Bismarck, they had in mind an international conference of the Madrid Convention signatories of 1880. They assumed that Britain would give France only platonic support, because of the dissatisfaction with French policy voiced in a section of the English press, the antipathy toward France of the English colony in Tangier, and the reports of Walter B. Harris, the Tangier correspondent of *The Times*. Also, Holstein assumed that Germany could hold Italy in line; that the Spaniards were already fearful that France would cheat them; and that Austria, the United States, and other signatories of the Madrid Convention would support Germany in order to maintain the open door in Morocco.

Holstein in addition contended that the principle of "contractual collectivity" justifying a conference would remove the appearance of German aggressiveness and would avoid injuring French pride. If France refused a conference, she would put herself in the wrong; and if the conference took place, it would not hand Morocco over to the French. A conference, moreover, would leave the door open for "an eventual settlement between Germany and France through an international agency," thus permitting Germany to evade her promises to Morocco and to receive her share of the Moroccan spoils.[6] Holstein's conference policy therefore precluded previous direct negotiations with France but envisioned the continuation of the policy already initiated of working on and through the sultan of Morocco.

Underlying this policy was Holstein's preoccupation, ever since his memorandum of 3 June 1904, with Germany's prestige, which to him was more important than the material interests emphasized by the German press and business. Germany had to prove that she was not a *quantité négligeable*. In so doing she would emerge from her threatened isolation and break up the Entente Cordiale. Holstein as-

6. Rich, *Holstein*, II, 700–02.

sumed that in a test of strength France would discover that the entente was useless and would therefore turn to Germany and join the continental alliance so dear to the kaiser's heart. Paralleling this objective was that of bringing about Delcassé's fall. The Germans believed that Delcassé had deliberately ignored Germany (as he had), and that he sought generally to oppose and humiliate her. The growing vocal criticism in Paris of Delcassé's policy encouraged the belief that he could be brought down.[7]

Though Germany had a good case against France on economic grounds and a legitimate grievance against Delcassé, her tactics undermined her position. Holstein and Bülow failed to foresee the effects of the sphinxlike attitude of the German diplomats and Foreign Office who were enjoined by Bülow, 24 March, to hold their tongues. Their silence when questioned left the rest of the world to indulge in all sorts of conjectures about German motives and ultimate goals. In view of the stress in all German public statements upon the protection of economic rights, it was assumed that Germany was seeking not only to maintain her juridical position under the Madrid Convention but also to get some Moroccan port, mining, and construction concessions, and, if she could not obtain them, compensation elsewhere. Along with this feeling of uncertainty came the fear that Germany might resort to arms to get what she wanted—a fear that was undoubtedly fostered in part by a renewed Anglo-German press war in February.

Against this background of suspicion and mistrust, the kaiser reluctantly rode a choppy sea and landed at Tangier in the forenoon of 31 March 1905. The anti-French elements there, encouraged by agitators, among them Walter B. Harris of *The Times*, had prepared an elaborate welcome and entertained high hopes of his visit. An uncle of the sultan received the kaiser as he landed and accompanied him to the German Legation, where he addressed the German colony, received the representatives of the powers, and spoke to the Moroccan delegation. His statement to the Sultan's uncle, however, was the speech that everyone examined for a key to German policy. The Havas news agency reported that he said:

> It is to the Sultan in his quality as an independent sovereign that I make my visit today. I hope that under the sovereignty of the Sultan, a free Morocco will remain open to pacific competition of

7. Otto Hammann, *World Policy of Germany*, p. 168; Ritter, *Schlieffen Plan*, pp. 114–15; Pierre Guillen, *L'Allemagne et le Maroc*, pp. 854–57; Samuel R. Williamson, *Politics of Grand Strategy*, p. 32.

all nations, without monopoly and without exclusion, on the footing of absolute equality. My visit to Tangier is intended to make known that I have decided to do everything in my power to safeguard effectively German interests in Morocco, since I consider the Sultan an absolutely free sovereign. It is with him that I want to agree on the proper means of safeguarding those interests.[8]

The kaiser's speech went beyond Bülow's directive of 26 March, drafted by Holstein, which was phrased in general terms concerning the sultan's independence and the freedom of trade, and said nothing of what Germany would do. The kaiser, however, had committed Germany to a more rigid policy than Holstein had intended. Paul von Schwabach reports that Holstein, when he read the kaiser's speech, became ill with anger and had to go to bed. On the other hand, the Moroccans were overjoyed at the kaiser's visit and words, and, according to the United States minister in Tangier, openly declared that the kaiser had been sent by God to deliver them from the French.

II.

Delcassé seems to have received the Tangier demonstration with the same *sang froid* he had counseled Taillandier to maintain. He sought support for a rejection of a conference of Madrid signatories that was being mooted as a means of settling the Moroccan question, and by mid-April had received heartening responses from Britain, Russia, Spain, and the United States. By this time, however, excitement was mounting in Paris, where Ambassador Radolin reported that quite serious people were asking whether it would come to war. Members of the government and of Parliament, including Rouvier, Étienne, Clemenceau, and Jaurès, had been urging Delcassé to open talks with Germany. In fact, Delcassé had sought to initiate conversations, but instead of forthrightly proposing to ask Germany for approval of his Moroccan policy by an accord similar to those with Britain and Spain, he took the position that he had given Germany explanations of his accords in both March and October 1904, and that, as he told the Chamber of Deputies, he was ready to dissipate every misunderstanding, "if, in spite of formal declarations, any could still exist."[9] He

8. The Havas news agency text: 2 *DDF*, VI, no. 222. Cf. Rich, *Holstein*, II, 695.
9. 2 *DDF*, VI, 325, note 2.

instructed Bihourd to raise the question with Bülow whether "misunderstandings" existed, and himself put the same question to Radolin after a German embassy dinner on 13 April. To all his efforts he met the sphinxlike attitude ordered by Bülow in March. Bihourd, failing to talk with Bülow, finally on 18 April talked with Otto von Mühlberg, undersecretary of state for foreign affairs, and learned the latter's personal opinion that Germany counted upon an international conference to eliminate the misunderstanding.

In the absence of any progress toward discussions with Germany, French antagonism toward Delcassé and his policies mounted to a climax in the third week of April. There was personal jealousy among former colleagues who had seen him surmount five cabinet crises. The socialists and radical-socialists, who had supported pacific penetration in Morocco, now turned against him as difficulties arose, and wanted an agreement with Germany which they believed Delcassé had spurned. The socialists, moreover, saw him as the man of the Russian alliance, no longer of any military value, and the radical socialists accused him of giving up Egypt in return for a "hazardous adventure" in Morocco. The colonial group was now bent upon an understanding with Germany. The nationalists, who had never liked the Entente Cordiale, blamed him for exposing France to German attack for the benefit of Great Britain. Most important for Delcassé's position was his incompatibility with Rouvier. In the Combes government they had clashed over the Bagdad railway and Russian loans. Now that Rouvier was premier, his banker's instincts to do business with Germany and his suspicions of Delcassé as a secretive and independent director of foreign policy made him a lukewarm suporter of his foreign secretary and ultimately led him to conduct negotiations with Germany behind Delcassé's back.

The first crisis arose on 19 April, when the deputies debated what action to take in view of the German danger and the desire for negotiations. Delcassé made an ineffectual declaration, repeating his previous statements that negotiations were proceeding satisfactorily at Fez and that he was entirely ready to dissipate any misunderstanding with Germany. The chamber received his statement coldly, and in all groups "Delcassé is condemned" was the verdict.[10] Had it come to a vote, Delcassé would have been overwhelmingly censured. Rouvier, however, intervened to say that Germany had changed her policy since April 1904 not because of Delcassé but because of Russian de-

10. Paléologue, *Un grand tournant*, p. 293.

feats, and to emphasize French readiness to treat with Germany. The whole government, not Delcassé alone, should take responsibility for the policy pursued. Rouvier's defense of Delcassé was surprising but may be explained by his fear that if he let Delcassé go, he would be accused of obeying orders from the kaiser. Delcassé tendered his resignation on 20 April, however, after further indications in the press that he lacked even moderate support. Although President Loubet and Rouvier persuaded him to withdraw his resignation, his position had been shaken and the debate of the 19th presaged his ultimate downfall.

Meanwhile Bülow had pledged German support to the sultan of Morocco if he refused to accept the French demands and made an appropriate proposal for a conference of Madrid signatories. He also began to sound the powers concerning the holding of a conference. At the Foreign Office there was some sentiment for dickering with France, but Holstein firmly excluded separate negotiations with her. Despite the lukewarm or negative responses to Bülow's testing of the powers concerning a conference, Holstein was still convinced that Germany would receive the support of the majority. German adherence to the Madrid treaty principle, he thought, would put France in the wrong if she refused a conference, and England would not back her.

Holstein's gift of prophecy, especially in regard to Great Britain, was notoriously poor and in this case strikingly wrong, for after the Tangier episode Britain publicly and privately supported France. At first Lansdowne did not take seriously the kaiser's Tangier performance, but soon changed his attitude, perhaps influenced by such anti-German advisers as Mallet at the Foreign Office and Ambassador Bertie in Paris. The press, with the exception of the *Morning Post* and the *Manchester Guardian*, saw the German policy as a challenge to the Entente and "definitely embraced the French cause."[11]

The British government could not believe that Germany was solely concerned about the open door and German prestige, and suspected that she wanted a port on the Atlantic coast of Morocco. Admiral Fisher with his usual vigor thought that such an acquisition "ought to be made a *casus belli, unless we get Tangier,* which would perhaps (but only perhaps) be a *quid pro quo.*"[12] On 22 April Lansdowne telegraphed Bertie to inform Delcassé that if Germany asked for a

11. Oron J. Hale, *Germany and the Diplomatic Revolution,* pp. 105–06, 115–16.
12. Arthur J. Marder, *From the Dreadnought to Scapa Flow,* I, 115.

port, the British government "would be prepared to join the French government in offering strong opposition to such a proposal," and to beg the French government to afford the British "a full opportunity of conferring with them as to steps which might be taken in order to meet it." The final paragraph of the telegram read: "German attitude in this dispute seems to me most unreasonable having regard to M. Delcassé's attitude and we desire to give him all the support we can."[13]

Bertie changed the order of topics in the telegram when he delivered a translation to Delcassé. By placing Lansdowne's last paragraph first, Bertie's *aide mémoire* gave the impression that Britain would give France, not just Delcassé, all the support within her power. Moreover, a change in wording with reference to a German demand for a port from "conferring" to "concert" gave a stronger tone to British intentions than the original.[14] This note reached Paris at about the same time as a message from Edward VII, cruising in the Mediterranean, in support of Delcassé. The two messages together were undoubtedly taken to mean more than was intended. Moreover, there had undoubtedly been British indiscretions, taken by the French to be assurances, in March and April by military and naval men that might well have been reinforced by Edward VII during an incognito visit to Paris, 29 April to 4 May, when he talked with President Loubet and Delcassé.[15] All the manifestations of sympathy and support convinced Delcassé and even Rouvier of Britain's complete backing of France.

After withdrawing his resignation, Delcassé twice sought without success to negotiate with Germany, although he did not share the view that Germany would go to war if she did not get what she wanted in Morocco, and believed that she was bluffing. On the other hand, Rouvier had developed a panic fear of a German attack, against which Russia could give no help whatever, and Britain would be of little use because her navy did not run on wheels. He accordingly initiated a series of personal and secret efforts through the German embassy in Paris and agents in Berlin. He let the Germans know that he would drop Delcassé if necessary, and proposed a general agreement similar to the Anglo-French accord, suggesting that boundaries in middle Africa and the Bagdad railway might be topics to be in-

13. Lansdowne to Bertie, 22 April 1905: *BD*, III, no. 90.
14. Bertie, Aide-mémoire: 2 *DDF*, VI, no. 347 (*BD*, III, no. 91).
15. Andrew, *Delcassé*, pp. 280–87.

cluded. While the Germans learned much from Rouvier's overtures about his fears and his almost abject desire to come to an understanding with them, Rouvier learned little except that Germany insisted upon a conference and that Holstein, at least, wanted Delcassé dismissed.

At the time of these clandestine maneuvers Count Tattenbach, former minister in Tangier and Lisbon who had accompanied the kaiser to Tangier, was ordered to Fez to consummate the work begun by Dr. Vassel. He won a decisive victory over Taillandier when, 30 May, the sultan confirmed his complete agreement with Germany by issuing invitations to a conference of the Madrid Convention signatories to be held at Tangier.

In Paris throughout May, Delcassé, suported by Paul Cambon and Barrère, who came to Paris for conferences at least twice during the month, struggled with Rouvier over the issues of whether Germany would risk war and what reliance France could place upon Great Britain and, to a lesser extent, upon Russia, Italy, and Spain. Both men wanted to deal with Germany, but Rouvier wanted a far-reaching agreement, while Delcassé wanted only to clear up misunderstandings. Despite their differences Rouvier retained Delcassé because of his warm support by Loubet and the marked favor of Edward VII. More important, however, was the possibility that Delcassé might successfully mediate between Russia and Japan. Rouvier felt that he could not dismiss from the Quai d'Orsay such an experienced man who might contribute greatly to peace in the Far East. In addition, Germany had not offered Rouvier any concessions in return for the removal of Delcassé.

Delcassé's close advisers, like him, were optimistic about the possibility of France winning out if she kept cool. Paul Cambon wrote his son that France had "a lot of trumps," the "assistance of England, the entente with Italy, Spain, and the Russian alliance," but had been betrayed by the "deficiency of Bihourd" and by the "unconscionable feebleness" of Rouvier.[16] Cambon, Barrère, and Delcassé believed that because Germany would not dare provoke an attack when European opinion was clearly against her, France should disregard Berlin's menaces and find out what material aid Britain might be ready to give her; if France and England were allied, Italy would certainly observe benevolent neutrality. Barrère, like the other two, had interpreted Lansdowne's statement of 24 April as indicating that Britain would

16. P. Cambon to his son, 13 May 1905: *Correspondance*, II, 194.

go with France "jusqu 'au bout."[17] Thus the triumvirs felt confident of British military support and, despite Rouvier's categorical opposition to further talks with them, agreed that Paul Cambon should seek Lansdowne's views.

Great Britain in May 1905 had other worries besides the Franco-German confrontation. The director of naval intelligence thought that they might be facing a continental alliance by August, and Lansdowne's major preoccupation was the renewal of the Japanese alliance. With reference to Germany there was anxiety over her possible demand for a coaling station not only in Morocco but elsewhere in the Atlantic and the Middle and Far East. Against this background Lansdowne discussed the situation with Cambon on 17 May. Wishing to prevent the kind of special deal that some British officials feared, Lansdowne emphasized the need for complete frankness in Anglo-French relations. In his own summary of the conversation he wrote that the two governments "should keep one another fully informed of everything which came to their knowledge, and should, so far as possible, discuss in advance any contingencies by which in the course of events they might find themselves confronted." Cambon on the other hand, conscious of the conflict between Delcassé and Rouvier over the possibility of a German attack and how to meet it, asserted that he would write Delcassé "that if circumstances required it, that if, for example, we have serious reason to believe in an unjustified aggression, the British government would be entirely ready to concert with the French government on the measures to take."[18] Thus the presumption of the French triumvirate that Britain was ready to ally with France gave a twist to Lansdowne's words that he had not intended.

On 21 May a crucial conference took place in Paris of President Loubet, Rouvier, Étienne, Delcassé, Barrère, and Cambon. The last gave the details of his talk with Lansdowne, which Delcassé apparently hoped would prove his contention that France could count upon British support. Far from convincing Rouvier, however, that France might call a German bluff, Cambon's presentation made the premier fearful that if the Germans got wind of Franco-British negotiations for an alliance, they would attack immediately. Consequently, instead of healing the breach between Delcassé and Rouvier, the conference widened it.

17. Camille Barrère, "Souvenirs diplomatiques," 8 RDM, X (1932), 614–15. Cf. Barrère to Delcassé, 30 April 1905: 2 DDF, VI, no. 376.

18. Lansdowne to Bertie, 17 May 1905: BD, III, no. 94; P. Cambon to Delcassé, 18 May 1905: 2 DDF, VI, no. 443.

One further step in the French misunderstanding of Britain's position came a few days later when Cambon on 24 May sent Lansdowne a note recording what he had written to Delcassé about Lansdowne's remarks of the 17th. Lansdowne at once saw that whereas he had been trying to prevent a Franco-German bargain at Britain's expense, Cambon had limited the appeal for frank discussions to the event of a German aggression. Lansdowne accordingly wrote Cambon on the 25th in order to make clear his point that he wanted "full and confidential discussion between the two governments not so much in consequence of some act of unprovoked aggression on the part of another power, as in anticipation of any complications to be apprehended during the somewhat anxious period through which we are at present passing." Cambon, however, interpreted the note as an extension of the statement on 17 May, and wrote Delcassé on 29 May that Lansdowne's note gave "a larger and more immediate meaning" than a case of aggression. Delcassé welcomed the note and instructed Cambon to tell Lansdowne that he, too, was prepared to examine all aspects of the situation, but Cambon held back, arguing that conversations would lead to an alliance and that any response to Lansdowne should have Rouvier's assent.[19] There the matter rested, but Cambon by his misinterpretations of Lansdowne's words had armed Delcassé with one of his principal means of defense against his critics.

These events within the Quai d'Orsay and French government circles paralleled a lively German activity on all fronts. The Germans pursued a policy of pressure upon Rouvier and discussion with Washington designed to prevent a successful Anglo-French mediation in the Russo-Japanese war and, if possible, to persuade Britain through President Roosevelt to accept the German conference proposal. Because they knew that Rouvier was retaining Delcassé in case questions of Russo-Japanese peace negotiations might arise, Bülow became more concerned to prevent a successful mediation by Delcassé than to obstruct his Moroccan policy, as Bülow's messages to Roosevelt indicated. On 16 May he urged the president to attempt mediation between Japan and Russia, and continued through the 31st to appeal to him to accept a conference on Morocco. While Bülow had the satisfaction of watching Roosevelt, rather than France or England, bring about Russo-Japanese peace negotiations, he failed in May to win the presidents' support of a conference.

19. Lansdowne to Cambon, 25 May 1905: *BD*, III, no. 95; Cambon and Delcassé exchange, 29 May to 1 June 1905: 2 *DDF*, VI, nos. 465, 470, 480.

After receiving Tattenbach's early reports from Fez, Bülow heightened the pressure on Rouvier to get rid of Delcassé. Holstein had been urging his removal since 8 May, when he wrote Radolin that, because Delcassé with Loubet's help might overturn Rouvier, it might be better to get rid of him at once. The Russian defeat at Tsushima on 27 May and the Moroccan invitation to a conference three days later brought the two issues of peace and the Moroccan question to a head and persuaded Bülow that Delcassé had to go at once. Between 30 May and 2 June Dr. Johannes Miquel of the Paris embassy hammered away at Rouvier, who refused at first to dismiss Delcassé because, he said, if he did so at German insistence he would "never, never" be forgiven; he apparently even considered his own resignation. Bülow prodded him again by directing Radolin to have a confidential agent tell him that, now that the sultan of Morocco had adopted the German program, "Germany would be compelled to follow out the consequences, if France . . . pursued the policy of intimidation and violence hitherto carried on by Delcassé . . ."[20] Rouvier's private secretary reported him as saying that he had the impression from Miquel's communication that it might be a preparation for a possible ultimatum. On the evening of 2 June Rouvier talked with Etienne and the minister of the navy and decided to take Delcassé's policy before the Council of Ministers, but had to await the departure of the Spanish king, who was visiting Paris 30 May to 4 June.

The 5th of June was a day of excitement in the Chamber of Deputies where the members were quaking with the fear of war. On the 6th the morning papers demanded Delcassé's resignation. At the Council meeting at 11 A.M., which had been preceded by a conference of Loubet, Rouvier, and Delcassé, the foreign minister rested his case on two points: Germany was bluffing, and France should accept the British overture to form an alliance. Rouvier countered him by asserting that Germany was not bluffing, but knew of the Anglo-French pourparlers and, if an agreement for common action were signed, would invade France without a declaration of war. He gave as his authority Bülow himself. French forces, he contended, were in no condition to fight, and although Britain could triumph on the seas, France would meanwhile engage in a very unequal, if not disastrous, struggle on land. When it came to a vote, there was a unanimous rejection of Delcassé's policy. Thereupon he resigned.[21]

20. Bülow to Radolin, 22 and 30 May, 1 June; Miquel, Memoranda, 30 and 31 May 1905: GP XX(2), nos. 6665, 6669, 6673–75.
21. For the Council meeting, see Joseph Chaumié, "Note sur la Conseil de Ministres," 6 June 1905: 2 DDF, VI, 601–04.

In France the press treated Delcassé's resignation not as a national humiliation imposed by Germany but as a result of his adoption of a bellicose policy that endangered France. In England both the press and the government regretted Delcassé's fall. Balfour told the Cabinet that his resignation under pressure from Germany "displayed a weakness on the part of France which indicated that she could not at present be counted on as an effective force in international politics," while Lansdowne commented: "The fall of Delcassé is disgusting and has sent the *entente* down any number of points in the market."[22] The German press, following a directive from Bülow, treated the event as an internal French concern and did not play it up as a German diplomatic victory. Privately, Bülow and Holstein gloated over it as a German triumph, but both were soon to discover that the diplomatic triumph was more apparent than real and that Germany had not bettered her diplomatic position; on the contrary she had alarmed the powers about her aims and now appeared in the role of international bully.

III.

The day before Delcassé's fall, 5 June 1905, Bülow notified the sultan of Morocco that Germany accepted his invitation to a conference, and in all discussions with France would insist rigidly upon French acceptance. Pursuing Holstein's line, Bülow had excluded any possibility of bargaining with France either over participation in the Moroccan pie or compensation elsewhere. Rouvier, on the other hand, was more than ready to come to an agreement with Germany, but regarded the acceptance of a conference as a humiliation for France. Radolin told him not only that Germany required it, but also that if it did not take place "it is the *status quo*, and you ought to know that we are behind Morocco with our entire strength."[23] This attitude, when Rouvier had assumed that after the fall of Delcassé Germany would be more conciliatory, left him and his government puzzled and anxious.

By mid-June the old fears had returned, and the press reflected them. After all, it was thought, Germany must be seeking ulterior ends, such as the destruction of the Entente Cordiale. The question of

22. Kenneth Young, *Balfour*, p. 248; Newton, *Lansdowne*, p. 341.
23. Rich, *Holstein*, II, 708; "Note du Ministre," 10 June 1905: 2 *DDF*, VII, no. 28.

accepting a conference therefore became linked with that of whether France should choose Germany or England. The sense of crisis was heightened by Professor Theodor Schiemann's article in the *Kreuz-zeitung*, 14 June, setting forth the "hostage theory"—that in case of war between Germany and England, France would lose out because Germany would war on her and thereby recover compensation by land for all damage England might cause by sea. Although there was no unanimity in the French press, resentment at what was taken to be the German policy grew, and many papers that had been critical of the Entente Cordiale began to accept it as an indispensable factor in French policy. During the war scare, which reached its highest pitch by 23 June and thereafter slacked off, Rouvier shared the perplexity of the press.

In Germany the press and government remained calm. At the Foreign Office Holstein was determined to follow a hard line, for he felt that if the French had their way in Morocco, they would thank the English, not the Germans; therefore France had to give in to German demands, although eventually Germany would gladly give France what she wanted in Morocco once the question had been "internationalized" by a conference. Furthermore, Holstein, and Bülow too, felt (quite rightly) that although Delcassé had gone, Rouvier was seeking to carry out his program under the influence of Delcassé's loyal supporters at the Quai d'Orsay and in the diplomatic service, and that if Rouvier were once convinced that France would get nothing from Germany before a conference was held, he would perforce yield and accept Germany's viewpoint. In the last days of June, Holstein sought to win France over by a "vision of the future," in which, after reforms recommended by the conference had failed, just as international reforms had failed in Turkey, Germany would be freed of her commitments to the Moroccan sultan and thus enabled to come to an understanding with France to the exclusion of third parties, and perhaps to get a share in southwestern Morocco. But the main aim of German policy was to demonstrate to the French *ad oculos* that it was better to treat Germany well than badly, since "perhaps better official relations than hitherto would then develop on the basis of mutual respect."[24]

Here, then was the issue: Rouvier wanted no conference but an accord with Germany similar to those with Britain and Spain. Bülow and Holstein, on the other hand, wanted to compel France to accept a

24. Rich, *Holstein*, II, 711–12.

conference and thereby to prove that she had better align with Germany than with Britain. Once the conference was over, deals might be made.

Radolin made the opening move, 14 June, by presenting the German position concerning a conference in general terms and as his personal view. If France accepted the invitation to a conference, Germany would come to an understanding with her on the program of the conference. Germany sought no particular advantage, and for her the question was one "de forme et d'étiquette."[25] The French ministers, to whom Rouvier submitted Radolin's remarks, decided to gain time; they might in the end be obliged to go to a conference, but only after further talks with Germany. Above all, they wanted to avoid war. Rouvier, however, remained unsure of the proper response to Radolin, feeling that he faced a genuine dilemma—a dilemma implicit in German thinking: he believed that a no to Germany would mean war; but a yes would mean a rupture with England. He finally left the drafting of his reply to Paul Révoil, former governor-general of Algeria and now at the Quai d'Orsay, Georges Louis, director of the political section at the Quai d'Orsay, and Paul Cambon, who came to Paris for the purpose. Not without reason, therefore, the note delivered on 21 June smacked of Delcassé, as Radolin interpreted it.

After a long review of the positions taken by France and Germany in the Moroccan question, the note argued in favor of an accord rather than a conference. If the conference met, the note concluded, a previous exchange of views would be the best way to insure its success and to second effectively the sincere efforts of the two governments to bring about the understanding that France wanted as much as Germany. Bülow rejected the note as unacceptable because it did not flatly commit France to a conference, and again talked vaguely about the future of France. Thus neither party was satisfied with the exchange: the Germans because France had accepted the conference only in principle, and the French because they had received no definite word concerning the future about which Bülow had hinted. Moreover, the French were puzzled by the contradiction between Radolin's "form and etiquette" and the refusal of Berlin to make its position clear and precise. In addition, reports of German pressure on other powers increased French uneasiness.

None of the other powers, not even Austria-Hungary, had flatly accepted the conference, but each had agreed to it if all others did so.

25. "Note du Département," 14 June 1905: 2 DDF, VII, no. 54.

Consequently Germany tried to persuade Italy and Spain especially to break their accords with France and support the German position. But nowhere did Berlin exert greater pressure than at Washington, where the kaiser hoped that President Roosevelt could be enlisted in the German cause. The Germans explained that if France were permitted to do what she pleased in Morocco, a dangerous precedent would be established; and furthermore should England join France in a war on Germany and annihilate German sea power, an isolated United States would hardly be able to prevent the partition of China by England, Russia, and Japan. A conference over Morocco would obstruct such schemes, and a word from Roosevelt in London and Paris would render a further service to the cause of peace.

French Ambassador Jean J. Jusserand was well aware of the importance of American support and sought to counter the German pressures by frequent contacts with Roosevelt. The latter told him that the United States would not go to a conference unless France was willing to do so, and would "take very strong grounds against any attitude of Germany which seemed to [Roosevelt] unjust and unfair." As a result of the president's apparent willingness to act as mediator, Rouvier appealed to him on 23 June to intervene in the interest of peace. In Jusserand's presence that evening Roosevelt dictated a note to Ambassador Speck von Sternburg, saying that he had been informed unofficially that France had ceased her opposition to a conference, and it seemed "as a matter of course that a program of the conference would be needed in advance." He concluded: "Let me congratulate the Emperor most warmly on his diplomatic success in securing the assent of the French Government to the holding of this Conference. . . . It is a diplomatic triumph of the first magnitude."[26] Roosevelt had, of course, jumped the gun, for France had said neither yes nor no to the Germans, but he had definitely supported the French contention that a program should be drawn up in advance of the conference. The president had based his statement about acceptance upon Rouvier's telegram of the 23rd, in which he had said: "we are ready to accept the conference."[27] Although Roosevelt's move was probably not decisive in bringing about an agreement between France and Germany, it undoubtedly paved the way. The gratitude for his help expressed by both France and Germany clearly exaggerated his role but was part of the game of trying to win the president's support.

26. Joseph Bucklin Bishop, *Theodore Roosevelt*, I, 478, 483–85.
27. Rouvier to Jusserand, 23 June 1905: 2 *DDF*, VII, no. 112.

While these maneuvers were occurring in Washington, the British attitude stiffened. Lansdowne had informed Ambassador Metternich more than once that Britain had not offered France an alliance, as alleged, but on 28 June told him that she felt bound to support France diplomatically. He added that in case of a Franco-German war, it was not to be foreseen "how far British public opinion would force the government to support France."[28] What disturbed Germany was not only the rumors of an alliance offer to France, but also the British refusal on 9 June to accept the sultan's invitation to a conference. Lansdowne told Metternich, however, that he would have to learn the result of the correspondence between France and Germany before he could reply to the German circular supporting the conference. By the end of June British confidence in the French government, at a low level after Delcassé's fall, was returning. Moreover, the Admiralty, the War Office, and the Committee of Imperial Defense were all considering the strategical implications of a possible Franco-British war with Germany.

Meanwhile, Rouvier and Radolin undertook their official discussion of the terms on which France would agree to go to a conference. Besides their direct discussions, Jean Dupuy, senator and publisher of the *Petit Parisien*, supplied Rouvier with notes of Radolin's talks which reflected telegrams from Bülow and Holstein. Dupuy and Radolin were convinced that Paul Cambon and the English were working to prevent Rouvier's acceptance of the conference. Cambon, to be sure, was concerned that no Franco-German understanding be of such a nature as to break the accords of 1904 with Britain and Spain. Although a definitive text for an exchange of letters and a declaration were submitted to Radolin on 1 July, it was not until the 8th that a final wording was agreed upon.

The letters asserted that France was convinced that Germany would not pursue at the conference any objective that would compromise the legitimate interests of France or would be contrary to her rights resulting from treaties or arrangements, and would act in harmony with the following principles: the sovereignty and independence of the sultan, the integrity of his empire, economic liberty without inequality, the utility of reforms of the police and of finances whose introduction would be regulated for a short period by means of an international accord, recognition of the situation of France in Morocco because of the contiguity, "on a vast extent," of Algeria and the Sherifian em-

28. Metternich to A. A., 27 and 28 June 1905: *GP*, XX(2), nos. 6859–60.

pire, as well as the special interest of France that order reign in Morocco. In consequence of this conviction France dropped her objections to the conference and agreed to attend it. Radolin confirmed the understanding that Germany would not pursue any objective that would compromise the legitimate interests of France and repeated the clauses about principles.[29] In short, Germany secured a conference and France got the right to decide what was to be determined at it.

The Franco-German arrangement, as Révoil remarked, represented not an arrangement but a truce. He and Paléologue agreed that Rouvier would soon reach the same outlook as Delcassé and that it was German diplomacy and methods that had "worked this miracle."[30] The parallel of this observation was Holstein's gloomy prediction that further negotiations would be certain to lead to serious quarrels, and his disillusionment with Rouvier, who, he felt, was weak and was being terrorized by the Delcassé group. Holstein's policy, curiously designed to bring about a rapprochement with France by proving that she could not get along without German consent, had had the opposite effect, and had served only to rally support for France, who had accepted the conference in the belief that she would have a majority on her side.

During the next two and a half months, France improved her relations with both England and Spain. With Britain it was not a matter of diplomatic activity but rather a question of restoring the cordiality and public confidence of the Delcassé era. This goal was largely reached by an exchange of fleet visits, arranged even before the kaiser's Tangier visit but now to take on added significance. As for Spain, her attitude at times gave rise to fears concerning her steadfastness, and convinced Jules Cambon, ambassador in Madrid, that France should discuss the conference agenda with her as well as Britain, because Spain's policy was to a considerable extent dependent upon England's. Cambon went to work in August with Montero Rios, the Spanish premier, and reached an understanding on their respective objectives at the conference that was recorded in an exchange of letters on 1 and 2 September 1905. By the accord France and Spain were to divide the instruction and command of native troops in five Moroccan ports; they likewise agreed upon their respective spheres within which to suppress the contraband arms traffic. They were to cooperate in public enterprises, but France was to hold the presidency of a state bank while Spanish participation in it was to surpass that of any other

29. Texts of letters and declarations: 2 *DDF*, VII, no. 209.
30. Paléologue, *Un grand tournant*, pp. 386–87.

power excepting France. They pledged each other to act in common accord at the conference. Lansdowne gave his blessing to the agreement in an exchange of notes with Paul Cambon on 6 and 9 September. The accord reaffirmed the close relations among the three powers.

Meanwhile, negotiations between Rouvier and Radolin made little progress. On 1 August Rouvier communicated a draft of the agenda but received no reply for more than three weeks while exchanges took place over a German concession to build a mole at Tangier and over a proposed German loan to the sultan, both of which Tattenbach had busily promoted. The French bitterly criticized the German activity, complaining that, as *Le Temps* put it, while Germany did not want France to make of Morocco another Tunis, France did not want Germany to make it another Turkey. In Germany, Holstein was annoyed by the concession for the mole because it offered fuel to the Delcassé party, but he believed that the loan was perfectly justifiable; it gave Germany "no special privileges in Morocco, nor had it been secured by promises of any kind." Since both matters were, in his judgment, insignificant, he could explain the uproar only as inspired by Britain.[31]

The revival in Germany of anti-British feeling, coupled with the implications of the kaiser's Björkö adventure, may well have helped to slow down the German pursuit of an agreement with France over the conference agenda. At times it appeared that perhaps Bülow was not unwilling to let the whole matter bog down. The announcement in July that the British fleet would visit the Baltic in late August for the first time since the Crimean war created a furor in the German press, while the personal relations of Edward VII and Wilhelm II could scarcely have been worse, to judge by expressions on both sides. From midsummer to the end of the year, Franco-German negotiations took place against this backdrop of Anglo-German tension. Under the circumstances Berlin was unsure about the tactics to be followed.

Holstein and Bülow could not agree upon how to proceed, while the kaiser quite clearly wanted to pursue a conciliatory policy toward France. Bülow felt that Morocco might be used as a bribe to win French adherence to the continental alliance envisioned at Björkö, or at least to avoid pushing her more firmly into the arms of the British. But Holstein disagreed, arguing that a German retreat would be regarded as a humiliation for the kaiser and a success for the Entente

31. Rich, *Holstein*, II, 719–20.

Cordiale; continued pressure on France would bring Rouvier around, and the tsar would help by refusing to support France in her Moroccan policy and by trying to bring her into the German-Russian alliance. But again, Holstein completely misjudged the situation. The Russians, contrary to his expectations, tried to persuade Germany to yield over Morocco. The French, early in August, had sought Russian support, explaining that if France was not reduced to the sole support of Britain, the Moroccan policy would lose the appearance of the intimacy with England which caused German resentment. Lamsdorff accordingly gave Ambassador Osten-Sacken in Berlin instructions to support the French conference agenda and also their protests over Tattenbach's activities at Fez.

Without giving up his purpose of forcing France to recognize her dependence upon German good will, Holstein moved close to Bülow's notion of winning France to the continental grouping by yielding in Morocco. But because an exchange of proposals, 26 August and 1 September, was still unsatisfactory, and because a number of technical questions were involved in the negotiations, Secretary Richthofen suggested that Dr. Friedrich Rosen be sent to Paris as a specialist on North Africa and a future minister at Tangier. At the same time Holstein, again ill, retreated to the Harz, leaving Bülow to enjoin upon Rosen a "very conciliatory" policy. Despite these instructions, much heated wrangling between the French and German experts and not a little hard feeling between Ambassador Radolin and Rosen ensued before agreement was reached.

While the negotiations were going on, Witte appeared in Paris on his way home from the Portsmouth peace conference, where he had acted as Russia's chief plenipotentiary, and talked with both Radolin and Rouvier. He had an ax to grind on behalf of Russia, a loan which Russia badly needed, but was told by Rouvier that there would be none until the French differences with Germany were settled. In talking with Radolin, Witte emphasized the desirability of a three-power coalition against England and urged a settlement with France at all costs. In Germany, where Witte had a long talk with Bülow on 25 September and with the kaiser at Rominton on the 26th and 27th, he repeated the arguments he had used with Radolin. How far Witte's intervention went in bringing about a German acceptance of French demands it is impossible to say, but on the very day of their meeting Bülow instructed his representatives in Paris virtually to accept the French proposals for the conference agenda. He insisted that there be no publicity, for he was willing to accept a diplomatic setback but not a humiliation.

The "Accord on the Program of the Conference," signed on 28 September by Radolin and Rouvier, incorporated the points upon which the French had insisted throughout the negotiations. The first topic, the organization of the police, excluded from the purview of the international gathering the frontier region that France maintained should be dealt with only on the basis of longstanding treaties between France and Morocco. On the second topic, the suppression of contraband traffic in arms, France also insisted that in the region of the frontier this was a matter exclusively between France and Morocco. The other points were not ostensibly circumscribed by French interests: financial reform, the nonalienation of any public service to the profit of particular interests, and the principle of allocating contracts for public works without regard to nationality. These last two points represented German insistence upon the open door and equality of economic activity. On the other hand, Germany yielded to France in agreeing upon Algeciras as the site of the conference.

In addition to the accord on the conference agenda and the site, Rosen and Révoil signed two accords dealing with the loan and the Tangier mole. French bankers secured a share in the "advance," as the loan was characterized, and established their right of preference for the future, while the Germans won on the Tangier concession. The accords of 28 September 1905, like the agreement of 8 July, were little more than a truce that was frankly recognized as such by Rouvier. On 25 September, while protesting his desire to avoid flagrant discord at the conference and to cooperate in such a way that there would be "neither victor nor vanquished," he asserted that "aside from the formula [i.e. the agreed program] which will be signed by the two governments, I consider that I am not bound on any point."[32] In other words he was going into the conference to gain for France whatever advantage in Morocco he could win.

Bülow, who had adopted a policy of conciliation in order to pave the way for a genuine rapprochement with France as part of the Björkö dream, must have sensed the French temper not only when interviews with French journalists early in October backfired, but also when he tried to follow up Rouvier's early suggestion of a more general accord. Radolin broached the subject on 18 October only to be rebuffed by Rouvier, who explained that he had offered a more far-reaching agreement when he had hoped to settle the Moroccan

32. Rouvier to Bihourd, 25 September, and circular, 28 September 1905: 2 DDF, VII, nos. 452, 467.

question "à nous deux" without a conference, but that now under the changed circumstances he would be ready to approach the subject only after the conference. In fact, from the time of the agreement of 28 September 1905 to that of the opening of the conference on 16 January 1906, Germany's prospects quite steadily declined, while France's position grew stronger in the *dessous politique* of continuing rivalry. She blasted the hopes of a German-Russian-French coalition,[33] succeeded in keeping both Italy and Spain loyal to her, and, most significant of all for the future, tightened the Entente Cordiale as a result of diplomatic and military talks with Britain.

Both Britain and France had reason to be uneasy in the autumn of 1905. On the one hand, a flare-up of Anglo-German tension occurred; the English suspected Germany of attempting an anti-British coalition, while German preparations for an increase in the fleet fanned ill will toward England. On the other hand, France became alarmed once more, as in May and June, over the possibility of a German attack. Rumors of German aggressive designs came from several directions, but the most significant was the warning of King Alfonso XIII of Spain, who told the French military attaché in mid-December that Germany was contemplating an attack on France in the not too distant future. He gave as evidence recent remarks to him by the kaiser as well as other signs of German war preparations. Rouvier sent the report to Paul Cambon and suggested that he talk with Edward VII, who might, through Ambassador Nicolson, influence King Alfonso to hold his ground against German proposals to cooperate in a war with France and to enter more completely into the Anglo-French entente.

In carrying out these instructions, Cambon pointed out that Spanish premier Moret was more than suspect. He asked if Nicolson might inspire King Alfonso to resist the Germanophil tendencies of his government. King Edward advised Cambon to talk with Sir Edward Grey and Sir Henry Campbell-Bannerman, respectively the foreign minister and the prime minister in the Liberal government that had been in office since the 11th. Although Cambon brought up the question of British military support for France and recalled Lansdowne's offer to concert with France, he did not discuss the question when he saw Grey and Undersecretary Sanderson after leaving the king, but talked only in general terms about exerting influence on Spain. On

---

33. See above, pp. 103–04; Rich, *Holstein*, II, 728–30; Hale, *Germany and the Diplomatic Revolution*, pp. 193–201; S. L. Mayer, "Anglo-German Rivalry," *Britain and Germany in Africa*, ed. Gifford Prosser and W. R. Louis, pp. 218, 220–21.

23 December, however, Rouvier shifted the emphasis from Spain to Anglo-French relations. He instructed Cambon to push farther his discussion with Grey and advised him that the question was not to arrive at a formal and immediate accord but rather to assure himself that, if the occasion should arise, such an accord could be concluded rapidly, or that British dispositions were so certain no accord need be made. This inquiry and the fear of German aggression sparked both diplomatic and military discussions.[34]

Several months before December the French and British military men had begun to face the problem of possible German aggression. In May 1905 British naval and military personnel, especially the Committee on Imperial Defense, had begun to mull over plans to uphold Belgian neutrality or to support France in case of war. In July the C.I.D. established a special subcommittee to examine the whole problem of war with Germany. The French general staff, through Commandant Huguet, French military attaché in London, learned in August something of the British studies and in November of the British capability of sending 100,000 to 120,000 men to the Continent within a month after the decalaration of war. Apparently the French took no steps formally to get in touch with British military and naval authorities until the war scare of December.[35]

On the 20th Huguet received from General Grierson, Director of military operations at the War Office, the details of studies that were being made there. This talk inaugurated a series of discussions involving Colonel Repington of *The Times*, members of the C.I.D., the War Office, and the Foreign Office. The Admiralty remained aloof because Admiral Fisher opposed joint naval action with France, although he disclosed to the French naval attaché the British naval plans. Fisher told him that if Germany attacked France, Great Britain would fight, and that Germany would not have a ship or a colony left at the end of the war.

Such unofficial assurances were not enough for Rouvier, for he asked Paul Cambon to find out what support Britain would give France in case she were attacked by Germany. Cambon talked with Grey on 10 and 15 January 1906 but received only a postponement of discussion until after the prime minister and members of the Cabinet returned from electioneering. Grey gave his private opinion, however, that public opinion would strongly support France in case of war. In

34. See 2 *DDF*, VIII, nos. 223, 227, 246, 262, 265.
35. Monger, *End of Isolation*, pp. 206–11, 228–32, 236–39; 2 *DDF*, VIII, no. 137.

his correspondence with Bertie in Paris, Grey stated his opinion flatly that in case of a Franco-German war arising from the Anglo-French agreement over Morocco, Britain had to take the part of France. As for the military discussions, which Cambon had mentioned, Grey told the ambassador that he had talked with Haldane, Minister of War, who had authorized him to say that communications might proceed "between the French Military Attaché and General Grierson direct; but it must be understood that these communications did not commit either Government."[36] Consequently military talks continued not only between Huguet and Grierson but also, at the latter's request, between the British military attaché in Belgium and the Belgian chief of staff.

While these military talks were going on, Paul Cambon returned on 31 January to the question he had put to Grey on the 10th concerning the support Britain would give France in case of war. Grey remarked that a promise of armed support would constitute an alliance and should be in writing, but this procedure would change the entente into an alliance and could not be kept secret from Parliament. He did not want to take the matter to Parliament or the Cabinet, for he was obviously fearful of the opposition that might develop among his fellow Liberals. He asked if the situation was so serious as to warrant an alliance, and Cambon agreed that there was no immediate danger of war, but felt that they should be ready for all contingencies. As a result of a conversation with Sanderson as well as with Grey, Cambon concluded that the English wanted to make a binding pledge only in case of absolute necessity, but that if it arose, France could count on them.[37]

These diplomatic and military exchanges, even though hedged by the elimination on both sides of the word "alliance," nevertheless constituted one of the most significant results of the Franco-German duel over Morocco. The official British sanction of military conversations meant that henceforth and down to 1914 Great Britain not only was tied to one of the European groups but also faced the possibility of making war in its support.

Meanwhile, France and Russia were sparring with each other over the question of a loan that Russia desperately needed. V. N. Kokov-

36. Grey to Bertie, 15 January 1906: *Twenty-Five Years*, I, 74 (*BD*, III, no. 215). P. Cambon erroneously ascribes authorization of military talks to Prime Minister Campbell-Bannerman: 2 *DDF*, VIII, no. 417.

37. For both the military and diplomatic talks of January 1906, see Monger, *End of Isolation*, pp. 236–56, 268–74. Cf. Marder, *Dreadnought*, I, 116–19; S. R. Williamson, *Politics of Grand Strategy*, pp. 81–88.

stov, Russian minister of finance, arrived in Paris early in January 1906 to make final arrangements for the loan that Witte had discussed with Rouvier in the previous September. He learned that the possibility of a credit operation was slight because of mistrust of Russia's domestic policy in the face of the revolutionary situation and fear of a collision with Germany over Morocco. Rouvier demanded in effect that Russia support France by putting pressure on Germany. Both Witte, who was now heading the Russian government, and Lamsdorff responded by pledges of loyalty to France and assurances that she had nothing to fear from Germany. Whether convinced by Russian arguments or persuaded that France willy-nilly had to come to Russia's aid, Rouvier arranged on 11 January for a credit by French banks of an amount up to 266 million francs. Sir Edward Grey, noting that the Spanish premier wanted French money to quiet the opposition to Spanish support of France, and that Russia was demanding a loan as the price of her support, commented to Bertie: "The mud of Foreign politics is deeper than any I have been in yet."[38]

While France was making strenuous efforts to rally support at the forthcoming conference, the Germans were doing little. One reason for their inactivity lay in the divergence of views between Holstein and Bülow. The former thought that they should seek to win Britain over to the German side, whereas Bülow, who agreed that the British attitude was the key to the outcome of the conference, felt that Germany could yet win over Italy and Spain and that Britain and the United States would eventually swing over to Germany, thus compelling France to grant Germany territorial compensation in Africa for her gains in Morocco. In any case he wanted to learn how far Britain would support France. Grey was equally anxious to make the British position clear, and on 1 January 1906 instructed Ambassador Lascelles to remind Germany of Britain's arrangements with other countries, especially Japan and France, and her determination to live up to them. Two days later Metternich had a long talk with Grey reviewing Anglo-German relations, and learned from Grey that in case of a war between Germany and France public opinion would make British neutrality impossible. Holstein thought it a mistake not to communicate Germany's conference policy to the United States and Britain, but after another temporary absence from the Wilhelmstrasse found on his return in mid-January that it was too late to achieve any results. Moreover, just as France feared German aggressiveness if she did not

38. Grey to Bertie, Private, 15 January 1906: *BD*, III, no. 216.

get her way, so Holstein thought France might provoke trouble in Morocco, in order to assure British aid. Grey's comment on this idea was to assert that Britain could not "deprecate any action on the part of France which comes within the terms of the Anglo-French declaration of April 1904."[39]

On the eve of Algeciras, France, by persistent efforts, had won the sympathy of the major powers, including the United States, whereas Germany, by her "failure to follow a well-defined line on the Moroccan question," had made an impression of "insincerity and dishonesty" and had thus incurred a handicap that was to render unlikely her diplomatic success.[40]

IV.

The Conference of Algeciras opened on 16 January 1906 with representatives of thirteen states: the six European great powers, Morocco, Spain, Portugal, the Netherlands, Belgium, Sweden, and the United States. The Duke of Almodovar, as foreign minister and first delegate of Spain, was chosen president. Almost at once it became apparent that the basic issue before the conference was that of a privileged position for France in Morocco versus internationalization and equal rights for all, for which Germany contended. Because there was little difficulty over the items on the agenda concerning smuggling, the increase of revenues, the regulation of customs, and public services and works, the points over which France and Germany fought were the organization of a state bank and a police force.

Germany entered the conference overconfident of her ability to win against France, but her delegates were instructed to take care that they were not left alone with Morocco by a coalition against them; the avoidance of isolation was to be their first concern. For more than a month after the conference opened, Holstein mainly directed German policy. He ruled out the possibility of war over Morocco and saw the alternatives to lie between the kaiser's declaration at Tangier and the status established at Madrid in 1880. There were to be no concessions concerning the open door. He wrote to

39. Mayer, "Anglo-German Rivalry," *Britain and Germany in Africa*, pp. 220, 222–27; Rich, *Holstein*, II, 732–33; Grey to Lascelles, 15 January 1906: *BD*, III, no. 243.
40. Rich, *Holstein*, II, 733.

Radolin that he thought Germany would emerge from the conference "decently and honorably as a result of the English elections and the attitude of America. After all we do not want to gain anything, only we do not want to lose anything either."[41]

France, on the other hand, felt more confident than in the days of June 1905. At home the government had pushed military preparations, and the press had recovered from its defeatist proclivities of the previous summer. Abroad, France could count upon Great Britain; upon Russia not only because of the alliance but even more because of her dire need for loans; and upon Spain, who jibbed occasionally during the conference but in the main stuck to her accords with France. Moreover, France had high hopes that the Italian delegation under the direction of Visconti Venosta would support her on the crucial points, and that the United States would favor her over Germany.

On the whole French expectations were fulfilled and the German were not. The personalities in the two delegations had something to do with this outcome. An elderly diplomat, Joseph von Radowitz, ambassador to Spain, headed the German delegation, but the active, indeed aggressive, second delegate, Count von Tattenbach, who had played a major role at Fez in the duel with France, pulled the laboring oar. He was known as a special favorite of Holstein's, and his stiffness, bluntness and bluster—rudeness, according to Sir Arthur Nicolson, the British delegate—tended to alienate the other delegates. On the other hand, Paul Révoil, the French delegate who had been at the Quai d'Orsay since the previous June, was the better diplomat, despite his stubbornness over crucial points, and impressed his colleagues as supple and cool-headed. He quickly established the closest relations with Nicolson and rapidly won the collaboration of Henry White of the United States, the Russian Count Cassini, and Visconti Venosta, in planning the tactics of winning his way.

British support of France, however, was not a matter of personalities, but a result of the subtle shift in policy that had occurred under the direction of Sir Edward Grey. Whereas Lansdowne had contemplated going to war to prevent the German acquisition of a port in Morocco, Grey cared little about the military and naval aspects of the Moroccan question but rather emphasized the entente, and was guided in his relations with France and Germany by his desire to preserve and strengthen it in the interests of the balance of power. This policy left Britain little freedom of action at Algeciras and con-

41. Ibid., 732–35.

stituted the main reason why German hopes of British support were founded upon a miscalculation. As Grey explained to Nicolson, if France succeeded in achieving a special position in Morocco, "with our help, it will be a great success for the Anglo-French Entente. If she fails the prestige of the Entente will suffer and its vitality will be diminished."[42] At the conference not only did the British support the French, even when Nicolson thought they were wrong, but also Grey sought to open the way toward an entente with Russia, a move that helped to loosen the ties between Russia and Germany. In Nicolson, Britain had a representative who was completely in accord with Grey's policy and was, moreover, a shrewd diplomat whose loyalty to France was heightened by Tattenbach's crude attempts to win him to the German side.

Although Russia sought to help France, she had no direct interest in Morocco and had enjoyed good relations with Germany. Lamsdorff, therefore, attempted the role of mediator, and wanted above all peace and a speedy conclusion of the conference in order to get the French loan that Russia so badly needed. Instead of conducting a genuine mediation, however, Russia again and again tried to persuade Berlin to yield to French desires, not only through the usual diplomatic channels but also through appeals of Witte and the tsar directly to the kaiser. These Russian efforts finally destroyed the Björkö fantasy to which the kaiser had clung so tenaciously.

More difficult than Russia's was the position of Italy, upon whom Germany exerted heavy diplomatic pressure with some hope of success when Sonnino, reputed to be a supporter of the Triplice, took over the government on 8 February. As it turned out, however, Germany overplayed her hand and permitted press condemnation of Italian policy that backfired by arousing Italian irritation. Also, the astute Barrère had a strong ally in the finance minister, Luzzatti, who was not only pro-French but also anxious to convert government bonds, which he could accomplish only if the Paris money market was open to him. Barrère advised his government to treat Italian overtures concerning the bonds with reserve until the conference was over. He welcomed and encouraged the trend of opinion that looked upon the Triplice as purely defensive, and the assurances even of Sonnino that Italy intended to follow the policy of amity with France. Barrère pointed out to the Italians that the accord of 1902 should be interpreted to mean Italian support of French penetration into Morocco

42. Harold Nicolson, *Carnock*, pp. 128–29.

just as France was already instructing her agents in Tripoli to support Italian policy there. Another imponderable in the Italian situation was the estrangement between Germany and Great Britain, Italy's old friend who was patently on the side of France. Therefore, despite German pressure, Rome left Visconti Venosta complete freedom at the conference. He tried to play a mediating role, but clearly furthered French desires and toward the end voted with the French group.

For Spain the link with France was even less ambiguous than Italy's, and while some in the government felt that Spain had not received her just deserts in the accords with France, the majority, including the king, stressed loyalty to France. Ojeda, undersecretary of foreign affairs and acting minister while Almodovar was at the conference, was reputed to be a Francophobe, but he told the German chargé d'affaires that as long as the British fleet was stronger than Germany's, there could be no close alliance between Germany and Spain.

Most interesting of all was the position of the United States, which claimed no direct interest in Morocco but was concerned that France receive a fair deal at the conference. From the outset Baron Speck von Sternburg sought to win President Roosevelt's support on the plea of the open door and equality for all nations. On the other hand, J. J. Jusserand held a higher place in Roosevelt's esteem and continued to maintain the confidential relations with him that had emerged in the previous June. At the conference Henry White tried to act the role of mediator and was better placed than anyone else to do so, yet his correspondence and the testimony of Révoil's journal[43] indicate that he tended to associate himself with the French viewpoint in the daily informal discussions of objectives and tactics.

Thus the only delegations upon which Germany could rely when the chips were down were the Moroccan and the Austro-Hungarian. The former hardly counted as an active participant, but Count Welsersheimb of the latter played an important part in formulating and presenting the compromises that led to a settlement at the end of March.[44] Among the smaller powers, Portugal sided with the British, while Belgium, the Netherlands, and Sweden, having little interest in Morocco and desiring to avoid offense to either protagonist, remained in the background. They abstained when the majority was not clear, and voted with the majority when the issues seemed largely resolved.

43. Paul Révoil, "Journal," 12 January to 9 April 1906: 2 DDF, IX, 857–969.
44. See Bridge, From Sadowa to Sarajevo, pp. 280–82.

The story of the conference, which will not be told here,[45] may be divided into two phases. In the first, from 16 January to 3 March, Germany still felt fairly confident, as the conference disposed of the matters of secondary important and launched into the two knotty problems of the Moroccan state bank and the police. Over these questions a deadlock developed by mid-February. Germany was willing to grant France concessions on the organization of the bank and other financial matters in order to induce her to yield on the police question. France, however, insisted that France and Spain be given a police mandate for all the Moroccan ports and their vicinity, while giving guarantees to maintain the open door and equality for all nations in competition for the construction of public works. Germany refused on the grounds that a police mandate would give France political as well as economic preponderance. Each played for time and the French won out, for a vote on a procedural question, 3 March, engineered by Nicolson, found Germany supported by only Austria-Hungary and Morocco. This situation, which Bülow found "hardly gratifying,"[46] convinced him that Germany had to make concessions on the police question.

In the second phase of the conference, 3 March to 7 April, Germany first tried to initiate direct negotiations with France but found the door closed. The fall of Rouvier's government on 7 March over a domestic issue hampered the French delegation, although Rouvier remained at the Quai d'Orsay until the establishment of the Sarrien government on 13 March with Léon Bourgeois as foreign minister. Germany continued to pursue a hard line until mid-March, but thereafter retreated concession by concession, as Bülow took the direction of policy from Holstein, who continued, however, to give advice until his resignation early in April. At length, and to a considerable extent as a result of the mediatory activity of White and Visconti Venosta, the French and Germans on 27 March agreed upon a solution of the police question. That same afternoon the conference acted upon the bank, and thus concluded all but minor details and the final drafting of the conference act. On 7 April the delegates signed the "General Act of the International Conference of Algeciras."

The Act, asserting respect for the independence and integrity of the sherifian empire, gave international sanction for the more press-

45. For more detailed accounts, see E. N. Anderson, *First Moroccan Crisis*, ch. XVII; A. J. P. Taylor, "La conférence d'Algesiras," *RH*, CCVIII (1952), 236–54.
46. Rich, *Holstein*, II, 739.

ing reforms in Morocco: the suppression of the trade in arms, the creation of new resources, and the organization of customs. It proclaimed freedom of trade and equal rights in the economic development of Morocco. Moreover, the principle of internationalization was applied to the provisions for the bank, to be supervised by France, Germany, Britain, and Spain. Although France failed to obtain as many shares in the bank as she had demanded, she obtained a preferential position and preserved the pledges of the maghzen to the French consortium of 1904. Also, in respect to the police, France and Spain enjoyed a special position. France and Morocco were jointly to carry out the regulations on the Algerian frontier, and Spain and Morocco were to exercise them in the Riff. The police were to be organized and instructed by France in Rabat, Mazagan, Safi, and Mogador; by Spain in Tetuan and Larache; and by both in Tangier and Casablanca, all under the eyes of a Swiss inspector-general. He could not intervene, but was to report to the maghzen at least once a year and remit a copy of his report to the doyen of the diplomatic corps at Tangier. Even though the diplomatic corps could demand a special inquiry into the administration of the police, if any legation asked for it, the terms of the Act had obviously reduced the "internationalization" of the police to a minimum and had virtually fulfilled the Franco-Spanish accord of 1905.

The Algeciras Act represented only a truce between France and Germany, for the Franco-German duel continued until 1911. Who was victor and who vanquished? Contemporaries, even the press, put little stress on the question. Bülow, publicly and privately, insisted that Algeciras vindicated the German championship of the open door and had "proven that even thorny questions which concern the prestige of great powers can be settled by peaceful negotiations at a conference table; we have avoided a war in which . . . we should have risked much, could lose a great deal, but gain little." Germany, he said, had proved that she was not to be treated as a negligible quantity.[47] On the other hand, the French, with perhaps greater cogency, argued that their special position in Morocco had been recognized even though limited in some degree by the organization of the bank and the supervision of their police forces outside the Algerian border.

But what both historians and contemporaries have stressed is the effect of the whole Moroccan crisis, including the conference, on the power relationships in Europe. Clearly Germany emerged from the

47. Bülow, *Memoirs*, II, 231–32, 253. Cf. Rich, *Holstein*, II, 742–45.

crisis in a weaker position than when she opened it. Italy had demonstrated her independence, at least in Mediterranean matters where France and Britain were involved. The kaiser's hopes of a continental alliance were shattered by the Russian display of loyalty to the Dual Alliance and by France's categorical refusal to contemplate closer ties with Germany.[48] Germany was therefore forced to look upon Austria-Hungary as her one true ally. The implications of this dependence Bülow ruefully recognized at the time.

In contrast, the Entente Cordiale emerged a strengthened and invigorated combination, while Britain and Russia began laying the ground work of their eventual understanding. These events cast long shadows before, because the swing of the power pendulum away from the central powers toward a grouping that enjoyed ties either of alliance or of friendship with Japan and the United States embodied a revolution that was to affect European and world relations through the war of 1914–1918. Considering the outcome of that war and the meager gains for Germany at Algeciras (*pace* Bülow), the Moroccan crisis ended in a fateful diplomatic defeat for Germany.

48. Russia's loyalty was mainly determined by her need for a loan from France. See Bernard F. Oppel, "The Waning of a Traditional Alliance: Russia and Germany after the Portsmouth Peace Conference," *CEH*, V (1972), 322–26.

Chapter 6

The Diplomatic

Revolution Consummated,

1906–1907

The negotiators of the Anglo-Russian conventions of 1907 were Alexander Petrovich Izvolsky, Russian foreign minister, 1906–1910, and Sir Arthur Nicolson, British ambassador to Russia for the same period. In London, Foreign Secretary Grey and the anti-German members of the Foreign Office—among them Senior Clerk Eyre Crowe and Permanent Undersecretary Sir Charles Hardinge, who replaced Sanderson in February 1906—worked for the entente with Russia, and Chancellor of the Exchequer Herbert H. Asquith, Secretary for India John Morley, and Secretary for War Richard Burdon Haldane also favored it. In Russia, V. N. Kokovstov, minister of finance, and the ambassador to Britain, Alexander Constantinovich Benckendorff, supported Izvolsky, while General F. F. Palitsyn at first doubted the value of a British entente. Involved in negotiating the other pacts of 1907–1908 were French Foreign Minister Stephen Pichon, Paul Cambon in London, and his brother Jules Cambon, ambassador to Spain till April 1907, when he went to Berlin. Among the Germans involved in the Baltic Pact of 1907 was Baron William Eduard von Schoen, ambassador to Russia until November 1907, when he replaced, at Berlin, Heinrich Leonard von Tschirschky as secretary of state for foreign affairs. On the Russian side Baron M. A. de Taube, legal counsellor in the foreign affairs ministry, was an active participant in the Baltic Pact negotiations.

The Russo-Japanese war and the First Moroccan crisis accelerated the shift in great-power relationships that constituted the final phase in the diplomatic revolution of 1902–1907. A significant factor in the shift was the Anglo-German tension that reached a high point in 1904–1905 and was never thereafter completely released. Likewise, the reorientation of Russian policy after the defeat in the Far East included a rejection of close ties with Germany and the substitution of reliance upon the western powers, France and Great Britain. This change in policy meant willingness if not eagerness to participate in the reshaping of great-power alignments on the Continent. Even without the First Moroccan crisis and the conference of Algeciras, events had been driving Germany and Britain apart and would have led sooner or later to antagonism between them.

I.

Undoubtedly Anglo-German naval rivalry was the most important reason for the rising tension. The British first became genuinely alarmed over German naval building in 1904. Among the events that contributed to uneasiness was the Kiel regatta in June, when the whole strength of the German navy came under the inspection of King Edward VII and British naval officers. At the same time, popular apprehension rose with the publication in English of August Niemann's novel under the title of *The Coming Conquest of England*. The First Sea Lord, Sir John Fisher, was becoming convinced that Germany meant to attack England, and talked of "Copenhagening" the German fleet before it could do so. Such remarks and the regrouping of British naval strength in the North Sea, announced in Parliament on 10 December 1904, heightened German fears of British policy, already aroused by rumors concerning the dreadnoughts under construction. The feeling of jitters among the kaiser and responsible Germans persisted after the first scare of November 1904, and flared up again in periods of diplomatic tension such as those in the spring and autumn of 1905.

The era of naval competition that was consequently inaugurated led to a British assessment of the problems involved in balance of power and to the further extension of alliances and alignments begun with the Japanese in 1902 and continued with the French in 1904. Inevitably, as the British shifted their thinking from the pro-German policy of the late nineteenth century to an anti-German posture, the importance of an entente with Russia began to be voiced in the press as well as among British statesmen who had flirted with the idea for a half dozen years. The conclusion of the Entente Cordiale had given rise as well, especially among Frenchmen, to the desire for an Anglo-Russian entente, but the Russo-Japanese war had brought to a halt

5. *Sir Edward Grey (Culver Pictures)*

the tentative steps toward it. When the British press and French statesmen in the autumn of 1905 began again to talk of an Anglo-Russian rapprochement, they gave it a clearly discernible anti-German twist. In the British foreign service, men like Sir Charles Hardinge in St. Petersburg and Sir Francis Bertie in Paris vigorously advocated an entente, the latter frankly expressing a desire to encircle Germany. At the Foreign Office both Lansdowne and T. H. Sanderson, permanent undersecretary of state, were doubtful of success in wooing Russia and failed to share the anti-German sentiments that were growing among the departmental personnel.

The Liberal Party, preparing in the autumn of 1905 to take office, advocated better relations with both Russia and Germany, but under the government that took office in December shifts in Foreign Office posts heavily weighted the staff on the anti-German side. Sir Louis Mallet, most extreme among the anti-German group, became Grey's private secretary; and in February 1906, Sir Charles Hardinge, who looked upon Russia rather than France as the effective check upon Germany, replaced Sanderson as permanent undersecretary of state. Thus anti-German sentiment became the "prevailing orthodoxy," and there was no longer at the foreign office "a powerful voice to dissent from the anti-German policy of the majority party."[1] In the course of 1906 Eyre Crowe, a senior clerk, was emerging as the ablest of those who were suspicious of every German policy development, and his famous memorandum of 1 January 1907 reflected clearly and cogently the prevailing attitude toward Germany. Involved in it was not only the recognition that Germany constituted a "threat to the European balance" and that there was need for a Russian agreement, but also that there was a change in the nature of the Entente Cordiale from a friendly settlement of differences to an instrument for the protection of France as a European power. Although Grey then and in his memoirs claimed that he had retained his freedom of action, in fact he was committed to an anti-German policy, in which the Admiralty, the War Office, and the India Office concurred. Under the circumstances, German attempts in the summer and autumn of 1906 to bring about a détente proved ineffective, and despite Grey's insistence that an understanding with Russia was directed toward no one, it, too, was in fact part of a tacit policy of curbing Germany.

In Russia at the same time a shift occurred away from the German

1. George Monger, *End of Isolation*, pp. 264–66; Zara S. Steiner, *The Foreign Office and Foreign Policy*, pp. 65–66, 75–76, 112–116.

orientation that had tended to prevail for a decade. The repudiation of the Björkö treaty in the autumn of 1905 and the pursuit of a pro-French policy at Algeciras in cooperation with the British were early symptoms of change that accompanied the reorientation of Russian objectives away from the Far East toward Europe and the Near East. Not only did Russia no longer need the German backing that she had enjoyed during the war with Japan, but also, in her new orientation, especially toward the Near East, she might well find Germany blocking her way. Moreover, because all Russian statesmen agreed that the alliance with France had to be maintained, some kind of agreement with Britain, rather than close ties with Germany, became imperative. Although Lamsdorff had himself favored an Anglo-Russian entente and had renewed his hopes of it after the Portsmouth peace treaty, it remained for his successor, Alexander Petrovich Izvolsky, to initiate the new Russian policy and to negotiate the entente.

Izvolsky became foreign minister in mid-May 1906 after a diplomatic career in the Balkan states, at the Vatican, Tokyo, and Copenhagen. Although the last post appeared to be a demotion after the Japanese capital, it was significant because of the tsar's family connections with the Danish court. The tsar's mother, daughter of King Christian IX, was one of Izvolsky's supporters and may well have helped to bring about his appointment as foreign minister. His contemporaries characterized him as able, intelligent, and ambitious; if they were admirers, they called him clever and adroit but sensitive and cautious; his detractors dubbed him subtle, crafty, and timid; all agreed that he was vain and snobbish. His career as foreign minister suggests that he was something of a timeserver and an opportunist.

Izvolsky wanted to liquidate the heritage of Russia's Asiatic adventures and return to Europe, where lay Russia's historic interests. This required the maintenance and strengthening of the French alliance, rapprochement with Japan in the Far East and with Britain, Russia's antagonist in middle Asia and France's friend. His attitude toward Germany appeared to be ambivalent: close friends thought him pro-German and anti-British, but his acts indicate that his new course meant an end of the Björkö fantasy as well as the dreams of a renewed *Dreikaiserbund*, and yet—at least while Russia was still weak in the aftermath of war and revolution—he could not afford to antagonize Germany. Thus, while convinced of the need for an entente with Great Britain and undoubtedly aware of its implications for balance-of-power politics, he sought to maintain good relations with Germany and her ally Austria-Hungary.

The task of Anglo-Russian rapprochement and eventual entente was a difficult one for both Grey and Izvolsky, however much they desired it, because of the legacy of antagonism they inherited. The chief points of friction had been China, Tibet, Afghanistan, and, above all, Persia. The outcome of the Russo-Japanese war had largely eliminated the first by the substitution of Japan for England as Russia's chief opponent in the Far East. Because of the Anglo-Japanese alliance, moreover, Russia had to come to an understanding with Japan as a condition for an entente with Britain; hence a Russo-Japanese rapprochement constituted a necessary corollary of an Anglo-Russian one.

Tibet was perhaps the least controversial point of friction, yet was a touchy one. Nominally a part of China and nowhere touching the border of Russia, the Buddhist Dalai Lama became the target of a Siberian Buddhist adventurer who in the late 1890's tried to establish Russian influence at Lhasa as part of a far-reaching scheme for Russian dominance in Asia. Lord Curzon, the ambitious and imperious British viceroy of India, could not brook such a development, and after a failure to secure satisfaction in border disputes and in communication with Lhasa, persuaded a reluctant British Cabinet to sanction the Younghusband mission to the Tibetan capital. Younghusband marched into Lhasa in the summer of 1904 and a month after his arrival signed a treaty that assured Britain of Tibetan independence of any other foreign power and of satisfaction in questions of boundaries, trade, and communications. Russia, helpless because of the war with Japan, protested British action, but had perforce to accept assurances that England sought no occupation of territory or intervention in Tibet's internal affairs.

Afghanistan, however, was a thornier problem. Bordering on both India and Russia, its freedom from Russian influence and its close ties with British India had been regarded by the British throughout the latter half of the nineteenth century as essential to the security of India from Russian expansion into middle Asia. About 1900, again as part of the dream of predominance in Asia, Russia began an attempt to establish direct relations with Afghanistan, alleging that the settlement of border problems required them and promising not to give such relations a political character. The Indian government, which had watched with concern the building of the Trans-Caspian railway into the area, objected to the Russian move but did nothing immediately. On the other hand, British efforts to counteract Russian commercial penetration into Afghanistan and to reaffirm the Amir's pledge to conduct foreign relations only through the Indian government, achieved in an agreement with the Amir, March 1905, aroused Russian fears that Britain intended an advance into Afghanistan, or at least to change her previous policy. The war with Japan again tied Russia's hands, while British statesmen became increasingly convinced that an understanding with Russia was preferable to continued antagonism and tension.

Of the three middle Asian problem areas, Persia was the most important to both Russia and England. Here, after the turn of the century, Russian penetration by the usual means of trade, finance, and concessions was most active and successful, even threatening to challenge British supremacy in the Persion Gulf. By 1904, however, Russia was becoming wary of further financial commitments.[2] Hampered by the Boer war, Britain could at first do little, but on 15 May 1903, almost a year after its termination, Lansdowne issued a declaration concerning the Persian Gulf which clearly warned any and all powers that while Britain would not exclude "the legitimate trade of others," she would resist by all the means in her power the "establishment of a naval base or a fortified port" there by any other power.[3] Moreover, the British countered as best they could Russian preponderance in the north of Persia by developing their own economic interests in the south, especially in Seistan, which they regarded as vital to the command of trade routes into India and to the security of both Afghanistan and India. Clearly the advantage of proximity gave to Russia preponderance in the north and to Britain dominance in southeastern Persia and along the Gulf, and suggested a possible ending of rivalry by partition of the country into spheres of influence.

Obviously for Great Britain the security of India as well as Afghanistan lay behind her policy in the region. The Liberal government, with its desire to reduce military expenditures, had a more immediate interest in an understanding with Russia than its predecessor. From July 1905 the government of India had been pressing for attention to the danger of a Russian advance into Afghanistan and Persia, and the Committee of Imperial Defense (C.I.D.) estimated that in the first year of a war with Russia, Britain would need to send 100,000 men to India. Because an understanding with Russia would

2. See the minutes of ministerial conferences in June 1904 and August 1905: A. L. Popov, ed., "Anglo-russkoe sopernichestvo v Persii v 1890–1906 gg. (Anglo-Russian Rivalry in Persia, 1890–1906)," KA, LVI (1933), 49–59.

3. Newton, Lansdowne, pp. 242–43.

obviate the anxiety and expense, John Morley, Secretary of State for India, was one of the staunchest supporters of an Anglo-Russian entente.

What urged both Russia and England toward an entente in 1906, however, was the expansion of German interests in Persia and the Gulf. The opening in 1906 of a regular Persian-Arabian steamship service, the development in the same year of commercial activity in the Gulf, the active German role in efforts to settle a Turkish-Persian border dispute, and rumors of negotiations for a loan to Persia and the opening of a German bank and schools at Teheran all led the British ambassador at Constantinople to warn Sir Edward that "it was very probable that if Great Britain and Russia do not very soon come to an agreement with regard to their respective interests in Persia, they may find themselves confronted there with Germany very much as did France in Morocco."[4] For Russia, as for Britain, a German thrust into Persia constituted an additional reason for an understanding with England, because Russia could not hope to oppose both powers, and the western orientation that Izvolsky sought clearly indicated a preference for a British entente.

Peripheral to the mid-Asian focus of Anglo-Russian interests was the Near Eastern question, in which Germany had become a much more important power factor than she was in Persia. Here the interrelated problems of the Macedonian question, the Straits, and the Bagdad railway were of major concern to Russia, and the last two to Britain as well. The Macedonian question and the tangled complex of Balkan politics were vital interests not of Germany or Great Britain but rather of Russia and Austria-Hungary, and will be dealt with in the following chapter.

The Straits question had been reopened when Russia sent out four destroyers in 1902 and some converted merchant vessels of her volunteer fleet in 1904. The question of the Straits, however took on a new aspect for Britain when the newly formed C.I.D., in February 1903, adopted the view that Russian control of the Straits would not fundamentally alter the existing strategic situation in the Mediterranean.

The Bagdad railway, however, was closely related to the Persian question because the German-Turkish convention of 5 March 1903 provided for the extension of the line toward the Persian Gulf. At first both the French and British governments had favored cooperation with the Germans in building and managing the railway. In

4. Sir Nicholas O'Conor to Grey, 24 April 1906: *BD*, IV, no. 328. Cf. D'Apchier le Maugin to Bourgeois, Teheran, 5 May 1906: 2 *DDF*, X, no. 42.

London, however, a strident anti-German press campaign and, more important, the German failure to offer a scheme for participation that would meet the British demand for equality led the Cabinet to reject cooperation. For a similar reason France likewise finally rejected participation, although undoubtedly Russia also exerted pressure against cooperation with the Germans. Russia from the first opposed the German enterprise, fearing that its development would enable Mesopotamia to compete with Russian grain and oil, that the railway line itself would offer dangerous competition to Russian trans-Caspian and Caucasian lines, and that it would open to the Germans the Persian market that Russia had chosen for her own exploitation. In 1900 Russia secured an agreement with Turkey by which the Sultan promised to award concessions for north Anatolian and Armenian railways only to Russians or to syndicates approved by the tsar. Despite the lack of cooperation, the Germans pressed forward with the construction of the Bagdad line, but after reaching Bulgurlu in October 1904, they faced much more difficult and costly construction through the Taurus and Amanus mountains and felt that they could not go on without substantial financial aid from both the Ottoman government and the great financial markets. Thus, in 1905–1906 the question of internationalization of the Bagdad railway again arose.

Consequently, paralleling steps toward an Anglo-Russian understanding and related to them were attempts to bring about a four-power agreement on the railway. Early in April 1906, when the question of a deal was raised with both the British and the French by an official of the Bagdad Railway Company, Grey approached Paul Cambon, saying that the British financiers were ready and that the Cabinet, thinking that the line would be constructed sooner or later with or without British cooperation, was disposed to participate in an international combination that would include France, Russia, and Britain. Grey not only asked France to persuade Russia that the line could not injure her economic and political interests, but also undertook on his own to win Russian cooperation. The Quai d'Orsay seized upon Grey's proposal as a means of rendering a service to both Russia and England by fostering an entente between them in return for their help at Algeciras, but pointed out that if the Bagdad railway question were to be taken up again, it could be done only in accord with Germany, and that England, who held a trump in the proposed terminus of the railway at Koweit, should make the first démarche in Berlin.

The Russians were divided in their attitude toward the Bagdad line. Although Izvolsky was personally well disposed toward Russian participation, the minister of finance, Kokovtsov, opposed it because

Russia was not in a position to cooperate financially. In the end nothing came of the intermittent talks of 1906–1907, except an understanding among Britain, France, and Russia that they would act together in dealing with Germany.

In the meantime, on 24 April 1906, Grey had counseled with Asquith, Morley, Haldane, and Nicolson concerning negotiations with Russia. Sir Arthur Nicolson was not optimistic about the prospects for agreement because of the mistrust of one another and the instability of the Russian internal situation. He also felt that "if the Emperor and the Russian government were free from any other political ties, they would gladly form an intimate alliance with Germany."[5] Nevertheless by May the stage had been set for active Anglo-Russian discussions. The ground had been tested over the previous three years, and in 1906 an approach had been made by cooperation at the Algeciras conference and by British participation in an international loan to Russia. Moreover, the establishment of the Russian Duma made an accord with Russia more palatable than before to the British Liberals. In mid-May Izvolsky replaced Lamsdorff at the Singers' Bridge in St. Petersburg, and in late May, Nicolson arrived to take the ambassadorial post vacated in February by Hardinge. Thus the two governments and the two principals in the subsequent negotiations were ready to go ahead.

II.

Nicolson, who visited Izvolsky on 29 May, pledged him to complete discretion concerning the important matters he had been instructed to bring up, for he feared that Izvolsky would communicate the progress of negotiations to the German ambassador. Despite Izvolsky's cordiality and that of the tsar, however, the timeliness of action and French encouragement, negotiations that were formally opened on 7 June moved excruciatingly slowly. Nicolson outlined British relations with Tibet and made proposals for an agreement, suggesting that after it had been reached he would make proposals concerning Afghanistan, but that Izvolsky should make Russia's proposals concerning Persia. To all of this Izvolsky agreed, and yet it was autumn before Nicolson could report that Izvolsky had taken a step or two in advance. Summer holidays, Isvolsky's effort to reorganize the foreign

5. Nicolson, *Carnock*, p. 153.

ministry, the need for time to study the subjects to be discussed, and the domestic difficulties of the Russian government accounted in large part for the delay. Nicolson, however, was anxious to continue negotiations in spite of difficulties, and felt that a reason for doing so was German activity in Persia.

In fact, Germany was never far from the minds of the Russians as well as the British. Count von Osten-Sacken, Russian ambassador in Berlin, on 8 July wrote Izvolsky that the bettering of Anglo-Russian relations had frightened Germany, who did not accept the assurances of St. Petersburg and London concerning the rapprochement. He thought that a German exchange of views with the Turks and German activities in Teheran were part of a plan to create on the Russian border a wall of powers subjected to German influence. But Izvolsky, who had been determined from the first not to give offense to Germany, apparently found good reason for going slowly with the British. During a trip to the West in October he told Bertie and the French that he was going to stop in Germany on his way home in order to find out what interests Germany had in Persia. When he told Bertie that he could not go further in negotiations with Britain until he had obtained the views of the German government, Bertie asked if he meant that an Anglo-Russian arrangement was subject to German concurrence. He said no, but that he wanted German views so that he could not be accused, like Delcassé, of a fait accompli behind their backs.[6]

After two days in Berlin, 28–30 October, Izvolsky was satisfied that he had overcome the German ill-humor dating from Algeciras. He declared to the Germans that the negotiations with England aimed only at removing points of friction and could not lead to Russia's joining a political combination hostile to Germany; and if negotiations touched German interests in any way, he would be ready to make explanations to Germany in order not to bear her any injury. In return Izvolsky received assurances that an Anglo-Russian accord, as he had represented it, would not create German resentment and would not lead to action to impede its effects; also he was assured again that Germany had no political interests in Persia, but only commercial objectives. Izvolsky thought, therefore, that his goal of preventing another Morocco had been attained and that the Berlin talks would facilitate his negotiations with Britain.

Meanwhile, despite the lack of progress in actual negotiations over

6. Bertie to Grey, 22 October 1906: BD, IV, nos. 230–31.

Persia, Russia and Britain had improved their relations in dealing with questions arising there. For example, in February 1906 Grey had let Russia know that he had rejected Persian requests for a loan because he did not want to change the status quo pending an understanding with Russia, and he hoped that Russia would take the same position. Izvolsky later referred to the exchange of February as a "tacit agreement," and indicated to Nicolson that he wanted "to act in harmony" with its spirit.[7] Nevertheless, while friendly and even cordial relations existed between the capitals, representatives of the two powers at Teheran failed throughout most of 1906 to cooperate with one another. Accordingly, Izvolsky instructed Nicholas Hartvig in Teheran to cooperate with his British colleague, and at the same time Grey gave similar instructions to Sir Cecil Spring-Rice, who went to Persia in September after having served for three years in the British embassy at St. Petersburg. Hartvig and Spring-Rice apparently fulfilled their instructions, for according to the latter they both wanted an Anglo-Russian entente.

At home Izvolsky was experiencing both encouragement and opposition from the members of the foreign service and the government. On 20 September he called a ministerial conference that included Kokovtsov and the chief of the general staff, General F. F. Palitsyn, along with representatives of the ministries of foreign affairs, trade, and the interior. Izvolsky pointed out that this was the first of ministerial conferences that would be held to deal with the negotiations with Britain and was occasioned by the need for a decision concerning joint Anglo-Russian aid to the Persian treasury. Kokovtsov took the lead in the discussion, pointing out that Russia had got very little as a result of her handouts to Persia, and that instead of additional gifts she should come to some agreement with Great Britain about financial assistance and spheres of influence (though aparently he did not use that phrase) and should exploit her rights in the North with capital from small neutral countries like Belgium. Since England should not go beyond certain limits in the South, the two powers should avoid conflicts and prevent involvement in the complications that would arise in Persia. All the members of the conference except Palitsyn expressed agreement with Kokovtsov, and the conference closed with a resolution authorizing plans for a loan to Persia on the basis of the British proposal, and for further financial activity there.[8]

7. Nicolson to Grey, 1 September 1906: ibid., no. 336.
8. Popov, ed., "Anglo-russkoe sopernichestvo," *KA*, LVI, 59–64.

Despite the encouragement that Izvolsky might have gained from this conference, he made no effort immediately to get down to brass tacks with Nicolson. He had yet to visit Berlin, and at home he faced stubborn opposition to compromises in Persia, mainly from the military. Although many in the Russian court and government opposed the policy of entente with Britain, most outspoken was the general staff, which adhered to the old dreams, talking of controlling Seistan (a key point on the road to India), the Persian Gulf, and access to the Indian Ocean. Benckendorff condemned the general staff for having learned nothing and forgotten nothing; they were talking as they had about Manchuria, Korea, and the Pacific before the war with Japan. Under the circumstances Izvolsky felt that the negotiation of an entente with Britain would take a long time. Grey recognized the situation and refrained from putting pressure on him, although he was uneasy over the almost complete stoppage of discussion throughout December 1906 and January 1907.

Quite apart from Izvolsky's expressed wish to study the questions before him—such wishes always meant long delays—he was involved at this time in negotiations with Japan over questions left undecided at Portsmouth. Besides conventions concerning commerce, railways in Manchuria, and the like, Izvolsky wanted a genuine entente cordiale. Though Nicolson and Grey recognized the significance of a Russo-Japanese settlement for the success of Anglo-Russian negotiations, Britain avoided direct involvement in them, only urging upon the Japanese the importance of an agreement. France, however, became associated with them. She had already begun discussions with the Japanese in order to safeguard her own interests in southern China and Indochina, and at the end of November 1906, when Izvolsky complained to French Ambassador Bompard of Japan's exorbitant demands, which had created a deadlock, France was ready to assist him. Because Japan had approached France for a loan in November, the French had a means at hand with which to put pressure upon the Japanese, who by mid-February 1907 were ready to discuss a general accord with Russia.

In the meantime France and Japan had pursued their own negotiations. They arranged a loan in mid-March after Russia had indicated that her own discussions with Japan were progressing satisfactorily. Paul Cambon seized upon the news of the loan to suggest a political understanding among Paris, London, St. Petersburg, and Tokyo, an idea that Sir Charles Hardinge approved. Grey, however, while favoring a general entente, suggested the impossibility of keeping Germany out of it because of her interests in the Far East, and pointed out that the inclusion of Germany would destroy the character they wanted to give the entente. If both Russia and France came to accords with Japan in addition to the Anglo-Japanese alliance and the Anglo-French entente, the cordial relations established among the four powers and the mutual communications exchanged would give to the combination the character of a general entente. Stephen Pichon, French foreign minister in the Clemenceau government since October 1906, did not pursue these ideas, but without serious difficulty completed the agreement with Japan, 10 June 1907, along the lines he had been following. The two powers accorded most-favored-nation treatment to their nationals in Japan and in Indochina respectively; they pledged their respect for the independence and integrity of China and for the open door, and mutual support to assure peace and security in those regions where they possessed rights of sovereignty, protection, or occupation.[9]

Russia and Japan took longer to draw up their conventions and agreements: they concluded a convention on the Manchurian railway in June, another on fisheries and a treaty of commerce and navigation in July, and finally signed a political and a secret convention on 30 July 1907. These carried the usual pledges to respect each other's territorial integrity and to recognize the independence and integrity of China and the principle of equal opportunity there. Secretly they delimited their spheres of activity and influence in Manchuria. Russia undertook not to interfere in Korea, and Japan recognized Russia's special interests in Outer Mongolia with which she pledged not to interfere.[10]

While the Japanese agreements with Russia and France may have been more advantageous to Japan than to the other two, those with Russia helped to facilitate Russia's return to Europe, a major French as well as Russian objective. Moreover, the agreements paved the way to the conclusion of the Anglo-Russian entente, and all the accords combined meant that Russia was linked with the Anglo-Japanese group as well as with France, thus fulfilling Grey's description of a general four-power entente. Little wonder that Germany again feared a quadruple alliance, and with more reason than she had had in 1904–1905.

To resume the story of the Anglo-Russian negotiations: Izvolsky

9. The text: 2 *DDF*, XI, no. 24.

10. The texts: Victor A. Yakhontoff, *Russia and the Soviet Union in the Far East* (New York, 1931), pp. 374–76.

held his second ministerial conference on Persia and related matters on 14 February 1907. The membership was the same as that of September 1906, except that Benckendorff, who was in St. Petersburg on leave from the London embassy, also attended. Izvolsky posed as the first question the British proposal to divide Persia into spheres of influence, pointing out that there was as yet no public opinion in favor of the idea, that some government circles were convinced that Persia should come entirely under Russian influence, and that Russia should strive for a free outlet on the Persian Gulf, which would involve the building of a trans-Persian railway and a fortified terminus on the Gulf. Because the events of the previous few years, continued Izvolsky, had shown this plan to be impossible and had brought to the fore the idea that a conflict with England had to be avoided at all costs, he was convinced that the best way to do so was to demarcate spheres of influence, but he wanted to learn the views of the conference on this point before turning to an examination of the British proposals. The conference accepted the principle of spheres of influence as the only possible basis for agreement with Great Britain.

In discussing the demarcation of the Russian sphere of influence, Kokovtsov and the military men were far apart. The former suggested a line far to the north of that suggested by Palitsyn, the chief of staff, and justified it on the grounds that the finance ministry regarded his line as delimiting an area where Russia had already established a solid commercial position. Palitsyn wanted a line farther south including all of Khorassan, so that Russia could secure the strategically important roads to Afghanistan. His line followed that finally agreed upon between Russia and Britain, except for the terminus on the Afghan border that was fixed farther north so that Russia's sphere would not touch the Afghan-Persian boundary. Palitsyn's assistant supported him, pointing out that Seistan had so much importance for Britain as the natural route to India that conceding it to England might enable Russia to get substantial concessions from her; and he suggested that Russia should try to get British consent to recognize Afghanistan as a "buffer state" rather than a place for future activities directed against Russia. Izvolsky reminded the conference that since his purpose was an agreement that would prevent clashes in Asia with Britain and other powers, he could not be guided exclusively by strategic considerations, but would use Palitsyn's line as Russia's maximum demand and as a basis for negotiation. Moreover, he admitted the possibility of obtaining greater concessions from Britain respecting Afghanistan if Seistan were included in her sphere.[11]

After the ministerial conference Anglo-Russian negotiations proceeded more rapidly, although some hard bargaining remained. The British draft on Tibet was virtually accepted four days after the conference, and Izvolsky offered portions of the first Russian draft on Persia and communicated the concession of Seistan to Great Britain. He asked for British proposals concerning Afghanistan that Nicolson had held back since the previous September. Nicolson complied on 23 February and thus completed the proposals on the three major topics under discussion. Two topics, however, entered into the exchange of views that were to be excluded from the final agreement: the Straits and the Persian Gulf.

On 15 March 1907 Benckendorff raised with Sir Edward the question of the Straits. The subject had never been far from the minds of the Russians and the English, and Izvolsky's great ambition was to open the Straits to Russian warships. Although Grey and Hardinge agreed with the C.I.D. that freedom of the Straits for Russia would not markedly affect the British position in the Mediterranean, they pointed out that the Straits were a European concern and that they would have to consider other powers, especially Germany and France. Grey felt that public opinion would make an agreement difficult, and suggested that Britain would need a quid pro quo for such a great concession. After further reflection, Grey informed Nicolson that it would be better not to bring the Straits into the Asiatic agreement, but if matters were settled favorably, "the Russians will not have trouble with us about the entrance to the Black Sea."[12] Izvolsky in a memorandum of 14 April 1907 noted with pleasure the British attitude but agreed with Grey that it would be inopportune to conclude special arrangements concerning the Straits. A further exchange in May and June clarified the British and Russian positions, and there the matter rested.

Following the agreement to give up the Straits question, Izvolsky made progress in securing support for his entente policy at a ministerial conference concerning Afghanistan, 27 April. The major result of this conference was a general agreement upon the necessity for an understanding with Britain, and the view that Afghanistan lay outside

11. Minutes of the conference: S. Pashukanis, ed., "K istorii anglo-russkogo soglashenya 1907 g.," *KA*, LXIX–LXX (1935), 19–25. Siebert and Schreiner, *Entente Diplomacy*, pp. 474–77, print an excerpt of the minutes.

12. Grey to Nicolson, 1 April 1907: *Twenty-Five Years*, I, 158–59.

the Russian sphere of influence. The principal concern of the conference was to ensure that Afghanistan would be truly a "buffer state," and that Britain would neither annex nor occupy it. The tone of the conference, including that of the military members, showed that Afghanistan was much less important in Russian eyes than Persia, over which there had been obvious conflicts of opinion in February, and that Izvolsky had gained ground in winning acceptance of the notion that Russia, because of her internal weakness, had to conclude an entente with Britain.[13]

After the conference, negotiations moved along quite smoothly, except for a belated British effort to include in the preamble of the Persian arrangement a statement that would assert Russian recognition of British preponderance in the Persian Gulf. What brought the matter up was the fear that Russia or Germany might build a railway to the Gulf, but Grey explained that after Lansdowne's declaration of 1903 no reference to the Persian Gulf in the agreement would badly impress public opinion and jeopardize the popularity of the agreement. In response Izvolsky turned the tables on the British and used the same arguments against the Persian Gulf proposal as Grey had used with reference to the Straits, that the Gulf did not concern Russia and Britain alone. Nicolson pointed out that Izvolsky was anxious not to offend Germany, who might consider the proposed clause as constituting a Russian obligation to oppose the extension of the Bagdad railway. After the third attempt to get Russian agreement to some statement, Izvolsky approved a declaration to be made in Parliament that Great Britain had "no reason to suppose that the maintenance of the *status quo* in the Persian Gulf would give rise to difficulties between the two governments." Accordingly Grey included in his despatch to Nicolson concerning the signature of the convention a statement designed to disarm criticism that the arrangement concerning Persia contained nothing about British interests in the Gulf. It expressly affirmed that the Russian government had stated that it did not deny the special interests of Great Britain there and concluded by declaring that H. M. Government would continue to direct all its efforts to the preservation of the status quo and the maintenance of British trade, while not desiring "to exclude the legitimate trade of any other Power."[14]

13. Pashukanis, ed., *KA*, LXIX–LXX, 25–32.

14. Briton Cooper Busch, *Britain and the Persian Gulf*, pp. 360–66, gives a detailed exposition containing the direct quotations above.

That the Foreign Office had reason for anxiety over the reaction of the public to an Anglo-Russian understanding had become clear by the summer of 1907. The Indian government in particular was opposed to the entente because of mistrust of Russia, but Morley staunchly supported Grey, pointing out to the Viceroy that the cost of defending India was "one fundamental argument" for the convention with Russia. In Persia, too, Spring-Rice, although he did not oppose the entente, had doubts concerning the loyalty with which the Russians would live up to it. The security of India, he said, depended upon men, not paper, and as for Persia, Grey was likely to be attacked for coming to terms with Russia, who had tried to destroy popular institutions there. He went on to assert, however, that "Persia is a damned hole and hardly worth an outside sheet of the *Times.* If he [Grey] can get *real* agreement with Russia, it is well worth sacrificing Persia."[15]

Izvolsky, too, still had to deal with critics in his government who did not like the Afghanistan convention because they felt that Britain was gaining too great commercial and political advantages and Russia was losing out. Izvolsky countered these arguments by asserting that a more general wording of the convention was better for the future than a detailed one that might prove to be restrictive, and that the British pledge to maintain the political status quo gave Russia the right to raise her voice if there were British interference in Afghan affairs. These views were aired at a special conference, 24 August 1907, chaired by Prime Minister Stolypin. He and Izvolsky stressed again the importance for Russia of securing peace in Asia by both the British and the Japanese ententes. Russia's hands had to be free in Asia, said Izvolsky, in order to raise her voice in Europe where "great upheavals . . . for instance, in Austria and the Balkan peninsula" might be expected. The conference in conclusion endorsed the agreement with England over Afghanistan that Izvolsky had submitted.[16]

Between the virtual settlement of the Persian arrangement in June and the conclusion of the Afghan convention at the end of August the last lull in negotiations occurred when Nicolson returned to London for a few weeks and Izvolsky accompanied the tsar to a meeting with William II at Swinemünde, 3–6 August. Izvolsky felt that because Germany feared isolation, he could not neglect any precaution to pre-

---

15. Spring-Rice to Chirol, 21 June 1907: *Letters and Friendships of Sir Cecil Spring-Rice,* II, 101–02.

16. Pashukanis, ed., *KA,* LXIX–LXX, pp. 32–39.

vent a German attempt at thwarting the Anglo-Russian entente. Considering all aspects of the situation, it is understandable that Izvolsky was anxious again to explain Russian policy to the Germans. To do him justice, good relations with Germany as well as with other powers were more a matter of practical politics in Russia's weakened condition than one of pro-German sentiment, as the French and English feared. As on the occasion of his visit to Berlin in October 1906, Izvolsky was happy over the Russo-German discussions at Swinemünde. The Germans had prepared a lengthy agenda. They claimed that the Björkö treaty was still valid, but Izvolsky disagreed with them, although he said that he wanted to honor its spirit. Other points covered were the second Hague conference, the Macedonian question, the draft of a Baltic pact (of which more below), the Russo-Japanese agreement, Persia, and the Bagdad railway, none of which raised any conflict of opinion. Upon his return home Izvolsky expressed his belief that he had brushed aside forever the misunderstanding over Björkö and had laid a solid foundation for a friendly arrangement over German economic interests in Persia. When Nicolson returned to his post, Izvolsky was ready to put the finishing touches upon the agreements concerning Persia, Tibet, and Afghanistan, all three of which he and Nicolson signed on 31 August 1907.

III.

The agreements, as signed, consisted of three parts: an "arrangement" concerning Persia, a "convention" regarding Afghanistan, and an "arrangement" in respect to Tibet.[17]

By the preamble of the first of these agreements, the parties pledged to respect the integrity and independence of Persia, expressed a desire for the preservation of order and the establishment of equal trade and industrial advantages for all other nations, and noted the special interests, in certain provinces, of Russia and of Great Britain by reason of geographical propinquity. By Articles I and II they demarcated their respective spheres of influence, Russia in the north and Britain in the southeast, by means of a pledge by each not to seek concessions in the other's territory. Article III provided that the two powers would not oppose, "without previous arrangement," any concessions to British or Russian subjects in the area between the two spheres, the so-called

17. The French texts: *BD*, IV, App. I.

"neutral zone." By Articles IV and V the arrangement made provision for the collection and control of revenues pledged by Persia for the amortization and interest on British and Russian loans. Furthermore, Grey's letter of 29 August constituted part of the public record of the British position respecting the Persian Gulf.

The Afghanistan convention never came into force, because its terms required the Amir's assent and he refused to give it. The terms are therefore of interest mainly as an indication of how far Russia and Britain were willing to go for the sake of an entente. Important for Russia was the British pledge not to change the political status quo or take any measures that would threaten Russia or encourage Afghanistan to do so. The British won Russia's recognition that Afghanistan lay outside her sphere of influence, and her engagement to conduct all political relations "through the intermediary of the British government." The Russians, however, might establish direct relations with designated Afghan authorities "for the settlement of local questions of a non-political character." Even though the convention remained a dead letter, both parties were guided by it in subsequent years.

By the "Arrangement concerning Tibet," Britain and Russia, "recognizing the suzerain rights of China in Tibet," and considering that Great Britain, because of her geographical frontier, had a "special interest in the maintenance of the *status quo* in the external relations of Tibet," engaged to respect its territorial integrity and "to abstain from all interference in its internal administration" (Preamble and Article I). They pledged not to enter into negotiations with Tibet except through China and except for the direct relations between British commercial agents and Tibetan authorities agreed upon in the Anglo-Tibetan conventions of 1904 and 1906. Other provisions permitted Buddhists to enter upon direct relations with the Dalai Lama on religious matters, and prohibited both Russia and Britain from sending representatives to Lhasa and from seeking concessions or other rights in Tibet or accepting any part of the revenues of Tibet as pledges or assignments.

The agreements were communicated to interested and friendly powers within a day after ratification on 23 September 1907, and were published on the 26th. The reaction to them in both Great Britain and Russia was a divided one. Critics found the provisions of the agreements one-sided, ascribing to the other country all the gains and bewailing the losses of their own. This dissatisfaction in both countries indicated that the agreements were, after all, a compromise.

In Great Britain the severest critics, both in the press and in the parliamentary debates of February 1908, were men who had had experience in Asian affairs, like Lord Curzon, former viceroy in India, H. F. B. Lynch of the famous Lynch Brothers family, and C. E. Yates, former chief commissioner of Baluchistan. Curzon called the Persian arrangement "deplorable," giving up there all that Britain had been "fighting for for years." Lynch particularly stressed the alienation from England of "the good opinion and sympathy of all Persians."[18] This point was made strongly and more than once by Spring-Rice, minister to Teheran, from within the government's own diplomatic circle. In addition, Radicals—Labor and Radical Liberals—attacked the convention as a bargain with the hated tsarist Russia, although most Liberals accepted it as a business deal.[19] On the other hand, Lord Cromer, famous for his work in Egypt, defended the agreement because it was important for Britain "in the increasingly difficult task of adjusting her relations with the peoples of the Orient" to be free from Russian interference, and because it was desirable to have understandings among the powers "who stood to lose most from German aggression."[20] Lord Lansdowne, though critical of some details, was so mild in his remarks that Grey called them "a summing up in favor of the Convention."[21]

In Russia the press agreeably surprised Izvolsky, who had expected a flood of criticism but had exerted pressure to secure a favorable reaction. In the government and diplomatic circles there were severe critics of the convention who believed that Russia had given up too much in order to win British friendship. Baron Taube, at the time a counselor in the foreign ministry, took that position, while the shrewd observer and foreign relations expert, Prince Trubetzkoi, felt that Russia had gained by the elimination of economic competition over a wide area of Persia. Curiously enough, Soviet commentators have tended to agree with the critics rather than the supporters of the Anglo-Russian understanding.[22]

18. Earl of Ronaldshay, Lord Curzon (London, 1928), III, 38–39; H. F. B. Lynch, "The Anglo-Russian Convention," 3 Asiatic Quarterly Review, XXV (1908), 316–17.

19. In a letter to The Times, 11 June 1907, Ramsay MacDonald, G. B. Shaw, and John Galsworthy, among others had condemned making an agreement with Russia because it meant taking the side of autocracy against the Russian people.

20. Zetland, Cromer, pp. 310–12.

21. As quoted by Rogers Platt Churchill, Anglo-Russian Convention, p. 328.

22. Taube, Politique russe, pp. 139–40; G. N. Trubetzkoi, Russland als Grossmacht (Stuttgart, Berlin, 1913), pp. 93–96. For a Soviet evaluation, see I. Reisner, KA, X, 54–66.

Among the other European powers, the public reception of the Anglo-Russian entente was on the whole favorable. The French were naturally pleased to have their ally and their friend settle long-standing differences. Germany, where the progress of negotiations had been anxiously watched out of fear of an emerging quadruple alliance, was outwardly calm, following Bülow's press directive to receive the agreement "quietly and objectively."[23] Yet beneath the surface Germany recognized that the understanding betokened a change in European international politics that was unfavorable to herself. Bülow's word "encircling" in his Reichstag speech of 15 November 1906 came increasingly into use in diplomatic and public statements. German feeling had been clearly expressed in instructions to the ambassador in Russia. He was to make it clear that Germany could understand the Russian desire to clear up disputed points with England but could not understand Russia's joining a coalition of Britain, Japan, and France, "which, however ostentatiously they advertise its purely defensive aims, yet in the nature of the thing is directly aimed at us and must threaten our position as a world power."[24]

Germany's attitude demonstrated that the major significance of the Anglo-Russian convention, taken together with the Russo-Japanese and the Franco-Japanese agreements of 1907, lay in its European rather than its Asiatic effects. Although the Germans talked of encirclement and the Anglo-Russian understanding constituted the second side, after the Entente Cordiale, of an anti-German combination, it was not in and of itself an aggressive alignment. From the Russian viewpoint it removed middle Asia from the area of conflict with Great Britain, and Izvolsky, by his refusal to recognize British preponderance in the Persian Gulf, had left the way open for a deal with Germany over the Bagdad railway in exchange for Russian preponderance in northern Persia. He hoped, however, to get British support for his Straits policy and perhaps for his Balkan policy as well. Britain, on the other hand, was freed from her generations-long worries over the security of India. Moreover, the effect of the agreement with Russia was to change the nature of the Anglo-Japanese alliance, which had been designed to meet a situation that no longer existed. Sir Edward Grey emphasized the potential rather than the actual significance of the entente when he wrote to Nicolson that he was pleased that events

23. Hale, *Publicity and Diplomacy*, pp. 300–01.
24. To Schoen, 2 June 1907, as quoted by Brandenburg, *From Bismarck*, pp. 261–62.

were bringing Britain and Russia together, but a combination of these two with France was presently weak. He added, however, that "Ten years hence, a combination of Britain, Russia and France may be able to dominate Near Eastern policy; and within that time events will probably make it clear that it is to the interest of Russia and us to work together; but we must go slowly."[25]

In other words, the convention did not establish an entente but, like the Anglo-French understanding of 1904, had to await developments in order to create a genuine Triple Entente. Those developments, however, grew out of European, not Asiatic, events.

IV.

Besides the entente with Russia, Great Britain in 1907 had entered a Mediterranean agreement with France and Spain that may also be explained by fear of Germany as an aggressive power.

In June 1905, at the height of the Moroccan crisis, Lansdowne made a first approach to an agreement with Spain. He suggested to Señor de Villa-Urrutia, who was accompanying the King of Spain on a visit to London, that a "mutually advantageous arrangement" might be made by which Spain would undertake not to alienate to a third power strategic points in her possessions, and Great Britain would undertake to support her. Nothing came of the suggestion immediately, but in December 1906, when the Liberal government had taken over and Villa-Urrutia was ambassador in London, Sir Charles Hardinge raised the subject again. Grey also discussed it with Prime Minister Campbell-Bannerman, and took it up in the C.I.D. Their primary concern was some arrangement by which they could assure the security of Gibraltar, especially from German threats.[26]

What brought the question to the fore was a German attempt to get Spanish consent to a cable from Vigo to the Canary Islands. Both the British and the French wanted to persuade Spain to refuse the German proposal for fear that the German cable might be extended to the Moroccan coast and be developed into a network that would compete with French and British systems. Behind these fears lay the ever-recurrent anxiety that Spain might be drawn into the orbit of German

25. Grey to Nicolson, 24 February 1908: *BD*, IV, no. 550.
26. Lansdowne to Cartwright (in Madrid), 8 June 1905: *BD*, VII, no. 1; Monger, *End of Isolation*, pp. 318–19.

influence, a concern frankly set forth by Bertie in Paris, who asked: "Does it not become necessary to take every possible precaution for the maintenance of the *status quo* and the preservation of the balance of Power in the European system?"[27]

The French were as disturbed as the British, although they felt that their interest in preventing the development of German enterprises in the direction of Morocco and the Balearics was no greater than British concern about the African coast and the Atlantic. It was Jules Cambon who triggered negotiations in Madrid, Paris, and London by submitting to the Spanish government a *Projet,* 2 January 1907, for an agreement designed to prevent any one of the three powers from ceding or granting concessions leading to an occupation of any of their respective possessions. The British Foreign Office, piqued by J. Cambon's failure to consult them in advance, preferred an Anglo-Spanish agreement rather than an accord *à trois,* because that would look too much like an alliance, and also they were anxious about Gibraltar, although they had to drop any reference to it because of Spanish susceptibilities.

A Spanish change of government in January delayed negotiations, but Maura, the new premier, favored a tripartite agreement and wanted to conclude it after the elections in March, but before Jules Cambon left his Madrid post for Berlin to which he had been appointed. Grey insisted, however, upon an exchange of notes with Spain, rather than a tripartite agreement, because of the necessity for parliamentary approval of the latter. In addition to the delays caused by the difficulty of convincing the Spanish ministers and king to accept an Anglo-Spanish exchange of notes, Spanish irritation at France arose over her occupation of Udja, upon which Spain felt that she should have been consulted in accordance with the secret agreement of 1904. The British succeeded in clearing up both points when Edward VII visited Alfonso XIII at Cartagena, 8 to 10 April. Although the eventual accord has been called the "Pact of Cartagena" and Edward VII's role represented as decisive, the discussions were but one phase of five months of negotiation, and Sir Charles Hardinge, rather than King Edward whom he accompanied, appears to have been the principal negotiator.

In the end, however, both the British and the other two parties had their way, for in addition to an exchange of notes between Grey and Ambassador Villa-Urrutia in London and between Pichon and Ambas-

27. Bertie to Grey, 3 January 1907: *BD*, VII, no. 8.

sador Castillo in Paris, 16 May 1907, Grey and Paul Cambon exchanged notes expressing their satisfaction over the identity of British and French policy respecting Spain, and recognizing that if it were necessary for either to communicate with Spain over any alteration of the territorial status quo, Britain and Spain would, as Grey put it, "be able to communicate with the French government also," or, as Cambon phrased it, the French government would be "ready to act in concert" with Spain and Britain.[28] The French were apparently not quite satisfied with this exchange, and on 8 June 1907 Paul Cambon asked Grey if France could count upon British support should Germany take a threatening attitude concerning the Mediterranean agreements, "as in 1905." Grey replied that the new accords only complemented the conventions of 1904, and that the British government considered itself linked with France at the same time as with Spain. "In a word," Cambon said, "if Germany seeks a quarrel with us, we could count on you?" "Yes," Grey replied. "As you could count on us," Cambon commented, "if Germany put herself between Spain and you."[29]

The final texts of the bilateral notes broadened the scope of the accords from that originally proposed. The three powers undertook to maintain the territorial status quo in the Mediterranean (instead of only the western basin) and "in that part of the Atlantic Ocean which washes the shores of Europe and Africa," thus including Spain's Fernando Po as well as the Canaries. Furthermore, in the final text the powers were afforded the opportunity "to concert, if desired, by mutual agreement the course of action" to be adopted "in common," should any power threaten the status quo.

Copies of the notes were communicated to the great powers on 15 June, with an advance explanation to Italy on the 12th. Because of the anti-German aspect of the negotiations, the signatories watched Berlin's reaction with special interest. The kaiser remarked that the exchange of notes, by freeing the English fleet in the Mediterranean, had "a point directed against Germany." Jules Cambon, now at Berlin, relying upon the impressions of the British ambassador as well as his own, reported that although the Germans were "evidently not content," they had not gone beyond the bad humor that was to be expected. He observed that the Foreign Office manifested more resentment than the chancellor, and concluded that "the pill is swallowed." Izvolsky, however, regretted the accords as "clouding" Franco-German

28. Texts of all exchanges, 16 May 1907: *BD*, VII, nos. 39–43.
29. P. Cambon to Pichon, 8 June 1907: 2 *DDF*, XI, no. 17.

relations, and "charging them anew with electricity," when he wanted to see them bettered.[30] Izvolsky, on the other hand, had his own scheme for maintaining, if not bettering, good Russo-German relations.

For some time Izvolsky had wanted to be freed from the terms of the treaty of 30 March 1856 with Great Britain and France that prohibited fortification of the Aaland Islands, and hoped to win German support for the nullification of the treaty. Perhaps he also looked upon an approach to Germany as one means of counteracting any German ill-feeling over his agreement with Britain. At any event, when he went with the tsar to Swinemünde in August 1907, he left with Bülow the draft of a secret protocol by which the two powers, "in recognizing the existence of a perfect community of interests in their policy respecting the regions of the Baltic Sea," and desiring to consolidate their "traditional friendship and good neighborliness," declared "that their general policy in those regions had the objective of maintaining the existing territorial *status quo* on the basis of the complete exclusion from the affairs of the Baltic Sea of all foreign political influence." Accordingly, the draft continued, Russia and Germany resolved to preserve intact their rights in their Baltic possessions, and not to recognize in the future any power interested in Baltic affairs except the riparian states of Russia, Germany, Sweden, and Denmark."[31] This proposal was a bold one considering the omission of Norway, separated from Sweden in 1905, and France and England, who had not only signed the Aaland Island treaty but also pledged to support the integrity of Sweden by a treaty of 21 November 1855; they were, moreover, respectively an ally and a friend of Russia.

Germany, undoubtedly mindful of the Mediterranean agreements of May 1907, was ready to agree to the maintenance of the status quo in the Baltic but did not consider the exclusion of other powers to be a German interest, because the Baltic had never been a closed sea and such an exclusion would seem to be directed against England, a point that the Foreign Office wanted to avoid. Accordingly the German counterproposal eliminated the exclusion clause and suggested that Sweden and Denmark be included in the accord. Izvolsky was willing to accept these modifications, whereupon the text of a "secret protocol" was agreed upon and signed at St. Petersburg on 29 October 1907

30. *GP*, XXI(2), 570–71, note**; J. Cambon to Pichon, 19 June and Bompard to Pichon, 27 June 1907: 2 *DDF*, XI, nos. 38, 51.

31. Secretary of State Tschirschky, Note, 7 August 1907: *GP*, XXIII(2), no. 8083.

by Baron von Schoen, who was about to return to Berlin to succeed Heinrich von Tschirschky as secretary for foreign affairs, and K. A. Gubastov, acting head of the Russian foreign office during the absence of Izvolsky on a trip to western Europe. Besides the pledge to maintain the status quo in the Baltic region, the protocol recognized the possibility of special accords with Sweden and Denmark. As for the Aaland Islands question, Germany promised not to oppose action favorable to Russia.[32] It was obvious, however, that if Russia was to get the restrictions upon the fortification of the islands removed, further negotiations were necessary, especially with Sweden as well as with Britain and France. Moreover, just what Izvolsky had gained by his secret protocol other than German good will, which hardly required such an instrument, is difficult to see.

Because rumors of the secret agreement reached Paris and London almost immediately after its signature, Izvolsky found himself on the defensive against the sharp reproaches of Pichon, who feared that the Baltic pact went farther than a pledge to maintain the status quo. Izvolsky, however, did not admit that there was a Russo-German accord but insisted that discussions with Germany had been only preliminary to negotiations with the riparian states of the Baltic. Germany, on the other hand, as early as September, when the secret protocol was still under discussion, began thinking of a proposal to Great Britain of a North Sea pact, and sent a draft to Ambassador Metternich for unofficial transmittal to Grey. It followed the same lines as Izvolsky's Baltic proposal. Thus on the one hand Izvolsky had to go forward with the negotiation of a Baltic pact with Denmark and Sweden, while on the other Germany was negotiating a parallel pact with Britain and other North Sea powers.

As a result of Sweden's opposition to the annulment of the Aaland Islands treaty of 1856 Izvolsky was compelled to drop the specific mention of the Aaland Islands in the final text of the declaration that was signed at St. Petersburg by Russia, Germany, Sweden, and Denmark on 23 April 1908. The agreement took the form of a declaration and a memorandum, both similar to those of the secret Russo-German protocol of October 1907. The declaration added that if the status quo in the Baltic were menaced, the four signatory powers would concert on measures to maintain it. The memorandum stated that status quo meant "territorial integrity," and that the pact could not be invoked

32. The negotiations and final text: ibid., nos. 8084–95; Taube, *Politique russe*, pp. 156–58.

in respect to the "free exercise of sovereign rights of the high contracting powers in their respective possessions mentioned above." Izvolsky had again failed to get explicit clearance, as far as the Baltic states were concerned, of Russia's right to fortify the Aaland Islands.[33]

Both Britain and France had wanted to participate in the Baltic pact. The British were worried that between it and the North Sea pact, under discussion since December 1907, the freedom of the waters between the two seas might not be assured, and suggested either a single Baltic-North Sea pact or a convention concerning the straits. The Germans took the position that a single pact would include so many powers that it would be of little value. The French finally suggested that at least the two pacts should be signed at the same time, and the British insisted that the two regions should be so defined that there would be no water gap between them.

Between the first German contemplation of a North Sea pact and the beginning of negotiations, the question of Norwegian integrity, raised at the time of her separation from Sweden, was settled. After a year of negotiation, Germany, France, Great Britain, Russia, and Norway signed a treaty, 2 November 1907, over Swedish protests, promising to recognize and respect Norwegian integrity, while Norway undertook not to cede, permit occupation, or make any kind of disposition of her territory. If Norway were menaced, the other four powers undertook to offer their support in order to safeguard her integrity. Russian *amour propre* was eventually satisfied by Anglo-French-Norwegian and Anglo-French-Swedish declarations, 23 April 1908, that the 1855 treaty had ceased to be in effect.[34]

A month after the signing of the Norwegian treaty, Schoen sent instructions to Ambassador Metternich to inform the English verbally and strictly confidentially that Germany had entered an agreement with Russia over the Baltic Sea strictly along the lines of the Mediterranean agreement of May 1907, that the other Baltic states were to be drawn in, and that Germany would be happy if England were ready to enter a North Sea status-quo arrangement that would include Denmark and the Netherlands. Though Britain was not eager to enter such a pact, Grey felt that it would not do to refuse Germany and thus give grounds for saying that Britain was seeking German isolation. He did insist, however, that France should be included as a North Sea riparian

33. Cf. Taube, *Politique russe*, pp. 161–71; *GP*, XXIII(2), nos. 8120–24, 8136–57; 2 *DDF*, XI, no. 336.

34. *GP*, XXIII(2), ch. 173A; *BD*, VIII, ch. 63; 2 *DDF*, XI, nos. 193–94, 284.

state, and subsequently that Sweden, bordering upon the straits, should be drawn in. After nearly five months of exchanges among the interested powers, Germany, France, Denmark, Great Britain, the Netherlands, and Sweden signed a declaration and a memorandum at Berlin, 23 April 1908, the same day as the signature of the Baltic pact at St. Petersburg. The two instruments affirmed the intention of the signatories to preserve their rights intact and to respect them reciprocally.[35]

What did the spurt of pactophilia in 1907–1908 signify? In each case there was, to be sure, a definite though often veiled objective in view: the Mediterranean declarations were intended to keep Spain from yielding to German imperialistic designs; the Baltic pact was to preserve Russo-German amity and win Russian freedom for the exercise of her "sovereign rights" in the Aaland Islands; the Norwegian treaty was to guarantee her territorial integrity; and the North Sea pact was to avoid the appearance of German isolation. Looking back, however, we can believe that these arrangements were much ado about nothing and justified the cynical remark attributed to the British minister at Copenhagen: "Few people would be found who were naive enough to attribute any worth to these paper arrangements."[36]

An equally cynical view might be taken concerning the second Hague conference, which met from 15 June to 18 October 1907. Although this second conference, like the first in 1899, spent the bulk of its time on matters of international law concerning land and sea warfare, the problems of armaments and of compulsory arbitration constituted the topics of major political significance. That was so primarily because of the growing naval rivalry between Great Britain and Germany.

Although the tsar of Russia had called the first Hague Conference in order to deal with the limitation of armaments, the Conference had been unable to take any action other than to adopt an innocuous *voeu* (desire) that the governments study the matter. By 1907 the peace movement had grown in size and strength, two wars — the Boer and the Russo-Japanese—had occurred, and these and other tensions had helped to boost the expenditure on armaments by Europe, the United States, and Japan from 251 to 320 millions of pounds, according to British estimates. Moreover, not only military men but also heads of

35. GP, XXIII(2), ch. 173B; BD, VIII, ch. 64; 2 DDF, XI, passim.

36. Schoen, Memorandum, 1 July 1908: GP, XXIII(2), no. 8159. Cf. David W. Sweet, "The Baltic in British Diplomacy before the War," HJ, XIII (1970), 476–77.

states treated the idea of arms limitation as "nonsense," as the kaiser put it, or "humbug" as King Edward VII was reported saying.[37] Yet the earnest drive of powerful public figures and of international organizations fostering the notion of a world "parliament of man" could not be ignored. President Theodore Roosevelt made the first move to summon a second peace conference but upon the conclusion of the Russo-Japanese war relinquished the honor of issuing invitations to the tsar of Russia, who sent them out in April 1906.

In preparing the program of the conference, Russia emphasized pacific settlement of disputes and omitted the armaments question. The British government, however, requested that the subject of armaments be put upon the program of the conference. As proof of its seriousness the government announced in July 1906 a considerable reduction in naval construction and promised even more if other nations responded. Germany at once looked upon the British proposal as an attempt to prevent the completion of her naval program, laid down in 1900 and expanded in 1906. The German attitude, reflected in a Reichstag debate of 30 April 1907, may be summarized as "First England isolates us and now seeks to disarm us."[38] Yet Britain was not alone, for the United States and Spain joined her in wanting a discussion of armaments, while Germany and Austria-Hungary declared that they would not participate in any such debate. The Rusisans sided with the central powers, refraining from adding the topic to the conference program. The British delegates introduced the subject of armament expenditures, but ended by proposing a resolution reaffirming the *voeu* of 1899 that it was desirable for all governments to "resume the serious study of this question." The Germans absented themselves from the twenty-five-minute discussion of the subject, and also opposed the principle of compulsory arbitration, another topic which interested the peace organizations and which failed to gain approval by the conference.

Despite the minimal achievements of the conference, the delegates resolved to hold another within seven years—a resolution destined to be voided by the outbreak of war in 1914. Like the first Hague Conference, the second tended to fasten upon Germany "the odium of driving back a work of peace for which the whole world was longing." This attribution was manifestly unfair to Germany, because "it was Germany's frankness rather than her policy that distinguished

37. Sir Sidney Lee, *King Edward VII*, II, 530.
38. Hale, *Publicity and Diplomacy*, p. 295.

her from the other great powers."[39] In contrast, Britain's championship of armament limitation suited her interests, because her naval superiority and lack of need for a standing army would have given general armament limitation a genuine practical value. Even so, the Admiralty, War Office, and Foreign Office were not advocates of any real diminution in armaments.

The Hague Conference of 1907 fitted the discussions of status quo in the Mediterranean, Baltic, and North Sea. All made a show of peace-loving policies but failed to affect the balance-of-power politics behind the façade. Only the Anglo-Russian understandings over mid-Asian points of conflict represented a true revolution in European alliances and alignments. And even that entente had still to be tested and hardened in the fires of the Bosnian crisis of 1908–1909.

39. Brandenburg, *From Bismarck*, p. 277; Merze Tate, *The Disarmament Illusion* (New York, 1942), p. 342.

Chapter 7

The Balkans and
the Bosnian Crisis,
1908–1909

Austro-Hungarians most active in Balkan affairs were Count Agenor Goluchowski, foreign minister until October 1906, his successor, Alois Baron Lexa Aehrenthal, and General Franz von Conrad von Hoetzendorff, Chief of the General Staff. Their ambassadors abroad were Count Laszlo Szögyényi in Berlin, Count Leopold Berchtold in St. Petersburg, Count Johann von Pallavicini in Constantinople, and Count Albert Mensdorff in London. The Russians who directed Balkan policy were Count Lamsdorff, foreign minister, and A. P. Izvolsky, who succeeded him in May 1906. Prime Minister Count Peter Stolypin held the latter in check. German Chancellor Count Bernhard von Bülow, Secretary for Foreign Affairs Baron William Eduard von Schoen, and Alfred von Kiderlen-Waechter, acting secretary during Schoen's illness from November 1908 to March 1909, directed German policy. General Helmuth von Moltke, Chief of the German General Staff, agreed with General Conrad von Hoetzendorff upon military cooperation in case of war. Sir Edward Grey, British foreign secretary, and Sir Charles Hardinge, permanent undersecretary at the Foreign Office, were aided in their efforts to avoid war by Ambassadors Sir Arthur Nicolson in Russia and Sir Fairfax Cartwright in Vienna. French Foreign Minister Stephen Pichon and his ambassadors, Philippe Crozier in Vienna and Vice-Admiral Charles-Philippe Touchard in St. Petersburg, played a minor part in the Bosnian crisis, as did Tommaso Tittoni, Italian foreign minister. Prime Minister Nicholas Pašić of Serbia, and Prince Ferdinand, later tsar of Bulgaria, were little more than pawns of the great powers.

While the completion of the Entente Cordiale, the Russo-Japanese war, the First Moroccan crisis, and the Anglo-Russian convention of-

6. *Baron Alois Lexa Aehrenthal (Culver Pictures)*

fered Europe centers of dramatic interest, the Balkans, especially Macedonia, provided an almost constant though lower-keyed cause of international concern from 1902 to 1908. Here was involved not only the perennial Near Eastern question of what was to become of the Ottoman empire, but also the latent great-power rivalries always associated with the solution of that question and the strident nationalism of the Balkan peoples themselves.

I.

The two major rivals for preponderance in the Balkans—Russia and Austria-Hungary—had agreed in May 1897 to maintain the status quo in the peninsula as long as possible. If that task became impossible, however, the two powers agreed to renounce any idea of conquest, to pursue "a policy of perfect harmony and to avoid in consequence everything which might engender between us elements of conflict or mistrust."[1] Once the Greco-Turkish war ended in the summer of 1897, the other powers, too, were preoccupied with events elsewhere. Far Eastern affairs, the Fashoda crisis, the Boer war, and other imperial conflicts and transactions pushed the Balkans and the Near East from the center of the stage.

Unfortunately, forces were building up in the Balkans which in a few years reached an explosive point. The scene was Macedonia, the ill-delimited area that lay between Bulgaria on the east and Lake Okhrida on the west, and between the Aegean Sea on the south and Serbia and the Sanjak of Novi Pazar on the north. There, populations were so intermingled that boundaries along national lines were impossible to draw. Over this land after the Congress of Berlin in 1878, peoples—mainly Bulgars, Serbs, and Greeks—backed by their respective states squabbled with one another and with their common foe the Turks with increasing intensity as the nineteenth turned into the twentieth century. Between 1898 and 1903 Bulgarian bands alone engaged Turkish troops no fewer than 130 times. For good measure the Kutzo-Vlachs, backed by Romania, began to push for recognition, while the Albanians within and west of Macedonia annually made trouble for their Turkish overlords.

By the opening of 1902 the conditions in Macedonia of insecurity, pillage, arson, and murder were beginning to cause uneasiness in the

1. Pribram, *Secret Treaties*, I, 184–95.

European chancelleries. By early spring a clearly revolutionary movement was emerging, and the Turks were responding by sending troops into the area with the usual consequences of increasing the violence and suffering among the inhabitants. Austria-Hungary, geographically closest to the disturbed area, was more alarmed over developments than Russia. Italy, long desirous of developing her influence (in opposition to Austria) in Montenegro and the Albanian coastal region, pressed for concerted great-power action, while Great Britain, free of the Boer war in May, began to urge effective reforms in Macedonia and, like Italy, to favor a European concert. In November, under pressure by Austria-Hungary and Russia, the sultan appointed a commission of inquiry and an inspector-general, Hilmi Pasha, to survey the situation and introduce palliative measures, but failed to act vigorously. Consequently, Lamsdorff and Goluchowski issued the "February Program" of reform, which the Porte accepted on 23 February 1903. Although the other powers approved the program, there was much dissatisfaction with it, mainly because there was no provision for any control by the powers over Turkish compliance with the program. Italy and Great Britain were notably critical of its inadequacy, and their reservations proved to be justified, for the situation in Macedonia went from bad to worse in the course of 1903.

Russia, whose conflict with Japan was developing, was more than ever determined to avoid involvement in the Balkans, while Austria-Hungary, fearful of a partition of the Balkans and the emergence of a great Serbia or Montenegro, was equally determined to maintain the status quo. Lansdowne urged that more effective measures of reform be worked out and made suggestions for them on the eve of a meeting between Tsar Nicholas II and Emperor Francis Joseph, accompanied by their foreign ministers. At the hunting lodge of Mürzsteg, 2 October 1903, they worked out a program that provided for the appointment of Russian and Austrian civil agents to be associated with Hilmi Pasha in watching over the introduction and application of reforms; the appointment of a foreign general to head the gendarmerie, and foreign officers to supervise, instruct, and organize it; each of the great powers except Germany, who refused to participate, was to be responsible for a specified district; after the pacification of the country Turkey was to delimit the administrative districts anew in order to establish a better grouping of the various nationalities; and the administrative and judicial machinery was to be reorganized to admit Christians as well as Mohammedans. The Porte accepted the program a month after its presentation, selected an Italian to organize the gen darmerie with the assistance of twenty-five foreign officers, and accepted the appointment of the Austrian and Russian civil agents. Because for more than a year efforts were concentrated upon the gendarmerie, the proposed financial and administrative reforms made little progress.[2]

Although the powers, some of them reluctantly, subscribed to the Mürzsteg reforms in order to make a show of unity, none, with the possible exception of Britain, was genuinely concerned to improve the lot of the Macedonians. The two "mandatories" of Europe, as Russia and Austria-Hungary considered themselves, were more interested in avoiding involvement than in bettering the condition of the Christians, but up to the end of 1907 they claimed the prerogative of directing the reforms. Their common interest in preserving their cooperation and in avoiding conflicts that might endanger it helped to prevent the Monarchy's worsening relations with Serbia from leading to a rupture with Russia.

Although Austria-Hungary along with Russia immediately recognized the accession on 24 June 1903 of Peter Karageorgevich to the Serbian throne after the assassination of King Alexander on the 10th, and extended the status quo policy in the Balkans to Serbia, relations with the southern neighbor deteriorated over the following years. Serbia, under the leadership of the nationalistic Radical party, which came into power with King Peter, embarked upon a pro-Russian policy. This shift from the former pro-Austrian line reflected a growing mistrust of the Dual Monarchy. At the same time the rising national feeling and the widespread establishment of patriotic organizations coincided with the development within the Danubian Monarchy as well as in Montenegro and Macedonia of a South Slav movement. Moreover, Serbia took an active part with Bulgaria and Montenegro in working toward the realization of the goal of "the Balkans for the Balkan people." Austria-Hungary watched these developments with growing uneasiness, and Goluchowski felt that they might well endanger the Monarchy.

A crisis in Austro-Hungarian relations with Serbia came early in 1906 over trade and armament issues. The trade treaty between them expired early in 1905, and in the negotiations for a new treaty the

2. Grey, *Twenty-Five Years*, I, 166, wrote in retrospect: "The various efforts to improve Turkish government in Macedonia have little interest and no importance now. They were intolerably wearisome, very disagreeable, and painfully futile."

Dual Monarchy made demands that Serbia regarded as incompatible with her position as an independent sovereign state. In order to better her bargaining position, Serbia began negotiations with other states. When a Serbo-Bulgarian treaty looking toward the eventual establishment of a customs union was revealed, Vienna immediately broke off negotiations with Serbia and refused to reopen them unless Serbia renounced the Bulgarian treaty, a demand that the Serbians regarded as a sign that Austria-Hungary wanted to show that "Serbia lay in her power."[3] The trade question was complicated by a dispute over orders for military equipment. Goluchowski insisted that Serbia buy big guns from Skoda, while the Serbians favored Krupp or Schneider-Creusot, eventually buying from the French firm with the aid of French loans. Suddenly, on 22 January 1906, the Monarchy stopped all imports from Serbia, having "discovered" that Serbian live stock was diseased. Thus began the "Pig War," which went on intermittently for four years. The effect was to weaken the Mürzsteg entente and at the same time to consolidate the Serbian government and opposition parties in resisting Austro-Hungarian demands. Also the break between the Dual Monarchy and Serbia accelerated the development of the South Slav movement. Here lay the germ of the conflict which eventually led to war in 1914.

At Vienna, Goluchowski did not long remain in office after the break with Serbia. Wearied by Hungarian baiting in the delegations and the press, and despite Francis Joseph's wish that he continue in office, he resigned in October 1906. He was succeeded by Alois, Baron Lexa Aehrenthal, who had been the Austro-Hungarian ambassador in St. Petersburg since 1898. This shift at the Ballhausplatz was no less significant than Izvolsky's replacement of Lamsdorff at the Singers' Bridge in the previous May. Aehrenthal was an experienced diplomat who had served in the Foreign Office and in the diplomatic service at Paris and Bucharest as well as at St. Petersburg. Though apparently not a brilliant man, he worked untiringly and tenaciously toward his chosen goals, aided by a faultless memory, a wide knowledge of history and constitutional law, and a mastery of logic. He was ambitious to play an independent role in European politics, and to enhance the prestige of the Dual Monarchy, which stood none too high in 1906.

A convinced supporter of the Triple Alliance, Aehrenthal felt that Austria-Hungary should be treated by Germany as an equal, not a

3. W. S. Vucinich, *Serbia between East and West*, pp. 136–50, 180–89. Cf. Bridge, *From Sadowa to Sarajevo*, pp. 277–80.

subordinate. His long years at St. Petersburg and his participation in formulating the Mürzsteg program and in preserving the entente with Russia made him appear to be a Russophile, especially in the eyes of Bülow, who never felt as confident of him as of the more passive Goluchowski. Aehrenthal, like Izvolsky in Russia, wanted to strike out on a new course more positive and more dynamic than his predecessor's. Although he may not have clearly understood the internal difficulties of the Dual Monarchy, he did recognize the dangers of the South Slav movement, and at first hoped to counter them by reorganizing the Slavs within the Monarchy in order to create a unit that would inevitably draw Serbia to it. Within a month of taking office, Aehrenthal had to encounter another strong-willed figure in Franz Baron Conrad von Hoetzendorff, who became chief of the general staff in November 1906. Conrad saw the chief enemy in Italy, with whom Aehrenthal hoped to live on friendly terms, and advocated an active Balkan policy in opposition to Russia, whereas the foreign minister sought to preserve the entente with Russia.

In dealing with Russia, Aehrenthal began with the advantage of high favor in Russian circles. Izvolsky, however, warned him that political pressures at St. Petersburg might create difficulties in continuing to cooperate with Austria-Hungary, especially if her relations with Serbia should worsen. Also, Izvolsky's hope of an entente with Britain raised Aehrenthal's fears that he might side with the British in seeking more radical Macedonian reforms. As the story of their relations indicates, both men were bound ultimately to clash, because each was pursuing a dynamic policy which in the last analysis centered upon achieving his country's interests even if it destroyed the cooperation envisaged in the Mürzsteg program.

Because by the end of 1906 the gendarmerie had been organized and the financial reforms in Macedonia had been as good as assured, there remained the reform of justice administration which the Mürzsteg program had originally proposed in principle. The negotiations that extended through 1907 and until the Young Turk revolution of July 1908 reflected not only the conflicting interests of the powers, but also the jockeying for alignments that would either preserve or replace the Russo-Austrian entente. Austria-Hungary and Germany, particularly the latter, wanted to offer reforms that would not weaken Turkey or lead to a Balkan upheaval. At the other extreme from these "conservative" powers was Great Britain, where Grey, pushed by public opinion and Parliament, proposed farther-reaching and more radical reforms than those upon which the powers had agreed. Britain sought the support of France, who tended to go along with her, and Russia. Izvolsky, increasingly ambitious to play a more active role in the Balkans as his negotiations with Britain and Japan progressed favorably, faced the difficult task of remaining on good terms with his neighbors and yet responding to the British desire to work with him in the Balkans. What made his position more difficult was a rising Pan-Slavic and anti-Austrian feeling in the Russian press to which he was always sensitive.

While nominally the two Mürzsteg powers were entrusted with the task of formulating a judicial reform plan that was to be approved by the European concert, Izvolsky and Aehrenthal were drawing apart over the conservative-radical issue, and Great Britain was gradually taking the lead in the concert that was becoming increasingly discordant. In this situation the ambassadorial conference at Constantinople, 5 February 1908, agreed to recommend to the great powers the provisional acceptance of a scheme of reform put forth by the sultan, and suspension of European action for a fixed number of years in order to give the Porte time to put its plan into operation. Because neither Britain nor Russia was happy over this failure of the powers to act, Grey and Izvolsky continued to formulate and discuss proposals for reform until the Young Turk revolution of July 1908 put an end, by common consent, to the whole experiment of solving the Macedonian question by international action—a sorry precedent for later efforts by the League of Nations and the United Nations to deal with trouble spots.

More significant in 1907, however, than the judicial reform question were the shaping of policy by Aehrenthal and his preliminary exchanges with Izvolsky over their goals in the Near East. After a failure in the spring to agree upon the procedure in dealing with the reform problem, Aehrenthal and Izvolsky in talks at Vienna, 25–28 September 1907, tentatively shaped a bargain by which Russia would get what she wanted in the Straits and Austria-Hungary would annex Bosnia and Herzegovina. Because neither was yet ready to push toward his goal, they were both noncommittal, agreeing only to communicate any contemplated steps in good time. Moreover, they again vowed loyalty to the Mürzsteg program, although within two months Aehrenthal was doubtful about maintaining the status-quo principle upon which Mürzsteg was based.

Aehrenthal, in fact, had been developing plans for expanding Austro-Hungarian economic interests in the Balkans and solving the South Slav problem within and without the Dual Monarchy. His scheme for accomplishing the first objective was to build a railway through the Sanjak of Novi Pazar to be linked at Mitrovitsa with the railway to Salonika as the first step toward his grand design of a commanding position in the Balkans for the Monarchy. His ultimate plans included drawing the Balkan nations to Austria-Hungary and making them economically and politically dependent upon Vienna. In July 1907 he obtained the approval by a ministerial council of the Sanjak railway, and in October he ordered Ambassador Pallavicini to request permission of the sultan to make preliminary studies and tracings, but then postponed action until late December. Although Aehrenthal's plans had been formulated when he saw Izvolsky in September, he had said nothing about them to him.

The South Slav question was more difficult to solve. Aehrenthal had hoped to rectify Goluchowski's mistakes in dealing with Serbia by pursuing a conciliatory policy in 1907 without offering anything concrete, for both Vienna and Budapest rejected Serbian wishes concerning terms of trade with the Monarchy. In Aehrenthal's mind, however, Serbian relations were linked with the South Slav problem, which he believed could be solved by his proposed reorganization of the empire along trialistic lines. In a memorandum of February 1907 he wrote of the annexation of Bosnia and Herzegovina as part of his scheme for a Serbo-Croatian unit, but seemed to think of annexation as a later step after he had made progress with his economic penetration of the Balkans. Yet, demands for it grew louder as time went on, and Conrad coupled with it the necessity for the annexation of the non-Bulgar part of Serbia. Although a council of ministers, 1 December 1907, agreed that the annexation should take place if conditions required or permitted it, Aehrenthal preferred to wait until other questions related to the Berlin treaty of 1878 should arise. Also he was primarily interested at the moment in forwarding the Sanjak railway scheme, the broaching of which in January 1908 marked a turning point in Balkan affairs and the relations of Russia and the Dual Monarchy.

II.

Although the grand vizier was at first disturbed by Aehrenthal's request for permission to survey the Sanjak railway route, the Porte finally granted it after German Ambassador Marschall had lent his support. Even before the issuing of the sultan's iradé of 31 January

1908 authorizing the survey, Aehrenthal presented the project to the Austrian and Hungarian Delegations in glowing terms as part of the Monarchy's mission in the Balkans of civilization and economic development. At the same time he declared that Austria-Hungary sought no territorial acquisitions. In answer to the objection that the project might jeopardize the Balkan agreement with Russia, Aehrenthal argued that the building of the Sanjak railway did not affect the political status quo, and that an extension of the Bosnian railway was a matter solely concerning Turkey and the Monarchy.

Upon the announcement of the Sanjak project there was something of an uproar in the European press. Because the Treaty of Berlin had empowered Austria-Hungary to build military and commercial roads through the Sanjak, no one could accuse Aehrenthal of exceeding the Monarchy's treaty rights. In Serbia, however, the project rearoused old resentments, and in Russia the Pan-Slavs were not only incensed at Austria-Hungary but also saw Germany behind the move. Izvolsky, who had not been perturbed when first informed of the railway plans, was surprised at the vehemence of the Russian press and became very angry, declaring to the German ambassador that Austria-Hungary had "hurled a bomb between his legs."[4] In the end he agreed with Aehrenthal that the entente of 1897 did not restrict economic activity in the Balkans, and promised not to put obstacles in the way of the Sanjak railway project. Izvolsky had undoubtedly been influenced to take a calm attitude toward it as a result of the conclusions of a ministerial council on 3 February 1908. He explained to the council the necessity for pursuing an energetic policy in the Balkans and the serious impairment of the entente with Austria-Hungary; he suggested that the way out of a situation damaging to Russian prestige might be sought in a close approach to Britain and perhaps in joint military measures against Turkey. The army and navy ministers, however, declared that Russia's forces were unprepared for an active policy, and Prime Minister Stolypin absolutely vetoed any kind of venturesome course of action. Izvolsky was therefore obliged to give up energetic measures, but did seek to cooperate with Grey in formulating further Macedonian reforms, and with Serbia in the promotion of her Danube-Adriatic counterproposal to the Sanjak project.

A trans-Balkan railway had been considered from time to time since the 1870's. Although there had been several projects, the one that

4. As quoted by Arthur J. May, "The Novibazar Railway Project," *JMH*, X (1938), 515.

Serbia revived in 1908 was for a line from the Black Sea to the Danube at Orsova, thence through Serbia, the vilayet of Kossovo, and down the Drin valley to the Adriatic. What appealed to Serbia was the prospect of opening up an East-West trade route free from control by the Dual Monarchy, whose territory it would not traverse. In March, Serbia formally asked the Porte to approve surveys through Ottoman territory. By this time Izvolsky was vigorously supporting the Serbian scheme; Romania, Italy, France, and, with some reluctance, Germany and the Dual Monarchy pledged their support. Like the Sanjak project, however, the Danube-Adriatic line failed to materialize. Its significance in 1908 lay in its exacerbation of Serbo-Austro-Hungarian antagonism.

As a result of the stir created by the rival railway schemes and the failure to agree upon a course of action in Macedonia, the Russo-Austro-Hungarian entente seemed to have crumbled in the spring of 1908, while Russia and Britain were drawing closer together. Their mutual desire to cooperate was dramatized by the meeting of Edward VII and Nicholas II at Reval on 9–10 June 1908. What made the occasion of a first visit of a British king to Russian shores seem the more significant was the retinue that accompanied him: Sir Charles Hardinge, Ambassador Nicolson, General Sir John French, and Admiral Sir John Fisher. Their presence and that of their opposite numbers on the Russian side and the warmth of the toasts exchanged at the state banquet helped to blow up the Reval meeting beyond its actual importance. The Germans, for example were convinced that England and Russia had come to an agreement at Reval to oppose Germany; the Turks were fearful that the two powers had subscribed to a Russian policy that might mean the end of Turkish rule in Macedonia, if not in Europe. Again, as on previous occasions when Anglo-Russian good relations were manifested, Izvolsky tried to assure both Berlin and Vienna that no secret conventions existed which were hostile to Russia's neighbors.

As far as published records go, the nearest that Izvolsky and Hardinge came to the strengthening of the entente occurred when the latter, in effect, invited Russia to stand by Great Britain in the face of a German threat to her security. After briefly describing British mistrust of Germany's naval program, Hardinge asserted:

> In seven or eight years' time a critical situation might arise in which Russia, if strong in Europe, might be the arbiter of peace and have much more influence in securing the peace of the world than at any Hague peace conference. For this reason it was abso-

lutely necessary that England and Russia should maintain towards each other the same cordial and friendly relations as now
exist between England and France, which, in the case of England
and Russia are moreover inspired by an identity of interests of
which a solution of the Macedonian problem was not the least.[5]

The three-hour discussion, however, was mainly taken up with the
Macedonian problem, Persian affairs, Crete, and the Balkan railways.
As for other matters, two highly placed Russian officials assert that
Izvolsky came away from the meeting with the promise, or at least the
conviction, that England would support Russia's desire for the free
passage of her fleet through the Straits. If the subject was discussed,
the available documents do not record it, not even Izvolsky's own report to Benckendorff.[6] Yet Izvolsky may have been confirmed by
Hardinge's words about close relations in his belief, fostered by the
discussions of 1907, that Great Britain would support his Straits policy.

Because the French press hailed the Reval meeting as the prelude to
the formation of a new triple alliance and the Russian press called it
"the visible sign of a new era in Anglo-Russian relations," there was
ground, despite Izvolsky's assurances, for German alarm over what
might have happened there.[7] Bülow not only expressed the German
cause for anxiety but also described the way to meet the situation
when he sent a circular to the Prussian ministers in the state capitals
on 25 June 1908. He explained that they had to assume that if Germany or Austria-Hungary should become involved in a serious conflict of interest with one of the entente powers, the hitherto loose ententes and understandings would become hardened into alliances that
might become aggressive. Because the situation was serious, both central powers should look to their armaments, financial and economic as
well as military and naval. As for the Near East, and especially the
Balkan peninsula, Bülow declared that "a loyal cooperation with Austria-Hungary must and shall remain the highest principle of German
foreign policy."[8] Thus a not insignificant result of the fears raised by
Reval was the renewed determination to stand by the Dual Monarchy

---

5. Hardinge, "Visit to the Emperor of Russia at Reval in June 1908," 12 June
1908: BD, V, no. 195.

6. Izvolsky to Benckendorff, 18/5 June 1908: Graf Benckendorffs diplomatischer
Schriftwechsel, I, 11–14; A. A. Polovtsev, "Dnevnik," KA, IV (1923), 128; Taube,
Politique russe, pp. 185–86, 187.

7. Wade Dewood David, European Diplomacy in the Near Eastern Question,
p. 62. Cf. Hale, Publicity and Diplomacy, pp. 309–10.

8. Bülow, Memoirs, II, 362–67. Cf. Bülow to Aehrenthal, Private, 23 July 1908:
OUA, I, no. 18.

and her interests in the Balkans, a commitment quite in contrast to Bismarck's policy and one fraught with danger for Germany's future, because of the loss of freedom to make decisions in Balkan affairs, in which, as Bülow pointed out, Germany had only economic interests. He had Ambassador Szögyényi call Francis Joseph's attention to the circular, and himself wrote privately to Aehrenthal of his views and his determination to stand by the Monarchy. Aehrenthal could but rejoice that his ambition to be independent of German dictation had been achieved.

At the same time Izvolsky was planning to forward Russian interests in the Near East according to the policy of "healthy egoism" which he had announced to the Duma in April, for without concern for the fate of the Balkan peoples he had decided to open the Straits question. Confident after Reval of British support, he had to strike a bargain with Austria-Hungary, whose interest in annexing Bosnia and Herzegovina he had known at least since the previous September. There was, moreover, an additional reason for acting after Reval, the desirability of proving to both Germany and the Dual Monarchy that he was not planning with the British to deal a telling blow to the Ottoman empire, as they suspected.

Accordingly, in an *aide-mémoire* of 2 July 1908, dispatched to Vienna, Isvolsky made a bid for the renewal of the entente of 1897 based upon a clarification of certain points: the inclusion of the Balkan railway projects in the status quo, and a territorial delimitation of the Sanjak of Novi Pazar, whose boundaries had hitherto been vague. Coming to the meat of his proposal, he stated that the annexation of Bosnia, Herzegovina, and the Sanjak, as well as the question of Constantinople and the Straits were "eminently European" in character and not "to be adjusted by a separate understanding between Russia and Austria-Hungary." Nevertheless, he asserted, "in view of the extreme importance to the two countries to see the two questions mentioned above adjusted in conformity with their reciprocal interests, the Imperial Government would be ready to enter upon a discussion in a spirit of friendly reciprocity." Isvolsky concluded with an affirmation of his anxiety "to preserve the most friendly and confidential relations" with the Dual Monarchy.[9]

Aehrenthal recognized the conciliatory spirit of the memorandum but took his time in making a reply. An unexpected cause of delay occurred when the Young Turk revolution brought about the restora-

9. Aide-mémoire, 2 July/19 June 1908: *OUA*, I, no. 9.

tion by Sultan Abdul Hamid II on 24 July of the 1876 constitution. For Austria-Hungary the establishment of a constitutional regime in Turkey immediately raised the question of Bosnia and Herzegovina. What if the Young Turks should try to reassert Turkish sovereignty? What if the Serbs in the provinces asked to be represented in the new Turkish Parliament? For some time Baron von Burian, the minister responsible for the administration of the provinces, had advocated the establishment of a diet, which, Aehrenthal declared, could not be done until annexation. In April 1908 Burian pressed for a permanent constitutional incorporation of the provinces in the Monarchy; and in the summer Joseph M. Baernreither, a member of the Reichsrat and the delegations, advocated the incorporation of the provinces as "a third portion of the Habsburg realm" in order to effect the reforms that he regarded as urgent.[10] Aehrenthal himself began planning the annexation after agreeing with Burian on 6 August that the time for it had come. He had reasons for acting in addition to the implications of the Turkish revolution, namely the relatively favorable international situation offered by German support and Izvolsky's readiness to strike a bargain. Besides the enhancement of the Monarchy's prestige, and his own, there was growing pan-Serb propaganda to cope with.

Aehrenthal, who had begun to take a different attitude toward the Serbs from that of the previous year, set forth his revised views in a memorandum of 9 August. Starting from the premise that in case of the break-up of the Ottoman empire, Austria-Hungary had to have secure southern boundaries, the memorandum concluded that security could only be achieved by backing the Bulgars against the Serbs and favoring the creation of a great Bulgaria that would annex the Serbian territory inhabited by Bulgars. At a favorable moment in the European situation and after proper diplomatic preparation, the Monarchy should seize the rest of Serbia. In addition, Aehrenthal envisaged an independent Albania under an Austro-Hungarian aegis and a friendly Montenegro. In short, his ultimate aim was a group of Balkan satellites with Serbia eliminated.[11]

On 19 August Aehrenthal submitted to a meeting of Austrian and Hungarian ministers his view of the urgency of annexing Bosnia and Herzegovina, explaining that he would seek an understanding with

10. Joseph M. Baernreither, *Fragments of a Political Diary*, pp. 19–32; David, *European Diplomacy*, p. 93.

11. S. Musulin, Memorandum, 9 August 1908: *OUA*, I, no. 32.

Russia. On 10 September the ministers made the final decision to annex the provinces and to withdraw from the Sanjak. As Aehrenthal had explained to Baron von Schoen, German secretary for foreign affairs, when telling him of his immediate plans, the ultimate goal of his Balkan policy was to destroy completely the "revolutionary Serbian nest."[12] Aehrenthal also revealed his plans to Italy, although less frankly. Foreign Minister Tittoni assured him that he wanted to proceed in "closest agreement" with Austria-Hungary and Germany. Having found his allies in a complacent mood in respect of his policies, and having no intention of sounding out Britain and France, Aehrenthal was ready to talk with Russia.

On 27 August 1908 he answered Isvolsky's *aide-mémoire* of 2 July. Without going into the question of the Balkan railways, the heart of the answer was his question if Russia would observe a "benevolent and friendly attitude" should the Monarchy annex Bosnia and Herzegovina and at the same time withdraw from the Sanjak of Novi Pazar. In return, Austria-Hungary would discuss the question of the Straits.[13] Following this communication, Leopold Count Berchtold, Austro-Hungarian ambassador in Russia, arranged a meeting of Aehrenthal and Izvolsky at Buchlau, his estate in Bohemia, on 15 and 16 September.

What passed at Buchlau in a day-long discussion has been a matter of controversy ever since. No records of the conversation were kept, and Aehrenthal's version differed from that of Izvolsky's various accounts in some important respects. Aehrenthal reported that Izvolsky had given Russia's consent to the annexation, and in return he had assured Izvolsky of the Dual Monarchy's benevolent attitude toward the opening of the Straits to Russia; both changes to be ratified by the Berlin treaty signatories of 1878; but Aehrenthal planned to make the annexation a *fait accompli,* and the conference action merely a rubber stamp. On the other hand, Izvolsky insisted that he had given a tentative consent to the annexation pending the approval of the tsar, and had envisaged taking both the annexation and the question of the Straits to a European conference where the Monarchy and Russia would support one another. Moreover, Aehrenthal claimed that he had informed Izvolsky of the imminent annexation of the provinces, and there is evidence that Isvolsky knew it was to take place fairly early in October, but he denied that he had been informed

---

12. Schoen to Bülow, 5 September 1908: *GP,* XXVI(1), no. 8927.
13. Aide-mémoire, 27 August 1908: *OUA,* I, no. 48.

of the timing of the event. Basically the two men saw the Buchlau meeting differently. To Aehrenthal it was the last stage in his preparations for annexation, while to Izvolsky it was a step in a series of continuing negotiations that had to involve the other European powers as well as Russia and Austria-Hungary before final action was to be taken. These differences were the elements in the bitter Aehrenthal-Izvolsky quarrel that followed the annexation proclamation.[14]

Another controversial subject, unrelated to the Buchlau meeting but constituting a source of misunderstanding and recrimination, was Aehrenthal's role in the Bulgarian declaration of independence. At Buchlau, Aehrenthal and Izvolsky agreed not to oppose Bulgarian independence (nor a Greek annexation of Crete). Aehrenthal had been encouraging Prince Ferdinand to believe that the Dual Monarchy would at least take a benevolent attitude toward Bulgaria, and the memorandum of 9 August indicated that he intended to play Bulgaria against Serbia. At Budapest, 23–24 September, after Ferdinand had withdrawn his agent from Constantinople on the pretext that he had been snubbed by the Porte, and after Bulgaria had seized a section of the Oriental railway, Aehrenthal by his own report encouraged Ferdinand to take the step of independence. When Aehrenthal denied to the British ambassador that he had any foreknowledge of the Bulgarian declaration, he may have been uttering a half-truth, but the British believed that he had lied to them.

Returning to the aftermath of Buchlau, Izvolsky spent a leisurely few days in southern Germany and then started on a round of visits to Italy, France, England, and Germany. He would scarcely have done so if he had known that Aehrenthal was proceeding at once to an annexation of Bosnia-Herzegovina. On the other hand, he was well aware that it would take place sooner or later, for he began to prepare with N.V. Charykov, his deputy at the Singers' Bridge, an elaborate campaign to win the approval of the contemplated action by both the Russian and the foreign press. The tsar, too, shared Izvolsky's optimism that the Buchlau bargain would enable Russia to gain the right of passage through the Straits.

Unfortunately for Izvolsky and the tsar, the Russian dream was to be turned into a nightmare by Aehrenthal's unexpectedly early action

---

14. For detailed analyses of the conflicting reports, see Bernadotte E. Schmitt, *Annexation of Bosnia*, pp. 20–26; Momčilo Ninčić, *La crise bosniaque*, I, 215–51. Cf. Berchtold's diary, as summarized by Hugo Hantsch, *Berchtold*, I, 120–25; Albertini, *Origins*, I, 206–10.

and the repercussions of the proclamation of annexation both in Europe and in Russia. Tittoni, it is true, when he met Izvolsky at Desio, 29 September, raised no objection to the Buchlau bargain, as Izvolsky reported it to him, and looked forward to an Italo-Austro-Russian agreement concerning the contemplated changes in the treaty of Berlin. After Izvolsky reached Paris on 4 October, however, he received two communications that altogether destroyed his complacency: A letter from Aehrenthal informed him that the annexation would be proclaimed on the 7th of October, only three days away, and a telegram from St. Petersburg within the next two or three days reported an upsurge of public indignation and the disapproval of his policy by Prime Minister Stolypin. The rest of his journey, therefore, was more concerned with what to do about the annexation than with Russian aspirations concerning the Straits. The conflict of testimony and viewpoints between him and Aehrenthal began at once.

III.

Although the European governments knew what was coming, the public learned with shock and dismay of the Bulgarian declaration of independence of 5 October and the Austro-Hungarian annexation of Bosnia-Herzegovina proclaimed on 6 October, a day earlier than originally planned. Outside the Dual Monarchy, where the annexation was generally approved, the initial comments were highly condemnatory of both the Bulgarian and the Austro-Hungarian actions.

Most directly affected by them were Serbia, Turkey, and Montenegro. The greatest excitement over the annexation occurred in Serbia, where the acquisition of Bosnia and Herzegovina in order to reconstitute national unity had been the object of Serbian aspirations for years. Moreover, the annexation of the provinces by the Dual Monarchy was interpreted as a forecast of Vienna's ultimate designs upon South-Slavic lands. While the people fitted out guerilla bands, sent emissaries into Bosnia, organized a boycott of Austrian goods, and founded the *Narodna Odbrana* (National Society), which was to figure prominently in the Austro-Hungarian accusations of July 1914, Foreign Minister Milovan Milovanović began a round of visits to European capitals to seek support for Serbian territorial compensation. Prince George and Nicholas Pašić, the leader of the dominant Radical party, went to Russia for aid.

Turkey, on the other hand, was disturbed not so much by the annexation at first—partly because of the Dual Monarchy's renunciation of rights in the Sanjak of Novi Pazar—as by the declaration of Bulgarian independence. On 10 October, however, a meeting of 10,000 people at Salonika protested the annexation, and a boycott of Austrian goods and stores began that increased in intensity and extent as the months rolled on. In consequence, the Turkish government refused to recognize the annexation, to the great disappointment of Aehrenthal, who had taken the position that the only power directly concerned was the Ottoman empire, from which he had expected little difficulty. The Porte did not immediately communicate its views to the other powers, but instead concentrated upon the illegality of the Bulgar proclamation and called for a conference to deal with the reestablishment of legal order and the safeguarding of Turkish interests as previously assured by treaties.

Montenegro's attitude was a minor problem compared with the other two. In announcing the annexation to Prince Nicholas, Aehrenthal had promised financial aid in building roads and his readiness to enter into negotiations concerning the modification of Article XXIX of the treaty of Berlin.[15] The Prince replied with a notice of the cancellation of Article XXIX and a request for frontier rectifications. Aehrenthal ignored this outburst and virtually ignored Montenegro altogether for several months.

The Dual Monarchy's allies received the news of the annexation with mixed feelings. Both the kaiser and Ambassador Marschall were indignant because they feared that Germany's position in Constantinople would be endangered by the action of her ally. Bülow, however, from the first inkling of Aehrenthal's plans had decided to support him, and the Foreign Office staff agreed with him, especially Alfred von Kiderlen-Waechter, who had been summoned from Bucharest because of the illness of Secretary Schoen, and Holstein, who, though no longer on the staff, kept in close touch with Bülow and Kiderlen. He phrased the argument neatly in advising Bülow to stand by Austria "calmly and resolutely, imposing no restrictions or conditions, for in

15. Article XXIX provided for the annexation by Montenegro of Antivari and its coast on the conditions that Montenegro could not have warships, Antivari would be closed to the warships of all nations, no fortifications could be built between the lake and the coast, Austria-Hungary would police the coast, Montenegro would adopt the maritime laws in force in Dalmatia, should come to an understanding with Austria-Hungary concerning the construction of a road and railway across the new territory, and should assure complete freedom of communications on the roads: *British and Foreign State Papers*, LXIX, 760.

defending her *own* cause she was fighting *our* battle against the encircling Powers, England, Russia and France (and Italy). This basic principle must take precedence over all other considerations, particularly consideration for Turkey."[16] Bülow stuck to this policy from the beginning to the end of the crisis, and the kaiser reluctantly acquiesced.

For Italy no such feeling of alliance loyalty existed, and the public and press were much more vociferous in denouncing the annexation than the German. Tittoni was at first complacent; by his talks with Izvolsky and Aehrenthal in September he fancied that he had established an entente among the three powers. But despite his efforts to convince the Italians that Italy's interests had been safeguarded, a belief in Parliament that he had been either ignorant of what was going on or incompetent nearly caused his overthrow. In view of the criticisms of his policy he felt compelled to reverse his earlier position and to come out for a European conference. At the same time he besought Vienna in vain to make some conciliatory gesture toward Italy. Although he had wanted to play a leading role in revising the Treaty of Berlin, he found himself sidetracked and was forced to play a minor one, trying to balance between the Triplice and the Triple Entente.

Among the Entente powers France was least indignant—both press and government—and in view of the Casablanca incident of 25 September, which they thought might well lead to a crisis in Franco-German relations, was particularly anxious to maintain peace. Premier Clemenceau denounced the annexation as "a gross breach of a treaty engagement and an offense to public morality,"[17] and favored a conference to be proposed by France, Russia, and Britain acting together, but he and Foreign Minister Pichon left the lead to Russia and England. Because they feared, moreover, that Anglo-German ill-feeling might heighten the tensions among the powers, they sought to maintain good relations with the central powers, an endeavor that was greatly promoted by the Monarchy's ambassador in Paris, Count Rudolf von Khevenhüller, and by the Austrophile French ambassador, Philippe Crozier, in Vienna.

British indignation at both the annexation and Bulgarian independence was sharply expressed in the press and forthrightly communicated by the government to the powers, but it was mainly the

16. *Holstein Papers*, I, 195. Cf. Rich, *Holstein*, II, 817–18.
17. As quoted by Schmitt, *Annexation*, p. 36.

Austro-Hungarian move that preoccupied the government. Grey decided to withhold British approval until the signatories of the treaty of Berlin had given theirs, in accordance with the Protocol of 1871 by which treaties were to be revised only by the consent of the signatories. At the same time he sought to calm the Serbians and the Turks. Several factors account for the stiff attitude that put Great Britain into a leading position throughout the crisis. Although the stand upon the proper method of treaty revision has been questioned as a genuine motive behind British policy, there is no doubt of the concern over the effects upon the Young Turk regime. "A cruel blow it seemed," wrote Grey in retrospect, "to the budding hopes of better things in Turkey."[18] Furthermore, Britain wanted peace and saw the two events of annexation and Bulgarian independence as concerted actions likely to lead to high tension, if not war. The growing consciousness of German naval rivalry and the anti-German sentiment in the Foreign Office fostered the assumption that the Austro-Hungarian move, at least, was inspired and supported by Germany. This assumption led to the support of Russia in the interest of balance-of-power politics. British policy was clear and consistent from the outset to the end of the crisis: support Turkey and Serbia in their resistance to the two treaty violations and cooperate with Russia in her backing of Serbia and her demand for a European conference to regulate the new order.

Russia, the leading protagonist in what was at bottom a diplomatic duel with Austria-Hungary, seethed with indignation over the blow to Slavdom by the annexation of Bosnia-Herzegovina. From Premier Stolypin and Finance Minister Kokovstov to the Pan-Slav circles and the press, there was little interest in Izvolsky's scheme for getting the freedom of the Straits as compensation. When Stolypin learned of the Buchlau bargain, he was enraged and threatened to resign if the tsar backed Izvolsky's policy. To make the situation worse, search in the archives revealed what neither Izvolsky nor the tsar had apparently known, that Russia three times over in the 1870's and '80's had promised the Dual Monarchy not to oppose the annexation of Bosnia-Herzegovina and the Sanjak of Novi Pazar. As the tsar wrote to his mother, 21 October, "You will understand what an unpleasant surprise this is, and what an embarrassing position we are in."[19] For Stolypin and his colleagues, however, the paramount concern was to

---

18. Grey, *Twenty-Five Years*, I, 169.
19. "Iz perepiski Nikolaya," *KA*, L–LI (1932), 185–86.

avoid war, lest revolution break out, and until military reforms could be carried through. For the tsar the blasting of Izvolsky's scheme was a bitter pill, and he reluctantly agreed to send new instructions to Izvolsky that did not prevent him from pursuing the Straits question, but apparently required him to oppose the annexation of Bosnia and Herzegovina. Receipt of these instructions on 6 or 7 October caused Izvolsky to change his tactics.

Izvolsky found himself in an impossible situation and talked of resignation. Repudiated at home, he could not effectively pursue the Russian goal of the Buchlau bargain; but on the other hand he could not forthrightly denounce that bargain and salvage Russian prestige in the eyes of Slavdom. Because of his memorandum of 2 July 1908, Aehrenthal held a whip hand over him if he sought to oppose the annexation. He did have an opening for an attack on Aehrenthal, however, for he had declared both in his memorandum and at Buchlau that the annexation and the Straits were European interests that should be approved by Europe; and Aehrenthal had agreed in principle. Furthermore, he had broached the idea of compensation for the annexation to Serbia and Montenegro, to which Aehrenthal had not agreed. A conference of the signatories of Berlin and compensation became the battleground between him and his opposite in the Monarchy.

Not that Izvolsky immediately abandoned his hope of achieving Russian freedom of the Straits. He talked of it to the Turkish ambassador in Paris while there between 4 and 9 October, and found that the Turks would uphold the law of the Straits unless the powers agreed to a change. The French deferred to Great Britain on the question and were worried over the very considerable French investments in the Ottoman empire. In London between 9 and 16 October, Izvolsky received flattering personal attention but a refusal to back his Straits objective, because, the British Cabinet decided, it was "inopportune." The British attempts to sugar the pill by talking about a later "voluntary agreement" between Russia and Turkey only emphasized the blasting of Izvolsky's hopes that his own government had already accomplished by its repudiation of his policy.[20]

Meanwhile, Izvolsky, like the French and the British, had attempted to quiet the Serbians. He tried to represent the renunciation of the Sanjak of Novi Pazar as a real gain for Serbia, because it opened the possibility of a common frontier with Montenegro. War, he told the

20. M. B. Cooper, *HJ*, VII, 268–69.

Serbian chargé in London, would be suicide. Making vague promises to obtain territorial compensation for Serbia, he declared that Russia could not go to war on account of Bosnia; the Serbian government should stop military preparations and restrain the people's bellicose feelings.

Izvolsky's one hope of doing anything for the Serbs and of getting revenge on Aehrenthal lay in the meeting of a European conference. Aehrenthal informed him, however, through Count Albert Mensdorff, his ambassador in London, that, while not opposing a conference in principle, the conditions upon which the Monarchy would attend were a previous Turkish recognition of the annexation and the acceptance by the conference of this act without debate. Germany was also opposed to any discussion of the annexation. On the other hand, Turkey, Montenegro, and above all Serbia wanted a European conference to debate and settle their grievances. Italy (from 8 October), France, and Great Britain looked upon a conference as the only way to settle the problems arising from the annexation and the Bulgarian declaration. On 13 October Izvolsky and Grey issued a statement that they had agreed to demand a conference, and on the 15th they drew up a nine-point program that included Bulgaria, Bosnia-Herzegovina, Article XXIX, and, point 7, "Advantages to be procured for Serbia and Montenegro," but did not mention the Straits. Grey also promised Izvolsky diplomatic support in demanding compensation for Serbia and Montenegro, but insisted that compensation for Turkey take precedence.[21]

Having enlisted British cooperation in demanding a conference, and undaunted by Aehrenthal's rejection of point 7 because it left the door open to demands for territorial compensation, Izvolsky visited Berlin on 24 and 25 October. Even before reaching Germany, Izvolsky had appealed to her through her ambassadors in London and Paris for assistance. He had argued that Serbia was entitled to compensation, and that he could not return to Russia with empty hands. In his hope that he might gain something by talks in Berlin, he again experienced disappointment, for Bülow and Schoen convinced him that Germany would support Austria-Hungary completely. Bülow made clear that Germany did not like Russian reliance upon France and Britain, and that in the face of a group consisting of Russia, France, England, and Italy, Germany had no choice but to support

---

21. Ibid., 270. On the difficulty of British cooperation with Russia, see Steiner, *The Foreign Office*, pp. 96–97.

her ally. Bülow did not miss the chance to indicate that Izvolsky's close relations with Britain had failed to bring him any satisfaction over the Straits question. Talks with Schoen delineated the areas of agreement and disagreement over a conference agenda, but on the whole Izvolsky reached home disappointed and in dread that the war party in Vienna would gain the upper hand and attack Serbia.

For the time being, however, a quarrel with Aehrenthal over the publication of documents highlighted the bitter personal feud between the two men. Izvolsky had been using strong language about Aehrenthal's "treacherous" behavior wherever he went, and had told Bülow that he had betrayed and insulted Russia. Aehrenthal for his part warned Izvolsky that if he made a public statement not in accord with the Buchlau agreement, he would be compelled to publish the secret protocol of 1878 and the memorandum of 2 July 1908. Izvolsky was not so much alarmed over the publication of the former as he was over the revelation of the exchanges in the previous summer. This threat of publication hung over him for the remaining months of the crisis.

Upon his return to St. Petersburg, Izvolsky communicated the conference agenda to Aehrenthal and sent a memorandum to Berlin outlining his position. Germany had already decided in accordance with Aehrenthal's views that there would be no discussion of Bosnia-Herzegovina and the Sanjak, and rejected point 7 out of hand. Aehrenthal, while still willing to exchange views with Russia, flatly stated his position in an answer of 14 November to Izvolsky: Bulgarian independence should be recognized after financial questions had been adjusted; there could be no conference discussion of the annexation on which Austria-Hungary would reach an agreement with Turkey; there were reservations concerning Montenegrin sovereignty; and as for point 7, the advantages to Serbia and Montenegro could only be economic, not territorial. In sticking to his original position, Aehrenthal was banking upon Russia's desire for peace and her military weakness. Also, he knew that France was grateful to Francis Joseph for putting in a word with William II over the settlement of the Casablanca incident, and was ready to repay the favor. Italy, too, although Tittoni still wanted a conference and suggested that it meet in Rome, was opposed to Serbia's territorial demands despite the sympathy of the Italian public, which saw Serbia as the "Piedmont" of the South Slavs.

After exchanges in early December, Izvolsky on 17 December, "in a spirit of conciliation," agreed with Aehrenthal that the powers should come to a preliminary understanding and that the conference should record the settlements already arrived at. In a circular to the powers of 19 December he set forth the Russian point of view and called upon Austria-Hungary to explain hers. When Aehrenthal promptly communicated the November-December exchange of notes to the powers, Izvolsky found himself cornered because of references in them to Russian initiative concerning Bosnia and promises of a friendly attitude. Taking offense at references to the understanding of 1897, Izvolsky notified the Austro-Hungarian chargé, 30 December, that by order of the tsar the Russian government would henceforth confine itself to strictly official communications with Vienna. Not only had the two powers reached a deadlock, but until 6 March 1909 there was no personal contact between Izvolsky and Ambassador Berchtold, and the subject of the conference was dropped for almost the same length of time.

The rift between Aehrenthal and Izvolsky was not, however, the only point of tension among the powers, for a sharp conflict between Austria-Hungary and Great Britain also occurred both in diplomatic exchanges and in the press. Aehrenthal accused the British of inciting Russia, Turkey, and Serbia in order to attack Berlin through Vienna, and told Sir Fairfax Cartwright, who replaced Goschen as British ambassador at Vienna, 10 December, that the British attitude was at the bottom of his troubles. In the face of the press war that raged throughout January 1909, Grey kept calm and let Aehrenthal know that he was supporting Russia's championship of Serbia and Montenegro, but approved the procedure of a preliminary understanding before a conference met and emphasized his desire for peace and agreement, however accomplished. At the same time he tried to relieve Izvolsky's anxiety by reiterating British support, for while he was not trying to break up the German-Austrian alliance or seeking an Anglo-Russian one, as Aehrenthal thought, he was determined to maintain the entente with Russia.

While Aehrenthal's relations with both Russia and Great Britain worsened, Germany stood staunchly by him. In a letter to Bülow of 8 December, Aehrenthal thanked him for his support and raised the question of the alliance in case of war, suggesting that Conrad and Moltke, Chief of the German General Staff, exchange views if Russia should attack Austria-Hungary. In reply Bülow discounted the possibility of war with either Russia or France, but readily agreed to an exchange of views between the two chiefs of staff. Accordingly, Conrad and Moltke began corresponding in January 1909, with the approval of their respective governments and sovereigns. By the exchange Moltke pledged Germany to support Austria-Hungary fully if she decided to invade Serbia and thereby incurred the active intervention of Russia. This pledge constituted another fateful commitment of a kind that Bismarck had explicitly avoided. Germany had not encouraged the Monarchy to attack Serbia, but she had given Aehrenthal another blank check supplementary to the diplomatic support he had long enjoyed.[22]

There were no such close ties among the Triple Entente powers, as Izvolsky bitterly observed more than once. To be sure, Great Britain had promised him diplomatic support, but Grey had made it clear that she would not go to war. France, on the other hand, was in a different position because of the alliance. On 2 February 1909 Izvolsky reminded the French Ambassador, Admiral Touchard, that if Russia were compelled to fight the Dual Monarchy as an invader of Serbia, Germany would support her ally and France would have to march. Touchard pointed out that France would have to bear the brunt of the German attack because of the slowness of Russian mobilization, and suggested talks about bettering the speed of mobilization by improving certain strategic roads. Pichon approved his language but instructed him not to return to the subject until further notice. As the situation became more and more tense during the month of February, Izvolsky lashed out at the ineffectual aid he had received from France; he believed in the good will of the government, but its diplomacy at Berlin and Vienna had not afforded Russia the support expected. Pichon, of course, denied the charges, insisting that France was faithful to the alliance but, like Russia, wanted peace. Izvolsky cooled down, and on 6 March the French military attaché reported a plan of the Russian general staff to speed up mobilization. Moreover, during March the attitude of France became firmer and the tone of the press more positive in its emphasis upon French obligations to Russia.

These exchanges among the powers were incidental to the mainstream of negotiations, which continued in parallel over an Austro-Hungarian-Turkish settlement, a Turkish-Bulgarian agreement, and the Serbian and Montenegrin demands upon the Dual Monarchy. For Aehrenthal the most urgent of these discussions was the Turkish settlement, for he insisted that once they had reached agreement, the

---

22. Cf. Schmitt, *Annexation*, pp. 94–99; Norman Stone, "Moltke-Conrad: Relations between the Austro-Hungarian and German General Staffs, 1909–1914," *HJ*, IX (1966), 206–11.

signatory powers of the Berlin Treaty had but to recognize the cancellation of Article XXV of that treaty. The negotiations with Turkey, however, were fraught with difficulties, largely because of Turkish demands for compensation for the loss of sovereignty over the annexed provinces. Aehrenthal at first refused to grant it, but the active pressure of Berlin and the hopelessness of overcoming Turkish obstinacy led him to offer the Porte £T 2,500,000 as compensation for the crown lands in Bosnia. Finally, 26 February 1909, Turkey and the Monarchy signed an agreement by which Turkey recognized the annexation of Bosnia-Herzegovina and the renunciation of the Sanjak of Novi Pazar. Besides the payment of compensation, the Monarchy consented to an increase in Turkish customs duties from 11 to 15 percent and to other Turkish demands. The Turks received almost everything they had demanded, and Aehrenthal came off second best in dealing with them. Also, Aehrenthal's desire to participate in the Turkish-Bulgarian settlement in order to maintain his influence in Bulgaria was to be thwarted by the Porte's disregard of him to the benefit of Izvolsky, who earned the gratitude that Aehrenthal had sought.

The negotiations of Turkey with Bulgaria were even more difficult than those with Austria-Hungary and involved greater tension, which sometimes verged upon open warfare. At the end of January 1909 Izvolsky submitted a project to the two contestants by which to meet the Turkish financial demands upon Bulgaria that would have well exceeded the 100,000,000 francs which France estimated to be Bulgaria's capacity to pay. The Bulgars accepted the plan in principle at once, and Turkey, upon British urging, also accepted it, but dickered over the sums proposed by Izvolsky. At length, 15 March, Russia and the Porte came to an agreement that provided for the renunciation by Russia of forty annuities of the war indemnity imposed upon Turkey in 1878, and for the right of the Porte to capitalize the remaining thirty-four at 4 percent. The 125,000,000 francs thus accounted for equalled the East Rumelian tribute demanded by Turkey, the payment for the Oriental railway and a minor line seized by Bulgaria in the previous September, and indemnification for the Turkish crown lands in Bulgaria and East Rumelia. Turkey received no cash, but she profited by an amount that Great Britain had considered to be an equitable compensation. Bulgaria and Turkey finally signed an agreement on 19 April. The Entente powers separately recognized Bulgarian independence on 23 April, and the Triplice collectively followed suit on the 27th. The settlement was a diplomatic triumph for Izvolsky, his only clear victory in the tortuous diplomacy of the crisis.

Aehrenthal, on the other hand, was to win out in his stubborn resistance to the Russian-backed Serbian demands that constituted the crux of the crisis from October 1908 to March 1909 for both Aehrenthal and Izvolsky. The latter, after the blasting of his hopes concerning the Straits, saw the only way of salvaging Russian and his own prestige to lie in helping Serbia to gain her objectives. He and Grey, too, who supported him, were handicapped by Russian military weakness and their refusal to go farther than diplomatic support of Serbia, whereas Aehrenthal could risk war, if he chose, knowing that Germany would give him all-out military support.

The Serbs also talked of war, if they did not get territorial compensation for the annexation, and consequently military activity on both sides of the Serbian border produced increasing tension. The powers tried to exercise a moderating influence at Belgrade, while Vienna contended that the Monarchy was more sinned against than sinning. It is true that there was a war party there, led by Chief of the General Staff Conrad, who advocated that the Monarchy wipe out the Serb state while Russia was too weak to interfere. But his patron, the heir apparent Francis Ferdinand, as well as the emperor, opposed war. Aehrenthal in his letter of 8 December 1908 to Bülow declared that the Monarchy's policy was "guided by the desire to seek no conflict with Serbia," but was "not of a mind to pursue the policy of patience and forbearance *in infinitum*." If in the next two months Serbia's attitude gave cause for serious complaint, the time would then have come to take a "decisive resolution."[23] Though he did not rule out eventual war at that time, in another month he had changed his mind about his ultimate objective. Whereas in September he had talked of wiping out the "revolutionary Serbian nest," he told Conrad on 17 January 1909 that the incorporation of Serbia into the Monarchy was not practicable; all he sought was to assure the annexation of Bosnia-Herzegovina, and his successors could do the rest.

After the failure of attempts in February 1909 at mediation, largely because of German backing of Aehrenthal's refusal to accept it, both the British and the French urged Izvolsky to give up his support of Serbian demands for territorial compensation. Responding to their pressure, he decided to modify his policy. At the same time he vigorously denounced a proposal concerted by Kiderlen and Jules Cambon

23. Aehrenthal to Bülow, 8 December 1908: *OUA*, I, no. 703.

which would have paved the way for direct negotiations between Vienna and Belgrade, instead of a settlement by the powers, because such a confrontation would put Serbia at the mercy of Austria-Hungary. The Serbs meanwhile had stated in a circular of 24 February that Serbia would refrain from any action leading to war and would follow the advice of the powers. Taking this statement as his cue, Izvolsky on the 27th requested Serbia to give up her demand for territorial compensation and to formally declare that she would rely upon the decision of the powers on all pending questions. By this act Izvolsky took his first step in retreat from his original position, but at the same time he hoped to prevent bilateral negotiations such as those between Austria-Hungary and Turkey, and to maintain the principle of a settlement by the powers, either through a conference, which Tittoni was again suggesting, or through other means.

By the opening of March 1909, a new Serbian government of 24 February had placed its fate entirely in the hands of the powers and had declared that it would make no categorical demands, either territorial or economic. On the other hand, Aehrenthal seemed as intransigent as ever in his insistence that Serbia must address Austria-Hungary directly, giving assurances that she would not raise territorial demands, that she would discontinue her increase in armament, and that she would promise neighborly conduct in the future. In return he would do his best to satisfy Serbia's economic wishes. He emphasized, however, that he would not permit mediation by the powers, and refused to recognize Russia's right to act as Serbia's protector. A Serbian note of 10 March, however, failed to fulfill Aehrenthal's demands and only helped to deepen an already acute crisis. Aehrenthal now added a new demand. He had called upon Izvolsky to recognize the annexation at the time the Turkish protocol was signed and now insisted that Serbia do so, too, and that Russia should exert her influence to bring about Serbian recognition. He declared that he would give Serbia until the end of March, but if she had not by then complied with his conditions, he would issue an ultimatum and march. Once more the question of secret documents cropped up to complicate the direct Austro-Russian relations that had been renewed on 6 March. When Izvolsky remonstrated about pressing the Serbs to acknowledge and accept the Turkish protocol, Berchtold informed him that Aehrenthal would be compelled to communicate to Belgrade, London, and Paris secret documents that would clarify the facts about the annexation. Izvolsky was understandably deeply disturbed by this turn of events.

Germany at this point began to take a hand by denouncing the Serbian note of 10 March, and by maintaining that a conference, for which Russia, Britain, and Italy were again calling, should deal only with questions upon which the powers had already reached an agreement. Certain of German support, Aehrenthal on 12 March also declared the Serbian note to be unsatisfactory, pointing out that since it was addressed to the powers, it was not an answer to his recent request, and in any case was not acceptable because it put the annexation question up to the decision of the powers. The next day a ministerial council decided to send additional battalions to the border if Serbia had not made a satisfactory answer by the 16th. On the 14th the Serbian government handed Count Johann Forgách, the Austro-Hungarian minister, a note that repeated the declarations of the 10th and then concentrated upon proposals for handling the commercial treaty and the *modus vivendi*, due to expire on the 31st. Not only Austria-Hungary and Germany, but also France, Britain, and Italy held this note to be unsatisfactory. Realizing that Serbia had to demonstrate greater good will than she had heretofore shown, Grey undertook on 17 March to draft a Serbian note that would satisfy Austria-Hungary. Because Aehrenthal did not reject Grey's mediation, negotiations ensued that ultimately brought about a peaceful outcome. Meanwhile Germany entered the scene.

Izvolsky himself gave Bülow the opportunity to intervene, for on 14 March he appealed personally to the German Chancellor to prevent Aehrenthal from publishing the documents he had threatened to reveal. Bülow, who was still being advised by the bluff and energetic Kiderlen, saw an opportunity to end the deadlock. Whether he and Kiderlen were motivated by a desire to demonstrate their diplomatic superiority over Aehrenthal's diplomacy and to recover the leading strings in the alliance or were jealous of British efforts is not clear, but undoubtedly such considerations along with a sincere desire to avoid what Kiderlen called a "silly war" and a European conference entered into their calculations.[24] Bülow therefore offered to help Izvolsky if Russia would force Serbia to remain quiet, and suggested that if the powers recognized the annexation by an exchange of notes, Russia would be in a better position to use firm language at Belgrade. If Russia refused to make use of this proposal and to give up her opposition to the *fait accompli* Germany would be obliged to let matters take their course. Pourtalès was to present the proposal as an

24. *Kiderlen-Waechter*, II, 11.

attempt to be helpful. Both Izvolsky and the tsar accepted it as "friendly" in intention and as a happy sign that Germany wanted a peaceful way out of the situation. Yet Izvolsky hesitated for fear that agreement upon an exchange of notes would eliminate the conference upon which he had insisted, and that the scheme would leave the Dual Monarchy free to deal with Serbia as she wished. Furthermore, Grey objected to his draft of a reply to Bülow because it did not mention a conference and because Grey believed that a pacific settlement between the Monarchy and Serbia should be achieved before recognition of the annexation. Although a Russian ministerial council on 20 March agreed that Russia could not go to war, Izvolsky was still trying to avoid a Russian recognition of the annexation. Hence he purposely made his reply to Bülow of the same day "a little obscure," as he told Nicolson. The kaiser regarded it as a refusal and an "insolent answer."[25]

Although Schoen thought it not wise to "bend the bow too tightly" in dealing with Russia, Kiderlen had no such compunctions.[26] He drew up the famous note of 21 March requesting a yes or no answer to the question whether Russia would consent to the abrogation of Article XXV; if the answer was no, Germany "would then draw back and let matters take their course"; but the question of a conference was not relevant at this juncture and could be discussed later.[27] Was this note an ultimatum, or was it simply a forthright attempt to cut through the Gordian knot that was tying up a peaceful settlement? Bülow, Schoen, and Pourtalès maintained that it was not an ultimatum but a friendly effort to clear the air, which would be necessary if Germany was to exert any influence upon Vienna, as Izvolsky had requested. Kiderlen, on the other hand, boasted of his strong language. Charykov, who was in charge of the Russian foreign office for a few days because Izvolsky was ill, asserted that the note was "couched, I must admit, in the most amiable form," and Taube, legal expert at the Singers' Bridge, called it "assez ultimatif," but since it contained no threat of military measures, "it could not be called an ultimatum."[28] The tsar in writing to his mother asserted that "the form and the method of Germany's action—I mean towards us—has simply been

25. Nicolson to Grey, 20 March 1909: *BD*, V, no. 729; the kaiser's marginalium, *GP*, XXVI(2), no. 9458.

26. Wilhelm von Schoen, *Memoirs of an Ambassador*, p. 84.

27. Bülow to Pourtalès, 21 March 1909: *GP*, XXVI(2), no. 9460.

28. Charykov, *Glimpses of High Politics*, p. 270; Taube, *Politique russe*, pp. 227–28.

rude and we won't forget it."[29] Izvolsky described the *démarche* as a "political ultimatum" in talking with Nicolson, but six months later confessed to Cartwright that Germany had acted in a friendly spirit. The interpretation of the note as an ultimatum seems to have developed among the British and French, who feared—none more so than Nicolson—that Russia, made aware by Germany of her helplessness and the inability of her friend and her ally to help her, might turn toward the central powers, as Izvolsky had hinted more than once, and thus return to a *Dreikaiserbund*.[30] Certainly, whether or not the note of 21 March was an ultimatum, Russia, whose ministers unanimously agreed to give assent to the annexation, was in no position to say no, especially because Izvolsky, who was thrown into a panic, was convinced that a rejection would mean an Austro-Serbian war and an invasion of Russia. The tsar put the situation less dramatically when he wrote his mother that there was nothing to do "but swallow one's pride. . . . If this sacrifice on our part will save Serbia from being crushed by Austria, then, in my opinion, this sacrifice was worth while."[31]

Needless to say, the Wilhelmstrasse was jubilant over Russian acceptance of the annexation, and notified Vienna of it on 24 March. When Aehrenthal asked the other powers to give theirs, however, Great Britain and France refused to do so until the Serbian conflict was settled. After all, Russia's humiliation did not affect the outcome of the negotiations between Grey and Aehrenthal over the form of the acceptable Serbian note to Austria-Hungary which Aehrenthal was stubbornly demanding. Nor did Russia's collapse prevent a decision in Vienna on 29 March to mobilize the army if its demands were not met. Undoubtedly both Berlin and St. Petersburg exaggerated the significance of the German move and of the Russian surrender.

It is true that Russia's action to a certain extent robbed Grey of the force he might otherwise have exerted in his attempt to get Aehrenthal's approval of a note that would not humiliate Serbia. Aehrenthal, on the other hand, had become more determined in his attitude toward Serbia, wanting to demonstrate that she had to yield to Austro-Hungarian wishes. At length on 26 March Aehrenthal submitted the text of a Serbian note, which Izvolsky approved and Grey accepted,

29. "Iz perepiski Nikolaya," *KA*, L–LI, 188–89.

30. Pourtalès to Bülow, Private, 1 April 1909: *GP*, XXVI(2), no. 9503; Crozier to Pichon, 1 April 1909: 2 *DDF*, XII, no. 152; Berchtold diary and memoirs summarized: Hantsch, *Berchtold*, I, 172.

31. "Iz perepiski Nikolaya," *KA*, L–LI, 188.

asking the powers to join with Britain in urging Serbian acceptance. At the same time Grey informed Aehrenthal, who was angered by his refusal to approve the annexation, that after Serbia had delivered the note agreed upon and Austria-Hungary had accepted it, Britain would assent to the abrogation of Article XXV.

Serbia, despite the Austro-Hungarian military preparations on her border, had not ordered mobilization, and on 26 March had made Alexander crown prince in place of his older brother George, who had been among the more violent advocates of resistance to Austria-Hungary. The Serbian government adopted the text of the note presented to it and sent it to Vienna on the following morning. The note represented a triumph for Aehrenthal. By it Serbia recognized that her rights had "not been affected by the *fait accompli* brought about in Bosnia-Herzegovina," and that she would comply with the decision of the powers concerning Article XXV. She would abandon "the attitude of protest and opposition" held since the previous autumn, and would undertake "to change the direction of her present policy toward Austria-Hungary in order to live henceforth on terms of good neighborliness with the latter." Moreover, she promised to reduce her army to the strength in the previous spring, "to disarm and dismiss the voluntary bands" and to prevent the formation "of new irregular units on her territory."[32]

Aehrenthal declared that the controversy was closed and friendly relations restored; he also ordered his minister, Forgách, to open negotiations with Serbia for a trade treaty. He was disappointed, however, not to receive Britain's assent to the abrogation of Article XXV, for Grey now included a settlement with Montenegro in his conditions.

Like Serbia, Montenegro had made known her desires and had sought Russian and Italian help. Italy was the more interested in her case and carried on negotiations with the Dual Monarchy, although Izvolsky resented Italy's initiative. Tittoni proposed to suppress the paragraphs in Article XXIX of the Berlin treaty which were obnoxious to Montenegro and to provide that Antivari, instead of being closed to the warships of all nations, should "retain the character of a commercial port." Aehrenthal accepted the proposal in principle but stipulated that Montenegro had to resume a correct attitude toward the Monarchy and to establish relations of good neighborliness. Finally, on 6 April Montenegro sent notes to both Italy and Austria-Hungary

32. Verbalnote der serbischen Gesandtschaft, 31/18 March 1909: *OUA*, II, no. 1425.

agreeing upon the proposed modifications of Article XXIX, and Aehrenthal accepted them. By the changes in Article XXIX, in addition to Antivari's new status, Montenegro won the right to possess warships and to build fortifications between Lake Scutari and the coast; she was also freed from Austro-Hungarian policing of the coast and from the other restrictions on her sovereignty. All the powers accepted the modifications in Article XXIX to which Aehrenthal had agreed and thus closed the books on all serious questions arising from the annexation of Bosni-Herzegovina.

Accordingly, the powers one by one formally recognized the abrogation of Article XXV of the Treaty of Berlin: Germany on 7 April, Italy on the 11th, Great Britain on the 17th, and France and Russia on the 19th. The crisis that had arisen in October 1908 had at last ended without the war that everyone dreaded.

IV.

The crisis of 1908–1909 was a dress rehearsal for that of July 1914, and in significant ways set the stage for it.[33] The Serbo-Austro-Hungarian confrontation involved the loyalty of Germany to her alliance partner, even the blank check to be filled in by the Dual Monarchy. Italy played a minor role but clearly a neutral one as far as the Triple Alliance was concerned. On the other hand, Russia championed the Serbs, Great Britain supported Russia, and France stood in the wings hopeful that she would not be compelled to face a showdown with the central powers. The Triple Entente emerged in opposition to the Dual Alliance of the central powers. The Entente had hardly existed in September 1908, but before very long, as William II wrote Nicholas II on 5 January 1909, "A Triple Entente between France, Russia, and England is being talked of by the whole world as an accomplished fact."[34]

Equally important were the legacies of hatred and mistrust left by the crisis. The most obvious was the conviction of the Serbs that their future lay in a triumphant confrontation of Austria-Hungary, who remained the hated enemy of their national goal. Although Aehrenthal had won the first round in compelling them and Europe to accept the

33. Cf. William L. Langer, "The 1908 Prelude to the World War," *FA*, VII (1929), 635–49 (also, *Explorations in Crisis*, pp. 76–90).
34. *GP*, XXVI(2), no. 9188.

annexation of the two Serbian provinces, he had paid the price of arousing Slavdom against his country. The subsequent failure to provide Bosnia and Herzegovina with the constitutional machinery that Aehrenthal had made the excuse for removing them from Ottoman sovereignty emphasized the incapacity of the Monarchy to deal effectively with the South Slav problem. Aehrenthal failed to implement his dreams of reform, and the governments after him, for reasons of both internal conditions and external events, such as the Balkan Wars, were unable to assuage the Serbian and South Slavic hatred of Habsburg rule. Therefore, while Aehrenthal had succeeded in "raising the international status of the Monarchy, proving its vitality, and strengthening national consciousness,"[35] his diplomacy had also succeeded in creating only a superficial covering of the wounds he had inflicted upon the South Slav spirit; he and his successors failed to cauterize them.

Izvolsky within six months after the end of the crisis claimed that German-Russian relations had returned to normal, and within ten months professed to have forgiven Aehrenthal, but the rift between Russia and the central powers remained unclosed. Russia had backed down in 1909 out of weakness, and her leaders resolved not to experience the humiliation again. A logical component of Izvolsky's policy after 1906 was a vigorous championship of Slavdom. The Dual Monarchy stood in Russia's way in the Balkans, and Germany at Constantinople and the Straits. To rearm and outplay Austria-Hungary in the Balkans, to tighten the French alliance and to foster the entente with Great Britain in the diplomatic duels with Germany— these were the imperatives that might be lost from sight from time to time but fundamentally remained the guidelines of Russian policy.

As for the western powers, the crisis confirmed and deepened the British conviction that Germany was pursuing an aggressive policy. Coinciding as the crisis did with the heightening of naval rivalry, all the protestations of Aehrenthal that he was independent of German dictation could not alter the British belief that he was but a pawn in a German game. The differences between Great Britain and Austria-Hungary were easily glossed over, but the British mistrust of Germany remained an almost constant factor in the international relations of succeeding years. For France, the consequences of the Bosnian crisis were less obvious because of her preoccupation with the Moroccan question and French awakening to the interlocking relationship of

35. Baernreither, *Fragments of a Political Diary*, pp. 64–65.

Morocco and the Balkans in the alliance with Russia was yet to come.

In summary, Aehrenthal had heightened the prestige of the Dual Monarchy, but at a cost that was out of all proportion to his gains. Germany had entered a path that Bismarck had carefully avoided and, except for a few months of hesitation, followed it through the fateful days of 1914. Russia, Great Britain, and France emerged in a Triple Entente which was tried and found wanting on more than one subsequent occasion, but which nevertheless represented a basic element in the balance of power over the next five years.

Chapter 8

Between Crises,

1909–1911

Between 1909 and 1911 changes occurred in diplomatic personnel in Russia, Germany, and Great Britain, while at Vienna Baron Aehrenthal remained at the Ballhausplatz and in Italy Tommaso Tittoni continued to be foreign minister until the end of 1909, when he became ambassador in Paris. In July 1909 Theobold von Bethmann Hollweg succeeded Prince Bernhard von Bülow as German chancellor, and in the following summer Alfred von Kiderlen-Waechter became secretary for foreign affairs in place of Baron William Eduard von Schoen, who became ambassador to France. At about the same time Sergei Sazonov succeeded A. P. Izvolsky, who went to Paris as ambassador. From March to December 1911 Anatole Anatolievich Neratov acted as foreign minister while Sazonov was ill. In the autumn of 1910 Sir Arthur Nicolson became permanent under-secretary at the Foreign Office in place of Sir Charles Hardinge, and was succeeded as ambassador at St. Petersburg by Sir George Buchanan. In the Anglo-German discussions of a naval agreement Admiral Alfred von Tirpitz and Kaiser William II greatly influenced German policy, while in London Eyre Crowe (knighted in 1911), senior clerk at the Foreign Office, took an increasingly active part in advising Sir Edward Grey. A change of British ambassadors at Berlin occurred at the end of 1908, when Sir Edward Goschen replaced Sir Frank Lascelles.

In the two-year period between the Bosnian and the Agadir crises the great powers conducted diplomatic relations at a lower pitch than the excited tones of 1908–1909 and 1911. To be sure, there were many problem areas that required sustained interchanges and inevitably gave rise to differences of opinion. In the Near East the Ottoman regime after the coup of 24 March 1909, when the Young Turks prevented a counterrevolution and enthroned Mohammed V in place of Abdul Hamid II, frequently aroused anxiety as to its stability and character. The Armenian massacre at Adana in April 1909 and the bloody suppression of the Albanian uprising, April-June 1910, emphasized the seeming return to Hamidian tactics. The Cretan movement for union with Greece, futilely proclaimed on 7 October 1908, tested the moderating influences of the four protecting powers— Britain, France, Russia, and Italy—who managed to prevent a Greco-Turkish crisis. They were powerless, however, to prevent the appointment of Eleutherios Venizelos as Greek prime minister in October 1910, an event of great significance for both the rejuvenation of Greece and the eventual union of Crete with Greece in October 1912. In addition there was the recurrent question of railways in Turkey, of which more later.

The most important concern in the Balkans and the Near East, however, was the great-power rivalry that the Bosnian crisis had engendered. Throughout the period of 1909–1911, Austria-Hungary played a passive role and Italy a very minor part, while Russia became the leading actor. In the West at the same time, Anglo-German naval rivalry and the futile attempts to end it or at least to reduce the tempo of ship-building were the major themes of the period. Thus there were two axes around which relations among the great powers revolved: the Near East on the one hand, and Anglo-German relations on the other. Inevitably there were overlapping areas, particularly whenever alliances or alignments seemed to be affected by policies pursued or ends sought.

I.

Although Izvolsky continued to smart over his diplomatic defeat at the hands of Aehrenthal, he reciprocated the German desire to restore good relations between Germany and Russia. At the meeting of the two sovereigns in Finnish waters, June 1909, Secretary of State Schoen sought, quite successfully to judge from Izvolsky's later remarks, to disprove the "legend," as Schoen put it, of a German ultimatum in March. Moreover, he tried without apparent success to reassure Izvolsky concerning Aehrenthal's Balkan policy. In view of the planned visits of the tsar to France and England later in the summer and the Anglo-German naval rivalry, Isvolsky emphasized the peaceful character of the entente with Britain and his determination, along with the French, not to transform the ententes into alliances or to give them an anti-German character. Izvolsky felt satisfied with the restoration of good feeling, but the Germans, especially William II

7. Sergei Sazanov (Culver Pictures)

and Chancellor Bethmann-Hollweg, who succeeded Bülow in mid-July, never quite trusted him.

They had reason for mistrust. Izvolsky pursued a policy designed to bar Austria-Hungary from any further Balkan expansion—an objective Aehrenthal repudiated but his neighbors continued to fear. Sharing Russian concern over further Austro-Hungarian moves southward was Italy, where Foreign Minister Tommaso Tittoni had long sought to strengthen his country's position vis-à-vis the Dual Monarchy. It is not clear who first broached the idea of an Italo-Russian agreement over the Balkans, but the Germans were probably correct in their suspicion that it was Izvolsky. In any event the long-deferred visit of Nicholas II with Victor Emmanuel III, who had gone to St. Petersburg in 1902, took place at Racconigi on 24 October 1909. Izvolsky and Tittoni utilized the occasion to draw up a very secret agreement designed to form the basis of cooperation in the Near East.

By this accord they agreed (1) to strive for the maintenance of the status quo in the Balkan peninsula; (2) to uphold the application of the principle of nationality in the development of the Balkan states, excluding all foreign domination; and (3) to oppose by common diplomatic action "any manoeuvre at variance with the above-mentioned aims." Also, (4) neither power was "to make fresh agreements with a third party outside those already existing in the European Near East . . . without the participation of the other"; and, most significantly, (5) Russia and Italy undertook "to view with goodwill, the one the Italian interests in Tripolitania and Cyrenaica, the other the Russian interests in the Straits question."[1]

The conflict between the maintenance of the status quo and the development of the Balkan states along national lines is obvious, as is the anti-Austrian intent of the third and fourth points. With number 5, Russian support of Italian ambitions in Tripolitania rounded out the great-power approval that the Triplice, Great Britain, and France had already given to Italy, while Italian good will toward Russia in the Straits question was intended to strengthen Izvolsky's hopes for a Russian solution. Izvolsky's single-mindedness in making the accord is clear, whereas Tittoni's position was ambivalent, to say the least, toward Austria-Hungary. He had sought throughout the summer, with German support, to win a pledge from Aehrenthal that if the Dual Monarchy were to reoccupy the Sanjak of Novi Pazar, Italy would be compensated through some previous agreement. At the time of the Racconigi meeting, however, agreement had not been reached

---

1. The text: *LN*, I, 357–58. Cf. Albertini, *Origins*, I, 306–11.

on the wording of the pledge. After the meeting Tittoni and Aehrenthal continued negotiations that led to an exchange of notes between Aehrenthal and Tittoni's successor, Count Francesco Guicciardini, on 30 November and 15 December 1909.

In addition to the understanding concerning the Sanjak, which in effect spelled out the application of Article VII of the Triple Alliance treaty to it, the two undertook "not to conclude with a third power any agreement whatsoever concerning Balkan questions without the participation of the other cabinet on a footing of absolute equality," and to communicate to each other "every proposition" made by a third power which ran "contrary to the principle of non-intervention and tending to a modification of the status quo in the regions of the Balkans or of the Ottoman coasts and islands in the Adriatic and of the Aegean Sea."[2] Presumably, because the Racconigi agreement had been made before the exchange of notes with the Dual Monarchy, the Italians did not regard it as a Balkan accord that had to be revealed to Vienna. For them it constituted a reinsurance that the Dual Monarchy would live up to its treaty obligations. Moreover, both Tittoni and Izvolsky asserted after Racconigi that they hoped all the powers would subscribe to the principles concerning the Balkans upon which they had agreed. Izvolsky represented Tittoni as desirous of a triple entente of Italy, Russia, and Austria-Hungary, and declared that he also wanted the same thing.

If Izvolsky meant what he said, his actions belied his avowed intentions, for he seemed to be primarily concerned to organize the Balkans in a pro-Russian league as a further bar to suspected Austro-Hungarian designs in the Peninsula. Although he did not subscribe to N. V. Charykov's plan to open the Straits through another Unkiar Skelessi, he went along with the idea of a Balkan league including Turkey, also part of Charykov's dream of a Russian-oriented Balkan bloc. Charykov went to Constantinople early in the summer of 1909 as the new ambassador to Turkey and was replaced as assistant foreign minister by Sergei Sazonov. Izvolsky, from the time of his public endorsement in his Duma speech of 25 December 1908 of a Balkan union, took every opportunity to encourage a Serbo-Bulgarian and Serbo-Montenegrin rapprochement. Despite some initial steps in 1909 and an abortive attempt to tie Bulgaria more closely to Russia, both his and Charykov's endeavors met with no success in 1909–1910.

At the beginning of 1910 Izvolsky at last turned to the problem of

2. Pribram, *Secret Treaties*, I, 240–43. Cf. Christofer Seton-Watson, *Italy from Liberation to Fascism, 1870–1925* (London, 1967), pp. 346–49.

a Russian-Austro-Hungarian détente, which Aehrenthal had professed to want ever since the ending of the Bosnian crisis. Despite the continuing suspicion of his aims in the Balkans, Aehrenthal had indeed renounced any further expansion southward and was pursuing a policy of conciliation and cooperation with other powers in maintaining the status quo. He still put a high value on independence from German leading strings, a posture that sometimes gave Berlin uneasiness. He favored the strengthening of Romania and Bulgaria, but resisted the incorporation of Serbia into the Monarchy, as Chief of Staff Conrad wished. He summed up his general policy in a memorandum of 15 August 1909: "In Europe to uphold the balance of power among the great powers, in the Near East not to oppose the natural development of the Balkan states, but also to favor the balance of power according to expediency, whereby naturally Rumania and Bulgaria are to receive special consideration."[3] There was nothing in such a policy to prevent his cooperation with Russia or Italy, and at times, such as during the Albanian crisis of 1911, he participated in a kind of triple entente, such as Tittoni had desired.

Although both Italy and Germany had sought to bring about a rapproachement of Vienna and St. Petersburg, no progress had been made up to the end of January 1910. On the contrary, two articles in the *Fortnightly Review* had seemed to lessen the chances of a reconciliation. An article in the September 1909 issue entitled "Baron Aehrenthal and M. Iswolsky's diplomatic enigmas," obviously inspired by Izvolsky, presented Russia's case against the Dual Monarchy in the Bosnian affair. A reply in the November issue, "Monsieur Iswolsky and Count Aehrenthal, a rectification," published over a pseudonym but written by E. J. Dillon, revealed some of the background of Buchlau, including Izvolsky's aide-mémoire of 2 July 1908. Characteristically, Izvolsky flew into a rage and suspected Berchtold of responsibility for the revelations. Dillon denied that Berchtold was the source of his article and told Izvolsky that the story was well known in the capitals of Europe, and that it came to him from a Russian Out of the exchanges over the *Fortnightly* articles came the negotiations over the restoration of normal relations.

From the first the views of Izvolsky and Aehrenthal differed over the form of the understanding that they both clearly wanted. At bottom Izvolsky wanted to score a triumph over Aehrenthal, as the latter suspected and sought in every way to avoid. Aehrenthal pro-

3. *OUA*, II, no. 1720.

posed a return to something like the understanding of 1897, but Izvolsky refused to resurrect it and suggested an exchange of notes in such a form as to make possible the participation of other interested powers. The upshot of the exchanges was the announcement in both capitals on 20 March that normal relations between them had been resumed. Izvolsky, however, without previous consultation with Aehrenthal, accompanied his notice to the other capitals with copies of seven aide-mémoires and telegrams covering the negotiations from 15 January to 14 March. This action constituted his revenge for the revelations by Aehrenthal in December 1908. Under the circumstances a genuine rapprochement was scarcely achieved, and nothing in the way of a concrete agreement concerning Turkey and the Balkans, but only imprecise statements of principles similar to those in the Racconigi agreement.

By March 1910 Izvolsky's days at the Singers' Bridge were numbered. His career up to the Buchlau meeting of 1908 had been on the whole successful, but from that turning point onward he played a sorry role, except for his mediation of the Bulgar-Turkish settlement and the Racconigi agreement. At the end of September he left St. Petersburg for the Paris embassy, where he was destined to play a significant but secondary part.

Sergei Sazonov, Izvolsky's successor, was a quite different kind of man. He had had a limited diplomatic experience before 1909 as counselor at the London embassy and head of the Russian legation at the Vatican, but was valued for his personal qualities. He had none of Izvolsky's faults, Taube testified, but also few of his good points; he was simple, modest, affable, and completely disinterested personally; he was profoundly religious, very orthodox, and very Russian. On the other hand, he was sickly and nervous, almost neurasthenic, and lacked stability of viewpoint, changing his mind as a result of impressions and intuitions. Maurice Paléologue, French ambassador in Russia from January 1914, had a kindlier opinion of Sazonov, whom he regarded as a scrupulously honest, most conscientious, and hardworking minister with a good knowledge of diplomatic problems and outstanding loyalty to the tsar. Sazonov was expected to reestablish the balance and stability which Russian foreign policy had lacked since the onset of the Bosnian crisis and to improve relations with the central powers, especially Germany.[4]

4. Taube, *Politique russe*, pp. 237, 248–49, 252; Albertini, *Origins*, I, 367 (quoting from a Paléologue letter); A. V. Neklyudov, *Diplomatic Reminiscences before and during the World War, 1911–1917* (London, 1920), pp. 32–33.

Even before Sazonov became minister, Russia (and Britain as well) had been worried over German economic and financial advances toward Persia. Germany, on the other hand, feared that Russia and Great Britain were trying to exclude her from the Persian market, and complained that the promises in the Anglo-Russian convention of 1907 to maintain the open door in Persia were not being kept. She offered to come to a friendly understanding over Persian questions. While Britain did not immediately respond to this offer, there were several reasons why Russia began to consider a general understanding with Germany. From the Balkans to the Far East Russia was facing problems the solution of which would be made easier if she were sure of German backing, or at least neutrality. Russia had never been convinced of Aehrenthal's pacific intentions; in Turkey naval armament with German help posed a threat in the Black Sea, and Turkish military measures on the Persian border aroused Russian suspicions; in China the renewal of a trade treaty had run into difficulties that the Russians proposed to overcome by a show of force on the Chinese border. Moreover, Izvolsky's departure at the end of September seemed to the tsar to be an appropriate time to seek improvement in Russo-German relations, a feeling which Germany reciprocated, because agreement with Russia might weaken or even break up the Triple Entente.

For Sazonov the crux of a Russo-German understanding lay in the Persian question, and in August 1910 he asked Ambassador Pourtalès if conciliatory Russian proposals might lead to an accord. German willingness to come to an agreement, the tsar's desire for better relations, the necessity of safeguarding Russian interests in Persia from German pressures, and the internal Persian "anarchy," as Sazonov described it, all pointed to the resumption of the talks of 1907 that had been broken off in July of that year. Germany had then proposed an arrangement by which Russia would make no opposition to the completion of the Bagdad railway, and would link future Persian railways with a branch of the Bagdad railway at Khanikin on the Persian-Turkish border, while Germany would not seek concessions for railways, roads, or telegraph lines in northern Persia but would enjoy equal economic freedom there. The problem for Russia, then and in 1910, was to avoid a one-sided arrangement that would enable Germany with her superior economic and financial resources to outstrip Russia in the Persian market. In preparation for a meeting at Potsdam of the tsar and Sazonov with the German emperor, the chancellor, and the secretary of state for foreign affairs, Alfred von

Kiderlen-Waechter,[5] Sazonov laid the problem before a special ministerial council over which Stolypin presided on 28 October. The result of the discussion was that, because better relations with Germany were important, the 1907 proposals should be discussed at Potsdam in very general terms, but that Russia should seek to safeguard her economic preponderance in northern Persia by building railroad links with Russia before establishing a link with the Bagdad branch at Khanikin which, in Sazonov's estimate, would not be constructed short of ten or fifteen years. While the council clearly preferred to avoid any link with the Bagdad line, the acknowledged financial weakness of Russia made an agreement with Germany a second best choice of policy.[6]

The meetings at Potsdam on 4 November and in Berlin on the 5th went off happily for both sides. The Germans were favorably impressed by Sazonov, whose policy, they believed, represented a Russian reorientation toward closer relations with Germany, and Austria-Hungary as well. The discussions, mainly at the level of generalities, were not recorded. Hence there are variations between the reports of Sazonov and Bethmann-Hollweg, and even greater differences between those two on the one hand, and the written agreement drafted by Bethmann and sent to Russia on 15 November, on the other.[7] Taking all three sources into account, the important declarations of policy were: With reference to Austria-Hungary, Sazonov believed that if Aehrenthal adhered to the principles agreed upon in the previous March, there would be no menace to peace, but if difficulties should arise, Russia would not refuse to treat with Vienna through Berlin. Germany would accept a mediatory role, said Bethmann and Kiderlen, and while they did not expect the Dual Monarchy to embark upon an expansionist policy in the Balkans, Germany would not support such a policy, being bound neither by treaty nor interests to do so. As for the Balkans, Sazonov and the Germans agreed upon a policy of peace, the maintenance of the status quo, and the peaceful development of the Balkan states; they would attempt to localize any conflagration that might occur there. In respect of Turkey, the kaiser and his ministers vigorously denied that they were encouraging

5. Kiderlen took office in August 1910, replacing Schoen who became ambassador to France.

6. Minutes, 28/15 October 1910: Erusalimski, ed., "K istorii," *KA*, LVIII (1933), 52–57.

7. Bethmann Hollweg to Pourtalès, 8 and 15 November 1910: *GP*, XXVII(2), nos. 10155, 10159; Sergei Sazonov, "L'entrevue de Potsdam," *LN*, II, 331–34.

panislamism or supporting an aggressive Turkish policy, especially toward Persia, and persuaded Sazonov to agree with them upon the support of a strong and stable Turkish government to maintain order internally and on the frontiers. Concerning Persia, Sazonov suggested that, in making difficulties for Russia, the Persians might be hoping for German support. The Germans branded such an idea "phantasy." They went on to discuss an understanding over Persia along the lines of the 1907 German draft, although details were to be worked out after the meeting. Sazonov, in his report to the tsar, omits his promise not to oppose the Bagdad railway, saying "the question of the Bagdad railway itself was not raised," but that he felt it necessary to declare "that in case of the partition of the line among the interested powers," Russia would want the Bagdad-Khanikin line. Even more curious was the omission by both Sazonov and Bethmann of the declaration that Russia was not pledged to support a hostile English policy toward Germany and had no intention of doing so. This assertion appeared in the German draft agreement of 15 November as Article II.

The Germans wanted the declarations and agreements of Potsdam-Berlin put into written form, and Ambassador Pourtalès found Sazonov ready to pursue further the "threads" that had been spun at Potsdam. But when Pourtalès suggested that Sazonov make a written declaration that Russia would not participate in an English policy that was hostile to Germany, Sazonov put him off by saying he would have to receive an order to do so from the tsar. Bethmann lost no time, however, in submitting a draft agreement and along with it a prepared statement to be read to the Reichstag on 10 December, for which he obtained Sazonov's approval.

Bethmann's draft included all of the declarations and agreements of Potsdam-Berlin concerning Austria-Hungary, the Russian pledge concerning English policy, the Balkans, Turkey, Persia, and the Bagdad railway. Sazonov, however, refused to accept the first four articles of the draft. He and the tsar asserted that verbal assurances made written ones unnecessary and that the declarations of the two emperors at Potsdam were worth more than an exchange of notes. Although irritated by the Russian refusal to put the declarations in black on white, Bethmann and Kiderlen proceeded to the consideration of a Persian and Bagdad railway convention, which Bethmann had already indicated was the essential thing. Negotiations went on over the next eight months. Sazonov became ill in February 1911 and was replaced in March by Acting Foreign Minister A. A. Neratov who, on 19 August 1911, at length signed the agreement with Pourtalès.

The final text began with a preamble upon which Russia had insisted over German objections, for, in addition to the principle of equal treatment in Persia of the commerce of all nations, it recognized special Russian interests and the German pursuit of only commercial aims there. Germany renounced any attempt to secure concessions in the Russian zone of Persia, while Russia undertook to secure from Persia a concession for a railway from Teheran to Khanikin where it would connect with a branch of the Bagdad line to be built from Sadijeh (outside Bagdad). If, however, Russia was unable to obtain a Teheran-Khanikin concession within a specified time, Germany was free to obtain it. Most important for Germany was the provision that Russia promised not to impede the completion of the Bagdad railway or to prevent the participation of foreign capital in it, on condition that no Russian pecuniary or economic sacrifice would be involved. Further provisions safeguarded Russian and German rights in the projected Teheran-Khanikin line.[8]

Even before the meeting at Potsdam, Great Britain and France had been concerned about the Russo-German discussion of Persia and the Bagdad railway. For Britain the shoe was on the other foot. Negotiations with Germany over the Bagdad railway had gone on in 1909–1910 as part of an Anglo-German understanding and had irritated and aroused the suspicions of both the Russians and the French. Grey had kept them informed, however, and had advised the Russians that they might well make a preliminary agreement with Germany before the Bagdad railway was taken up à quatre, as had been agreed upon in 1907. Both Britain and France let Sazonov know that they wanted to be fully informed of anything said at Potsdam about Persia and the Bagdad railway, and to be consulted before the conclusion of any agreement. Sazonov, believing that he would need Anglo-French capital in order to control the Teheran-Khanikin line, was the more willing to keep in touch with the western powers. Accordingly, he and Neratov communicated to France and Britain the major steps in the negotiations and the final text of the agreement. Nevertheless the French were angry at what they regarded as a breach of the understanding that none of the entente powers should negotiate unilaterally with Germany over the Bagdad railway. Grey took the same view as the French and also feared that the Russo-German agreement greatly weakened the position of Britain in future negotiations with Germany. The only excuse offered by the Russians was that their consent to the completion of the railroad applied only as far as Bagdad, which

8. The text: BD, X(1), no. 741.

would be constructed regardless of the attitude of the other powers, and that Russia was left free in respect to other sections.

The significance of the Potsdam meeting and the subsequent accord is difficult to assess. They did bring about a temporary détente in Russo-German relations, which were better in the short run than at any time since Björkö. On the other hand, they loosened the ties between Russia and her entente partners and between Germany and Austria-Hungary, because of the mistrust aroused among the respective friends and allies. France and Britain regarded the Russo-German understanding as a triumph for Germany, especially in the Russian acceptance of the Bagdad railway and in the weakening of the Triple Entente. Austria-Hungary was suspicious of the German oral assurances concerning the Dual Monarchy and the Balkans. From what Kiderlen told the Austrian chargé Aehrenthal concluded that the days of *Nibelungentreu* were over, as indeed they were for the time being. The Agadir crisis of 1911, however, and the Balkan wars of 1912–1913 wiped out the effects of Potsdam upon Russo-German relations. In the long run the parallel Anglo-German negotiations, although negative in their results, were more significant in the developments eventually leading to the war of 1914 than was Potsdam.

II.

In the first decade of the twentieth century, Anglo-German relations fluctuated between calm and high tension. After the failure of alliance talks at the end of 1901, the formation of the British ententes aroused German irritation and fear of encirclement. The first Moroccan crisis, Algeciras, and the Bosnian crisis of 1908–1909 convinced the British of Germany's aggressive designs. The Bagdad railway from 1903 became a recurrent bone of contention. The basic issue, however, especially from 1904, was the naval rivalry, which aroused mutual distrust, fear, and consequent tension at both the governmental and popular levels.

In England the anti-German group in the Foreign Office and service interpreted every German move and every German proposal to Britain with a suspicion that deepened as the years went by. The British public, too, came to regard Germany as an aggressive and hostile power. Grey wrote:

> The economic rivalry (and all that) with Germany do not give much offense to our people. . . . But they do resent mischief

making. They suspect the Emperor of aggressive plans of Welt-politik, and they see or think they see that Germany is forcing the pace in armaments in order to dominate Europe, and is therefore laying a horrible burden of wasteful expenditure upon all other powers.[9]

On the other hand, in Germany William II, with his set purpose of developing German naval power and his almost psychopathic mistrust of his Uncle Edward VII, found support among such like-minded advisers as Admiral Tirpitz, who could never be persuaded that it was not trade rivalry but naval competition that lay at the bottom of Anglo-German tension. Bülow knew better but rarely had the courage to follow the advice of such percipient counselors as Ambassador Wolff-Metternich in London and Holstein at the Wilhelmstrasse, and to oppose the big navy policy of the kaiser.

Admiral von Tirpitz's purpose, according to the memorandum attached to the law of 1900, was to protect Germany's sea trade and colonies by a "battle fleet so strong that even for the adversary with the greatest sea power a war against it would involve such dangers as to imperil his position in the world."[10] This was the famous "risk" theory. A further purpose in the minds of the kaiser and his advisers was to achieve alliance value, and bring about a British recognition of the need for agreement with Germany, or, if Britain did not respond as they hoped, to make Germany an attractive ally for France and Russia. Neither expectation was fulfilled, and England had reacted in a quite different way from that hoped for.

In 1904 the conclusion of the entente with France removed British fears of her navy. This change and the advent of Sir John Fisher as First Sea Lord both contributed to the real beginning of British war-planning against Germany. The laying down of the first dreadnought in October of the following year inaugurated a new stage in naval rivalry. Because its higher tonnage, greater speed, and increased fire-power made all other battleships obsolete, it offered Germany the possibility of building a navy on more equal terms with Britain. An additional factor in the growing Anglo-German rivalry was the

9. Grey to Roosevelt, December 1906: George Macaulay Trevelyan, *Grey of Fallodon*, p. 132.

10. "Memorandum Appended to the German Navy Bill, 1900," Archibald Hurd and Henry Castle, *German Sea Power* (London, 1914), p. 348. Cf. Tirpitz, *My Memoirs*, I, 123–24; Steinberg, *Yesterday's Deterrent*, pp. 20–21, 201; Berghahn, *Der Tirpitz-Plan*, pp. 593–94.

Cawdor program, put through by the Conservative government, providing for four large armored ships—dreadnoughts and battle cruisers —a year.

These events aroused a genuine fear in Germany of a British attack and thus helped Tirpitz and his ardent supporters in the Navy League to win Reichstag approval of a new naval bill in May 1906, to be supplemented by a law passed in February 1908, which together enhanced the fighting power of the German fleet by increasing the tonnage and cost of battleships under the 1900 law, by providing for the replacement of battleships after twenty years, instead of twenty-five, with dreadnoughts, and by adding to the number of large cruisers and destroyers. The net result was the planned construction of three dreadnoughts and one battle cruiser each year from 1908–1909 to 1911–1912, instead of three ships a year before the amendments. Also, the Kiel canal was to be deepened in order to accommodate the larger dreadnoughts. The provisions of the new bills, especially that of 1906, did not in themselves arouse so much British alarm as the strident propaganda that accompanied their discussion. Gottlieb von Jagow, who became secretary for foreign affairs in 1913, believed that it was the agitation even more than the actual fleet-building that made British antagonism so acute.[11]

Sir Eyre Crowe, in his famous memorandum of 1 January 1907, declared that "the union of the greatest military with the greatest naval Power in one State would compel the world to combine for the riddance of such an incubus."[12] Because the British believed that Germany was building a fleet in order to reach the goal of world hegemony, they could not take calmly the emergence of Germany from fifth place to second in naval power in less than a decade. In short, by 1906 Tirpitz's "risk" fleet had become the threat in British eyes that he had intended to make it.

The Liberal government that came into power in December 1905 at first accepted the Cawdor program and put through his estimate of costs for 1906–1907, but then under the leadership of Campbell-Bannerman and with the support of the radical wing of the party, sought to reduce naval expenditures in order to underwrite the social reforms of the Liberal party platform. The government argued that it was safe to mark time, because as yet no one else had any dreadnoughts. They struck one big ship from the 1906–1907 estimates and

11. *Ursachen und Ausbruch des Weltkrieges* (Berlin, 1919), pp. 25–26.
12. *BD*, III, 416 (in Appendix A).

proposed to reduce those for 1907–1908 still further unless the Second Hague Conference of 1907 failed to reduce armaments. There was a vigorous reaction to these reductions which produced a minor naval scare in the late summer and autumn of 1906, triggered by the German announcement that their first dreadnought would be larger and more heavily armed than the British. Moreover, there was little prospect that the Hague Conference would bring about any limitation of armament.

Meanwhile, efforts to bring about better Anglo-German relations through exchanges of visits among journalists and trade unionists and an overture of the German government failed to affect the basic problem of naval rivalry. Grey rejected proposals for the discussion of an Anglo-German understanding on the grounds that there were no conflicts between Britain and Germany, such as the ones that had existed between Britain and France and Britain and Russia, over which an entente might be formulated. In short, within two years of office the Liberal government had completely adopted the attitude of the Conservatives. Nevertheless, a high point in good feeling occurred with the visit of William II to England in November 1907. In both public speech-making and private talks a spirit of conciliation and friendship prevailed, as attested by both Grey and Bülow in public pronouncements and by the press in both countries.

There was apparently no formal discussion of naval matters, but the introduction of the German naval bill of 1908 into the Reichstag at the time of the kaiser's visit sounded a discordant note that created British resentment. In characteristic fashion, the kaiser later contributed to it and went far to cancel the favorable impression of his November visit. In February 1908 he wrote privately to Lord Tweedmouth, First Lord of the Admiralty, that Great Britain need not be apprehensive about the German navy because it was not aimed at Britain and did not challenge British naval supremacy. The kaiser's intentions were good, but the British, when the receipt of the letter was revealed in *The Times*, looked upon it, in the words of *The Times* correspondent, as an "attempt to influence, in German interests, the Minister responsible for our naval estimates" just before they were to go to Parliament.[13] Though Asquith in England and Bülow in Germany tried to calm excited spirits, the episode left a bad taste in the mouth. Sir John Fisher was so convinced that the kaiser's assurances masked an aggressive German design that he suggested to King

13. 6 March 1908, p. 11.

Edward a plan for "Copenhagening" the German fleet. Needless to say, the king refused to consider such an idea.

On the other hand, German mistrust was heightened when King Edward VII visited Nicholas II at Reval in June. The emptiness of press reports left room for the conjecture that the Anglo-Russian entente was being expanded by military and naval talks of European significance. The German press by its scare headlines contributed to what became another war scare, although German officialdom remained calm.

In the same month, however, unofficial talks were undertaken by Sir Ernest Cassel, a prominent British financier and friend of Edward VII, and Albert Ballin, managing director of the Hamburg-American steamship line and friend of the kaiser. Cassel explained that the king regarded the rapid development of the German navy as a threat to England and that fear was the compelling motive of his entente policy. He pointed out that England and her friends might ask Germany when she intended to call a halt to her increases in armaments. Ballin, doubtless acting on official information, replied that Cassel would render a great service to Britain and to peace if he left no doubt that such a move would involve war. Bülow confirmed this view in a circular of 25 June in which he stated that Germany would not discuss an agreement limiting her armament. "A power which demands such an agreement," he wrote, "must clearly understand that such a demand means war with us."[14] Although no doubt informed of this view, leading Englishmen discussed the naval question with Ambassador Metternich at various times during the summer—Hardinge, Grey, Lloyd George (Chancellor of the Exchequer), and Balfour (leader of the opposition). Metternich's reports of British desires for an understanding that would lessen the burden of armaments aroused the ire of William II, who commented on Metternich's despatch of 30 June 1908 that "the simplest solution is an entente or alliance with us; then all anxiety would be ended." Later and more sharply the kaiser wrote on a report of 16 July that the ambassador "must be made to feel that a good understanding with England is not desirable at the cost of the completion of Germany's fleet. If England only intends graciously to offer us her hand on condition that we reduce our fleet, that is an enormous impertinence and a gross insult to the German people and their emperor, which the ambassador must reject *a limine.* . . . If they want war, then they may begin it; we are not afraid of

14. *GP*, XXV(2), 478 (in no. 8820).

it."[15] The British government, however, was determined to raise the question of naval limitation.

What the government looked upon as a suitable occasion for discussion came when King Edward visited the kaiser at Cronberg in August 1908. Grey prepared two memoranda to guide Sir Charles Hardinge in broaching the naval question with William II. They presented the argument that the best way to improve Anglo-German relations was to stop the increase in naval spending; the British did not presume to question the right of Germany to build as large a navy as she thought necessary, but at the current rate of building, Germany in a few years would surpass Britain in the most powerful battleships; a slackening of naval expenditure on both sides would be followed by a feeling of friendliness and security, and would be welcomed everywhere, not in Germany and England alone. Hardinge carried out the instructions on 11 August and met with William II's sharp declaration that the German shipbuilding program could not possibly be modified, and that discussion of it could not be allowed, because it was a matter of national honor. This attempt to open the way to the negotiation of a slowdown marked a turning point in British diplomacy. Coupled with the Bosnian crisis that began in October 1908, the failure to win German cooperation in the limitation of shipbuilding meant that henceforth Great Britain strove the harder to strengthen the ententes as a means of maintaining the balance of power.

The drive in Great Britain for an increase in naval building in order to maintain a clear superiority over Germany developed in the winter of 1908–1909 to a hysterical climax by March 1909. The movement may have been accelerated by the *Daily Telegraph* article of 28 October 1908. It reported the Kaiser's attempt during his visit in November 1907 to prove to Colonel E. Stuart Wortley how absurd were the British fears of Germany and what a friend of England's he had been over the previous decade, particularly during the Boer war when, he asserted, he had thwarted attempts of Russia and France to create an anti-British coalition, and had made suggestions for the campaign against the Boers that led to the final British victory. The subject of a plot against England had been well aired in the press before the *Daily Telegraph* revelations, but the sensation created by the article in both Britain and Germany arose in considerable measure because of the timing in the midst of the first phase of the Bosnian crisis. Both the

15. As quoted by Brandenburg, *From Bismarck*, pp. 282, 284.

kaiser and Wortley had thought that the publication of the kaiser's remarks might help to promote Anglo-German friendship, but, as in the case of the Tweedmouth letter, it had the opposite effect. While some British newspapers, especially the *Manchester Guardian*, took a calm view of the Kaiser's "impulsive declaration," the Conservative press sought to make capital of his indiscretions in order to promote its campaign for building more dreadnoughts. In Germany the *Daily Telegraph* story led to sharp criticism of the kaiser's irresponsibility and the demand by the Social Democrats for legal changes that would limit his personal rule. Bülow in characteristic fashion, evaded most of the critical questions put to him in the Reichstag, but ended by promising that while he remained in office, such incidents would not recur. The kaiser, badly shaken by the outcry, came to terms with Bülow but never forgave him for his unenthusiastic defense of his sovereign and let him go at the first opportunity. Grey believed that the episode had shaken and shocked the pro-Germans, and that opinion had never been so wide awake and on guard with respect to Germany.

Part of the British press reacted to this awakening by demanding at least seven dreadnoughts, and the Navy League asked for eight. The government tried to remove anxiety by clarifying the two-power standard as "ten percent preponderance over the two strongest powers, whoever they might be," although Asquith, now prime minister, in the following May excluded the United States.[16] On the other hand, Field Marshal Lord Roberts told the House of Lords in November 1908 that the forces should be strengthened to meet a possible German invasion, which was "becoming every day more threatening and the undertaking every day more practicable."[17] Major attention, however, was fastened on fleet building.

When Grey told Metternich in January 1909 that at the present rate Germany would have thirteen dreadnoughts by 1912, Metternich denied the accuracy of that figure, but admitted a second point raised by Grey, that materials were being collected in advance for four capital ships. These ships, he explained, were part of the naval program for which appropriations had not yet been voted, and were not additions. Yet rumors of secret acceleration of German shipbuilding contributed to the scare of March when the naval estimates came up for debate. The furor arose not over the current situation but over the

16. Marder, *Anatomy of British Sea Power*, p. 514.

17. 23 November 1908: 4 *Parliamentary Debates*, Vol. 196, cols. 1679–95.

future. Convinced as the British were of German aggressiveness—a conviction that grew as the Bosnian crisis reached its climax in the same month—and of British sea power as the major bulwark against Germany's far-reaching designs, it followed that the bulwark should not be allowed to crumble. Britain had laid down only two dreadnoughts in 1908, but in view of the revised German program of four capital ships annually over the next four years and of German refusal to make a limitation agreement, Great Britain had to increase the number of her ships in order to keep up the standard of naval power she had set.

The panic in March was created by a complex of rumors, suspicions, mistrust, and politics, to which must be added the ardent ambition of armament manufacturers to recoup the low income of 1908. The Admiralty demanded six and wanted eight dreadnoughts in 1909–1910, the last to be laid down in March 1910. The Cabinet was at first unwilling to go that far, split as it was between the "economists," led by Lloyd George and Winston Churchill, who wanted four, and those who wanted six. But, as Churchill later wrote, it came to a "curious and characteristic solution: the Admiralty had demanded six ships; the economists offered four; and we finally compromised on eight."[18] The Liberal government, in making a strong case for increased building in order to win the approval of the Radicals, succeeded in convincing the Conservatives that the Liberal plans were inadequate. All sorts of wild statements about German shipbuilding fed the country's fears and spread the sense of panic. The upshot of the parliamentary debate was the authorization immediately of four dreadnoughts, to be supplemented in July by four more if needed. The additional four were ordered in July, making a total of eight. The program initiated in 1909 gave Britain eighteen dreadnoughts in 1912, whereas Germany, whose construction program was delayed in order to match the increased firepower of the new British ships, had only nine, instead of the thirteen predicted by Asquith or the seventeen or twenty-one that were wildly foretold during the parliamentary debate. The editor of the Navy League's *Annual* commented that the dreadnought panic of 1909 was "one of the most portentous pieces of parliamentary humbug ever practiced on the electorate."[19]

The furor in England inevitably made an impression on the German government, which tried during March to correct the erroneous figures

18. Winston S. Churchill, *The World Crisis*, p. 33.
19. As quoted by Hale, *Publicity and Diplomacy*, p. 364.

and rumors that were bandied about in England. The British received their corrections with skepticism, and Grey three times suggested that the naval attachés be permitted to visit shipyards and make reports on the actual progress of construction in order to allay suspicions, but Tirpitz refused. Others in Germany noted the British fever with growing alarm, among them Holstein, whose last bit of advice before his death was a note of 6 April 1909 to Bülow urging him to push through a rapprochement with England. Even Tirpitz became willing to negotiate with Britain in the hope of limiting her dreadnought program. The kaiser, however, remained obdurately opposed to naval talks until April 1909, when he authorized them along lines proposed by Tirpitz. Kiderlen-Waechter, still at the Foreign Office before returning to his post at Bucharest, unofficially talked with the British ambassador about the possibility of a political agreement that would obviate naval rivalry, but the British thought his suggestions were incompatible with the French and Russian ententes and made no reply. At the same time another factor entered British calculations: the announcement that both Austria-Hungary and Italy were planning to increase the size of their fleets. The Austrian addition to Mediterranean naval power was looked upon as a supplement to the German fleet. In announcing the decision to make the four contingent dreadnoughts a part of the 1909–1910 program, the British government emphasized the Austro-Hungarian and Italian plans.

Despite the lack of response to Kiderlen's feeler, Bülow persisted in seeking an understanding with Britain. Schoen drew up a sketch of a broad agreement covering political, trade, colonial, naval, and Bagdad-railway accords, and Wilhelm von Stumm, director of the political section at the Wilhelmstrasse and former secretary of embassy in London, visited England, 28 April to 6 May, to explore the ground. Although he did not deem it advisable to broach the details of a treaty, he made it clear that there could be no slowdown in shipbuilding without a general political understanding. In concluding his report on his trip to London, Stumm was of the opinion that England would be ready for a far-reaching rapprochement if it were possible to make concessions on the fleet question of such importance as to allay genuinely and lastingly mistrust of official circles and public opinion. Bülow, on his part, pushed for a naval agreement in May and June, arguing that since the Liberal government might be overturned because of the expense of the shipbuilding program, and the Conservatives might come into power on the promise of ending the German menace, Germany must do her best to keep the Liberals in office. Tirpitz, on the other hand, did not believe in the danger of a preventive war and reasoned that there must first be a political détente, then an entente, and only after that an agreement on the limitation of armaments; but Bülow made no headway toward an understanding before his resignation in July.

Before Bethmann Hollweg became chancellor on 14 July, another fruitless unofficial attempt at Anglo-German naval talks was initiated by Albert Ballin, who wanted to bring Admiral Tirpitz and Sir John Fisher together, arguing that the responsible heads of the respective fleets might come to an agreement more readily than the diplomats. With the approval of the kaiser and Tirpitz, he secured the agreement with his scheme of his friend Cassel, but Tirpitz was not pleased with the results he had obtained, and Bethmann Hollweg canceled any further moves, insisting that naval discussions should be conducted through regular diplomatic channels and should not even include Tirpitz.

The new chancellor, according to Otto Hammann, head of the press bureau at the Foreign Office, was firmly convinced that friendly relations with Great Britain had to be established by means of a naval truce, and regarded this goal as his chief task in foreign affairs. He was supported in his objective by Kiderlen-Waechter, whom he consulted in Bucharest; by the kaiser; and to a certain extent by Tirpitz, who in August agreed to talks involving a British pledge that her treaties and ententes were not directed against Germany. Kiderlen expatiated upon the need for a general understanding, for, since Britain could cause Germany trouble in many areas, Germany had to avoid the situation that France had faced at Fashoda, and could not satisfy her needs by a purely naval agreement. Moreover, there had to be a general political understanding in order to win public opinion, which would not accept a fleet restriction alone; to begin with political relations would be easier than making a naval agreement that would run into technical difficulties certain to be raised by both admiralties. Kiderlen's thinking reflected the conclusions to which Bülow and members of the Foreign Office had come, and to which Bethmann himself subscribed.

Even before he received Kiderlen's advice Bethmann had opened discussions with Ambassador Goschen, 21 August, saying that in response to England's repeated declarations in favor of a limitation of naval expenditures, he would shortly make a proposal, but that a discussion would be useless unless it formed part of a general political understanding that would preclude any possibility of an Anglo-

German war. This point of view was already well known in London, where the Cabinet decided to encourage negotiations while recognizing the difficulties in seeking a political agreement. They replied to Bethmann's overture that they would cordially welcome naval proposals and would receive sympathetically proposals for a political understanding, but intimated that a naval agreement had to precede a political understanding. Grey, in a private letter to Goschen, explained that there was nothing in the British agreements with France and Russia directed against Germany and hence nothing to prevent a friendly arrangement with her. He continued:

> But we have no general political understanding formulated either with Russia or France; and to do with Germany what has not been done with Russia and France would look as if we were intending to change friends. I want a good understanding with Germany, but it must be one which will not imperil those which we have with France and Russia.

He thought the best solution would be some "formula to which they might also be parties," though he recognized that France could not participate in anything that appeared to confirm the loss of Alsace-Lorraine.[20]

Hence, even before Bethmann made his formal proposals to Goschen, Germany and Great Britain were poles apart on the content and procedure of an understanding. Germany wanted a political agreement involving neutrality in case of war as a condition for a naval agreement, whereas Britain envisaged a naval accord first and such a political agreement as would not jeopardize her ententes with France and Russia. These differences in outlook and approach doomed the intermittent discussions of two and a half years to failure. Furthermore, through exchanges in October and November 1909 another contradiction in viewpoints emerged. Whereas Bethmann declared that there could be no reduction in the ship-building program, but only a retardation, Grey made it clear that an agreement must provide for a definite reduction in the program and in expenditure. Bethmann countered by representing a retardation of building to be a great concession and proposed an agreement by which the two powers would declare that neither contemplated aggression and that in case either were attacked by a third party, the other would observe neutrality.

20. 1 September 1909: *BD*, VI, no. 195. Cf. Hardinge to Goschen, 26 April 1910: Lowe and Dockrill, *Mirage of Power*, III, 431.

The British government, however, disappointed in Bethmann's position, dropped further negotiations in view of the parliamentary crisis and impending elections.

During the lull in discussions of the naval question the Bagdad railway problem arose because of British efforts to obtain from Turkey a concession for a railroad in Mesopotamia where British interests lay. When the Turks appealed to Germany for aid in dealing with the British requests, Arthur von Gwinner, director of the *Deutsche Bank*, undertook to find a formula that would satisfy British, German, and Turkish interests. In December 1909 he suggested to Sir Ernest Cassel the creation of a new company to construct the line from Bagdad to the Persian Gulf, in which British interests would have virtual control. The British government found the proposal unsatisfactory, mainly because they believed that the proposed 50 percent share in the new Company was not enough to assure control. Moreover, Grey insisted that any Anglo-German agreement concerning the Bagdad railway had to have the approval of both Russia and France, who had agreed that a settlement with Germany had to be made *à quatre*. When in March 1910 Grey suggested that a preliminary arrangement over the Bagdad and Persian railways might be made, Bethmann asserted that these questions should form part of the general political agreement he had proposed in the previous year. He pointed out that he could not withstand the Pan-Germans and the press unless he could get something in return for such a valuable concession as the line from Bagdad to the Gulf. Again, he maintained that the Bagdad and Persian railways questions should be incorporated in a political understanding. The anti-German group in the British Foreign Office received Bethmann's statements with great indignation and no doubt influenced Grey to look upon them as an unsatisfactory basis for further discussion. Accordingly, he failed to answer Bethmann, and once more explained to Goschen that Britain could enter no political agreement that would separate her from France and Russia, that no understanding with Germany would be acceptable unless it meant the cessation of increases in naval expenditures, and that, while England did not want to deprive Germany of the Bagdad concession, she did not want to let Germany have the only door for trade in Mesopotamia.

After the brief exchanges of March and April 1910, Bethmann opened the way for a resumption of negotiations in July when he told Goschen that he feared remarks of Prime Minister Asquith in the debates on the naval budget would mislead the public by giving the impression that Germany had rejected British proposals for a reduc-

tion in armaments, whereas Germany had made clear that some allevi-
ation could be brought about by temporarily reducing the rate of
construction. Upon receipt of these remarks the British government
reconsidered the whole question and shifted its position in a memorandum of 29 July that was sent to Germany. The government was
now prepared to abandon its previous insistence that an agreement
had to be based upon a reduction of the German naval program; it
was ready to discuss retardation in the rate of construction, and to
negotiate on the basis that the existing German program should not
be increased and that an exchange of information would assure each
country of knowing the actual progress in shipbuilding by the other.
As for a political agreement, the memorandum stated:

> There would be difficulty in accepting any formula which would
> give the impression of an understanding different in kind from
> that which exists between His Majesty's Government and any
> other European Power, and might therefore affect adversely the
> relations between His Majesty's Government and certain other
> Powers, unless these Powers could also be parties to it. His
> Majesty's Government have, however, always been ready to give
> assurances that there is nothing in any agreement between them-
> selves and any other Power which is directed against Germany,
> and that they themselves have no hostile intentions respecting
> her.[21]

In communicating these statements Goschen asked the chancellor
what precisely was meant by a retardation of the rate of construction, but got the impression that Bethmann himself was not clear
about it, for, he said, the question was best left to the naval experts.

Bethmann, in his formal reply of 12 October, reiterated his willingness to discuss a retardation but offered no suggestions concerning
the exact nature of an arrangement. With reference to a pledge not
to enlarge the German program, he asked what equivalent engagement the British would make. As for the proposal to exchange naval
information, he accepted it in principle but was very skeptical of its
practical value. He still believed that a political agreement could be
formulated, and impressed Goschen with his sincere desire to establish better Anglo-German relations. On the other hand, he complained
that the British had often opposed German interests even when the

21. Memorandum, 29 July 1910: *BD*, VI, no. 387.

interests of both countries were identical. He added that if the British people had not been taught by their government to regard Germany as their enemy, the expansion of the German fleet would have caused no more concern than that of the United States.

Like his declarations of the previous April, Bethmann's memorandum of October drew forth vitriolic comments in the British Foreign Office. Sir Eyre Crowe agreed with Bethmann that "it is not merely or even principally the question of naval armaments which is the cause of the existing estrangements," for the building of the German fleet "is but a symptom of the disease. It is the political ambitions of the German government and nation which are the source of the mischief."[22] While new general elections in England again deferred consideration of the chancellor's communication, Grey in November made a preliminary reply in which he reported a favorable impression of the German willingness to exchange information but deep resentment of Bethmann's allegation that the British government had taught the people to look upon Germany as an enemy. Grey asserted that "German complaint of English unfriendliness has been practically chronic." Moreover, Germany had recurrently made demands upon Britain as the price of continuing friendship. Grey would lose all hope of bettering Anglo-German relations if Bethmann seriously expected that "His Majesty's Government should abandon the protection of British interests whenever their maintenance is looked upon by the German Government as an obstacle to some enterprise or ambition of their own."[23]

In January 1911, after the elections, Goschen communicated to the German government the views of the Admiralty concerning an exchange of information. The British wanted to treat the subject independently of negotiations over naval and political questions, hence did not raise the matter of a pledge not to increase the German naval program. At length, in March, the British position concerning a political agreement went to Berlin as a formal reply to Bethmann's memorandum of October and as a basis for further negotiation. The British memorandum again reiterated the familiar line that British arrangements with other powers were not directed against Germany and that such an agreement as Bethmann had suggested would go farther than any accord Britain had made with other powers. The British government felt that

22. Memorandum, 20 October 1910: ibid., no. 404.
23. Grey to Goschen, 23 November 1910: ibid., no. 414.

in any general formula care must be taken to avoid on the one hand undue vagueness and on the other the risk of possible misunderstanding. With this object [in mind] His Majesty's Government think that an endeavor to come to an agreement upon certain specific questions should form part of the negotiations.[24]

The Bagdad and Persian railways were suggested as examples of specific questions. Thus the British had assented to the German view that a wider agreement than one dealing with naval expenditures was necessary, but declared that they assumed that discussion of the subject would not be delayed and would proceed so as to bring about an accord simultaneously with the political understanding.

The German reply in the form of an aide-mémoire of 9 May 1911 seemed to represent a step backward concerning a naval understanding, for it asserted that the slow progress in negotiations had not only prevented any retardation in German shipbuilding up to the current year, but also compelled Germany to forego for the future the original intention of retarding the execution of the naval laws. Despite this shift in intentions, however, Germany would be happy to continue an exchange of views over a naval agreement beyond the proposed exchange of information. Moreover, the German government still believed a political agreement to be a necessary corollary of a naval arrangement. The tone of the mémoire was friendly, but the content, as Grey minuted, was "most unsatisfactory." Nevertheless, after long negotiations Britain and Germany did finally agree, in January 1912, upon how to exchange information about shipbuilding, the one achievement of their three-year debate over the naval question. The "Panther's spring" at Agadir on 1 July 1911, however, prevented further conversations about a general naval and political agreement until the Haldane mission of 1912.

The failure to achieve concrete results in the negotiations of 1909–1911 can be attributed to both governments. Bernadotte Schmitt has put the reasons succinctly:

The British insisted on both their naval supremacy and their diplomatic combinations, for thus the balance of power was turned against Germany. To restore the balance in their favor the Germans wished to retain their freedom in the matter of armaments or to break the Triple Entente. The position of each was

24. Same to same, 8 March 1911: ibid., no. 468.

logical, so long as the theory of equilibrium was the mainspring of European diplomacy.[25]

It must also be noted that in both countries there were powerful political and public-opinion factors that hampered the negotiations. In Germany, except for occasional conciliatory gestures, the kaiser and Admiral von Tirpitz tied the chancellor's hands when it came to matters of naval expenditure. They were backed by "the Navy League, the Defense League, the Conservatives and National Liberals, and the rest of the Pan-Germans, the participating heavy industries and their allies of the press," who were not willing to sacrifice a single battleship for the sake of British friendship.[26] Bethmann and Kiderlen, moreover, repeated in 1911 the mistake that Bülow and Holstein had made in 1905, and in the Agadir crisis destroyed any chance of a genuine betterment of Anglo-German relations.

On the other hand, the British were no more flexible or conciliatory. They were, if anything, even more suspicious and mistrustful than the Germans. Crowe's minute of 24 October 1910 that the kaiser, Bethmann, Tirpitz, and the rest "are none of them to be believed on their word" reflected the atmosphere of the Foreign Office.[27] The March 1909 dreadnought panic had molded the stereotypes of German behavior that persisted and became hardened as the years went by. Sir Charles Hardinge, permanent undersecretary of state for foreign affairs, 1906–1910, well expressed the gospel: "I fully believe in the theory of Germany's intention if possible to dominate Europe, to which we are the only stumbling block." As for the navy, "The only thing we can do is to go on building, and to make our position so absolutely secure that no sane man could ever dream that he would gain an advantage by attacking us."[28] Grey, however, translated these ideas into the language of politics when he told Metternich in June 1909 that keeping Germany in check "was a question of preventing the balance of power from being destroyed."[29] Consequently, the British could not yield what was necessary for a genuine Anglo-German understanding. To have done so would have meant the reversal of the diplomatic revolution, to the completion of which German naval building had provided a major stimulus.

25. The Coming of the War, I, 56.
26. Theodor Wolff, The Eve of 1914, p. 28.
27. BD, VI, 533.
28. As quoted by Steiner, Foreign Office, p. 101.
29. Grey to Goschen, 9 June 1909: BD, VI, no. 182.

Chapter 9

The Agadir

Crisis, 1911

The resolution of the Franco-German conflict over Morocco centered in Berlin, where French Ambassador Jules Cambon dealt with Baron William Eduard von Schoen, secretary for foreign affairs, and his successor, Alfred von Kiderlen-Waechter. The French ministers of foreign affairs concerned with the problem were Stephen Pichon in 1909 and 1910–1911; Jean Cruppi, March to June 1911; and Justin de Selves, in the government of Joseph Caillaux. Chancellor Bethmann Hollweg was involved on the German side, as were Kiderlen's assistants: at the Foreign Office, Arthur Zimmermann and Langwerth von Simmern; in Paris, Ambassador Schoen and Embassy Counselor Oskar von der Lancken; and in London, Ambassador Metternich. Frenchmen who took minor parts in the conflict were Georges Louis, head of the political section at the Quai d'Orsay, Théophile Delcassé, minister of marine, and André Tardieu, foreign editor of Le Temps. *British statesmen involved in the Moroccan affair were Foreign Secretary Sir Edward Grey, Chancellor of the Exchequer Lloyd George, and Prime Minister Herbert H. Asquith, with Sir Arthur Nicolson, permanent undersecretary at the Foreign Office, acting as counselor. Russia's diplomats were Ambassador Alexander Petrovich Izvolsky at Paris, Count Benckdorff at London, and Count Osten-Sacken at Berlin, all under the direction of A. A. Neratov, acting foreign minister.*

Although France had hailed the outcome of the Algeciras conference because it demonstrated her strong diplomatic position, the policy to be pursued in Morocco encountered greater difficulties than before. Not only did most Frenchmen want peace and the avoidance of conflict, but a small minority, led by Jean Jaurès, spokesman of the socialists, roundly condemned the imperialistic policy that had brought about the conflict with Germany. On the other hand, for many Frenchmen the Act of Algeciras meant nothing if it did not make possible, under the cover of "internationalization," the continuing expansion of French influence in the sherifian empire. Delcassé had succinctly summarized the significance of Morocco, and his words supplied the grounds for seeking preponderance there: "Morocco, placed under our influence, is our North African empire fortified. Subjected to a foreign influence, it is for the same empire a threat and paralysis."[1]

I.

At every turn, however, France found that her obligations in Moroccan finances and police could not well be fulfilled without the accusation that she was stepping beyond the bounds of the Algeciras Act. If France remained true to the international formula, she had to sacrifice special interests that she had been seeking; if she served those interests, she violated the Act and gave other powers, notably Germany, grounds for complaints and fresh conflicts. Germany, on the other hand, was determined to maintain the rights of equal economic opportunity under the Act and tried to exercise them in seeking economic concessions. For both France and Germany the basic question often arose as to when economic activity became political, to which each frequently gave a contrary answer. Also, given the state of unrest and near-anarchy in Morocco, acts of France often seemed to overstep the police powers that had been granted her.

Although the Clemenceau government (October 1906 to July 1909) was opposed to the "national solution" of the Moroccan question, the conditions inside Morocco and the German rivalry there made very difficult, if not impossible, the implementation of the Act of Algeciras. The country was virtually bankrupt, the maghzen saturated with corruption, and the regular troops, the *méhalla*, created in 1877 by the French, an ineffective force. French efforts at reform turned the natives against them, and French reprisals for assassinations and mob violence gave rise to German accusations that France was violating the mandate of Algeciras. Both Frenchmen and Germans, especially business interests, urged an understanding between the two countries, but efforts in 1907 to arrive at one were fruitless, although France and Germany did finally agree at the end of 1908 to recognize Mulay Hafid, who had rebelled against his brother, as the new sultan. The

1. Quoted by Joseph Caillaux, *D'Agadir à la grande pénitence*, p. 15.

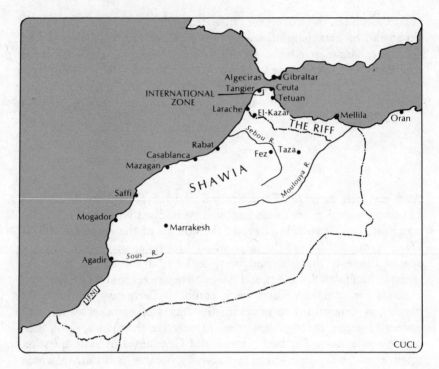

I. Morocco, 1911

Casablanca affair of September 1908 and the Bosnian crisis of October, however, finally forced the two powers to face squarely the problem of Morocco over which they had been sparring since 1906. For France the situation in the late summer of 1908 was the more stressful because of her anxiety over Britain's inadequate military preparations and her own luke-warm relations with Russia. On the other hand, the Bosnian crisis, the continued pressure of German business circles interested in the Sherifian empire, and the pro-French attitude of Austria-Hungary undoubtedly influenced Berlin in the direction of an agreement with France.

At Casablanca on the morning of 25 September 1908 the French harbor commandant arrested five deserters from the French Foreign Legion who were attempting with the aid of the German consul to escape on a German steamer lying off the port. Germany at first demanded the release of the three Germans among the deserters, but later proposed arbitration that France accepted. Though tension mounted again in the autumn when Germany returned to her demand for the release of the three Germans, France stubbornly insisted that they await the arbitral award. Great Britain and Russia loyally supported the French stand, and Francis Joseph urged the kaiser to settle the affair amicably. The German government gave up its demands and agreed with France to exchange notes of regrets and to refer the question of fact and of law to the Hague Tribunal. The Tribunal handed down a judgment in May 1909 that censured the German consul for aiding the escape of non-German legionaries and the French authorities for needless violence in the arrest of the deserters.

The Casablanca incident, however, failed to deter the efforts of both Germans and Frenchmen to reach an understanding that would assure the French of political preponderance in Morocco and the Germans of an open door there. The kaiser, upon the onset of the Bosnian crisis, urged Bülow to settle the Moroccan affair quickly and finally; Morocco would be French, he asserted, and Germany should get out of it with good grace in order to end the frictions with France now that "great questions are at stake."[2] In addition Foreign Office memoranda helped to move Bülow toward an agreement. He was the more willing, moreover, to establish good relations with France in order to lessen the possibility of her intervention on the side of Russia in the Bosnian controversy. Men in France also favored an understanding: Georges Louis, head of the political section at the

---

2. William II to Bülow, 6 October 1908: *GP*, XXIV, 441, note **.

Quai d'Orsay, pushed for it, and André Tardieu, foreign editor of *Le Temps,* ardently worked for it. French Foreign Minister Pichon, although he had no desire to become embroiled in the Russo-Austro-Hungarian conflict, wanted to avoid the appearance of disloyalty to Russia in coming to an understanding with Germany. Accordingly, when at last, 6 January 1909, Secretary of State Wilhelm Eduard von Schoen suggested an exchange of ideas to Ambassador Jules Cambon, Pichon instructed the ambassador to take Schoen's remarks as the resumption of the 1907 discussions, because a negotiation opened in 1907 "would not have any apparent link with the events in the East."[3]

The proposals and counterproposals that followed during January indicated that the principal stumbling block was the insistence of France that her preponderant political influence in Morocco be recognized by Germany. Finally, 27 January, Schoen conceded the point, although to the end he refused to write a flat statement of French political preponderance into the text of the agreement. In drafting the text, Cambon worked mainly with Kiderlen-Waechter, who had been called to the Foreign Office from Bucharest during Schoen's illness in December. Cambon and Kiderlen completed their work by 3 February, and after the French government gave its approval, Cambon and Schoen signed the accord on 9 February.

The significant points in the agreement were the French resolve to "safeguard economic equality in the Sherifian empire," and the German declaration that she was "pursuing only economic interests" there, and her recognition of the "special political interests of France." Furthermore, both declared that "they would seek to associate their nationals in affairs for which they were able to obtain concessions," but that Germans would "not be candidates for the functions of directors or counsellors" or instructors in public services having or likely to have a "political character." It is noteworthy that although Germany did not renounce a political interest explicitly, the circumlocutions of the declaration were made precise in a letter of explanation by Cambon that formed the basis of French policy until Agadir. Furthermore, Germany, in accepting the letter, recognized the superior economic position of France even in cooperative ventures.[4] Germany had taken a long step toward the recognition of French predominance in Morocco, a position incompatible with a strict interpretation of the Act of Algeciras.

3. Pichon to J. Cambon, 9 January 1909: 2 *DDF,* XI, no. 604.
4. The texts: *GP,* XXIV, nos. 8490–92.

The French reception of the agreement, though generally favorable because of the relaxation of tension after the Casablanca affair, was mixed. The colonial group regarded it as removing the major obstacle to French preponderence in the Sherifian empire, and the commercial and industrial groups who had already veered toward closer cooperation with German businessmen were pleased. On the other hand, staunch upholders of the Triple Entente, like Paul Cambon and Camille Barrère, distrusted German motives and good faith, while officials in Morocco and with some exceptions at the Quai d'Orsay opposed the agreement. Clemenceau seems to have grudgingly approved the accord, not because of any enthusiasm for French progress in Morocco, but because of the European situation in which he wished to safeguard France from a too exclusive dependence upon either Russia or Britain, as the tensions mounted in the one case over Bosnia and in the other over naval rivalry.

Because the agreement was basically the result of the European rather than the Moroccan situation, the reaction of other powers was predictable. Izvolsky voiced Russian resentment, declaring that Austria-Hungary would now feel that she had a free hand in the Bosnian affair. Aehrenthal rejoiced over the accord, as did Tittoni with less reason. Although London initially received the news of the agreement cordially, largely because of the relaxation of Franco-German tension, there was an undercurrent of skepticism concerning the effect upon others of the envisaged Franco-German economic association and, on Grey's part, some fear of a slackening of French loyalty. Grey was also concerned over what he thought was shabby treatment of Spain by the French. Spain herself felt aggrieved that the agreement had been negotiated and concluded without any communication with her; but in order to quiet Spain's fears of being pushed aside, Pichon drew up a protocol stating that in view of assurances given by France and Germany, the Spanish government would accept with satisfaction "an act destined to bring about definitively . . . a harmony with which the prosperity of the Sherifian empire" was "closely linked." Germany, at length, yielded to requests from both Great Britain and France and signed the protocol.[5]

The Franco-German agreement enjoyed a honeymoon until the end of 1909. By the next year, however, the difficulty of making satisfactory arrangements for economic collaboration and the mistrust that accompanied the negotiations brought about a failure to achieve the

5. 2 *DDF*, XII, nos. 80, 186.

anticipated results. The three major areas of failure were mining, railroad construction in both Morocco and central Africa, and exploitation of the Congo. In all three types of enterprise, private industrial and trading companies tried to create consortia and to involve the governments in their schemes; where the initiative lay in each case is often difficult to decide. Tardieu asserted that Morocco showed how hard it was to mix politics with business without compromising business enterprises, and a French diplomat emphatically declared that it was not business men and financiers who kept the accord of 1909 from working.[6] Nor was it always French versus Germans, for in the case of mining concessions a Franco-German group opposed a German group that had drawn in French collaborators.

Especially complicated were attempts at collaboration in building public works. In February 1910 business firms, with the approval of their governments, formed the Moroccan Society of Public Works. The proposed projects came to naught, however, because of disagreement between France and Germany over procedures and over railroad construction and management. A major issue arose over a proposed railroad line that the French insisted was for military purposes hence was to be built only by French military engineers, but that the Germans believed should be built and operated by the Moroccan Society. Operation of the line was a stumbling block to agreement, for a French minister declared: "We don't want German station masters in Morocco."[7] Nevertheless agreement was almost reached in early March 1911, when the Briand government fell, but the Monis cabinet which followed temporized until the Panther's spring on 1 July relegated such matters to the scrapheap of unfulfilled expectations.

Yet another venture, not connected with Morocco but projected as a result of efforts at Franco-German collaboration, was the Ngoko Sangha affair. Without going into all the details, the enterprise was an attempt, first discussed in 1909, to create a consortium of French and German companies to exploit the resources of a vast concession held by the Ngoko Sangha Company in the French Congo. Germans and British had infiltrated the area, and the Company tried to get an indemnity from the French government because of its failure to keep

6. Eugene Staley, *War and the Private Investor*, p. 483, note 2. Pierre Guillen claims that it was British opposition that blocked Franco-German cooperation in railway concessions: "Les questions coloniales dans les relations franco-allemandes," *RH*, CCXLVIII (1972), 90–91. But Lowe and Dockrill, *Mirage of Power*, I, 37–39, blame the French.

7. André Tardieu, *Le mystère d'Agadir*, p. 82.

out the interlopers and because of loss of territory through a frontier rectification in 1908. The Company made the payment of the indemnity a condition of its entry into the proposed consortium. Although the Briand government in 1910 agreed to the payment of the indemnity and favored the projected consortium, opposition arose in the Chamber of Deputies where Caillaux, for political reasons, condemned the proposed indemnity as a "job" of the worst description. A new project for Franco-German collaboration in the Congo, May 1911, was approved by Caillaux, now minister of finance in the Monis government, and won the interest of Kiderlen-Waechter. It languished at the Quai d'Orsay, however, until the events of July buried it along with the project for Moroccan railroads.

The failure of efforts at economic collaboration within and without Morocco, accompanied in the first half of 1911 by French military advances in Morocco, convinced the Germans that they were getting the short end of the stick and would lose out altogether, despite the agreement of 1909, if they did not make a dramatic stand for some kind of compensation. Up to the fall of the Briand government in March 1911 they had some hope of achieving cooperation, but Jean Cruppi, foreign minister in the Monis government (March to 23 June 1911) seemed to change course from that followed by his predecessor with respect not only to collaboration but also the French policy pursued in the Sherifian empire.

II.

By 1911 the situation in Morocco was rapidly going from bad to worse. A French loan contracted with Mulay Hafid in May 1910 covered a multitude of unpaid past obligations but so encumbered the revenue and at the same time so entrenched the French in military and financial management that Mulay Hafid clearly became a French puppet. Moreover, efforts of the maghzen to raise additional revenue to meet current needs added fuel to the flames of unrest which by January 1911 had led to the open defiance of the sultan by several Moorish chieftains. French efforts to contract a new loan in February were blocked by Spain and Germany because they felt that the terms of the loan gave the French increased power without offering them any compensation. Thus the sultan found himself in the same hopeless position as his predecessor, Abdul Aziz, whose plight had enabled Mulay Hafid himself to gain power. Without an effective mili-

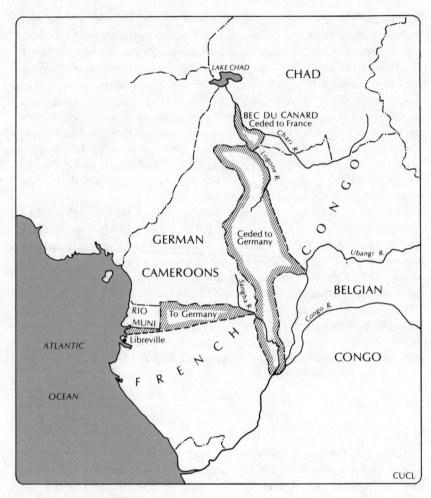

II. The Franco-German Congo Agreement, 1911

tary force he could not successfully crush the growing rebellion; without adequate income he could not support a military force. His use of the *méhalla*, instructed and officered by the French, only increased the resentment against him as subservient to the hated foreign power.

The French government, too, faced a difficult problem, especially after the middle of January, when an attack by the Zaer tribe on a French army unit in the Shawia, the hinterland of Casablanca, caused the death of Lieutenant Marchand and four other officers. Two opposing pressures developed: on the one hand, a group led by Jaurès demanded the withdrawal from the Shawia, and, on the other, the *Comité du Maroc* and its supporters stridently insisted that Marchand's killers be promptly punished and that an energetic policy in the whole of Morocco be pursued. Time, moreover, was running out for the exercise of French police power in Morocco, for the Act of Algeciras provided that France (and Spain) should organize police in eight ports for five years from the ratification of the Act, namely, until 11 December 1911. Already France had overstepped the Act by occupying the Shawia for three and a half years. Could she expect the acceptance, especially by Germany and Spain, of a further extension inland of her police powers? In March came news of an alliance among the tribes of the Gharb (north of the Shawia) against Mulay Hafid, and fast upon it the request for reinforcements by General Moinier commanding the French forces in the area. By mid-March the French faced the question of whether or not to succor the sultan in his capital city of Fez, whence *méhalla* had been despatched against a rebellious tribe, leaving only a small force in the city.

The French government claimed that it was responsible for the protection of Europeans in the capital city, although the provisions of Algeciras could hardly be stretched that far. Throughout March, moreover, conflicting testimony filtered out concerning the extent and even the existence of danger at Fez. The German consul there consistently reported that there was none, and his view was corroborated by most European agents, including the Russian. Early in April Cruppi informed the powers that if the situation did not improve, France would be compelled to assure the safety of the European colony at Fez by military measures. After further alarming reports on 18 April that Fez was isolated and communications broken off, Cruppi and War Minister Berteaux decided to send a flying column of French troops from Casablanca to Fez in order to reinforce the weak *méhalla* forces, which were inadequate for the relief of the allegedly belea-

guered city. The Council of Ministers ratified the decision on 22
April, but it was not until the 28th, after reports of a worsened situation and the sultan's request (upon French prompting) for French aid,
that a French company began the fateful march to Fez.

Among the powers to whom Cruppi had communicated French
actions, Austria-Hungary, significantly, adopted a waiting attitude and
failed to criticize France, whose assurances of respect for the Act of
Algeciras the Ballhausplatz seemed to take at face value. Italy received the news of the march to Fez with "sympathy and good will,"
reported Barrère, but was nevertheless nervous over developments in
the Mediterranean because of fear that some power might lay hands
on her promised land of Tripoli. Russia watched the French action
with some concern, and although she made only mild representations
at Berlin on behalf of France, Acting Foreign Minister Neratov instructed Izvolsky to express the hope in Paris "that we may be supported if necessary in like fashion by France."[8] More forthrightly
than Russia, Great Britain supported the French policy and action,
even though the Foreign Office recognized that France was acting
beyond the limits of her obligations under the Act of Algeciras; Sir
Arthur Nicolson, undersecretary for foreign affairs since October
1910, told Paul Cambon as early as 5 April that if France went to
Fez to protect Europeans, "you will arrive too late, and if to assure
the sultan's throne, you will be obliged to stay there because once
your troops leave they will cut off his head."[9]

Repercussions from the march to Fez concerned the British: in
respect to Germany, of course, for the failure of their own effort
to achieve a naval agreement had heightened the suspicion and mistrust that colored the interpretation of every German move; and in
relation to Spain, because from the time of the Entente Cordiale,
Britain had acted as umpire between the Latin sisters. In mid-April
Cruppi himself recognized the possibility of a Franco-German crisis,
and accordingly suggested that "it behooved the French and British
governments to carry matters further as regards possible co-operation in certain eventualities than had hitherto been done." He wanted
not a convention but an understanding on "what the joint action
should be in case they had to co-operate." His suggestion had been
anticipated if not inspired by a talk between the British military

8. Neratov to Izvolsky, 5 May/22 April 1911: Siebert and Schreiner, *Entente
Diplomacy*, no. 675.

9. P. Cambon to his son, 5 April 1911: *Correspondance*, II, 313.

attaché and General Foch. The latter expressed his conviction of the urgent necessity for an understanding concerning the "form which joint action should take in the event of a war between France and Germany." Grey called Cruppi's suggestion to the attention of Prime Minister Asquith, and approved, at least tacitly, the military conversations that were ultimately concluded in July.[10] Grey's basic principle in dealing with Morocco was to support France for the sake of the Entente, and he did so both publicly and in discussion with the German ambassador.

Spain presented a more troublesome problem than Germany up to the end of June. She was suspected by both the French and the British, without specific evidence, of acting as a tool of the Germans. After the Franco-German agreement of 1909, Spain had watched French moves in Morocco with growing apprehension. She warned France early in April 1911 that an occupation of Taza (near Fez) or Fez, even if temporary, would upset the balance in Morocco, and would lead Spain to occupy her zone as agreed upon in 1904. Later, on the eve of the march to Fez, Perez Caballero, the Spanish ambassador at Paris, reminded Cruppi of the possible repercussions upon the situation in northern Morocco. Spain's attitude was ominous, for if Spain carried out her threat to move into Morocco, the French contention that the Act of Algerciras was still in force would be proved false.

Cruppi, in his efforts to restrain the Spaniards, called upon Russia and Britain for help. While Izvolsky advised Cruppi to come to an agreement with Spain in order to keep her from Germany's arms, Grey responded by advising Spain to await developments before acting. "It would be most unwise," he said, "for Spain to force partition of Morocco; the political consequences would be deplorable."[11] A lively three-way exchange ensued, mainly in an effort to find some compromise in the face of Spain's insistence upon her rights under the 1904 secret treaty, but Spain went her way. She moved troops near Tetuan in mid-May and occupied Larache and El-Kazar on 8 and 9 June. Like France, and later Germany, Spain justified her action by the need to protect her nationals, two of whom had been killed. The Spanish move alarmed the French because of its possible effect upon

10. Bertie to Grey, 13 April 1911: *BD*, VII, no. 207; Colonel Fairholme to Bertie, 8 April 1911: *BD*, VI, no. 460; Grey, *Twenty-Five Years*, I, 91–93. Cf. S. J. Williamson, *Politics of Grand Strategy*, pp. 136–41, 170–77; Paul G. Halpern, *The Mediterranean Naval Situation, 1908–1914* (Cambridge, Mass., 1971), pp. 9–11.

11. Grey to Bunsen (in Madrid), 1 May 1911: *BD*, VII, no. 238.

German policy, and irritated Grey, who warned Spain that "if Spain by tearing up the secret agreement with France forces a partition of Morocco there is no certainty that her zone will be recognized."[12] The big question, however, was how Germany would behave.

When Jules Cambon told Secretary of State Kiderlen on 4 April, and repeated his words in writing the next day, that France might have to send a column to Fez in order to facilitate the departure of Europeans, and to occupy Rabat from which to punish the Zaers for the death of Marchand, Kiderlen warned that such moves would disagreeably affect German public opinion, and that the occupation of Rabat would be regarded as a step toward the destruction of Algeciras. He cautioned Jules Cambon that France should go slowly and suggested an exchange of ideas with Germany should the contemplated steps be regarded as necessary. He went further than that on the 6th, however, declaring that "if the sovereignty of the sultan should happen to disappear, Germany would leave you free to do what you like with Morocco, provided that you concede her a port, Mogodor, for example, and not more. Meanwhile it is necessary to maintain the present state of things."[13]

Cambon, who had no authority to go into the implications of Kiderlen's hint about compensation for French freedom of action, stressed the temporary character of the contemplated action in Fez and Rabat, but met with skepticism. The exchange of notes in Berlin and the full report of the discussions between the 4th and the 8th should have alerted Cruppi to the complications that might arise if France followed the course of action he had in mind. He declared to Izvolsky on 13 April, however, that a "completely friendly exchange of ideas" between Cambon and Kiderlen was taking place in Berlin.[14]

On 17 April Cambon reported to the German Foreign Office the disquieting news that Paris had received from Fez and the decision of the government to reinforce its troops in Casablanca. Undersecretary Zimmermann protested that Germany had received satisfactory news and hoped that France would not resort to military measures within the Moroccan interior. Upon further news from Paris of the encirclement of Fez and the sultan's appeal for aid, Bethmann asserted that

12. Grey to Rennie (in Madrid), 15 June 1911: ibid., no. 323.

13. Jules Cambon, "Premier conversation avec M. de Kiderlen Waechter," 6 April 1911: 2 DDF, XIII, no. 222, Annexe II. The mention of Mogador was omitted from the Yellow Book, Affaires du Maroc, at Germany's request: J. Cambon to Poincaré, 20 January 1912: 3 DDF, I, no. 493.

14. Izvolsky to Neratov, 13 April/31 March 1911: LN, I, 76–77.

Germany could not encourage the sending of troops. On the other hand, the kaiser on the 22nd and 26th thought that France should be allowed to do what she pleased as far as Germany was concerned; an expedition to Fez would weaken France on Germany's western border. The Pan-German press, however, began to agitate for a partition of Morocco, as they continued to do throughout the crisis. Kiderlen himself may well have encouraged their views, for Dr. Heinrich Class, President of the Pan-German League, declared under oath in a libel trial of January 1912 that Kiderlen had told him on 19 April 1911 that he supported the policy of partition; "We shall stick to Morocco. . . . I am as Pan-German as you are." Although Kiderlen denied the truth of Class's testimony, his denials were not convincing, especially because others testified to similar statements as late as 10 July.[15] Whatever the truth, the remarks of German statesmen and the demands of the press boded ill for France when the expeditionary force started for Fez on 28 April 1911.

Already Bethmann had expressed doubts to Cambon that France would ever leave Fez if she reached it. Kiderlen on the 28th declared that if the French could not leave Fez and the sultan needed their bayonets, Germany would not regard him as the sultan of the Algeciras Act; hence, because she would not consider the Act in force, Germany would regain her liberty of action. The warning was publicly repeated on 30 April in the official *Norddeutsche Allgemeine Zeitung*, and was reprinted in the leading newspapers throughout Europe. Both Jules Cambon and Joseph Caillaux took the warning seriously, but Cruppi seems still to have been more worried about Spain than Germany.

While these warnings were being issued, the Wilhelmstrasse was preparing a memorandum for Kiderlen on German policy, that was issued on 3 May over his signature. After reviewing the history of the Moroccan question, the memorandum sketched future German policy on the assumption that the French would be unable to withdraw from Fez as they had promised to do. Germany would then regard the Act of Algeciras as nullified and would send warships to Mogador and Agadir to hold them as pledges while awaiting a French offer of compensation in the colonial area in return for a withdrawal of Germany from Morocco. There was no mention of partitioning Morocco or of German retention of a port.[16] The kaiser approved the program on

15. *The Times*, 20 January 1912, p. 5, and 19 February 1912, p. 8.
16. Memorandum, 3 May 1911: *GP*, XXIX, no. 10549.

5 May. The question immediately arises as to what Kiderlen really wanted, because he had undoubtedly talked of staying in southern Morocco, and members of the Foreign Office continued to do so. Whatever he had in mind, and his mind may not have been made up completely, his main concern, as he told Oscar von der Lancken, counselor at the Paris embassy, was to secure a pledge-in-hand (a *Faustpfand*) that would bring the French to the negotiating table and secure for Germany a price for her renunciation of Morocco. After the failure to bring about Franco-German collaboration, he said to Lancken, it was necessary to pound the fist on the table.[17]

In France, Caillaux recognized the German desire for compensation and held confidential talks with Lancken over the possibility of a deal involving the French Congo in return for a German renunciation of Morocco. Ambassador Schoen was unable to follow up any kind of overtures, for he was instructed on 9 May to treat the Moroccan question with the greatest possible reserve—a tactic reminiscent of Bülow's silence after the kaiser's Tangier visit in 1905. Because Kiderlen had left Berlin early in May on vacation, Jules Cambon, on instructions from Cruppi, approached Bethmann on 10 and 11 June to assure him that events—mainly the Spanish occupation of Larache and El-Kazar—had not modified French intentions, and to suggest that France and Germany come to a full understanding, as France and Britain had done in 1904, except that there was one question between France and Germany (obviously meaning Alsace-Lorraine) that could not be solved. Cambon said that Germany could not prevent Morocco from falling to France like ripe fruit, but an agreement would obviate German perturbation over that eventuality. He also mentioned that Cruppi wanted to renew negotiations over Moroccan railways. Bethmann promised to think about what Cambon had said and ended by advising him to see Kiderlen soon at Kissingen. Cruppi himself talked a few days later with Schoen about the Cameroon-Congo railway project and suggested a general discussion about Africa, on which, he said, the French government was disposed to seek an accord. Schoen of course, could not respond, although he expressed doubts about the possibility of an agreement.

These French feelers over renewing discussions concerning railways scarcely satisfied Kiderlen, who regarded them as trifles in the game foreshadowed by the memorandum of 3 May. Moreover, in a memorandum of 12 June Zimmermann asserted that the Spanish advance

17. Lancken, *Meine dreissig Dienstjahre*, p. 96.

offered an occasion for throwing off the previous German reserve. He urged a declaration to the powers that Algeciras had become insupportable, and the sending of ships to Mogador and Agadir.

French efforts to initiate discussions and the German determination to "pound the fist on the table" constituted the background for the talks between Jules Cambon and Kiderlen at Kissingen on 20 and 21 June. Kiderlen, after pointing out that neither Algeciras nor the accord of 1909 provided for the protectorate over Morocco that France was "in the process of organizing," agreed with Cambon that they should come to an understanding. He suggested that they not confine themselves to Morocco, for "it was useless to replaster" what had been done on that subject. Cambon agreed, but then issued a significant warning: he recalled to Kiderlen that he had at another time mentioned Mogador, and vigorously asserted that if Germany wanted any part of Morocco, it would be better not to begin conversations; since French opinion would not accept a German share of the land, "one may seek elsewhere." Obviously neither man wanted to take the first step toward a concrete proposal, but Cambon promised to carry the ideas they had discussed to his government, and Kiderlen said: "Bring us something from Paris." Cambon, in concluding his report on the talks, strongly recommended an accord with Germany, because if there were none, she would open her arms to Spain. Therefore it was important to go ahead and study the bases for future conversations.[18]

The day after Cambon drew up his report, the Monis government fell. The new government of Joseph Caillaux was not formed until 28 June and scarcely had time to give Kiderlen "something from Paris" when the Agadir coup caught everyone by surprise.

While Paris was without a government, Langwerth von Simmern, an undersecretary at the Wilhelmstrasse, was preparing for an all-important interview on 26 June of Kiderlen and Bethmann with the kaiser, whose approval for despatching a ship, or ships, to the Moroccan coast had to be obtained. Because there had been no disturbances in southern Morocco and there were few Germans there—not even one at Agadir—Langwerth arranged with Dr. Wilhelm K. Regendanz, managing director of the Hamburg Morocco Society, to present a petition from Hamburg firms for government action to protect German interests. Curiously, Regendanz obtained nearly a dozen signatures to the petition without letting the signers know the contents. In addition to the petition, Albert Ballin also helped to get the kaiser's

18. J. Cambon to Cruppi, 22 June 1911: 2 DDF, XIII, no. 364.

reluctant consent to send ships. Why but one ship was sent and why to Agadir rather than Mogador are not clear. The one ship may well have been a matter of availability. The *Panther*, on her way home from Southwest Africa, could be diverted to Agadir by the target date of 1 July. It is possible that Agadir was chosen because it was not an "open port" under the Act of Algeciras, and therefore had no French or Spanish police in residence who might cause complications if a German gunboat suddenly showed up. In order to overcome the obvious falsehood in the announcement of the *Panther's* leap, that it was sent to protect the life and property of "some German firms, established in South Morocco, and especially at Agadir and its environs," Langwerth asked Regendanz to send an employee of the Hamburg Morocco Society from Mogador to Agadir. Since he arrived four days late, however, there was not even one "endangered German" in Agadir when the *Panther* cast anchor in the harbor on 1 July. Nevertheless, it cannot be denied, as Theodor Wolff remarked, that "our people made long preparations for their mistakes and went about their frivolous moves without any precipitation."[19]

Now that Kiderlen had his *Faustpfand*, the question in everybody's mind, including that of many Germans, was what did he want? Uncertainty and mistrust were consequently added to the universal surprise over the Agadir coup.

III.

The official German explanation of why the *Panther* was sent to Agadir—that it was "to lend, in case of need, aid and succor to its subjects and protégés as well as the considerable German interests" in Agadir and its vicinity[20]—was received with great skepticism. Gradually, however, over the next two months some of the true reasons filtered out. Zimmermann on 2 July told the Spanish ambassador that in addition to the danger of disturbances, public opinion would not allow Germany to stand by while other nations were dividing the country. Metternich told Sir Arthur Nicolson much the same thing. Inevitably, Germany was suspected of wanting a port in Morocco, although Richard von Kühlmann, counselor at the German

19. *The Eve of 1914*, p. 43.
20. "Aide-Mémoire Communicated by Count Metternich," 1 July 1911: *BD*, VII, no. 338.

embassy in London, denied it. Weeks later Zimmerman explained that the despatch of the ship to Agadir was really to make it easier for the French government to defend any compensation they might be ready to give. At no time, however, did Kiderlen explain his desire for a pledge-in-hand in order to assure Germany of her just deserts.

In Paris Ambassador Schoen made it clear that a return to the status quo was impossible, but declared that the German government was ready for an amicable exchange of views concerning a solution of the Moroccan problem. Fortunately, the leading newspapers tended to take a moderate attitude, expressing surprise and irritation over the German move, rather than indignation. Some, to whom the Kissingen talks were known, even blamed France for acting too slowly; they all expressed bewilderment over the objective of the *Panther's* spring. Foreign Minister Justin de Selves, new in office, asked for the opinion of London and St. Petersburg and, suggesting to London that France might send a warship to Mogador, asked if Britain would be disposed to take similar action. Even before London could reply, however, Premier Caillaux, who took over the Quai d'Orsay temporarily from the 3rd to the 7th while Selves was absent, canceled the question, determined, with the support of Delcassé, minister of the navy, not to send ships to Morocco.

Selves, under the influence of "Young Turks" at the ministry, like Maurice Herbette, his principal private secretary, and Edmond Bapst and Alexander Conty in the department of political affairs, was inclined to deal high-handedly with the Germans and even to risk war rather than to yield to German desires. On the other hand, Caillaux, who, it will be remembered, had approached the Germans two months before with the idea of compensation for a French free hand in Morocco, wanted above all to make a deal with Germany in a spirit of conciliation. A few weeks later he was confirmed in his determination to avoid war when he pointed out to General Joffre that Napoleon allegedly refused to engage in battle unless he thought he had a 70 percent chance of victory, and asked Joffre if France now had such a margin over Germany. When Joffre said no, Caillaux declared: "We will negotiate."[21] He was as determined as Selves to get Germany out of Morocco, but better appreciated the need to bargain. Besides this significant divergence in outlook, Caillaux had little confidence in Selves, who was a choice forced upon him by the refusal of abler men to take over foreign affairs. This unfortunate

21. Marshall Joffre, *Memoirs* (2 vols. London, 1932), I, 14–15.

situation in a time of crisis often left France's friends uncertain as to what policy she was pursuing, and Caillaux's resort to confidential agents outside the diplomatic personnel complicated negotiations with Germany.

Returning to the events of early July: the first reaction of Russia to the Agadir coup was a desire to adjust her views to those of Great Britain. At the same time, Neratov on 4 July instructed Osten-Sacken to ask Berlin in a friendly talk how far its action was compatible with the Act of Algeciras and the Franco-German accord of 1909. Neratov thought it possible to take the position that France through her communication to the powers concerning the expediton to Fez had received silent consent for her action, and asked Osten-Sacken at Berlin to seek an assurance that the Agadir coup had no political character. Kiderlen in two conversations explained at length that because France had gone beyond the Act of Algeciras, Germany wanted a new arrangement that would avoid every conflict over Morocco in the future. Apparently Osten-Sacken made no comment, and Russia had no intention of putting pressure upon Germany, with whom Neratov was still negotiating the convention over Persia and the Bagdad railway. Jules Cambon characterized the Russian action at Berlin as "extremely feeble."[22]

In England both the press and the Foreign Office received the German explanations of the *Panther's* spring with grave doubts. Grey, after consulting the Cabinet and proceeding in accordance with its instructions, warned Germany that Britain, too, had interests in Morocco, even greater commercially than Germany's Morever, Britain could not recognize any new arrangement that was arrived at without her. Grey's statement to Ambassador Metternich of this position, 4 July, was intended to elicit German recognition of Britain as a power to be taken into consideration, but, as Grey told the Commons in November, only silence ensued on the part of Berlin. To France, Grey promised the fulfillment of all British obligations, and said that discussions among Germany, France, Spain, and England were inevitable, although it was essential to agree beforehand on a solution of the Moroccan problem which France would consider reasonable, practical, and conformable with her interests. Grey also gave Benckendorff the substance of his communication to Metternich and added, among other points, that if Germany wanted some compensation for French advances, neither France nor England would object. Grey's

22. J. Cambon to Selves, 10 July 1911: 2 *DDF*, XIV, no. 54.

desire for discussions *à quatre*, however, was doomed to disappointment, for neither Germany nor France wanted them.

Although France had received only feeble support from her ally Russia, Germany fared even worse with her allies. Aehrenthal was piqued that he had been given no advance notice of the *Panther's* leap, and was still smarting over the German promise to Russia at Potsdam concerning the Balkans. He made it clear that Austria-Hungary's only interest in Morocco was the preservation of the open door and that he could not promise support until he knew what Germany wanted. Moreover, he failed to curb the critical comments of the press or the statement of the Hungarian premier that the Dual Monarchy was not bound by the Triplice with respect to Morocco. Privately he told Joseph Redlich that "the whole German Moroccan policy is Krupp and Mannesmann," and agreed with Redlich that the alliance was not intended to protect such interests. Later, he remarked that Austria-Hungary would always fulfill her alliance duties, "but after Agadir I cannot follow Kiderlen."[23] Italy was even more negative, pointing out that her accord with France obliged her not to oppose French action in Morocco. The Wilhelmstrasse, however, could draw some comfort from the Spanish attitude that continued to be influenced by mistrust of France. Spain concurred in the German view of the necessity for a new arrangement and of the loss of the sultan's independence as a result of the march to Fez.

In Germany, the nationalist and Pan-German press exulted in a move that it interpreted as a show of determination to get southwestern Morocco. German public opinion, however, was split between the views of the colonialists and financiers on the one hand, who were interested in the Congo, and the industrialists who wanted the Sous area of Morocco for its reputed iron ore.

In Paris, Caillaux and Jules Cambon, who stayed in the city from 22 June till 8 July, were in agreement that they had to talk with Germany to the exclusion of Russia, Britain, and Spain, because they envisaged a settlement involving compensation to Germany in the Congo and perhaps other parts of the world where the three powers were not concerned. Cambon concluded a long despatch of 6 July to Caillaux by suggesting that if the pledge taken by Germany at Agadir had to be bought from her, a rectification of the Congo frontiers might be sufficient. A conference on 7 July of President Fallières, Caillaux, Delcassé and himself failed to give him clear directions other

23. Joseph Redlich, *Schicksalsjahre Osterreichs*, I, 92, 95.

than that, if they had to make large concessions to Germany to get her out of Agadir, "the establishment of our empire in North Africa is worth some sacrifices."[24]

At the first meeting of Cambon and Kiderlen, 9 July, they made little progress toward serious negotiations, each waiting in vain for the other to make a proposal. Cambon hinted at compensation to Germany in the Orient, but Kiderlen rejected that. Cambon reiterated his Kissingen declaration that France would not tolerate a German acquisition of part of Morocco, to which Kiderlen replied that nothing up till then had indicated that Germany intended to acquire possessions there. They touched upon the Congo as an object of a bargain, and agreed that negotiations should be conducted at Berlin à deux. The tone of the conversation encouraged Cambon to believe that they had made a good start. In a private letter to Selves, Cambon again urged that France seize the opportunity to get Germany out of Morocco, and made the same point in a private letter to Caillaux in which he also represented Kiderlen as believing that Caillaux was the strong man with whom he could do business. This idea undoubtedly encouraged Caillaux to take a hand in the negotiations with Germany, even over the head of his foreign minister.

Both at Paris and at Berlin the French pressed the Germans to state their wishes, while expressing satisfaction that the question of compensation had veered to the Congo rather than to a partition of Morocco. The kaiser at the same time was urging speed upon the chancellor and the Foreign Office. A meeting of Cambon and Kiderlen on 13 July got nowhere, but another on the 15th had explosive results in both Germany and France. Kiderlen, calling for a map, indicated that Germany wanted the Congo from the ocean to the Sangha River. Cambon, taken aback, declared that such a demand could not be met and asked if Germany offered anything in exchange. Kiderlen then suggested that perhaps Togo, although the Colonial Office was against it, and the northern Cameroons might be offered. On 17 July, Selves confirmed Cambon's view and refused to concede the region demanded. Paul Cambon reflected French thinking when he pointed out that the area outlined by Kiderlen was larger than the whole of Morocco, only part of which was valuable and the rest desert.

Kiderlen's report of the discussion with Cambon set off a violent reaction in William II, who was cruising in Norwegian waters. Kiderlen said that if France obstinately rejected his Congo proposal, Ger many had to proceed "forcibly," which the kaiser took to mean that his secretary of state would go to war. He felt that he had to go home immediately in such an emergency and let the chancellor know that he would not consent to a procedure that might lead to war. Kiderlen, on the assumption that he had lost the kaiser's confidence, sent his resignation to Bethmann, who refused to accept it. But Kiderlen persisted, and in a second letter of resignation spelled out his view that in order to break French obstinacy, Germany had to convince them that she was determined to take the most extreme measures, although he declared that he did not intend to make war. The chancellor attempted to persuade the kaiser that the best way to avoid both a diplomatic defeat and war was to authorize Kiderlen to proceed as he thought best. William II yielded on 21 July.

Meanwhile, incomplete accounts of the German demands, omitting the possible offer of Togo and part of the Cameroons, leaked to the press on 19 July. This breach of secrecy put Kiderlen in a bad temper, and at his next meeting with Cambon on 20 July he not only complained of the news story—because of the agreement on secrecy and because the news had inflamed French public opinion—but also threatened that if the negotiations broke down, Germany would demand the strict enforcement of the Act of Algeciras and would go, if need be, "to the very end (*jusqu'au bout*)." Cambon stood his ground and declared that France would go as far as Germany.[25] It seemed that tension had almost reached the breaking point. What made the situation the more serious was the conjecture in Paris and London that Kiderlen had expected his Congo claim to be turned down and to use the refusal as an excuse to keep Agadir and southern Morocco. At this point what Kiderlen had not foreseen occurred: Britain intervened.

Nowhere, not even in Paris, had the news of Kiderlen's proposal concerning the Congo aroused more indignation and alarm than in England. *The Times* was particularly vociferous in its condemnation of German designs and its conclusion that British interests were directly involved should Germany get a seacoast in central Africa. Britain had already made clear that she had interests in Morocco that were not to be ignored, but despite Crowe's suspicion that France might make a deal with Germany behind England's back, Grey had accepted British exclusion from negotiations and had trusted the French to keep him informed. What troubled the English Foreign Office was the nagging suspicion that Germany wanted a partition of

25. J. Cambon to Selves, 20 July 1911: ibid., no. 90.

Morocco, despite official denials. Beyond that, however, was doubt concerning French firmness in opposing Germany. As Nicolson and Crowe saw the situation, it boiled down to a trial of strength; whereas Britain in 1909 had given Russia only diplomatic support, she had to back France to the limit in 1911, else the Entente Cordiale might be destroyed.

It seemed imperative, therefore, to find out what Germany intended, the more so since Grey feared that Germany would interpret Britain's silence as a sign that she did not care what happened. Consequently, Grey asked Metternich to see him on 21 July. After stating his fears that, because German demands were so excessive they might lead to a breakdown of negotiations, and again bringing up the question of Agadir, he asserted that although he did not know what was going on there, Agadir was well suited to become a naval base and therefore was a British interest. Accordingly, if negotiations over the Congo should break down, Great Britain would become involved and would have to be admitted to the negotiations. Metternich could give no information about Agadir and had the temerity to criticize British policy for using a double standard in dealing with France, who had gone so far in Morocco, and Germany, who had done so little. He knew, however, from Grey's remarks that outside of Agadir and Morocco, Grey would give his blessing to negotiations over other areas.

At this juncture Lloyd George's Mansion House speech on the evening of the 21st proclaimed to the whole world the substance of Grey's warning about Morocco. Lloyd George had been alarmed over developments as described in the press. Both Grey and Asquith, whom he consulted about the statement he proposed to make, were undoubtedly aware of the internal political significance of a warning to Germany by the Chancellor of the Exchequer, who belonged to the radical, anti-imperialist wing of the Liberal party. The usefulness of Lloyd George in healing party rifts and ending antagonism toward Grey's policy undoubtedly helps to explain the approval of his words, the international repercussions of which were evidently not foreseen.

Lloyd George at the Mansion House, 21 July, said:

> I believe it is essential in the highest interests, not merely of this country, but of the world, that Britain should at all hazards maintain her place and her prestige amongst the Great Powers of the world. . . . But if a situation were to be forced upon us in which peace could only be preserved by the surrender of the great and beneficent position Britain has won by centuries of heroism and

achievement, by allowing Britain to be treated, where her interests were vitally affected, as if she were of no account in the
Cabinet of Nations, then I say emphatically that peace at that
price would be a humiliattion intolerable for a great country like
ours to endure.[26]

Although the statement by itself was a moderate one, and might
well have been directed both to Germany and to France, whose weakness the British feared, the press next day stridently proclaimed it as a
warning to Germany. The *Daily Chronicle*, whose editor was close to
Lloyd George, headlined its report of the speech: "Britain Warns Germany—National Honour is at Stake." *The Times* and others, except
the *Manchester Guardian*, took the same line, interpreting the speech
to mean that Britain would be loyal to France. Thus Grey's entente-
balance-of-power policy received the support of all parties until after
the Moroccan settlement, when the Radicals renewed the attack.

Germany's reaction to the speech, at first moderate, became vehement both at the Wilhelmstrasse and in the press, because of the interpretation of it by the British and French press. The Germans thought
that the British intended to veto Germany's attempt to procure compensation for withdrawing from Morocco and thus to block her legitimate expansion. On 24 July, Metternich replied to Grey's comments
of the 21st by assurances that Germany had no designs upon Morocco,
and by protests against the "chauvinistic tone" of the French and part
of the British press that did not help negotiations. When Grey asked
if he could tell Parliament Metternich's declaration that not a man
had been landed at Agadir, Metternich requested that no public statement be made until he had communicated with his government. The
next day, however, Metternich's statements and Grey's replies revealed a high state of tension. Metternich said that after Lloyd
George's speech, Germany could not authorize the use in Parliament
of his statement about Agadir, because it would appear that Germany
had made a declaration of her intentions in Morocco in consequence
of the speech. Moreover, Metternich read a statement that Germany
was trying to vindicate her rights under the Act of Algeciras, and
"German dignity as a Great Power would make it necessary to secure
by all means, and, if necessary, alone full respect by France of German

26. David Lloyd George, *War Memoirs* (6 vols. Boston, 1933–1937), I, 41–42.
Cf. Keith Wilson, "The Agadir Crisis, the Mansion House Speech, and the
Double Edgedness of Agreements," *HJ*, XV (1972), 513–32; Lowe and Dockrill,
Mirage of Power, I, 39–42, and III, 433–34.

treaty rights." He went on to describe the bad impression in Germany of the Mansion House speech, and to suggest that it would have been better if England had expressed her views through the usual diplomatic channels. He was right; the British government could not have chosen a better means of embroiling the political situation and leading to an explosion. Grey repeated what he had said before, that the speech claimed only that Britain was entitled to consideration as one of the great powers. He added that if it was beneath the dignity of the German government to explain what was going on at Agadir, "the tone of their communication made it not consistent with our dignity to give explanations as to the speech of the Chancellor of the Exchequer." He did assure Metternich, however, that Britain sincerely desired the success of the Franco-German negotiations, and he would make that clear to the Commons.[27]

Grey was so alarmed by the tone of Metternich's communication that he warned the Admiralty of the danger of a German attack "at any moment." Both the Admiralty and the War Office hummed with the activity of preparing for a possible war with Germany in which they would send an expeditionary force to France. Here lay one of the major consequences of the Agadir crisis, the completion of plans for military cooperation with France—a further step in the consolidation of the entente. Moreover, the press in England, France, and Germany was aware of British special Cabinet meetings, the cancellation of the fleet's visit to Norwegian waters (to avoid contact with German activity there), a sag in the security market, and a run on Lloyd's war-risk insurance. All these events contributed to a war scare that subsided in a few days but left the British government fearful of a possible war throughout August and September, when the feasibility of war was discussed in Berlin but rejected by civilians and military, with the possible exception of Chief of Staff Moltke.

In Berlin the government was not alone in its indignation over the excesses of the press. Jules Cambon was furious at the French government's indiscretions, which he attributed to the underlings at the Quai d'Orsay who hated him; he thought the press publicity would ruin all chances of a settlement. Kiderlen, however, although he had talked big in his instructions of 25 July to Metternich, had come to recognize his miscalculations with respect to the British attitude, and on 26 July modified his previous stand by authorizing a British parliamentary statement that Franco-German negotiations did not affect British

27. Grey to Goschen, 24 and 25 July 1911: *Twenty-Five Years*, I, 218–22.

interests; he also requested a definite statement by the British government of Grey's assurance that it wanted a successful conclusion of the negotiations. As a result, Grey and Metternich met on the 27th in a more cordial atmosphere, and Asquith's statement on the same day made clear the British position and cooled excited spirits. On the basis of his explanations no one doubted, however, that if negotiations broke down, Britain would actively participate in the discussion, and that she would support France. The speech made a good impression in Berlin. According to the British ambassador Cambon's spirits rose enormously, and the speech would "give Kiderlen a much desired opportunity to climb down a little."[28] Certainly, although there was much rough water ahead, the British intervention had helped to channel Franco-German negotiations into their ultimately successful course. For one thing, if indeed Kiderlen had still harbored thoughts of gaining southwestern Morocco, he had to give them up or face a combined Franco-British opposition.

Meanwhile, in Paris, Caillaux had not been idle. His desire to avoid war and his recognition after 15 July that a few "scraps" by way of compensation would not satisfy Germany came into collision with Selves and the Herbette-Conty clique, who wanted to demand Morocco and refuse all compensation. On the 18th Caillaux participated in discussions with Selves, Paul Cambon, and others without as yet having made up his mind what course to follow. Cambon helped him decide to offer Germany a part of the Congo without the seacoast. Caillaux's disagreement with Selves and his mistaken belief that Lancken at the German embassy represented the kaiser's views led him to welcome discussions beginning on 25 July between Lancken and Alphonse Fondère, explorer and director of river navigation on the Congo, who had already served as a go-between in Caillaux's sub-rosa contacts with the Germans in May.

Kiderlen authorized secret discussions on 23 July, and told Lancken that Lloyd George's speech would please everybody in France but Caillaux; he thought that peace and compensation might be more easily achieved through secret discussions than through official channels. The talks between Lancken and Fondère, however, failed to bring about agreement on what part of the Congo France should cede to Germany. Caillaux wanted a worldwide settlement, which Kiderlen rejected, and at the end of July, Caillaux "buttoned up," as Lancken put it. Without a doubt Caillaux's change of attitude toward the talks

28. Goschen to Nicolson, Private, 27 July 1911: *BD*, VII, no. 431.

arose because the Quai d'Orsay had deciphered telegrams from the German embassy to Berlin which revealed the secret negotiations and, Caillaux avers, misrepresented his position.[29] Nevertheless, he continued to keep in touch with Kiderlen throughout the subsequent negotiations, especially after 17 August, when he virtually took them over; and Kiderlen utilized the services of such financiers as Paul von Schwabach, head of the banking firm of Bleichröder, to communicate with Caillaux.

The major reason why the Lancken-Fondère talks had gotten nowhere was that Kiderlen was still talking big, as Goschen had put it, apparently influenced by the Pan-German press, which touted him as the new Bismarck, and together with the mouthpieces of big industry opposed any settlement that did not give Germany a slice of southern Morocco. The Wilhelmstrasse appears to have been sufficiently impressed by the clamor to send Regendanz to Morocco in late August to report on the potentialities of southern Morocco. Regendanz came to the conclusion that the economic resources of the region had been greatly overrated. Long before his report, however, Kiderlen had modified the truculent tone that had dismayed Jules Cambon in July. On 1 August the two men established the bases of further negotiations: in Morocco, Germany would give France a free hand politically, although Kiderlen advised against the use of the word "protectorate" in the agreement; as for the Congo, Germany would revise her demands, but Kiderlen insisted as a *sine qua non* that Germany be given access to the Congo River, and he wanted to reach the sea between Spanish Rio Muni and the port of Libreville. He preferred not to offer a part of Togo in exchange, and eventually definitely refused to do so. The Bec du Canard in the northern Cameroons, however, remained a pawn in the play. Nevertheless, tense days lay ahead because of rumors that Germany was landing troops at Agadir, and Kiderlen's announcement of a holiday during the latter part of August, which Selves suspected was to give Germany a chance for further advances in Morocco while negotiations were suspended. Caillaux, irritated by Selves' reaction to the situation, took over the direction of policy from 17 August and created a lasting schism between himself and Selves which worried Delcassé and the Cambons.

While the atmosphere was becoming clouded by continuing press agitation and recrimination in Germany and France and a slowdown

29. Lancken, *Meine dreissig Dienstjahre*, pp. 101–05; "Notes de M. Fondère": 2 *DDF*, XIV, no. 105; Caillaux, *Mémoires*, II, 157–59.

occurred in negotiations, Russia, at the behest of Ambassador Georges Louis, took a renewed interest in the situation. On 30 July Neratov again instructed Osten-Sacken to approach Kiderlen and let him know, in the "mildest possible form" that Russia anxiously desired quiet progress in negotiations. Little wonder that Kiderlen paid tribute to Russia's correct attitude, and asserted that had Britain followed her example the negotiations would have advanced much farther. Grey worried about Russian loyalty to France, and suggested to Benckendorff that much depended upon what Berlin thought about Russia's attitude in case of complications. In contrast to Osten-Sacken's "mildness" in Berlin, Izvolsky at Paris earnestly worked on Selves to exercise "prudent compliance" with Germany's wishes. He compared the situation to that of February 1909, when France had counseled him to do everything possible to avoid a war that would find little sympathy in France. Now Russia had the right to advise prudence "in a similar friendly way." Izvolsky also talked with Caillaux and Delcassé along the same lines, and from them and others concluded that there was an upswing of nationalist sentiment in French political, military, journalistic and financial circles. Neratov and the tsar approved Izvolsky's language and asked him to enlighten the French government once more concerning the necessity for conciliation, because Russia would have no sympathy with a colonial war and because Russia's military reforms were not yet complete. Benckendorff, who had disagreed with Neratov's tactics, pleaded in vain that moderating pressure was more needed at Berlin than at Paris, and suggested that Russia get in touch with England about the means to be employed "in the last resort."[30]

Izvolsky's communication hardly dampened the ardor of the war party at the Quai d'Orsay, for Jules Cambon on a visit to Paris between the 20th and 31st of August felt that Selves, under the influence of Herbette, opposed even the principle of negotiation with the Germans. Fortunately, Caillaux had taken decision-making out of his hands. In a round of conferences that included the war and colonial ministers, Delcassé, Cruppi, Barrère, and the Cambon brothers, the French position on details of the Moroccan settlement and on the Congo concessions was worked out. Even so, Jules Cambon found that the Quai d'Orsay in drawing up his instructions had failed to follow some of the decisions agreed upon in conference.

30. Izvolsky to Neratov, 16/3, 18/5, 21/8, and 22/9 August 1911: 3 *IBZI*, I, nos. 328, 341, 350, 354; Neratov to Izvolsky, 30/17 August 1911: ibid., no. 368; Benckendorff to Neratov, 12 Sept/30 August 1911: ibid., no. 423.

Upon returning to Berlin, Cambon found the French proposals unacceptable to Kiderlen, whose counterproposals looked to the French like an attempt to gain advantages in Morocco through economic arrangements that were incompatible with the interests of other powers and with Kiderlen's repeatedly expressed willingness to leave Morocco to France. Caillaux told Schwabach, whom Kiderlen sent to talk with him, that all of a sudden Kiderlen was taking back the greater part of what he had promised, and had thus raised the suspicion that he did not want the negotiations to succeed. Caillaux wrote to Cambon that he would like to conclude immediately but that public opinion prevented him from new conciliatory steps. He accused Germany by her proceedings and delays of bringing about in France and even in Germany an atmosphere almost incompatible with an accord. He directed Cambon to continue to be firm.

Whether it was the firmness of Caillaux and Cambon, or the September crash on the Berlin bourse, or even the realization that Germany had got all she could expect, as Schoen suggested, Kiderlen began to yield ground from the middle of September. Cambon attributed the change in attitude to the financial crisis. He believed that Kiderlen had seen that when he spoke of war, he unchained a crisis that he did not expect, and Cambon suggested to Caillaux that "we have a certain interest in seeing that the crisis continues."[31] Whether or not he was correct in his conjecture concerning the influence of the stock market slump, he found a reason a few days later why it was important for France to conclude the agreement on Morocco. He pointed out to Caillaux that the danger of an Italian occupation of Tripoli and the possibility that Germany might yet seize the Sous region in southern Morocco meant that if these events should occur, the French position in North Africa would be compromised. Therefore, Cambon felt that the conclusion of an accord with Germany for the sake of France's future in the Mediterranean was a far greater necessity at this time than all the previous considerations had indicated. Thus the sensitivity in Germany, as evidenced by the market slump, to the uncertainties engendered by protracted negotiations, and the possibility of complications arising from the outbreak of an Italo-Turkish war (declared on 29 September) influenced both parties to hasten toward a settlement concerning Morocco which they reached by the middle of October.

In the Cambon-Kiderlen negotiations over the Congo, beginning on 15 October, both of the principals were handicapped by public opinion.

31. J. Cambon to Caillaux, 16 September 1911: 2 DDF, XIV, no. 326.

The French felt that Morocco belonged to them "by a sort of historical imperative," as Binion puts it, and although Germany was entitled to some consolation, she deserved no "compensation" for getting out.[32] On the other hand, the Pan-Germans were demanding greater territorial concessions than Kiderlen appeared to be winning. Two major points were stumbling blocks to progress: Kiderlen's demand for access to the Congo River, and for the cession to Germany of French option rights to the Belgian Congo. Kiderlen won his access to the Congo River. The Belgian question was another matter, involving the susceptibilities of Belgium and the interests of other powers. Kiderlen had to yield on this point. At length, on 2 November, he and Cambon reached the end of the rough road to a territorial settlement, and on the 4th signed the two conventions and accompanying notes.[33]

With respect to Morocco, the two powers agreed to conditions that would enable France to establish a protectorate, although the word appeared only in an explanatory note. For her part, France promised not to permit any inequality in taxes, customs duties, and the like, to provide for the development by others of mines and public works, and to continue to respect fishing rights in Moroccan waters. Germany agreed to renounce her right of consular jurisdiction when a new judicial system was established. The state bank was to remain as set up at Algeciras. In short, the Franco-German accord of 1909 was superseded by an arrangement that put France in control of Morocco but left the door open for Germany and other powers to carry on economic enterprises. The letter accompanying the convention also recorded French acquiescence in a German acquisition from Spain of specified possessions, and German assurance of nonintervention in any Franco-Spanish agreement over Morocco. Finally, disputes over the interpretation or application of the convention were to be arbitrated under the Hague Convention of 1907.

The convention concerning the Congo opened by stating that it followed that on Morocco and, "by reason of the rights of protection over the Sherifian empire recognized to France," provided for "territorial exchanges in Equatorial Africa." France ceded to Germany a corridor from the sea south of Rio Muni but north of Libreville to the Congo River and thence northward in an arc to the Ubangi River, a tributary of the Congo. Thus, although France retained the valuable southern part of her central African colony, including Gabon, which

32. Rudolf Binion, *Defeated Leaders* (New York, 1960), p. 42.
33. Texts: 3 *DDF*, I, no. 19.

Kiderlen had at first demanded, her remaining territory was trisected by German prongs at two points on the Congo River and the Ubangi. The "exchange" consisted of the cession to France of the Bec du Canard, a triangular strip of land in the northern Cameroons. The rest of the convention provided for French communications between her divided lands, equality of treatment of nationals, railroad building, river transportation, and freedom of commercial enterprise. With reference to French reversionary rights in the Belgian Congo, if the territorial status of the basin of the Congo were modified by either France or Germany, they had to confer with each other and with the signatory powers of the Act of Berlin of 1885. The supplementary letter again referred disputes to an arbitral tribunal, and in addition welcomed the creation of Franco-German enterprises in either the French or the German possessions involved in the convention.

Who won in the final settlement? A case could be made out for either country if the square miles of territory exchanged are computed. The vehement criticism of the treaties in both Germany and France, however, was based more on political and prestige factors than upon square mileage. In Germany, where the secretary for colonies resigned in protest, the discussion of the settlement reflected not only the disappointment of the Pan-Germans and industrialists over the failure to get a foothold in Morocco, but also party jockeying with an eye to the parliamentary elections scheduled for early 1912. Kiderlen had been prepared for the outcry, for he told Osten-Sacken early in October: "You will see that once the text of the arrangement is known, the result will be an explosion of indignation in the press of both countries who will cry of deception and call it treason. . . . As for me, I don't care."[34] Kiderlen's disregard of public opinion may well have contributed to the unfavorable reception of the settlement, for his policy of secrecy permitted a build-up of tension and an attitude of skepticism toward the government and toward Kiderlen himself. On the other hand, Tirpitz profited by the increasingly loud demand for a larger navy in order to ensure safety against a surprise British attack, for the most striking aspect of both the press and the parliamentary debates was the bitter criticism of Great Britain. In fact, the rancor toward England overshadowed that toward France. Theodore Wolff of the *Berliner Tageblatt* wrote: "The German people are united on two points that figure in the debate; the one, that Britain's will shall not pass for law throughout the entire world, and the other, that

34. Osten-Sacken to Neratov, 6 October 1911: 2 *MO*, XVIII(2), no. 543.

German policy of the past months has been a chain of fateful mistakes."[35]

In France, much more than in Germany, politics colored the parliamentary and press debates. Those who placed a high value upon the completion of France's North African empire rejoiced over the conventions. Jules Cambon waxed lyrical in his praise of Caillaux's government for completing the work begun in 1830. Caillaux himself adopted Cambon's theme in defending the settlement. Fortunately for Caillaux the attack on the conventions in Germany helped in persuading the French to approve them. On the other hand, there were those on the right who attacked the settlement as a humiliation for France, because she had yielded to the Agadir threat and might better have gone to war. Although this was an extreme view, it was symptomatic of the nationalist spirit that the crisis engendered and that helped to explain the downfall of Caillaux in January 1912. He was not only accused of dealing underhandedly behind his foreign minister's back but also of seeking an agreement with Germany to the detriment or destruction of French friendship with Britain. In short, as Kiderlen predicted, Caillaux was guilty of treason. His government was replaced in mid-January by that of Raymond Poincaré. Fortunately, saner heads who recognized the value of a clear title to Morocco carried the vote in both the Chamber of Deputies on 20 December 1911 and the Senate on 10 February 1912. The condemnation of Caillaux and his work, however, partly arising from personal political animus, meant that the conclusion of the settlement failed to lead to a rapprochement with Germany, and, on the contrary, contributed to the rise of national fervor already on the upswing during the crisis.

In Great Britain the settlement, the Reichstag debates, the revelations in November of the secret Anglo-French and Franco-Spanish agreements of 1904 concerning Morocco, and a speech by Captain Faber concerning the military preparations during the summer revived the Radical-Liberal attacks upon the policy pursued by Grey and the government. Grey's defense of his policy in the House of Commons on 27 November satisfied the Conservatives but failed to quiet the Radicals in his own party. In the main they criticized Grey and Prime Minister Asquith because they had countenanced Russian "ruthlessness and bad faith" in Persia, because of their secrecy in the conduct of foreign relations and the consequent lack of parliamentary control, because of the steady "worsening . . . of their relations with Germany"

---

35. As quoted by Hale, *Publicity and Diplomacy*, p. 411.

almost to the point of war, and because of "the turning of a friendly understanding with France into an alliance without the approval or knowledge of Parliament.[36] The criticism failed to change the outlook of Grey and the Foreign Office but undoubtedly spurred them to renew naval discussions with Germany in the following February.

Because the Franco-German settlement left Spain untouched, France had to negotiate with the Spanish government. The details of the relationship between the two powers in administration and influence respecting such matters as customs, railroads, and advisory roles vis-à-vis the sultan took months to settle. Britain took a decisive hand in the delimitation of the Spanish zone in the north, for she refused to accept the French request for the Atlantic coast as far as Ceuta, and insisted that Spain get the coastal section as laid down in 1904. Elsewhere England acceped the principle of compensation to France for her sacrifices in coming to the agreement of 4 November 1911 with Germany. In the convention that was finally completed on 14 November 1912, Spain obtained a little less territory than she had been promised in 1904 but was given virtually a free hand in her sphere. Tangier was placed under international control.

Long before the Franco-Spanish settlement France had established her protectorate over her share of Morocco by a treaty of 30 March 1912. The signatories of the Act of Algeciras, to whom France and Germany had submitted the convention of November 1911, in due course accepted the changes brought about by the agreement, and Morocco, after two crises and only five years after she had been solemnly recognized as independent and sovereign, became a French dependency.

In retrospect, Morocco had offered the last opportunity for a working agreement between France and Germany that, despite Alsace-Lorraine, might have so modified the relationship between them as to postpone, if not prevent, the war of 1914. On both sides statesmen like Kiderlen and Caillaux and business and financial circles sincerely wanted to establish genuinely friendly relations. But the mistakes on both sides turned events, beginning with the failure of economic collaboration and the march to Fez, into challenges and resentments. Kiderlen's *Panther's* spring was a blunder that heightened mistrust of Germany, not only in France and England but even among his allies. Similarly, Lloyd George's Mansion House speech and the less

---

36. Ibid., p. 415. E. D. Morel, *Morocco in Diplomacy*, with its criticism of Grey's policy and defense of Germany, is an example of the Radical position.

dramatic but persistent and clearly enunciated British policy of backing France infuriated the Germans. The constant factor throughout 1911 which made accommodation and a genuinely satisfactory solution of the Moroccan problem impossible was the expression of public opinion. Not only in France but in Germany and England as well, a chauvinistic press created popular anxieties and excitement that put a heavy burden upon negotiators seeking acceptable compromises.[37]

Agadir, instead of leading to friendship, heightened enmities; and instead of weakening the Triple Entente, as Kiderlen had hoped, cemented the ties, at least of France and Britain, thus depriving the latter of much of her previous flexibility of maneuver. Though it is not true that the crisis immediately accentuated the European split into two camps, because Russia on the one side and Austria-Hungary and Italy on the other did not close ranks with their ally, the aftermath led to a consolidation of the two groups. Finally, Agadir started a chain reaction in the Mediterranean area—the Italo-Turkish war over Tripoli, the abortive attempt of Russia to open the Straits, the Balkan wars, and ultimately the war of 1914. In this sense, Agadir marked a watershed between the comparative calm of the first decade of the twentieth century (despite the first Moroccan and the Bosnian crises) and the quick pile-up of events that led to July 1914.

37. A. J. P. Taylor, *Struggle for Mastery in Europe, 1848–1918* (Oxford, 1954), p. 473, aptly asserts: "The conflicts of 1905 and 1909 had been crises of diplomacy; in 1911 nations faced each other in a 'pre-war' spirit."

Chapter 10

From Agadir to
the Balkan Wars,
1911–1912

In 1911–1912 the heads of governments were: in France, Joseph Caillaux until January 1912, followed by Raymond Poincaré; in Germany, Theobald von Bethmann Hollweg; in Great Britain, H. H. Asquith; in Italy, Giovanni Giolitti; and in Russia, V. N. Kokovtsov, formerly finance minister. The men responsible for foreign policy were Alois Baron Lexa Aehrenthal in Austria-Hungary, Justin de Selves (till January 1912) and Raymond Poincaré in France, Kiderlen-Waechter in Germany, Grey in Britain, Marquis San Giuliano in Italy; and Neratov (until December 1911) and Sazanov in Russia. The active ambassadors were, for France, Maurice Bompard in Turkey (1908–1914), Paul Cambon in England, and Georges Louis in Russia (1909–1913); for Germany, Baron Adolf von Marschall at Constantinople, and Count Metternich at London: for Britain, Sir Francis Bertie in Paris and Sir Edward Goschen in Berlin; for Italy, Tommaso Tittoni in Paris; and for Russia, Izvolsky at Paris, N. V. Charykov in Turkey, A. V. Neklyudov in Sofia, Nicholas Hartvig in Belgrade, Benckendorff at London, and Osten-Sacken in Berlin. In the Anglo-German negotiations Admiral Alfred von Tirpitz, Albert Ballin, Director of the Hamburg-American lines, Sir Ernest Cassel, British financier, Winston S. Churchill, first lord of the British Admiralty, Richard Burdon Haldane, minister of war, and Sir Arthur Nicolson at the Foreign Office shouldered varying degrees of responsibility.

I.

The first country to react to the changed situation in the Mediterranean as a result of the Agadir crisis was Italy, who had long cast eyes at Tripoli and Cyrenaica. Like France in Morocco, Italy at first had chosen the path of "peaceful penetration" in the two Turkish provinces, uti-

8. Admiral Alfred von Tirpitz (The Bettmann Archive)

lizing the cultural and economic tools familiar in imperialistic endeavors. Peaceful penetration, however, was not as successful as the Italians had hoped, partly because of the poor resources of the country, and partly because of the resistance of the Turkish government to exploitation, especially after the Young Turks came into power in 1908. Nevertheless, having been encouraged by the Italian government to establish "un-economic 'economic interests' in Tripoli," the Bank of Rome, which had become the principal agent of economic development, pressured the government to adopt more aggressive tactics.[1]

A factor of equal, if not greater, importance than economic interest in forcing Italy into war with Turkey over Tripoli was the rise of nationalist feeling, with its stress upon the need for the acquisition of colonies. The nationalist movement had developed into a powerful force after the Austro-Hungarian annexation of Bosnia-Herzegovina. That act was regarded in Italy as a humiliation, because again, as in 1878, Italy received no compensation for her neighbor's gains. By 1911 the Nationalists were represented in Parliament and especially in the press. From among the nationalist leaders, Luigi Federzoni went to Tripoli in the spring of 1911 with a half dozen other journalists and carried on active propaganda in the Italian press, which emphasized even the smallest misdeeds of the Turks and whipped up feeling for aggressive measures. Other elements in the background of the war were the increasing prosperity that Italy was enjoying and, even more important, the balance of about 400 million lire in the state treasury. Italy was therefore in an excellent position to undertake an active foreign policy.

Up to July 1911 the Italian government had sought to calm public excitement and had refused to resort to force in order to bring about Turkish compliance with its demands. Two factors, however, operated to change Italian policy after the midyear: the Agadir crisis, and fear that other powers might step into Tripoli ahead of Italy. If France established a protectorate over Morocco, as seemed not unlikely by September 1911, then Italy had every reason to cash the promissory notes of France and the other nations. Moreover, as early as June there had been talk of American, German, and other concessions in Tripoli, and of a French threat to the hinterland through the occupation of Ghadames on the border between Tripoli and Tunis. While the Marquis of San Giuliano, foreign minister in the Giolitti government, which had taken office in March 1911, sought to calm the public

1. Eugene Staley, *War and the Private Investor*, pp. 62–70.

in a speech of 9 June, scarcely two months later, after the *Panther's* spring and further rumors of German activity in Tripoli, he became convinced that Italy should act.

Diplomatic preparations for an occupation of Tripoli-Cyrenaica began in late July when the ambassador in London learned that Grey was sympathetic with Italy in her grievances against the Turkish obstruction of Italian enterprises in Tripoli. In August and early September both Russia and France promised their support of Italy, the former on the assumption that the Balkan situation would not be changed. Austria-Hungary and Germany were in a difficult position because they, especially Germany, were friends of Turkey and at the same time allies of Italy. Aehrenthal, though fearful of repercussions in the Balkans, where he hoped to maintain the status quo, was glad to see his troublesome ally involved in Africa. The Germans, however, were more hesitant, hoping up to the last moment that an expressed willingness of Turkey to grant Italy all desired concessions short of monopoly might lead to further discussions short of war. They tried in various ways to keep the peace, but failed, for the Italians rejected their proposals and sent an ultimatum to Turkey on 28 September, declaring war the next day.

The reaction of the European press to the war was, on the whole, unfavorable, although the Austrian press was less caustic than the German, and the leading French newspapers recognized French engagements to Italy and pledged loyalty to them. In view of the interests at stake, however, it is not surprising that the war created uneasiness and irritation among the great powers. The effect upon the Ottoman empire as a whole concerned Germany. The possibility of provoking the Balkan states to action preoccupied Austria-Hungary and Russia, while the repercussions, if the war were extended to the Aegean and the Dardanelles, concerned all the great powers, especially Russia and Great Britain. The powers with large Moslem populations in their empires, like Britain and France, dreaded a possible Moslem uprising in support of the Ottoman government. Yet no one was in a position to intervene. The best that could be hoped for was a localization of the conflict and possibly mediation.

Aehrenthal took the lead in proposing to the great powers that they try to prevent the war from spreading to the Balkans. His determination to achieve this objective was put to the test within several hours after the declaration of war, when Italian naval vessels went into action off Prevesa. He sharply reprimanded Italy and wrung from San Giuliano the promise to avoid naval action in the Adriatic and Ionian seas.

Nevertheless, despite his anger, he continued to seek the preservation of the Triplice and to avoid a break with Italy. In this policy he was vigorously opposed by General Conrad, who advocated ousting Italy from the Triplice and the settlement of old scores. Aehrenthal bluntly opposed such a policy, and the Emperor not only backed him up but also dismissed Conrad from his post at the end of November, replacing him as chief of the general staff by Count Blasius Schemua. At a ministerial meeting early in December, Aerhenthal justified his position on the ground that, because the Italian king and government had decided to renew the Triplice, any move other than granting them a free hand in Tripoli would further the plans of the western powers to push Italy out of the alliance. Furthermore, Aehrenthal anticipated a crisis in Anglo-German relations in which the Monarchy would be compelled to support its ally. In such circumstances its interests lay in retaining Italy in the alliance, even though it could not count upon her loyalty. Except for his continued efforts to keep the war out of European waters, Aehrenthal as well as Leopold Count Berchtold, who succeeded him in February 1912, consistently adhered to this policy.

Germany was in the same position as Austria-Hungary, although even more concerned over the effect of the war on the Ottoman Empire. Marschall at Constantinople, after the outbreak of war as before, sought in vain some means of bringing about peace. In Berlin, Kiderlen took an optimistic view of the situation and hoped for an Italian landing in Tripoli as soon as possible in order to satisfy Italy's *amour propre* and to give Turkey a pretext for listening to the counsels of her friends. "In reality," he said, "this whole war is not a war; it is a diplomatic negotiation preceded by a *prise de gage*." He believed that Turkey, weak at sea, was ready to make great sacrifices if the nominal sovereignty of the sultan over Tripoli could be maintained, but the time was not yet propitious for intervention by the powers.[2] The German government, meanwhile, sought to influence the press to take a more friendly attitude toward Italy for the sake of the alliance.

Among the Entente powers France adopted a cordial attitude, and the British government adhered to the position taken by Grey at the end of July. Most cordial of all was Russia, because of the Racconigi agreement, whose authors, Izvolsky and Tittoni, were now fellow ambassadors in Paris. Izvolsky recognized the danger of repercussions in the Balkans and approved Tittoni's suggestion that St. Petersburg, Vienna, and Rome should exchange views about the situation there. He was

2. J. Cambon to Selves, 2 letters, 4 October 1911: 2 *DDF*, XIV, nos. 398–99; Osten-Sacken to Neratov, 6 October/23 September 1911: 3 *IBZI*, I, no. 544.

also anxious that Italy reiterate her pledge to Russia respecting the Straits now that she was establishing her own rights in Tripoli. On the other hand, Neratov, acting foreign minister, seemed primarily concerned to establish agreement with France and England over the policy to be pursued and to forestall Germany in any attempt at mediation. He was seconded in both objectives by Selves and, less enthusiastically, by Grey, though all three believed that the time had not yet come for intervention.

Although Italy was able to occupy five ports in Tripoli and Cyrenaica between 4 and 21 October, she could make little headway into the interior. The Turkish government, at first anxious to make peace, gradually gained greater confidence and, while continuing to formulate peace proposals, failed to offer anything that Italy would accept. The Italian government, on the other hand, was determined to annex Tripoli and Cyrenaica and, probably to forestall any European mediation on some other basis, proclaimed the annexation of the provinces on 5 November, naming them Libya. This unusual step, representing hopes rather than accomplishments, was accompanied by rumors that Italy might extend her naval operations to the Red Sea and the Aegean. Consequently, on 18 November, the Ottoman government appealed to the powers to prevent an extension of the war to the Aegean and threatened to close the Straits if they refused to intervene at Rome. While France, Austria-Hungary, Germany, and Britain took no action, Russia notified Turkey and Italy that she would regard any measures endangering the free passage of the Straits by neutral merchant vessels as a violation of Article III of the 1871 London treaty, by which the Black Sea should remain accessible to the merchant vessels of all nations. On 22 November, Neratov proposed collective action by the powers to prevent the closure of the Straits. Again the powers failed to respond to such a proposal, mainly because at this time it appeared that the necessity for it would not arise. The Russian move, in any case, was but a minor episode paralleling Russia's attempt to gain the freedom of the Straits for her warships, which was stimulated by the outbreak of the Italo-Turkish war but by no means caused by it.

II.

Until the outbreak of the war Russia had pursued a conservative policy in the Balkans and the Near East. In the spring and early summer of 1911 she had, at first by her own efforts and later in cooperation with Austria-Hungary and Italy, restrained Montenegro from a conflict with

Turkey over the Malissori, the rebellious Albanian highlanders many of whom had fled to Montenegro for asylum. At the same time, two developments in the Ottoman empire had led Russia to reassess her position in the Near East and her relations with Turkey. Most important was the increase of the Turkish fleet by the purchase in 1910 of two almost obsolete battleships in Germany and the contract in the following year for two dreadnoughts to be built in Great Britain. If Turkish naval plans were completed, Russia might find herself surpassed in the Black Sea. The Ottoman government was also considering the construction by American or French interests of railways in Asia Minor reaching the Black Sea and the Russian and Persian borders. Again, if such plans were realized, enabling Turkey to move troops rapidly toward the Caucasus, Russia would face a security problem on land as well as at sea. The Russian foreign ministry, the army, and the admiralty discussed the problem intermittently from the spring of 1910. It became clear that the naval question could scarcely be solved satisfactorily unless passage through the Straits would permit the cooperation of the Black and Baltic seas fleets. As for the railway problem, Russia could not financially afford to buttress her defenses in the Caucasus by building railroads on her side of the border.[3]

Because Russia was handicapped financially and geographically in meeting her security problem, her only recourse was diplomacy. On the railway issue, the Minister of Foreign Affairs had long since given up the notion that Russia could maintain the agreement of 1900 with Turkey by which, if the Turkish government could not itself construct railways in northeastern Asia Minor, Russia would have the exclusive right to do so. Although German and American interests canceled plans to build railways in the area of the Russo-Turkish agreement, French financial groups dickered with the Porte to construct lines in both Asia Minor and across the Balkans. In April 1911, Ambassadors Charykov and Bompard at Constantinople drew up a protocol embodying the railway projects and the views of Russia and France; and early in August the Porte and the French signed a declaration of intent to contract for the proposed lines. Because Russia was not in a position to thwart plans that had the support of her French ally, Neratov decided to attempt a revision of the 1900 agreement by providing for a junction of Turkish and Russian lines as one step toward a Russo-Turkish rapprochement that might pave the way for an opening of the Straits.

3. See Edward C. Thaden, *Russia and the Balkan Alliances*, pp. 30ff.; George W. F. Hallgarten, *Imperialismus*, II, 164ff.

Concerning the Straits and the problem of Russian naval superiority in the Black Sea, discussions took place, beginning in May 1911, among the ministries of foreign affairs, navy, and war, and on 7 August, Neratov proposed to Finance Minister Kokovtsov that Turkey be asked to open the Straits to Russian war ships in return for Russia's consent to the building of the Eastern Anatolian railways; if the Porte agreed in principle, the question of the Straits could later be referred to international deliberation. Kokovtsov opposed both the raising of the Straits question and the linking of the railway problem with it. Nevertheless, upon the outbreak of the Italo-Turkish war, Neratov went ahead with plans for negotiations with Turkey.

Although both Izvolsky and Charykov urged that Russia take advantage of the outbreak of war to forward her interests in Turkey and the Balkans, Neratov had undoubtedly prepared his instructions of 2 October to Charykov before receiving either plea. His instructions conformed in the main with his proposal of August to Kokovtsov, except that he stressed the pursuit of the Anatolian railway question first and the broaching of other points only if the reception of the railway proposal was favorable. With his directive to Charykov he included drafts of four agreements: on the railways, the opening of the Straits to Russian warships, an increase in Turkish customs duties, and the transfer to Russia of Turkish contracts with Armstrong of England for the building of dreadnoughts. Neratov, like Charykov, felt that in addition to the outbreak of war the change in the Turkish government by which Said Pasha had become grand vizier made the moment a favorable one for negotiations, because Said was expected to turn from Germany toward Great Britain. Neratov followed his despatch of the 2nd with telegrams urging the opening of talks with the Turks and conveying the tsar's approval.

At the outset, vagueness on the part of Neratov and overeagerness on that of Charykov bedeviled the diplomatic enterprise. Charykov, in his letter of 30 September, had emphasized the importance of the preliminary approval of France and Italy before approaching the Porte, and when Neratov assured him that the ideas in his letter had been carried out, apparently meaning that he had informed France and Italy, Charykov assumed that they had given their approval. This was not true of France, whose acquiescence in the Russian proposal Neratov requested on 5 October, and Italy promised her loyalty to the Racconigi agreement only on the 13th. On the other hand, Charykov wanted to add to Neratov's proposals the promise that Russia would use her "good offices to facilitate the establishment—on the basis of the status quo—of firm, good-neighborly relations between the Imperial Ottoman Government and the Balkan states." He also proposed a Russian offer to discuss the capitulations. Assuming French consent to the Russian move, he took the French ambassador, Bompard, completely into his confidence. Although Neratov, perceiving that Charykov was exceeding his instructions, warned him to proceed with the greatest caution, Charykov as early as 12 October had given a "personal" letter to Said Pasha outlining Russian proposals.[4] In his letter Charykov included Neratov's offers concerning the Anatolian railways and the Straits, but substituted his own ideas about the status quo in the Balkans and the capitulations in place of Neratov's offer to support tariff increases and his request for the transfer of dreadnought contracts. He did stress to the grand vizier that his letter represented his own private views.

During the remainder of October the outlook for Turkish acceptance of the Russian proposals looked bright. Assim Bey, the foreign minister, told Charykov that he wanted a rapprochement with Russia and Said Pasha asserted that Turkey could not remain isolated; he hoped to conclude an entente, not an alliance; and to strengthen Turkish relations with all the powers, especially the Balkan states. Charykov thought Said might first approach Germany but on conditions that Germany could not accept, and he would then turn to England rather than to Russia or France; a Turkish understanding with England could lighten the way for Russia to achieve her objectives. The Ottoman government fulfilled Charykov's predictions by approaching Great Britain with a proposal for an alliance at the end of October, but was promptly turned down until after the end of the war with Italy. This failure was a serious if not fatal blow to the success of Russo-Turkish negotiations, because Turkey was fearful that the Russian proposals meant Russian domination, a second Unkiar Skelessi, if Turkey were not protected by a broadening of the rapprochement to include Great Britain and perhaps France. But there were other reasons, too, why Ottoman statesmen began to cool toward Charykov's proposals. While interested in establishing friendly relations with the Balkan states on the basis of the status quo, they were suspicious of a Balkan league that would be dominated by Russia and would inevitably arouse the implacable opposition of Austria-Hungary. Said Pasha, therefore, in November resorted to dilatory tactics.

Meanwhile, Neratov had been disturbed by the wording of Charykov's letter to the grand vizier, for he had made the opening of the Straits dependent upon the previous consent of the other signatories of the Convention of 1871, whereas Neratov wanted to make an agreement with Turkey and then notify the other signatory powers, just as France and Germany were doing in respect to Morocco. Moreover, Neratov was worried over the complications that the inclusion of Turkey in a Balkan league might create, because Russia was already fostering the Serbo-Bulgarian steps toward an alliance. Yet, though he chided Charykov on 22 October, he went along with him by informing Neklyudov in Sofia and Hartvig in Belgrade that the Serbo-Bulgarian alliance should be so framed that Turkey could adhere to it, and subsequently forwarded instructions to that effect. Because both Russian diplomats rejected the idea, the proposed shift in the character of the Balkan alliances was dropped. Neratov, however, was as eager as ever to push the negotiations with the Porte and on 2 November urged Charykov to take advantage of the rumor that Italy might extend the war to the Aegean and attack the Dardanelles in order to press the Porte to complete the negotiations.

While Charykov optimistically continued his efforts at Constantinople, Neratov renewed his attempt to get the support of the great powers. Selves on 14 October had given a general assurance that Russia could count upon the full assent of France, but wanted to find out British views. When Benckendorff approached Grey on 23 October, the latter asserted that Great Britain would stand by the declaration to Izvolsky on 14 October 1908, but any "new" formula would have to be considered by the Cabinet. Neratov, dissatisfied with the attitude of Britain and France, asked on 2 November for written statements from both powers. From France he wanted "entire liberty of action," and from England a written opinion concerning Russia's proposed agreement with the Porte. Great Britain failed to answer the request, because Grey was unwilling to comment until after the Porte had given its consent, and France finally replied on 4 January 1912, long after the "Charykov kite" had fallen to the ground.

Germany seemed less hesitant than Russia's partners. When Osten-Sacken, who had been reluctant to broach the question, finally asked Kiderlen his views and requested his support in Vienna, Kiderlen replied that Germany would not oppose in any fashion a Russian arrangement with the Porte concerning the Straits, but he hedged with reference to Austria-Hungary, saying that Vienna wanted to know the details of the proposed agreement. In fact Kiderlen and Aehrenthal disagreed, for the latter opposed the Russian proposals, while Kiderlen thought there was little risk in trying to win Russian gratitude and thus to sow discord among the entente partners, for he doubted if Britain would support Russia. Marschall in Constantinople, to whom the Turks appealed for support early in December, vigorously opposed Kiderlen's position, even threatening to resign, and in the end won out. Both the Austrian and German ambassadors, in mid-December when Charykov had already been ordered to drop negotiations, declared to the Ottoman foreign minister that their countries supported the status quo.

Meanwhile, without awaiting instructions, Charykov had resubmitted his proposal of 12 October on 27 November, this time "officially." At this point Sazonov stepped in. He had recovered his health, and on his way home gave an interview in Paris to the *Matin* that was published on 9 December. In it he declared that Russia had "asked for nothing, has not begun negotiations of any sort, and had not sought to undertake any step." At the same time he telegraphed Neratov to instruct Charykov "to establish clearly the completely private character of his exchange of ideas with the Turks . . . and by no means to give these discussions the signification of official negotiations."[5] Obviously, on the basis of talks in Paris with Izvolsky and Benckendorff and with the French, Sazonov had grasped the hopelessness of the attempt to come to an understanding with the Porte. Clearly the Turks had made an about-face after the British rejection of their advance at the end of October, and were privately and publicly resisting any opening of the Straits to Russia. "No government, no Turk," declared a Turkish newspaper on 6 December, "could for a moment entertain the idea that the Ottoman Empire might fall to the level of a Russian vassal."[6]

Also, Foreign Minister Sazonov was aware that there was little foundation for including Turkey in a Balkan confederation, and he himself favored a Serbo-Bulgarian alliance. The second day after he returned to the Singers' Bridge, Sazonov ordered Charykov to tell Assim Bey that "we are compelled now to suspend the further exchange of views, but would always be ready to listen privately to the views of Turkey concerning the questions mentioned." For Charykov's personal orientation, Sazonov added that the receipt of an official Turkish answer to

<hr>

5. Sazonov to Neratov, Paris, 9 December/26 November 1911: 3 *IBZI*, II, no. 186, and 215, note 1.

6. As quoted by Langer, "Russia, the Straits Question, and the Origins of the Balkan League," *PSQ*, XLIII (1928), 352.

his proposals was undesirable.[7] Nevertheless, Assim Bey on 21 December handed Charykov a declaration that the Ottoman government could not authorize the exclusive passage of the Russian fleet through the Straits in either peacetime or wartime. This categorical rejection of Russia's démarche brought an inglorious end to Charykov's efforts, and his failure cost him his post, although he was not recalled until March 1912.

Although Charykov's own later statement loyally represented the official Russian view that he undertook negotiations with the Porte on his own initiative, the "Charykov kite" is a misnomer for the diplomatic episode, because, despite his freewheeling interpretation of instructions, the Russian government after months of deliberation had authorized the *démarche* in the hope that the exigencies of the Italo-Turkish war offered a golden opportunity to achieve at least two objectives: a revision of the railway agreement with Turkey of 1900, and the freedom of the Straits. It is true that Charykov added a third, the creation of a Balkan confederation including Turkey, but from the viewpoint of St. Petersburg the aim of establishing a Russian-directed bloc of Balkan states was already in process of realization, owing to the efforts of Ambassadors Neklyudov and Hartvig in Sofia and Belgrade. Charykov, however, was not alone in bungling the negotiations with the Turks. Neratov had been just as guilty in failing to procure the support of the powers in advance, as Charykov had advised, and in failing to keep Charykov properly informed of the attitude of his diplomatic colleagues and of the great powers. After the moment in October 1911, when Said Pasha's government wanted to come to terms with the entente powers, the doubtful support of Britain and France and the resistance of Austria-Hungary and finally of Germany rendered any hope of success illusory.

Though Sazonov grasped the hopelessness of the situation, whereas Neratov had muddled along, Sazanov did not give up the idea of revising the railroad agreement with Turkey, returning to the subject in January 1912. Other developments, however, such as the problem of the Serbo-Bulgarian alliance, the questions raised by the continuation of the Tripolitan war, and the Persian crisis absorbed his attention to the exclusion of Anatolian railways.

7. Sazonov to Charykov, 15/2 December 1911, 3 *IBZI*, II, no. 207.

III.

Although the Russian attempt to open the Straits, because of its secrecy and unofficial character, failed to arouse great public interest in England, the British government's policy in the Agadir and Persian crises brought Radical-Liberal and Labor opposition to Sir Edward Grey's foreign policy to a head. The two aspects of British foreign policy were interrelated, but the crucial question in the press and parliamentary debates in November and December was Persia.

Without going into details, we may note that the crisis there arose over Russian determination to hamstring the work of W. Morgan Shuster, Treasurer-General, in reforming Persian finances and putting Persia on her feet as an independent nation. Russia looked upon his creation of a Persian gendarmerie under British officers and his disregard of Russian interests in northern Persia as a threat to her determination to dominate her sphere of influence there both economically and politically. Two ultimatums to the Persian government at the beginning and end of November and the sending of Russian troops into the country aroused such a storm in England that Benckendorff feared for the life of the Anglo-Russian entente and of the British government. Undoubtedly his pleas for Russian consideration of the serious situation in London helped to prevent a Russian occupation of northern Persia, although they did not save Shuster from the dismissal in which Grey himself had acquiesced.

In opening the parliamentary debate on foreign policy, 27 November 1911, Grey explained the government's policy respecting Germany and sought to defend his Persian policy. On the latter he took the position that the Anglo-Russian convention had ended "constant friction" between the two nations, as it was intended to do; and that the "independence of Persia must take account of the interests of her neighbors. . . . Without the Anglo-Russian agreement the independence of Persia would have been infinitely more threatened than today, and the relations of England and Russia imperilled."[8] By the time the debate was renewed, 14 December, tension had eased somewhat and Grey, pursuing the same line as before, made it clear that his basic policy was friendship with Russia come what might in Persia. Between the two

8. Grey's speech: *BD*, VII, 725–35. For the debate see John A. Murray, "Foreign Policy Debated," *Power, Public Opinion and Diplomacy* (Durham, N.C., 1959), pp. 140–71.

dates, however, his views had helped to modify Russian demands upon the Persian government. His critics were not satisfied but by mid-February 1912 were quieted by the restoration of cooperation between the Persian and Russian governments.

As for Germany, Grey himself had voiced the thought that perhaps Great Britain had been too hard on her, and in his November speech he declared that he did not want to oppose German expansion in Africa. Through December 1911 and January 1912 his critics continued to demand some form of agreement with Germany and thus spurred Grey and the government to attempt once more a naval-colonial deal with Germany, picking up where the previous negotiations had left off before the *Panther's* spring at Agadir.

German resentment at what was regarded as British intervention in the Agadir crisis found an outlet in the demand for a bigger navy. Admiral Tirpitz was quick to capitalize upon this sentiment, and upon his own conclusion that the Moroccan settlement was a diplomatic defeat for Germany. Accordingly, he planned a supplementary naval bill, the *Novelle*, which would provide a third squadron for the high seas fleet, more rapid replacement of obsolete armored cruisers, and a building program of six dreadnoughts over the next six years in addition to the two each year in the existing naval law. His objective was no longer a "risk" fleet but a ratio of 2:3 in comparison with the British, in order to ensure Germany against attack and to create a new power relationship that would compel political and colonial concessions in the future and even a shift of British alignment from France to Germany. He had no difficulty in persuading the kaiser to approve the plan, but ran into the obstinate resistance of Bethmann Hollweg, who, along with Ambassador Metternich, envisaged the dire effects of the *Novelle* on relations with Great Britain. In mid-November, however, Bethmann agreed to provide for the *Novelle* in the next budget. He feared dismissal if he did not, but he sought also to establish the primacy of the army over the navy, and won his point with the kaiser in January 1912. He had in mind not only a modification of Tirpitz's plans in agreement with England, but also a far-reaching colonial accord with her.

Even before Grey's conciliatory remarks in his speech of November, Bethmann moved to reopen naval discussions by reminding Ambassador Goschen that the British government had never replied to the German proposal of the previous spring. The Christmas holidays and the German Reichstag elections of January 1912, however, delayed a British reply until 28 January, when the subject of an exchange of fleet information became lost to view because of the Haldane mission. Meanwhile, Grey and Metternich opened talks about possible colonial agreements, on the assumption that something like the bases of the Anglo-French and Anglo-Russian ententes might be worked out which would lead to better Anglo-German relations. On Bethmann's instructions, Metternich touched upon the Belgian Congo, the Portuguese African colonies, the Persian Gulf, and the Bagdad Railway.

The kaiser, however, was scornful of the notion that Germany should acquire additional colonies, and Tirpitz and his supporters stubbornly insisted that the way to attract England and thus weaken her ententes with France and Russia was to build a larger fleet. Ambassador Metternich eloquently pleaded for the dropping of the *Novelle*, which, in his judgment, would only convince the world that Germany was intending war and would spur the British to meet the challenge with increases in their fleet. The *Novelle*, he firmly believed, would prevent any kind of agreement with England, whereas to increase the army, for which plans were already being prepared, would not endanger good relations with England and would give Germany advantages on the Continent, where the ultimate decision for her "must always take place."[9] In the midst of this conflict of opinion the cooperation of Ballin and Cassel brought about a renewal of naval discussions and led to the Haldane mission.

As in 1909, again in 1912, Albert Ballin and Sir Ernest Cassel undertook to bring about a resumption of Anglo-German negotiations over their naval rivalry. Ballin apparently took the initiative early in January by writing to Cassel, who approached Winston Churchill, first lord of the Admiralty since the previous October. As a result of his talks in London, Cassel went to Berlin, where he met Ballin, Bethmann, and the kaiser. His report led to the decision of the British Cabinet, 5 February, to send Haldane, secretary for war, to Berlin. They chose Haldane rather than Grey, who was skeptical that an understanding could be achieved and fearful of the effect of a mission to Berlin upon Paris, because they wanted the mission to be "private and informal, so that, if nothing came of it, there would be no sensation and little disappointment to the public." Because Haldane frequently visited Germany and was friendly with the kaiser and other important personages, his going to Berlin was "more natural and less artificial" than that of any other member of the Cabinet. Moreover, his brother,

9. Paul von Wolff-Metternich, "Meine Denkschrift über die Flotten novelle von 10 Januar 1912," *EG*, IV (1926), 57–71.

a well-known scholar, accompanied him to help disguise the nature of his mission.[10]

Grey had good reason for doubting the success of the Haldane mission, because, despite the exchanges that had occurred through Ballin and Cassel, the British and German governments were working at cross-purposes. The British position that Cassel had carried to Berlin was stated to be the acceptance of English superiority at sea and a reduction as far as possible of the German naval building program in return for promotion of German colonial ambitions and mutual declarations that neither power would take part in aggressive plans or combinations against the other. In replying on 3 February to the German response through Cassell, the British government warned that an increase in the German building program would entail a "serious and immediate increase of British expenditures," but if the

> German naval expenditures can be adapted by an alteration of tempo or otherwise so as to render any serious increase unnecessary to meet the German programme, [the] British Government will be prepared at once to pursue negotiations on the understanding that the point of naval expenditure is open to discussion and that there is a fair prospect of settling it favourably.[11]

On the other hand, Bethmann, agreeing with Metternich's view of the serious consequences if the *Novelle* went through, succeeded after great difficulty in persuading Tirpitz to accept a discussion of tonnage, but only on condition that Britain give sufficient guarantees of a friendly disposition toward Germany. An agreement not to participate in combinations against each other would make possible an understanding about expenditures on armaments. If Britain agreed with these views, Germany was "ready to continue the discussion in a friendly spirit."[12]

Although these bases for discussion covered much the same ground, the emphasis was different, just as it had been in the negotiations of 1909–1911. Britain wanted a naval agreement first, to be followed by political understandings, whereas Germany made political agreements the condition for naval discussions. This difference in approach

10. Grey, *Twenty-Five Years*, I, 241–43. See Randolph S. Churchill, *Winston S. Churchill*, II, 1901–1914, 541–43, for Cassel's contacts with Churchill and the latter's approval of talks.

11. W. S. Churchill, *The World Crisis*, pp. 99–100.

12. As quoted by B. E. Schmitt, "Lord Haldane's Mission to Berlin in 1912," *The Crusades*, pp. 252–53.

plagued the negotiations throughout their duration. Furthermore, the British government envisaged Haldane's mission as purely exploratory, whereas the Germans treated his visit as that of a plenipotentiary, and afterward when the British raised objections to points that he had seemed to accept, the Germans, especially the kaiser, believed them guilty of perfidy and double dealing. The British, on the other hand, felt that the Germans deliberately misrepresented Haldane's mission and words.

In addition, neither government was united in its attitude toward the negotiations. In Germany, Tirpitz and the "navy clique," including the kaiser most of the time, wanted above all to put through the *Novelle* in order to achieve a ratio with Great Britain of 2:3 and only grudgingly accepted a discussion of their program, while Bethmann, supported by the Wilhelmstrasse, wanted a political agreement providing for British neutrality if Germany were involved in war, and was ready to pay for it by a reduced naval building program. In England, the government approved the Haldane mission in part because of public pressure arising from dissatisfaction with the Agadir and Persian policies, and in part to head off an increase in the German navy that would entail a heavy financial burden for the British taxpayer. A few members of the Cabinet—among them Morley, Harcourt, Loreburn, and Haldane—sincerely wanted an understanding with Germany, but the professionals in the Foreign Office and diplomatic corps—Crowe, Nicolson, Goschen, and Bertie most prominently—were too mistrustful of Germany and too concerned to maintain and even to strengthen the Triple Entente to support wholeheartedly efforts directed toward an Anglo-German understanding. Moreover, they were naturally suspicious of the "amateur diplomacy" represented by Haldane, who admittedly had little knowledge of the intricacies of previous negotiations over the naval problem. While Haldane was in Berlin, Churchill, who supported the mission, talked in Glasgow on 9 February in a way that enraged the Germans and angered some of his colleagues, for he spoke of the British navy as a necessity and referred to the German navy as "more in the nature of a luxury." He went on to declare that Britain would meet any competition without "whining," and by increasing her margin of superiority would prove to other naval powers that they would be outdistanced "in consequence of the measures which we ourselves will take."[13] This pronouncement hardly contributed to a cordial atmosphere for Haldane in Berlin.

13. W. S. Churchill, *The World Crisis*, pp. 101–04.

Haldane spent three days at the German capital, 8–10 February, and talked with the chancellor, the kaiser, and Tirpitz. Though Haldane and Bethmann discussed colonial questions, they were of secondary importance. The focus of the talks was upon shipbuilding and a political agreement. Haldane did not accept a ratio of 2:3 but did agree that Germany needed a reorganization of her fleet and did not seem disturbed over the establishment of a third squadron. What he proposed was a slowing down of the dreadnought construction until the climate of Anglo-German feeling improved through the establishment of better relations.

The Germans made it clear that there could be no modification of their naval program without a political agreement, and Bethmann discussed with Haldane a draft convention that would pledge the two powers not to attack one another or participate in any combination directed against the other; in case either became "entangled" in a war with one or more powers, the other would observe benevolent neutrality. Tirpitz was willing to drop one dreadnought from the *Novelle* as the price of such an agreement. Here was the crux of the whole matter. As the Germans saw it, they were being offered a British pledge not to attack them and some colonial possessions of little value in return for a naval limitation that would leave them facing a greatly superior British fleet that might be thrown into the balance should Germany become embroiled with France and Russia. On the other hand, the British felt that Germany was offering only a retardation of their building plans in return for a pledge that would break the ententes with France and Russia, and would permit a German thrust to the Channel that, in case of war, would threaten British security. The essential point for Britain was a reduction in German naval building; for Germany it was relief from the threat of an Anglo-French-Russian combination against her.

While Bethmann Hollweg in Berlin struggled against Tirpitz and an increasingly mistrustful and angry kaiser to postpone the official publication of the *Novelle*, Metternich in London carried on discussions with Grey, Haldane, and others. The British Admiralty discovered features in the *Novelle*, the text of which Haldane had brought back with him, that had not entered previous discussions, but when called to the attention of the Germans, the kaiser and Bethmann felt that, because Haldane had not objected to the aspects of the *Novelle* now being criticized, he was being disavowed and the bases of discussion were being changed.

Nevertheless, when Bethmann on 12 March telegraphed Metternich that the *Novelle* was still being held back in the hope that Britain would meet German wishes concerning a political agreement, Grey, who had been preoccupied with a threatening coal strike, drafted a declaration that was approved by the Cabinet and handed to Metternich on 14 March. It ran:

> England will make no unprovoked attack on Germany, and pursue no aggressive policy toward her. Aggression upon Germany is not the subject, and forms no part of any Treaty, understanding, or combination to which England is now a party nor will she become a party to anything that has such an object.

Metternich felt that because this formula did not contain the word "neutrality," it would not be acceptable. Next day he suggested an addition, to the effect that "England will therefore observe at least benevolent neutrality should war be forced upon Germany," or alternatively, "England will therefore as a matter of course remain neutral if a war is forced upon Germany." Grey defended his formula by saying that it described the situation exactly, for if France attacked Germany, England would not support her, whereas the German addition "might be taken to mean that under no circumstances, if there was a war on the continent, could anything be expected of us."[14] On 16 March Grey discussed with Metternich the rewording of phrases, but it was perfectly clear that Britain would make no pledge of neutrality, and Germany would accept nothing else.

From 16 March to 10 April, when Bethmann gave up the search for an acceptable formula, the Anglo-German exchanges amounted to little more than the threshing of old straw, except for renewed attention to colonial questions that were not followed up. Meanwhile, Churchill presented naval estimates to Parliament, 18 March, explaining that Britain would no longer pursue a two-power naval standard, but rather a 60 percent superiority over Germany. Also, he suggested a naval building holiday. On 22 March the German government published a summary of the *Novelle* in the semi-official *Norddeutsche Allgemeine Zeitung*. Bethmann's final word of 3 April, communicated to Grey on the 10th, was that the English refusal "to offer us a satisfactory agreement about neutrality means that we can no longer hope to meet British wishes by modifying our supplementary naval law." He was ready, however, to continue the discussions of colonial and territorial questions. On 10 April, Asquith came to the same conclu-

14. Grey to Goschen, 14 and 15 March 1912: *BD*, VI, nos. 537, 539; Metternich to Grey, 14 March 1912: ibid., no. 538.

sión as Bethmann, writing to Grey about the discussions with Germany: "Nothing, I believe, will meet her purpose which falls short of a promise on our part of neutrality: a promise we cannot give. And she makes no firm or solid offer, even in exchange for that."[15] The British and undoubtedly Tirpitz and his supporters breathed a sigh of relief that the fruitless negotiations had come to an end. Metternich, who had incurred the wrath of the kaiser for his failure, as the kaiser saw it, to stand up to the British, lost his post, to be succeeded in June by the redoubtable Alfred Baron Marschall von Bieberstein, whose sudden death in August prevented a renewal of Anglo-German negotiations under his auspices.

During the negotiations in February and March, Grey or Nicolson had informed Cambon and Benckendorff about them. Ten days after the deadlock of 16 March and nearly a week after Grey had told Cambon that Britain had refused to promise Germany her neutrality, Ambassador Bertie asked Foreign Minister Poincaré to take a strong stand against a British pledge to Germany. The French protests that ensued were represented by Izvolsky some months later, when Poincaré told him about them, as the reason why England rejected the German proposals; and revisionist historians seized upon the story as an explanation for the failure of the Anglo-German negotiations. The chronology of the deadlock and the French protests indicates clearly, however, that Britain and German had both taken a stand that rendered further negotiations futile long before Ambassador Bertie prompted Poincaré to protest against a pledge of British neutrality.

The failure of the attempt, initiated by the Haldane mission, to reach an Anglo-German understanding lay in the irreconcilability of the British and German positions as imposed by balance-of-power politics. The Germans could not logically give up their armament plans as long as they had to face a potential Anglo-French-Russian combination in case of war. Where they failed, however, was in their insistence upon building sea power that inevitably ranged Britain against them, whereas land power was the crucial issue for a nation in the heart of Europe, as Metternich pointed out at the time. In the end Tirpitz' *Novelle* only ranged England more solidly against Germany and caused her to build and reorganize her fleet in such a way as to nullify the advantages that Tirpitz had sought.

Great Britain was pursuing a logical course, too, because Germany

15. Bethmann Hollweg to Metternich, 3 April, and Metternich to Bethmann, 10 April 1912: *GP*, XXXI, nos. 11440–41; Asquith to Grey, 10 April 1912: *BD*, VI, no. 571.

had asked for a pledge that was more far-reaching than any Britain had made to any other power in Europe, except Portugal—as Grey pointed out more than once during the negotiations. The British insistence upon free hands in the event of a European war was an old tradition not lightly to be given up. Where logic failed them was in approaching an Anglo-German détente over naval competition as if they were dealing with the same kind of problem that the ententes with France and Russia had solved. The points of imperialistic rivalry settled with those powers were much more easily resolved than competition in armaments, which involved security, prestige, and national honor. As Bethmann pointed out, the German offer to limit naval expenditure was "unprecedented in history."[16] Moreover, the British set against Germany had become too firmly established. Nicolson had been uneasy lest Britain make some engagement that would offend France and, indirectly, Russia. He explained to Goschen that it was far more disadvantageous to have an unfriendly France and Russia than an unfriendly Germany, although he believed that relations with Germany had "cleared considerably" and there was no reason for unfriendliness.[17] In fact, the Haldane mission and its aftermath did ease Anglo-German relations sufficiently to make possible a collaboration during the Balkan wars and eventual arrangements concerning the Portuguese colonies and the Bagdad railway, the latter being the only point of serious imperialistic rivalry between the two powers. On the other hand, the failure to reach an Anglo-German naval agreement led immediately to a tightening of the bonds between Britain and France.

IV.

Although Great Britain and France had concerted plans for the cooperation of their armies in case of war, their naval staffs had never reached explicit agreements, nor even kept in close touch with each other. Yet leading French statesmen and soldiers like Delcassé and General Joffre were convinced that war was inevitable and might even come in the spring of 1912. Sir Francis Bertie, playing his occasional role as prompter to the French, urged Poincaré early in February 1912 that in view of the alarming European situation, France and England

16. Grey to Goschen, 10 April 1912: *BD*, VI, no. 573.
17. Nicolson to Goschen, 15 April 1912: ibid., no. 575. Lowe and Dockrill, *Mirage of Power*, I, 48–52, add information about Cabinet attitudes and activities respecting the Haldane Mission.

should get together at once. The French acted upon this advice only in April when Paul Cambon suggested to Nicolson a declaration of the British position in case of a Franco-German war. Nicolson, however, who was certainly in favor of whole-hearted cooperation with France, advised the ambassador that he thought it doubtful if His Majesty's government would tie its hands in any way. Therefore technical arrangements for military cooperation remained, but naval and political commitments were still lacking.

Circumstances on both sides, however, led to an Anglo-French naval understanding within a year. On the British side, the failure of negotiations with Germany necessitated a reorganization of the British fleet. Plans had been adumbrated by Churchill on 18 March 1912 and were finally authorized by the government after a naval-military conference at Malta in late May. In order to counter the threat of an expanded German naval force, a home fleet of three squadrons was created, with a fourth squadron to be located at Gibraltar instead of Malta. This squadron was to cruise in the Mediterranean but be available in the Atlantic in case of a conflict with Germany. Because this arrangement left at Malta only some battle cruisers and armored cruisers augmented by submarines, the Malta conference recognized that a definite agreement with France would be necessary in order to maintain control of the Mediterranean. By mid-July the British Cabinet had approved this reorganization but had not yet acted upon an overture by Paul Cambon early in May concerning naval talks.

Churchill, after the Cabinet decision, opened discussions with the French naval attaché on 17 July and shortly thereafter submitted the draft of a naval convention, but the government was still reluctant to tie its hands by a definite agreement. In the meantime France had made the decision to shift her Brest squadron to Toulon, news of which leaked out prematurely in September. The British and French relocation of their naval forces required some kind of agreement if the security of the British in the Mediterranean and of the French in the Channel and the Atlantic were to be safeguarded. But even Churchill was reluctant to give up British freedom of action and the "consequent power to influence French policy beforehand," as he put it in a letter to Asquith, 23 August 1912.[18] Nevertheless, naval discussions went slowly forward to a conclusion in February 1913, providing for a division of responsibilities in the Mediterranean, the Channel, the Dover straits, and the Far East.

Long before the naval arrangement, the deadlock between the Brit-

18. W. S. Churchill, *The World Crisis*, pp. 115–16.

ish and French concerning a political agreement was finally broken through the suggestion of Paul Cambon of an exchange of letters between himself and Grey that would define the nature of the entente. With the approval of the Cabinet, Sir Edward wrote a note to Cambon, 22 November 1912, in which he began by recalling the understanding that naval and military consultations did not restrict the freedom of either government to decide "at any future time whether or not to assist the other by armed force"; but Cambon had pointed out that in case of attack by a third power it might prove "essential" to know if one could count upon the other. Grey therefore concluded:

> I agree that, if either Government had grave reason to expect an unprovoked attack by a third Power, or something that threatened the general peace, it should immediately discuss with the other whether both Governments should act together to prevent aggression and to preserve peace, and, if so, what measures they would be prepared to take in common. If these measures involved action, the plans of the General Staffs would at once be taken into consideration, and the Governments would then decide what effect should be given to them.

In his reply of 23 November, Cambon in slightly different language repeated the substance of Grey's statement that amounted to a pledge to consult with one another in case of an attack.[19]

Nicolson's (or his son's) comment upon the Grey-Cambon letters correctly affirms their signinficance:

> In eliciting this document from the Cabinet, M. Cambon had obtained something beyond his most optimistic expectations. It seems incredible that the British Government did not realize how far they were pledged. They had, in fact, committed themselves to a guaranty which would involve England either in a breach of faith or a war with Germany. And it was the Novelle of Admiral von Tirpitz which produced this curious result.[20]

19. Grey, *Twenty-Five Years*, I, 94–96. Grey implies that until this exchange most of the Cabinet members were ignorant of the military plans, but ministers knew of the talks as early as August 1911. See S. R. Williamson, *Politics of Grand Strategy*, pp. 196, 198.

20. Nicolson, *Carnock*, pp. 271–72. On the Grey-Cambon exchange and the naval talks, see Halpern, *The Mediterranean Naval Situation*, ch. IV; Lowe and Dockrill, *Mirage of Power*, I, 52–58.

While Anglo-French relations thus became more closely knit, those between Britain and Russia remained precarious, for when it became clear that the Haldane mission had failed, Russia returned to a harsh policy toward Persia that scarcely met with the approval of England. Moreover, the development of the Balkan alliances under Russian aegis in the spring of 1912 seemed to betoken an anti-Turkish policy that ill suited either England or France because of their concern for Moslem feeling and financial interests. Yet the Russians counted upon the Triple Entente to support their Balkan policy and upon British fear of the German navy to guarantee loyalty to Russia.

Both the Russians and the British hoped for better relations as a result of Sazonov's visit to England in late September, when he was entertained at Balmoral Castle and talked not only with the king and Grey but also with Bonar Law, leader of the opposition, Lord Crewe, secretary for India, and others. The official reception was cordial enough, but the London crowds and some newspapers gave vent to their ill-feeling toward Russia. This show of anti-Russian feeling led Sazonov to tell Nicolson at the end of his visit that he did not know if Anglo-Russian relations would remain intimate and cordial. Sazonov's report to the tsar indicated that he and the British statesmen had discussed a wide variety of subjects, ranging from the question of British naval aid in the Baltic in case of a Russo-German war to Tibet and Mongolia. The major emphasis was on Persia; they reached a consensus to keep Germany out of the neutral zone. As for the Balkans and Turkey, Sazonov and Grey discussed proposals for maintaining peace, but Grey, to Sazonov's disappointment, seemed more anxious over the reaction of the Moslem world to Turkish difficulties than over the fate of Ottoman Christians. Sazonov concluded that Russia could not count upon British support if a further deterioration of the Balkan situation required energetic pressure upon the Turkish government.

St. Petersburg was greatly disappointed over Sazonov's visit to England because so much attention had been paid to Persia and so little to the Balkans. A brother of the late Premier Stolypin warned Russians in the *Novoye Vremya* not to put much faith in the entente with Britain, and Ambassador Buchanan reported on 9 October an "outburst of resentment against England." Public opinion, he wrote, attributed the aggravation of the Balkan crisis "to the lack of support given Russia by her partners in the Triple Entente." One newspaper, formerly a supporter of the entente, recommended its abandonment and a rapprochement with Germany. Nicolson, one of the architects of the Anglo-Russian entente, minuted Buchanan's despatch to the effect that they might have to make up their minds whether to take up the Balkan cause with Russia and risk offense to the Moslems and Turks, or to placate the latter and imperil the Triple Entente, "and probably break it."[21] A week later he was appealing to Paul Cambon to cooperate in applying themselves to the maintenance of the Triple Entente, to strengthening the ties of England and France, and to working together in St. Petersburg in order to dissipate the suspicions there of the English government and its policy. He argued in a letter to Buchanan that the entente with Russia was of more vital interest to England than to Russia; if it should break up, Russia would have a free hand in the Middle and Far East; also, relations with France would not remain so intimate; and finally, England would have to become the "subservient friend" of Germany, who could offer no help in stopping Russian encroachments in Asia.[22]

France, too, had had her difficulties with Russia in 1912, although of a different kind from Britain's. In Franco-Russian relations, the fear of a European war, perhaps even in 1912, the continuing and apparently unending Italo-Turkish war, and the unmistakable signs of increasing Balkan unrest and truculence all formed a significant background. Moreover, the mood of heightened confidence in French military power and of patriotic fervor inspired a bolder conduct of foreign relations. The German military attaché concluded that "the French people have gradually fallen into a kind of ecstacy which has led to a substantial enhancement of national self-consciousness."[23] In this situation Poincaré reflected the aims endorsed by Frenchmen in that he was concerned for the security, the influence, and the prestige of France. In pursuit of these ends and in keeping with his precise, legal approach to problems, he wanted to know where France stood, not only with Britain, as noted above, but also with Russia, hoping to tighten the bonds of the Triple Entente in its opposition to the Triple Alliance. The relations with Russia were particularly important because France had not forgotten the Potsdam agreement of 1910–1911, about which Russia had not consulted her, and the lukewarm support during the Agadir crisis. To be sure, Cruppi and Selves, Poincaré's predecessors at the Quai d'Orsay, had not been men to inspire confidence in the perspicacity or vigor of French policy, but, as Izvolsky observed, Poin-

---

21. Buchanan to Grey, 6 and 9 October 1912: *BD*, IX(1), nos. 808, 811.
22. Nicolson to Buchanan, 22 October 1912: *BD*, IX(2), no. 57.
23. Winterfeldt Report, Paris, 19 February 1912: *GP*, XXXI, no. 11515. Cf. Schoen to Bethmann, 22 March 1912; ibid., no. 11520.

caré was a man of a quite different stripe, with whom discussion was not only useful but necessary.

Shortly after taking office, Poincaré agreed with Izvolsky that France and Russia should keep in very close contact, and especially should come to agreement concerning the anticipated complications in the Near East. Ambassador Louis attributed to Sazonov the notion that the allies need only inform each other in advance of contemplated action. Poincaré, greatly irritated, emphasized to Izvolsky that the alliance obligated the two allies to "consult previously" with reference to any general policy not constituting a response to a German attack. Izvolsky tried to excuse Sazonov, suggesting that Louis had not understood him, or that he had carelessly used the word "inform" (*se prévenir*) for "consult" (*se concerter*). Poincaré was obviously not yet ready to discuss specific aspects of the Near East and Balkans, as suggested by Sazonov, but asserted that France remained firmly attached to her traditional policy in the Near East, i.e. the integrity of the Ottoman empire and the maintenance of the status quo in the Balkans.[24]

Although the question of a near-eastern policy was left hanging in the air, France and Russia took up the matter of a naval convention, which was finally agreed upon by the chiefs of the naval staffs on 16 July 1912. Like the military convention, it provided for close cooperation in planning naval operations and strategy, and for annual conferences of the chiefs of staff.[25]

Poincaré, obviously still mistrustful of Russian policy, deprecated the meeting of William II and Nicholas II at Baltic Port, 4–6 July, and long before it, decided to have a full-scale discussion with the Russians. Arriving in St. Petersburg on 9 August, he spent a week of sightseeing and of conferences with Premier Kokovtsov and Sazonov. Poincaré's notes on these discussions do not reveal significant details, but Sazonov recorded the important exchanges over obligations of the alliance in words that Poincaré himself asserted were accurate. Poincaré told Sazonov that French public opinion would not permit France to undertake military action for purely Balkan questions if Germany did not take part and if she did not "provoke on her own initiative the application of the *casus foederis*"; in case of war France would fulfill her treaty obligations. Sazonov, in response, reiterated

24. Poincaré to Georges Louis, 27 January, 14 March, 8 April 1912: 3 *DDF*, I, no. 539, and II, nos. 202, 310; Izvolsky to Sazonov, 14/1 March 1912: *LN*, I, 216–20.

25. The text: 3 *DDF*, III, no. 206.

what the tsar had told Ambassador Georges Louis in 1911, that Russian public opinion would not justify "taking an active part in military operations provoked by extra-European colonial matters, as long as the vital interests of France were not affected."[26] These statements represented no more than the traditional interpretation of the alliance obligations. If there were any further discussions that tended to modify them, there is no record of them.

An equally significant topic was the Balkan situation. When Poincaré learned for the first time the terms of the Serbo-Bulgarian treaty of March, he rightly judged them to constitute a "convention of War." Sazonov sought to remove his fears by insisting that Russia held a veto over the actions of Balkan states, and wanted to prevent the outbreak of war. In other matters, Poincaré sought to tighten the ties of the Triple Entente. When he and Sazonov exchanged letters, 15 and 16 August, formally approving the naval convention of the previous month, Poincaré urged that Russia seek agreement with England concerning cooperation in the Baltic as a complement to French naval assistance to Russia in the Mediterranean, where France would contain the Austrian navy and prevent its entry into the Black Sea. Poincaré also informed Sazonov of the military arrangements with Britain. With reference to Italy, they agreed that her membership as a "dead weight" in the Triple Alliance was useful to them both. Other matters, such as the Anatolian railways and the question of Georges Louis' recall, were of minor importance in their talks.[27]

Throughout the autumn, and especially after the outbreak of the Balkan war, October 1912, Poincaré maintained his attitude of watchful vigilance over French relations with Russia. He was in a difficult spot because French financial interests in the Balkans and the Ottoman empire clashed with Russian ambitions in the area. Nevertheless, he reiterated to Izvolsky his position on French obligations to Russia, and insisted upon previous consultation over Russian policy in the Balkans. He refused, moreover, to take the responsibility of suggesting policy, because Russia as the directly interested power should take the initiative. He reserved the right to examine proposed measures but would not agree with them or discuss them until he knew what they were. He believed that an Austro-Russian conflict over Serbia would involve German support of her ally and based his pledge to support Russia on

26. Sazonov, "Le voyage de Poincaré," 17/4 August 1912: LN, II, 338–45; "Notes de M. Poincaré," 3 DDF, III, no. 264.

27. Poincaré, Au service de la France, II, 119–20.

that premise. His position was that announced publicly at Nantes, 27 October: "France does not desire war, but it is not afraid of it." Schoen thought the statement an accurate reflection of the French temper, and a month later Moltke concluded that there were no signs that France was harboring bellicose designs.[28] The French position vis-à-vis Russia was not unlike that of Germany vis-à-vis Austria-Hungary: neither quite trusted her partner, but neither could fail to act if the *casus foederis* should arise.

As for the "broadening" of the Franco-Russian alliance, attributed by so many writers to Poincaré, it can scarcely be interpreted to mean that either power assumed new obligations. Rather, Poincaré's efforts were directed toward achieving a tighter relationship than that of 1910–1911, when each power ignored the other in formulating and acting upon policy. Poincaré by the autumn of 1912 knew full well that a Russo-Austrian conflict might provoke a European war in which France would inevitably be involved, because he assumed that Germany would support her ally and thus bring about the *casus foederis* stipulated in the Franco-Russian convention. He accepted this eventuality, but sought to make sure that "the conflict would not be unchained lightly [*à la légère*]."[29] Neither Poincaré nor Izvolsky planned to bring about war in 1912.

V.

While the powers of the Triple Entente were busily attempting to strengthen their ties and black clouds were gathering over the Balkans, Italy and Turkey continued to wage their indecisive war. Italian activities, however, created side effects for the great powers. In January 1912 Italian seizure of two French merchant ships, the *Carthage* and the *Manouba*, caused sharp exchanges between the two governments which, although ending in a settlement, left ill feeling on both sides. Germany and Austria-Hungary seized the opportunity offered by

28. Poincaré, 27 October 1912, as quoted by Schmitt, *The Coming of the War*, I, 66; Moltke Report, *GP*, XXXI, 416, note **.

29. See Izvolsky to Sazonov, 12 September/30 August and 5 December/22 November 1912: *LN*, I, 323–27, 362–68; Poincaré to Izvolsky and to Georges Louis, 16 November, and to Louis, 19 November 1912: 3 *DDF*, IV, nos. 468–69, 494. Cf. Hermann Kantorowicz, *Gutachten zur Kriegsschuldfrage 1914*, pp. 114–17, 173–75.

Franco-Italian tension to boost the loyalty of Italy to the Triplice, which became more popular in Italy than for a long time.

Efforts at mediation having failed, Italy in an attempt to bring Turkey to terms extended the war to the Aegean and bombarded the outer forts of the Dardenelles. This activity raised the question of compensation to Austria-Hungary under Article VII, but Count Berchtold, who had succeeded Aehrenthal in February 1912, finally agreed that Italy might take Rhodes and other islands on an Italian pledge that the occupation would be temporary. By the end of May Italy had seized all the Dodecanese, the permanent possession of which all the powers opposed. Except for one more bombardment of the Dardenelles in July, war activities simmered down, and secret and unofficial Italo-Turkish pourparlers got under way beginning in mid-June. The gathering storm in the Balkans and the outbreak of war in October hastened the conclusion of peace by the signature of a secret treaty on 15 October and a public treaty on the 18th at Ouchy, a suburb of Lausanne.

By the first treaty Italy and Turkey agreed upon a complicated face-saving procedure that provided for the transfer of Libya to Italy. The public treaty arranged for the cessation of hostilities, the removal of Turkish soldiers and civilians, the exchange of prisoners, and the like. Italy promised to recall her forces from the Dodecanese when Turkey had completely evacuated Libya, to conclude commercial treaties, to support Turkey in her effort to abolish the capitulations and increase customs duties, and to pay an annual sum of not less than 2,000,000 lire.[30]

The establishment of peace between Italy and Turkey cleared the way for the renewal of the Triple Alliance which had been hanging fire for more that a year. In the autumn of 1912, after the signature of Ouchy, San Giuliano proposed to Berchtold that they settle the matter of renewal as quickly as possible, for Italy's policy remained that of the previous decade: cordial relations with the Triple Entente, but membership in the Triplice in order to have a check on the Dual Monarchy in the Balkans. The renewed negotiations did not go smoothly, however. Berchtold objected to the supplementary protocol that San Giuliano proposed, by which the Italo-Austro-Hungarian agreements of 1900–1901 and 1909 were to be regarded as an integral part of the treaty. At length Kiderlen and San Giuliano worked out two protocols by which Italy gained the substance of her demands and Berchtold the

30. The texts: BD, IX(1), no. 466.

form. The unexpected victory of the Balkan states over Turkey and the advance of Serbia toward Albania persuaded Berchtold to accept the compromise. The three parties signed the treaty on 5 December 1912 at Vienna.[31]

The text of the treaty remained unchanged from that of 1902; the first of two protocols embodied the provisions of the 1902 protocol respecting most-favored-nation treatment in economic matters, the accession of England to the provisions for the status quo in Tripoli, Cyrenaica, and Tunis, and Italian action in these territories. The second protocol brought the treaty up to date by recognizing that the status quo implied Italian sovereignty over Libya, and satisfied Italy's demands with respect to her agreements with Austria-Hungary concerning Albania and the Sanjak of Novi Pazar by the understanding that they were "not modified by the renewal of the Treaty of alliance between Austria-Hungary, Germany, and Italy."

Although the Triple Alliance was thus renewed until 1920, with a possible extension to 1926, and Italy seemed more sincerely loyal to it than had been the case for several years, the structure was by no means solidly based, because the conflicts of interest between Italy and the Dual Monarchy still remained, and the relations between Germany and Austria-Hungary were by no means smooth. Kiderlen's determination to keep the leading strings of the alliance in the hands of Berlin, and Austro-Hungarian resentment over what they regarded as limitations upon their Balkan policy and as German flirtations with Russia, ever since Potsdam, remained close to the surface.

In brief, 1912 was a paradoxical year. On the one hand, the relations among the Entente powers and among the members of the Triplice had been tightened. On the other hand, there were still unresolved differences between Great Britain and Russia, France and Russia, and among all three of the Triplice members, while areas of interpenetration continued to exist. Russia and Germany, as indicated by the Baltic Port meeting, enjoyed a cordial atmosphere. Despite the failure of the Haldane mission, Germany and Britain experienced a feeling of détente that enabled them to cooperate during the first Balkan war. Although irritation existed on both sides between France and Italy, the new "status quo" in the Mediterranean, as a result of the Tripolitan war and the shift in naval power there from British to French hands, failed to arouse the kind of antagonism that had existed up to the turn of the century. Moreover, British insistence upon five-

31. Pribram, *Secret Treaties*, I, 245–59, and II, 168–73.

power rather than "group" action in dealing with Libyan and Balkan problems, with which the other powers at different times acquiesced, presaged a revival of the concert of Europe, even though the balance-of-power concept still compelled the maintenance of awkward alignments. The first Balkan war was to highlight these paradoxes and put the "two-camp" relationships of Europe to the test.

Chapter 11

The Balkan Wars,

1912–1913

During the Balkan wars a major change in the direction of great-power foreign policy occurred—the death of Kiderlen-Waechter on 30 December 1912 and the appointment in his place of Gottlieb von Jagow. In France Raymond Poincaré was elected president of the Republic, but here the change was slight because he continued to influence the premiers and foreign ministers who succeeded him. Significant changes occurred at other levels, however. In ambassadorial staffs Théophile Declassé replaced Georges Louis as French ambassador to Russia, Prince von Lichnowsky became German ambassador in London, and the Russian ministers in Sofia (Anatole Vassilievich Neklyudov) and Belgrade (Nicholas Hendrikovich Hartvig) became far more active than before. In Austria-Hungary, Count Blasius Schemua stepped down as Chief of the General Staff at the end of 1912 upon the reappointment of General Conrad von Hoetzendorff. In the Balkan states the veteran Nicholas Pašić again became Serbian premier in 1912, and in Bulgaria the Geshov-Danev ministry of 1911–1913 dissolved in June 1913 when Stoyan Danev became premier, only to be supplanted in July by Vasil Radoslavov.

The Balkan League that made war on Turkey in October 1912 owed its conception to the Bosnian crisis of 1908–1909. Count Leopold Berchtold, commenting upon the proposal of General Blasius Schemua, the Austro-Hungarian chief of staff, to mobilize in Bosnia and Herzegovina and Dalmatia in early October 1912, rightly declared:

> We may not give ourselves any illusion over [the fact] that our manner of advance in the annexation of Bosnia and Herzegovina not only has given the first impulse to the league of Balkan states, but also unavoidably has awakened the mistrust of all the great-power chancelleries against the Monarchy and thereby

created a bond of understanding, not existing before, in respect of their posture toward our eastern policy.[1]

But the progress toward the league that confronted Turkey in 1912 was slow and fitful.

I.

Three factors explain the difficulties and delays. First of all were the divergent interests among the Balkan states. Serbia, feeling that her future had been jeopardized by the Austro-Hungarian annexation of Bosnia-Herzegovina, and fearful that the Dual Monarchy would continue its southward expansion, sought an anti-Austria alliance under the slogan "The Balkans for the Balkan people." On the other hand, Bulgaria was primarily concerned with the Macedonian problem, which might be solved with Serbian and Greek help against Turkey or by a rapprochement with Turkey but in any case was not to be complicated by anti-Austrian objectives or by Greek aspirations to acquire Crete. Montenegro under the ambitious Nicholas, who assumed the title of king in 1910, though aggrieved by the annexation of Bosnia-Herzegovina, was less hostile to the Dual Monarchy and more anti-Turkish than Serbia. The rivalry for Balkan-Slav leadership between Nicholas and King Peter I remained a source of ill-feeling until 1912. Romania, still firmly tied to Austria-Hungary and the Triplice, had no interest in either anti-Austrian or anti-Turkish schemes, and was mistrusted by the other Balkan states, especially Bulgaria.

A second complicating factor, closely related to the first, was the Macedonian question. The wishes of the Internal Macedonian Revolutionary Organization to establish an autonomous regime with the motto "Macedonia for the Macedonians" hardly suited the three neighbors, although Bulgaria regarded it as a second-best solution after Bulgarian annexation. The alternative, partition, had never been agreed upon because of the conflicting ethnic and economic claims. The Macedonian riddle had baffled negotiators before 1909 and continued to thwart efforts at alliance or rapprochement from 1909 to 1911; it nearly caused the breakdown of Serbo-Bulgarian alliance negotiations in 1912.

The third factor was Russian policy, which was inconstant and

1. Berchtold, Memorandum, 2 October 1912: *OUA*, IV, no. 3928.

9. Count Leopold Berchtold (The Bettman Archive)

never really informed by a consensus among the officials and diplomats responsible for formulating and carrying it out. While Izvolsky remained foreign minister (until September 1910), the principal Russian objective in the Balkans was to form a confederation that would serve as a bulwark against Austria-Hungary and a solid source of support for Russia. There were differences of opinion, however, about who should be included in the confederation and about the pivot of the combination. Charykov wanted to include Turkey in the Balkan alliance. On the other hand, the most energetic and forceful Russian diplomat in the Balkans, Nicholas Hartvig, minister in Belgrade from 1909, hated Austria-Hungary as the arch-enemy of Slavdom and envisaged a Balkan alliance centering upon Serbia. His counterpart in Sofia from March 1911, Anatole Nekyludov, shared his views about the exclusion of Turkey from a Balkan bloc, but was pro-Bulgarian in his sympathies. St. Petersburg tended to share Nekyludov's views and particularly his opposition to an offensive alliance, but both Neklyudov and Hartvig felt the lack of a clear-cut policy at home.

Although Russia encouraged the Balkan states to unite under her aegis, 1909–1910, she made little progress until the autumn of 1911, after a series of events in the spring and summer helped to prepare the way for the alliances that Russia desired. Perhaps the most important was the coming into power in March of the Geshov-Danev Bulgarian government, more ardently pro-Russian than its predecessor. At the same time the idea of Balkan alliances was once more in the air, and the outbreak of the Italo-Turkish war turned aspirations into deeds, because the uncertainties of the war's outcome, the fear of Austro-Hungarian action in the Balkans, and of turbulence in Macedonia and Albania compelled cooperation among the Balkan states.

Contacts established at Belgrade by Bulgarian diplomats resulted in an agreement in October 1911 upon the bases for negotiations. To ensure the remarkably well-kept secrecy, negotiations were carried on in Sofia where only four members of the government knew of them. Neklyudov and Hartvig kept in close touch with the negotiators and intervened to hasten progress and to make sure that the Russian insistence upon a defensive rather than an offensive alliance was observed. By the end of December the terms had been settled except for the problem of Macedonia. Bulgaria wanted an autonomous regime there, but yielded to Serbia's demand for a division. Throughout January and February they haggled over their shares of the region in case of a victorious war with Turkey. While the northwestern part of Macedonia was to go to Serbia and the central and southern part to

Bulgaria, the area around Struga at the mouth of the Black Drin on Lake Ochrida remained in dispute. Hartvig, Neklyudov, and Romanovsky, Russian military attaché in Sofia, sought to bring about an agreement. When Bulgaria refused to accept Romanovsky's proposal to divide the area at the Drin River, Sazonov authorized Neklyudov to promise Geshov orally that Russia would consider Bulgaria's wishes in a future demarcation of Macedonian boundaries. Thus, while Serbia and Bulgaria had agreed to the tsar's arbitration if they could not come to an agreement between themselves, Sazonov had secretly committed Russia in advance to a judgment in favor of Bulgaria. This step cleared the way for the final drafting of the treaty of alliance, which was signed on 13 March 1912.[2]

The treaty provided for mutual guarantees of political independence and territorial integrity, and for mutual help if either were attacked, or if any great power should seek to annex or occupy, even temporarily, any part of the Balkans under Turkish rule and if one of the parties declared this act to constitute a *casus belli*. The military convention, signed on 12 May, spelled out the implications of this last provision of the treaty, and a secret annex to the treaty of alliance, signed the same day, trespassed upon the "defensive" character of the alliance and dealt with the disposition of Macedonia. The parties were obligated to refer any difference of interpretation of the treaty, the annex, or the military convention to Russia for her final decision.[3]

The Serbo-Bulgarian alliance constituted the first and most elaborate of the alliances that formed the Balkan League. As soon as the Bulgarians completed the terms of the Serbian alliance, they took up negotiations with Greece. Neither party kept Russia informed, although on 29 May 1912, a fortnight before the Greco-Bulgarian treaty was signed, Neklyudov received a summary of it. It provided for aid if either were attacked by Turkey, but by a military convention of 5 October the alliance would become operative in case of an attack upon Turkey, if both parties agreed to strike.[4] Although there was apparently an oral agreement between Greece and Serbia, there was no

2. Thaden, *Russia and the Balkan Alliances of 1912*, pp. 86–93. The notion, mainly based upon Ivan Geshov, *The Balkan League*, that the partition of Macedonia envisaged a large "contested" zone between uncontested Serbian and Bulgarian zones, has to be revised in the light of 2 *MO*, XIX. The "contested" zone was a small area around Struga: Philip Mosely, *JMH*, XII, 75–76.

3. The texts: Geshov, *Balkan League*, pp. 112–22.

4. Ibid., pp. 127–33.

written treaty, nor was there any understanding with either Bulgaria or Serbia concerning the partition of Macedonia. Montenegro was the last to complete agreements with the other Balkan states, for it was not until the end of August, when Bulgaria had decided to make war on Turkey, that she accepted King Nicholas' offer to begin the war in return for financial support and the pledge of as much territory as he could conquer. Serbia followed suit by signing an alliance, 6 October, providing for the conduct of military and political action against not only Turkey but also the Dual Monarchy. The agreements with Montenegro completed the series of bilateral treaties and agreements that formed the Balkan League.

The great powers throughout the summer of 1912 reacted in characteristic fashion to events in the Balkans. Except for Russia and Great Britain, they had only an imperfect knowledge of the Serbo-Bulgarian alliance and of the other agreements, about which even Russia was not fully informed. Accustomed to look upon the Balkan states as weak minor powers whose destiny was under the control of the concert of Europe, if it could be harmonized, or was dependent upon the will of one or another "most-interested" great power, none, least of all Russia, appreciated the determination of the Balkan allies to make war upon Turkey and drive her out of the territories they coveted. Despite the warnings of Neklyudov and other Russian diplomats abroad, Sazonov and Premier Kokovtsov were confident that Russia exercised a genuine veto power over the Serbo-Bulgarian alliance provisions. There is no doubt, moreover, that Russia wanted to maintain peace and the status quo in the Balkans, as did all the other powers. There the consensus ended, however, for as unrest and disturbances increased and as the internal crisis of the Ottoman government deepened, "narrow-mindedness and rivalry" prevented agreement on how to deal with the situation.[5]

While the Italo-Turkish war dragged on, the endemic turbulence of the Albanians erupted in the summer of 1912. A new Turkish government on 23 July which sought to make peace with the Albanians made little headway, and a massacre in Kočana, 1 August, was followed a few days later by the Albanian seizure of Üsküb. About the same time, Montenegro appealed to the powers to settle a boundary dispute with Turkey, and IMRO appealed to Bulgaria for aid of a general Macedonian uprising. Thus the Balkan pot had reached the boiling point when Berchtold, in order to prevent any other power

5. Hantsch, *Berchtold*, I, 306.

from taking the lead, tried twice in August to bring about concerted action at Constantinople and the Balkan capitals. He wanted to support the Porte in inaugurating reforms and to keep the Balkan states from disturbing the peace, but failed to win the cooperatioñ of the other great powers who mistrusted his motives.

Berchtold's efforts were followed by attempts of Sazonov and Poincaré to maintain peace and the status quo in the Balkans. Sazonov, before his visit to London on 20 September, had proposed great-power pressure on Turkey, but did not ask, as Berchtold had done, for action at the Balkan capitals. Instead he admonished the Balkan states on his own to keep the peace. While Sazonov was in England, Poincaré tried his hand at concerted action. After sounding out his entente partners and gaining the approval of Kiderlen-Waechter, who failed to inform Berchtold, to the latter's annoyance, Poincaré issued a call for the joint action of Russia and Austria-Hungary, who were to speak for all. They were to warn the Balkan states to keep the peace, and to say that if they did not, Europe would not tolerate territorial changes in the Balkans. At the same time the two powers were to impress upon Turkey their interest in reform. Early in October both Berchtold and Sazonov agreed to the proposal, modified by Russia and Britain, and on 8 October presented Europe's note to the Balkan states. Two days later the powers collectively notified Turkey that they were willing to assist in carrying out the reforms already announced. This time the concert that had been established was helpless. The Turks resented the offer of assistance as interference, and on 8 October Montenegro declared war, to be followed ten days later by the other Balkan allies. The Balkan states had taken the bit between their teeth, and no amount of tugging on the reins by Sazonov or anyone else could stop them.

II.

No one was surprised that war broke out, but the swiftness with which the Balkan allies drove the Turks before them upset all calculations and caused unexpected shifts in policy. Within little more than a month the Bulgars had reached the Chatalja lines, the last defense of Constantinople, but had been stopped there; the Greeks had spread over southern Macedonia, entered Salonika, and occupied nine Aegean islands; the Serbs had taken Monastir, reached Durazzo on the Adriatic, and overrun the Sanjak of Novi Pazar along with the Montenegrins, who had also surrounded Scutari but had been unable to take it. In short the Balkan allies had pretty well taken possession of European Turkey with the exception of a few strongholds. The armistice of 3 December among Turkey, Bulgaria, and Serbia ended the first phase of the war and paved the way for a peace conference that opened in St. James' palace in London on 16 December 1912. The Greeks also attended, although they had not signed an armistice.

Most directly concerned over the outbreak of the war was Russia, but for whose encouragement of the Serbo-Bulgarian alliance the Balkan states might not have been able to compose their differences. Though Russia had sought to prevent the outbreak of the war, she could not well persuade her protégés that she would not in the last resort support them. Moreover, as usual, Russia spoke with more than one voice, that of Kokovtsov, Sazonov, and the tsar, who wanted peace, and that of the military and representatives abroad, of whom Hartvig was so vociferous in support of Serbian aspirations that Sazonov eventually had to counsel moderation. At the very outset of the war, when its outcome and the policy of Austria-Hungary were still unclear, Sazonov was not certain of the course to follow. His major fear was of an Austro-Hungarian action against Serbia or occupation of the Sanjak, and as early as 9 October he had informed Berchtold that as long as the Dual Monarchy refrained from such actions Russia would not move. Russia had already, 30 September, set in motion a trial mobilization in Russian Poland which involved calling up reserves and the retention of the third-year levy beyond the normal date of its dismissal. Sazonov explained the action as long planned, and apparently satisfied Germany and Austria-Hungary that they need not be alarmed, but the retention of the third-year levy contributed to the severe tension that soon developed over Austro-Russian disputes concerning points of settlement.

Besides her own resources, Russia hoped that France and England would support her views at least diplomatically, but as the war rapidly developed into a triumphal march for the Balkan allies, both powers insisted that Russia should state her aims and interests. Early in November Sazonov sketched his ideas of an acceptable peace settlement. A major point was the denial of Constantinople to Bulgaria and a retention by Turkey of a hinterland to protect the city. He favored a Serbian expansion southward as far as Okhrida and westward to the Adriatic, providing a corridor to the sea. He would accept an autonomous Albania and a Montenegrin acquisition of the Sanjak, and he thought that Bulgaria should rectify her frontier with Romania in the Dobruja. Salonika might become a free port and Mt. Athos be neutralized. Sazonov was to shift his emphasis and some of his objectives from time to time, but in the main was able to resist the most rabid demands of the Pan-Slavists and to pursue a moderate line.

In regard to the other "most-interested" power, Austria-Hungary, Berchtold faced three problems: (1) what looked like Russian mobilization on the frontier, a problem that did not become acute until the conflict of views over Serbia; (2) his dependency upon Germany if a crisis developed; and (3) cooperation with the European powers, which seemed to him indispensable in view of the experience in the Bosnian annexation crisis only four years before. He had participated in concerted action before the outbreak of the war, but afterward he had to act in a different framework—decide what the Monarchy's interests were and how to protect them. He knew that a reoccupation of the Sanjak of Novi Pazar or a threat to Serbia would arouse Russian opposition, hence destroy any hope of a European concert. He also knew that Germany was opposed to intervention in the Balkan conflict but at the same time was demanding a statement of his policy.

After a series of Ballhausplatz conferences from 16 October till near the end of the month, when the rapid progress of the Balkan allies changed the prewar conditions and asumptions, Berchtold successfully rejected General Schemua's proposal to mobilize on the Serbian border and was able to assure Russia that the Dual Monarchy would not take military steps in the direction of the Sanjak. In fact, the ministerial conferences decided that the Sanjak was not a vital interest and that Austria-Hungary should seek no territorial acquisitions with the exception of such frontier rectifications as the Lovčen mountain, commanding the Bay of Cattaro, and the Danubian island of Ada Kaleh. The council agreed that the one vital interest lay in the prevention of any power from establishing itself on the eastern shore of the Adriatic or Ionian seas; but a positive goal to be achieved, if the status quo could not be maintained, was the creation of an independent and viable Albania. This state was to safeguard the coast of the Adriatic and limit the expansion of Serbia and Montenegro, who were to be drawn into economic association with the Dual Monarchy. In the eastern Balkans, Berchtold cared little about what Bulgaria did, but wanted Romania compensated for Bulgarian gains. Finally, the conferences agreed upon the maintenance of important markets for Austrian industrial products in the former Turkish territory and the safeguarding of such economic interests as lay in Salonika and railway communications with it.

Both Russia and Austria-Hungary had to take their allies into account in laying down any line of policy, but for the latter this was a more serious consideration than for the former. Italy, who had made her peace with Turkey on the day the Balkan war broke out, offered little difficulty. San Giuliano assured Berchtold, who visited Italy 21–23 October, that Italy would work in unison with her allies toward the localization and speedy ending of the war. He gave the impression that he would like a condominium or a partition into spheres of influence of Albania, but Berchtold did not pursue the topic. A few days later San Giuliano approved the October program that Berchtold communicated to him on 3 November. Although the Italians were in sympathy with Serbia's aspirations, the government's negotiations for the alliance renewal, nearing completion, dictated an accommodation with the Dual Monarchy.

Germany's attitude was far more significant for Austria-Hungary than Italy's. When the war clouds began to gather in September, Kiderlen told Bethmann that Germany was not obliged to support the Dual Monarchy's eastern policy, and should decide what attitude to take from case to case. In order to avoid saying no to Austria some day, Kiderlen declared, "we must ask Austria to consult us before taking decisions. . . . We will not be her satellite in the Near East."[6] The rivalry for leadership of the alliance, which had existed from Aehrenthal's time, may well have been accentuated by a personality clash between Kiderlen and Berchtold. Bethmann, too, after visiting Berchtold at Buchlau, 7 September, agreed that Austria-Hungary needed to be watched. The Germans, including the kaiser, saw no reason to intervene in the Balkan fight and wanted Europe to keep out and hold the ring. Kiderlen therefore seconded Poincaré's efforts to bring about a concerted policy toward the Balkans, and fostered the idea of close cooperation with Britain. Believing that Russia did not want war, he was much more complacent about the outbreak than was Berchtold, upon whom he urged discussion of peace terms. When Berchtold presented his program at the end of October, Kiderlen approved it as reasonable and moderate, but differences between the allies cropped up from time to time, and early in November the kaiser, Bethmann, and Kiderlen agreed that Germany should not give her ally carte blanche. Nevertheless, despite Kiderlen's determination to hold the whip hand, the development of tension between the Monarchy and Russia brought the realization that Germany had an interest in the preservation of Austria-Hungary as a great power and should support

6. As quoted by G. P. Gooch, *Before the War*, II, 246.

her if she had to fight to maintain her position. Meanwhile, Germany's policy was one of peace and the smoothing away of antagonisms among the powers.

Russia's ally, France, though concerned to maintain the alliance, was anxious along with Germany and England to establish and maintain the European concert. No one worked harder than Poincaré to stave off the Balkan war and, after its outbreak, to localize it. He believed that the more solid the Triple Entente ties, the more likelihood that Russia would stick to a policy of peace and the status quo, but at the same time he let Russia know that if she had to intervene in the Balkans to thwart Austro-Hungarian military moves, France would stand by the alliance. Far from giving Russia carte blanche, however, he insisted that only if Germany attacked Russia would France become involved. Thus Poincaré, though ever mindful of the Russian alliance, supported the concert as the means of preserving peace.

Great Britain, even more than France or Germany, wanted to keep the peace among the great powers, believing that she had no direct interest in what happened in the Balkans. Grey wanted to preserve the Triple Entente but believed that a British role of mediator was not inconsistent with it, because he felt that Germany would influence Austria-Hungary to be moderate, and they could therefore avoid a confrontation of the Dual and the Triple alliances. Even before the outbreak of the war he made tentative approaches to Germany to cooperate in keeping the peace, and although Kiderlen was evasive, wanting to make cooperation with England a means of breaking up the Triple Entente, Grey enjoyed German support in his efforts to localize the war, and continued to hope that Germany, France, and England could keep out of trouble.

By the opening of November all the powers recognized that the status quo ante could not be restored, although Berchtold was the first to admit it publicly, which he did on the 5th. He told the Hungarian Delegation that the Monarchy had no expansionist ambitions—a renunciation of territorial acquisitions which he communicated to Russia the same day—but that its interests must not suffer injury through new arrangements in the Balkans. Berchtold made clear to the powers what those interests were by communicating his October program to Rome, London, Paris, and St. Petersburg at the same time. Although Berchtold rejected Poincaré's proposal that the powers declare their disinterestedness (because, he said, Austria-Hungary had very important interests in the Balkans), he subscribed to a formula offered by Kiderlen that the powers mediate between the belligerents if requested to do so by one of them. Already, however, the major issue that was to cause tension between Russia and the Dual Monarchy had arisen. The Serbs were marching toward the Adriatic, and although they did not reach Durazzo until the end of the month, their aim of acquiring a port on the Adriatic was clear. On 3 November Berchtold asked Italy to join in preventing Serbia from getting such a port, and at the same time warned Russia of his position. With Italian support promptly assured, Berchtold was applying one of the major points in his program that also included an independent and viable Albania whose creation would keep Serbia from reaching the sea. Sazonov tried in vain to get Berchtold to modify his policy, but informed Hartvig, 11 November, that Russia would not go to war for a Serbian port on the Adriatic, thus reducing the likelihood of war but at the same time laying himself open to Pan-Slavic abuse. Because the Russian aim was to secure "the minimum for the Bulgars, the maximum for the Serbs," and because Austrian objectives were the reverse, "grave tension was inevitable."[7] The task of the allies of the two protagonists was to prevent a humiliation such as Russia had suffered in 1909, and to induce the Dual Monarchy to pursue a moderate and wise course. At the same time the powers, especially France and Britain, counseled Serbia to accept alternatives to an Adriatic port, as Berchtold himself had suggested, but the Serbian port problem dragged on until late December.

The tension engendered by this question was heightened by disputes between Serb army officers and Austrian consuls in Macedonia, and by military measures in both Russia and Austria-Hungary. The Austro-Hungarian government had nervously watched the Russian trial mobilization, but aside from strengthening the forces in Bosnia-Herzegovina and along the Serbian border in November and December, it did not make counter moves on the side of Russia until 19 November, when it decided to strengthen the Galician corps as a measure that would test Russia's attitude toward the Austro-Serbian situation. The kaiser and Moltke, 22 November in Berlin, assured General Schemua of their full support if Russia threatened Austria-Hungary. A day later a Russian crown council rejected War Minister Sukhomlinov's proposal to mobilize part of the Warsaw and all of the Kiev military districts, but decided to retain with the colors the third-year levy for an additional term of six months. This measure meant an increase in the size of the army by 350,000 to 400,000 men as opposed

7. Ibid., II, 328.

to approximately 224,000 called to the colors by Austria-Hungary. A further cause of anxiety in all the great-power capitals was the reappointment on 12 December of Conrad von Hoetzendorff as chief of staff in the Dual Monarchy. Rumors spread of an Austrian planned attack on Serbia, whom Russia would support and thus bring into play the *casus foederis* of the rival alliance systems.

Berchtold, however, not only resisted the pressures of the war party, but also in a curious and futile way sought to open the door to conciliation and cooperation with Serbia, one of the objectives of his October list of interests. In response to an article in *Semuprava*, a Pašić organ, which announced that Serbia sought a rapprochement with the Dual Monarchy and that Pašić was ready to make far-reaching concessions if Serbia were permitted an outlet on the sea, Berchtold instructed Stephen de Ugron, minister at Belgrade, that Austria-Hungary would not oppose Serbia's territorial expansion in case the powers no longer upheld the status quo, and that the stronger the bonds between Serbia and Austria-Hungary, the more compliant Vienna would be. A few days later Berchtold asked Joseph Redlich to undertake a mission to Belgrade in order to probe the possibility of establishing friendly relations with Serbia. Berchtold instructed Redlich that he had nothing against Serbian expansion and the partition of the Sanjak between Serbia and Montenegro, but would insist upon the noninfringement of Albanian territory; if necessary, Austria-Hungary would go to war to preserve her own integrity. Redlich reluctantly undertook the mission and spent the 4th to the 6th of November in the Serb capital. He talked with several ministers, including Pašić, who stressed the Serbian determination to be independent and the necessity to reach the sea; if the Dual Monarchy were friendly toward Serbia, then eventually a customs union might be possible, but presently Austria-Hungary was pursuing a false policy concerning Albania, which might better be partitioned among the Balkan allies than established as an independent nation. Redlich on his return to Vienna formally proposed yielding an Adriatic port to Serbia, but was unable to convince Berchtold and his officials.[8]

Pašić, on the other hand, did not drop the question of better relations with Austria-Hungary, and in December outlined to Thomas Masaryk a quite comprehensive plan for peace and friendship with the Danubian Monarchy. He proposed a visit to Vienna in order to discuss the subject with Berchtold, but the latter—on 12 December, when

8. See Redlich, *Schicksalsjahre*, I, 166–78.

III. The Balkans, 1912–1913

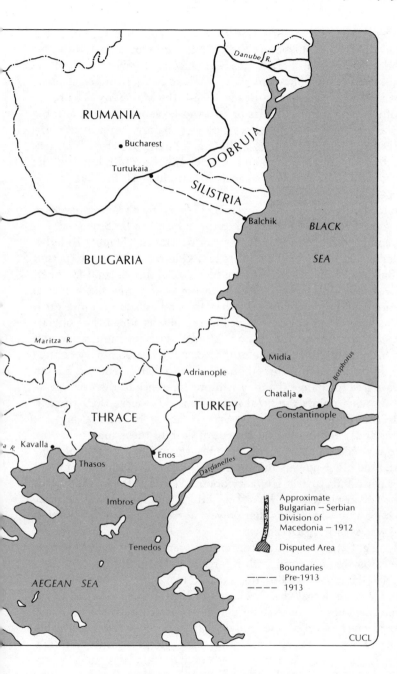

RUMANIA

Bucharest

DOBRUJA

Turtukaia

SILISTRIA

Danube R.

Balchik

BLACK

SEA

BULGARIA

Maritza R.

Midia

Adrianople

Bosphorus

Chatalja

TURKEY

Constantinople

THRACE

Kavalla

Enos

a R.

Thasos

Dardanelles

Imbros

Approximate
Bulgarian – Serbian
Division of
Macedonia – 1912

Disputed Area

Tenedos

Boundaries
——·—— Pre-1913
———— 1913

AEGEAN SEA

CUCL

Masaryk reported to him—refused to invite Pašić, on the ground that the subject had been put before the powers who would deal with it at the London conference. Berchtold's real reason, however, was that he could not reverse his policy on what he felt to be an insufficient guarantee of a change in Serbia's attitude toward the Monarchy. The result of the official and unofficial missions was to leave the Serbian and the South Slav questions exactly where they were before, unresolved problems that Berchtold and others, including Aehrenthal before him, recognized but were unable to resolve. To Berchtold's credit, however, he continued, with the support of Francis Joseph, to resist the war party's solution—war upon Serbia.

As noted by Berchtold, the powers had agreed by 12 December to an ambassadorial conference and also to the subjects to be discussed. On 18 November, when the war scare was nearing its height, Kiderlen suggested a conference of the powers to decide what changes to permit in the Balkans. Poincaré had proposed a conference in mid-October, which was rejected as premature. Even now Grey opposed a formal conference and suggested instead that the ambassadors of the great powers at Paris should discuss issues informally as a means of obviating the time-consuming and often misunderstood communications by telegraph. In a note to Berlin he proposed that the preliminary conference begin by discussing three points: (1) to what extent the Balkan allies were free to change the map without reference to the great powers; (2) on what points the great powers should reserve their right to make decisions—perhaps Albania, Serbian access to the sea, and the Aegean islands; and (3) the settlement of each of these topics that the great powers could accept. Grey's proposal won the approval of Germany and the other powers during the early days of December, except that Germany and Austria-Hungary opposed Paris as the meeting place because of their mistrust of Izvolsky, Tittoni, and Poincaré. They proposed London, to which the other powers agreed. The date for the first meeting was set for 17 December.

While negotiations over the conference were going on, two important developments occurred with reference to the positions of Russia and Austria-Hungary. About the 23rd of November, when plans of the military were defeated in the tsar's council, Sazonov began to retreat from the support of Serbian demands for access to the Adriatic. He warned Hartvig on 27 November that Russia wanted a peaceable solution, but because Serbian policy was likely to prevent it, Hartvig's duty was to dampen Pašić's ardor and to advise him to behave in accord with Russia's peaceful policy. On 10 December, Sazonov counseled the Serbs to accept the decision of the Triple Entente, to which they agreed on the following day. Moreover, persistent rumors of Austrian military measures, though they worried Poincaré, left Sazonov undisturbed. Berchtold remarked: "One could not believe that this mild, conciliatory, equable little man had gotten onto his high horse only shortly before and had run stormily against our position like a wild Don Cossack."[9] The change in Russian policy was attributed to the return of the tsar from a hunting party at Spala, where he had been surrounded by Pan-Slav enthusiasts, to Tsarskoe Selo and the more peaceful counsels represented by Kokovtsov. Perhaps more important was Sazonov's conviction that Berchtold would stand by his declared policy, that Russia would have no support from Italy, and that neither France nor Britain wanted an armed conflict over Balkan issues.

On the other hand, Kiderlen watered down the Viennese hopes of German support which grew out of the meetings of the kaiser and Moltke with Archduke Francis Ferdinand and General Schemua on 22 and 23 November. Bethmann, however, told the Reichstag on 2 December that if the Austro-Hungarians in securing their interests, were "attacked from a third side and thereby threatened in their existence, we, true to our duty as an ally, would have to stand resolutely by their side. And then we should fight for the preservation of our position in Europe, for the defense of our own future and safety."[10] Coming as this declaration did in the midst of negotiations for a conference and fears of an Austro-Russian conflict, it alarmed the Entente capitals, to whom it looked like sword rattling. The British had already paid tribute to Berchtold for his discretion and patience, and since early November Grey had warned Prince Lichnowsky, the German ambassador, that if Russia and Austria-Hungary went to war, all of the great powers might be drawn in. After Bethmann's speech Grey again warned Lichnowsky, asserting that the declaration might endanger the peace policy pursued by both Britain and Germany. Also, Haldane told the ambassador that Britain would be unable to remain neutral in a continental war arising from an Austrian invasion of Serbia, because she was committed to the balance of power and could not permit France to be crushed. These messages from London sent the kaiser into a paroxysm of anger, for the principal reason why he had allowed himself to be persuaded to back the Dual Monarchy in a war over Serbia

9. Hantsch, *Berchtold*, I, 353.
10. As quoted by Gooch, *Before the War*, II, 249.

was the argument that England would remain neutral in such a war. He called a conference of his military and naval chiefs on 8 December, in which he urged immediate preparations for a war with England. Moltke agreed that war was unavoidable, and that the press should prepare the public for it. Tirpitz, however, preferred to postpone a fight for another eighteen months. Although Bethmann was not involved in this conference, the kaiser a week later thought he had accustomed himself to the idea of war. Nevertheless, German policy remained pacific, for Bethmann agreed with Tirpitz that Germany was not ready for war, and he still hoped to win British neutrality.[11]

In anticipation of the ambassadorial conference, Lichnowsky had correctly interpreted Grey's thinking: through the conference no one should appear to be victor or vanquished, but all questions should be settled by mutual concessions. The key to Grey's policy, he believed, was balance of power. Grey wanted to prevent a war in which Britain might become involved in protecting France from a crushing defeat, and beyond that to avoid the humiliation of Russia by a repetition of her diplomatic defeat of 1909. Grey saw the means of achieving his goals to be an informal give-and-take at the conference table.

The conference met for the first time on the afternoon of 17 December 1912 at the London Foreign Office. Present were Mensdorff for Austria, Lichnowsky, Imperiali for Italy, Benckendorff, and Paul Cambon, with Sir Edward Grey in the chair. This gathering began a series of meetings lasting until August 1913 and convening whenever agreed upon in the discussions outside the conference, where most of the negotiations took place. Although no minutes were kept, Paul Cambon prepared a summary of discussions. While Grey sought to emphasize "concert," the members, as Ernst Helmreich has pointed out, were "representatives of the Triple Entente and the Triple Alliance as well, and this fact was to dominate their actions." Taking exception from time to time were Lichnowsky, whose occasional failures to support Mensdorff earned him criticisms from Vienna and reprimands from Berlin, and Grey, who in general sided with Russia but "still maintained a neutrality which received full recognition [and] won the confidence of all."[12]

At the first three meetings the Austrian view regarding the Serbian

---

11. Cf. J. C. G. Röhl, *HJ*, XII, 659–66; Fritz Fischer, *Krieg der Illusionen*, pp. 231–41.

12. *Diplomacy of the Balkan Wars*, pp. 249–51.

expansion to the sea, which had been accepted by all the powers even before the conference, was recorded. Serbia was to have a commercial outlet to the Adriatic through a free and neutral Albanian port by means of an international railway under European control, and was to enjoy freedom of transit for all merchandise, including munitions of war. Furthermore, it was agreed that Albanian autonomy under the sovereignty of the Porte was to be guaranteed and controlled by the great powers, and Austria-Hungary and Italy, the sponsors of Albania, were to draw up a plan of government. Albanian boundaries were to extend from Greece to Montenegro, thus effectively preventing a Serbian coast on the Adriatic. An Austro-Russian conflict over the boundaries, however, blocked further progress in December. The Dual Monarchy championed the nationalist principle of "Albania for the Albanians," but because Russia, backed by France, protested against it on the grounds that such cities as Ipek and Scutari would be denied to Montenegro by such a rule, months were to go by before a consensus on Albanian boundaries could be reached. The conference also opened the subject of the Aegean islands, Grey's third point on his earlier list, but came to no agreement except on Crete, which was to go to Greece.

January 1913 witnessed a series of futile negotiations within and without the ambassadorial conference. Austria-Hungary and Russia failed to agree on the disposition of Scutari. A renewed war scare brought the danger of a Russo-Austro-Hungarian confrontation to the fore again. Romania, preparing to attack Bulgaria, was held back by Sazonov and Berchtold. The peace conference between Turkey and the Balkan allies broke down. The ambassadorial conference considered coercive action at Constantinople, but Grey was not in favor of proposed naval action, and Germany—under the guidance of Bethmann, the kaiser, and Gottlieb von Jagow since the death of Kiderlen-Waechter on 30 December 1912—opposed it. On 22 January a Turkish council voted to conclude peace, but the next day the Young Turks, led by Enver Bey, overthrew the government by a coup d'état and reestablished the authority of the Committee of Union and Progress. They proposed a division of Adrianople at the Maritza River but accepted the cession of the Aegean islands. The Balkan states denounced the armistice, however, and resumed war on 3 February 1913.[13]

13. Another event of January 1913 was the election of Raymond Poincaré to the presidency of France on the 17th. Louis Barthou succeeded him as premier and Charles Jonnart as foreign minister, but Paul Cambon believed that Poincaré continued to direct foreign policy: Correspondance, III, 39, 43, 66.

III.

The resumption of war occurred in a situation of deadlock among the great powers and of anxiety over the Albanian boundaries, the disposition of the Aegean islands, and the claims of Romania against Bulgaria. In the eyes of Sir Fairfax Cartwright, British ambassador in Vienna, Serbian ambitions were the greatest danger, for if the Serbs, encouraged by Russia and France, became aggressive toward Austria-Hungary and the latter were provoked into taking action against them, war would be unavoidable. "Servia," he wrote prophetically, "will some day set Europe by the ears and bring about a universal war on the continent. . . ."[14] What made the crisis particularly menacing was the continuing military posture of both the Dual Monarchy and Russia, which led to dire predictions of a European war.

To prevent such a development, Berchtold attempted a détente by sending Prince Gottfried zu Hohenlohe-Schillingsfürst to Russia with a message to the tsar from Emperior Francis Joseph. Hohenlohe, who had been well liked in Russia while serving as military attaché there, was cordially received by Nicholas II, and found Sazonov, Kokovtsov, and War Minister Sukhomlinov voluble in expressions of peaceful intentions. He failed, however, to bring about an understanding on reductions of armaments. The Hohenlohe mission was nevertheless useful in clarifying the views of the two powers. It was clear that the tsar and Premier Kokovtsov wanted no war; in Vienna, Francis Ferdinand and the clerical party wanted peace at almost any price.

Though Conrad still insisted upon a state of preparedness in case of a war with Serbia, and Minister of War Krobotin was convinced of the necessity for it, Berchtold received a strong letter from Bethmann urging him to control the war party and to reach a modus vivendi with Serbia. As Berlin saw it, a conflict with Serbia would enable the Pan-Slavists in Russia to gain the upper hand and probably to throw out those who wanted peace. As a result, a war between the Triple Entente and the Triple Alliance would ensue in which Germany would have to bear the brunt of a French and British attack, and Italy would be a doubtful partner. Bethmann argued that whereas in 1908–1909 England had supported Russia, she was now a mediating force, and there was hope that she might reorient her policy if the present crisis could be passed. Moreover, Moltke wrote to Conrad urging restraint,

14. Cartwright to Nicolson, Private, 31 January 1913: BD, IX(2), no. 582.

although he was convinced that "a European war must come sooner or later," and it would be a war "between Germanentum and Slaventum"—not a happy thought for Conrad, who pointed out that his country was 47 percent Slavic.[15] Berchtold, who took a gloomy view of the outlook for Austria-Hungary, was impressed by her isolation and at length, on 22 February, proposed to Russia a reduction of troops. As a result the two powers issued identical press communiqués, 11 March, announcing reciprocal troop reductions. By these measures Berchtold hoped to ease the tension over the Albanian borders, but was to be disappointed.

Meanwhile, in the ambassadorial conference, Grey and Lichnowsky had attempted to work out a compromise between the Austrian and Russian positions. It was obvious by the beginning of February that the basic difficulty was not which town should be incorporated in Albania and which in Serbia or Montenegro, but rather the preservation of prestige in the Balkans. Though Germany, as Bethmann and Moltke indicated, would not fight over the assignment of this or that village, she did want to support the great-power status of Austria-Hungary. On the other hand, France supported Russia for similar reasons. Grey believed that France, reluctant to go to war over the Balkans, was working upon Russia to prevent a conflict there, and asserted: "We on our side can be no party to France precipitating a conflict for the revanche."[16] Signs in London and Berlin of Anglo-German cooperation, which had encouraged Bethmann to hope for a reorientation of British policy, worried Sazonov. Benckendorff believed, however, that because London was convinced of Germany's desire for peace, a cooperation had developed that was advantageous to Russia; Grey could insist that Berlin influence Vienna, and the solidarity of the Triplice in the ambassadorial conference was not as complete as the protocols might indicate.

By February the chief points in controversy were Djakova, center of the Albanian Malissori, and Scutari, under siege by both Montenegrin and Serbian troops. Various proposed compromises proved to be unacceptable to one side or the other, and on 9 February Serbia threatened resistance to the decisions of the ambassadors if she did not get Djakova and Dibra. Sazonov, however, warned her that Russia would

---

15. Bethmann to Berchtold, 10 February 1913: *GP*, XXXIV, no. 12818; Norman Stone, "Moltke-Conrad . . . *1909–1914*," *HJ*, IX (1966), 213–14.

16. Grey, Minute on Nicolson to Grey, 24 February 1913: *BD*, IX(2), no. 656. His allusion to "revanchism" may have been prompted by Ambassador Bertie's feeling that it was rising: To Grey, 19 February 1913: *BD*, X(2), no. 461.

not support her, because Russia had won Prizren, Ipek, and Dečani for her, and Djakova and Dibra were purely Albanian towns. Pašić made an angry retort, declaring that Djakova, Dibra, and Scutari were not the question, but rather: "Is Russia and its friends stronger or weaker than Austria and its friends?" Sazonov, nevertheless, stuck to his advice to be moderate and await the future. He counseled that "it would be best to be satisfied with the great achievements and organize the new Serbia in order at a later moment, when the time has come, to open up the Austro-Hungarian sore, which today is not as ripe as the Turkish."[17]

The ambassadorial conference was unable to reach a decision up to 22 March. Grey threw up his hands in mid-March when Berchtold raised another issue, that of the enforcement of conference decisions. He warned that the Dual Monarchy might be compelled to put Serbia and Montenegro in their places. He still lacked the support of Berlin, however, for Jagow, the new secretary for foreign affairs, suggested that he should try to placate Serbia. Nor was Italy any more willing than Germany to back Berchtold. In this situation the influence of the war party at Vienna again began to grow, and public opinion criticized Berchtold as too lenient. Responding to these pressures, the Austro-Hungarian government decided on 18 March to demand that Montenegro stop the bombardment of Scutari until civilians could withdraw from the city, and on the 19th to make a naval demonstration and blockade the coast if Montenegro refused. If these measures were ineffective, Austria-Hungary was to mobilize against both Montenegro and Serbia.

At this point Berchtold contributed to the lessening of tension by a decision to give Djakova to Serbia, for he saw no other way out of the blind alley in which the Albanian problem had become entrapped. Francis Joseph, too, advised giving way. When Berchtold announced the decision on 21 March, he made the condition that the rest of the northern Albanian border be drawn in accord with Austrian wishes. This meant that Scutari was to go to Albania. Furthermore, Berchtold wanted effective protection of Albanians and Catholics who were to be incorporated in Montenegro and Serbia, and six-power action to assure the immediate cessation of hostilities and the evacuation of territory assigned to Albania. Russia (after some pressure from Grey) and the other powers accepted Berchtold's stipulations, and on 22 March the London ambassadors recorded them. They also invited Belgrade and Cetinje to raise the siege of Scutari, end hostilities, and pro-

17. As quoted by Helmreich, *Balkan Wars*, pp. 284–85.

ceed to a rapid evacuation of Albanian territory. The actions ended the long-drawn-out squabbles over boundaries by what was in effect a bargain, in which Russia got her way over Djakova and Dibra and the Monarchy won out on Scutari, but new problems now came to the fore.

The first and most serious issue arose when Austria-Hungary prepared to carry out the decisions of 18 and 19 March. Berchtold telegraphed Cetinje, 22 March, to stop the bombardment of Scutari. The next day he notified the powers that he intended to use peaceful measures of coercion if Montenegro refused to act in accord with the decision of the powers. Sazonov, visibly shaken, remonstrated with the Austrian ambassador that such a move was contrary to the principle of concert; Russia would have to recall her reserves and, if Montenegro were coerced, the Dual Monarchy would have to prepare for war. In a second conversation on the same day, 24 March, Sazonov lamented that his policy had been wrecked, pointing out that he had admonished Montenegro and Serbia to heed the will of the powers. Berchtold defended his own action in a circular of 25 March, arguing that Austria-Hungary was not trying to break the concert but was acting in the spirit of the conference decisions; some kind of energetic action had to be exercised if the battle of Scutari was to cease; time was pressing, for fresh Serbian troops were arriving and a renewed attack upon Scutari was imminent. There was reason on both sides. Berchtold could not afford to let Montenegro seize the city for fear that Europe would be too divided to force her out, and Scutari could easily become an outlet to the sea for Serbia should close relations with Montenegro—or the union that was much talked about—be established. For Sazonov the prestige of Russia in the eyes of the two Slavic states was at stake if Austria-Hungary forced her views upon them. Scutari therefore had become a cardinal point in the rivalry of the two powers. While the war party in Vienna clamored for the landing of troops in Montenegro, Berchtold held back lest the action arouse both Italy and Russia.

Because no one wanted Austria-Hungary to act alone, the powers, including Russia, approved Grey's proposal of a common naval demonstration at Antivari. The renewed bombardment of Scutari on 30 March spurred the powers into action, though France was reluctant to participate unless St. Petersburg gave permission, and Great Britain did not want to participate alone with the Triplice. Sazonov, now out of patience with King Nicholas, begged both powers to join the demonstration, in which Russia could not take part for lack of ships in the region. Admiral Sir Cecil Burney, senior officer of the assembled ships, established a blockade of the coast after Nicholas refused to comply with the wishes of the powers. This move paved the way for the withdrawal of Serbian forces, announced on 11 April. Stubborn King Nicholas achieved his goal on the night of 22–23 April when Scutari surrendered to his forces. What Berchtold had feared had now occurred, and while there was great rejoicing in the Slavic capitals, gloom descended upon Vienna.

A little more than a fortnight before Scutari fell, Berchtold had again appealed to Berlin for an understanding of his position. He painted a gloomy picture of Pan-Slavism at high tide, and asserted that if the powers failed to enforce their decisions, the Dual Monarchy would be compelled to force the evacuation of Albania, even though it might involve war with Serbia, Montenegro, possibly Greece, and perhaps Russia. He felt that the Monarchy's demands had been modest and its concessions far-reaching. If it now sacrificed its minimum, Berchtold argued, "merely for the sake of peace, this would in my judgment involve catastrophic reactions on our position in the Balkans and jeopardize our Southern Slav territories." Unless St. Petersburg persuaded Cetinje and Belgrade to yield to the decisions of the ambassadors they would not give way, and Austria-Hungary would be compelled to take her own line. Bethmann this time responded, for, as he wrote the kaiser, the Albanian buffer state was "Austria's only gain from the shipwreck of her Balkan aspirations," and Germany could not let this modest gain slip from her hands. "To avert the weakening of Germany through the humiliation of Austria is our chief task at the moment."[18] On the other hand, the Dual Monarchy's other ally, Italy, was more doubtful. When approached for support, Italy hesitatingly agreed to parallel action by sending forces into southern Albania at Valona while Austria-Hungary secured Scutari. Berchtold would not agree, foreseeing a possible partition of Albania; and the Entente powers opposed the scheme as useless in dealing with the main problem of Scutari. Sazonov proposed that Great Britain and France join Austria in military action, but France refused without a public Russian mandate, and Britain would not act alone for fear she would seem to be separated from the Entente. At a ministerial council in Vienna, 2 May, the government, deciding to take the risk of war, approved mobilization in the South in preparation for military measures against Montenegro and voted the necessary credits.

At this juncture, the defiant attitude of Cetinje, maintained as late as

18. Quotations from Gooch, *Before the War*, II, 253–54, 409–10.

30 April, began to change to panic upon the news that Austria-Hungary was about to send troops across the border. All the great-power representatives urged Montenegro to give way before she received an Austrian ultimatum. The hope of economic assistance, discussed by the ambassadors as early as the 11th of April, and the fear of Austro-Hungarian action at length led King Nicholas on 4 May to announce his decision to evacuate Scutari. In the following days the Dual Monarchy canceled the military preparations, and on 14 May detachments from the international fleet took over Scutari from the Montenegrin troops. The crisis was over without a war, and all Europe heaved a sigh of relief. The moderation of both Austria-Hungary and Russia and international cooperation centering under Grey's leadership in the concert at London had postponed a continental conflict for another fourteen months.

Another issue, far less serious than Scutari, engaged the attention of the powers at the same time. Romania demanded that Bulgaria cede Silistria as compensation for Bulgar gains in the first Balkan war, but Bulgaria refused, despite strong pressure from Russia, supported by France and Great Britain. In February both Romania and Bulgaria asked the powers to mediate, and they entrusted the problem to the ambassadors at St. Petersburg, where a conference began meeting on 31 March. By this time Bulgaria had added Adrianople to her war trophies, much to the pleasure of Russia and France, and Georges Louis had been replaced as French ambassador to Russia by Théophile Delcassé. Sazonov, Delcassé, and Buchanan worked closely together, but the Triplice ambassadors were divided. Berchtold wanted to support Bulgaria in order to draw her out of the Russian camp but at the same time could not well sacrifice the close ties with Romania that had been renewed by the prolongation of the Austro-Hungarian-Romanian alliance on 5 February. Therefore he backed the cession of Silistria to Romania and suggested that Bulgaria receive Salonika. Germany flatly rejected such a scheme, for she wanted Salonika to go to Greece, and anyway did not approve the idea of exchanging a trustworthy Romania for an uncertain Bulgaria. On 7 April the Entente ambassadors suggested a settlement, the major feature of which was the cession of Silistria to Romania with compensation to the Bulgarians who might leave the area. Berchtold's efforts to secure territorial compensation for Bulgaria, although supported by Germany and Italy, were defeated. After a month's delay the ambassadors signed the final protocol on 8 May.

By this time peace terms between Turkey and the Balkan states had been under consideration for more than two months. Turkey had accepted the mediation of the powers on 28 February, but the Balkan states did not accept the principle of mediation until 14 March. All except Montenegro agreed to an armistice in mid-April. Terms and counterterms passed back and fourth between the belligerents and the ambassadorial conference until 5 May, when Grey submitted a draft treaty that had been worked out by Paul Cambon. The powers accepted it and passed it to the Balkan and Turkish delegates, who reached London in mid-May to reopen peace talks. In the wrangling that ensued, open rifts began to appear between the Bulgarians on the one hand and the Serbs and Greeks on the other. At length Grey, weary of the haggling, called all the chief delegates except the Montenegrin into his office one by one on 27 May and in effect told them to sign or go home. With the approval of their home governments, they signed the peace on 30 May, the text of which was the same as the draft of 5 May.

After a pious word about perpetual peace among the contracting parties once the treaty had been ratified, Turkey ceded to the allies all territory in Europe west of a line from Enos on the Aegean to Midia on the Black Sea; the delimitation of Albania and all other matters concerning it were left to the great powers to settle; Turkey ceded Crete to the allies, renouncing sovereignty and other rights in the island, and left the fate of the Aegean islands in the hands of the great powers; financial questions were left to an international commission to meet in Paris; and the usual postwar problems of prisoners, trade, and the like were to be settled by special conventions. The Balkan allies, who agreed that the London treaty was final, officially ended their peace conference on 9 June, leaving the special conventions provided for in the treaty to direct negotiations between the respective allied governments and Turkey. "Perpetual peace," however, lasted less than a month.

IV.

Long before the peace of 30 May 1913, the Balkan allies had fallen out over the division of Macedonia. The fortunes of war and the great-power decision to establish Albania had greatly changed the conditions foreseen in the provisions of the Serbo-Bulgarian treaty and military convention. There had been no agreement concerning the Greek share of the coveted Macedonia, but Greek troops had taken Janina and other points in southern Macedonia and had shared Salonika with Bulgarian forces. While Bulgaria was conquering Thrace, the Serbs had occupied northern and central Macedonia, including Monastir, which had been earmarked for Bulgaria. Although Bulgaria was more interested in Macedonia than in Thrace, she had pursued the Turks there because of military exigencies, while her allies were taking over the region she most coveted. Serbia, who held not only the zone assigned to her in the treaty of 1912 but also most of the Bulgarian zone, asked Bulgaria in February and again in May to agree upon a revision of the partition clauses.

On 30 May 1913, in the midst of the wrangling over Macedonia, Geshov, under whom the Serbo-Bulgarian agreement of 1912 had been negotiated, resigned, to be succeeded in June by Stoyan Danev, who was thoroughly in sympathy with the strong Macedonian party in Sofia and who rigidly opposed any revision of the treaty. Although there was justice on both sides, Serbia had the advantage of holding the territory she demanded. Moreover, the common interest in opposing Bulgaria brought Serbia and Greece together after intermittent parleying that began in January. Their negotiations progressed rapidly in May, when they drew up a military convention and a treaty of alliance that included an agreement on the partition of Macedonia. They signed the documents on 1 June. They also sought other allies. Romania held back from a formal commitment, awaiting an outbreak of war, but Montenegro pledged loyalty to the alliance with Serbia if war with Bulgaria occurred. The Turks made no formal agreement, but were obviously interested in recouping their losses to Bulgaria.

Among the great powers Russia was most anxious to prevent a split between Serbia and Bulgaria. Sazonov at the end of April notified Belgrade and Sofia that they must submit their dispute to Russian arbitration and that Russia expected them to settle all disagreements according to the stipulations of the treaty of 1912, not by armed force. When it became obvious that the two states were making no progress toward an agreement, Nicholas II on 8 June sent a personal message to the two sovereigns that he would not be indifferent to a "criminal war" and that the instigator would be held responsible "before the Slav cause." Encouraged by the responses of Kings Peter and Ferdinand, Sazonov invited representatives of Serbia, Bulgaria, and Greece to St. Petersburg to settle their differences, and on 21 June, thinking the replies were satisfactory, he asked for a memorandum supporting their respective claims. By this time, however, Danev was convinced that war was unavoidable, although he went along with a ministerial council that demanded a Russian arbitral award within seven days. Danev's sharp note to Russia angered Sazonov, who replied in effect, 25 June, that Russia washed her hands of Bulgaria—a significant turning point in Russian relations with the Balkan rivals.

At the same time emotions in Sofia were building up to a high pressure for the "freeing" of Macedonia, and on 28 June General Savov, the Bulgarian commander-in-chief, on authorization of King Ferdinand and Danev, ordered an attack upon the Greek and Serbian positions the next day. Sazonov tried to stop a counterattack without success, and the Bulgarian government, which learned of the order only on 1 July, demanded a halt. It was too late, however, for Greece and Serbia were glad to enter a fight which Bulgaria had put herself in the wrong by starting. Montenegro's troops were already on their way to join Serbia when Bulgaria attacked. Neither Russia nor the concert could stop the second Balkan war, and behind the scenes Austria-Hungary tried to make capital of the shattering of the Balkan League..

Berchtold felt isolated and also threatened by the emergence of a greater Serbia and by the role Russia was trying to play as arbitor of Balkan disputes. He refused to go along with a proposal for a collective great-power pressure on the Balkan states to demobilize, because he resented the tsar's allusion to the "Slav cause" in his note of 8 June. In the absence of concert he sought to promote Austro-Hungarian interests by drawing Bulgaria out of the Balkan league and thus setting up a counterweight to Serbia. The major difficulty lay in the relations of Romania with Bulgaria, for Berchtold could not afford to alienate his ally for the *beaux yeux* of Sofia. After much backing and filling, Danev sought to win Berchtold's support by declaring, 21 June, that Bulgaria was not bound to fight the Monarchy and would pursue a friendly policy in the future. To this gesture Berchtold replied on the 24th that the Monarchy would follow a Bulgarophil policy as long as Danev's promise held good, since the strengthening of Serbia was not in the interest of Austria-Hungary, but he made the condition that Bulgaria take Romania's wishes into consideration and offer her such compensation as would make it possible to bring pressure on Bucharest for an agreement between them. But Berchtold's efforts since mid-April to bring Bulgaria and Romania together were no more successful in June than before, for Romania, dissatisfied with the award of Silistria, now demanded the line of Turtukaia-Balchik as the price of her neutrality, and Bulgaria failed to offer it despite Berchtold's prodding. When Danev wanted to resign on 2 July, the Austro-Hungarian minister at Sofia reported that not a single party leader would disgrace himself by ceding more territory to Romania. In any case, hoping to win more by war than by peaceful negotiations, Romania mobilized on 3 July and entered the war on the 11th. By this time she had become a focal point of rivalry between the Triplice and the Triple Entente, each trying to outbid the other in seeking her favors.

Berchtold recognized the meaning of the Romanian attack on Bulgaria, for from that time he believed that she was lost to the Triplice, not only because she had taken the side of Serbia, the Dual Monarchy's enemy, but also because with her awakened nationalism she would develop a drive for the Romanian *irredenta* of the Siebenbürgen in Hungary. What discouraged him even more was his failure to convince his allies, especially Germany, to accept and support his aim of winning the allegiance of Bulgaria. But Berlin failed to respond to his pleas. Germany agreed upon the closest possible relations with Romania, but also wanted to pull in Greece, of whom Berchtold was very doubtful. Germany did not share Berchtold's strictures against Russia, whose support of Balkan Slavdom he regarded as the root of his difficulties. On 25 June Berchtold appealed to Berlin in vain for support of his efforts to reconcile Bulgaria and Romania, and threatened that if there were a war between Bulgaria and Serbia the Monarchy might have to intervene in order to prevent an excessive strengthening of Serbia at Bulgarian expense. Germany feared that efforts to win Bulgaria might throw Romania into Russia's arms, and regarded attempts to support both Romania and Bulgaria as the height of folly.

The kaiser, 30 June, roundly denounced Bulgaria for starting a new Balkan war and hoped she would be thrashed. Now was the time, he told the Austro-Hungarian naval attaché, to make a lasting agreement with Serbia, whereas Bulgaria could not be trusted. Berchtold turned to Italy for help in modifying the German attitude, but only awakened the fear that Austria-Hungary would intervene in the Balkan struggle and let loose a European war. Although Berchtold did not intend to intervene, his efforts to convince his allies of the serious threat to the Monarchy of a victorious Serbia and his occasional references to the necessity of attacking Serbia led Ambassador Tschirschky, like San Giuliano, to fear that Austria-Hungary might become involved in the Balkan struggle. Berchtold painted a gloomy picture to Francis Joseph on 5 July, asserting that he could get nowhere alone and that his appeals to Berlin to put pressure upon Bucharest had been fruitless. The emperor agreed that they stood alone at a time when to be or not to be was the question before them. He and Berchtold were obviously more worried over their isolation than over the events unfolding in the Balkans. The next day Berlin reaffirmed its refusal to dissuade Romania from going to war, and Bethmann sought to soothe his ally's feelings by emphasizing the Austro-Hungarian achievement in establishing Albania. He suggested that the Monarchy should be glad to see Bulgaria and Serbia weakened by war and strongly advised against any idea of "gobbling up Serbia, which would only weaken the Monarchy." Little wonder, after such frank talk in Berlin and the futility of trying to keep Romania out of the war, that Berchtold now adopted an attitude of watchful waiting. He admitted that a war against Serbia, who had Romanian cooperation, in order to help Bulgaria, who always turned to Russia for help, would be sheer nonsense.[19]

As early as 8 July Bulgaria, beset on three sides by Serbia and Greece and on 11 July by Romania and the next day Turkey, turned first to Russia. She accepted Sazonov's proposal to send delegates to St. Petersburg to establish the bases of peace, but Serbia and Greece wanted peace preliminaries signed on the battlefield. After a second fruitless appeal to Russia on 14 July, Danev threw up his hands and resigned on the 15th, to be replaced two days later by Vasil Radoslavov. The shift betokened disillusionment with Russia, for the new government was reputedly pro-Austrian. In fact, feelers had been put out in Vienna, and Ferdinand on 15 July had appealed to Francis Joseph for aid. Berchtold advised a direct appeal to King Carol to stop the Romanian advance and to persuade Serbia and Greece to conclude an armistice, a step that Ferdinand followed. The upshot of these maneuvers was a general agreement on 18 July upon a peace conference to convene in Bucharest.

At this point Berchtold tried once more to influence the course of events. He sent Alexander Hoyos, his principal secretary, to Bucharest on the 19th to explain that he wanted Bulgaria to surrender to Romania, who in turn was to abandon Serbia and Greece. Hoyos was to impress the Romanian government that it would be impossible for Austria-Hungary to pursue her former policy toward Romania if she should ally with Serbia. Premier Titu Majorescu listened to Hoyos courteously but made it clear that Vienna could expect little from Bucharest. Shortly after this discouraging discussion, Radoslavov proposed an alliance to Berchtold, who assured him that Austria-Hungary would follow a Bulgarophil policy and accepted the notion of an alliance in principle, but could not hurry into it because he had to consult his allies; meanwhile Bulgaria should come to a full accord with Romania.

19. Hantsch, *Berchtold*, II, 452–53.

The turn of events now linked Berchtold and Sazonov in a common cause. On 22 July, Turkey recaptured Adrianople. Both men notified Turkey that they could not permit her to recover territory inhabited by Christians, and the ambassadorial conference approved an identical démarche at the Turkish capital. The Turks refused to give up their conquest, however, even though Sazonov threatened to march into Armenia and tried to get support for a financial boycott and a naval demonstration. Berchtold supported him, but the great powers failed to agree, and the firmness of the Turks enabled them to keep Adrianople.

Although several of Berchtold's advisers advocated a march into Serbia if Russia moved into Armenia, Berchtold turned them down, declaring that "we never wanted to attack Serbia." His objective, he said, was to secure and maintain the existing Austro-Hungarian boundaries.[20] Besides, Germany was as indifferent to the Monarchys' special interests as before, and still differed from her by championing the cause of Greece. Yet Berchtold tried once more to explain his views to Berlin. In a long memorandum of 1 August he asserted that the South-Slav, "or better said the Serbian" problem was the one that most concerned the Monarchy. A great-Serb development would jeopardize its very existence, because the Radical party in power at Belgrade aimed at incorporating all Serbs in one national state, thus making the opposition to the Monarchy lasting and unbridgeable. Furthermore, behind Serbia lay a powerful Pan-Slavic movement in Russia that made highly probable Russo-Serbian cooperation. Now that Serbia had freed her fellow nationals from Turkey, she would turn to the West as soon as she had incorporated her newly acquired territories into the Serbian state. The Monarchy was therefore compelled to adopt farsighted policies and enter into close relations with Bulgaria, as well as Romania, and thus establish a counterweight to Serbia. As for Greece, he believed that close ties with her were not desirable because the central powers would have to take on the Mediterranean interests of Greece, whose active support in any case could not be relied upon. Berchtold explained that he did not want an alliance with Bulgaria immediately, but to see to it that Bulgaria was not completely eliminated as a power factor and that a close understanding between Romania and Bulgaria be established which could later serve to draw Bulgaria into the Triplice.[21] What Berchtold obviously wanted was not only approval of his

20. Ibid., 465.
21. Ibid., 466–68.

proposed Bulgarian policy but also support in trying to intervene on behalf of Bulgaria in the peace negotiations at Bucharest.

The conference of Bucharest which opened on 30 July made more rapid progress than might have been expected. The great powers were divided on whether to reserve the right to make the final decisions concerning peace terms. Because Russia and Austria-Hungary were strongly in favor of it, their representatives at the Romanian capital were most active in trying to influence the outcome of the negotiations. Germany was just as strongly opposd to great-power revision of the peace, and her representative, along with those of Great Britain and France, kept himself in the background. The peace treaty, signed on 10 August, reflected the outcome of the war and the wishes of the victorious coalition rather than those of the great powers. Romania secured the Turtukaia-Balchik line that she had demanded; Greece acquired Crete and the lower Vardar and Struma River valleys together with Kavalla, a port on the Aegean that Bulgaria hotly contested without success; Serbia was to have the Upper Vardar valley, including Monastir, Štip, and Kočana, all three of which had been allotted to Bulgaria in the treaty of 1912.

Besides Bulgaria, whose gains by the first Balkan war had been greatly reduced, both Russia and Austria-Hungary felt that their interests had been injured—the former because she had wanted to retain Bulgarian loyalty and had tried to have Kavalla assigned to her, and the latter because of a greater Serbia at Bulgarian expense. Sazonov, who along with Berchtold tried to get the powers to agree to revision, soon weakened and gave up. Perhaps he was partly convinced by Izvolsky's argument that the treaty of Bucharest was advantageous to Russia because it relieved her of the impossible task of dividing Macedonia. In addition, Sazonov had separated Romania from Austria-Hungary, who now stood alone. Berchtold did indeed stand alone, for none of the great powers supported his push for revision. Germany in fact virtually killed his chances of any success by publishing an exchange of telegrams between the kaiser and King Carol, 10 August, in which the former had put the stamp of approval on the work of the Bucharest conference, credit for which the German Foreign Office assigned to Carol. The unfinished task of drawing a Bulgar-Turkish boundary offered the two dissenting powers another chance to attempt intervention on behalf of Bulgaria. They tried to save Adrianople from Turkey, but here again the lack of unity among the powers enabled the Turks to gain their point. The boundary agreement of 18 September, incorporated in the Bulgar-Turkish peace of Constantinople of 30

September, gave Turkey not only Adrianople but Kirk Kilisse as well, thus returning to her a good part of Bulgaria's gains in the first Balkan war. The result was not only an embittered Bulgaria, whose quarrel with her neighbors keyed Balkan politics for a generation to come, but also a highly alarmed Austria-Hungary, whose divergence in policy from Germany had become public knowledge. The feelings of the Monarchy about the threat of a greater Serbia formed a significant background for the crisis of July 1914; and the rift with Germany constituted an equally important factor, by inversion, in 1914.

During the second Balkan war the ambassadorial conference in London continued to debate the unsolved problems of Albania's government and southern boundary, and the disposition of the Aegean islands. The conference rejected the Austro-Italian draft of an Albanian constitution in May 1913, but after two months of discussion it agreed upon the form of government for Albania as an independent neutral state under a prince to be designated by the great powers. At length, in December 1913, the powers named Prince William of Wied, sponsored by King Carol of Romania, as the sovereign prince of Albania. The unhappy prince accepted the throne on 6 February 1914 but left the country shortly after the outbreak of war in 1914, never to return.

The Albanian boundary problem was more difficult to solve because it became involved in the disposition of the Aegean islands. While France championed the Greek claims, Italy at first led the opposition. Germany, however, came to the fore in the discussion of the Aegean islands because she wanted to safeguard her interests in Asia Minor by assuring security to the Ottoman empire. The Italian occupation of the Dodecanese also complicated the situation. France wanted Italy to cede them to Greece, but Italy refused. Grey, who had come to the conclusion that the ambassadors could not solve the two problems soon and wanted to end the tiring conference debates, proposed an arrangement that the powers agreed upon: Albania's southern boundary was left to an international commission; Greece was to acquire the Aegean islands inhabited by a Greek majority, except Imbros, Tenedos (guarding the Dardanelles), and Thasos (subsequently assigned to Greece); and Italy was to reiterate her promise in the treaty of Ouchy to give up the Dodecanese upon the withdrawal of Ottoman troops from Libya; the powers were to settle the fate of these islands in a final settlement. The agreement was far from definitive, and the international commissions had not completed their work when war came in 1914.

Despite loose ends, the ambassadorial conference stopped meeting after 11 August 1913 without any protocol of dismissal, votes, or farewell speeches. Grey commented in his memoirs:

We had not settled anything, not even all the details of Albania boundaries; but we had served a useful purpose. We had been something to which point after point could be referred; we had been a means of keeping all the six Powers in direct and friendly touch. . . . When we ceased to meet, the present danger to the peace of Europe was over; the things that we did not settle were not threatening that peace; the things that had threatened the relations between the Great Powers in 1912–13 we had deprived of their dangerous features.[22]

This statement is true, and no little credit for preventing war went to Grey himself, and to a certain extent to the cooperation of Germany with him. But over many crucial questions there had been no concert, because, as the tsar put it to his mother, "there is no such thing as European unity—merely great powers distrusting each other."[23]

Equally important in hampering a European concert were the Balkan states themselves, who frequently disregarded the advice of friendly powers, let alone the wishes of the ambassadorial conference. In making final peace terms they, too, failed to settle all questions left over by the ambassadors and by the peace of Bucharest. Montenegro and Turkey, for example, failed to conclude a peace of any kind. Serbia and Montenegro, however, by an agreement of 7 November 1913 divided the Sanjak of Novi Pazar between them. Bulgaria and Turkey, as already noted, made peace on 30 September, and Greece and Turkey concluded the treaty of Athens on 14 November 1913. Finally, Serbia and Turkey made peace at Constantinople on 14 March 1914. While negotiations over these settlements dragged on, the Balkans remained a diplomatic battle ground among the Balkan states and the great powers right up to the cataclysm of 1914.

The Balkan wars of 1912–1913 and the tenuous peace settlements afterward constituted the matrix out of which the war of 1914–1918 developed. That a European war did not come in 1912–1913 was owing less to the concert, to which many commentators have given the

22. Grey, *Twenty-Five Years*, I, 262–63.
23. Nicholas II to Maria, 13 July 1913: *Secret Letters of the Last Tsar* (New York, 1928), pp. 286–87.

credit, than to the rifts within the two alliance systems. These rifts were less serious in the Triple Entente than in the Triplice. Although France emphasized her loyalty to her alliance obligations if Germany attacked Russia, she never gave Russia carte blanche in pursuing an anti-Austrian policy, while at the same time she sought diplomatic advantages for herself, notably in her championship of Greece. In the case of Kavalla, French backing of Greece ran directly counter to her ally's wishes.

In the Triplice, on the other hand, the German attitude constituted a sharp break with Austria-Hungary, despite German public declarations, such as Bethmann's on 2 December 1912, that Germany would be true to her alliance obligations. The second Balkan war especially brought the failure of Berlin to support Vienna into clear focus, leaving the reestablishment of Austro-German agreement about Balkan policy a major task of the next ten months. Italy supported her ally vigorously when it suited her own interests, as in the Adriatic and Albanian questions, but was as cautious as Germany when she feared that Austro-Hungarian aims ran the risk of bringing about a war.

Both Russia and Austria-Hungary suffered a loss of prestige during the wars.[24] Russia's inability to avert a clash between Serbia and Bulgaria in May–June 1913 betrayed her helplessness to control her protégés, just as the outbreak of the war in 1912 had revealed her inability to direct the coalition she had helped to create. On the other hand, the positions of both Serbia and Romania, that Russia would continue to turn to her own advantage, compensated to a certain extent for the defection of Bulgaria. Conversely, the emergence of Serbia and Romania was a blow to Austro-Hungarian interests and, in the case of Serbia, revealed the bankruptcy of the Monarchy's policy toward the South Slavs both within and without her borders. Aehrenthal's hopes of pursuing a policy of conciliation after 1909 had been frustrated, and Berchtold was even less able to conceive and follow such a policy. Both had been hampered by Hungarian resistance to peaceful coexistence with the South Slavs.

In the ten months between the peace of Bucharest and the murder of Archduke Francis Ferdinand the alliance systems gained solidarity, while the aftermath of the Balkan wars witnessed the darkening rather than the brightening of the prospects for peace.

24. Paul Cambon remarked that Sazonov and Berchtold were "poor brains" who were preoccupied with escaping responsibilities and were changing their minds every minute: *Correspondance*, III, 44–45.

Chapter 12

Uneasy Peace,

1913–1914

In the months before the July crisis of 1914 the heads of governments and the foreign ministers remained the same as before, except that Vladimir Nikolaievich Kokovtsov lost his post as Russian premier in February 1914 and for a brief period A. A. Neratov again acted as foreign minister in Sergei Dimitrievich Sazonov's place. In the frequent changes of French ministries, Stephen Pichon in 1913 again served as foreign minister. In Austria-Hungary, Hungarian Premier Stephen Tisza began strongly to influence foreign policy. Likewise, Eleutherios Venizelos, Greek premier since 1911, was rising into prominence. In the diplomatic world Maurice Paléologue replaced Théophile Delcassé as French ambassador to Russia and as Entente colleague of the British ambassador, Sir George Buchanan; the German ambassador to Turkey, Baron Hans von Wangenheim, began to play a major role in the Near East, while Prince von Lichnowsky in London continued to work for entente with Britain although he was not entirely trusted by Secretary for Foreign Affairs Gottlieb von Jagow. Like Wangenheim, the Russian ambassador in Constantinople, M. N. Giers, carried a heavier burden in 1913–1914 than before. In the British Foreign Office, Sir Eyre Crowe had been promoted to assisant undersecretary, seconding Sir Arthur Nicolson, the permanent undersecretary. Among the active military men were General Conrad in Austria-Hungary, Helmut von Moltke, German chief of the general staff, and V. A. Sukhomlinov, Russian minister of war.

After the peace of Bucharest in August 1913, the great powers faced a set of new problems in the Near East that tested the alliance systems, exacerbated old rivalries, and, despite agreements such as those between Germany and Great Britain and Germany and France over the Bagdad railway, left relations among the powers no better than before. First and most significant was the Austro-Hungarian-Serbian crisis of October 1913, and next in chronology and importance was the complex

10. Raymond Poincaré (Culver Pictures)

of conflicting aims and interests that centered around the Liman von Sanders mission to Turkey at the end of the year.

I.

Berchtold, after his failure to revise the Bucharest treaty, found himself a lonely and discouraged man, but in a test of strength with Serbia recouped something of his lost position. An Austro-Hungarian-Serbian crisis arose over Serbian occupation of territory awarded to Albania by the ambassadorial conference. In mid-August, in response to a great-power demand, Pašić promised to withdraw Serbian troops, but when he failed to do so, Berchtold asked the powers to make a further protest. Russia, however, saw no need for additional advice to Serbia. In mid-September, despite a Serbian statement that orders to pull back had been issued, the Austro-Hungarian military attaché in Belgrade learned that the Serbian troops had not withdrawn behind the London line of demarcation. A few days later a revolt broke out among the Albanians, and Serbian troops moved back into the Albanian area while suppressing the revolt.

Lacking a concert among the great powers, Berchtold sought the support of his allies in making a further warning to Belgrade, for he was convinced that Serbia was bent upon upsetting the London decision and threatening to push to the Adriatic. His fears seemed to be supported by the Paris *Temps* publication of an interview with Pašić in which he expressed hope for a strategic rectification of the London boundary line. Vienna sent a warning to Belgrade on 1 October not to infringe upon Albanian territory. Although Germany had favored such action, Italy had opposed it, and the Dual Monarchy took the step alone. Berchtold, who had discussed with Conrad possible military action, laid the situation before a crown council on 3 October. There both the emperor and Archduke Francis Ferdinand opposed military action, although Berchtold represented the European outlook as favorable because of better Anglo-German relations and French and Russian need of peace. He depicted the future as dark, for the Balkan league might conceivably be reestablished against the Monarchy; the armament race and French financial activity in the Balkans might turn the scales against Austria-Hungary. Tisza, who had become Hungarian premier in June and was increasingly influential in foreign policy decision-making, argued for firmness in dealing with Serbia: if energetic protests failed to move her, then send an ultimatum to be followed by military action if necessary; a humiliation of Serbia was a condition of life for the Monarchy, but under no circumstances should Austria-Hungary annex any Serbian territory. Berchtold, who had been unconvinced by Pǎsić's friendly assurances that Serbia had no designs on Albanian territory, doubted if Germany and Italy would support the course advocated by Tisza, but nevertheless adopted it.

After two further messages to Belgrade warning against advancing into Albania, and unsatisfactory Serbian replies, Berchtold framed a mildly worded ulimatum in the form of a *note verbale* on 17 October that was delivered the next day. He expressed the hope that the Serbian government would immediately proceed to a total evacuation of Albanian territory as delimited by the ambassadors in London. If not completed within eight days, the Imperial and Royal government would be compelled to take "the proper means to assure the carrying out of its demands."[1] Berchtold had already procured German approval, and he circulated the note to all the other powers. None of them liked this procedure, although surprisingly, Sazonov made little fuss about the Austro-Hungarian démarche. Serbia, therefore, had no alternative but to yield to the Monarchy's demands, and gave notice of her withdrawal from Albania on 25 October within the eight-day time limit. The successful thrust, which took a form resembling that of July 1914, was significant as a model not only for handling the later crisis, but also as encouragement for the argument that Serbia should be handled with firmness and that Russia would not intervene.

At the same time, the most encouraging aspect of the episode for Berchtold was the attitude of Germany. The kaiser, who had failed throughout the Balkan wars to look with sympathy upon the Austro-Hungarian anxiety over the Serbian menace, now went overboard in his condemnation of the Serbs and his protestations of support of Austria-Hungary even in the case of war. In addition to talks with Conrad and Francis Ferdinand, he expounded his views to Berchtold in Vienna on 26 October, when the two men had a long discussion of future policy. Berchtold outlined his strategy of playing the Balkan states against one another, for the success of which the Bulgar-Serb conflict was of "decisive importance." The attitude of Romania, however, was a great difficulty, in which Germany could perhaps help. In response the kaiser launched into a tirade against the Slavs in general and the Serbs in particular, who were born to serve, not to rule, and were waxing stronger in a way to give "food for reflection" to Ger-

1. Berchtold to Storck (in Belgrade), 17 October 1913: *OUA*, VII, no. 8850.

many and the Dual Monarchy. Moreover, the proper position of the Serbs was one of dependency on the Monarchy, which should establish its hegemony over all the states in the Balkans. Even more significant was the kaiser's reiterated assurance that he would stand behind Austria-Hungary and was ready to draw the sabre if the Monarchy's action made it necessary. In closing, recorded Berchtold, the Kaiser "was pleased to assure me that whatever came from the Vienna foreign office was for him a command."[2]

Yet the discussion of details revealed that there were still differences between the allies, notably with reference to Bulgaria. The kaiser still criticized and mistrusted King Ferdinand, and failed to endorse Berchtold's proposed policy of creating a Balkan bloc, including Bulgaria. On the other hand, the kaiser promised help in persuading Romania to exert pressure on Serbia to comply with Austro-Hungarian demands, although, be it noted, not to make friends with Bulgaria, which was Berchtold's principal problem. He also ruled out a return to the Holy Alliance or the Three Emperors' League, a concept still cherished by Francis Ferdinand, but optimistically predicted that there need be no anxiety about Russia for the next six years, since her army would not be ready until then and the revolutionary specter was again reappearing. Berchtold's suggestion that consideration should be given to the monarchical principle was brushed aside by the kaiser, for he envisaged a life-and-death struggle one day in which Germany and Austria-Hungary would stand together against a common foe.

Although these outpourings of the kaiser's should be discounted in view of his well known tendency to flights of fancy, they cannot be dismissed as totally eccentric. For one thing he may well have been inspired to talk of Serbian subordination to the Monarchy by Conrad, who discussed wih him early in September an Austro-Hungarian-Serbian-Montenegrin federal union. Moreover, Bethmann told Ambassador Szögyény a few days after the kaiser's return from Vienna that the latter wanted henceforth a completely unified procedure between Germany and the Monarchy in Balkan questions. Bethmann also reported in vague terms the kaiser's wish to establish close, trustful relations with the non-Slav states, which Szögyény took to mean Romania and Greece. Bethmann himself claimed that he understood completely Austria's need to maintain and develop her relations with Bulgaria, but, significantly, offered no encouragement. As late as mid-

2. Berchtold, Memorandum, 28 October 1913: ibid., no. 8934 (in translation, *SEER*, VII [1928], 24–27).

December the Kaiser still harped on the theme, which by now had become almost a stereotype, of Serbian subservience to the Dual Monarchy by enticement or by force. He still thought, however, that it was more important to win the Serbs than the Bulgars, whose king was untrustworthy.

How little hope there was of winning Serbia at this late date is revealed by the plans of Pašić, who wanted peace until the new Serbian acquisitions could be organized and the nation could recuperate from the exertions of the Balkan wars. He and the tsar agreed in a discussion on 2 February 1914 that Serbia must foster the alliance with Greece and widen that with Romania, whose fellow nationals in Transylvania were more nationalistic than the Romanians themselves. The tsar was confident that the Romanian government would attach itself as closely as possible to Russia. As for Bulgaria, a restoration of good relations with Serbia might be brought about if Bulgaria were willing to help solve the Serbo-Croat question. And Pašić envisaged a union of Serbia and Montenegro in such a way as to assure the existence of the Montenegrin monarchy. At the close of the interview, Nicholas II declared: "For Serbia we shall do everything; greet the king for me and tell him: for Serbia we shall do all."[3]

Thus in the winter of 1913–1914 the line-up of July 1914 had already been formed, but undoubtedly the calculations of Pašić and the tsar were more realistic than those of Conrad and the kaiser when they talked of solving Austria-Hungary's South-Slav problem by winning over the Serbs. Little wonder that the aged Francis Joseph remarked: "The peace of Bucharest is untenable, and we are faced by a new war. God grant that it may be confined to the Balkans."[4]

II.

It was neither Serbia nor another Balkan state, however, that increased the tension between Germany and Russia in the winter of 1913–1914, but the Ottoman empire and the Straits question. Although the major cause of the rift between them was the Liman von Sanders military mission to Turkey, the mission itself was only one aspect of a complex of rivalries that involved all the great powers. The issues arose out of

3. Miloš Bogičević, *Die auswärtige Politik Serbiens*, I, 421. Cf. Hartvig to Sazonov, 24/11 February 1914: 1 *IBZI*, I, no. 314.
4. Ottokar Czernin, *In the World War* (London, New York, 1919), p. 6.

Turkey's defeat by the Balkan states that had followed so closely
the loss of Libya to Italy and the consequent fear that the Ottoman
empire was disintegrating.

The first to move was Russia, who in the winter of 1912–1913 took
up the cause of the Armenians and demanded reforms in the Turkish
provinces they inhabited. Some of the Russian Armenians asked that
Russia annex the neighboring Turkish provinces. Sazonov rejected
such a policy but promised to seek reforms in Turkey. Although Russia had repudiated annexation, she wanted to control a reform administration in what might become autonomous provinces, and, if it were
necessary in order to effect reforms, to occupy the region. Like all the
other great powers, Russia wanted to guarantee a sphere of influence
for herself if the Ottoman empire should disintegrate.

Sazonov gave the Turks warning of the Armenian situation in December 1912 and vaguely referred to intervention. France and Britain,
whom he approached, wanted to postpone action until the Balkan
problems were settled. The Germans learned of Russian moves early
in 1913 and reacted vigorously, demanding that Germany be consulted
because her Bagdad railway extending the length of Anatolia included
areas inhabited by Armenians. The Germans realized, however, that
the Armenian complaints against Turkey were justified, and advocated
German cooperation with Turkey to effect reforms. At the same time
Foreign Secretary Jagow agreed with Ambassador Wangenheim that
Germany should attempt to increase her influence over a 400 kilometer
strip along the Bagdad railway in order to safeguard her interests.
Referring to a possible break-up of the Ottoman empire, Secretary of
State Jagow declared: "To go away empty-handed would be a second
Morocco for us."[5] In the spring of 1913 suspicion mounted on all sides.

By this time the Turks had begun to plan a reform program, and
in March they proposed a reorganization of vilayet administration. In
the following month they asked for English officials to help carry out
the new reforms in the Armenian vilayets, and based their request on
the Cyprus Convention of 1878. Russia, as was to be expected,
strongly protested such an arrangement on the grounds that the Armenian provinces were a paramount interest for her and that her
promises to the Armenians dictated that Russia assume the leadership
in promoting Armenian reforms. Accordingly, Grey in July 1913 postponed sending any officers to Turkey pending a conference of the
powers to take up the reform question.

5. Jagow to Lichnowsky, 31 May 1913: *GP*, XXXVIII, no. 15317.

Already plans for a conference had been discussed. Sazonov wanted the Triple Entente to freeze out the Triplice in solving the Armenian reforms, but Grey countered that to be effective a program had to be formulated by the six powers, and the French pointed out that if the Entente acted alone there might be a crisis without any hope of preventing war. Accepting these arguments, Russia called a conference at Constantinople, which began its deliberations in July but came to no conclusion because of a conflict of views between Russia and Germany. Attempts to draw up a compromise between the two positions were at first blocked by the Turks, who refused to accept a reform program worked out by Ambassadors Giers and Wangenheim. Modifications in their proposal seemed to be making some headway by early December, when the Liman von Sanders crisis turned the focus of attention to Constantinople and the Straits.[6]

The initiative for the Liman von Sanders military mission, perhaps with German prompting, was taken by the Turks, who wanted to rebuild their army and defenses after the ignominious defeat by the Balkan states. The French military mission to Greece under General Eydoux, served as a model for their plans. In April the grand vizier requested the German military attaché, Major von Strempel, to send a Prussian officer to oversee the rebuilding of the Constantinople defenses. The kaiser wanted to grant the request and noted that the officer might be useful in obtaining orders for German materials. The Foreign Office had no objection to sending an officer once peace was made, and thereafter seems to have had little to do with negotiations over the military mission, which grew in size and duties far beyond the initial conception. Undoubtedly Ambassador Wangenheim and Major von Strempel had much to do with the elaboration of plans for the mission, the objectives of which extended beyond simply military considerations to economic and political matters.

In fact, Grand Vizier Mahmud Shevket Pasha himself, a Germanophil and one of the Young Turk leaders, envisaged a complete reorganization of the Ottoman empire through British direction of civil administration and the navy, and German reform of the army and the system of education. A French general was already in charge of the gendarmerie. Although Mahmud was murdered in June 1913, his successors perpetuated his ideas, with the active support of Wangenheim,

6. See Roderic H. Davison, "The Armenian Crisis, 1912–14," *AHR*, LIII (1948), 481–505, upon which my treatment of the subject above and below is mainly based.

who laid before his government in late May the conditions in Asiatic Turkey and the policy Germany should pursue. The question was, he said, could Asiatic Turkey "maintain itself any longer by its own strength?" He feared that foreign powers would demand reforms and that their intervention would lead to the partition of Turkey, for which Germany was unprepared. The only way to save it was to establish a real control over the Ottoman government by foreign officials and military men whose orders would be obeyed by their subordinates—in short a kind of Egyptian regime.[7]

As a spur to German planning, the rivalry of financiers and armament makers, already a well established feature of *dessous politique* in the Balkans and Turkey, was revived by the helplessness and the needs of the defeated Turkey. In financial power France outranked all the others, a factor that often put her at odds with her ally Russia and made her sympathetic with the German opposition to partition. On the other hand, as the kaiser noted, the supply of arms and equipment was directly related to the question of a military mission. The appointment in 1912 of British Admiral Limpus to head the Turkish navy demonstrated that point, for at the time of the Liman von Sanders crisis Armstrong-Vickers procured a contract to renovate workshops and docks at the Golden Horn and to build new ones at Ismid, while British firms procured all orders of the fleet administration. Also at this time Krupp and Schneider-Creusot were hotly contesting the high stakes of army orders. Armament and financial rivalry and plans for railroad building and exploitation of oil constituted a tangled skein of interests that formed the background for the political ambitions of the powers. In this situation Germany sought a commanding position by which to hold the Ottoman empire together, or to get her share if dissolution came.[8]

With the formal request of the grand vizier, transmitted to Berlin on 22 May, for a "leading German General" to take over the reorganization of the Turkish army, planning for the mission went on apace. On the occasion of the marriage of the kaiser's daughter, 24 May, William II informed the tsar and King George V, who were attending the wedding, of the Turkish request, and believed that both had completely agreed that he should grant it. Though details still had to be worked out, the appointment of Lieutenant-General Otto Liman von

7. Wangenheim to Bethmann Hollweg, 21 and 29 May 1913: *GP*, XXXVIII, nos. 15312, 15318.

8. On the eve of the war in 1914 Germany was still far from the dominant power in Turkey. See Ulrich Trumpener, *Germany and the Ottoman Empire, 1914–1918*, pp. 7–13.

Sanders to head the mission to Turkey was announced on 30 June. By September his powers had been defined as head of some forty-two German officers who were to accompany him to Turkey, inspector-general of the army throughout all Turkey, director of the military schools, commander of the first army at Constantinople, and member of the supreme war council with control of promotions to the rank of general in the Turkish army. Instead of a two-year term, like that of Admiral Limpus, General Liman was to serve for five years in order to guarantee continuity of military developments. Whereas previously the total annual budget for German officers in Turkey had been less than 30,000 marks, the new mission was to be provided with about a million.

Although the planning and the negotiations had been carried on secretly pending the conclusion of peace between Turkey and Bulgaria, and Sazonov upon visiting Berlin in October had not been informed of them, rumors led Neratov, acting foreign minister, to tell the German chargé d'affaires on 7 November that Russia could not conceive of the projected mission "in any other way than as directed against herself." He explained that "every thing that transpires in Constantinople and the Straits is of the highest importance for Russia." He accordingly asked the chargé immediately to procure a report from the German Foreign Office.[9] Sazonov, returning to St. Petersburg from Livadia on 17 November, reiterated Neratov's words of alarm, stressing the political aspects of the mission and the unacceptable command by a German general of Turkish troops at Constantinople. He was chagrined that no word about the mission had been breathed to him at Berlin, and asked Premier Kokovtsov, who was stopping there from 17 to 20 November to take up the matter with Bethmann and the kaiser. They defended the mission as a continuation of the policy of German military advisers to Turkey that had been going on for years, and pointed out that a British admiral was commanding the fleet and a French general was guiding the gendarmerie. The only "new" feature was the command of an army corps at Constantinople, a proper measure because of the military schools located there. The kaiser stressed his notice to the tsar and King George, both of whom later testified that his remarks had been casual and had given the impression that the Liman mission was simply a continuation of previous military missions.

Kokovtsov protested that Constantinople had to remain a Turkish

9. Robert J. Kerner, "The Mission of Liman von Sanders," *SR*, VI, 25, quoting *GP*, XXXVIII, no. 15445.

capital and that a German command there put all embassies under German protection and gave Germany the major responsibility for order and security. He asked for either a modification of the German general's powers or his transfer to another city, such as Adrianople, but he seems to have given Bethmann the impression that he would not insist upon his request. In any event, the chancellor and the kaiser approved Jagow's proposal that they refuse any modification in the terms of Liman's contract, negotiations for which were too far advanced for change. In fact the contract was signed with Turkey on 27 November, and the terms published on 5 December.

Sazonov in the meantime talked with O'Beirne, the British chargé d'affaires, about the possibility of compensations, such as Russian officers in Armenia and British elsewhere. Both Grey and Pichon (again French foreign minister) objected to asking for compensations because of the implications of partition, and suggested that the first step be an inquiry for further information. Grey at first accepted the Russian view of the dangers inherent in the Liman mission, but later came to feel that the matter was not as important as Sazonov had made out. He was supported in this view by Nicolson, who thought that Sazonov had "completely lost his head." Moreover, Grey found reason to be cautious when he learned that Admiral Limpus, not Liman von Sanders, commanded the Straits, and that Turkish newspapers were playing up the Armstrong-Vickers contracts at the Golden Horn and Ismid. The French were anxious not to disrupt the favorable negotiations with Germany over railways in Asia Minor, and Lieutenant Maucorps, military attaché at Constantinople, told the Turks that there was no objection to the German mission if France was not entirely excluded from orders for military supplies. Under these circumstances Sazonov found little encouragement for vigorous Triple-Entente action, although he was thoroughly aroused over the terms of the Liman von Sanders appointment, insisting that the matter was a test of the Triple Entente. He was nevertheless compelled to accept Grey's proposal of an official request to the Porte for information, which the three ambassadors delivered on 13 December. Russia received little consolation from the reply of the grand vizier. All that he would say was that the Straits were not under Liman's command and that the minister of war, not the German general, was directly responsible for order in Constantinople.

On 13 December 1913 General Liman von Sanders arrived in Constantinople amid a great fanfare arranged by the Turks, and formally took up his post on the 20th. Sazonov continued to press for a modification of his terms of command, but the Germans found that the Turks were unwilling to make them. The Russian and German military attachés sought a solution of the problem but were unable to agree. On 21 December Wangenheim sketched out what became the ultimate solution, a promotion of Liman von Sanders and a Turkish commander of the Constantinople army corps. He felt that Germany should offer Russia a "sop," although the kaiser had already declared that nothing should be done that looked like a retreat before Russia or the Triple Entente. Sazonov appreciated the German efforts to find an acceptable change in the Liman set-up, but soon gave up hope of progress and again appealed to Britain and France, 27 December, to ask Berlin what further course Germany envisaged; an evasive answer, he said, would create a serious situation requiring new and more determined Triple-Entente steps in Constantinople. Sazonov and his Triple-Entente partners seemed to be still in much the same position that Nicolson had described earlier: "the difficulty always in dealing with Sazonov is that one never knows precisely how far he is prepared to go." Although Nicolson was willing to admit that the Liman appointment was a serious matter, "still we would look rather foolish if we took the question up warmly and then found that Sazonoff more or less deserted us." Crowe was of the same mind, for he refused to assure the Russian chargé d'affaires of action in Berlin and instead posed three questions: "What exactly did Russia demand or desire to obtain?" If her demands were rejected, "what means did Russia propose to employ to exact either compliance or reparation?" Finally, would Russia "press her demands to the point of war with the Triple Alliance?" Gaston Doumergue, who had replaced Pichon as French foreign minister, raised similar questions at the Russian embassy in Paris.[10]

In order to deal with the problem of the Liman von Sanders mission and to answer the questions posed by both France and Britain, Sazonov called a special ministerial conference, which met on 13 January 1914 with Kokovtsov in the chair. The ministry of foreign affairs had drawn up an agenda for discussion, including the question of what measures might be taken, such as the occupation of some place in Asia Minor if Germany did not yield to Russian demands. Sazonov pointed out that if Liman were removed from the command in Constantinople, the discussion would become academic, and Kokovtsov recalled that he

10. Nicolson to Mallet, Private, 2 December, and Crowe's Minute, 29 December 1913: *BD*, X(1), nos. 393, 452; Doumergue, Note, 30 December 1913: 3 *DDF*, VIII, no. 689. Cf. Izvolsky to Sazonov, 15/2 January 1914: 1 *IBZI*, I, no. 12; Fischer, *Krieg der Illusionen*, pp. 494–98.

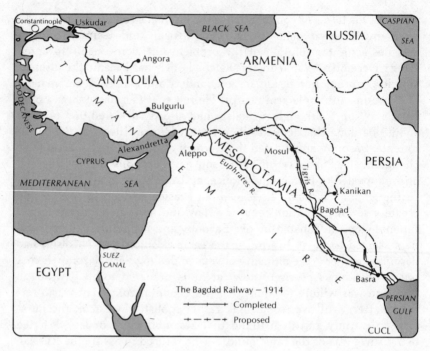

The Bagdad Railway – 1914
Completed
Proposed

IV. Turkey in Asia, 1914

had established the basis of negotiations with Germany in Berlin and thought that Russia should not be driven from that basis. After considering the proposals before them, the conference agreed to maintain opposition to the command of a German general in Constantinople but to accept a general inspection of the Turkish army; to negotiate with Berlin till failure became obvious; in that case to concert with France and England; and, unless sure of the active support of both, not to apply coercive measures that might lead to war.[11]

Much has been made by revisionist historians in contrasting the peace-loving Kokovtsov with Sazonov's readiness to go along with the "militarists," mainly Sukhomlinov and Minister of the Navy Grigorovich, in risking a European war.[12] Yet Kokovtsov himself has asserted that Sazonov was not under the influence of the minister of war and the Admiralty in January 1914, because "he was well aware of our unpreparedness," and in any case the Admiralty "never showed the least aggressiveness in its policy, and was conspicuous for its extreme caution." Kokovtsov has explained that he succeeded in winning consent to his views at a time when everyone knew his days in office were numbered, "because no member of the conference, and certainly not Sazonov, was contemplating the starting of a world war."[13]

Fortunately, the German effort to find a sop for the Russians achieved success in January 1914 when Enver Pasha, who had just become minister of war, agreed on 10 January to name Liman von Sanders a marshal and thereby automatically remove him from command of the Constantinople army corps, if he was promoted in Germany to General of Cavalry. At the same time he would be Inspector-General of the whole Turkish army, the position that the Germans had originally sought for him. Bethmann Hollweg notified St. Petersburg, 15 January, of these arrangements and expressed the view that by them Germany had met Kokovtsov's wishes. Sazonov grumbled, but Kokovtsov was satisfied. For Russia the settlement was an empty diplomatic victory because Germany had successfully defended the substance of the Turkish army control through Liman von Sanders. Sazonov drew two conclusions: the Triple Entente whose weakness he blamed for the failure to win a complete victory over Germany,

11. Minutes of the conference, 13 January 1914/31 December 1913: Friedrich Stieve, *Isvolsky and the World War*, pp. 228–29.

12. For example, Sidney Bradshaw Fay, *Origins of the World War* (1929), I, 535–36.

13. Kokovtsov to Michael T. Florinsky, 23 April 1929: *FA*, VIII (1929), 139–40. Cf. Kokovtsov, *Out of My Past*, pp. 401–03.

should be transformed into a genuine alliance; and Russia had to face up once more to the problem of the Straits, no longer an academic question, "but a serious practical problem of diplomacy and military strategy in which great powers were concerned," for Asiatic Turkey was crumbling and unless Russia acted, Germany might well reap the harvest.[14]

Even before the Liman von Sanders affair had reached an acute stage, Sazonov had written a long memorandum, 6 December 1913, on the Near Eastern problem and the question of the Straits, and had called for a council to discuss Russian policy. He argued that the Ottoman empire was in a state of dissolution, but that Russia wanted no territory and wanted peace. Nevertheless, if the status quo were upset, she could not accept a solution of the Straits question contrary to her interests. Both economic and strategic considerations raised the question whether the Russian army and navy could seize Constantinople and the Straits in case of need. In conclusion Sazonov wrote:

> I reiterate my desire expressed above that the status quo remain unchanged as long as possible. Furthermore I must repeat that the question of the Straits can hardly advance a step excepting by way of European complications. . . . The difficult and complicated questions set forth here require an on-going study in order to make foreign-policy decisions consonant with our means.[15]

Sazonov's memorandum served as the basis for other memoranda by the naval general staff, which recommended various measures in order to counter the possible increase of the Turkish fleet, and approved Sazonov's proposal that Russia get Romania and Bulgaria to cooperate in future operations at Constantinople and the Straits.

The conference Sazonov had asked for took place on 21 February 1914, eight days after Kokovtsov had relinquished the post of premier to the aged Ivan L. Goremykin. Sazonov took the chair and opened the conference by stating that while no grave political complications seemed probable at the moment, the status quo might be upset at any time, even in the near future. Russia in that case had to occupy the Straits rather than let any other power take them. Consequently he wanted to know what had been done and what more was needed in order to effect a successful operation. In the course of discussion

14. Kerner, "Mission," SR, VI, 560.
15. Sazonov, Memorandum, 6 December 1913: LN, II, 363–72.

Sazonov noted that a seizure of the Straits could not take place "without a European war," but Zhilinsky, Chief of the General Staff, pointed out that in case of such a war no separate army could be sent to the Straits, for Russia would have to put all her forces on her western front. Others indicated that because 95 per cent of Russian trade was carried in foreign bottoms, Russia lacked ships to transport troops to the Straits. The conference agreed to take several measures intended to remedy such weaknesses, to strengthen Russia's position in the Caucasus, and to recommend to departments that they take the necessary technical measures for an eventual seizure of the Straits. Yet although Sazonov and others seemed to think that a conflict in the near future was not improbable, they could not get around the basic dilemma that without war there could be no seizure of the Straits, but that with war Russia lacked the resources to take them and to fight on her western front at the same time. In view of this helplessness the technical discussion of troop transport and the like was a far cry from a sinister plot to bring about a European war.[16]

The Armenian reform question, meanwhile, had reached a happier conclusion. After negotiations had seemed to produce an agreement at Christmas time in 1913, Sazonov unexpectedly demanded new concessions, but after a brief period of tension and of unfounded rumors of an imminent massacre in Armenia, he yielded after obtaining minor concessions and signed an accord with the Porte, 8 February 1914. By this agreement the powers were to nominate two inspectors-general who were to have fairly extensive control over Armenian affairs. There was little satisfaction over the settlement by either Turkey or the Armenians, but the diplomatic tension was relaxed. Germany regarded the accord as a defeat for Russia, whereas the Russians considered it a victory over Turkey and Germany, because the agreement was between Russia and Turkey, and in their judgment Germany had lost caste by her efforts to please both the Turks and the Armenians. Moreover, friendlier relations developed between Turkey and Russia in the succeeding months, the high point of which was a special Turkish delegation to visit the tsar at Livadia in May. At the same time, German-Turkish relations cooled, because of German inability to help the Turks financially, and both Germany and Austria-Hungary were worried by the Russo-Turkish rapprochement.

A more significant aftermath of the Liman von Sanders crisis was the rancor harbored by Sazonov and the deterioration in Russo-Ger-

16. Minutes of the conference, 21/8 February 1914: Stieve, *Isvolsky*, pp. 230–46.

man relations. This worsening of relations was revealed in a virulent press war of February and March 1914 that was climaxed on 2 March by an article in the *Kölnische Zeitung*, considered to be a mouthpiece of the Foreign Office. Russia, the St. Petersburg correspondent wrote, was not yet ready for war but would be in 1917, and he implied that Russia would attack Germany when she was prepared to do so. Sukhomlinov inspired a reply that stressed the great improvement in the Russian army, but asserted that it would displease no one who was not aggressive. Sazonov declared that no Russian seriously intended to attack Germany, but the Russian military attaché in Berlin reported that there was a widespread fear of a German-Austro-Hungarian preventive war on Russia. The press war undoubtedly reinforced Sazonov's determination to shore up his diplomatic position in the Balkans and to tighten the bonds of the Triple Entente, objectives that he pursued over the first six months of 1914 as a defensive rather than an aggressive strategy.

III.

While Russia was dealing with the question of Constantinople and the Straits and winding up the Armenian reform problem, France and Great Britain were separately pursuing negotiations with Germany and the Porte over railroads and other projects in Asiatic Turkey. The Russo-German agreement of 1911, by which Russia withdrew her opposition to the Bagdad railway, broke the deadlock of nearly a decade. Henceforth both France and Britain felt free to pursue their own interests. The German-Turkish convention of March 1911 added another factor of flexibility in that Turkey, while agreeing to the extension of the Bagdad railway from Bulgurlu to Bagdad, induced the Germans to surrender their rights to build from Bagdad to the Persian Gulf and to give up a claim to any funds that might accrue from an increase in Ottoman tariffs. These two points had been major stumbling blocks to British acquiescence in the extension of the Bagdad railway and to the raising of Turkish tariffs. They spurred French aspirations to secure railroad concessions in Syria and Anatolia.

The French, however, were held up by Germany, who had no objection to financial agreements between French and German bankers but did not want to involve the governments. Moreover, Jagow did not want to discuss Syria until he knew how negotiations with Great Britain might come out. When he realized that failure to negotiate

with France might jeopardize discussions with Britain, who wanted
an all-around settlement, he yielded to French overtures of May 1913.
A round of discussions among financiers and representatives of the
foreign offices resulted in an agreement on 15 February 1914 between
the Imperial Ottoman Bank (French) and French interests in Asia
Minor on the one hand and the Deutsche Bank and German railroad
interests on the other. Both the French and the German foreign offices officially recognized the agreement and exchanged notes ratifying
the terms. By them the French acquired the right to build railway lines
in northern Anatolia and in Syria from Tripoli to Homs and eastward
to the Euphrates; but the Germans reserved Alexandretta, Aleppo, and
the area in Anatolia through which the Bagdad railway ran as their
sphere of activity. The agreement also indicated measures—such as a
rise in Turkish tariffs in order to increase Ottoman revenues—which
would provide guarantees for the French and German railways. In
accord with this arrangement, a Franco-Turkish agreement of April
granted a loan to Turkey and provided for railway concessions in the
French spheres of influence and for ports on the Mediterranean and
Black Sea coasts.

Concurrently, Germany and Britain were carrying on discussions
that took place within a framework of efforts on both sides to better
their relations. Africa as well as Turkey figured in their negotiations,
which had been foreshadowed by the Haldane talks in Berlin of February 1912 and were taken up by Prince Lichnowsky when he arrived
in London as ambassador in November 1912. On the German side,
Jagow and Bethmann agreed, with the kaiser's approval, that the best
way to maintain peace and to counter the encirclement of Germany
was to improve relations with England. On the British side, Grey had,
to a considerable extent, adopted the policy advocated by his critics
in the winter of 1911–1912. He was not sanguine over the possibility
of a genuine rapprochement with Germany but was ready to cooperate
with her and to favor German expansion in the Ottoman Empire and
Africa.

The first of the agreements to emerge was that on the Portuguese
colonies. German bankers had developed grandiose schemes for a
Mittel-Afrika involving not only Portuguese possessions but also the
Belgian Congo, and the German government wanted to update the
agreement with Britain of 1898. Grey was willing to do so in order to
prove that Great Britain did not begrudge Germany her colonial
aspirations. After nearly a year of negotiations, Grey and Lichnowsky
initialed an agreement, 20 October 1913, by which Britain was to

receive a little more of Mozambique than before and a smaller strip of Angola, bordering on Rhodesia, while Germany was to get the rest of Angola, giving her a long frontier with the Belgian Congo.[17] Grey wanted to publish the agreement along with the declaration to Portugal of 1899 by which Britain promised to defend her integrity, but Jagow refused, fearing that the "good atmosphere" desired would be destroyed by publication of the two documents, since the German public would never understand the inconsistency between them. Because the matter was still unsettled when war came in 1914, the agreement over the Portuguese colonies was never signed.

Similarly, the Anglo-German convention concerning the Bagdad railway and related matters was never signed, although it was initialed in June 1914. The questions involved were far more complicated than those relating to the Portuguese colonies. Without going into details, Great Britain wanted to dominate the Persian Gulf, to be assured of fair treatment for British trade, and to secure the interests of British enterprises in the navigation of the Tigris and Euphrates rivers and in oil and irrigation projects in Mesopotamia. Germany wanted to safeguard her interests in the Bagdad railway and the districts as far as Basra, through which the line was to run. Turkey hoped to secure a rise in tariffs from 11 to 15 percent. Agreements between Britain and Turkey of July 1913, recognizing Britain's special position in southern Mesopotamia, cleared the way for the completion of Anglo-German negotiations—contingent, however, upon new conventions between Germany and Turkey. As in the case of the Franco-German agreement of 1914, the bundle of Anglo-German ones involved bankers and businessmen on both sides, but in contrast, the convention of 15 June 1914 was initialed by Grey and Lichnowsky. German-Turkish delays in completing their accord held up the signature of the documents, although steps were taken in late July to sign them. Because the July crisis forestalled the formal conclusion of the agreement, the terms, which satisfied both the British and German desires are of academic interest only.[18]

The British-German-French-Ottoman agreements and conventions amounted to a peaceful partition of Asiatic Turkey into spheres of influence. As for the relations of Germany and the two entente powers,

17. The text: *BD*, X(2), no. 341. For the background and negotiation of the agreement, see Richard Langhorne, "Anglo-German Negotiations concerning the Future of the Portuguese Colonies, 1911–1914" *HJ*, XVI (1973), 361–87.

18. Texts of the Anglo-Turkish and Anglo-German agreements: *BD*, X(2), nos. 124, 249. For both agreements, cf. Fischer, *Krieg der Illusionen*, pp. 431–39.

the effect of the agreements was virtually nil in the case of France and Germany, and superficial in that of Great Britain and Germany. To be sure, their cooperation during the Balkan wars and their African and Turkish agreements were accompanied by a relaxation of the tensions that had developed over naval rivalry. These better relations undoubtedly contributed to the German expectation that Britain would remain neutral in case of war—a disastrous calculation in the July crisis of 1914. The Germans, and many Englishmen too, failed to note that the problem of naval armaments remained unsolved and that of the balance of power untouched.

The relations within the great-power blocs, however, were by no means completely harmonious. In the Triple Entente, Russia and France were uneasy over the better relations between Britain and Germany, and Russia especially wanted to transform the Entente into an alliance. Sazonov argued that an Anglo-Russian alliance, or something equally definite and public, would deter Germany from aggression. He professed that he did not care about the form of the agreement, but that it must be such as to publicize the solidarity of the Triple Entente. The tsar used much the same language, except that, after French prompting, he suggested a naval understanding. The French, of course, backed Russia's desire for more definite Anglo-Russian commitments.

While the British government could not contemplate an alliance with anybody, much less with Russia, of whom the Radicals were still especially critical, both Buchanan in St. Petersburg and Nicolson at the Foreign Office felt that something had to be done to consolidate Anglo-Russian relations. Nicolson feared that the "whole Anglo-Russian convention was about to totter in fragments to the ground." He shared with Buchanan the view that "Russia is rapidly becoming so powerful that we must retain her friendship at almost any cost" and that if she became convinced of British unreliability and uselessness, she might strike a bargain with Germany and regain her liberty in Turkey and Persia. Buchanan commented: "Our position then would be a very parlous one." Sir Eyre Crowe could see no objecttion to a naval understanding similar to that between Britain and France, but Grey was reluctant to enter into naval discussions with the Russians, hoping to postpone them as long as possible.[19] Nevertheless, despite

19. Nicolson, *Carnock*, pp. 294–96; Crowe, Minute: *BD*, X(2), 783. For the conflict of views concerning British policy, see Lowe and Dockrill, *Mirage of Power*, I, 119–21 and III, Documents, nos. 66–69.

grievances against Russian behavior in northern Persia, Grey, like his advisers, was so imbued with the fear of what harm Russia might do in the Middle East and India, and so impressed with her growing military power, that he acquiesced in the Russian and French-backed requests for the closer naval ties that were conveyed to him on his visit to Paris with King George V in April 1914.

Upon receiving authorization by the Cabinet, Grey's first step, 19 May, was to communicate to Benckendorff his letter of 22 November 1912 to Cambon, leaving it to the French to reveal Cambon's answer of 23 November. Although Sazonov wanted an arrangement for cooperation in the Baltic and the Mediterranean and even for a landing in Pomerania, Grey rejected the notion of operations in the Baltic, and left the whole matter of a naval understanding to negotiations between the two admiralties. The Russian naval attaché in London was authorized to begin discussions, but Churchill discovered that he was not well enough informed to carry on useful conversations. Instead, Prince Louis of Battenberg, First Sea Lord, planned to visit Russia in August to discuss naval cooperation with the Russian chief of the Admiralty and the minister of the Navy.

Meanwhile the German Foreign Office learned of the *pourparlers* through the Russian diplomatic correspondence, copies of which were regularly forwarded to Berlin by Benno de Siebert, secretary of the Russian embassy in London. By arrangement with editor Theodor Wolff, the *Berliner Tageblatt* on 22 May and 2 June revealed the proposed Anglo-Russian naval understanding and called attention to the dangers, inherent in such a development, of jeopardizing an Anglo-German rapprochement and encouraging renewed naval agitation in Germany. The hoped-for response came on 11 June, when a Liberal member of the House of Commons asked Grey whether Britain and Russia had made a naval agreement and whether negotiations were pending. Grey replied with an evasive answer that amounted to a falsehood, for he reminded the House of Asquith's statement of the previous year that there were no unpublished agreements that would hamper the freedom of the government or of Parliament to decide the British course of action in case of war, and then declared that "no negotiations have since been concluded. . . . No such negotiations are in progress, and none are likely to be entered upon, as far as I can judge." Grey's answer did not deceive the Germans, who had the Russian documents before them, and it heightened mistrust of Grey at the Wilhelmstrasse. On the other hand, the parliamentary question and answer destroyed any British desire for haste in carrying on negotiations with the Russians. Also, Grey had second thoughts about his denial of negotiations, and on 9 July informed Lichnowsky that he could not deny that "conversations had taken place between the naval and military authorities on the two sides." Tirpitz believed that a naval convention had been concluded, but the only change that occurred in Anglo-Russian relations was Russia's great satisfaction over British willingness to negotiate a naval agreement, which Sazonov regarded as of great importance "in a general political sense."[20]

Between France and Britain and France and Russia no serious divergence of views occurred in the last months before the July crisis. The cordiality of Anglo-French relations was attested during the visit of George V to Paris in the latter days of April. France and Russia had tightened their military cooperation in the staff talks, annual since 1911, of August 1913. The negotiation of a French loan in 1913 for Russian railway construction ran into difficulty because of Kokovtsov's objection to the French condition that the strategic lines, planned in collaboration with the French, be begun at once, and that the effective strength of the Russian army be considerably increased. When Kokovtsov finally conceded the French condition, the French government approved a maximum loan of 500 million francs annually over a period of five years, providing for the building of strategic railroads as soon as possible. In February 1914 Maurice Paléologue, a long-time friend of Poincaré and since January 1912 director of political affairs at the Quai d'Orsay, replaced Delcassé as ambassador to Russia. If we may believe his own interpretation of his mission, he was assigned to a "contradictory" task: "On the diplomatic terrain, I should constantly restrain the Russian government, whereas on the terrain of military preparations and plans I should constantly stimulate them." Because, he added, in case of war, "the Russian armies should mobilize with the briefest delay; that is, for France, a question of life and death."[21]

The Triple Alliance, like the Triple Entente, was also concerned with military and naval agreements in the last years of peace; unlike the Triple Entente the Triplice discussions were often quite divorced from political and diplomatic realities. The most striking illustration is the series of talks concerning the role of Italy in case of war. As a result of the war with Turkey and the cooling of relations with France, Italy evinced a desire to tighten her ties with her allies. The first fruit of

20. Sazonov to Benckendorff, 28/15 May 1914: Siebert and Schreiner, no. 850 (also 1 IBZI, III, no. 109). For a convenient summary of Anglo-Russian relations, 1912–1914, see Lowe and Dockrill, Mirage of Power, I, 133–38.

21. Paléologue, Au Quai d'Orsay . . . 1913–1914, p. 284.

this change in the Italian attitude was a naval convention (23 June, revised 2 August 1913) designed to gain control of the Mediterranean and thus to protect the Adriatic and to prevent France from drawing troops from North Africa. Furthermore, in February 1914, the Italian general staff renewed the arrangement with Germany by which Italy was to send her third army corps to the Rhine in case of war. An additional surprising development was the willingness of General Alberto Pollio, chief of the general staff, to aid Austria-Hungary in a two-front war with Russia and Serbia. There is no doubt of General Pollio's devotion to the Triple Alliance, but his political wisdom and his knowledge of foreign relations were scarcely commensurate with his lavish promises. His death on 28 June 1914 ended the brief revival of close military cooperation between Italy and her allies.

Similarly the relations of Moltke and Conrad lacked contact with and control by civilian authorities. It is true that the exchange of 1909 was sanctioned by Bülow and Aehrenthal, but the Moltke-Conrad discussions then and afterward took place in a political vacuum. The two chiefs of staff were mainly concerned to coordinate their military operations. Moltke was especially desirous that Austria-Hungary launch an attack on Russia that would prevent her from overwhelming the weak German forces left in the East while the main forces were engaged against France. Conrad, on the other hand, wanted Germany to pin the Russians down on the Narew River in order to prevent their deployment against the Dual Monarchy. Neither Moltke nor Conrad was ever fully satisfied with the promises of the other; both in fact promised more than they could deliver, with the result that the operations on the eastern front were a gamble, and that neither Conrad nor Berchtold was certain of effective German cooperation in a war with Russia. In their last meeting before the July crisis, 12 May 1914, Moltke and Conrad talked in generalities about the political situation, the question of Italian and Romanian loyalty, the increasing strength of Russia, the likelihood of British participation in a continental war, the Balkans, and military matters like reserves and guns. When Conrad asked how long in a war with Russia and France before Germany could turn against Russia, Moltke optimistically replied: "We hope to be finished with France in six weeks after the commencement of operations, or at least so far that we can transfer our main strength to the east."[22]

These unsatisfactory and inconclusive discussions neither bound

22. Conrad, *Dienstzeit*, III, 669–73. Cf. Stone, "Moltke-Conrad," *HJ*, IX, 214–15.

Germany to back the Dual Monarchy against Serbia, as has been alleged,[23] nor adequately provided for unified action. Far more significant were the talks about the danger arising from Russia's growing military strength. Intermittently from the autumn of 1913 Conrad raised the question of why they should wait until Russian military preparations were completed before risking a war in which the probability of winning would steadily decrease. Moltke in May 1914 agreed that to wait was to lessen the chances of victory. Afterward he talked with Secretary of State Jagow about the necessity of a preventive war. Jagow was not prepared to conjure one up, although he thought that if war appeared to be inevitable, one should not let the enemy dictate the timing, but should decide that for himself. Yet despite the forebodings of the military and the talk of preventive war, when the German government on 5 July 1914 had to decide whether to back Austria-Hungary, Moltke was not even consulted. The background of that event lay not in military plots to start a war but in the realm of diplomacy, and involved primarily the problem of the Balkans.

V.

The Balkans, no less than Turkey, continued to be a theater of great-power rivalry from the end of the second Balkan war to the July crisis of 1914. Here Russia and France were pitted against Austria-Hungary in both diplomacy and finance. Italy, too, vied with the Dual Monarchy over the Adriatic and Albania. Russia was anxious to maintain and expand the victorious combination of Serbia, Montenegro, and Greece, while Austria-Hungary sought to preserve the loyalty of Romania and to win over Bulgaria and perhaps Turkey in order to prevent the formation of an iron ring around the Monarchy. Although France ably seconded Russia, Germany proved to be a dubious ally from the viewpoint of Vienna. On the whole, Russia was more successful than the Monarchy.

Aside from the consolidation of Russia's ties with Serbia and Greece through the visits of Pašić and Venizelos to St. Petersburg in February 1914, Sazonov persistently sought to win over Romania. Relations had been good after the peace of Bucharest, but with the coming of Ion Bratianu to power in mid-January 1914 they became

23. See Schmitt, *Coming of the War 1914*, I, 14–17; and cf. Max Montgelas, "Professor Schmitt über den Ursprung des Weltkrieges," *KBM*, IX (1931), 434.

warmer, for the Liberal party, of which he was head, was anti-Hungarian because of the treatment of fellow nationals in Transylvania. At the end of March the visit of the Romanian crown prince and princess with their son to St. Petersburg indicated a rapprochement. A return visit of the tsar along with Sazonov took place on 14 June at Constantsa. There the sovereigns and their ministers found that they had common interests. Foremost was the freedom of the Straits, should Turkey in her still unsettled conflict with Greece over the Aegean islands go to war and close them. Then, too, Romania's attachment to the peace of Bucharest was the same as that of Greece and Serbia, sharers in the spoils, whose conquests Russia approved and wanted to see consolidated.

At the meeting in June, Sazonov assured Bratianu that Russia was supporting Romania's interests and had modified her former pro-Bulgarian policy. He wanted to know if Romania had any foreign ties that would prevent cooperation. Bratianu declared that Romania had no obligations to take part in a war in which her interests were not directly concerned—an obvious *suggestio falsis* in view of her ties with the Triplice. When Sazonov tried to pin him down more explicitly concerning a war between Russia and Austria-Hungary, Brantianu still evaded a flat answer, declaring that Romania's attitude would depend upon the circumstances and also upon Romanian interests. In his turn Bratianu quizzed Sazonov on the possibility of war, and learned that a Russian move against the Dual Monarchy was likely only if the latter attacked Serbia; in that case Russia could not stand aside. Bratianu then assured Sazonov that it was not in Romania's interests to see Serbia weakened. From this discussion Sazonov concluded that in case of war Romania would take the side of the stronger and the one who promised her the greater profits. On the whole, he felt that the tsar's visit had been a great success and had permitted hope of "neighborly relations" with Romania.[24]

France had contributed to the winning of Romania by an active propaganda campaign there in favor of the Triple Entente, but her main contributions in the Balkans were financial. Upon Russian recommendation, France lent 40 million francs to Montenegro in December 1913. After a visit of Venizelos to Paris in January 1914, France promised a loan of 500 million francs to Greece. Serbia was not only the center of much Franco-Russian activity, but also the battleground of Franco-German armament rivalry. Despite a French loan of 250 million francs in January, German and Austrian munition makers managed

24. Sazonov to the tsar, 24/11 June 1914: *LN*, II, 377–84.

to get orders for guns along with those of France. The major Russo-French failure, however, lay in Bulgaria, whose desire for revenge and whose flirtations with Austria-Hungary led Russia to veto much-needed loans in late 1913. Through the efforts of the German minister in Sofia and the Austro-Hungarian government Berlin banks were persuaded early in 1914 to negotiate a 500-million-franc loan. Russia and France did their best to prevent the German loan but failed, for in the end the Sobranje in a turbulent session on 16 July approved it. This action was a significant step toward the ultimate Bulgarian alliance with the central powers, although the Berlin banks canceled the loan upon the outbreak of war.

The triumph of Russo-French diplomacy highlighted the failures of Austro-Hungarian policy. Berchtold, early in January 1914, raised the question of his resignation with Francis Joseph for the third time since August 1913. He argued that the German frustration of his efforts to revise the peace of Bucharest had prejudiced his position, but the emperor disagreed with him and asked him not to resign. Though torn between going and staying, Berchtold again yielded to the emperor. Ambassador Mensdorff told Crowe in London: "Count Berchtold is a polished man who doesn't like to say No brutally"; and his biographer adds that he equally disliked to say Yes forthrightly.[25] Quite apart from Berchtold's diplomatic humiliations, however, the Dual Monarchy was economically in a bad position in 1914. Prices were rising and industry and commerce were feeling the effects of a slump in foreign trade because of French and German competition in the Balkan market.

Austria-Hungary's ultimate cause of anxiety, however, was Russia, with whom relations were outwardly correct. Mistrust of Russia arose not alone from stories in the Pan-Slav press of a new Balkan federation and from fear of Russian aims in the Balkans, but also because of propaganda within the Monarchy, especially among the Ruthenes, and fear of Russian armaments. The failure of Austria-Hungary to solve the South-Slav problem and to placate the Romanians also meant that the enlarged Serbia, with Russia at her back, became the most hated neighbor at the Ballhausplatz, with Romania in second place. The question was how to build up most effectively an anti-Serbo-Russian and pro-Austro-Hungarian bloc, but the Monarchy's allies were either hostile or completely impervious to Vienna's proposed policies.

For example, in April 1914 rumors of a contemplated union of

25. Hantsch, *Berchtold*, II, 520–21.

Serbia and Montenegro greatly disturbed Berchtold, but he found that both Germany and Italy opposed his proposals for preventing Serbian access to the sea by such a union. Even more serious was the Austro-Italian rivalry in Albania. The arrival in Durazzo early in March of the Prince of Wied sparked an open contest between the Austrian and Italian ministers in Albania for predominance in the affairs of the fledgling nation. But there were other points of conflict, as Riccardo Bollati, Italian ambassador in Berlin, pointed out to San Giuliano. After calling attention to them, he wrote: "In fact, there is, perhaps, not one single question where the interests of Italy coincide with those of Austria; where the policy of the one is not jealously watched and guarded against by the other."[26]

If there was little hope of cordial relations with Italy, the prospect of a pro-Austro-Hungarian federation in the Balkans was no brighter. The obvious candidate for the pivot of an anti-Serbian combination was Bulgaria, who had emerged from the second Balkan war with a thirst for revenge. Her first endeavor was to ally with Turkey as a step toward the Triplice, but hesitations arising from the risks involved, should a Turkish-Greek conflict occur, and over the attitude of Romania, without whose support Bulgaria could not hope for a rapprochement with Berlin and Vienna, prevented the consummation of a Turkish alliance that was opposed by Germany in any case. The situation therefore boiled down to this: the hope of an anti-Russo-Serbian coalition in the Balkans lay in Sofia and Bucharest, but they were at odds with one another, because the one wanted revision of the Bucharest peace and the other its maintenance. Furthermore, Austria-Hungary could not make any headway toward resolving her problem without hearty German support, which she lacked, despite the kaiser's bombastic promises of October 1913 to follow Vienna's Balkan policy. Yet Berchtold tried to square the circle of antagonisms from November 1913 to July 1914.

In order to hold Romania fast, Berchtold sent Count Ottokar Czernin as minister to Bucharest. He belonged to Francis Ferdinand's circle and was a member of the Austrian House of Lords; he was an outsider in diplomacy but a specialist in the nationality problems of the Dual Monarchy. Berchtold laid the situation before him realistically. He recognized the need for reform in the treatment of the Romanians in Hungary, but felt that their grounds for grievances were no worse, if as bad, as those under the Russians in Bessarabia. Basically the worst fault of Romania was to cooperate with Serbia, a cooperation that had

26. Antonio Salandra, *Italy and the Great War*, p. 38.

been represented as a wartime measure but had not diminished after the end of the war. Berchtold flatly named Serbia as the enemy of the Monarchy and castigated cooperation with her as incompatible with the Romanian-Austrian alliance. Czernin's task was to realign Romania with the Triplice, although the tenor of Berchtold's instructions offered a dark outlook for his success.

After Czernin's first interviews in Bucharest, November 1913, he declared that Austria-Hungary stood at the parting of the ways. He urged the need of Hungarian reforms and suggested that the Austro-Romanian treaty of alliance, known only to the prime minister and the king, be revealed to the public at once. Berchtold, however, felt that the time was not yet right. He placed his hopes upon the reforms in Hungary, upon which Tisza was working, and upon the intervention of the German kaiser.

In Berlin there was little understanding of the Dual Monarchy's problems, or sympathy with its policy. At the Wilhelmstrasse no one could understand why Austria-Hungary had not come to terms with Serbia, and Jagow told Joseph Baernreither in March 1914 that the Monarchy should join a Romanian-Greek-Serbian group in which the non-Slavs would constitute a majority. Such talk emphasized the truth of what Berchtold had said a year earlier: "The Germans are working to secure Bulgaria's encirclement, we Serbia's."[27]

William II, in a round of talks at Vienna, Miramar, and Konopischt, helped very little to bring about a concerted policy. In discussions with Francis Joseph, Berchtold, and Tisza in March, the kaiser tried to reassure them concerning both Romania and Russia. Francis Joseph and Berchtold agreed with him that "Romania must now look more to Berlin to be the connecting link between her and the Triple Alliance," and hoped that "Berlin would do all that was possible in that direction." As for Russia, the Kaiser did not believe that belligerence toward Austria or Germany was mainly responsible for her war preparations, but that in part they were a condition of French loans and in part protective measures in case of eventual action against Turkey. Tisza, who impressed the kaiser very favorably, represented his efforts to conciliate the Romanians as progressing favorably and hoped that in time their dissatisfaction with Hungarian rule might die out.[28]

---

27. Joseph M. Baernreither, *Fragments of a Political Diary*, p. 193. Cf. Gerard E. Silberstein, *Troubled Alliance*, pp. 16 ff., for Austro-Hungarian-German relations with the Balkan states.

28. Tschirschky to Bethmann, 23 March 1914: *GP*, XXXIX, no. 15715 (also Max Montgelas, *The Case for the Central Powers* [London, 1925], pp. 229–31).

It is noteworthy that neither Berchtold nor Tisza broached the subject of a Bulgarian alliance, according to the kaiser's report. This omission is the more remarkable in Tisza's case because he had just drawn up a memorandum (on 15 March) dealing, among other things, with Bulgaria. In the memorandum he recommended the adoption of a long-term policy aiming at the creation of a Balkan group that should be supported by Germany for the sake not only of the Dual Monarchy but also of Germany herself. The position of Russia, assisted by the "mad ambition" of Romania and Serbia and by the endangered position of Bulgaria, was the Monarchy's greatest problem. With Germany's help Romania should be led to renounce the lure of Transylvania, and in alliance with the Monarchy to assure her possessions and her independence and thus to avert the danger of becoming a Russian protectorate. But the main thrust of the memorandum lay in a plea for the support of Bulgaria lest she be forced to throw herself into Russia's arms. With German cooperation, close relations should be encouraged with Bulgaria, Greece, Romania, and Turkey, thus creating a Balkan bloc favorable to the Triplice. There was no time to be lost, Tisza emphasized, but the attainment of the objective he advocated would require years of peace.[29]

So far as Romania and Greece were concerned, Archduke Francis Ferdinand, whom the kaiser visited at Miramar after leaving Vienna, agreed that they should constitute "a wall in the Balkans to protect the Triple Alliance against the Slavs." Turkey, too, should be brought in if possible. Although the Archduke hated Tisza, he listened to the kaiser's praise of him, and only emphasized that Hungary should deal with her Romanian problem, as Tisza had evidently tried to do and intended to continue doing. When William II visited the Archduke at Konopisht, 12–14 June, no progress had been made toward winning back Romania, but the two men agreed that King Carol should be consulted about the tense Greco-Turkish situation and encouraged to intervene in order to prevent any infringement of the peace of Bucharest. Both expressed their dislike for Ferdinand of Bulgaria. They also agreed that Russia was not to be feared, because she was not ready for action, and they discussed Italy, whom the Archduke mistrusted and the kaiser defended. The kaiser also urged a forthright advance against Serbia. Francis Ferdinand frankly expressed his antipathy toward Hungary, "absolutely anachronous and medieval," and Tisza whose deeds did not "coincide with his words." The kaiser, however, thought Tisza

29. Tisza, Memorandum, 15 March 1914: *OUA*, VII, no. 9482.

"such a strong and exceptional man" that he should not be thrown overboard but "kept under iron-handed control," and he promised to instruct Ambassador Tschirschky "to go on perpetually saying to Tisza: 'Sir, remember the Romanians!' "[30]

In view of the Austro-Hungarian conviction that the major enemy was Russian-backed Serbia, the complacency of the Germans from Jagow to the kaiser about Serbia and Romania and their elimination of Bulgaria as a potential ally could but discourage policymakers in Vienna. Berchtold, to be sure, had not entirely given up Romania, nor energetically pushed for an alliance with Bulgaria, although he was promoting the German loan for her. But the cumulative effect of Czernin's pessimistic reports from Bucharest, the impracticability without Romania of all the Balkan groupings discussed or suggested, and the obvious significance of the tsar's Constantsa visit in mid-June seemed at last to have moved Berchtold to take a positive position. The upshot was a memorandum which was intended to win firm German support for a reorientation of Austro-Hungarian policy. On 17 June Berchtold went to work with Baron Franz von Matscheko and Count Johann Forgách to draw up the memorandum. The first draft, completed 24 June, embodied ideas already included in Berchtold's memorandum of 1 August 1913, some of Tisza's thoughts in his memorandum of 15 March, and especially those of Hans von Flotow of May 1914. Matscheko reworked the first draft following Berchtold's directives between the 24th and 28th, after which a brief supplement was added on 1 July.

In a balancing of the books after two years of upheaval, the memorandum found only three items on the credit side: the creation of an independent Albania as a counterweight to Serbia; a greater Greece, who, despite ties with Serbia, need not be regarded as hostile; and, most important, Bulgaria, who was no longer a Russian satellite. On the other hand, the debits outweighed the credits: Turkey, whose interests were identical with those of the Triplice, had been driven from Europe and weakened; Serbia, "wholly subject to Russian influences," had expanded beyond her own expectations and might be further enlarged by union with Montenegro; and Romanian relations with the Triplice had been "materially altered." Moreover, Russia and France were far from satisfied and were aiming at extending their advantages. While the policy of the Monarchy and Germany—to a certain extent,

30. Treutler to A. A., 27 March, and to Zimmermann, 15 June 1914: GP, XXXIX, nos. 15720, 15736 (also Montgelas, The Case, pp. 231–35).

Italy as well—was conservative and defensive, that of the Franco-Russian alliance was opposed to the status quo and had an "offensive character." Its main aim was to unite the Balkan states against the central powers by offers of territorial expansion, and one of its persistent efforts was directed toward forcing Bulgaria into its camp. Thus far Russia and France had failed, but the only way to prevent their eventual success was to take action that "would stiffen Bulgaria's backbone . . . and would secure the nation against isolation."

Turning to Romania, the memorandum noted the success of Russia and France in directing public opinion there against Austria-Hungary, and the adoption by the government of a free-hand policy. Yet despite the admitted Romanian rapprochement with Russia, King Carol would try to prevent Romanian participation in a war against the Monarchy, with what success was dubious. Although the memorandum left the door open for a faint hope that Germany might yet win back Romanian loyalty, it declared that circumstances excluded the possibility of using Romania longer "as the pivot of the Monarchy's Balkan policy." Austria-Hungary had not only to prepare militarily for the contingency of Romanian neutrality, perhaps even hostility, in a war with Russia, but also to show Romania that the Monarchy was able to find other pillars of support for her Balkan policy.

The only way to achieve this objective was to accept Bulgaria's offers, repeated over the previous year, to establish relations that would in practice amount to an alliance. Also the Monarchy should seek to bring about a Bulgar-Turkish alliance. But these moves had to be made soon and could not be undertaken before a full understanding with Germany, a matter of the greatest importance. In conclusion, the memorandum sought to convince Germany that her interests were as directly involved as those of the Monarchy, and that Russian policy, as manifested in military preparations and in traditional expansionist aims, was as inimical to Germany as to Austria-Hungary.[31]

There was little that was new and much that was erroneous in the analysis of the situation, but what was new was the elimination of Romania as a "pivot" of Austro-Hungarian Balkan policy, and the pleas for the support of Bulgaria as a new pillar of a pro-Triplice group. With reference to both points, the language was guarded and less than forthright—out of consideration, no doubt, for Berlin's well-known attitude toward the two states. Yet the argument for change was clear and constituted the first energetic step toward winning German sup-

31. Memorandum, 3rd draft, 1 July 1914: *OUA*, VIII, no. 9984 (also, KD, no. 14).

port for the Dual Monarchy's revamped policy. What effect the memorandum might have had in Berlin without the impact of the Sarajevo crime can only be conjectured. That event lent weight to the document, for the supplement, written after 28 June, pointed up the Austro-Hungarian determination to tear asunder the net being woven about the Dual Monarchy.

VI.

The European pattern of international relations on the eve of the July crisis of 1914 was not black and white, but varicolored. The blackest section was that of the Russo-Austro-Hungarian rivalry in the Balkans. Even here, as Berchtold's memorandum testified, there was no thought of an immediate armed conflict, but rather a diplomatic contest over the loyalties of the Balkan states, which was envisaged as a continuing one over the years to come. Nor were the lines between the alliance groups as yet clearly drawn. Italy and the Dual Monarchy within the Triplice were more actively opposed to each other than France and Germany, or Russia and Germany. Ambassador Schoen, in a long despatch of 5 February 1914, testified to the pacific sentiments in France and declared that no one "was disposed to risk his or his son's bones for the question of Alsace-Lorraine."[32] Bethmann Hollweg doubted if Russia was planning a war against Germany. British-Russian relations within the Triple Entente were again on the verge of a serious conflict over Persia. On the other hand, Anglo-German relations were better than at any time since the height of the naval rivalry in 1912. Bethman wrote to Lichnowsky, 16 June:

If we should both stand forth with determination as the guarantors of European peace, an attitude which, as long as we sought this object from the beginning on the basis of a common plan, neither the Triple Alliance nor the Entente obligations could prevent us from assuming, war could be avoided.

Grey responded, 24 June, with similar sentiments, while stressing Britain's intimate relations with France and Russia.[33] In short, there

32. Schoen to Bethmann, 5 February 1914: GP, XXXIX, no. 15667.
33. Bethmann to Lichnowsky, 16 June, and Lichnowsky to Bethmann, 24 June 1914: KD, nos. 3, 5. Fritz Fischer interprets Bethmann's letter as part of an effort to localize a threatening Greco-Turkish war and to separate Britain from the Entente: Krieg der Illusionen, pp. 611–12.

was little apprehension of an immediate European war and no plans for one.

On the other hand, there was an underlying current of uneasiness and anxiety, fostered in considerable measure by the armament race. In 1913 both France and Germany had increased their forces by the three-year service law in France and the German army bill that provided for an increase in the peacetime army from 544,000 to 870,000 at a cost of about a billion marks. While the French law yielded an immediate increase in the army to about 770,000 men, the full goal of the German bill was not to be realized for some years. What was as significant about the French army as the three-year service law was the spirit of self-confidence that pervaded the armed forces after the Agadir crisis.

A similar situation existed in Russia, who planned in October 1913 to expand her army to a peacetime strength of about 2,300,000 men. This development along with her plans for strategic railways to the western front gravely worried the central powers over the prospects in the years to come. What deepened their anxiety was the new confidence of the Russian military, who up to 1914 had stressed their lack of preparedness. In that year, however, as part of a public dialogue with their French counterparts, they began boasting of their strength. The most notable example was the article in the *Birsheviya Vyedomosti* of 13 June, inspired by General Sukhomlinov and headed: "Russia is ready, France must also be ready." The article was intended to help assure the retention of the French three-year service law that was threatened by the victory of the Left in the elections of May 1914, but it heightened the fear in Berlin of Russian aggressive plans. The kaiser commented in characteristic fashion: "Well! At last the Russians have shown their hand! Whatever German still refuses to believe that in Russo-Gaul they are working at high pressure for an early war with us, or that we should adopt the necessary measures for self-protection, deserves to be sent at once to the mad-house at Dalldorf."[34]

While predictions of war recurred throughout the first six months of 1914, no one saw it as an immediate eventuality. Usually the prophecy served as a stimulus to preparedness, as in the case of the debate over the renewal of the three-year service law in France, or as an argument for diplomatic action, as in Berchtold's memorandum. Colonel House, who visited London, Berlin, and Paris in May and June to discuss armament limitation characterized the situation as one of "nervousness"

34. A report of the Russian article and the kaiser's comments: KD, no. 2.

and "fear."[35] Another witness, Winston Churchill, writing several years after 1914, testified to the "strange temper in the air," the "national passions" beneath the surface, the men "everywhere eager to dare," and the military preparations. His nostalgic epitome of the 1914 world, however, omitted the uncertainties and fears that were current:

> The world on the verge of its catastrophe was very brilliant. Nations and empires crowned with princes and potentates rose majestically on every side, lapped in the accumulated treasures of the long peace. All were fitted and fashioned—it seemed securely—into an immense cantilever. The two mighty European systems faced each other glittering and clanking in their panoply, but with a tranquil gaze. A polite, discreet, pacific, and on the whole sincere diplomacy spread its web of connections over both. A sentence in a dispatch, an observation by an ambassador, a cryptic phrase in Parliament seemed sufficient to adjust from day to day the balance of the prodigious structure. Words counted, and even whispers. A nod could be made to tell. . . . The old world in its sunset was fair to see.[36]

35. *Intimate Papers of Colonel House* (ed. Charles Seymour. Boston, 1928), I, 258.

36. *The World Crisis*, pp. 198–99.

Chapter 13

The July

Crisis, 1914

The principal actors in the July crisis, listed by their countries, were: For Austria-Hungary, Emperor Francis Joseph, Foreign Minister Count Berchtold, Austrian Premier Count Karl Stürgh, Hungarian Premier Stephen Tisza, War Minister Alexander Baron Krobatin, Finance Minister Leon von Biliński, and Chief of the General Staff General Conrad; their advisers at the foreign ministry were Count Alexander Hoyos (Berchtold's chief secretary), Johann von Ghymes und Gács Forgách, and Karl Baron von Macchio; the ambassadors were László Count Szögyényi-Marich in Berlin, Kajetan de Mérey in Rome, Count Albert Mensdorff in London, and Friedrich Count Szápáry in St. Petersburg. In France, Raymond Poincaré was president and René Viviani was both premier and foreign minister, while Paul Cambon in London and Maurice Paléologue in St. Petersburg were ambassadors. For Germany, Kaiser William II, Chancellor Bethman Hollweg, Secretary for Foreign Affairs Gottlieb von Jagow, and his under-secretary Arthur Zimmermann; German ambassadors were Heinrich von Tschirschky at Vienna, Carl Max Prince von Lichnowsky at London, Hans von Flotow at Rome, and Count Pourtalès in Russia. Great Britain's personnel were King George V, Prime Minister Asquith, Foreign Secretary Sir Edward Grey, and at the Foreign Office Permanent Undersecretary Arthur Nicolson and Assistant Under-secretary Sir Eyre Crowe; her ambassadors were Sir Maurice de Bunsen in Vienna, Sir Edward Goschen in Berlin, Sir Rennell Rodd in Rome, and Sir George Buchanan in St. Petersburg. In Rome, Premier Antonio Salandra and Foreign Minister Antonio Paterno-Costello Marquis of San Giuliano directed policy. For Russia, Tsar Nicholas II and Foreign Minister Sergei Sazonov (whose secretary was Baron Moritz Shilling) were the decision-makers, and the ambassadors were Nicholas Shebeko at Vienna, A. P. Izvolsky at Paris, and Count Benckendorff at London.

11. *Archduke Francis Ferdinand and Wife at Sarajevo*
    (The Bettmann Archive)

On 28 June 1914, about 11 A.M., Gavrilo Princip fatally shot Archduke Francis Ferdinand and his consort on the Appel Quay in Sarajevo. Oceans of ink have been spilled over the origins of the plot to kill the archduke, the motives, and the official and unofficial responsibility for it. While many details are still obscure and the truth has not yet been completely distilled from the conflicting testimonies of contemporaries and the monographs of researchers, the main outlines are clear concerning the reasons for the plot, its organization, and the course of events leading up to the assassination.

I.

The backgrounds of the Sarajevo plot lay in the turbulent youth movements of Bosnia-Herzegovina, Croatia, and Slovenia within the Austro-Hungarian empire. Their objective was freedom from Habsburg rule and some kind of unity among the South Slavs—cultural for some, cultural and political for others—although in the many secret societies among the youth there was little unanimity concerning ultimate aims and even concerning means. On the whole, however, hatred of Habsburg rule engendered an anarchistic recourse to terrorism and acts of individual violence that increased in number after the annexation of Bosnia and Herzegovina in 1908. In Bosnia, where the youth movement was given the generic name of "Young Bosnia" (*Mlada Bosna*), although there was no such formal organization, the Balkan wars added fuel to the flames, especially among the Serbs, many of whom joined the *komite* (comitadji), the irregular troops that had been fighting the Turks for years, and thus formed links with Serbian activists. Before 1914, a notable terrorist attempt was that of Bogdan Žerajić upon Governor Varešanin at Sarajevo in June 1910, a few days after the visit of Emperor Francis Joseph there. After his failure to kill the governor, Žerajić committed suicide and thereafter became venerated by young Bosnians as a hero and martyr in the anti-Habsburg cause. Princip and his fellow conspirator Čabrinović testified at their trial that they often visited Žerajić's grave, and Princip added: "At his grave I swore to myself that I would do as he had done at all costs."[1]

The agitated university and even secondary-school youth of Bosnia offered fertile soil for Serbian propaganda directed from Belgrade. The principal agencies were the *Narodna Odbrana* (National Defense),

---

1. "The Sarajevo Murder Trial," *SR*, IV (1926), 647.

founded in 1908, and *Ujedinjenje ili Smrt* (Union or Death), familiarly known as the Black Hand and organized in 1911 by former participants and their sympathizers in the 1903 murder of King Alexander. The head of the organization was Colonel Dragutin Dimitrijević, known as Apis. Although the organization was heavily military in its membership, there were able civilians among the leaders, one of whom founded *Pijemont*, a periodical that was the mouthpiece of the society. Both organizations were patriotic societies, but differed in their objectives. *Narodna Odbrana*, at first a paramilitary society, became mainly concerned with cultural matters after the Serbian capitulation to Austro-Hungarian terms in April 1909, and maintained contacts with the South Slavs of the Dual Monarchy through a network of confidential agents. On the other hand, the constitution of the Black Hand stated that its purpose was the unification of Serbdom through revolutionary action "in all territories inhabited by Serbs . . . with all the means available."[2] Inevitably there was much duplication of membership, the Black Hand often finding it advantageous to work under the cover of the older and better known *Narodna Odbrana*. For example, Apis, as chief of the military intelligence section of the Serbian general staff, built up a spy ring in Bosnia and elsewhere and utilized agents of the *Narodna Odbrana*. The complex of wheels within wheels that characterized propaganda, spying, and conspiracy accounts for much of the conflicting testimony and interpretation of the Sarajevo plot and its background.

In the plot to kill Francis Ferdinand Bosnians decided upon the deed, but agents of the Black Hand supplied the weapons and helped three of the conspirators to reach Sarajevo. It should be noted, however, that the ultimate goal of the Young Bosnians was not the expansion of Serbia, which was the objective of the Black Hand, but a Jugoslav union. The origins of the plot lay in the minds of the youthful Bosnians who had been talking for months of a deed of terrorism against some Austrian official. When news came of the archduke's planned visit to Sarajevo in connection with maneuvers to be held southwest of the city in June, he became the target. A plot to murder him was no new idea, for over the previous dozen years there had been many rumors and at least three attempts upon his life. To the young Bosnians his character and politics mattered very little; it was enough that he was a "top personage" of the hated Austria.

When news of the archduke's plan to visit Sarajevo was published,

2. Vladimir Dedijer, *The Road to Sarajevo*, p. 374.

Gavrilo Princip was in Belgrade preparing for school examinations and associating closely with Nedeljko Čabrinović, a fellow Bosnian and former *komita*, and Trifko Grabež, another Bosnian. The three agreed to attempt the death of the archduke, and through Milan Ciganović, a former *komita* and a friend of Major Vojin Tankosić, himself a Bosnian and commander of all *komite* units, they obtained revolvers and bombs from the Serbian Kragujevac arsenal. The three conspirators, after practicing with the revolvers under the direction of Ciganović and others, and procuring money, set out on 28 May for Sarajevo along a route that would enable agents of the secret underground to aid them upon the orders of Tankosić.

Meanwhile, before leaving Belgrade, Princip had enlisted the aid of a long-time friend and former school teacher in Sarajevo, Danilo Ilić, who readily agreed to help and enlisted three more conspirators who had been active in plots and in school-boy radical groups. Also, it was Ilić who assigned the six plotters their places on the Appel Quay beside the Miljacka river, along which the archduke and his party were to ride to the town hall for an official reception.

Before the approach of the archduke the conspirators mingled freely among the crowds that lined the street without incurring any suspicion on the part of the few gendarmes and police on duty. Had the same precautions been taken as those for Francis Joseph's visit in 1910, the conspirators would have had little opportunity to fire upon the archduke. As it turned out, however, only two of them had the presence of mind or the nerve to act. As the archduke rode toward the town hall, Čabrinović tossed a bomb at his car, but had failed to allow the necessary time to elapse after pulling the firing pin with the result that the bomb rolled off the back of the car and exploded under the next one, wounding several people including the aide-de-camp of General Oskar Potiorek, governor of Bosnia. Upon leaving the town hall, Francis Ferdinand insisted upon visiting the wounded officer, which meant a change in the planned return route. The archduke's car, however, began to take a wrong street when Potiorek ordered it to stop and turn back. This pause, which occurred a few feet from where Princip was standing, enabled him to fire almost point blank at the archduke. Princip had two fortuitous circumstances to aid him. In addition to the halting of the archduke's car, a bystander kicked a policeman in the knee throwing him off balance when he tried to intercept Princip as he raised his revolver. Dedijer concludes that the Sarajevo assassination "was one of the most amateurish regicides of modern times. Despite their number, their single-mindedness of purpose, and the coolheadedness of their leader Princip in the most decisive minute of the day, the success of the conspiracy was due mainly to sheer luck."[3]

Because the assassination was seized upon by Austria-Hungary as an outrage for which Serbia was ultimately responsible, an important question is: What was the culpability and responsibility of Belgrade? Belgrade here covers two separate elements: the Apis-Black Hand apparatus on the one hand, and the Pašić government on the other. While all the details of the situation have not been established, it is clear that Apis knew of and approved the plans of Princip and his companions. Tankosić would scarcely have dared to render the aid that he did without the approval of his superior. As for the government, there was a bitter and open conflict going on between Apis and Pašić. The latter's Old Radical party looked upon the group around Apis as "pretorians who were threatening the whole political system of Serbia." *Pijemont* charged the party with corruption, even mentioning Pašić by name. The Old Radicals retaliated with the charge of militarism and were responsible for dubbing *Ujedjenje ili Smrt* as the Black Hand. In the spring of 1914 tension was particularly acute, for a struggle had developed in the newly acquired Macedonian lands over who was to have the upper hand there—the civil or the military authorities. On 2 June the Pašić government resigned, but with the backing of Russia and Prince Alexander, Pašić returned to power. On 24 June he dissolved the Skupština and set elections for 1 August. On the same day King Peter turned over the throne and the command of the army to Alexander as Prince Regent. Thus the Sarajevo plot coincided with a bitter struggle between Apis and Pašić, who could not afford politically to appear openly as an opponent of such a popular cause as the anti-Austrian drives of the young Bosnians.

Nevertheless, he took action when he learned indirectly through the *Narodna Odbrana* of the crossing into Bosnia of armed men. He ordered an investigation by civilian officials at the border and an inquiry concerning Apis by military authorities. Whether he warned Vienna is not clear, but *apparently* Jovan Jovanović, Serbian minister in Vienna, had gone to Leon von Biliński, finance minister whose department administered Bosnia and Herzegovina, on 23 May and told him "in a friendly manner" that if Francis Ferdinand went to Sarajevo on Vidovdan (28 June, St. Vitus day, a Serbian national holiday), both his visit and the maneuvers would be considered by the people to be a provocation, and no one could be certain that a "sharp missile" might not go

3. Ibid., p. 323.

astray toward an "undesired target."[4] This friendly admonition was obviously very vague, and did not mention a plot. It could not be regarded as an official warning, and Biliński apparently paid no attention to it.

On the basis of the evidence available, neither the Pašić government nor *Narodna Odbrana* can be accused of instigating or furthering the plot. In the midst of a political crisis and on the eve of general elections, the last thing the Serbian government wanted was a crisis in relations with the Dual Monarchy. As for Apis and the Black Hand, they clearly did not instigate the plot, though without their aid Princip and Ilić might well have lacked the arms and bombs that they needed, and Princip and his companions would have had great difficulty in making their way to Sarajevo without being apprehended. It is also fairly clear that the political situation and the uncertainty of the conspirators' success explain why Pašić probably did not warn Vienna. In that failure lies his sole responsibility.

Likewise attempts to put the blame for Sarajevo on Austria-Hungary and Russia are fruitless. It is true that security precautions were extraordinarily lax, but General Potiorek and the military who had complete charge of the archduke's visit can scarcely be accused of anything more than gross overconfidence in their meager precautions and lack of appreciation of the dangers inherent in the Young Bosnian movement. As for Russia, while Apis and the Russian military attaché, Colonel V. A. Artamanov, were in close touch with one another, the latter supplying information and providing money for some of the expenses of the Serbian spy network in Austria-Hungary, there is no reliable evidence that either Artamanov or Hartvig had any knowledge of the Princip conspiracy. Apis himself declared at the time of his trial in 1917 that he had not told Artamanov of the plot.[5]

II.

The news of the Sarajevo crime shocked Europe and evoked sympathy with Austria-Hungary and the house of Habsburg. Nobody thought of

---

4. Jovan Jovanović, in *Politika*, 4 December 1926: *KBM*, V (1927), 85.

5. Cf. Albertini, *Origins*, II, 82–86; and Uebersberger, *Osterreich zwischen Russland und Serbien*, pp. 287–90, who think Artamanov knew of the plot; Dedijer, *Road to Sarajevo*, pp. 432–34; and Schmitt, *Coming of the War 1914*, I, 236–40, who think he did not.

an Austro-Serbian war, let alone a world war. In France, Poincaré indirectly warned the Austro-Hungarian ambassador against anti-Serbian excesses, although the French press suspected that the Dual Monarchy would make Sarajevo a pretext for reprisals. The Russian reaction was much the same as the French. In Germany, where the kaiser was especially incensed at the murder of his friend, whom he had visited only two weeks before, the responsibility for the crime of Pan-Serbian agitation was taken for granted, but there was no agreement concerning the guilt of the Serbian government, or the measures that Vienna might legitimately take. At the Foreign Office, Zimmermann, acting head while Jagow was absent on his honeymoon, advised Belgrade not to be imprudent and Vienna to be restrained. As late as 4 July he admonished Ambassador Szögyény that while vigorous action against Serbia would be understandable, Vienna should exercise great prudence and not make humiliating demands upon Serbia.

In Austria-Hungary the reaction to the archduke's death was a mixed one. "Despite the embarrassing discrepancy between official horror and the the 'third class funeral' on the one hand," writes Geiss, "and public indifference and internal relief over the disappearance of the heir apparent on the other, the assassination aroused in many Austrians a desire to force a showdown with troublesome Serbia."[6] Bunsen, the British ambassador, testified that all sections of the population were now "blindly incensed against the Servians" and that "sensible persons" thought that the Monarchy had to prove its strength "by settling once and for all her long-standing accounts with Servia, and by striking such a blow as will reduce the country to impotence for the future."[7] The significance of the outburst against Serbia lay in the encouragement of the government to take the vigorous action which Conrad had long advocated, but which Berchtold had resisted as long as Vienna had not been dominated by a war mood. The virulent demands for the punishment of Serbia and Serbians represented an irrational remedy for the Monarchy's failure to deal in time with the nationalistic struggle of the South Slavs that was threatening to tear the empire apart.

Uncertainty characterized the atmosphere at the Ballhausplatz, where Joseph Redlich found the planlessness and anxiety that, he as-

6. Imanuel Geiss, *July 1914*, p. 56.

7. Bunsen to Grey, 5 July 1914: *BD*, XI, no. 40. Because this chapter is based primarily on the documents in *ARB* or *OUA*, VIII, *BD*, XI, 3 *DDF*, X, 1 *IBZI*, V, and *KD*, I shall not document quotations unless the provenance is unclear or they come from an outside source, and shall omit 1914 from document dates.

serted, was always present there. A group composed of Count Hoyos, Count Forgách, and Baron Macchio supported the notion of a show- down with Serbia. Conrad argued for immediate action, although in his interview with Berchtold on 29 June he confined his suggestion to mobilization against Serbia. Berchtold agreed that the time had come to settle the Serbian question, but wanted to await the results of an investigation. He was in the middle between, on the one hand, the war party joined by Alexander von Krobotin, minister of war, and, on the other, Tisza, who staunchly opposed war with Serbia, and coun- seled caution from the outset. In a letter to Francis Joseph of 1 July he had denounced the intention to settle accounts with Serbia; if war came, it would be a "large-scale war," for Russia would intervene, Romania would not aid the Monarchy, and Bulgaria, the only state to be relied upon, was exhausted. Tisza urged peace while winning back Romania and negotiating with Bulgaria; war could be brought about later if necessary. The emperor, when Berchtold talked with him on 2 July, thought war was unavoidable, but the time for military action had not yet come. Berchtold, on the other hand, feared that delay might permit a favorable atmosphere to evaporate. He agreed, how- ever, that two conditions for action were proof of Serbian complicity, and the certainty of support at least by Germany and eventually by Bulgaria.[8]

At this point contradictory advice was coming from German sources. On 30 June Tschirschky had advised "quietly but very impressively and seriously against too hasty steps."[9] No doubt he assumed, like Zimmermann, that the policy of restraint, pursued by Germany in 1912 and 1913, was still being followed. The next day, however, Victor Naumann, close to the Bavarian prime minister and to Wilhelm von Stumm in the Wilhelmstrasse, expatiated to Count Hoyos upon the situation in Berlin, where not only military and naval circles but also the Foreign Office and the kaiser no longer completely opposed a pre- ventive war against Russia as they had the year before. Public opinion in Germany, Naumann assured Hoyos, would force the Foreign Office to support the Monarchy. While his estimate of public opinion was a dubious one, Naumann was quite right about the kaiser, who had written on Tschirschky's report of the 30th: "It is none of his busi- ness, as it is solely the affair of Austria, what she plans to do in this

---

8. Norman Stone, "Hungary and the Crisis of July 1914," *1914: The Coming of the First World War*, p. 160; Hantsch, *Berchtold*, II, 563.

9. Tschirschky to Bethmann, 30 June: KD, no. 7.

case . . . Serbia must be disposed of, *and* that right *soon!*" He had prefaced this statement with the laconic "Now or never." Either because of a hint from Berlin or because of further reflection, Tschirschky changed the emphasis of his remarks when he talked with Francis Joseph and with Berchtold on 2 July. With them he stressed the need for a clear and well-thought-out policy, and privately assured them that Germany would support a program to defend Austria-Hungary's vital interests. Moreover, on the 4th Tschirschky let the Ballhausplatz know, through a newspaper correspondent, that Germany would support the Monarchy through thick and thin, whatever it decided to do about Serbia, and the sooner Austria let go the better.[10]

Whatever effect such pronouncements may have had, they could not suffice for the Viennese statesmen. All agreed, from Conrad and Berchtold to Tisza and the emperor, that Austria-Hungary could not take the risk of European complications by punishing Serbia without official assurance of Germany's approval and support. In view of Tisza's attitude there had been no agreement as yet concerning what the Monarchy should do or how to proceed. No one, not even Tisza, doubted that something had to be done and that the Sarajevo crime had provided the provocation that had been lacking in 1913, when Berchtold had sought in vain Germany's support of an anti-Serbian policy. In short, the key to a final decision lay in Berlin, and thither Count Hoyos went on 4 July with the memorandum that had been completed on 1 July and a letter from Francis Joseph to Emperor William. Neither document explicitly mentioned war against Serbia, but the intent of eliminating Serbia "as a factor of political power" and the destruction of "this hearth of criminal agitation at Belgrade" was clear. Also, Berchtold instructed Hoyos to explain to Ambassador Szögyény that the moment had come to settle with Serbia; certain guarantees would be required for the future, upon the refusal of which military action would be considered. The ambassador was to find out the attitude of Berlin before Vienna followed out such plans.

Szögyény presented the memorandum and Francis Joseph's letter to the kaiser at luncheon on 5 July. The kaiser asserted that he had expected "some serious step" against Serbia, but confessed that the letter made him "regard a serious European complication possible and that he could give no definite answer before having taken council with the imperial chancellor." After lunch, however, he went farther and authorized Szögyény, as the latter put it, "to inform our gracious Majesty

10. Notes on Naumann and a German journalist: *OUA*, VIII, nos. 9966, 10038.

that we might in this case, as in all others, rely upon Germany's full support." Although the kaiser had to find out what the chancellor would say, he had no doubt that Bethmann Hollweg would agree with him, "especially as far as action against Serbia was concerned." Furthermore, the kaiser expressed the opinion "that this action must not be delayed." Russia would no doubt be hostile but he had long been prepared for this, and if an Austro-Russian war was unavoidable, Germany would stand by her ally. Again he stressed the need to seize the moment for a march on Serbia. He would see to it that King Carol of Romania and his councillors would observe a correct attitude. While he did not trust Tsar Ferdinand, he would not object to a treaty between the Monarchy and Bulgaria as long as it contained nothing to offend Romania.[11]

In the afternoon of the 5th, William II saw Bethmann, Zimmermann, Falkenhayn (Prussian minister of war), Aide-de-camp Plessen, General Lyncker (chief of the military cabinet), and Captain Zenker (representing the navy). On the following morning before leaving for Kiel and a voyage in Scandinavian waters, the kaiser talked briefly with Admiral von Capelle (acting secretary of the navy), and General von Bertrab, Moltke's deputy on the General Staff. With all these men, excepting Bethmann Hollweg, there was nothing like a consultation, but rather a statement of views similar to those he had expressed to Szögyény, although the kaiser seemed more confident on the morning of the 6th that there would be no war with Russia and France because they were not ready for it. Besides, the tsar would not side with "prince murderers." There was therefore no pressure from the military at this point to commit the country to a war policy; its representatives merely learned of a pledge to Austria-Hungary. Bethmann Hollweg, of all the men with whom the Kaiser talked, had the constitutional duty of ratifying the kaiser's pledges. This he did on 6 July.

On that day Bethmann and Zimmermann talked with Szögyény in the presence of Hoyos. In words that closely paralleled those of the kaiser, Bethmann Hollweg spoke of the dangers that Austria-Hungary was facing and approved an alliance with Bulgaria as long as it did not violate obligations toward Romania, whom he would advise to stop agitation against the Monarchy and to take account of the impossibility of Austro-Serbian friendship. As for Serbia, in the words of Szögyény's report "the German government is of opinion that we must judge what is to be done to clear the course; whatever way we

11. Szögyény to Berchtold, 5 July: ibid., no. 10058.

decide, we may always be certain that we will find Germany at our side, a faithful ally and friend of our Monarchy." Like the kaiser, the chancellor

> considers immediate action on our part as the best solution of our difficulties in the Balkans. From an international point of view he considers the present moment as more favorable than some later time; he agrees with us that we need inform neither Italy nor Romania beforehand of an intended action against Serbia.

Bethmann's report of the conversation differed only in his ascribing to the kaiser the views and pledges communicated to Szögyény, and in the omission of the phrase "under all circumstances" from the pledge to stand by Austria-Hungary.[12] This omission from the draft by Zimmermann suggests that the chancellor had some reservations concerning the "blank check" or did not want explicitly to call attention to the unlimited character of the German obligation that "His Majesty" had assumed.

Among the assumptions upon which Germany pledged her support to Austria-Hungary was the crucial one held by the kaiser, the chancellor, and the men at the Ballhausplatz that Russia was not ready for war and that France and Britain would exert a pacifying influence upon her. Also, they believed that the tsar would not support regicides, and that all the world condemned the Sarajevo crime and would understand if Austria-Hungary held Serbia responsible for it. Therefore the time was propitious for the Dual Monarchy to wipe out the Serbian "nest of conspirators" and restore its power and prestige. Yet there were lingering doubts about the situation. First of all, would Austria-Hungary rise to the occasion and act decisively? If she delayed too long the favorable atmosphere would evaporate. Knowledge of the Anglo-Russian naval discussions and Grey's patent evasion of queries about them raised doubts of Britain's reliability in a showdown. Zimmermann believed that in case of war Great Britain would side with Germany's enemies in order to prevent the loss of France's power position. As Jagow put it after the war: "We fluctuated between fears and hopes."[13] Yet if worse came to worst and a world war was engendered by Austro-Hungarian action, the kaiser, the military, and the industrialists were convinced of German military superiority for

---

12. Same to same, 6 July: ibid., no. 10076. Hoyos wrote this telegram: Albertini, *Origins*, II, 147. Cf. KD, no. 15.

13. *Front wider Bülow*, ed. Friedrich Thimme (Munich, 1931), p. 219.

the time being, although Bethmann Hollweg and others believed that the situation would be reversed in two or three years. Moreover, all except Prince Lichnowsky believed that the Dual Monarchy was facing a crisis involving her vital interests, and that in such a situation Germany had to support her ally whatever the risks involved. This was no new concept, for Chancellor Hohenlohe had taken that position in 1896.

The kaiser and the chancellor, while in general agreement concerning the "blank check" to Austria-Hungary, were moved by slightly different considerations. Since October 1913, the kaiser had accepted Vienna's view that Serbia was an implacable enemy of the Monarchy and had, in fact, given a blank check to both Conrad and Berchtold which they had not cashed. Undoubtedly the murder of the archduke had affected the highly emotional kaiser deeply, and he viewed it as a princely affair to be handled by Francis Joseph as he saw fit. That the decision to back Austria-Hungary was primarily the kaiser's is indicated by Bethmann's report to Tschirschky of 6 July concerning the discussion with Szögyény, for he referred to the decisions and statements of "His Majesty" eight times in as many sentences.

Bethmann Hollweg, although he had agreed with the kaiser to back the Dual Monarchy, realized that Germany was taking the risk of a European war. Pessimistically he saw no alternative except as he said in his memoirs, German "self-emasculation," for Austria-Hungary, he told his confidant, Kurt Riezler, was growing weaker and more immovable, while the military might of Russia was growing rapidly. In view of his obsessive brooding over the growth of invincible Russian power, he was shaken by the revelation of Anglo-Russian naval discussions, and fancied that in case of war Germany might be threatened by a landing in Pomerania of Russian troops from British ships, as Sazonov had suggested to Grey. Furthermore, if Germany did not back Austria, he thought that the latter might gravitate toward the open arms of the western powers. He believed that there was no time to be lost, for there was a chance that if the Monarchy moved quickly, it and Germany could face Europe with a fait accompli and could then have a "friendly talk" with the Entente powers. If the Monarchy did not move quickly, the chances of avoiding war would become narrower and narrower. These considerations meant that Germany had to work to localize the Balkan conflict, if possible divide the Entente, and above all prevent closer Anglo-Russian ties lest the iron ring, as Jagow later put it, should close more tightly around her. If it came to war, it was better now than later, and in this thought the chancellor, as he admitted in February 1918, was espousing "in a certain sense . . . a preventive war." Thus Bethman, having weighed all the factors involved, took the "calculated risk" of backing Austria-Hungary, and admitted to Riezler, when he learned of her decision to send an ultimatum to Serbia, that it was a "leap in the dark."[14] In view of what we now know of Bethmann's calculations, the German blank check to Austria was neither "levitous" nor "careless" nor "silly," as various interpreters have alleged, but carefully weighed and almost desperately signed.

Unfortunately for the success of Bethman Hollweg's gamble, Austria-Hungary was incapable of moving rapidly despite the urgings of the German government conveyed by Tschirschky and Szögyény. The ministerial council of 7 July showed that there was still a difference of opinion between Tisza and the other ministers concerning how to proceed with Serbia. Berchtold, now that he was certain of German support, came out forcefully for military action against Serbia, because the experience of 1909 and of October 1913 had demonstrated that diplomatic triumphs had made no change in the relations with Serbia; a "radical solution" of the question raised by the propaganda for a greater Serbia was "only possible through an energetic intervention." Biliński, Krobatin, and Count Karl Stürgkh (Austrian premier) argued in favor of immediate war upon Serbia. Tisza, however, would hear of no such procedure, wanting to prepare the ground diplomatically by winning over Bulgaria, who would keep Romania in line. Berchtold asserted that there was no hope of a Bulgarian alliance immediately. Tisza finally modified his attitude to the extent of admitting the possibility of warlike action, but "would never consent to a surprise attack upon Serbia without a previous diplomatic action." The members of the council discussed the possibility of Russian intervention, which Berchtold thought might not necessarily mean war, and Romania's position. They called in Conrad and the Deputy Chief of the Naval Staff for questioning concerning the military situation, and while the minutes of the meeting do not record what they said, we know that Conrad was none too happy about the chances in a war with Russia if Romania were neutral or took part in it. The council, whatever its knowledge of military possibilities, decided upon a compromise between Tisza and the others: all agreed that there should be a speedy decision concerning Serbia, whether of a warlike or of a peaceful character, and that mobilization was not to take place until after con-

14. Egmont Zechlin, "Deutschland zwischen Kabinettskrieg und Wirtschaftskrieg," HZ, CIC (1964), 354.

crete demands had been made upon Serbia and, if refused, until an ultimatum had been sent. Nevertheless, because of Tisza's attitude, a final decision had yet to be made concerning the demands on Serbia, and whether they should be such as to preclude Serbian acceptance.

Between the 7th and the 14th of July the main drive in Vienna was to bring Tisza around. In a letter to the emperor Tisza stuck to his view that a war with Serbia would "provoke Russian intervention and thus world war," with Romania on the side of Russia; the cooperation of Germany with reference to Bulgaria and Romania improved the outlook for diplomatic action. He repeated his threat to resign if Serbia were not permitted the chance to avoid war by accepting a humiliation. Berchtold at the same time wrote Tisza stressing the point made by Stürgkh at the council that Berlin expected action and would not understand it if the opportunity were allowed to pass without a blow. Also, Germany had guaranteed that Romania would not attack. Germany, thought Berchtold, would regard compromising with Serbia as an evidence of weakness which would affect the Monarchy's position in the Triplice and in future German policy. Berchtold obviously hoped that by stressing German expectations, he could persuade Tisza to change his mind. At the same time, Stephan Burián and General Conrad were discussing with Forgách, Macchio, and Hoyos at the Ballhausplatz the character of an ultimatum to Serbia. They concluded that the terms should be such as to preclude acceptance. Burián's adherence to the war party was of great significance, for he was one of Tisza's closest advisers, whose views probably had a greater influence in convincing Tisza that war was necessary than had Berchtold's.

On 9 July Berchtold discussed with Francis Joseph the alternatives open to Austria-Hungary in dealing with Serbia, and learned to his satisfaction that the emperor did not agree with Tisza but was ready to go forward along the lines of the council's decision. Berchtold himself was not inclined to make a hasty decision, for he was under pressure by both pushers and those who like Tisza wanted to put on the brakes. Among the former were his advisers at the Ballhausplatz and Tschirschky, who continued to press for quick action, saying that Austria-Hungary had to make up her mind whether she wanted to remain a great power, and if not, Germany would have to ponder alternatives to supporting her. On the other hand, Count von Lützow, former ambassador to Italy, told Berchtold that "localization" of a conflict with Serbia was a chimera, and if they made demands upon Serbia that could not be fulfilled, then there would be a world war, and Berchtold would risk the existence of the Monarchy.

In the meantime Councillor Friedrich von Wiesner had been sent to Sarajevo on 11 July to gather evidence upon which an ultimatum to Serbia might be based, but his first report of 13 July declared that there was "nothing to prove or even to suppose that the Servian government is accessory to the inducement of the crime, its preparation or the furnishing of weapons." On the other hand, the evidence indicated, he said, that the crime was resolved upon at Belgrade and that Serbian officials supplied the weapons and bombs, and smuggled Princip and his companions across the border. Thus the war party in Vienna had material upon which to press charges, even though Wiesner could not report the Serbian government's involvement.

By this time, however, the drafting of an ultimatum was well along, although not yet completed, and on 14 July at a meeting with Berchtold, Stürgkh, and Burián, Tisza gave up his objections to war with Serbia and approved the formulation of an ultimatum that would be unacceptable to her. Finally, it was agreed that the ultimatum was to be delivered on 25 July, the day when President Poincaré's planned visit to Russia was expected to end, in order to avoid an affront to Russia, and the personal influence of Poincaré and Izvolsky upon Russian decisions. Why Tisza shifted his position is not clear, but certainly the German pressure upon the Monarchy to act energetically and quickly, accompanied by the half-veiled threat to seek other allies if Austria-Hungary did not do so, were major factors in the decision. As head of Hungary he regarded the dictates of Berlin as more imperative than Vienna's. In addition, he had made no headway with Francis Joseph, and had apparently become convinced by the Serbian behavior and press that the Monarchy had to proceed against Serbia.

On 19 July, when the wording of the ultimatum had been completed, a ministerial council made the final decisions concerning it. Tisza made his approval conditional upon a unanimous declaration that "in the procedure against Serbia no plans for conquest by the Monarchy are involved and that the Monarchy does not wish to annex any part of Serbia except as regards frontier rectifications required by military considerations."[15] Although there were objections and reservations by other ministers, Tisza got his way, arguing that self-denial of expansion might obviate the provocation of Russia. The council set the delivery of the ultimatum at 5 P.M. on 23 July, the day on which Poincaré would leave Russia. Almost everyone concerned took the decisive step of 19 July with the conviction that Russian intervention

15. OUA, VIII, no. 10393, as quoted by Stone, "Hungary," 1914, p. 163. .

was inevitable. The decision to act in spite of the likely consequences was an act of desperation, for the very existence of the empire was believed to be at stake. "Better a fearful end than endless fears," one minister exclaimed.[16] Also, the hope of localizing the conflict with Serbia had dwindled with the extended delays in coming to a decision, in collecting the evidence on which to justify the ultimatum, and in timing its delivery.

No one was more conscious of the delays than the men in Berlin who had been kept informed of Austro-Hungarian deliberations and were unhappy over their slowness. Although Berlin did not receive the final text of the ultimatum until 22 July, it had known its character and intent for at least a week before the 19th. Had the Wilhelmstrasse wanted to soften the terms, it had plenty of time to make its influence felt. On the contrary no one had any desire to do so. As Berchtold testified in his memoirs, "Actually the Vienna and Berlin cabinets judged the situation in the July days of 1914 in the same way and in harmonious agreement strove after one and the same goal . . . the diplomatic work in Vienna and Berlin had perhaps at no time been so closely parallel as in those days."[17] Germany's principal worry down to 21 July was that Austria-Hungary would not act vigorously enough.

Other than that anxiety, Germany was concerned to prepare the ground for the localization of the conflict once the terms of the ultimatum became known. The first move was to publish a notice, drafted by Jagow, in the *Norddeutsche Allgemeine Zeitung* of 19 July to the effect that the European press increasingly recognized that the Monarchy's desire to clear up its relations with Serbia was justified. Hoping that a serious crisis would be avoided by Serbia's "giving way in time," the notice concluded by asserting that "the solidarity of Europe . . . demands and requires that the settlement of differences which may arise between Austria-Hungary and Serbia should remain localized."[18] Following up this expression of views, Bethmann Hollweg on 21 July sent a circular dispatch to St. Petersburg, Paris, and London arguing that because Greater Serbian propaganda, which had resulted in the outrage at Sarajevo, could no longer be tolerated by Austria-Hungary, unless she wished to "dispense forever with her standing as a great

16. Pribram, *Austria-Hungary and Great Britain*, p. 229.
17. Hantsch, *Berchtold*, II, 599, note 15.
18. Geiss, *July 1914*, no. 36.

power," her demands upon Serbia and their enforcement by military means, if necessary, were moderate and proper. It was solely for Austria and Serbia to deal with the problem, and the powers should leave the solution to the two immediate participants. "We earnestly desire the localization of the conflict," wrote the chancellor, for otherwise the consequences might be "inestimable." To Sazonov alone he made a plea to stand by Austria-Hungary for the sake of the "monarchical idea," because Serbian radicalism made rulers' families victims of its criminal tendencies. Inasmuch as passages in the dispatch implied knowledge of what the Monarchy was going to do, and the German government was asserting that it knew nothing of Vienna's demands and had exercised no influence on its decisions, Jagow telegraphed Paris and London on 23 July not to follow the instructions in the dispatch of the 21st until the wording of the note to Serbia had been made public through the press.

The chancellor, at Hohenfinow until late on the 25th, was brooding over what might happen after the delivery of the ultimatum. He told Riezler that a lasting understanding with Russia was preferable to an agreement with England, but more difficult. An accord with Russia, however, would mean the sacrifice of Austria-Hungary, a consequence that he immediately rejected. If the Serbian quarrel passed without a Russian mobilization, he conjectured that, once Austria was satisfied, Germany could come to an understanding with the tsar, who would be disappointed in his western allies. But should war break out, it would come from a Russian mobilization, and then they could sit and talk no longer. He believed that England would not immediately enter a war. As for the situation in Germany, he was concerned over two groups: the noisy Pan-Germans, whose blustering, encouraged by the crown prince whom Bethmann asked the kaiser to restrain, might destroy the posture of a defensive policy; and the Social Democrats, whose support of the government he hoped to win.[19]

While Bethmann Hollweg was pondering these problems, Jagow at the Wilhelmstrasse, like the kaiser in Norwegian waters, was uneasily awaiting the outcome of the ultimatum to Serbia with an outward show of confidence. He advised Vienna that Poincaré was not leaving St. Petersburg until 11 P.M. on the 23rd and might learn the terms of the ultimatum if it were delivered at 5 P.M. He also arranged to take over the Monarchy's affairs in Serbia if its minister left Belgrade.

19. Konrad H. Jarausch, "The Illusion of Limited War," *CEH*, II (1969), 62–64.

III.

The Entente powers had little information concerning Vienna's plans, because the secrecy of its deliberations was well kept. Moreover, both Germany and Austria-Hungary purposely kept up the appearance of peaceful complacency by uninterrupted vacation plans and, in the latter case, by giving leaves to the minister of war and chief of the general staff, "on purpose, in order to prevent any disquiet."[20]

Russia was most concerned over what might happen following the Sarajevo crime. After sending condolences to Vienna, Sazonov warned the Serbian government on 7 July to be "extremely careful" about events likely to increase the Serbophobia that he noted in Austria. At the time of Hartvig's sudden death at the Austro-Hungarian legation in Belgrade, 10 July, Sazonov urged Belgrade to avoid anti-Austrian demonstrations. Similarly he urged moderation upon the Dual Monarchy but plainly revealed his feelings to Pourtalès, the German ambassador, severely criticizing the Monarchy's authorities for permitting excesses against the Serbs within its borders. He also declared that it was unjustifiable to hold Serbia responsible for the Sarajevo crime, which was the act of "individual and immature young men." While Sazonov failed to warn the ambassador that Russia would not tolerate an attack upon Serbia, he seemed to reflect the hatred of Austria-Hungary that Pourtalès found in Russian society and that boded ill for the hope of Russian nonintervention in an Austro-Serbian conflict.

The first alarm over Austrian intentions came on 16 July. In a discussion between Marquis Carlotti, Italian ambassador in Russia, and Baron Shilling, head of the Foreign Office chancellory, Carlotti asked what Russia would do if Austria took action against Serbia, and Shilling replied that Russia would not tolerate a blow at Serbia's integrity and independence. Thereupon Carlotti advised that Vienna should be warned at once, for the Monarchy might take some irrevocable step. On the same day Ambassador Shebeko in Vienna learned that the Austrian government was drafting an extremely stiff note to Serbia containing demands that would be unacceptable to an independent state. When Sazonov returned on 18 July from a holiday and learned of Shilling's talk and Shebeko's telegram, he decided to give Austria Hungary his views. But in talking with Ambassador Szápáry, he found the ambassador so friendly and reassuring concerning the Monarchy's policy toward Serbia that he felt no need to issue the warning he had

20. Tschirschky to A. A., 10 July: KD, no. 29.

intended.[21] Although disquieting news continued to reach St. Petersburg, Sazonov still refrained from warning Vienna, but instead again vented his wrath to Pourtalès, 21 July. He declared that Russia could not be indifferent to a move aiming at the humiliation of Serbia, and "in no case should there be any talk of an ultimatum." Pourtalès closed his report by quoting what Sazonov had told Carlotti: " 'The policy of Russia is pacific, but not passive.' "

By this time President Poincaré, accompanied by his premier and foreign minister, René Viviani, had arrived in Russia. While there is no official record of the conversations that took place between 20 and 23 July, there can be little doubt that Austro-Serbian relations stood high on the agenda. Moreover, Poincaré undoubtedly gave his Russian hosts assurances of French loyalty to the alliance in case of complications. After he had left for home Sazonov and Paléologue gave Buchanan the three points upon which they had agreed:

1. Perfect community of views on the various problems with which the Powers are confronted. . . .

2. Decision to take action at Vienna with a view to the prevention of a demand for explanations or any summons equivalent to an intervention in the internal affairs of Servia which the latter would be justified in regarding as an attack on her sovereignty and independence.

3. Solemn affirmation of obligations imposed by the alliance of the two countries.

As Sir Eyre Crowe observed upon reading Buchanan's report: "The moment has passed when it might have been possible to enlist French support in an effort to hold back Russia."[22] This restraint the kaiser and others in Berlin had hoped to count upon. Berchtold no doubt drew the same conclusions as Crowe when he learned that at the diplomatic reception of 21 July Poincaré told Szápáry that Serbia had "some very warm friends in the Russian people. And Russia has an ally, France. There are plenty of complications to be feared."[23] Yet these words and Buchanan's account do not justify the revisionist argument that France had given Russia the same kind of blank check that Germany had

21. *How the War Began in 1914*, pp. 25–27.

22. Buchanan to Grey, 24 July: *BD*, XI, no. 101.

23. Paléologue, *Ambassador's Memoirs*, I, 19. Cf. Szápáry, 21 July: *OUA*, VIII, no. 10461, whose wording is not so blunt.

given Austria-Hungary. Poincaré and Sazonov did not yet know what the Monarchy was going to do, and had merely reaffirmed the alliance. Following Point 2 of their conclusions, however, and very belatedly, Sazonov issued a warning to Vienna during the night of 22–23 July, instructing his ambassador to tell Berchtold "cordially but firmly" of the dangerous consequences to which a step might lead if it was "of a character unacceptable to the dignity of Serbia." Both his warning and a later French one reached Vienna too late to have any effect there.

The attitude of their partner in the Triple Entente, Great Britain, was less clearly defined. At first there was little sympathy in the British press for Serbia or the Pan-Serbian movement. In mid-July both *The Times* and the *Westminster Gazette* advocated Serbian action to alleviate the reasonable anxiety of the Monarchy. These articles along with British preoccupation with the Irish question, rendered acute by the threat of armed revolt in Ulster, encouraged the central powers to count upon British neutrality. Grey, although not oblivious of the possibilities of a crisis, including one arising from German fear of Russia, counseled Austro-Russian discussions. As for an Austro-Serbian conflict, Grey was prepared to do his utmost to smooth away any difficulties, no doubt counting upon the experience of the London conference of ambassadors, 1912–13, as a guide to keeping the peace. Perhaps Grey shared Nicolson's doubts that Austria-Hungary would "take any action of a serious character," and his expectation that the storm would "blow over."[24]

If Grey's optimism did rest on such expectations, he should have been disillusioned by Sir Maurice de Bunsen's telegram of 16 July that Berchtold had told a friend of Bunsen's about the preparation of an indictment of Serbia and of specific demands. If Serbia failed to comply with them, the Monarchy would resort to force. On the same day, the counsellor at the Austro-Hungarian embassy in London gave Crowe much the same views. Bunsen did not reveal the name of his friend in his telegram, but only in a private letter of 17 July to Nicolson. Had Grey known that it was Count von Lützow, former ambassador to Italy, he might have been more impressed by Bunsen's telegram. As it was, the contents contradicted all that had come to him officially from Vienna, and scarcely revised the British opinion that the Dual Monarchy might take some action.

Nevertheless, Grey now began to think more seriously about how to keep the peace. He telegraphed Buchanan in St. Petersburg and

24. Nicolson, Minute, *BD*, XI, 33.

talked with Lichnowsky on 20 July, declaring that if the Monarchy's demands on Serbia were kept "within reasonable limits" and if "justification for making them" were produced, every effort should be made to keep the peace. He suggested that it was "very desirable that Austria and Russia should discuss things together if they become difficult." Even so, Grey did not tell his ambassador to discuss these ideas with Sazonov, but only to speak about them, "if occasion seems to require it." On 22 July, however, he urged upon Benckendorff direct Russo-Austrian talks, and revealed that he did not regard it as British "business to take violent sides in this matter" of Austrian charges against Serbia; Serbia should give Austria-Hungary "the utmost assurances" that in the future she would prevent such plots as the Sarajevo assassination. Meanwhile, Buchanan had reported Grey's views to Poincaré, who declared that negotiations à deux "would be very dangerous at the present moment," thus scotching Grey's suggestion.[25]

The report from Berlin, 22 July, that Jagow reaffirmed the attitude expressed in the Norddeutsche Allgemeine Zeitung of the 19th led Crowe to conclude that Germany knew what Austria-Hungary intended to do and had promised support. He also conjectured that the German government did not believe in "any danger of war" and relied upon Great Britain "to reinforce the German and Austrian threats at Belgrade." If Britain did that, wrote Crowe, or addressed admonitions to St. Petersburg, "the much desired breach between England and Russia would be brought one step nearer realization."[26] Herein lay the British dilemma. No one in England, least of all Grey, wanted a war, and even less wanted British involvement in it. Grey therefore hoped that Austria-Hungary might be led to moderate her demands upon Serbia and that Russia would display patience and forbearance. He took a very relaxed attitude toward the burgeoning crisis, probably not realizing the significance of some of the information that came into his office, and was careful not to make any move that would irritate Russia or France. On the other hand, his counsellors, Crowe and Nicolson, were already calling attention to the desirability of remaining friendly with Russia and the dangers that would arise from a break with her. Sincerely desiring to preserve peace, Grey and his chief advisers felt that they had to maintain the Entente, come what might. But the two objectives were not always compatible. As early as 24 July, Crowe concluded that "France and Russia are decided to accept

25. Ibid., nos. 67, 68, 76, 79.
26. Crowe, Minute; ibid., no. 77.

the challenge thrown out to them." They consider, he continued, "that the bigger cause of Triple Alliance versus Triple Entente is definitely engaged."[27] Whether conscious of this dilemma or not, Grey was not prepared for the kind of ultimatum delivered to Serbia on 23 July, nor the determination with which Russia and France were ready to oppose Austro-Hungarian objectives.

The power that should have known what those objectives were but was deliberately left on the side lines was Italy. Berchtold chose, at the time of Hoyos' mission to Berlin, not to communicate his plans to either Romania or Italy, and received Berlin's approval. His reasons in the case of Italy were his fear that she might warn St. Petersburg and Belgrade of what was brewing, and that she would demand compensation for any change in the Balkan status quo. Jagow in Berlin also mentioned Italian Serbophilia as a reason for keeping Rome in the dark. Hoyos felt that withholding information from Italy would make no difference, because Italy would remain neutral in any case.

Another possible reason for Berchtold's decision might well have been the unsatisfactory relations with Italy, arising from their rivalry in Albania and the Adriatic. The volume of Italian documents covering the July crisis is filled with correspondence on these points, giving the impression that at least until 20 July the Italian Foreign Office was almost fully preoccupied with them. At the same time, both Bollati, ambassador in Germany, and Foreign Minister San Giuliano seriously discussed whether Italy should break away from the Triplice. San Giuliano hoped that Germany would make possible Italian loyalty to the Triplice by satisfaction of her interests.

He was in a difficult position, however, to carry out a vigorous policy. Internally, Italy was experiencing socialist outbreaks and a virtual paralysis of parliamentary government. Of the key figures who decided upon foreign policy, Premier Salandra was heading a caretaker government and knew little of foreign affairs. Giolitti was out of the country until August, and San Giuliano himself was ill and residing at Fiuggi, fifty miles from Rome. Yet he made it clear that Italy would not support demands upon Serbia that violated the principle of nationality or the liberal concepts of Italy. He feared that the Dual Monarchy might seek to crush Serbia, and he claimed the right of compensation under Article VII of the Triple Alliance treaty for any change in the Balkans advantageous to Austria-Hungary. Jagow was anxious that the Dual Monarchy should come to an understanding with Italy

27. For Crowe, ibid., 63, 81; for Nicolson, ibid., 53.

and offer compensation, perhaps the Trentino. He argued that an Italian pro-Serb policy would greatly encourage Russia's "lust for strife,"
and that Italy had a right to claim compensation. His suggestions to
Vienna, however, fell on deaf ears.

Berchtold intended to present Italy with a fait accompli, and was
very optimistic about Italian acceptance of Austrian procedure. He
did, however, instruct Ambassador Mérey, 20 July, to talk with San
Giuliano, assuring him that a peaceful outcome of the démarche in
Belgrade was possible, that the Monarchy counted upon Italian loyalty,
and that if peace failed, Austria-Hungary would not acquire Serbian
territory. If San Giuliano raised the question of compensation, Mérey
was to deny any grounds for it. In talking with Mérey, San Giuliano
declared that he would support the demands upon Serbia if their fulfillment seemed equitable. He apparently did not dare raise the question of compensation, but argued in vain for a healing of the breach
between the Monarchy and Serbia by conciliation. In the following
days, however, San Giuliano recapitulated Italy's position in telegrams
to Berlin and Vienna, and forthrightly declared that Italy would not
condone attacks on Serbia, and that Russia, Romania, and Italy had
an identical interest not to see Serbia crushed.

IV.

In Belgrade on 23 July there was only a handful of ministers, because
Pašić himself and several others were away campaigning for the elections that had been set for 1 August. When Baron Giesl, the Austro-
Hungarian minister, reached the Serbian Foreign Office at 6 P.M. to
deliver the ultimatum, he was received by Laza Paču, the finance minister, who had replaced Pašić during his absence and who hesitated to
receive the note. Giesl told him that he would leave it on the table and
he could do with it what he pleased, but the time limit for a reply was
6 P.M. on the 25th; if there were no answer or if it were unsatisfactory,
he would leave Belgrade with his whole staff. Needless to say, Paču
and the secretary-general of the ministry, Slavo Gruić, read the note
and communicated it to the two ministers waiting outside.

The note was, as Grey remarked when he saw it, "a most formidable
document." Prefacing the demands upon Serbia, the note recalled the
Serbian pledge of 1909 and the failure of the Serbian government to
live up to it in the following years. The depositions and the confessions of the "criminal authors of the outrage of 28 June" showed that

the Sarajevo murders had been planned in Belgrade, that Serbian officials "belonging to the *Narodna Odbrana*" had provided the arms and
bombs, and Serbian frontier "organs" had conveyed the murderers
into Bosnia. The Monarchy's patience was exhausted, and it "had the
duty to put an end to such doings" that were a constant threat to its
peace. Accordingly the imperial and royal government demanded of
Serbia an official assurance that it condemned the propaganda directed
against the Monarchy and that it pledged to suppress it. To give a
"solemn character" to these assurances, Serbia was to publish a declaration on the 26th of July condemning propaganda directed against
Austria-Hungary, regretting the participation of Serbian officials in
such activity, and warning that in the future the Serbian government
would deal severely with anyone found guilty of so doing. In addition,
Serbia would pledge: (1) to suppress publications likely to inspire
hatred and contempt of the Monarchy, or directed against its integrity;
(2) to begin immediately to dissolve *Narodna Odbrana* and all similar
societies and associations engaged in propaganda against the Monarchy; (3) to eliminate everything in public instruction serving the
same end; (4) to remove from military service and the administration
all who were guilty of participating in such propaganda, whose names
Austria-Hungary would communicate; (5) "to consent that Imperial
and Royal officials assist in the suppression of the subversive movement directed against the territorial integrity of the Monarchy"; (6) to
institute a judicial inquiry of all who took part in the plot of 28 June;
the Austro-Hungarian government would "delegate organs" that
would take "an active part in these inquiries"; (7) to arrest at once
Major Tankosić and Milan Ciganović; (8) to effectively prevent smuggling of weapons and explosives across the frontier; to dismiss and
severely punish those of the frontier service at Šabac and Lognica who
helped the Sarajevo criminals to reach Bosnia; (9) to explain the unjustified remarks of high functionaries who spoke hostilely of Austria-
Hungary in interviews just after 28 June: (10) inform the Imperial
and Royal government without delay that the measures in the above
points had been carried out. In addition to these demands a supplement gave particulars concerning the conspirators and those who had
helped them, as revealed in the Sarajevo investigation.[28]

The ultimatum, it should be noted, accused the Serbian government
not of knowing about or promoting the Sarajevo crime but rather of
tolerating anti-Austrian propaganda, which led to the crime, and in so

28. Berchtold to Giesl, 20 July: *ARB*, I, no. 27.

doing of failure to live up to its promises of good-neighborliness. Surprisingly, the ultimatum failed to mention the Black Hand, although the Ballhausplatz had extensive information in its archives on the society. As for the vague term in point 6 of "organs" to participate in the investigation of the Sarajevo plot, Berchtold explained that no derogation of Serbian sovereignty was intended, but that term meant only the establishment of a secret *bureau de sûreté* in Belgrade similar to that which Russia maintained in Paris to shadow anarchists.[29] At the time points 5 and 6 were generally regarded as the demands most harmful to Serbian independence and sovereignty. Apologists have concluded, however, that they were necessary if the Monarchy was to expect any genuine search for the culprits who had taken part in the Sarajevo plot. They contend that Serbia's past performance and her inactivity after 28 June justified the Austro-Hungarian demands.

On 24 July the Austro-Hungarian ambassadors communicated the ultimatum together with a note of explanation to the great powers. Also on 24 July the German pleas for localization of the Austro-Serbian quarrel reached the great powers, while the men at the Wilhelmstrasse told newsmen that Russia would not move because of military weakness.[30]

Nowhere was the reaction to the Austrian and German communications more immediate and decisive than at St. Petersburg. When Sazonov learned of the ultimatum to Serbia, he exclaimed: "C'est la guerre européenne." He set to work to rally the Entente powers and Romania to support him, and to secure decisions for action from a ministerial council at 3 P.M. After depicting the Austro-Hungarian demands upon Serbia as "quite unacceptable to the Serbian government as a sovereign state," he secured the assent of his colleagues to attempt an extension of the time limit of the ultimatum, to advise Serbia not to offer any armed resistance to an invasion, but to entrust "her fate to the judgment of the great powers," to get the assent of the tsar in principle to a mobilization of four army districts that might be involved in a conflict with Austria but not with Germany, and of the Baltic and Black sea fleets; to proceed immediately to gather stores of war materials; and to diminish the funds held in Germany and Austria. After the council meeting Sazonov advised the Serbian minister that Serbia should use extreme moderation in her reply to Vienna. Meeting Pour-

---

29. Gottlieb von Jagow, *Ursachen und Ausbruch des Weltkrieges*, pp. 105 note, and 117.

30. Wolff, *Eve of 1914*, pp. 451–53.

talès in the evening, Sazonov rejected the German pleas for localization of the conflict and criticized the Monarchy not only for the character of its note to Serbia but also for the lack of courtesy shown the great powers, who had not been given an opportunity to consider the questions at issue and make observations before the expiration of the time limit for a Serbian reply.[31]

Earlier in the day Sazonov had been given Paléologue's pledge that France would fulfill her alliance obligations, but failed to obtain from Buchanan the firm statement of the British attitude that he desired. The next day, 25 July, the tsar approved the decisions of the ministerial council, and a crown council ordered the initiation of the "period preparatory to war" to begin on the 26th. Also the council authorized the drafting of an imperial ukase, to be published when Sazonov should decide, ordering the mobilization of 1,100,000 men. Although the general staff opposed the partial mobilization, adopted in principle by the ministerial council, the crown council approved it.[32] Again, on 25 July, Sazonov urged upon Buchanan a firm stand by Britain on the side of Russia and France, and instructed Benckendorff to do the same in London. That evening a demonstration in favor of war by the young cadets, who had just been promoted ahead of time to officer rank, offered a dramatic evidence of war fever. Sazonov, in answer to Buchanan's counsels of prudence, declared that he did not want to precipitate a conflict, but if Germany could not restrain Austria, the situation would be desperate; Russia could not let Serbia be crushed and, "secure of support of France, she will face all the risks of war."[33] In short, Russia was taking a position that, if continued, would destroy one of the assumptions upon which the kaiser had based his blank check of 5 July. If Austria-Hungary, backed by Germany, had taken the first step toward war, Russia was bent upon taking the second.

Her ally, France, was badly hamstrung, not only on the 24th and 25th but also until the morning of the 29th, because the president and prime minister, who was also foreign minister, were at sea on their way home from Russia, and the Foreign Office was in the hands of the minister of justice, Bienvenu-Martin, and the acting director of political affairs, Philippe Berthelot. Bienvenu-Martin was obviously ill-prepared to take any decisive action in the name of the government and gave the ambassadors of Austria-Hungary and Germany the im-

31. *How the War Began in 1914*, pp. 28–31.
32. Minutes of the council meeting, 25/12 July: I *IBZI*, V, no. 42.
33. Buchanan to Grey, telegram, 25 July: *BD*, XI, no. 125.

pression of a benevolent attitude toward the Monarchy and agreement with the idea of localization. He advised Serbia to yield as much as she could in her reply to Vienna, suggesting that she seek to gain time and declare her readiness to submit to the arbitration of Europe. Berthelot was more perceptive than his superior, sensing that the Austro-Serbian question concerned all Europe, and that if Russia decided to oppose the Dual Monarchy, France would be obliged to stand by her side. The Quai d'Orsay, however, was ill-informed of what was going on in St. Petersburg, where Paléologue assured Sazonov of France's loyal support without taking the trouble to tell Paris what decisions Russia was taking.

Great Britain occupied a key position in the emerging conflict between the central powers and the two great powers in the East and West. On the one hand, Russia felt that the only way to moderate the policy of Germany and Austria-Hungary was a solid Triple-Entente front, established by the prompt and declared support of England. On the other hand, Germany and her ally expected that the neutrality of Great Britain would help to further the localization of the Austro-Serbian conflict and perhaps deter Russian intervention. Sir Edward Grey seemed to fulfill the hopes of the central powers when he distinguished between the Austro-Serbian issue, in which he professed to have no interest, and an Austro-Russian conflict, which he correctly foresaw even before he knew Sazonov's attitude. He was clear that his first and most important task was to prevent the outbreak of war among the great powers, but, as he told Paul Cambon, if Russia took the view of the ultimatum that any power interested with Serbia would take, he felt quite powerless "to exercise any moderation." Accordingly he told him, and later Lichnowsky, that the only chance of mediating or of exerting moderating influence was that Germany, France, Italy, and Britain should act in the cause of peace simultaneously at Vienna and St. Petersburg. When Lichnowsky tried to justify the language of the ultimatum on the grounds of Serbia's lower standards than those of European "civilized nations," Grey doubted that Russia would accept such reasoning, and, offering his four-power mediation proposal, hoped that Germany might join him in pleading for a prolongation of the brief time limit, which he deplored as much as he did the tone of the ultimatum. At the same time Grey instructed his minister in Belgrade to urge upon the Serbian government a favorable reply to the Dual Monarchy on as many points as possible, although Crackenthorpe should consult his French and Russian colleagues before executing his instructions.

In the evening of the 24th Grey received two communications that influenced his further steps. One was an explanation by Count Mensdorff that the note to Serbia was not an ultimatum but a "démarche with a time limit," and, more important, that if the Serbian reply were unsatisfactory, Austria-Hungary would break off diplomatic relations and begin military preparations, but not operations. Grey felt that the delay in military action offered greater hope of preventing an Austro-Russian confrontation. The other message was the telegram from Buchanan relaying the three-point Franco-Russian agreement during Poincaré's visit to Russia, and the insistence of Sazonov upon British support. According to this telegram, Sazonov could not state what measures Russia would take, but made it clear that Russia would act, and personally thought that she would mobilize. Here was confirmation of Grey's forecast of the afternoon. Crowe, in a long minute of the 25th, recommended that at the first mobilization by any power Britain should mobilize her fleet in order to show that she would participate in the war. In characteristic fashion he declared: "Our interests are tied up with those of France and Russia in this struggle, which is not for the possession of Servia, but one between Germany, aiming at a political dictatorship in Europe, and the Powers who desire to retain individual freedom." Nicolson added that Russia would regard British action "as a test, and we must be careful not to alienate her." However much or little Grey might have sympathized with these views, he thought it "premature to make any statement to France and Russia."[34]

In his reply to Buchanan on the 25th, Grey approved his explanation concerning Britain's position, in which among other things he had asserted that "it would be difficult for England to remain neutral" in a general war, and presented his four-power mediation proposal. In talking with Lichnowsky, Grey was certain that Austria's mobilization would be followed by Russia's. He repeated that the Austro-Serbian conflict did not concern him, but that Austro-Russian strife would lead to a "world war, such as we had jointly managed to avoid the year before by the Ambassadorial Conference." Therefore he wanted to go hand-in-hand with Germany, whose cooperation would be essential for the success of four-power mediation because her counsels alone would have weight with Austria. Benckendorff, whom he saw in the afternoon, like Cambon was cool toward the proposal for four-power

34. Communication of the Austrian ambassador, 24 July; Buchanan to Grey, telegram, 5:40 P.M., 24 July: BD, XI, nos. 104, 101. Cf. Steiner, Foreign Office and Foreign Policy, p. 163.

mediation. He reported to Sazonov that Great Britain would not show her hand until war began and the balance of power became involved; nobody had indicated that she seriously intended to remain neutral, and his observations pointed strongly in the opposite direction.

Up to the evening of Saturday, 25 July, Grey had received no word from Berlin in answer to his proposals, but at length, after Lichnowsky had thrice urged a reply to the four-power mediation proposal, Jagow replied to Lichnowsky late in the evening, noting with obvious satisfaction that Grey, like Germany, made a distinction between an Austro-Serbian conflict, which had to be localized, and an Austro-Russian one. He hoped that Russia would not intervene, but if an Austro-Russian conflict arose, Germany, "with the reservation of our known alliance obligations," was ready to inaugurate with other great powers mediation between them. A little earlier in the evening Sazonov, to whom Buchanan had communicated the British advice to Serbia and Mensdorff's statement concerning Austria-Hungary's intentions, declared that if Serbia appealed to the powers, Russia would stand aside and leave the question in the hands of England, France, Germany, and Italy. Grey's mediation proposal was fruitless, because unless the Austro-Serbian issue were resolved, there was little that could be done about an Austro-Russian confrontation. By failing to face up to the former, Grey had encouraged the central powers in their hope of localization but at the same time had not deterred Russia from taking the path that was to lead to war.

While the great powers were exchanging views of what might be done, the Serbian government was wrestling with the reply to Austria-Hungary, Pašić, upon his return to Belgrade at 5 A.M. on the 24th, thought that Serbia could neither accept nor reject the demands but had to gain time. In her reply she should indicate the acceptable and the unacceptable points and meantime appeal to the powers to protect Serbian independence. He even thought of a special appeal to the prince regent's uncle, the king of Italy, to attempt mediation at Vienna, an idea later approved by the ministerial council but not carried out. Inevitably an appeal for Russian aid went out in the form of a telegram from the prince regent to the tsar, saying that Serbia was unable to defend herself against attack. As already noted, Britain and France counseled moderation, and Sazonov suggested that if Serbia was helpless, she had better draw back in case of an Austrian attack without resisting, and at the same time make a solemn appeal to the powers.[35]

35. Strandtmann to Sazonov, three telegrams, Belgrade, 24/11 July: 1 *IBZI*, V, nos. 35–37; Sazonov to Strandtmann, 24/11 and 25/12 July: ibid., nos. 22, 49.

By noon, 25 July, the Serbian government had formulated the reply to Austria-Hungary. As Pašić told the newly arrived French minister, Jules August Boppe, it was to accept most of the demands but to ask for explanations concerning the participation of Austrian officials in the judicial inquiry (point 6). If the Austro-Hungarian government were not satisfied with the reply, Serbia would be ready to submit the matter to the Hague Tribunal, or to the great powers who had taken part in drawing up the declaration of 31 March 1909. At 3 P.M. the government ordered general mobilization and during the afternoon made plans to withdraw, along with the foreign legations, to Nish. At about 5:45 P.M., Pašić carried the text of the reply to Giesl at the Austro-Hungarian legation. As outlined by Boppe earlier, the major reservations concerned points 5 and 6. "The collaboration in Serbia of organs of the Imperial and Royal government" in suppressing subversive movements was accepted only insofar as it corresponded with the principles of international law and criminal procedure. As for the judicial inquiry, Serbia would open one, but could not accept the participation of "organs" delegated by the Monarchy, because that would violate the constitution and the law of criminal procedure.[36]

Many historians have argued that a change came over the attitude of the Serbian government between noon and 5:45 P.M. from willingness to accept the demands completely to the formulation of reservations in the final text. They attribute the shift to promises of support by Russia, or at least to knowledge of the measures adopted by Russia on the 24th and 25th. The Russian documents contain no messages of encouragement that could have reached Belgrade, for the tsar's reply to Prince Alexander's plea for aid, which promised it, did not leave St. Petersburg until the 27th. What Minister Spalaiković may have sent from St. Petersburg has thus far not been revealed. Although a good case can be built up on the basis of testimony by men in Belgrade, the assumption of Russian pressure to reject the Austro-Hungarian demands lacks any proof from the Serbs themselves or the Russians, and is questionable. After all, the reply did follow the lines indicated vaguely by Pašić at 5 A.M. on 24 July, and conformed closely with what he had told Boppe sometime before 3 P.M. on the 25th. The change in public spirit, to which some observers attested, could well have been a patriotic upsurge following the mobilization decree.

Be that as it may, shortly after 6 P.M., 25 July, Giesl declared in a

36. The text of the Serbian reply together with the Austro-Hungarian comments of 28 July: Albertini, *Origins*, II, 364–71.

note to the Serbian government that because the reply was unsatisfactory, he was leaving Belgrade with all the legation personnel. He caught the 6:30 train northward. Vienna learned of the break in diplomatic relations a little before 8 P.M., and in consequence of the emperor's decision, Conrad, an hour and a half later, sent out the order for the mobilization of eight army corps to begin on 28 July. At the same time that the news from Giesl reached the Ballhausplatz, a telegram from Szögyény arrived carrying Berlin's regret that Austria-Hungary did not intend to begin military operations immediately upon breaking off diplomatic relations. The Foreign Office there, he reported, sees in every delay a great danger of intervention by other powers. "They advise us," he said, "most urgently to proceed immediately and put the world before a fait accompli." He said in conclusion that he completely shared this view.

Whatever the intentions of Vienna and the irritations of Berlin, the first phase of the July crisis had ended. The next was to witness the extension of the Austro-Hungarian-Serbian quarrel to an Austro-Hungarian-Russian conflict and the beginning of a European war.

Chapter 14

The Outbreak

of War

In addition to the names listed in chapter 13 the following appear
in this chapter: French Minister of War Adolf Messimy and Chief of
Staff General Joseph Joffre; in Germany, Albert Ballin, director of
the Hamburg American line, Chief of Staff General Helmuth von
Moltke, and Admiral Alfred von Tirpitz; in London, William G.
Tyrrell, who was Grey's principal secretary, and John Viscount
Morley, Lord President of the Council; also the Russian Chief of Staff
(since March) General Yanushkevich, and War Minister Sukhomlinov.

On Sunday, 26 July 1914, the feeling of crisis deepened. Serbia was
mobilizing. Austria-Hungary had ordered the mobilization of eight
army corps on the Serbian border. Russia was making all preparations
for mobilization during the period "preparatory to war" and thus
raising rumors that especially disturbed Germany, who ordered her
fleet to concentrate off the Norwegian coast. The British Admiralty
ordered the first and second fleets, which had been on maneuvers, not
to disperse, and Grey the following day diverted his Cabinet colleagues
from the Irish question to outline calmly the possibility of war. France
recalled officers and soldiers on harvest leave and after further measures assured the Russians, 28 July, that France was fully and actively
ready to carry out her responsibilities as an ally. All of this activity
was initiated before anyone knew the text of the Serbian reply to
Austria, which reached the foreign offices through Serbian communication on the 27th but was not published by Austria-Hungary until
the 28th, a delay that helped to create the feeling of uncertainty and
foreboding.

I.

In Grey's absence, Sir Arthur Nicolson at the Foreign Office decided
on the 26th to send out a proposal that they had agreed should be

12. *Theobald von Bethmann Hollweg arriving at the Reichstag*
   (The Bettman Archive)

made if the outlook became darker. By telegrams to Berlin, Paris, and Rome, the British proposed a conference at London of the ambassadors and Grey "to endeavor to find an issue to prevent complications" and at the same time to ask the suspension by Austria, Serbia, and Russia of "all active military operations" pending the results of the conference.[1] This proposal was, in effect, an implementation of Grey's earlier suggestion of a mediation *à quatre* between Vienna and St. Petersburg, but was no longer limited to that issue, for Nicolson and Sir William Tyrrell, Grey's principal private secretary, hoped that through the conference, as they told Lichnowsky, "it would be possible to get full satisfaction for Austria, as Serbia would be more apt to give in to the pressure of the powers and submit to their united will than to the threats of Austria." San Giuliano had a similar idea and later proposed that Serbia be induced to accept the Austrian demands on the advice of the powers invited to the conference. He explained to the British ambassador, Sir Rennell Rodd, that Austria would not accept any modification of her demands, but his suggestion would enable "Serbia to save her face in allowing her to think she had yielded to Europe and not to Austria alone." Unfortunately, little attention was paid to San Giuliano's proposal, nor was Grey's four-power conference approved.

Italy accepted Grey's proposal promptly. France, after some hesitation, accepted it, but Germany refused to consider it. Bethmann Hollweg informed Lichnowsky on the 27th that Germany could not participate in such a conference because she could not summon Austria-Hungary before a European court of justice. Her mediation activities had to be confined to a possible Austro-Russian clash. At about the same time as the German chancellor was composing this telegram, Grey was making a further proposal to Lichnowsky. Knowledge of the Serbian answer to Austria, communicated to the British Foreign Office in the forenoon, which Grey characterized as an acceptance of the demands upon her "to an extent such as he would never have believed possible," led him to ask Germany to persuade Vienna to accept it either as satisfactory or as the basis of a conference. If Austria occupied Belgrade, he said, that would indicate that she was seeking an excuse to crush Serbia and thus to strike at Russia and her influence in the Balkans through Serbia. Russia would have to take such action as a challenge, the result of which would be "the most frightful war

---

1. Again, as in Chapter 13, I shall not document quotations if their provenance from one of the collections of documents is clear, and shall omit 1914 from document dates.

that Europe has ever seen." Lichnowsky commented that Grey was "irritated" for the first time, and went on to predict that in case war came "we should no longer be able to count on British sympathy or British support, as every evidence of ill-will would be seen in Austria's procedure." Everybody was convinced, he continued, that the key to the situation lay in Berlin, and that "if peace is seriously desired there, Austria can be restrained from prosecuting" what Grey called "a fool-hardy policy." Later in the afternoon Lichnowsky sent a very explicit warning to Berlin that if Austria's intention to overthrow Serbia became more and more apparent, "England, I am certain, would place herself unconditionally by the side of France and Russia. . . . If it comes to war under these circumstances, we shall have England against us."

If the retention "on the ready" of the British first and second fleets had not alerted Berlin to the British temper, Lichnowsky's clear warning should have done so. Unfortunately, Lichnowsky's credibility was rated low at the Wilhelmstrasse, and other evidence seemed to contradict him. Prince Henry of Prussia, who had visited George V over the weekend, reported that the king had declared: "We shall try all we can to keep out of this and shall remain neutral." Albert Ballin, who had gone to London on a fact-finding mission for Jagow, concluded that England was absolutely pacific, although he did indicate that she would support France, if attacked, and would never permit Germany to march through Belgium. He asserted that "a fairly capable German diplomat might even then succeed in bringing about an understanding with Great Britain and France which, by preventing Russia from striking, would result in preserving the peace."[2] But more than a "capable diplomat" was needed in view of Germany's determination to stick to the course adopted on 5–6 July. Jagow in the afternoon of the 27th echoed what Bethmann had telegraphed to Lichnowsky earlier. In addition he asserted he had received news that Sazonov intended to exchange views with Berchtold, and thought this procedure would lead to a satisfactory result.

Meanwhile, Germany had pressured Russia to take no step that would endanger peace, and had warned that her mobilization would mean war. Bethmann Hollweg pointed out that, because Austria-Hungary had declared that she would not put Serbian integrity in question (a statement that hardly corresponded with the facts), it seemed possible "to arrive at a common basis of agreement even at a further stage of the affair." Ambassador Pourtalès reported that these telegrams had

2. Bernhard Huldermann, *Albert Ballin*, pp. 215–16.

made a good impression on Sazonov, who was ready to go the limit in accommodating Austria-Hungary. The moment had come, Sazonov thought, "to build a golden bridge for Austria." He hoped that a modification of some of the demands upon Serbia might be brought about, and asked for German cooperation; it should be possible to give Serbia her "deserved lesson," but to spare her sovereign rights. Sazonov had already discussed the Austrian ultimatum with Ambassador Szápáry, indicating that he had no objection to a number of points, but suggesting that others might be acceptable after an alteration of form. He had asked Pourtalès for some proposal. Speaking personally, Pourtalès suggested that if Vienna were willing to modify the form of certain demands, Russia might advise Serbia to accept them on the basis agreed upon between Russia and Austria. He urged Sazonov to get into immediate touch with Vienna along these lines. Accordingly Sazonov had instructed Ambassador Shebeko to discuss with Berchtold the question of modifying some of the points in the note of the 23rd, and also the authorization of Szápáry to enter into a private exchange of thoughts in order to come to an agreement that might be acceptable to Serbia and yield satisfaction in principle of the Austro-Hungarian demands.

When Benckendorff again, on 27 July, deplored the impression in Berlin and Vienna that Great Britain would "stand aside in any event," Grey pointed out that the orders to the first fleet not to disperse "ought to dispel this impression," although he added the caution that this order was not to be interpreted "as meaning that we promised anything more than diplomatic action." On the other hand, Viviani telegraphed Paléologue that evening from shipboard to tell Sazonov that France, understanding the importance of affirming the entente with Russia and of not neglecting any effort for a peaceful solution of the conflict, was "ready to second entirely, in the interests of general peace, the action of the imperial government." In the afternoon of the same day Grey learned indirectly that Sazonov had decided to propose direct conversations with Vienna, news that was confirmed on the following day. Nicolson minuted that Sazonov's decision was "confusing," for he had made one suggestion and two proposals in three days. Nicolson concluded: "One really does not know where one is with M. Sazonof." Sir Eyre Crowe, however, on the 28th saw the move as the first ray of hope, and Grey sanctioned it as "most satisfactory," informing Berlin that as long as there was a prospect of a direct exchange of views between Austria and Russia, he would suspend other suggestions.

Sazonov's proposal was doomed, however, from the start. First of all, he had no intention of changing his own stand on the ultimatum, and wanted Austria to alter the unacceptable points. Because Berchtold had already made it clear that Serbia had to accept the demands as formulated, there was little likelihood that he would retreat before Russia. Moreover, he was planning to declare war on Serbia, a move that caused Sazonov to cancel his proposal even before Berchtold formally rejected it on 28 July.

After the rupture of diplomatic relations with Serbia and the order to mobilize against her, Berchtold hesitated before declaring war. The original plan, favored by Conrad, was to declare war only after the completion of mobilization, scheduled for 12 August. Moreover, Berchtold believed that it was yet possible for Serbia to yield completely to his demands, and that as long as Austria-Hungary kept in touch with Russia, localization of the conflict was possible, even though the chances for it looked slim. He wanted to avoid everything that might draw Russia in. He therefore kept saying: "This is still not war."[3] In a conference wih Conrad and Ambassador Tschirschky at noon on the 26th, when Conrad adhered to the date of 12 August for the declaration of war, Berchtold declared that "the diplomatic situation will not hold as long as that." On the 27th, however, when Hoyos was sent to Conrad to raise the question again, he yielded, "so far as it appeared necessary from the diplomatic standpoint." Tschirschky was therefore able to report on the afternoon of that day that Austria-Hungary would declare war on Serbia on the 28th or 29th, "chiefly to frustrate any attempt at intervention."[4]

By the 27th of July, Bethmann Hollweg was beginning to have doubts about Russian nonintervention and British neutrality, two premises upon which he had taken his "calculated risk." Nevertheless, when he saw the kaiser at Potsdam in mid-afternoon of the 27th, following the latter's return from Norwegian waters, he had apparently regained his confidence. Whatever the results of the conference, in which military chiefs participated, Admiral von Müller, chief of the kaiser's naval cabinet, noted that the mood at Potsdam was decidedly milder; that the calm attitude of England was having a cooling effect upon Russia and France; and that the direction of German policy was "to keep quiet, letting Russia put herself in the wrong, but then not shying away from war." But the later arrival of Lichnowsky's telegrams, bringing Grey's request to influence Vienna to accept the Serbian reply either as satisfactory or as a basis for conferences, and his own warning that England might support Russia and France, appar-

3. Hantsch, *Berchtold*, II, 609–10.
4. Conrad, *Dienstzeit*, IV, 131–32; Tschirschky to A. A., 27 July: KD, no. 257.

ently changed the outlook. The chancellor now feared the grave "danger that France and England will commit their support to Russia in order not to alienate it, perhaps without really believing that for us mobilization means war, thinking of it as a bluff which they answer with a counterbluff." Grey's new position—mediation between Austria and Serbia rather than between Austria and Russia, as at first—threatened to prevent Anglo-German cooperation in limiting the spread of a Balkan conflict, as in 1913, and thus to render the localization program difficult if not impossible of achievement. "This development," recorded Riezler, "created immense commotion in the Wilhelmstrasse. Nobody sleeps. I see the Chancellor only for seconds."[5]

The upshot of the "commotion" in the evening of the 27th was two communications to Vienna concerning Grey's proposal that the Serbian reply be accepted as satisfactory or the basis for conferences. In the first, Jagow told Szögyény that shortly a British proposal would be transmitted to Berchtold, but the German government decidedly did not "identify itself with these propositions," and advised against considering them; they had to be passed on in order to satisfy the English government, because it was very important to prevent Britain from siding with Russia and France and consequently "to prevent the wire still working well between Germany and England from being broken." The second communication, passed to Tschirschky on the kaiser's instructions, reproduced Lichnowsky's telegram conveying Grey's proposal. Bethmann Hollweg explained that Germany could not waive the suggestion because, "by refusing every proposition for mediation, we would be held responsible for the conflagration by the whole world, and be set forth as the original instigators of war." The situation was the more difficult, he went on to say, because Serbia had apparently yielded to a very great degree. Accordingly, he requested Berchtold's opinion of Grey's proposal as well as his views about Sazonov's desire for direct negotiations. Although the chancellor already knew of Vienna's decision to declare war on the 28th or 29th, there is no reference to it, nor urgency expressed. One idea appears that had already been voiced in the afternoon at Potsdam, and was to recur again and again: that Germany had to avoid the responsibility for instigating war. Bethmann, moreover, was at least disingenuous, if not downright deceitful, in telegraphing London: "We have at once inaugurated a move for mediation in Vienna along the lines desired by Sir Edward Grey."

5. Riezler's diary, 27 July: Jarausch, CEH, II, 64–65; Röhl, HJ, XII, 669.

Quite different from the chancellor's was the kaiser's reaction to the Serbian reply, when he read it on the morning of the 28th. Bethmann saw it as making the situation more difficult, whereas the kaiser found it "a capitulation of the most humiliating kind, and as a result, *every cause for war* drops away." In view of Serbian "trickery," however, the kaiser proposed that Austria-Hungary "receive a *pledge-in-hand* (Belgrade) as a guaranty for the enforcement and carrying out of the promises, and should occupy it until the *petita* had *actually* been complied with." He envisaged a temporary military occupation, similar to that of the German troops in France in 1871, which would give the Austrian army, being mobilized for the third time, "a visible *satisfaction d'honneur*," a prerequisite for the mediation that the kaiser was ready to undertake. Because the kaiser did not apparently know that Vienna had decided to declare war on Serbia, he did not urge haste, but expected Jagow to check with him a proposal formulated along the above lines, before sending it to Vienna.[6]

Whether or not this procedure was followed, Bethmann Hollweg instructed Tschirschky, twelve hours after the kaiser had composed his note, to discuss with Berchtold the Halt-in-Belgrade proposal. He made one significant change and a considerable elaboration of the kaiser's thoughts. The change, which has been described as a deliberate falsification of the kaiser's proposition,[7] was to propose that Austria-Hungary hold Belgrade until her demands, instead of Serbia's promises, had been fulfilled. The kaiser's wish to proceed "as sparingly of Austria's nationalistic feeling . . . as possible," became an injunction to Tschirschky

> to avoid very carefully giving rise to the impression that we wish to hold Austria back. The case is solely one of finding a way to realize Austria's desired aim, that of cutting the vital cord of the Greater-Serbia propaganda, without at the same time bringing on a world war, and if the latter cannot be avoided in the end, of improving the conditions under which we shall have to wage it, in so far as possible.

What this last clause meant had already been spelled out when the chancellor wrote: "It is of utmost necessity that the responsibility for the expansion of the conflict to other powers should in all circum-

6. William II to Jagow, 28 July: KD, no. 293. Cf. Fischer, *Germany's Aims*, pp. 71–72.
7. Brandenburg, *Vom Bismarck zum Weltkrieg* (1939), pp. 559–60; Fischer, *Germany's Aims*, pp. 72–73.

stances fall upon Russia." If Austria-Hungary repeated to Russia her declaration that she did not want to take any territory from Serbia, and declared that her mobilization was solely for the purpose of a temporary occupation of Belgrade, and if then the Russian government failed to recognize "the justice of this point of view, it would have against it the public opinion of Europe." Basically what this telegram meant was: Let Austria-Hungary go ahead; perhaps Russia will accept her objective; but if not, everybody will recognize that Russia is responsible for the war.

II.

The Austro-Hungarian declaration of war upon Serbia at 11 A.M., 28 July, was received in Vienna with "wild enthusiasm." Berchtold told British Ambassador Bunsen shortly afterward that he could no longer negotiate on the basis of the Serbian reply, for the prestige of the Dual Monarchy was at stake and nothing could prevent war from being fought to a finish. Both Berchtold and Bethmann Hollweg argued that because Austria-Hungary had declared her territorial disinterestedness, Russia should not oppose her action against Serbia, but both Crowe and Nicolson in the British Foreign Office displayed little sympathy for this viewpoint. Nicolson felt that if the war were extended, Great Britain would side with her friends, and Crowe recognized that mobilization was now becoming the issue. Grey persisted, however, in hoping that a European war could be avoided.

Russia was the more immediately concerned, and Sazonov recognized at once that the declaration of war marked a new phase in the Austro-Serbian conflict. He had consistently refused to accept it as a "local" affair. The question before the Russian government on 28 and 29 July was whether to put into effect the decision of the 25th to mobilize partially on the Austro-Hungarian border, because it appeared that the attempt to discuss the ultimatum and the Serbian reply was now frustrated, and also there had been no progress in gaining acceptance by either Germany or Austria of Grey's conference proposal that Sazonov himself did not accept until the 29th. Sukhomlinov, minister of war, from the outset had looked upon war with Austria-Hungary as "almost inevitable," and the army was reported to be "clamoring for war."[8] For Sazonov mobilization on the Austro-Hun-

---

8. Paléologue to Viviani, 29 July: 3 DDF, XI, no. 274; Wilson to Secretary of State, St. Petersburg, 26 and 28 July: Papers Relating to the Foreign Relations of the United States, 1914 Supplement, pp. 15–17.

garian border was a reply to the declaration of war on Serbia and a means of pressure upon Vienna to negotiate. Because Jagow had given assurances that Germany would not move if Russia limited her military preparations to the Austrian frontier, the risk of war seemed small.[9]

But when Sazonov faced General Yanushkevich, chief of staff, late in the afternoon of the 28th, he ran into stubborn opposition to partial mobilization and insistence upon general mobilization. What he apparently did not realize and had not been told was the impossibility of a partial mobilization, because the army had no plan for it. If the railway timetables were modified to permit the mobilization of four military districts facing Austrtia-Hungary, and if afterward general mobilization ensued, the movement of troops would be likely to be so jumbled as to invite a major catastrophe. The conflict between Sazonov and the army was not resolved, for two decrees were prepared, one for partial and the other for general mobilization, both of which the tsar signed.

Events on the 29th, however, as well as the insistence of the general staff, led Sazonov by the evening to agree to general mobilization. Two talks with Pourtalès not only failed to reduce his fears of Vienna's aims, but also convinced him of German complicity. About mid-day, when Pourtalès asserted that Germany was attempting to persuade Vienna to have a frank discussion with Russia, and that the declaration of war need not make any difference, Sazonov questioned Austria's good faith, for there was no evidence that she would negotiate directly with Russia. He declared that the Austrian mobilization of eight army corps compelled Russia to mobilize the military districts on the Austrian border, and explained that this move did not mean war. Late in the afternoon, on orders from Berlin, Ambassador Pourtalès declared to Sazonov that the continuation of preparations would force Germany to mobilize, thus making a European war hardly preventable. Sazonov, greatly excited, sharply remarked that he no longer had any doubt of the true cause of Austrian intransigence, meaning that it was German support. After Pourtalès, Szápáry saw Sazonov and tried to reassure him concerning Austrian objectives, declaring that although Berchtold had refused to discuss the texts of the Austrian and Serbian notes, he would always be ready to exchange views on "a far broader basis" concerning Austro-Hungarian and Russian interests. Sazonov, however, was not to be placated, for as he saw it the enforcement of Ausstrian demands "meant Serbian vassalage." With reference to military

9. For Jagow's assurances, see BD, XI, no. 185; 3 DDF, XI, no. 134.

apprehensions, Szápáry advised Sazonov that it was necessary to end "the military competition which threatened to establish itself on the strength of false information." While discussing the mobilization question, Sazonov learned of the bombardment of Belgrade and became so agitated and vituperative that Szápáry left him, because he could not continue "a calm interview."[10]

Following these interviews and hot upon the news of the Belgrade bombardment, Sazonov was authorized by the tsar to hold a conference with Sukhomlinov and Yanushkevich. All three agreed upon general mobilization, believing that war with Germany as well as with Austria-Hungary was inevitable, and that Russia should prepare for it in good time.[11] Just before the order for general mobilization went out, however, the tsar canceled it, and accordingly an order for mobilization of the four military districts on the Austrian border went out instead. What had changed the tsar's mind was the receipt of a telegram from the kaiser declaring that a direct understanding between Russia and Austria was possible, and that his government was working to promote it, but that Russian military measures would jeopardize the kaiser's position as mediator, which he had accepted upon the tsar's appeal for help. Baron Fredericks, minister at the court, whom the tsar consulted, told him that general mobilization meant war. Whereupon, greatly disturbed, the tsar decided that he had to do everything possible to preserve peace and could not take the responsibility for the carnage of war. While the tsar was obviously unwilling to mobilize if there were any hope of a peaceful solution of the conflict with Austria-Hungary, Sazonov had given up hope and had yielded to the generals, although he assumed that mobilization did not mean war, but only "armed neutrality," as he had told Pourtalès.[12] The decision to be taken on 30 July, however, had only been postponed, hanging on the thread of the tsar's will, but the order for partial mobilization against the Dual Monarchy shifted the emphasis from Serbia to an Austro-Hungarian-Russian confrontation. Whether or not war could still be avoided or postponed depended upon a shift in the postures of the three empires.

In Berlin and Vienna, as in St. Petersburg, the military were begin-

10. *How the War Began in 1914*, pp. 48–49; Szápáry, 2 telegrams, 29 July: *OUA*, VIII, nos. 10999, 11003.

11. *How the War Began in 1914*, pp. 49–50; Sazonov to Izvolsky, 29/16 July: 1 *IBZI*, V, no. 221.

12. *How the War Began in 1914*, pp. 50, 55; "Graf Fredericks und die russische Mobilmachung 1914," *KBM*, IX (1931), 869–72.

ning to exert pressure on their governments. Contrary to Jagow's views, Conrad in Vienna urged on the 27th that Russia should be warned that her military preparations in the South and Southeast (i.e., on the Austrian border) were so threatening as to require counter-measures. On the 29th the Austro-Hungarian embassy in Berlin noti-fied the Foreign Office that the Russian mobilization of the four mili-tary districts facing Austria had led Conrad to consider that it was absolutely essential "to determine with certainty whether we can ad-vance against Serbia in full strength or whether we shall have to turn our main forces against Russia." Therefore Berchtold proposed that Germany frankly tell Russia that mobilization of the four military districts would compel extensive German and Austrian countermeas-ures.[13]

General von Moltke, too, warned Bethmann Hollweg on the 29th of dangers not only to the Dual Monarchy, but also to Germany, arising from the continuing Russian military preparations, and especially from her partial mobilization. He emphasized that Germany had to support Austria-Hungary, and wholeheartedly approved the latter's determination to cauterize a "cancer" that continually threatened to "poison the body of Europe." Russia, however, had intervened in Austria's "purely private quarrel" with Serbia and thereby risked the peace of Europe, for, he predicted, a partial mobilization of Russia would lead to a chain of mobilizations—Austria-Hungary, Germany, and ultimately France—and that meant war. Moltke asked Bethmann for a clear picture of the situation, because if France and Russia wanted to risk a war with Germany, she could under no circumstances allow those countries to gain a head start. As he saw it, both were already making preparations dangerous for Germany. General von Falkenhayn, minister for war, went even farther than Moltke, and when the two talked with the chancellor on the 29th, he advocated the proclamation of the "threatening danger of war." The military chiefs were worried lest Russia's measures during her "period prepa-ratory to war," begun on 26 July, and rumored French military prepa-rations were robbing Germany of advantages to be gained from her more rapid and efficient mobilization, and therefore pressured the government during the next two days. Clearly the military competition arising from false information, about which Szápáry had spoken to Sazonov, had begun.

Despite the pressure of the military, Bethmann refused to declare a

13. Austro-Hungarian Embassy to A. A., 27 July: KD, no. 349.

"threatening danger of war," which would authorize preparations for mobilization, although the Foreign Office forwarded to the German minister in Brussels the demand that German troops be permitted to cross Belgian territory, which Moltke had prepared on the 26th but which was not to be delivered to the Belgian government until explicitly ordered. The chancellor, however, was now convinced, after the bombardment of Belgrade and the disquieting news of Russian military preparations, that the mediation for which England had been pressing had to be undertaken. He had not yet, apparently, given up all hope that the Austro-Serbian duel could be localized, although Riezler remarked as early as the 27th that the chancellor saw "a fate, greater than human might, lying over the situation of Europe and over our people."[14] His reasoning in both resisting the military and shifting his tactics toward pressure upon Vienna was to avoid a situation in which the socialists at home and the powers abroad could accuse Austria-Hungary and Germany of starting a war.

Bethmann Hollweg's major efforts on the 29th were therefore directed toward preserving British cooperation and neutrality and persuading Austria-Hungary to show a more accommodating attitude. During the day he tried to convince Ambassador Goschen that Germany was doing her best in Vienna to prevent the dangers of European complications, and to support Grey's efforts in the cause of peace. He mentioned that an exchange of telegrams was taking place between the kaiser and the tsar, but did not, of course, reveal that he had suggested it—for a telegram to the tsar, "should war prove to be inevitable, would throw the clearest light on Russia's responsibility." Had he done so, the skepticism of the British Foreign Office concerning the sincerity of his efforts to moderate Vienna would have been even more pronounced than it was. Nicolson supposed, quite rightly, that what Germany wanted was Russian cooperation with the other powers "in keeping the ring while Austria strangles Servia." Grey on the 29th took a very serious view of the situation and again urged mediation, believing that a suitable basis for it might be provided, "if Austria, after occupying Belgrade, for example, or other places, should announce her conditions."[15]

Before receiving this British proposal, which paralleled the kaiser's Halt-in-Belgrade suggestion, Bethmann Hollweg made a direct appeal

14. Hillgruber, "Riezlers Theorie," HZ, CCII (1966), 348.
15. Crowe and Nicolson, Minutes on Goschen to Grey, 28 July: BD, XI, no. 249; Lichnowsky to A. A., 29 July: KD, no. 357.

for British neutrality should war break out. In the evening of the 29th he talked with Ambassador Goschen about the situation in case of a European conflagration caused by a Russian attack upon Austria. He judged that Great Britain would never allow France to be crushed, and accordingly offered a German assurance that, if Britain remained neutral, "Germany aimed at no territorial acquisitions at the expense of France." He could not give the same pledge respecting French colonies, but could do so concerning Holland; if Belgium did not take sides against Germany, "her integrity would be respected at the end of the war." The chancellor went on to say that these assurances might form the basis of a further understanding with England, and suggested that it might take the form of a neutrality agreement. The reception of such a proposal at the British Foreign Office can well be imagined. Crowe noted that by Bethmann's words, Germany "practically admits the intention to violate Belgian neutrality." Grey shared the indignation of his counselors, terming British acceptance of such a proposal, which amounted to a bargain with Germany at the expense of France, a "disgrace from which the good name of this country would never recover." Nor would England bargain away her obligation and interest respecting Belgium.[16]

Bethmann, in effect, received his answer long before Goschen formally conveyed it on the 30th, for after seeing Goschen, the chancellor received telegram no. 178 from Lichnowsky in which Lichnowsky reported Grey's statement to him that Britain could stand aside in a conflict confined to Austria and Russia, but if Germany and France were involved, "the British government would, *under the circumstances, find itself forced to make up its mind quickly. In that event it would not be practicable to stand aside and wait for any length of time.*" Here was the plainest talk about the possibility of British intervention that Grey had yet held. Though it struck a blow at one of the pillars of Germany's policy, the telegram also reported that Grey had told the Italian ambassador he believed, "if mediation were accepted, that he would be able to secure for Austria every satisfaction," and thus get for her "guarantees for the future" without war.

The events of the 29th, culminating with this warning, convinced Bethmann Hollweg that he had to exert more pressure on Austria-Hungary than he had yet applied. Quite apart from his aim of acting so as to put the blame for war on Russia, reiterated in the evening

16. Goschen to Grey, 29 July, and Grey to Goschen, 30 July: *BD*, XI, nos. 293, 303. Cf. Jarausch, *CEH*, II, 68–69.

discussions with Moltke and Falkenhayn, he had been irritated by Lichnowsky's report that the members of the Austro-Hungarian embassy in London, including the ambassador himself, had never concealed Austria's sole concern with the destruction of Serbia, parts of which were to go to Bulgaria and probably Albania. The chancellor commented:

> This duplicity of Austria's is intolerable. They refuse to give us information as to their program . . . at Petersburg they are lambs with not a wicked thought in their hearts, and in London their embassy talks of giving away portions of Serbian territory to Bulgaria and Albania.

Although he informed Tschirschky of the report and his own attitude toward it, he asked the ambassador to keep to himself his suspicions that Austria was pursuing secret plans.[17] On the other hand, he "expected" that Tschirschky should carry out at once his instructions concerning the kaiser's proposed Halt-in-Belgrade plan that he had so diffidently presented the night before. He next forwarded to Vienna the telegram conveying Grey's discussion of possible mediation, and suggested a basis for negotiation "if founded on an occupation of a portion of Serbian territory as a hostage." The chancellor followed this telegram with one reporting Russian partial mobilization and explained that this did not mean war. He concluded with an urgent request that "in order to prevent a general catastrophe, or at least to put Russia in the wrong," Vienna inaugurate and continue conferences with Russia according to the Halt-in-Belgrade proposal of the 28th. Meanwhile, Tschirschky reported that he had carried out the instructions concerning the Halt-in-Belgrade plan but had not received any further answer than thanks for the suggestion. This reply could but irritate Bethmann the more, especially because it must have arrived after Lichnowsky's telegram 178. The chancellor now forwarded it to Vienna and added, with reference to the threat of British intervention:

> As a result we stand, in case Austria refused all mediation, before a conflagration in which England will be against us, Italy and Romania to all appearances will not go with us, and we shall be opposed to four Great Powers. . . . Austria's political prestige,

17. Lichnowsky to A. A., 28 July: Bethmann to Tschirschky, 29 July: KD, nos. 301, 316.

the honor of her arms, as well as her just claims against Serbia, could all be amply satisfied by the occupation of Belgrade or of other places. . . . Under these circumstances we must urgently and impressively suggest to the consideration of the Vienna cabinet the acceptance of mediation on the above-mentioned honorable conditions. The responsibility for the consequences that would otherwise follow would be an uncommonly heavy one for Austria and for us.

A few minutes later Bethmann in another telegram concerning Sazonov's report that Vienna had refused to enter into direct conversations, declared that a refusal would be a serious' error and that Germany "must decline to be drawn wantonly into a world conflagration by Vienna, without having any regard paid to [her] counsel." Tschirschky was to talk to Berchtold at once "with all impressiveness and great seriousness." In these telegrams lay a change of course. Yet, if the shift were to carry conviction in Vienna, it required a forthright recognition that they had miscalculated on 6 July, and in addition a refusal to honor the alliance obligations if Vienna failed to change its course. Bethmann, however, took neither of these steps.

On 30 July, Bethmann, still awaiting an answer to his pleas, found himself beset by the kaiser and the military. In the forenoon the kaiser received the tsar's telegram that Russia's military measures had been decided upon five days before for reasons of defense against Austria's preparations. He also received word of Russian partial mobilization, a copy of Lichnowsky's telegram 178 of the 29th, and a report from the naval attaché in England that in case Germany went to war with France, England would attack immediately. These communications sent the kaiser into paroxysms of anger, mostly directed toward Great Britain but also, because of his misinterpretation of the tsar's words, against Russia, who, he assumed, had been mobilizing since the 24th. He declared that Germany had to mobilize immediately and that his role as mediator, which the tsar had asked him to assume, had failed, "since the tsar, instead of loyally awaiting its results, had already mobilized behind my back and without giving me a hint!" The chancellor, however, persuaded the kaiser not to give up his role as mediator as long as Vienna's decision was pending, but to warn the tsar that Russian mobilization against Austria had endangered it, if not made it impossible.

Although Moltke in the morning of the 30th still supported Bethmann's calm attitude toward Russian military measures against Austria, he changed his mind about noon, not so much because of the kaiser's dictum concerning the need for German mobilization as the intelligence reports concerning the extent of Russian mobilization. In a talk shortly after 2 P.M. with the Austrian military attaché, Baron von Bienerth, who reported that the general was "more agitated than I have ever seen him before," Moltke advised that Austria mobilize against Russia immediately in order to prevent her from gaining a head start. He obviously wanted Vienna to turn from its Serbian campaign toward Russia, and promised that Germany would "unconditionally participate" in resisting the imminent Russian attack. Later, in the evening, Moltke sent a telegram directly to Conrad urging immediate general mobilization. Such advice was clearly contrary to the chancellor's shift in policy adopted the previous night, and he still resisted the renewed demands of Moltke and Falkenhayn that he declare a state of emergency which would sanction the first steps toward mobilization. In the evening Bethmann Hollweg at length yielded so far as to promise to make a final decision not later than noon on the next day, 31 July.[18]

Yet Bethmann Hollweg himself was fast losing hope that war could be avoided. At 5 P.M. he laid his policy before the Prussian ministry, declaring that Germany and England had taken "all steps to avoid a European war" but admitting that "control had been lost and the stone had started rolling." He would not give up all hope, however, as long as Vienna had not repelled his démarche.[19] In the evening of the 30th the kaiser telegraphed Francis Joseph urging him to make a decision as soon as possible about the Halt-in-Belgrade proposal to which Austria-Hungary had not yet replied. Bethmann himself telegraphed a strong note to Tschirschky declaring that if Vienna rejected all mediation, especially the latest proposal of Grey, "it is hardly possible to place the blame of a threatening European conflagration any longer on Russia." But, a couple of hours afterward the chancellor canceled the telegram, later alleging that he did so because of a message from King George V, but more likely because Moltke had persuaded him that the military preparations of Germany's neighbor had made such protests to Vienna unwise and too late.

The dilatoriness of Vienna in responding to Bethmann Hollweg's proposals betokened a lack of understanding of the seriousness of the

18. Szögyény, 30 July: *OUA*, VIII, no. 11033; Ritter, *Sword and Scepter*, II, 256–59.
19. Protocol of the session, 30 July: KD, no. 456.

situation, or of the earnestness of the German chancellor's pleas. Undoubtedly Tschirschky was partially to blame for the disregard of the Kaiser's Halt-in-Belgrade scheme, because in talking with Berchtold he stressed Bethmann's wish not to put pressure upon Austria-Hungary nor restrain her from action, but only to improve the conditions under which they might have to fight a world war.[20] By the 30th, however, Berchtold and the Austrian prime minister, Stürgkh, were becoming uneasy over the possibility of a two-front war, although Conrad tried to reassure them that war was not inevitable because the Russians might stay behind their lines. On the afternoon of the same day Berchtold talked with Ambassador Shebeko and telegraphed Szápáry to talk with Sazonov, explaining the note to Serbia and asking him what subjects relating to Austro-Russian relations he would like to discuss. About noon Tschirschky had communicated Grey's proposals for mediation after an Austrian-Hungarian occupation of Belgrade. He had also talked with Hoyos and Forgách at the Ballhausplatz, who expressed the opinion that restrictions upon military operations would be out of the question, but said that Tisza would have to be consulted when he returned to Vienna the next day.

Berchtold's expressed willingness to discuss Austro-Russian relations with Sazonov was a meaningless gesture, because it would scarcely satisfy the Russians who wanted to discuss, not merely get an explanation of, the Serbian note and to halt the military operations against Serbia. His conciliatory attitude hardly touched the core of the problem. The march of events, however, was rapidly outstripping any pacificatory efforts, for in the evening of the 30th Francis Joseph approved general mobilization to begin on 4 August, and the next morning, 31 July, the ministerial council moved the date to the 1st. Also, at the suggestion of Tisza, the council approved an equivocal reply to Grey's proposal of mediation after the seizure of Belgrade, declaring that the prerequisites for acceptance were the continuing military action against Serbia "for the time being," a Russian halt in mobilizing troops against Austria-Hungary, and acceptance of the demands on Serbia of 23 July without change. The emperor rejected the kaiser's plea of the previous evening on the grounds that he had already ordered general mobilization. By this time the voice of Moltke was stronger than Bethmann Hollweg's, and Conrad was calling the

20. See the Austrian record of Tschirschky's communication, 29 July: *OUA*, VIII, no. 10939. His diplomatic colleagues suspected him of instigating the aggressive decisions of the Ballhausplatz: 3 *DDF*, XI, no. 284.

tune in Vienna. Also Russia had taken the step that made war inevitable.

What influence Great Britain and France may have had on Russian policy is problematical. While Britain had certainly not pushed Russia toward mobilization or war, Grey had not energetically restrained her. Conscious of the balance of power, he wanted to avoid a breakdown in entente solidarity, but he consistently refused to promise support of Russia, as the French and Sazonov several times wanted, because, as Sir Francis Bertie put it, "if we gave assurances of armed assistance to France and Russia now, Russia would become more exacting and France would follow in her wake." Besides, Grey could not make promises which only the Cabinet and Parliament had the power to give. Consequently, instead of forthright pressure upon Russia, such as Bethmann had sought to exert on Austria-Hungary, Grey was content to "earnestly hope" for Russian cooperation in working toward peace.[21]

On the other hand, the French position was clear. From the first day of the crisis, Paléologue had assured Sazonov of French solidarity with Russia. Because the heads of the French government were at sea until the morning of 29 July, and the acting premier was proceeding very cautiously, Paléologue at times acted without instructions, as when on the 28th he declared to Sazonov that France would fulfill her alliance obligations. The military, too, because of the stipulations of the military convention, were anxious not only to take all preliminary precautions at home, but also to make sure that in case of war with Germany, Russia would live up to her promise to launch an attack upon East Prussia. Adolph Messimy, minister of war, and General Joffre, chief of staff, urged this action upon the Russian general staff through the French military attaché and the ambassador on the 27th. On the 28th they reassured Count Ignatiev, Russian military attaché in Paris, of French readiness to fulfill the terms of the alliance. Viviani, too, after his return on the 29th, assured Izvolsky of the government's determination to act in complete unity with Russia, but in contrast to the military he had in mind collaboration for peace rather than for war.[22]

As already noted, Viviani had sent a message to Sazonov on 27 July combining a pledge of loyalty to the alliance with an expression

21. Nicolson, Minute; Bertie to Grey, Private, 30 July; Grey to Buchanan, 30 and 31 July: BD, XI, nos. 101, 320, 309, 335.

22. The day's record of Russian foreign ministry, 28/15 July; Ignatiev to Quartermaster-General, 28/15 July: 1 IBZI, V, nos. 172, 180.

of French readiness "in the interest of the general peace to second the action of the imperial government." Poincaré has pointed out that "this statement has to be taken as a whole," and as such was clearly concerned with collaboration in a "solution of the conflict" and the "general peace."[23] Even so, either Paléologue failed to convey the whole statement (which is not unlikely, for he played a role in St. Petersburg similar to that of Tschirschky in Vienna) or Sazonov misunderstood the message. In either case, Sazonov in the night of 29–30 July telegraphed Isvolsky the warning by Pourtalès that Germany would mobilize if Russia did not stop her military preparations. Sazonov asserted that because of Austria's mobilization of eight army corps and refusal to settle her dispute with Serbia pacifically, "Russia could but hasten her armaments and envisage the imminence of war." He expressed his thanks for the particularly "precious" declaration by the French ambassador that Russia could count completely on the aid of her French ally, and added that it was extremely desirable that England join them without loss of time in order to avoid a dangerous rupture of the European balance.

At 3 A.M., 30 July, Isvolsky communicated this telegram to Viviani, who at once conferred with Poincaré and Messimy. They agreed that Viviani should send a telegram to St. Petersburg and London, confirming that of the 27th with regard to seconding Russian action "in the interest of general peace," and asserting the French government's resolve to fulfill all the alliance obligations.

But [the telegram continued] in the very interest of the general peace and given that a conversation has begun among the less interested powers, I believe it would be opportune that in the precautionary and defensive measures to which Russia believes she is obliged to resort, she not immediately take any measure which might offer Germany a pretext for a total or partial mobilization of her forces.

Isvolsky received a copy of Viviani's telegram, and he and Count Ignatiev immediately sought clarification of the advice not to give Germany a pretext for mobilization. Jacques de Margerie, political director at the Quai d'Orsay, told Isvolsky that the French government, without wishing to meddle in Russian military preparations, recommended that they be of a character as little obtrusive as pos-

23. Poincaré, *Au service de la France*, IV, 384–85.

sible. At the same time Messimy suggested to Ignatiev that in the interests of peace Russia could slow down her mobilization measures without hindering the pursuit of military preparations as long as she refrained from transporting troops *en masse*.[24] All in all, the French advice to Russia was of the same character as Bethmann's to Vienna on the same night; both breathed loyalty to the ally, but if anything the French admonitions were much weaker than the German.

Although Paléologue reported that he had communicated Viviani's message to Sazonov before noon, it is doubtful if the tsar had learned of it before he ordered general mobilization. On a copy of Izvolsky's telegram reporting Viviani's instructions to Paléologue is recorded, probably by the tsar, "This telegram has come too late. Peterhof, 31/18 July 1914."[25] Paléologue, however, reported that in the forenoon of the 30th, probably about 12 o'clock, he had recommended to Sazonov that Russia avoid every military measure that might offer Germany a pretext for mobilization. Sazonov replied that during the previous night the general staff had postponed some secret measures, the revelation of which might alarm the German general staff. Did he have in mind the cancellation of general mobilization, or something else? In neither his telegram of the 29th to France nor in his talk with Paléologue had he been completely frank.

From the night of 29/30 July to the afternoon of the 30th, Sazonov wrestled with Pourtalès over the question of how to get Austria-Hungary to make concessions that would satisfy Russia, while the military chiefs pressed him ever more urgently to procure the tsar's order for general mobilization. At midnight Sazonov had summoned Pourtalès for a talk that lasted an hour and a half, but got nowhere. The Russian foreign minister wanted Germany to take part in four-power deliberations in order to move Austria "by friendly means" to drop those demands that infringed upon the sovereignty of Serbia, while the ambassador sought to convince Sazonov that the declaration of disinterestedness should suffice to permit the Dual Monarchy to

24. Viviani to Paléologue and P. Cambon, telegrams at 7:00 and 7:10 A.M., 30 July: 3 *DDF*, XI, no. 305; Izvolsky to Sazonov, 2 telegrams, 30/17 July; Ignatiev to Quartermaster-General, 30/17 July; 1 *IBZI*, V, nos. 289, 291, 293. The editors of 3 *DDF* found no records of these conversations at the Quai d'Orsay, and only cryptic notations among private papers: 3 *DDF*, XI, 262–63, note 2. Poincaré, *Au service de la France*, IV, 386, 408, casts doubt on the accuracy of Izvolsky's report.

25. 1 *IBZI*, V, no. 289. See the long and carefully reasoned discussion of these telegrams, the honesty of Viviani, and the untrustworthiness of Paléologue by Albertini, *Origins*, II, 602–27.

"be let alone" in settling her quarrel with Serbia. He also stressed the danger of a European war as a result of Russia's partial mobilization. Again, in the morning of the 30th, Sazonov repeated his declaration of the previous night that Austria-Hungary's assurances of territorial disinterestedness did not satisfy Russia. Upon a request by Pourtalès for a formula that would be acceptable to Russia, Sazonov wrote:

> If Austria, recognizing that her conflict with Serbia has assumed the character of a question of European interest, declares herself ready to eliminate from her ultimatum those points that infringe on Serbia's sovereign rights, then Russia agrees to suspend all military preparations.[26]

By late morning, however, Sazonov had become more concerned with the pressure of the generals than with peace conditions.

At 11 A.M. he met with General Yanushkevich and War Minister Sukhomlinov and agreed with them that the information the previous night supported their opinion that they had to prepare immediately for war, and consequently to order general mobilization. Sazonov, supported by the minister of agriculture, arranged for an audience with the tsar at 3 P.M., fully determined to obtain his order for general mobilization. His major argument was that because war was now unavoidable on account of the German attitude expressed the previous day by Pourtalès and evidenced by her alleged military measures, Russia had to be ready for it under the most favorable circumstances; for technical reasons the longer the partial mobilization orders ran, the greater the danger of catastrophe in trying to shift to general mobilization. Moreover, partial mobilization constituted a betrayal of the alliance with France. The tsar, appalled by the responsibility of "sending hundreds of thousands of Russian people to their death," at last after an hour of Sazonov's pleading gave in. As Sazonov explained, he could not capitulate before the central powers, "a thing that Russia would never forgive to the tsar, for it would cover with shame the good name of the Russian people." Sazonov immediately phoned Yanushkevich, who set General Dobrorolski to work securing the necessary signatures of the mobilization order and sending it out by telegraph. The fateful telegrams to the commanders of the military

26. Pourtalès, to A. A., 2 telegrams, 30 July: KD, nos. 401, 421. Grey asked Sazonov to amend his formula to conform with the Halt-in-Belgrade proposal, and the latter rewrote it: BD, XI, nos. 309, 393.

districts began to go out shortly after 6 P.M. In Dobrorolski's words, "the prologue of a great historic drama had begun."[27]

There is little doubt that Sazonov, whose nervous temperament and instability ill-suited him to bear the strain of crisis, had let himself be convinced by the generals that Russia was facing an imminent war and had to protect herself, and that he had persuaded the tsar to believe it, too. Yet they both thought that Russian mobilization would not automatically bring war. Sazonov declared to Paléologue: "Up to the last moment I will negotiate." The tsar had assured the kaiser by telegram just before his talk with Sazonov that as long as negotiations with Austria continued, "my troops shall not take any provocative action." General von Chelius, German military plenipotentiary at the Russian court, speaking of the partial mobilization, got the impression that "they have mobilized here from a dread of coming events without any aggressive intention," and even Moltke admitted that "the habitual Russian mobilizations and demobilizations had a different meaning from Germany's."[28] Yet, whatever the intent, mobilization in the Europe of 1914 did mean war because no country could sit back and wait after mobilization while its enemy completed its concentration of troops, as General Boisdeffre and Tsar Alexander III had agreed in 1892,[29] and because the Schlieffen plan, of which Sazonov and the tsar were probably ignorant, would not permit Germany to let Russia complete her mobilization before taking action. German civilian officials and military alike knew that their mobilization meant war. Whatever the assumptions upon which the Russians made their decision, they had taken the step that made a European war inevitable.

From the morning of 31 July, when Germany learned that Russian general mobilization was being put into effect, the continuing discussion of how to avoid war became meaningless. The die had been cast, for Germany declared the "threatening danger of war" (*Kriegsgefahrzustand*) at 1 P.M., thus initiating preparations for mobilization. At the same time Bethmann Hollweg telegraphed to Vienna that this declaration "inevitably means war. We expect from Austria immediate active participation in the war with Russia." From this point onward the major decisions were to be taken in Berlin by the military. Upon

27. *How the War Began in 1914*, pp. 62–66; Sergei Dobrorolsky, *Die Mobilmachung der russischen Armee* (Berlin, 1922), p. 29.

28. Chelius to A. A., 30 July: KD, no. 445; Moltke to Conrad, 30 July: Conrad: *Dienstzeit*, IV, 152.

29. 1 DDF, IX, 680.

Moltke's urging that there was no time to lose in putting into effect the timetable of the Schlieffen war plan to strike France through Belgium first and then to turn on Russia, Bethmann with undue haste sent off his demands upon Russia and France in the afternoon of the 31st. He gave Russia twelve hours in which to suspend every war measure against both Austria-Hungary and Germany, else German mobilization would follow. Curiously he did not explain to Russia that mobilization meant war, as he did in the telegram to Paris, in which he inquired if France intended to remain neutral in a Russo-German war. He expected a reply within eighteen hours, and instructed Ambassador Schoen that if the answer were affirmative, Germany would demand the fortresses of Toul and Verdun to be returned to France at the end of the war.

Even though there was no intention of striking at Russia at once, the German Foreign Office, anticipating a Russian refusal to stop her mobilization, began drawing up a declaration of war on Russia even before the delivery of the ultimatum, and Jagow sent it to Pourtalès a little before 1 P.M., 1 August. Pourtalès delivered it at 7 P.M (6 o'clock, Berlin time), apparently emotionally overcome by the implications of this first breach of European peace. When news reached Berlin that two Cossack squadrons had crossed the border of East Prussia in the district of Johannisberg about 8 P.M., 1 August, Moltke and Falkenhayn went to the chancellor to prevent the premature declaration of war and thus to make political profit of the Russian aggressive act, but it was too late. Nevertheless Bethmann and Jagow sought to represent the Cossack foray as the cause for the declaration of war.

At 5 P.M., an hour before the delivery of the declaration of war on Russia, the kaiser signed the order for general mobilization. The deliberations a little later at the palace concerning how to proceed against France were thrown into confusion when two telegrams from Lichnowsky arrived that seemed to indicate the possibility of securing French and British neutrality if Germany refrained from attacking along the western front. The kaiser and the chancellor took up the news with Moltke, Falkenhayn, and Tirpitz. Moltke was beside himself when Bethmann and the kaiser suggested that he abandon the plan to attack in the West and that he shift his main forces to the East. Such a sudden reversal of mobilization and deployment schedules would have meant chaos, and Moltke vigorously opposed it. As Ritter has commented: "What actually raised this entire debate to so high a pitch was the profound discrepancy between the 'purely military' Schlieffen plan and Germany's real needs, on which that plan cast such a stark light—the rigidity with which German policy was tied to a great western offensive, with all its political consequences."[30] Tirpitz helped the kaiser compose a telegram to George V, saying that he could not stop mobilization but if France offered neutrality and it was guaranteed by the British army and fleet, Germany would not attack France. The conference further agreed to delay the opening of hostilities with France, and the kaiser halted the invasion of Luxemburg, which had been scheduled to take place at once in preparation for the invasion of Belgium. Early in the morning of 2 August, Lichnowsky telegraphed that Grey had abandoned his suggestion as hopeless. Grey had had no authorization from France to make it, and Lichnowsky had not understood that he had proposed German neutrality toward a Russo-Austrian war as well as toward France.

Even before the final collapse of hopes for French and English neutrality, a debate in the early morning hours of 2 August took place among the top three military men, the chancellor, and German Foreign Office representatives about how to proceed toward France, who had replied to the inquiry of the 31st concerning neutrality that she would consult her own interests, and had ordered mobilization at 3:55 P.M. on 1 August (4:55 P.M., Berlin time). The civilians insisted that a formal declaration of war should be served upon France before opening hostilities, but the military men contended that a formal declaration of war was unnecessary and should be left to the French, who, they expected, would be forced to make it. The problem arose because the invasion of Belgium had been planned for 4 August and could scarcely be undertaken until Germany and France were at war. A declaration of war was agreed upon but was to be delayed, along with the presentation of demands upon Belgium, as long as possible in order to give Tirpitz time to mobilize the fleet.[31]

The Foreign Office began drafting a declaration of war on France and sent instructions in the afternoon to the minister in Brussels to present the German demands for passage through the country at 8 P.M., while assurances were sent to Luxemburg and to London that military activity in the duchy was for the purpose of protecting German-operated railways against threatening French attacks. The conflict of views between the military and the Wilhelmstrasse over the declaration of war on France was finally settled between Moltke and Jagow in the morning of 3 August by a compromise, which, it was hoped,

30. Ritter, *Sword and Scepter*, II, 268–69.
31. Ibid., II, 270–73.

would avoid the charge against Germany of aggression. The draft of a dignified declaration that had been completed was replaced by one alleging that French hostilities on German soil (most of the incidents cited proved to be false) had forced Germany to declare war on France. The statement was to be delivered at 6 P.M.

While Berlin was debating how to proceed without incurring the charge of aggression in the eyes of the world and above all in England, Paris was pursuing the same objective. Because of military information from Germany, Joffre in the afternoon of 31 July urged the immediate calling up of reserves and *couverture* of the northeastern border. The ministerial council at 5:15 P.M approved the covering operation but not the calling up of reserves. Soon, however, the government apparently decided that war was inevitable, for on the morning of 1 August, after Joffre had again pleaded for mobilization, the council approved it, to be ordered as late as possible in order to begin it on 2 August. They hoped that Germany would mobilize first, but the French order went out five minutes before the German. When Izvolsky, near midnight on the first, brought news of the German declaration of war on Russia, Poincaré declared that he and the whole Cabinet were resolved firmly to fulfill French obligations under the alliance, and the ministerial council, summoned immediately, confirmed his pledge. But Poincaré and the ministers did not want to declare war at once because it was thought best not to begin military operations before mobilization was more advanced, and Poincaré, especially because of Britain, wanted the declaration of war to come from Germany, who, he expected, would attack at once. In this game of trying to throw the responsibility for both Russian and French mobilizations and war upon the central powers, both Viviani and Poincaré gave false information at the time and in subsequent recollections, but they did outplay the Germans in declaring war. As noted above, Schoen presented the declaration shortly after 6 P.M. on the 3rd, and German troops opened hostilities an hour later. The European war had begun.

III.

Through the latter days of the July crisis both Germany and France had been anxious about the attitude of Italy, the one fearful that she would not be loyal to the Triplice, the other unsure of her neutrality. From 24 July, when the ultimatum to Serbia became known, Italy's policy was made clear to her allies. Premier Salandra and Foreign Minister San Giuliano took the position that Italy had no obligation to support Austria-Hungary because she had not been consulted; that her allies should accept the application of Article VII of the Triple Alliance treaty by which in case of a temporary or permanent occupation of Balkan territory by either Austria-Hungary or Italy a previous agreement should be negotiated providing for compensation and satisfying the "interests and well-founded claims of the two parties"; and that Italy should make sure of compensation for any territorial gains of the Dual Monarchy and minor compensations for any diplomatic support of her allies. German Ambassador Flotow thought that Salandra and San Giuliano wanted to make use of the occasion to acquire the Trentino, and that they took the position they did from fear of Italian public opinion and consciousness of their military weakness.

San Giuliano lost no time in informing Berlin and Vienna that Italy considered the Austro-Hungarian démarche in Belgrade to be a violation of Article VII and therefore reserved her liberty of action. The kaiser and Bethmann at once insisted that Vienna come to an understanding with Rome, but the Austrians were not convinced of the seriousness of the situation, and procrastinated in characteristic fashion. German pressure, however, finally persuaded Berchtold on 1 August to accept the Italian interpretation of Article VII in principle, but only on condition that Italy fulfill her duty as an ally. Berchtold's last-minute concession had come too late and was too indefinite about compensation to satisfy the Italians. San Giuliano had already told Flotow, 31 July, that because the Austrian attack on Serbia had to be regarded as an act of aggression the *casus foederis* had not arisen, and therefore Italy had to declare her neutrality. Cabinet meetings that evening and in the morning of 1 August confirmed San Giuliano's position. After a further meeting on 2 August, the official text of the declaration of neutrality was drawn up; it was published on the third.

The defection of Italy was followed by that of Romania, of whom Bethmann on 2 August requested immediate mobilization and an advance on Russia. Although King Carol vigorously advocated the observance of the alliance with the central powers, a crown council on 3 August decided that because Romania had been neither advised nor consulted concerning the Dual Monarchy's action against Serbia, the *casus foederis* had not arisen. The kaiser gloomily commented: "Our allies are already before the war falling away from us like rotten apples. A total collapse of both German and Austrian diplomacy. This could and should have been avoided."[32] The German treaty of alliance with the Ottoman empire, which Germany had urgently sought since 28 July and which was signed on 2 August, was scarcely a compensation for the loss of both Italy and Romania.

These two defections and one addition for the Triplice roughly coincided in time with Great Britain's decision to enter the war on the side of France and Russia. Britain's path was not an easy one, because she had to follow at the same time two lines of policy: to make clear to Germany that under certain circumstances she might come in, and at the same time to make France and Russia understand that she was free either to come in or to stay out. Grey, like his counselors Nicolson and Crowe, was always conscious of the "group" situation in the international politics of Europe and could not be expected to upset the balance of power for the *beaux yeux* of Germany. But Grey and the Foreign Office were not free to do as they pleased, because they were bound by public opinion, the Cabinet, and Parliament.

After 27 July, when Germany rejected Grey's proposal for a conference, Grey became increasingly pessimistic about the possibility of avoiding war. In Cabinet discussions, serious differences of opinion emerged concerning whether Great Britain should intervene in the approaching war. Lord Morley asserts that this question was uppermost in the Cabinet debates and that Belgian neutrality was treated "as less urgent than France." Grey insists that he made no effort to counteract the antiwar party because he felt that "if the country went into such a war, it must do so whole-heartedly, with feeling and conviction so strong as to compel practical unanimity."[33] In these circumstances Grey had to pursue a negative policy. He declared in retrospect that after Germany refused his conference proposal, he "could not put pressure on Russia. . . . If I had tried to hold back her military preparations, Sazonov would at once have said: Then will you help us if war comes?"[34] And Grey could pledge to fight for Russia even less than for France. To Paul Cambon's pleas for a commitment to France, which became increasingly urgent after 29 July, Grey could make no promises, although he personally favored intervention in a war between Germany and France. He told the Cabinet that he was

---

32. Marginalium on KD, no. 811.
33. Morley, *Memorandum on Resignation, August 1914*, p. 3; Grey, *Twenty-Five Years*, I, 324–26.
34. Trevelyan, *Grey of Fallodon*, p. 287.

not the man to carry out a policy of neutrality. The Cabinet, however, put the "precautionary measures on land and sea" into operation.[35]

By 31 July the British were becoming increasingly uneasy over Belgian neutrality. Grey told Paul Cambon that although he could make no promises to France, the preservation of Belgian neutrality might be an important though not a decisive development which might alter the situation and cause the government and Parliament to decide upon intervention. Late that same day he sent an inquiry to both France and Germany asking if they would pledge to respect the neutrality of Belgium. Early the following morning he learned that France would do so but that Jagow could not answer for Germany and doubted if the chancellor and the kaiser could either, alleging that Belgium had already committed hostile acts toward Germany. Grey called Lichnowsky's attention to the importance of the question, for if Germany violated Belgian neutrality, opinion would make it difficult for the British government to take an attitude of friendly neutrality.

By 1 August the contending parties in the Cabinet and the country were feverishly working to prevent or to promote intervention. Grey's advisers in the Foreign Office were forthrightly advocating that England stand by her friends. On the other hand, business and financial circles in the City were trying to prevent intervention against Germany. News of Russian general mobilization and the German declaration of *Kriegsgefahrzustand* created great excitement among the Cabinet members and officials, some of whom persuaded George V to send a personal telegram to Nicholas II appealing to him to stop mobilization. On the 1st of August, Grey made his ill-considered proposal to Lichnowsky that if Germany promised neutrality in an Austro-Russian war, Britain and France would remain neutral. This befuddled attempt to avoid intervention in the war that was now only a few hours away suggests that Grey was experiencing a state of nervous exhaustion, for he surely could not have been unaware of the alliance obligations of both Germany and France. But he was no nearer the ragged edge of a breakdown than Paul Cambon, who again asked for a British pledge of assistance to France, pointing out that as a result of Anglo-French naval dispositions in 1912 the north coast of France lay undefended. Again he received no commitment, but only a promise that the Cabinet would consider the matter at its meeting on the morrow. Cambon, "white and speechless," staggering into Nicol-

---

35. Cameron Hazlehurst, *Politicians at War*, p. 80. On the situation in the Cabinet, 30–31 July, ibid., pp. 82–86.

son's office, could only mutter: "They are going to leave us in the lurch."[36]

The decisions of the next day, 2 August, represented a breakthrough for the interventionists in the government. The Cabinet met in the morning knowing that Germany had declared war on Russia and had entered Luxembourg. It authorized Grey to give France the assurance that if the German fleet undertook "hostile operations against the French coast or shipping," the British fleet would "give all the protection in its power." The Cabinet also approved the mobilization of the fleet, which Churchill had ordered the previous evening on his own responsibility, but could not decide upon what to do about a violation of Belgian neutrality.[37] Nevertheless, even the positive actions were regretted by the neutralists at a noon luncheon, and that night Burns and Morley resigned from the government. Meanwhile, Lichnowsky reported to his government a talk with Prime Minister Asquith in which the latter had stressed the unfavorable effect upon English opinion of a violation of Belgian neutrality and of an attack on the northern coast of France. The next morning, 3 August, Jagow wired that Germany would not threaten the northern coast of France as long as England remained neutral—a pledge that was given scant attention by Grey in his speech to Parliament that afternoon.

Grey, following lines agreed upon by the Cabinet in the morning and knowing of the German ultimatum to Belgium and its rejection, spoke to Parliament at 3 o'clock. He revealed the military talks with France in 1906 and the exchange of letters with Paul Cambon in November 1912. Coming to the existing situation, he quoted his assurance to France that the fleet would protect her northern coast, and characterized the German assurance that they would not attack the coast as "far too narrow an engagement for us," because of the more serious question of Belgian neutrality. He reviewed the treaty of 1839 and the British action in 1870 and read King Albert's appeal for diplomatic intervention to safeguard the integrity of Belgium. Sketching the British interest in Belgian neutrality and the dire consequences of nonintervention, he explained that the government had rejected a declaration of neutrality, and closed with the confident assumption that the House of Commons and the country would support whatever

36. Nicolson, *Carnock*, pp. 304–05.

37. Grey to Bertie, 2 August: *BD*, XI, no. 487. For Cabinet feelings and actions, 1–4 August, see Hazlehurst, *Politicians at War*, pp. 92–102; and for a peace proposal by Samuels, see Lowe and Dockrill, *Mirage of Power*, I, 150–51, and III, no. 77.

action the government decided to take. In his memoirs, Grey pithily summarized what he had tried to convey in his parliamentary speech:

> The real reason for going into the war was that, if we did not stand by France and stand up for Belgium against this aggression, we should be isolated, discredited, and hated; and there would be before us nothing but a miserable and ignoble future.[38]

The dénouement came on 4 August when the situation in respect to both France and Belgium was clear. Germany had declared war on France the previous evening, and her troops had entered Belgium early that morning. At 2 P.M. Grey telegraphed Goschen to repeat the request of 31 July that Germany give assurance to respect Belgian neutrality and if there was not a satisfactory answer by midnight, (11 P.M. London time) to ask for his passports. At 11 P.M., since no answer had come from Berlin, Great Britain was at war with Germany.

Paradoxically, Austria-Hungary was still not at war with any of the great powers, even though Germany had gone to war with Russia on 1 August because of the Austro-Russian conflict of interest. At length, on 6 August, Austria-Hungary declared war on Russia, but it was not until the 12th that France and Great Britain went to war with the Dual Monarchy. Thus the circle was completed, and five great powers found themselves engaged in a combat that everybody expected to be over by Christmas. They had to wait another four years before the First World War came to an end.

38. Grey, *Twenty-Five Years*, II, 15–16; and for the speech ibid., Appendix D. Cf. Hazlehurst, *Politicians at War*, pp. 43–48.

Chapter 15

Conclusion

In reviewing the dozen crucial years from 1902, we are struck first of all by the diplomatic revolution that overturned the international alignments of the Bismarckian period. Then a dominant Germany, guided by a statesman who had set limited objectives for his country, enjoyed the security of the Triple Alliance, the cooperation of Russia to the east, and the benevolent neutrality of Great Britain to the west. Between the fall of Bismarck in 1890 and the end of the Boer war in 1902, a transitional period was highlighted by imperialist rivalries. The Bismarckian configuration began to crumble with the establishment of the Franco-Russian alliance in 1894, but, much more important, Germany with her booming industrial and commercial development emerged from the essentially continental politics of Bismarck's era into *Weltpolitik*, at the same time loosening the ties with St. Petersburg that Bismarck had carefully maintained and failing to preserve the friendly attitude of Great Britain. In this changing situation the astute Delcassé began to build a rival alignment that constituted the first step toward the diplomatic revolution. He achieved the consolidation of the shaky alliance with Russia and in 1902 consummated the reconciliation with Italy that gave her a partnership in the Mediterranean balance of power and weakened the Triple Alliance by offering her a freedom of choice in her allegiances.

In the second phase of the diplomatic revolution Great Britain became a key figure along with France. Convinced that security compelled a settlement of colonial points of conflict with one or more of the other imperialist powers, and that the "splendid isolation" of the Salisbury era was no longer tenable or safe, Britain turned first to an alliance with Japan that lightened her responsibilities in the Far East, and then, having failed to come to an understanding with Germany, turned to France to achieve the Entente Cordiale in 1904. From this time onward, although seeking to preserve her freedom of choice in European conflicts, Great Britain, step by unconscious step, incurred the moral obligations of alliance without the carefully contrived conditions of the Bismarckian prototype. The first such step was the planning of military cooperation with France in the event of a German attack upon her. The military talks of 1906 were inaugurated after the first Moroccan crisis, in which Germany sought to establish her right to be consulted in colonial areas that concerned her, and to break up the Anglo-French entente, which had confounded German predictions that the two powers could never compose their differences and that England in a pinch would be compelled to seek German support at a price set by Germany.

A factor that by this time had emerged and was to remain a constant element in the British balance-of-power policy was the building of the German fleet, which the British began in 1904 to regard as a menace to British sea power. This menace, which increased in British eyes with the introduction of the dreadnought in 1905 and the new German naval law of 1906, intensified the already well-developed drive toward a settlement with Russia in 1907 which removed the Russian threat to India and to other British interests in the Middle East. Again, the intention was not an alliance nor the encirclement of Germany, which the Germans themselves now began to regard as a menace to their security.[1] Nevertheless, as in the case of the Entente Cordiale, the Anglo-Russian entente became for the British a commitment to favor Russia on crucial issues. Thus the Triple Entente, as it began to be called in 1908, became a rival camp of the Triple Alliance, although the alignments down to the July crisis of 1914 were not so rigid as to prevent interpenetration among the members of the two groups and discord within them.[2]

Throughout the crucial years there were two poles of conflict in Europe, one in the west and the other in the east. In the west one underlying problem that proved to be insoluble was the Franco-German antagonism arising over Alsace-Lorraine. The issue was virtually overlaid and partly driven underground by the rivalry in Morocco. This rivalry, like most imperialistic conflicts, was at length settled in 1911 without war; the two protagonists made a deal by which France exchanged central African lands for dominance in Morocco. The settlement might have gone far to eliminate the older Alsace-Lorraine issue had parties who favored rapprochement in both France and Germany not been thwarted by an upsurge of nationalist feeling in both countries and the ineptitude of German procedure. In the two Moroccan

1. Cf. Paul W. Schroeder, "World War I as Galloping Gertie," *JMH*, XLIV (1972), 325–31.

2. Pierre Guillen, "Les questions coloniales dans les relations franco-allemandes," *RH*, CCXLVIII (1972), 103–05, asserts that the French mistrusted Britain and Russia in the Middle East as much as they did Germany.

crises Bülow's bullying in the first and Kiderlen-Waechter's hard-fisted tactics in the second confirmed the French and British belief that Germany was an aggressive power who had to be contained.

During the crucial years the press in entente countries and men in high office like Sir Eyre Crowe exaggerated Germany's aggressiveness in her striving for "a place in the sun," but the behavior of the Germans themselves gave grounds for such a judgment. Bethman Hollweg ascribed the outbreak of war in 1914 to popular feeling in which Germany had her share. As he put it, "a strident, pushing, elbowing, overbearing spirit had been produced in our people. They really were a mass of conceit, and totally ignorant of other countries."[3] Both the spirit and the ignorance were reflected in German foreign policy. Germany's emergence into Weltpolitik required a circumspect, stable, and far-sighted policy that Bismarck's successors were incapable of pursuing. Again to quote Bethmann Hollweg in his analysis of Germany's predicament during the July crisis of 1914: "The earlier errors: simultaneously Turkish policy against Russia, Morocco against France, the navy against England—challenge everybody, put yourself in everybody's path, and actually weaken no one in this fashion. Reason: Aimlessness, the need for little prestige successes and solicitude for every current of opinion."[4] This diagnosis fails, however, to note the negative aspect of Germany's huckstering tactics. By virtue of her position in the center of Europe she was constrained from playing the game of Weltpolitik with the same freedom as other great powers. Her fault was not so much "aimlessness" as her bothersome insistence upon being paid for doing nothing: for benevolent neutrality in the Russo-Japanese war, for nonpenetration of Persia, for suffering French activities in Morocco, for nonbuildng of more battleships. The deepseated suspicions of Germany, especially in Great Britain, obscured recognition of her failure to utilize the power and wealth at her command.[5] She succeeded only in acquiring a few thousand square miles of African territory and in convincing the entente powers that she was a threat to the balance of power.

Despite Franco-German irreconcilability and Anglo-German naval rivalry, détente was in the air after the Agadir crisis of 1911. Yet the effort to bring about a relaxation of the naval rivalry through the

---

3. Theodor Wolff, *The Eve of 1914*, 620–21.

4. As quoted from Riezler's diary, 20 July 1914, by Fritz Stern, "Bethmann Hollweg and the War," *Responsibility of Power*, p. 265.

5. Schroeder, *JMH*, XLIV, 331–34.

Haldane mission of 1912 proved fruitless, because the British conviction that their sea power was their only security against starvation in case of war and the dogged determination of the Germans to stick to their naval building plans unless Great Britain pledged neutrality in case of a European war prevented agreement upon naval limitation. On the other hand, the upshot of this failure and of the consequent relocation of the British fleet to meet the German naval menace was another step in the forging of British commitments to France by way of the naval agreement embodied in the Grey-Cambon exchange of letters in November 1912. The Anglo-German agreements over the Portuguese colonies and the Bagdad railway and the Franco-German arrangements over railways in Asia Minor in 1913–1914 were delayed, but ineffectual steps toward détente that came too late to have any effect upon the crisis of 1914.

Meanwhile, the western pole of international tension had become secondary to that of the east, where a Russo-Austro-Hungarian conflict was developing. The conflict of interests between Russia and Austria in the Balkans had existed since the eighteenth century, but bargaining and compromises had prevented war between them when both were strong, and the weakness of one or the other had kept the peace at other times. In Bismarck's day the two protagonists had been led by his adroit diplomacy to divide their spheres of influence. Then the preoccupation of Russia with the Far East and the domestic troubles of Austria-Hungary had led to an agreed policy of hands off in the Balkans. With the Japanese defeat, however, the party in Russia that had deprecated the Far Eastern push and conceived of Russia's true interests as lying in the Near East and the Balkans gained the upper hand and found its proponent in Izvolsky. At the same time, the drive in Austria-Hungary for a vigorous foreign policy that would resuscitate the decaying Habsburg Monarchy found a champion in Aehrenthal. The two men sought a bargain by which the Dual Monarchy would annex the largely Serbian inhabited Bosnia-Herzegovina and Russia would seek compensation in the freedom of the Straits. In the crisis of 1908–1909, however, Austria-Hungary grabbed her part of the deal and Russia found herself empty-handed and her Pan-Slavs indignant at the betrayal of their fellow Slavs, the Serbs. The stubbornly pursued goals of the Dual Monarchy, fully backed by Germany, not only resulted in the humiliation of Russia, who out of weakness had to accept the annexation of Bosnia-Herzegovina without compensation, but in addition the triumph over Serbian opposition threw coals on the fire of the South-Slav movement toward unification which now appeared to be possible only through the division and probable collapse of the multinational Habsburg empire.

Here was the kind of problem that in the traditions of the modern sovereign state could not be solved short of war. The Serbs, for their own nationalist objective of a greater Serbia, fostered South-Slav ambitions and could not be expected to give up their national goal any more than the Italians in the mid-nineteenth century, whose example the Serbs cherished, could have been expected to cease fighting the Austrian tyrant. On the other hand, Austria-Hungary could not be expected to graciously invite the South Slavs within her borders to secede and unite with their brethren of the Balkans. Nor, given the conflicting forces within the Dual Monarchy, could reforms such as trialism, which would bring about Slav contentment with Habsburg rule, be achieved. Aehrenthal dreamed of them but found himself thwarted in his efforts to conciliate the Serbs. Long before his death he had given up, and neither his successor, Berchtold, nor any of his colleagues even attempted the task. At best, conciliation could have achieved little more than the postponement of the ultimate showdown between virulent nationalism and the dynastic principle on which the Habsburg empire rested.[6]

After the Bosnian crisis the next stage in the East European pole of conflict was reached in the Balkan wars of 1912–1913. Russia and Austria-Hungary were kept from coming to blows by the mediatory efforts of Germany and Britain in the London conference of ambassadors and by German restraints upon her ally. One of the results of the wars was the ousting of the Turks from their major holdings in the Balkans, which meant a narrowing of room for maneuver between Russia and Austria-Hungary. More important for European politics were the considerable expansion of Serbian territory and the heightening of Romanian irredentism, which helped to loosen her ties with the Triple Alliance. The Dual Monarchy now faced a greater menace to her integrity than ever before. The greater Serbian size and prestige helped to increase the ferment among the South Slavs in the Dual Monarchy. In the autumn of 1913 Vienna became convinced that the future security of the Monarchy required the crushing of Serbia, but as yet the occasion and the enthusiastic support of the public were lacking.

6. For a less pessimistic view of Austria-Hungary, see Joachim Remak, "The Healthy Invalid: How Doomed the Habsburg Empire?" *JMH*, XLI (1969), 127–43. Cf. Bridge, *From Sadowa to Sarajevo*, pp. 370–73.

The Liman von Sanders affair at the turn of the year helped to increase irritation and tension, particularly between Russia and Germany, and both the civilian governments and the military in Germany, Russia, and France were filled with forebodings about the future. The passage of Germany's great army bill and France's three-year service law, both in 1913, intensified the armament race. In 1914 the Russians and the French tried to persuade Great Britain to tighten the Triple Entente but succeeded only in getting British consent to make a naval agreement with Russia. The initial negotiations, when revealed to Berlin, caused grave anxiety there over Anglo-Russian cooperation and the dangers of Russian rearmament that had already been touted in the Russian press as a means of needling the French to retain their three-year service law. In the Balkans the Serbs, although they were concentrating upon the consolidation of their gains in the Balkan wars, had obtained Tsar Nicholas II's pledge to support them in a future struggle with the Dual Monarchy.

On all sides (except perhaps in Britain; she was preoccupied with the Irish question) peace was considered precarious. French military men had predicted a war early in 1912, and news of the kaiser's bellicose language at the end of that year confirmed them in the belief that war was coming. The German military and naval men talked of a coming war at the end of 1913, and General von Moltke in May and June 1914 expressed his apprehensions to Conrad and to Jagow. Although the Russian war minister had published his boast that Russia was ready for war, German military intelligence reported that Russia and France were not yet prepared for it and thus encouraged the German belief that they would not risk war for another two or three years.

Moreover, Europe on the eve of the Sarajevo crime, although uneasy and anxious, had not yet drawn rigidly fixed battle lines. Great Britain and Germany, on the one hand, were experiencing a détente and Grey and Bethmann Hollweg both hoped that in case trouble arose they could cooperate to keep the peace. France and Russia, on the other hand, were more closely tied together than in either the Bosnian or the Agadir crises, for each had come to recognize that he had to support the other even if his own interests were not at stake. On the Triple Alliance side, Italy's military men had renewed their pledges of loyalty to the alliance, but the diplomats were wondering how long Italy could remain in it. Romania had obviously become a dubious ally of the central powers. Also Germany and Austria-Hungary were still at odds over the policy to be pursued in the Balkans. Outside the two alliance groups, Great Britain remained an uncertain factor for both sides. Had each of the two camps stood solidly united in opposition to the other, it is quite possible that war might not have occurred, because its outbreak is attributable in part to the uncertainties in the situation that led decision-makers in Germany and the Dual Monarchy to gamble.

In this picture of European international relations on the eve of the July 1914 crisis, I have purposely omitted the economic competition so important to the Marxists. It was, like the rivalry of armament manufacturers, a phenomenon that caused irritation, but not to the point of war.[7] Most frequently mentioned was the trade rivalry between Great Britain and Germany. Admittedly it was a talking point in the anti-German propaganda of the British publicists and a cause for conflict in the thinking of Admiral Tirpitz, who ascribed British antagonism to trade rather than to naval building. But the truth was that England was Germany's best customer and vice versa, and that the most stubborn resistance to intervention in the war against Germany came from the City of London, the heart of British finance. French and British armament makers vied with German and Austrian in selling arms to the Balkans and Turkey, and the French and Russians tried to bind the Balkan states to them with chains of gold. They succeeded with Serbia, who was tied to them anyway, but lost with Bulgaria, whose political interests lay with the central powers. Competition was there, but the businessmen on both sides characteristically resorted to bargains rather than war, as illustrated by the Franco-German deals over railway building in Asia Minor.

Furthermore, I have omitted the revisionist stories of a Poincaré-Izvolsky plot to bring about war, and of a Russian girding to seize the Straits when a European war should come about through her efforts. These exaggerated and biased interpretations, often based upon insufficient or dubious sources, were an outcome of the heated controversies over war guilt that raged in the first postwar decade. The more recent charge of the so-called Fischer school, that the German general staff and government had decided to wage a preventive war when Russia and France were not ready and when Germany still had a chance to win, belongs to the same category as the plots discovered by the revisionists.[8] To be sure, the evidence is much more convincing, but it still lacks the concrete proof required to clinch the allegations. That

7. A most convincing refutation of the economic cause of war is that of Jacob Viner, "Peace as an Economic Problem," *New Perspectives on Peace*, ed. George B. Huszar (Chicago, 1944), pp. 85–114.

8. Cf. Klaus Epstein, "Gerhard Ritter and the First World War," *1914: The Coming of the First World War*, pp. 188, 191; Martin Kitchen, *The German Officer Corps, 1890–1914* (Oxford, 1968), pp. 4, 113–114.

Moltke talked of war and the sooner the better, and that the kaiser uttered the phrase "Now or never!" there is no doubt. But that such utterances prove a determination to bring about a preventive war is another matter. The same thing is true of the allegation that Germany was planning a war for the hegemony of Europe or for the aggrandizement of Germany. What the talk about war and aggrandizement boils down to, whether in Paris, St. Petersburg, Berlin, or Vienna, is the anxiety of worried men who feared that their security was being endangered by the trends of the time. The statesmen and the public were reflecting a mood that was widespread in Europe by the spring of 1914: better war than this uneasy peace, better a decision one way or another than recurring crises whose settlements fail to bring about rapprochement or friendship. This atmosphere is a significant part of the situation on the eve of the July crisis in 1914.

Into this unsettled situation the Sarajevo crime came as a thunderbolt. Everywhere it was regarded as shocking, but nowhere as a portent of war. Nevertheless, the murder of Archduke Francis Ferdinand was one of the immediate causes of the war of 1914, because it acted as a catalyst upon the elements that had been gathering toward a decision about the Serbian problem. Here was the occasion and along with it the public mood in Austria-Hungary of anger and resentment that was required for crushing out the Serbian "nest of vipers." Vienna could not move, however, without the promise of German support, and, contrary to the policy of restraint up to this time, Berlin promised it even to the test of arms. Thus Germany and Austria-Hungary took the step that made a European war probable. Bethmann Hollweg himself regarded it as a "leap in the dark." Vienna especially and Berlin, too, made their decisions out of a sense of desperation. Vienna felt that the integrity of the Austro-Hungarian empire was at stake, and that it was better to fight than to sit back and passively wait for the disintegration to come. Berlin, gambling upon localization, felt that this time Germany had to support her one sure ally, come what might; if war came, better now than two or three years later, when Russia might have become an unbeatable power.

Russia, from the first inkling of Austria-Hungary's aims, declared that she would not stand aside and see Serbia crushed. The failure of the Dual Monarchy and Germany to respond to the first suggestions for talks and mediation and on top of that the declaration of war on Serbia and the bombardment of Belgrade convinced the Russian civilians and military that Russia had to act. Her partial mobilization was intended to put pressure upon the Dual Monarchy; the general mobilization was a preparation for the war that the Russians were convinced by 30 July was coming. They, too, were acting from a sense of desperation: they felt that they could not again back down as in 1909 before the determination of Austria-Hungary to attack Serbia. Moreover, this time, unlike 1909, they had the pledged support of France. Like Austria-Hungary and Germany, they were ready to risk war in order to prevent an Austro-Hungarian triumph in the Balkans and to maintain their prestige at home and among the Slavic peoples. Their decision made war inevitable.

Once Russia ordered mobilization, the wheels of war inexorably began to turn. Although Bethmann Hollweg tried to maintain control in Berlin in order to avoid any step that might throw the blame for starting the war upon Germany, the exigencies of the Schlieffen plan gave the military a priority in making decisions. The belief that the only hope of German victory in a two-front war lay in a rapid defeat of France, which strategically required a march through Belgium, meant that Germany had to be at war in order to move to the West. Moltke recognized in 1913 that the march through Belgium would bring in not only the Belgian army, but also Great Britain, and yet he felt that he had to fight the war that way. The rigid military timetable therefore eliminated freedom of maneuver and dictated the political moves. This aspect of Germany's position is the major ground for labeling her "militaristic."

Why the war of 1914? The Austro-Hungarian decision that Serbia had to be eliminated as a threat to the empire could only be implemented by force. Here was the basic fact from which the chain of events leading to war developed. Given the Russian determination that the Dual Monarchy should not have her way with Serbia, and given the loyalty of Germany on the one hand and of France on the other to their allies, there was no peaceable outcome possible. Only if Russia, as in 1909, accepted the humiliation and destruction of Serbia could Europe avoid war. Once the wheeels were set in motion on 30 July by Russia, nothing but Austro-Hungarian renunciation of her decision would have saved the peace, and no more than Russia could the Dual Monarchy be expected to forfeit her prestige and perhaps even her existence to yield at that late date. Germany could not force such a decision upon Austria-Hungary excepting at the price of losing her last faithful ally in Europe and facing isolation. France, for similar reasons had to support Russia. In this way the alliance system assured the involvement of Europe in the quarrel between Austria-Hungary and Russia.

As for Great Britain, the whole course of the previous ten years had demonstrated to her satisfaction that the major threat to the balance of power in Europe came from Germany, and that the crushing of France would leave Britain alone to face German preponderance on the Continent. Without the invasion of Belgium, and given the vital interests of the national sovereign state, she, too, had to join the opponents of the central powers. Belgium gave the British government the support of Parliament and the populace that would undoubtedly have been lacking if it had decided to intervene, as Grey wanted to do, to save France from being crushed.

Put in general terms, the nationalist drive of the South Slavs to achieve self-determination, spearheaded by Serbia, and the decision of Austria-Hungary, supported by Germany, to end the Slavic threat to her existence by war constituted a Gordian knot to be cut only by the sword.[9] The friends of Serbia took up the challenge and thus spread the local issue to Europe. Britain for the sake of the balance of power and the safeguarding of her own interest in preventing Germany from dominating the Belgian channel coast joined the fray. No peace machinery, such as the London conference of ambassadors or any since invented, could have prevented the war once the initial step had been taken by Austria-Hungary and Germany. The world war broke out because of a problem familiar since the Italian struggle for independence and unity in the mid-nineteenth century. The reason why in 1914 war engulfed the Continent instead of being limited to two great powers, as in 1859, lay in the evolution over the previous crucial years of the alliance system, designed to give the nations security, but operating in the end to bring all into the catastrophe.

9. Cf. Bridge, *From Sadowa to Sarajevo*, pp. 381–84. On the Dual Monarchy's plight and the responsibility of others for it, see Schroeder, *JMH*, XLIV, 334–45. Cf. Arthur Zimmermann, "Fürst Bülows Kritik am Auswärtigen Amt," *Front wider Bülow* (Munich, 1931), pp. 229–31.

Bibliographical Essay

In this essay I have made no attempt to compile a complete bibliography on European international relations, 1902–1914, nor to include all the works I have studied. Rather I have dealt with those most important for this book in two parts: I, the works most often used for the whole period or significant parts of it, and II, those which in addition supplied material for each chapter. In Part II works that appear in more than one chapter have been cited in full at the first entry, and thereafter by short titles. Whenever available, translations of foreign-language studies have been cited for convenience of students unfamiliar with the languages, although in many instances I have used the originals.

The most recent and best bibliographical essay on Europe in the period here studied is that of Oron J. Hale, *The Great Illusion, 1900–1914* (New York, Evanston, London, 1971), pp. 315–55. It begins with a valuable discussion of guides to the historical literature and thereafter covers all aspects of European life and politics.

Part I. General

1. PUBLISHED DOCUMENTS

Among the earliest publication of documents after the war of 1914–1918 were the *Austrian Red Book: Official Files Pertaining to Pre-War History* (3 parts, London, 1920), on the July crisis and outbreak of war; and Alfred Francis Pribram, *The Secret Treaties of Austria-Hungary, 1879–1914*, English edition by Archibald Cary Coolidge (2 vols. Cambridge, Mass., London, 1920–21). Except for Pribram's work there is no postwar publication of Austro-Hungarian documents until 1908, but thereafter see *Österreich-Ungarns Aussenpolitik von der Bosnischen Krise bis zum Kriegsausbruch 1914* (8 vols. Vienna, Leipzig, 1930), a collection edited by Ludwig Bittner and Hans Uebersberger.

After occupying the Belgian capital during the war, the Germans issued under the editorship of Bernhard Schwertfeger *Zur Europäischen Politik, 1897–1914* (5 vols. Berlin, 1919). These documents present events as seen through the eyes of Belgian diplomats who were on-lookers rather than active participants.

Germany began the flood of documentary publications concerning the background of the First World War in an effort to refute the war-guilt clause of the Versailles treaty. *Die gross Politik der europäischen Kabinette, 1871–1914* (40 vols. in 53, Berlin, 1922–27) was edited by Johannes Lepsius, Albrecht Mendelssohn, and Friedrich Thimme, who were influenced in the selection of documents by the objective of the publication. Bernhard Schwertfeger, *Die diplomatischen Akten des Auswärtigen Amts, 1871–1914: ein Wegweiser . . .* (5 vols. Berlin, 1927) is a useful guide to the collection. Documents on the July crisis were collected by Karl Kautsky and edited by Max Montgelas and Walter Schücking as *Die deutschen Dokumenten* (4 vols. Berlin, 1919; new and enlarged ed., 5 vols. Berlin, 1927). The first edition has been translated by the Carnegie Endowment for International Peace, Division of International Law under the title of *Outbreak of the World War* (New York, 1924), cited as KD.

The German publications spurred other nations to act. France established a Commission that issued *Documents diplomatiques français* (1871–1914), of which the second series covers the period of 1901–1911 (14 vols. Paris, 1930–55), and the third for 1911–1914 (11 vols. Paris, 1929–36), cited as 2 DDF and 3 DDF. The documents are arranged by date rather than topic as in the German and British collections, but are indexed by topics in the "Table Methodique" of each volume.

The British collection is entitled *British Documents on the Origins of the War, 1898–1914* (11 vols. London, 1926–38) and was edited by G. P. Gooch and Harold Temperley. The French and British collections together eliminate the need to study most of the "Yellow Books" and "Blue Books" that were issued from time to time on current events.

Italy planned an extensive publication similar to the French but has thus far issued only one volume in the period of study: *I Documenti diplomatici italiani*, fourth series, XII (28 giugno–2 agosti 1914) (Rome, 1954).

Likewise Russia has failed to complete her plans. On the period of 1900–1914, the *Mezhdunarodnye Otnosheniya v Epoku Imperializma* (International Relations in the Epoch of Imperialism), second series, XVIII–XX (Moscow, 1938–40) cover the period from mid-May 1911 to mid-May 1913; and the third series, I–X (Moscow, 1931–38) runs from January 1914 to 1916. (These documents are cited as 2 or 3 MO.) Both series have been translated into German under the editorship of Otto Hoetzsch as *Die internationalen Beziehungen im Zeitalter des Imperialismus* (Berlin, 1931–43), but with different series numbers. In addition to the official publications, the most important collections in translation are *Un livre noir*, ed. René Marchand (3 vols. in 5, Paris, 1929–31), containing correspondence of Izvolsky and other ambassadors and minister from 1911; *Entente Diplomacy and the World, 1909–1914*, tr. B. de Siebert, ed. George Abel Schreiner (New York, London, 1921), cited as Siebert and Schreiner; and Konrad G. W. Romberg, *Falsifications of the Russian Orange Book* (New York, 1923), which gives correct texts of documents issued in 1914 on the July crisis. The serial *Krasnyi Arkhiv* published documents that have been noted below in Part II. See also Benckendorff and Izvolsky in the subsection following.

The only publication in a western language of Serbian documents is that of Miloš Bogičević, *Die auswärtige Politik Serbiens, 1903–1914* (3 vols. Berlin, 1928–31). This collection by a former member of the Serbian diplomatic service is none too reliable.

2. MEMOIRS, BIOGRAPHIES, AND LETTERS

Only books by or about men who were active throughout all or most of the period under study will be noted here. Others will be discussed in the chapters for which they are relevant.

For Austria-Hungary a prime source for both military and political events is Franz Graf Conrad von Hötzendorf, *Aus meiner Dienstzeit, 1906–1918* (5 vols. Vienna, 1921–25). It is interlarded with official documents as well as private papers. The best biography of Emperor Francis Joseph is by Joseph Redlich, *Emperor Francis Joseph of Austria* (New York, 1929). Redlich was active in politics and a historian of note who has left a personal record of events and policies in *Schicksalsjahre Osterreichs, 1908–1919* (2 vols. Graz, Cologne, 1953–54). Another prominent Austrian, particularly interested in the South Slavs and relations with Serbia, was Joseph M. Baernreither, whose *Fragments of a Political Diary* (London, 1930), edited by Redlich, throws light on Austro-Hungarian foreign policy. Although Berchtold failed to publish his memoirs, his biographer has used his notes and private papers to produce a well-grounded and on the whole favorable picture of him and his policies: Hugo Hantsch, *Leopold Graf Berchtold, Grandseigneur und Staatsmann* (2 vols. Graz, Vienna, Cologne, 1963). This is an indispensable source for 1908–1918.

Among German public figures, Bernhard Prince von Bülow has left the most voluminous record: *Memoirs of Prince von Bülow* (4 vols. Boston, 1931–32). They are important but even less reliable than most memoirs are, although they may be checked by reference to *Die Grosse Politik* for his years as foreign secretary and chancellor. Equally important, to 1909, are the papers and biography of Holstein: *The Holstein Papers*: I, *Memoirs and Political Observations*; IV, *Correspondence, 1897–1909* (Cambridge, Eng., 1955, 1963); and Norman Rich, *Friedrich von Holstein* (2 vols. Cambridge, Eng., 1965). These works of outstanding scholarly editing and study replace the older studies of Holstein and contribute new insights into German policy. Among earlier indispensable works are *Kiderlen-Waechter, der Staatsmann und Mensch*, ed. Ernst Jäckh (2 vols. Berlin, Leipzig, 1925); *The World Policy of Germany, 1890–1912* (New York, 1927), by Otto Hammann, head of the press bureau in the Foreign Office; and Grand Admiral Alfred von Tirpitz, *My Memoirs* (2 vols. London, 1919) and *Politische Dokumente*: I, *Der Aufbau der deutschen Weltmacht* (Stuttgart, Berlin, 1925). These last two are basic for an understanding of German naval policy. Important for German-Russian relations are *The Kaiser's Letters to the Tsar*, ed. N. F. Grant (London, n.d.), and *The Willy-Nicky Correspondence, Being the Secret and Intimate Telegrams . . .* ed. Herman Bernstein (New York, 1918). Most of these documents are also printed in *Die Grosse Politik*. The leading Berlin banker, Paul H. von Schwabach, has printed correspondence with English, French, and Italian friends which reflects currents of German opinion, in *Aus meinen Akten* (Berlin, 1927).

Few French statesmen or diplomats have left memoirs pertinent to the whole period of this study. Joseph Caillaux, *Mes Mémoires* (3 vols. Paris, 1942–47) extends over the period, but while enlightening and for 1911 indispensable, it is a highly biased and often gossipy account. Of the greatest importance is Paul Cambon, *Correspondance, 1870–1924* (3 vols. Paris, 1940–46), which often significantly supplements the published French documents. A short but informative biography, *Paul Cambon, un Ambassadeur de France par un Diplomate* (Paris, 1937), was written by Henri Cambon, his son, who also edited the *Correspondance*. Keith Eubank's *Paul Cambon, Master Diplomatist* (Norman, Okla., 1960) is another good biography. The biography of Delcassé by Charles W. Porter, *The Career of Théophile Delcassé* (Philadelphia, 1936), is still the best but in need of revision because of private papers now available. Alberic Neton, *Delcassé* (Paris, 1952), offers some insights by a friend and admirer. The most extensive corpus of private records is that of Maurice Paléologue, who occupied high posts in the ministry of foreign affairs and the diplomatic service: *Un grand tournant de la politique mondiale, 1904–06* (Paris, 1934); *Au Quai d'Orsay à la veille de la tourmente: journal, 1913–1914* (Paris, 1947); and *An Ambassador's Memoirs*: I, *July 1914 – June 1915* (6th ed. New York, 1924). Although these works claim to be from diaries kept from day to day, internal evidence suggests that they were probably touched up for publication, especially for 1904–1906 when Paléologue was a close associate of Delcassé and for 1913–1914 when he worked closely with his old friend Poincaré. Although Poincaré led an active political life before he became premier in 1912, he devoted his memoirs to his premiership and presidency: *Au service de la France* (Vols. I–IV [to 1914], Paris 1926–27). Because he was under fire by his contemporaries and historians, Poincaré's memoirs are patently a defense of his policies but are none the less valuable if used in the context of the controversies he aroused.

In Great, Britain, King Edward VII, though not the policymaker foreigners believed, was at the center of foreign relations. His authorized biography by Sir Sidney Lee, *King Edward VII*, II, *The Reign, 22 January 1901 to 6 May 1910* (London, 1927), is a reliable record; and André Maurois, *King Edward and His Times* (London, 1953), occasionally adds important points. Among the statesmen, most valuable testimony for foreign relations is contained in Randolph S. Churchill, *Winston S. Churchill*, II, *1901–1914, Young Statesman* (Boston, 1967); Viscount Grey of Fallodon, *Twenty-Five Years, 1892–1916* (2 vols. New York, 1925); Richard Burdon Haldane, *An Autobiography* (New York, 1928), and *Before the War* (New York, London, 1920); Lord Newton, *Lord Lansdowne: A Biography* (London, 1929); Harold Nicolson, *Portrait of a Diplomatist: Being the Life of Sir Arthur Nicolson, First Lord Carnock* (Boston, 1930), cited as *Carnock*. In addition to Grey's memoirs, two biographies give valuable information: Keith Robbins, *Sir Edward Grey* (London, 1971), and George Macaulay Trevelyan, *Grey of Fallodon: The Life and Letters* (Boston, 1937). The latter is the more valuable and informative.

Only two Italians have left materials of importance for the whole period: Giovanni Giolitti, *Memoirs of My Life* (London, Sydney, 1923); and Francesco Tommasini, *L'Italia alla vigilia della guerra: La politica estera di Tommaso Tittoni* (5 vols. Bologna, 1934–41). Giolitti's recollection are as brief as the Tittoni corpus is extended.

Extensive Russian diplomatic correspondence is contained in *Graf Benckendorffs diplomatischer Schriftwechsel*, ed. B. de Siebert (3 vols.; rev. ed. Berlin, Leipzig, 1928); Izvolsky, *Au service de la Russie . . . Correspondance diplomatique, 1906–1911* (2 vols. Paris, 1937); *Der diplomatische Schriftwechsel Iswolskis, 1911–1914*, ed. Friedrich Stieve (4 vols. Berlin, 1924). Both of these collections are duplicated in part, along with selections from other sources, in Siebert and Schreiner and in *LN*. Among the memoirs, neither Izvolsky's *Recollections of a Foreign Minister* (Garden City, Toronto, 1921) nor Sergei Sazonov's *Fateful Years, 1909–1916* (New York, 1928) contains significant revelations. *Out of My Past: The Memoirs of Count Kokovtsov* (Stanford, 1935) is meatier but mainly concerned with financial and domestic affairs. More revealing and pertinent to foreign policy is the work by the legal councillor in the ministry of foreign affairs, M. A. Baron de Taube, *La politique russe d'avant-guerre . . . Mémoires* (Paris, 1928).

3. HISTORICAL STUDIES

Most thorough in dealing with the backgrounds of the war is the study by Luigi Albertini, *The Origins of the War of 1914* (3 vols. London, New York, Toronto, 1952–57), of which the first volume covers the period from 1879 to June 1914, and the other two, much more detailed and heavily supported by quotations from the documents, deal with the July crisis and outbreak of the war. This is the best single work in English on the subject. Among the earlier studies, Erich Brandenburg, *From Bismarck to the World War* (London, 1927; rev. German ed., *Vom Bismarck zum Weltkrieg*, Leipzig, 1939), is critical of German policy but moderately revisionist, whereas Sidney Bradshaw Fay, *Origins of the World War* (2 vols. New York 1929; rev. ed. 2 vols. in one, New York, 1935), is the classic revisionist work in English, but written before many of the British and French documents were available. A collaborative French work under the direction of Henri Hauser, *Histoire diplomatique de l'Europe, 1871–1914* (2 vols. Paris, 1929) is narrative history that is handy for reference purposes, but is now in need of revision. The anti-revisionist classic in English, Bernadotte E. Schmitt, *The Coming of the War 1914* (2 vols. New York, 1930), like Fay's work, was published before many French and British documents were printed and has been superseded by such works as Albertini's which are more extreme than he was in blaming Germany for the war. A later and more extensive treatment of the war backgrounds is George Peabody Gooch, *Before the War*, (2 vols. London, New York, Toronto, 1936–38), which is organized around the foreign ministers of the great powers, thus dealing with crises in a repetitive way. It is, however, a solid, scholarly treatment of the policies pursued by each of the great powers, without attempting to prove a thesis concerning the origins of the war. The dean of French authorities on international relations, Pierre Renouvin ,has also produced a balanced and comprehensive account in *Histoire des relations internationales*, VI, Part II: *De 1871 à 1914* (Paris, 1955). Shorter and more popular studies of the war origins are: Laurence Lafore, *The Long Fuse* (Philadelphia, New York, 1965), and Joachim Remak, *The Origins of World War I, 1871–1914* (New York, 1967). More recently L. C. F. Turner, *The Origins of the First World War* (New York, 1970), deals cogently with the period of 1911–1914. In the field of public opinion, two men have published outstanding studies: E. Malcolm Carroll, *French Public Opinion and Foreign Affairs, 1870–1914* (New York, 1931) and *Germany and the Great Powers, 1866–1914* (New York, 1938); and Oron J. Hale, *Publicity and Diplomacy with Special Reference to England and Germany, 1890–1914* (New York, London, 1940)—the best work on the subject in any language. A unique study is that of George W. F. Hallgarten, *Imperialismus vor 1914* (2 vols.; rev. ed. Munich, 1963), with emphasis upon economic and financial factors in imperialistic rivalry. Welcome and significant additions in the field of great-power foreign policies are F. R. Bridge, *From Sadowa to Sarajevo: The Foreign Policy of Austria-Hungary, 1866–1914* (London, Boston, 1972); C. J. Lowe and M. L. Dockrill, *The Mirage of Power: British Foreign Policy, 1902–1922* (3 vols. London, Boston, 1972); and Zara S. Steiner, *The Foreign Office and Foreign Policy, 1898–1914* (Cambridge, Eng., 1969).

Part II. Chapter Bibliographies

CHAPTER 1. Basic for this whole chapter is the incomparable study by William L. Langer, *The Diplomacy of Imperialism* (2 vols. New York, 1935), chs. XIV–XXIII, which carries the story of European international relations through the Anglo-Japanese alliance in 1902.

In addition, on the character and policy of Delcassé is the monograph of Christopher Andrew, *Théophile Delcassé and the Making of the Entente Cordiale* (New York, 1968). This reappraisal of French foreign policy, 1898–1905, breaks new ground with the aid of hitherto unused private papers, including Delcassé's. Other sources are Joseph Paul-Boncour, *Entre deux guerre*, I (Paris, 1946); Caillaux, *Mes mémoires*, I; Emile Combes, *Mon ministère* (Paris, 1956); and Paléologue, *Un grand tournant de la politique mondiale*.

Witte's financial policy and plans are well described by Jacob Viner, "International Finance and Balance of Power Diplomacy," *International Economics* (Glencoe, Ill., 1951); and by Hallgarten, *Imperialismus vor 1914*, I, 456ff. Light is thrown upon Russian personalities and politics by A. A. Polovtsev, a senator and state councillor, in his "Dnevnik (Diary)," *KA*, III (1923), 75–172, 319–26; IV (1923), 63–128, 435–42; and also by Boris Nolde, "Les desseins politiques de la Russie," *Monde Slave*, new series, VIII (Jan. 1931), 161–92.

J. C. G. Röhl, *Germany without Bismarck . . . 1890–1900* (Berkeley, Los Angeles, 1967), ch. VII, breaks new ground respecting the kaiser and the fleet program; Jonathan Steinberg, *Yesterday's Deterrent: Tirpitz and the Birth of the German Battle Fleet* (London, 1965) also revises former treatments of the subject in a full-length account of the backgrounds and objectives of the 1898 naval bill. One of the best and fullest recent studies of William II is that of Michael Balfour, *The Kaiser and His Times* (London, 1964). The work by Johannes Haller, *Philip Eulenberg, the Kaiser's Friend* (2 vols. New York, 1930), throws light on the views of both the kaiser and Bülow.

The literature on Austria-Hungary is less detailed and extensive than that on Germany but is creditably represented in English by Arthur J. May, *The Hapsburg Monarchy, 1867–1914* (Cambridge, Mass., 1951); Alfred F. Pribram, *Austria-Hungary and Great Britain, 1908–1918* (London, New York, Toronto, 1951), broader in scope than the title indicates; and Redlich, *Francis Joseph*.

British foreign relations have been well presented by George Monger, *The End of Isolation, 1900–1907* (London, 1963), who utilized unpublished public and private papers to make significant revisions of previous interpretations. Julian Amery, *The Life of Joseph Chamberlain*, IV, *1901–03* (London, 1951); and E. W. Edwards, "The Japanese Alliance and the Anglo-French Agreement of 1904," *History*, XLII (1957), 19–27, likewise offer new facts and interpretations. On Anglo-German tensions at the turn of the century two studies are indispensable: Pauline R. Anderson, *The Background of Anti-English Feeling in Germany, 1890–1902* (Washington, 1929); and Oron J.

Hale, *Publicity and Diplomacy*, chs. VIII, IX. *The History of the Times*, III, (New York, 1947), 335ff., reflects the views of "The Thunderer" and throws light on British policy.

CHAPTER 2. Italy's situation on the eve of negotiations in 1902, her commitments and policies are set forth in Langer, *Diplomacy of Imperialism*, II, passim; A. William Salomone, *Italy in the Giolittian Era* (Philadephia, 1960), pp. 43ff.; Herbert Feis, *Europe the World's Banker* (New Haven, 1930), pp. 241–42; Maggiorino Ferraris, "Public Debt of Italy," *North American Review*, CLXXV (1902), pp. 423–32; and René Pinon, *L'Empire de la Méditerrané* (Paris, 1904), an excellent contemporary exposition, still valuable, of western Mediterranean politics. Recent thorough studies, based upon archival as well as published sources and basic for this whole chapter, are two works by Enrico Serra, *Camille Barrère et l'intesa italo-francese* (Milano, 1950), and *L'intesa mediterranea del 1902* (Milano, 1957); also Andrew, *Théophile Delcassé*. A survey by a scholarly specialist in Italian foreign policy which depicts Italy's relations with her ally is William C. Askew's "Austro-Italian Antagonism, 1896–1914," *Power, Public Opinion and Diplomacy*, ed. L. P. Wallace and Askew (Durham, N.C., 1959), pp. 172–221. Among general studies of the Triple Alliance, an Italian interpretation is that of Luigi Salvatorelli, *La triplice alleanza* (Milano, 1939); and a German narrative history is by Arthur Singer, *Geschichte des Dreibundes* (Leipzig, 1914).

Contemporary testimony concerning Italian statesmen and foreign relations is contained in Luigi Albertini, *Venti anni di vita politica* (2 vols. Bologna, 1950); Maximilian Claar, press chief of the Austro-Hungarian embassy in Rome, "Die Abkehr Italiens vom Dreibund . . . 1901–1903," *EG*, VIII (1930), 425–39, "Tommaso Tittoni (1855–1931) und die Dreibundpolitik Italiens," *KBM*, IX (1931), 417–29, and "Zwanzig Jahre habsburgische Diplomatie in Rome (1895–1915): Persönliche Erinnerungen," *KBM*, XV (1937), 539–67. Also Camille Barrère, "Lettres à Delcassé," *Revue de Paris*, 44th year, II (1937), 721–63, "Le prélude de l'offensive allemande de 1905," 8 *RDM*, VII (1932), 634–41, and "Les responsibilités du Prince de Bulow," 8 *RDM*, III (1931), 89–101; and James Rennell Rodd, *Social and Diplomatic Memories*, third series, *1902–1919* (London, 1925). Later, critical discussions of the Franco-Italian accord that differ in their conclusions are Italicus [E. E. Berger], "Italiens Rückversicherung, 1902, ein Vertragsbruch?" *EG*, VIII (1930), 440–50; and J. Victor Bredt, "Die italienische Rückversicherung," *KBM*, VI (1928), 1166–76.

Anglo-Italian relations are set forth in great detail by James Linus
Glanville, *Italy's Relations with England, 1896–1905*, (The Johns Hopkins University Studies in History and Political Science, Series 52, no.
1, 1934), and are clarified by George Monger, *End of Isolation*.
Amery, *Joseph Chamberlain*, IV, 176ff., and *The History of the Times*,
III, 289ff., supply light upon both British and Italian policies. The
Russian revelation of Italian military commitments to Germany,
briefly noted by Albertini, *Origins*, I, 126–27, are presented through
pertinent documents in "Agressivnye plany Italii v sviazi a pere-
govormi o vozobnovlenii troistvennogo soiuza (Italy's Aggressive
Plans in Connection with the Negotiations over the Renewal of the
Triple Alliance)," *KA*, LXXXVII (1938), 64–88. Léon Noël, *Camille
Barrère* (Paris, 1948), and Jules Alfred Laroche, *Quinze ans à Rome
avec Camille Barrère, 1898–1913* (Paris, 1948), make a few contributions to the portrait of that extraordinary ambassador and his rivalry
with the Germans.

CHAPTER 3. The monographs essential for this chapter are Andrew,
Théophile Delcassé; Monger, *End of Isolation*; and P. J. V. Rollo,
*Entente Cordiale: The Origins and Negotiation of the Anglo-French
Agreement of 8 April 1904* (London, New York, 1969), designed for
students and general readers but an excellent synthesis based upon
printed primary sources. A supplement to Andrew's work is the scholarly study by Bertha R. Leaman, "The Influence of Domestic Policy
on Foreign Affairs in France, 1898–1905," *JMH*, XIV (1942), 449–79.
A thoroughly documented study of French colonialism that is indispensable for the background and objectives of French policy in Morocco and other areas of the Anglo-French agreement is that of Henri
Brunschwig, *Mythes et réalités de l'imperialisme colonial français,
1871–1914* (Paris, 1960; tr. as *French Colonialism*, London, 1964). An
older, useful work is Henri Cambon's *Histoire du Maroc* (Paris,
1952). A monograph, which well utilizes British, French, and German
printed sources is that of Herbert Emil Brenning, *Die grossen Mächte
und Marokko . . . 1898–1904* (Berlin, 1934). The role of Egypt and of
Viceroy Lord Cromer is convincingly presented by Joseph J. Mathews,
Egypt and the Formation of the Anglo-French Entente of 1904 (Philadelphia, 1939). The admirable monograph by Eugene N. Anderson,
The First Moroccan Crisis, 1904–1906 (Chicago, 1930), although written before the publication of the *DDF*, uses the French Yellow Books
and contains a well-organized and reliable treatment of the backgrounds of the crisis.

Besides the memoirs and biographies previously noted and the references in the footnotes, the studies of public opinion by E. Malcolm Carroll and Oron J. Hale, and the scholarly article by E. W. Edwards on "The Japanese Alliance and the Anglo-French Agreement of 1904," (noted under Ch. 1, above) all contribute to the subject of this chapter. To them should be added the well-grounded and presented work by Oron J. Hale, *Germany and the Diplomatic Revolution: A Study in Diplomacy and the Press, 1904–1906* (Philadelphia, 1931); the exposition of French foreign relations by the renowned French journalist André Tardieu, *France and the Alliances: The Struggle for the Balance of Power* (New York, 1908); and an essay on Paul Cambon's use of the German bugbear as a persuasive device, by Hans Hallmann, "Methoden Paul Cambons," *HZ*, CL (1934), 290–305.

CHAPTER 4. The Russian policies and actions before and during the Russo-Japanese war are authoritatively set forth in B. A. Romanov, *Russia in Manchuria, 1892–1906* (Ann Arbor, Mich., 1952), based upon the Russian archives but wretchedly and confusingly organized; and Andrew Malozemoff, *Russian Far Eastern Policy, 1881–1904* (Berkeley, Los Angeles, 1958), a thorough treatment of the causes of the war. An earlier, brilliant essay that puts Russian policy in perspective is B. H. Sumner's "Tsardom and Imperialiam in the Far East and Middle East, 1880–1914," *Proceedings of the British Academy, 1941*, pp. 25–65. Contemporary witnesses of importance are General A. N. Kuropatkin, *The Russian Army and the Japanese War* (2 vols. London, 1909), and "Iz Dvenik" (From the Diary), *KA*, II (1922), 5–177; VII (1924), 55–69; and VIII (1925), 70–100, which vividly record the Chief of Staff's anxieties and the conflicts within the Russian government to 1906; E. J. Dillon, *The Eclipse of Russia* (London, Toronto, 1918), the observations of an outstanding journalist, inspired in part by Witte; and A. Savinsky, *Recollections of a Russian Diplomatist* (London, n.d.), who was at the ministry of foreign affairs during this period. The Japanese side of the story is carefully presented, with attention to the press, by a contemporary, K. Asakawa, *The Russo-Japanese Conflict* (Boston, 1904), but is best interpreted by Ian H. Nish, *The Anglo-Japanese Alliance: The Diplomacy of Two Island Empires, 1894–1907* (University of London Historical Studies, XVIII, 1966), whose research in Japanese primary sources corrects and enriches previous interpretations.

The best exposition of the outbreak and the diplomacy of the war is the skilful monograph by John Albert White, *The Diplomacy of the*

Russo-Japanese War (Princeton, 1964), but earlier treatments are still useful: William L. Langer, "The Origins of the Russo-Japanese War," *Explorations in Crisis: Papers on International History*, ed. Carl E. and Elizabeth Schorske (Cambridge, Mass., 1969), pp. 3–45, first published in 1926; and David S. Crist, "Russia's Far Eastern Policy in the Making," *JMH*, XIV (1942), 317–41. British policy is best delineated by Nish, and by Monger, *End of Isolation*, while bits of information are supplied in addition to the biographies of Lansdowne and Edward VII by Kenneth Young, *Arthur James Balfour* (London, 1963), and *The Letters and Friendships of Sir Cecil Spring-Rice*, ed. Stephen Gwynn (2 vols. London, 1929). Spring-Rice was a close friend of the Roosevelts and secretary at the St. Petersburg embassy. French involvement in the war is brought out with new facts and interpretation by Andrew, *Théophile Delcassé*, and documented in addition to the *DDF* by Paul Cambon's *Correspondance*, his biography by his son, and by Paléologue's *Un grand tournant de la politique mondiale* (see above Part I).

The close German relations with Russia, revealed in *GP*, XIX, and the memoirs of Bülow and Holstein are best interpreted by Jonathan Steinburg, "Germany and the Russo-Japanese War," *AHR*, LXXV (1970), 1965–86, and in part explained by Kwang-Ching Liu, "German Fear of a Quadruple Alliance, 1904–1905," *JMH*, XVIII (1946), 222–40. Walter Hubatsch, *Der Admiralstab und die obersten Marinebehörden* (Frankfurt-am-Main, 1958), notes Tirpitz's reservations about an alliance in 1904. Russian documents on the Björkö episode, first published in *KA*, are translated with an introduction by Alfred von Wegerer in "Björkoe," *KBM*, II (1924), 453–501, and the story of the fiasco is ably told by Eugene N. Anderson, *First Moroccan Crisis*, ch. xv. The effects on naval policy of the war scares in 1904–1905 are described by Arthur J. Marder, *From the Dreadnought to Scapa Flow*, I, *The Road to War, 1904–1914* (London, 1961), 107ff., and E. L. Woodward, *Great Britain and the German Navy* (Oxford, 1935), 52ff.

The position and policy of the United States are explained by Alfred L. P. Dennis, *Adventures in American Diplomacy, 1896–1906* (New York, 1928), chs. xiii, xiv; and Tyler Dennett, *Roosevelt and the Russo-Japanese War* (New York 1925), both of which were based upon unpublished sources. A more recent brief but sound study is that of Luella J. Hall, "A Partnership in Peacemaking: Theodore Roosevelt and William II," *Pacific Historical Review*, XIII (1944), 390–411.

CHAPTER 5. The best study of the crisis through the Conference of Algeciras is Anderson's *First Moroccan Crisis*, and it is complemented by Hale's *Germany and the Diplomatic Revolution* (see above, Ch. 3), with emphasis on the press. Two contemporary accounts are by E. D. Morel, *Morocco in Diplomacy* (London, 1912), which portrays the wickedness of Anglo-French diplomacy and, André Tardieu, *La Conférence d'Algesiras* (Paris, 1907), which treats the subject in great detail. German policy to 31 March 1905 is best set forth by Pierre Guillen, *L'Allemagne et le Maroc de 1870 à 1905* (Paris, 1967), whose painstakingly researched work, based upon archival as well as published material, replaces previous treatments, although Francis T. Williamson, *Germany and Morocco before 1905* (The Johns Hopkins University Studies in History and Political Sciences, LV, no. 1, 1937), is still valuable for German commercial activities. The *Holstein Papers*, IV, and Rich, *Friedrich von Holstein*, II, 682ff. clarify and revise former interpretations of German policy during the crisis, while source materials supplementary to the *GP* are provided by Friedrich Thimme, "Aus dem Nachlass des Fürsten Radolin," *KBM*, XV (1937), 725–63; and "Graf Monts und Luzzatti," *EG*, IX (1931), 449–78. Hallgarten, *Imperialismus vor 1914*, I, 599ff., analyzes the *dessous politique* of armament manufacturers and businessmen; and Gerhard Ritter, *The Schlieffen Plan* (New York, 1958), critically examines the military. On the French side, the most important works are Andrew, *Théophile Delcassé*, to his fall in June 1905; and Paléologue, *Un grand tournant de la politique mondiale*. Also useful are Neton, *Delcassé*, and *Paul Cambon* by Henri Cambon for the defense of Delcassé's policy. Special studies include August Bach, "Delcassés Sturz," *KBM*, XV (1937), 1070–1112, which defends German policy; Pierre Muret, "La politique personnelle de Rouvier et la chute de Delcassé," *RHGM*, XVII (1939), which in condemning Rouvier, on the basis of both unpublished and published sources, completely catalogues contemporary and subsequent revelations concerning Delcassé's fall; and Leaman, "Influence of Domestic Policy on Foreign Affairs in France," (see above, Ch. 3) which brings out the forces opposing Delcassé.

British involvement in the Moroccan crisis is best described by Monger, *End of Isolation*. An article that throws new light on Anglo-German relations before and during the Conference of Algeciras is by S. L. Mayer, "Anglo-German Rivalry at the Algeciras Conference," *Britain and Germany in Africa*, ed. Gifford Prosser and William Roger Louis (New Haven, London, 1967), pp. 215–44. The Anglo-French and Belgian military talks were first soundly described by George Aston, "The Entente Cordiale and the 'Military Conversations'," *Quarterly Review*, CCLVIII (1932), 363–83, on the foundations of research and close personal association with the principals. J. D. Hargreaves, "The Origin of the Anglo-French Military Conversations in 1905," *History*, XXXVI (1951), 244–48, is a "revision" that is now in need of revision in the light of Monger's study. Jonathan E. Helmreich, "Belgian Concern over Neutrality and British Intentions, 1906–14," *JMH*, XXXVI (1964), 416–27, utilizes archival sources to clarify Belgian policy. Samuel R. Williamson, Jr., *The Politics of Grand Strategy: Britain and France Prepare for War, 1904–1914* (Cambridge, Mass., 1969), has searched archives and private papers to produce a definitive study of the political and strategic development of the Entente Cordiale.

Both Dennis, *Adventures in American Diplomacy*, ch. xix, and Joseph Bucklin Bishop, *Theodore Roosevelt* (2 vols. New York, 1920), are still indispensable for Roosevelt's mediation between France and Germany and for the United States at the Algeciras Conference.

CHAPTER 6. A reliable framework for the major portion of this chapter is Rogers Platt Churchill's *Anglo-Russian Convention of 1907* (Cedar Rapids, Iowa, 1939), which analyzes the background as well as the negotiations in a well-organized exposition. An earlier work that utilized all available documents, including the Russian, and summarized them faithfully, is that of Ludwig Poltz, *Die anglo-russische Entente, 1903–1907* (Hamburg, 1932). Russian documents pertaining to the negotiation of the convention are in S. Pashukanis, ed., "K istorii anglo-russkogo soglashenya 1907 g. (On the History of the Anglo-Russian Agreement of 1907)," *KA*, LXIX–LXX (1935), 3–39; I. Reisner, ed., "Anglo-russkaya konventsiya 1907 g. i Razdel Afganistana (The Anglo-Russian Convention of 1907 and the Partition of Afghanistan)," *KA*, X (1925), 54–66. Special studies on aspects of the negotiations are Briton Cooper Busch, *Britain and the Persian Gulf, 1894–1914* (Berkeley, Los Angeles, 1967), developed from a dissertation with the aid of materials in London, India, and the United States to be a compendium of information on the subject; another very thorough study using archival sources, Jens B. Plass, *England zwischen Russland und Deutschland: Der persische Golf in der Britischen Vorkriegspolitik, 1899–1907* (Hamburg, 1966), puts more emphasis on the press and commercial policy; a dissertation by William Habberton, *Anglo-Russian Relations concerning Afghanistan, 1837–1907* (Illinois Studies in the Social Sciences, XXI, no. 4, 1937) is a handy survey; similar but more recent is Firuz Kazemzadeh's *Russia and Britain in Persia, 1864–1914* (New Haven, London, 1968). On the Bagdad railway, the classic study by Edward Mead Earle, *Turkey, the Great*

Powers, and the Bagdad Railway (New York, 1923), is still useful but has been supplanted in large part by John B. Wolf, *The Diplomatic History of the Bagdad Railroad* (University of Missouri Studies, XI, no. 2, 1936), written mainly on the basis of the British and German documents. Additional sources in the *DDF* are used, for example, by Hallgarten's *Imperialismus vor 1914*. Richard M. Francis throws new light on the British attitude toward the railway in "The British Withdrawal from the Bagdad Railway Project in April 1903," *HJ*, XVI (1973), 168–78. A scholarly and well documented study by E. W. Edwards, "The Far Eastern Agreements of 1907," *JMH*, XXVI (1954), 340–55, brings out their relationship to the Anglo-Russian agreement.

On the policy and position of the powers, Wilhelm Schüssler, *Deutschland zwischen Russland und England . . . 1879–1914* (3rd. ed. Leipzig, 1940), deals briefly with the situation in 1906–1907. Monger, *End of Isolation*, brings to an end his brilliant study of British policy with the conclusion of the Russian convention. An essay that stresses the Indian security problem is that of Beryl J. Williams, "The Strategic Background to the Anglo-Russian Entente of August 1907," *HJ*, IX (1966), 360–73. Among the British biographies and memoirs, Nicolson's *Portait of a Diplomatist . . . Carnock* and Grey's *Twenty-Five Years* are most important for the subject of this chapter. On the side of Russia, most illuminating is Taube's *La politique russe*, for he was directly involved in the negotiation of the Baltic and North Sea pacts. A. V. Neklyudov, "Souvenirs diplomatiques," 6 *RDM*, XLIV (1918), 127–44, thinks that Björkö was a turning point in the Russian attitude toward Britain. For Izvolsky and his policies the best interpretation is that of W. M. Carlgren, *Iswolsky und Aehrenthal vor der bosnischen Annexionskrise: Russische und österreichisch-ungarische Balkanpolitik, 1906–1908* (Uppsala, 1955), although its main thrust is toward the Balkans. On the Russian Straits policy, William L. Langer, "Russia, the Straits Question, and the European Powers, 1904–1908," *EHR*, XLIV (1929), 59–85 (reprinted in *Explorations in Crisis*, pp. 46–75), is still the best guide to the complicated problem.

CHAPTER 7. A very brief treatment of Macedonia in the twentieth century is by Elizabeth Barker, *Macedonia: Its Place in Balkan Politics* (London, New York, 1950); and an excellent exposition of ethnic complexities and the events of 1902–1908 is by H. R. Wilkinson, *Maps and Politics: A Review of the Ethnographic Cartography of Macedonia* (Liverpool, 1951). A contemporary account of events up to 1904 is the Maxwell Memorandum, 1 February 1904: *BD*, V, 51ff.

Erich Rathmann, *Die Balkanfrage, 1904–1908, und das Werden der Tripelentente* (Halle, 1932), is a competent dissertation that overemphasizes conscious planning, especially by British diplomats; and Wade Dewood David, *European Diplomacy in the Eastern Question, 1906–1909* (Illinois Studies in the Social Sciences, XXV, No. 4, 1940), is another dissertation that, although poorly written, embraces a mass of material, including Turkish, and makes a useful contribution. M. S. Anderson, *The Eastern Question, 1774–1923* (London, New York, 1966), is an excellent synthesis that briefly treats of 1902–1909. The Serbian aspect of the Balkan scene is best set forth, stylistically and substantively, by W. S. Vucinich, *Serbia between East and West: The events of 1903–1908* (Stanford, 1954). An indispensable work that contributes fresh interpretations of personalities and policies is W. M. Carlgren's *Iswolsky und Aehrenthal vor der bosnischen Annexionskrise*. A Russian viewpoint is well represented in the memoirs of Taube, *La politique russe*. Soloman Wank has added to our knowledge and understanding of Aehrenthal in "Aehrenthal and the Policy of Action" (Dissertation, Columbia University, 1966); "Aehrenthal and the Sanjak of Novibazar Railway Project," *SEER*, XLII (1964), 352–69; and "Aehrenthal's Program for the Constitutional Transformation of the Habsburg Monarchy," ibid., XLI (1963), 513–36. A documentary contribution is that of Eurof Walters, "Unpublished Documents: Aehrenthal's Attempt in 1907 to Re-Group the European Powers," ibid., XXX (1951), 213–51. Additional source material as well as sober interpretations of Austro-Hungarian policy is supplied by Hantsch, *Berchtold*, using his diary and unpublished memoirs. Additional studies on the Balkan railway projects are Arthur J. May, "The Novibazar Railway Project," *JMH*, X (1938), 496–527; and "Trans-Balkan Railway Schemes," *JMH*, XXIV (1952), 352–67. The relationship of Reval to the Young Turk revolution is put in correct perspective by Ernest E. Ramsauer, *The Young Turks* (Princeton, 1957).

Coming to the Bosnian crisis, two studies form the framework for any synopsis: Bernadotte E. Schmitt, *The Annexation of Bosnia, 1908–09* (Cambridge, Eng., 1937), a thorough exposition in great detail; and Momčilo Ninčić, *Le crise bosniaque (1908–1909) et les puisances européennes* (2 vols. Paris, 1937), which complements Schmitt's work, bringing to a thorough study the benefit of experience as a onetime foreign minister of Yugoslavia. N. V. Charykov affords some sidelights on Izvolsky and the tsar in "Reminiscences of Nicholas II," *Contemporary Review*, CXXXIV (1928), 445–53; and *Glimpses of*

High Politics through War and Peace (New York, 1931). The tsar's letters to his mother are poorly translated in Edward J. Bing, ed., *Secret Letters of the Last Tsar* (New York, Toronto, 1938), and are best consulted in "Iz Perepiski Nikolaya II i Marii Feodorovny, 1907–1910 gg." (From the Letters of Nicholas II and Maria Feodorovna, 1907–1910), *KA*, L–LI (1932), 175–93. Kokovtsov, *Out of My Past*, pp. 214ff., describes the government's reaction to Izvolsky's policy, and W. L. Langer, "Russia, the Straits Question, and the European Powers" (see above Ch. VI) analyzes Izvolsky's failure to win the Straits. On Austria-Hungary, two sources are important for a grasp of informed public opinion: Baernreither, *Fragments of a Political Diary*, and Redlich, *Schicksalsjahre Österreichs*. Also a valuable study is that of the renowned historian, A. F. Pribram, *Austria-Hungary and Great Britain*. British policy has been freshly and convincingly interpreted by M. B. Cooper, "British Policy in the Balkans, 1908–1909," *HJ*, VII, (1964), 258–79. For Germany an essential source and an illuminating interpretation are *The Holstein Papers*, I and IV, and Rich, *Holstein*. French attitudes and policy are best gleaned from *DDF*, and Italian from Albertini, *Origins*, I, 219ff.

CHAPTER 8. There are no outstanding special studies on the relations of Russia with Austria-Hungary and Germany, 1909–1910, which must be studied mainly in published documents, of which Siebert and Schreiner (*Entente Diplomacy*) and the *Livre noir* become important sources in this period, supplemented by A. Popov, ed., "Turetskaya revolutsiya, 1908–1909 gg." (Turkish Revolution, 1908–1909), *KA*, XLV (1931), 27–52; and A. Erusalimski, ed., "K istorii Potsdamskogo soglashenya 1911 g." (On the History of the Potsdam Agreement, 1911), *KA*, LVIII (1933), 46–57. Aspects of Russian and Austrian policy are treated briefly in William L. Langer, "Russia, the Straits Question, and the Origins of the Balkan League," *PSQ*, XLIII (1928), 321–63 (also in *Explorations in Crisis*, pp. 91–127), a sound treatment, but in part revised by later studies; Ernst C. Helmreich, *The Diplomacy of the Balkan Wars, 1912–1913* (Cambridge, Mass., 1938); and Hans Uebersberger, *Österreich zwischen Russland und Serbien* (Cologne, Graz, 1958), based upon Austrian, Russian, and Serbian sources but obviously written to defend the policy of the Dual Monarchy. On Balkan and Turkish affairs the old and painfully detailed work of William Miller, *The Ottoman Empire and Its Successors* (rev. ed. Cambridge, Eng., 1923), is a valuable reference; and on economic rivalries in Persia, Eugene Staley, *War and the Private*

Investor (New York, 1935), pursues his theme that politics, not economics, governs the decision-makers, while Hallgarten, *Imperialismus*, II, 179ff. takes the opposite view.

The Anglo-German naval rivalry is portrayed in studies of the naval policy of each country. A recent work on German plans, Volker R. Berghahn, "Zu den Zielen des deutschen Flottenbau unter Wilhelm II," *HZ, CCX* (1970), 34–100, analyzes the previous studies and charts a new approach based upon archival research that he has himself pursued in *Der Tirpitz-Plan* (Düsseldorf, 1971). Cf. the critical review by Jonathan Steinberg in *HJ*, XVI (1973), 196–204. The work of Gerhard Ritter, *The Sword and the Scepter*, II (Coral Gables, Fla., 1970; tr. from the 2nd ed., *Staatskunst und Kriegshandwerk*, Munich, 1965), 162ff., critically describes the German policy and position in the face of British opposition. The works of Arthur J. Marder, *The Anatomy of British Sea Power* (New York, 1940), and *From the Dreadnought to Scapa Flow*, I, *The Road to War, 1904–1914*, are masterly expositions of British policy and accomplishments, while E. L. Woodward, *Great Britain and the German Navy*, though lacking many sources available to Marder, well delineates the diplomacy of the conflict from the British viewpoint. The role of Ballin in Anglo-German negotiations is brought out in two biographies: Lamar Cecil, *Albert Ballin: Business and Politics in Imperial Germany, 1888–1918* (Princeton, 1967), a reexamination in the light of archival sources; and Bernhard Huldermann, *Albert Ballin* (London, 1922), by one of Ballin's intimate co-workers who had access to his private papers.

CHAPTER 9. Two books deal exhaustively with the Agadir crisis and its background: André Tardieu, *Le mystère d'Agadir* (Paris, 1912), a detailed treatment by an active participant as a journalist and entrepreneur which has the shortcomings of contemporaneity and personal involvement; and Irma Barlow, *The Agadir Crisis* (Chapel Hill, N.C., 1940) a comprehensive study stretching from the aftermath of Algeciras to the resolution of the crisis, but requiring corrections in some details and interpretations in the light of material in 2 *DDF*, XI–XIV (Paris, 1950–1955). The other major French source is Joseph Caillaux's three works: *Agadir* (Paris, 1919), *D'Agadir à la grande pénitence* (Paris, 1933), and *Mes Mémoires*, II, *Mes audaces—Agadir, 1909–1912* (Paris, 1943). Considering the time lapse, there is a surprising congruity in these three, but the *Mémoires* contain the fullest account of Agadir and are, on the whole, consistent with the published documents. On the German side the most important memoirs are those of Oscar Freiherr von der Lancken Wakenitz, *Meine dreissig Dienstjahre, 1888–1918* (Berlin, 1931); Wilhelm Freiherr von Schoen, *The Memoirs of an Ambassador* (London, 1922), which are less revealing than Lancken's; and *Kiderlen-Waechter*, ed. Ernst Jäckh. The principal German primary source, however, is *GP*, XXIV and XXIX.

A special study of the 1909 agreement which, is based upon both the German and British archives and makes a genuine contribution to our knowledge of it is E. W. Edwards, "The Franco-German Agreement on Morocco, 1909," *EHR*, LXXVIII (1963), 483–513. The background and consequences of the agreement are treated in great detail by Raymond Poidevin, *Les relations économiques et financières entre la France et l'Allemagne de 1898 à 1914* (Paris, 1969), pp. 439–47, 458–510, 609–11. On the attempts to establish Franco-German cooperation, 1909–1911, both Eugene Staley, *War and the Private Investor* (see above, Ch. 8), and Hallgarten, *Imperialismus*, have unearthed a wealth of detail but often differ in their interpretations of it. On the crisis itself, two early German studies without benefit of the *DDF* but stimulating in their analyses are Fritz Hartung, "Die Marokkokrise des Jahres 1911," *APG*, VII (1926), 54–117; and H. E. Enthoven, "Kiderlen-Waechter und die deutsche Agadir-Politik," *EG*, X (1932), 192–208. F. W. Pick illuminates the planning of the *Panther's* leap and subsequent policy in *Searchlight on German Africa: The Diaries and Papers of Dr. W. CH. Regendanz* (London, 1939), while more recently Joanne Stafford Mortimer has added a scholarly study using the German archives in "Commercial Interests and German Diplomacy in the Agadir Crisis," *HJ*, X (1967), 440–56. Fritz Fischer, *Krieg der Illusionen: Die deutsche Politik von 1911 bis 1914* (2nd ed. Düsseldorf, 1969), ch. 5, expands the critical and provocative analysis of German policy that he first presented briefly in *Griff nach der Weltmacht* (2nd ed. Düsseldorf, 1962; translated as *Germany's Aims in the First World War*, New York, 1967). Samuel R. Williamson, Jr., *Politics of Grand Strategy* (see above Ch. 5), pp. 141ff, and ch. 7, well analyzes and interprets the repercussions of the Agadir crisis upon Anglo-French military and naval cooperation. Nabil M. Kaylani, "British Policy toward France and Germany in the Moroccan Question, 1909–1912" (dissertation, Clark University, 1967), contributes significant sidelights from the British Foreign Office papers.

CHAPTER 10. The only first-rate study of the Italo-Turkish war and its repercussions is that of William C. Askew, *Europe and Italy's Acquisition of Libya, 1911–1912* (Durham, N.C., 1942), which in its sober and comprehensive analysis of the subject takes into account all of the primary sources. The economic and domestic backgrounds are well treated in Staley's *War and the Private Investor*, and A. William Salomone, *Italy in the Giolittian Era*. The essential materials on the Russian attempt to open the Straits are more extensive. The earliest study in English is W. L. Langer, *PSQ*, XLIII, 321–63 (also in *Explorations in Crisis*, pp. 91–107), but the later publication of Russian documents (2 *MO*) made some revisions necessary that were first noted by Philip Mosely, "Russian Policy in 1911–12," *JMH*, XII (1940), 69–86, and treated in greater detail by Edward C. Thaden, "Charykov and Russian Foreign Policy at Constantinople in 1911," *JCEH*, XVI (1956), 25–44. He has dealt with the same subject more briefly in *Russia and the Balkan Alliances of 1912* (University Park, Pa., 1965), using the Russian documents to throw new light on Russian policy in 1911–1912. Feroz Ahmad, *The Young Turks* (Oxford, 1969), adds helpful information about the Turkish attitude toward both the "Charykov Kite" and the war with Italy.

The Haldane Mission and the Anglo-French understanding of 1912 are dealt with by E. L. Woodward, *Great Britain and the German Navy*, whose early account has been updated in the light of sources available since 1935 by Richard Longhorne, "The Naval Question in Anglo-German Relation, 1912–1914," *HJ*, XIV (1971), 359–70, and by Marder, *From the Dreadnought to Scapa Flow*, I. Sources of prime importance are Winston S. Churchill, *The World Crisis* (London, 1923), essentially memoirs of his post at the Admiralty; Sir Frederick Maurice, *Haldane, 1856–1915* (London, 1937), who quotes Haldane's letters to his mother from Berlin, thus supplementing his own account in *Before the War* (New York, London, 1920). Cecil's and Huldermann's books on Ballin (see above, Ch. 8) tell of the *pourparlers* of the Haldane mission, and Ritter, *The Sword and the Scepter*, II, and Fritz Fischer, *Krieg der Illusionen*, assess German policy. J. C. G. Röhl, "Admiral von Müller and the Approach of War, 1911–1914," *HJ*, XII (1969), 651–73, distills the contributions from Müller's diary and other sources that help to clarify German thinking. Special articles still useful in interpreting the Haldane mission are B. E. Schmitt, "Lord Haldane's Mission to Berlin in 1912," *The Crusades and Other Historical Essays* (ed. Louis J. Paetow, New York, 1928), pp. 245–88; and Ernst C. Helmreich, "Die Haldane Mission," *KBM*, XII (1934), 112–43. The most recent and the best study of Anglo-French relations and negotiations in 1912–1913, researched in archives and private papers, is Williamson, *Politics of Grand Strategy*, chs. 9–12.

The revisionist literature of the 1920's on Franco-Russian relations and the policy of Poincaré and Izvolsky is too restricted in its foundation of primary sources and too biased in interpretation to be a reliable guide, but reflects views that must be analyzed and weighed. Most important are: Harry Elmer Barnes, *The Genesis of the World War* (New York, 1927), Alfred Fabre-Luce, *The Limitations of Victory* (New York, 1926), and Friedrich Stieve, *Isvolsky and the World War* (London, 1926). Besides Poincaré's defense in his memoirs, contemporaries who countered the revisionists are Hermann Kantorowicz, *Gutachten zur Kriegsschuldfrage 1914* (Frankfurt-am-Main, 1967), Bernadotte E. Schmitt, *The Coming of the War*, I, and G. P. Gooch, *Before the War*, in his chapter on Poincaré.

CHAPTER 11. The thorough and comprehensive study of the Balkan wars by Ernst C. Helmreich, *The Diplomacy of the Balkan Wars*, remains the best exposition of the subject, despite the lack of revision in details concerning the Balkan League which subsequent publication of Russian documents shows are necessary. Ivan Geshov, *The Balkan League* (London, 1915), must also be supplemented by the Russian documents. The diaries of Baernreither and Redlich are valuable for Austro-Hungarian policy, and the monograph by Hans Uebersberger, *Osterreich zwischen Russland und Serbien*, utilizes Serbian and Russian as well as Austrian sources, but the most important study is Hantsch's *Berchtold*, which by summarizing and quoting Berchtold's unpublished papers and memoirs fills a previous gap in primary source material and makes more intelligible, if not excusable, Austro-Hungarian policy. Nothing on Russia provides equally significant data, but in addition to Taube's memoirs, Paul Miliukov, *Political Memoirs, 1905–1917* (Ann Arbor, Mich., 1967), and Horst Jablonski, "Die Stellungsnahme der russischen Parteien zur Aussenpolitik der Regierung," *Forschungen zur osteuropäischen Geschichte*, V (1957), 60–92, contribute some bits of information, as do the memoirs of such Russian and British diplomats as Neklyudov and Sir George Buchanan, *My Mission to Russia*, Vol. I (Boston, 1923). An important biographical essay on Hartwig by a Serbian who knew him well is Marco [Božin Simić], "Nikolaus Hartwig," *KBM*, VI (1928), 745–69. Alfred F. Pribram, *Austria-Hungary and Great Britain, 1908–1914* (see above, Ch. 7), presents excellent accounts of the London ambassadorial conference within the context of Anglo-Austrian relations. On the Balkans, Herbert Adams Gibbons, *The New Map of Europe, 1911–1914* (New York, 1911) is still valuable for the testimony of a contemporary journalist, and on Albania a recent account of her establishment is included in Stavro Skendi, *The Albanian National Awakening, 1878–1913* (Princeton, 1967).

CHAPTER 12. Ernst C. Helmreich, *Diplomacy of the Balkan Wars*, ably deals with the Austro-Hungarian-Serbian conflict in the autumn of 1913. The fullest and still the best exposition of the Liman von Sanders crisis is by Robert J. Kerner, "The Mission of Liman von Sanders," *SR*, VI (1927), 12–27, 344–63; (1928), 543–60; and VII (1928), 90–112. He has also touched upon it in "Russia, the Straits, and Constantinople, 1914–15," *JMH*, I (1929), 400–15. Michael T. Florinsky adds a footnote in defense of Sazonov in his introduction to a letter from Kokovtsov, "Russia and Constantinople: Count Kokovtsov's Evidence," *FA*, VIII (1929), 135–41. A later account and interpretation of the crisis by Hans Herzfeld, "Die Liman-Krise and die Politik der Grossmächte in der Jahreswende 1913/14," *KBM*, XI (1933), 837–58, 973–93, still lacked the evidence on Franco-Russian relations in 3 *DDF*, VIII and IX, and thus erroneously interpreted them.

The negotiations in and about Turkey, 1913–1914, are thoroughly studied and interpreted with the aid of Russian as well as western Europe documents (except the French) by Harry N. Howard, *The Partition of Turkey* (Norman, Okla., 1931). The Bagdad railway negotiations are summarized by both Earle and Wolf (noted above, Ch. 6), and the Anglo-German talks about the Portuguese colonies are clarified in a study that breaks new ground, by William Roger Louis, "Great Britain and German Expansion in Africa," *Britain and Germany in Africa* (see above, Ch. 5), pp. 3–46. Herbert Butterfield, *History and Human Relations* (London, 1951), pp. 211–15, calls attention to fear of Russia as a feature of British policy. The treatment of Entente diplomacy, 1913–1914, by Hermann Lutz, *Lord Grey and the World War* (London, 1928), like that of Stieve, *Isvolsky and the World War*, is not supported by the British and French documents that came out later than either publication. Theodor Wolff, *The Eve of 1914* (New York, 1936), as former editor of the *Berliner Tageblatt*, tells the story of the German discovery of Anglo-German naval discussions, while John C. Cairns, "International Politics and the Military Mind: The Case of the French Republic, 1911–1914," *JMH*, XXV (1953), 273–85, reveals the underlying doubt of Russian military capabilities, as well as confidence in their own strength, of the French military. Both Gerhard Ritter (*Sword and Scepter*) and Fritz Fischer

(*Krieg der Illusionen*) give much attention, with differing emphases, to the Moltke-Conrad exchanges and the question of preventive war on the eve of the July crisis. Recent works that contribute to our knowledge of events in 1914 are Gerard E. Silberstein, *The Troubled Alliance: German-Austrian Relations, 1914 to 1917* (Lexington, Ky., 1970), and Ulrich Trumpener, *Germany and the Ottoman Empire, 1914–1918* (Princeton, 1968).

CHAPTERS 13–15. The fullest and most recent treatment of the Sarajevo crime that replaces most of the previous literature is Vladimir Dedijer, *The Road to Sarajevo* (London, New York, 1966), the main conclusions of which are condensed in "Sarajevo, Fifty Years After," *FA*, XLII (1964), 569–84. Dennison I. Rusinow, "Assassination at Sarajevo: The Fiftieth Anniversary," American University Field Staff, *Reports Service*, Southeast Europe series, XI, no. 6 (Yugoslavia) (1964), 779–96, points out how Serbian and Yugoslav party and personal interests, as well as other national biases, have distorted studies of the crime. A popularly written account that uses the results of research in unpublished sources is Joachim Remak, *Sarajveo, the Story of a Political Murder* (London, 1959). The court record of the trial of Princip and his fellow conspirators was published by Albert Mousset, *Un drame historique: L'attentat de Sarajevo* (Paris, 1930); and interesting revelations of Princip's motivations are recorded by his physician and translated by H. F. Armstrong in "Confessions of the Assassin whose Deed Led to the World War," *CH*, XXVI (1927), 699–707. Classic interpretations of the plot are R. W. Seton-Watson, *Sarajevo: A Study in the Origins of the Great War* (London, n.d.), a sound analysis; and Edith Durham, *The Sarajevo Crime* (London, 1925), rabidly anti-Serbian.

On the July crisis the older works, such as Fay, Renouvin (*The Immediate Origins of the War*, New Haven, 1928), Schmitt and Albertini, are useful for their meticulous recording of day-to-day events, rather than their interpretations. Of the recent studies, Fritz Fischer, *Griff nach der Weltmacht* (2nd ed.), ch. 2, and *Krieg der Illusionen* (2nd ed.), ch. 22, add archival material and spell out the thesis of German war guilt by virtue of the decision to wage a preventive war in the drive for world power. Imanuel Geiss has rendered a service to students of the crisis in his *Julikrise und Kriegsausbruch 1914* (2 vols. Hannover, 1963–1964), by publishing the significant primary sources, mostly documents, of all the powers. His introductions interpret the sources as proof of the Fischer thesis. He has published about a third of the sources, with rewritten introductions, in translation, *July 1914: The Outbreak of the First World War* (New York, 1967). He also edited a unique study by the German jurist Hermann Kantorowicz, *Gutachten zur Kriegsschuldfrage 1914*, suppressed when written in the 1920's, which contains a penetrating analysis of the crisis that supports the anti-revisionist view of German war guilt. James Joll, *The Unspoken Assumptions* (London, 1968), stresses the importance of knowing the presuppositions of statesmen, and suggests ways of discovering them.

The role of Austria-Hungary is illuminated by the memoirs of Conrad, Redlich, Wladimir Giesl, *Zwei Jahrzehnten im Nahen Orient* (Berlin, 1927), Heinrich Graf von Lützow, *Im diplomatischen Dienst der K. und K. Monarchie* (Munich, 1971), Alexander Freiherr von Musulin, *Das Haus am Ballplatz: Erinnerungen* (Munich, 1924), and by Hantsch's *Berchtold*. Jan Opocénský, "A Wartime Discussion of Responsibility for the War," *JMH*, IV (1932), 415–29, published correspondence between Hoyos and Mérey, putting the blame for the war on Germany. An early revealing exposition of Austro-Hungarian procedure is Roderick Gooss, *Das Wiener Kabinett und die Entstehung des Weltkrieges* (Vienna, 1919). A recent collection of papers presented at the Budapest historical conference of 1964 which offers critical Marxist interpretations of the Monarchy's policy and relations is *Österreich-Ungarn in der Weltpolitik, 1900 bis 1918* (Berlin, 1965). A recent study by Norman Stone, "Hungary and the Crisis of July 1914," *1914, the Coming of the First World War* (ed. Laqueur and Mosse, New York, 1966), pp. 147–64, adds new insights, with the aid of unpublished sources, into Tisza's views.

Germany's decisions have been most thoroughly reviewed in the literature of the 1960's, with much emphasis upon Bethmann Hollweg because of the discovery of his friend Riezler's diary. Among the most important studies are Karl D. Erdmann, "Zur Beurteilung Bethmann Hollwegs," *Geschichte in Wissenschaft und Unterricht* (1964), pp. 525–40 (inaccessible to me and used at second hand); Imanuel Geiss, "Zur Beurteilung der deutschen Reichspolitik im ersten Weltkrieg," *Hamburger Studien zur neueren Geschichte*, II (1965), 49–82; Andreas Hillgruber, *Deutschlands Rolle in der Vorgeschichte der beiden Weltkriege* (Göttingen, 1967), a modification of the Fischer thesis with emphasis upon Bethmann's responsibility, and "Riezlers Theorie des kalkulierten Risikos und Bethmann Hollwegs politische Konzeption in der Julikrise 1914," *HZ*, CCII (1966), 333–51; Konrad H. Jarausch, "The Illusion of Limited War: Chancellor Bethmann

Hollweg's Calculated Risk, July 1914," *CEH*, II (1969), 48–76, an excellent analysis after unrestricted access to the Riezler diary; and Fritz Stern, "Bethmann Hollweg and the War: The Limits of Responsibility," *The Responsibility of Power* (ed. Leonard Krieger and Fritz Stern, Garden City, N.Y., 1967), pp. 252–85, who also had access to Riezler's diary. One of Fischer's principal critics has been Gerhard Ritter in "Eine neue Kriegsschuldthese?" *HZ*, CVIC (1962), 657–68, also tr. in *The Outbreak of the First World War: Who or What Was Responsible?*, (ed. Dwight E. Lee; 3rd ed. Lexington, Mass., 1970), pp. 103–09; and "Bethmann Hollweg im Schlaglicht des deutschen Geschichts-Revisionismus," *Schweizer Monatshefte*, Jahrgang 42 (1962), 799–808, but his own treatment of the July crisis in *The Sword and the Scepter*, II, has its share of errors, as pointed out by Geiss, *Julikrise*, I, 25–26, and by Norman Stone, "Gerhard Ritter and the First World War," *HJ*, XIII (1970), 158–71. A supporter of Ritter's viewpoint is Egmont Zechlin, "Deutschland zwischen Kabinettskrieg und Wirtschaftskrieg," *HZ*, CIC (1964), 347–458. Two articles that well summarize the debate from differing viewpoints are Imanuel Geiss, "Le déclenchement de la première guerre mondiale," *RH* CCXXXII (1964), 415–26; and Wolfgang J. Mommsen, "The Debate on German War Aims," *1914: The Coming of the First World War*, pp. 45–70, who criticizes the Fischer thesis and suggests further research. An excellent review that points out the contributions and faults of Ritter and Fischer is that of Klaus Epstein, "Gerhard Ritter and the First World War," *1914*, pp. 186–203.

British policy has been illuminated by Cameron Hazlehurst, *Politicians at War, July 1914 to May 1915*, Part I (New York, 1971). The older works by the Earl of Oxford and Asquith, *Memories and Reflections, 1852–1927* (2 vols. Boston, 1928), and David Lloyd George, *War Memoirs*, I (Boston, 1933), must be added to those by Grey and Nicolson. John Morley, *Memorandum on Resignation, August 1914* (London, 1928), is an important source. The studies of British policy by Herman Lutz, *Lord Grey and the World War*, and Max Montgelas, *British Foreign Policy under Sir Edward Grey* (New York, 1928), are penetrating but often misleading analyses. The influence of Crowe and Nicolson upon Grey has been convincingly reassessed by Zara S. Steiner in *The Foreign Office and Foreign Policy, 1898–1914*.

France has not been recently studied in depth. The defense of her policy has been best presented by Poincaré in his memoirs. Raymond Recouly, *Les heures tragique d'avant guerre* (Paris, n.d.), offers testimony on events as gleaned by a journalist.

Russia's decision to mobilize is critically examined by Gunter Frantz, *Russlands Eintritt in den Weltkrieg* (Berlin, 1924), and "Wie Russland 1914 mobilmachte," *KBM*, XIV (1936), 277–318; Michael T. Florinsky, "The Russian Mobilization of 1914," *PSQ*, XLII (1927), 203–27, attempting to justify it; and Alfred von Wegerer, "The Russian Mobilization of 1914," *PSQ*, XLIII (1928), 201–28, answering Florinsky's statement. A recent study, L. C. F. Turner, "The Russian Mobilization in 1914," *JCH*, III (1968), 65–88, seems to me to exaggerate the influence of France upon Russian decisions. A primary source for Russian policy and events is *How the War Began in 1914, being the Diary of the Russian Foreign Office* (London, 1925), kept by M. F. Schilling.

A major source for Italian policy is Antonio Salandra, *Italy and the Great War* (London, 1932); and brief summaries of Italy in the July crisis are presented by René Albrecht-Carrié, *Italy at the Paris Peace Conference* (New York, 1938), and Leo Valiani, "Italian-Austro-Hungarian Negotiations, 1914–1915," *1914: The Coming of the War*, pp. 108–31. Fuller studies are by Roy Pryce, "Italy and the Outbreak of the First World War," *CHJ*, XI (1954), 219–27; and by William A. Rienzi, "Italy's Neutrality and Entrance into the Great War: A Re-Examination, *AHR*, LXXIII (1968), 1414–32. Serbia's ordeal of 23–25 July is depicted by H. F. Armstrong, "Three Days in Belgrade, July 1914," *FA*, V (1927), 267–75, based on the recollections of Slavo Gruić, the secretary-general of the Foreign Office.

Two books that offer broad perspectives on the events of July 1914 are Raymond Aron, *The Century of Total War* (Garden City, N.Y., 1954), and Ludwig Dehio, *Germany and World Politics in the Twentieth Century* (New York, 1959). Alfred von Wegerer's "Kriegswille und Kriegsausbruch," *KBM*, XIV (1936), 927–45, is a thoughtful and well-balanced essay.

Index